Strategic Management
Canadian Cases

Strategic Management
Canadian Cases

Mark C. Baetz
and
Paul W. Beamish

Both of
Wilfrid Laurier University

1987

Homewood, Illinois   60430

All cases were prepared as a basis for class discussion
rather than to illustrate either effective or ineffective
handling of an administrative situation.

The Wilfrid Laurier University cases are distributed through
the LAURIER INSTITUTE, School of Business and Economics,
Wilfrid Laurier University, Waterloo, Ontario, Canada N2L 3C5.

ISBN 0-256-05987-X

Library of Congress Catalog Card No. 86–83135

Printed in the United States of America

1 2 3 4 5 6 7 8 9 0 K 4 3 2 1 0 9 8 7

To our wives:
Jeanie and Maureen

PREFACE

This book was possible only because of the academic and intellectual support from colleagues at Wilfrid Laurier University (WLU) and across the country and financial support from WLU. The primary stimulus for this book was our own on-going need for new Canadian material.

Having made the decision to produce a book of Canadian cases in strategic management, a number of other decisions were made: (1) to bring together Canadian cases written not just by ourselves but by faculty across North America; (2) to include only decision-oriented cases since we feel these provide the best training for future managers; (3) to include cases dealing with aspects of general management, that is, international business and government relations, which are particularly important to managers in Canada, a country with a small domestic market, and extensive levels of government involvement in business; (4) to provide some text material including a basic conceptual framework for use with all the cases; and (5) to include a section on how to do case and financial analysis.

We are indebted to several groups of people for assisting in the preparation of this book. First, we are grateful to the case contributors from both WLU and other institutions. At WLU we wish to thank Larry Agranove, David Blenkhorn, Tupper Cawsey, David Gillen, Hugh Munro, and Alex Murray. Colleagues from 15 other institutions also contributed as follows:

John Barnett, *University of New Hampshire*
Christopher Bartlett, *Harvard University*
Robert Blunden, *Dalhousie University*
Alan DeRoo, *University of Guelph*
Willard Ellis, *Concordia University*
Jonathan Foster, *London School of Economics*
Raymond Gaudette, *Concordia University*
Gary Gerttula, *Harvard University*
Harold Gram, *Concordia University*
Kenneth Harling, *University of Guelph*
Kenneth Hatten, *Harvard University*
Ross Henderson, *University of Manitoba*
Randy Hoffman, *York University*
Richard Knudson, *University of Manitoba*
Isaiah Litvak, *York University*

Henry Mintzberg, *McGill University*
Stella Nkomo, *University of North Carolina at Charlotte*
Tae Oum, *University of British Columbia*
Suzanne Otis, *McGill University*
Thomas Poynter, *Massachusetts Institute of Technology*
William Preshing, *University of Alberta*
Philip Rosson, *Dalhousie University*
Jamal Shamsie, *McGill University*
Howard Stevenson, *Harvard University*
Mark Teagan, *Harvard University*
Donald Thain, *University of Western Ontario*
Michael Tretheway, *University of British Columbia*
J. Frederick Truitt, *University of Washington*
James Waters, *York University*
Richard von Werssowetz, *Harvard University*

From the above list it is clear that the effort to produce the book has been both a national and international effort.

With regard to the textual material, we have borrowed many of the concepts and frameworks from others. While the footnotes at the end of each chapter indicate the sources of the material in the chapter, we wish to acknowledge, in particular, the assistance of Arthur Thompson and A. J. Strickland of the University of Alabama. In exchange for three of our cases for use in the next edition of their casebook, they have permitted us to borrow from various sections of their text. We look forward to a productive and continuing relationship with them.

Second, we are indebted to the policy area group at Wilfrid Laurier University and, in particular, Larry Agranove, John Banks, and Tom Diggory for helpful comments during all stages of the manuscript preparation. Third, we are grateful for the secretarial assistance at WLU. In particular, we wish to thank the group in the Word Processing Centre—Elsie Grogan, Susan Kirkey, and Maureen Nordin. In addition, our own secretaries—Jane Osborne and then Helen Hillier—were extremely helpful and patient. A fourth group which was instrumental in the preparation of this book were the reviewers used by our publisher. These included Chris Bart, George Lane, John Mundie, Carolyne Smart, Megeed Ragab, and William Taylor. They helped ensure quality standards were achieved.

We also wish to thank a number of our colleagues who assisted in various ways. For example, Nick Fry provided helpful feedback on the IKEA case as did Peter Killing on the Grand Theatre case; Robert Sexty and Joseph d'Cruz gave suggestions on how to organize the material; and David Newman and Ray Suutari provided advice on pedagogical approaches.

In addition, we wish to thank the various executives who gave us the required access to complete the cases in this book. Finally, we wish to recognize our students on whom we tested the cases for classroom use. Some of these students served as research assistants—in particular, Jeanne McDonald, Rosemary Pell,

Rick Rigby, Ralph Trochske, and William Webb helped in many ways in the production of the cases.

Any errors or omissions in this manuscript remain our responsibility. We look forward to feedback from the various users of this book.

Mark C. Baetz
Paul W. Beamish

CONTENTS

SECTION TWO: CASES 101

SECTION ONE

TEXT

CHAPTER 1

Strategic Management—
An Overview

Most battles are won—or lost—before they are
engaged, by men who take no part in them; by their
strategists.

Carl von Clausewitz
On War (1832)

Strategic management/business policy is the capstone course in most university
and college business administration programs in Canada and the United States.
Management schools teach strategic management—which integrates the material
about the functional areas—in order to prepare students as administrators capable
of seeing important relationships at a strategic level.

The study of strategic management has been steadily evolving. Original
emphasis was on the functions of the general manager—still an integral part of the
field. Exhibit 1–1, for example, provides an overview of the functional roles of the
general manager.

More recently, the strategic management field has broadened to include the
study of:

> The organizational systems and processes used to establish overall organizational
> goals and objectives and to formulate, implement, and control the strategies and
> policies necessary to achieve these goals and objectives.[1]

This text reflects this broadening in scope by providing case studies dealing
with most of the major subfields of strategic management. Eighteen major
subfields are summarized in Exhibit 1–2 under five headings: major reference
groups; conceptualizing strategic management; elements of strategy formulation;
elements of strategy implementation and review; and organizations.

The common element in discussions of strategic management is an emphasis
on strategy. The word *strategy* has become one of the most overused terms in
recent years, often indiscriminately used in an attempt to add importance or
significance to a variety of topics.

Derived from the ancient Greek *strategos* or "the art of the general,"[2]
strategy has military roots. In fact, not surprisingly, strong similarities exist

---

Exhibit 1–1: The Functional Roles of the General Manager

Three interpersonal roles:

— Figurehead role—representing the organization on ceremonial occasions.
— Liaison role—interacting with other managers and groups outside the organization unit.
— Leader role—establishing relationships with subordinates (motivating, supervising) and exercising formal authority within the organizational unit.

Three informational roles:

— Monitor role—receiving and collecting information from both inside and outside the organizational unit.
— Disseminator role—transmitting information to members within the organization unit.
— Spokesman role—informing those outside the organization unit.

Four decision-related roles:

— Innovator role—initiating change.
— Resource allocation role—deciding where efforts and energies will be directed.
— Negotiator role—dealing with situations involving negotiations on behalf of the organization.
— Disturbance-handler role—taking charge when crises arise and the organization is threatened.

Source: Adapted from Table 2 (pp. 91–93) in *The Nature of Managerial Work* by Henry Mintzberg. Copyright © 1973 by Henry Mintzberg. Reprinted by permission of Harper & Row, Publishers, Inc.

---

between the responsibilities of the military general and the general manager of an organization. Their definitions of strategy overlap as well. In a military context, strategy has been defined as "the employment of the battle as the means to gain the end of the war."[3] In a corporate setting, strategy could be defined as the implementable management scheme for achieving corporate ends. Alternately, corporate strategy has been viewed as "the pattern in the organization's important decisions and actions, and consists of a few key areas or things by which the firm seeks to distinguish itself."[4] Finally, in a broader context, strategy has been defined as "that which has to do with determining the basic objectives of an organization and allocating resources to their accomplishment."[5]

Understanding the role of resource allocation in the strategic management process is critical. Resource allocations serve to interpret and apply the firm's strategy. One can go so far as to say, "Resource allocation across businesses and over time is the essence of the strategy of a company."[6]

A firm grasp of the resource allocation process is necessary to appreciate its role in the strategic management process. As the matrix in Exhibit 1–3 indicates, the resource allocation process has three phases and three subprocesses. The first of three phases is the initiating phase—where many product/market ideas and proposals originate. This is the level where many new business graduates will spend their first years of employment. The other two phases are corporate (senior management level) and integrating. It is through the integrating phase—or what

Exhibit 1–2: Some Major Subfields of Strategic Management/Business Policy

Groups:

1. Board of directors.
2. General management.
3. Stakeholder analysis.

Conceptualizing strategic management:

4. The strategy-structure-performance linkage.
5. Corporate-level strategy (including mergers, acquisitions, and divestitures).
6. Business-level strategy.

Elements of strategy formulation:

7. Organizational goals.
8. Corporate social policy and management ethics.
9. Macroenvironmental analysis.
10. Strategic decision making (choice of strategy).

Elements of strategy implementation and review:

11. The design of macroorganizational structure and systems.
12. Strategic planning and information systems.
13. Strategic control systems.
14. Organizational culture.
15. Leadership style for general managers.

Organizations:

16. The strategic management of small businesses and new ventures.
17. The strategic management of not-for-profit organizations (including governments).
18. The strategic management of international business.

might be called the middle management level—that the goals and plans defined by corporate management will be conveyed down through the organization. It is also through the integrating phase that operational proposals (from the initiating phase) will be first screened and, if deemed promising, conveyed up through the organization to the corporate level.

The three subprocesses in the resource allocation process are definition, commitment, and organizational context. In the definition process, the underlying economic and technical considerations of a proposed investment (resource allocation) are determined. In order to understand how proposals that have already been defined move toward funding, the second of the three subprocesses—commitment or impetus—comes into play. It is at this stage that a senior manager must commit (or not) to sponsor a project. Because the general manager's reputation for good judgment may rise or fall depending on the outcome of the investment, the required commitment will be given only after careful consideration of the various demands at the corporate and operational

Exhibit 1–3: The Resource Allocation Process

Process / Phase	Definition — Goal/plan/result Definition and measurement	Commitment — Project/plan impetus	Organization — Determination of organizational context
Corporate (senior management)	— Macro strategy — Company environment aggregate system	Terminal decision, yes or no	— Design of corporate context — Overall structure, personnel assignment and development, incentive and control systems, style
Integrating (middle management)	— Financial aggregate goals — Strategic thrust → ← Product-market strategies	Filtered company needs (the company "wants") → ← Filtered product/market needs (the businesses "wants")	— Corporate needs — Implementation (differentiation integration) → ← — Subunit needs — Interpretation, adaptive needs
Initiating (operating level)	— Product-market strategies — Operational plans and execution	— Competing plans/proposals — I've got a "great" idea.	Product/market not served by structure

Source: Adapted from Joseph L. Bower, *Managing the Resource Allocation Process: A Study of Corporate Planning and Investment.* Boston: Division of Research, Harvard Business School, 1970, p. 80. Used with permission. (Republished as a Harvard Business School Classic: Boston: Harvard Business School Press, 1986.)

levels. Not surprisingly, this second subprocess can be viewed primarily as a political one.[7]

The final subprocess is context, which is the set of organizational elements—including formal structure, information and control systems, and reward systems—which influence both definition and impetus. This flow from the definition or formulation of a potential resource allocation through commitment to how it will ultimately affect, and be affected by, the organization begins to move us toward an understanding of the basic framework which underlies the study of strategic management.

Before examining the underlying paradigm, the components of business strategy will be discussed.

The Major Components of Strategy

Every firm has a strategy. Implicit or explicit, effective or ineffective, as intended or not—whenever a firm allocates the resources of people or capital, it is making a statement about its strategy.

Three components are present in a strategy: (1) mission or purpose, (2) goals and objectives (including product/market emphasis), and (3) basis of competition.

Mission / Purpose

In many of the more successful organizations there is a clear sense of who we are and where we are going. In deriving a notion of mission or purpose, managers must confront questions such as: What kind of organization/business is it? What will it become if it stays on its present path? What does it want to be? What should it be? From this basic vision follows a second, more-tangible component of strategy—the goals and objectives.

Goals / Objectives

The organization's mission or purpose can be translated into specific measurable performance targets. These objectives typically relate to profitability, growth, return on investment, market share, technological strength, and so forth. In addition, there are "soft" goals and objectives. These might include such things as benefits to society, employee welfare, and management autonomy. Knowledge of the existence of a "soft" counterpart to "hard" terms is essential if one is to have a more complete understanding of an organization. This distinction is discussed in detail in Chapter 5.

At the simplest level, the firm's goals and objectives can be specified in terms of products/services and markets. Both the existing and potential range and focus of product/service and market alternatives must be considered (see Exhibit 1–4).

The term *market* refers to both geographic (that is, local, regional, national,

Exhibit 1–4:   Product/Service and Market Alternatives

		Market Alternatives		
		Existing Market	*Expanded Market*	*New Market*
	Existing Products/ Services			
Product/ Service Alternatives	*Modified Products/ Services*			
	New Products/ Services			

international) and customer groups. There are any number of ways of defining customer scope and focus. In fact, there is a view that a business can be more accurately defined by focusing on the customer.[8] Specifically, the view holds that a business can be defined in terms of (1) customer groups (who is being satisfied), (2) customer needs (what is being satisfied), and (3) alternative technologies (how customer needs are satisfied).

Basis of Competition

The third component of strategy is basis of competition. Although discussed in greater detail in Chapter 3, Porter's "Five Forces" Model of Competition (see Exhibit 1–5) states that the competitive forces that shape strategy arise from suppliers, customers, substitute products, new entrants, and the moves and countermoves of rival firms.[9] This framework for analyzing competitors (and industries) is useful for understanding how a firm presently and potentially can compete. With this background on the components of strategy complete, it is now possible to place it in the context of a conceptual framework for understanding strategic management.

A Conceptual Framework for Strategic Management

All organizations are concerned with performance. Whether it is a not-for-profit organization, a multinational corporation, or the corner store, all must act in such a way as to remain viable. The strategies which organizations adopt in an attempt to achieve satisfactory performance are varied. Similarly, the organizational structures which are chosen to reflect these strategies differ as well.

The underlying paradigm in the strategic management area for the past 25 years has been the strategy-structure-performance relationship.[10]

Exhibit 1–5: The "Five Forces" Model of Competition

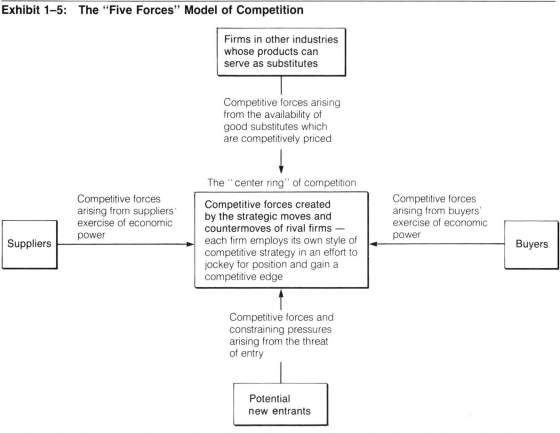

This relationship tells us two things—one which is immediately obvious and one which is not. The first and obvious point is that strategy affects performance. Whether one is attempting to organize a fund-raiser, increase sales, start a business, or allocate resources in a large organization—strategy matters.

The second, perhaps less obvious point is that organizational structure matters, too, as it can support or hamper the strategy. To implement any strategy, certain organizational actions must be taken: certain tasks must be carried out; reward and information systems put in place; people hired, trained, and managed; and reporting relationships established. An unlimited number of potential organizational actions exist. However, they are not all equally appropriate in all situations. Depending on the strategy chosen, some organizational structures are more appropriate than others. In fact, possibly the greatest challenge in the strategic management area is fitting an appropriate organization to the strategy which has been formulated.

Exhibit 1–6:   The Underlying Paradigm in Strategic Management

```
   ( Strategy )  ───▶  ( Structure )  ───▶  ( Performance )
```

In the balance of this chapter, we review several well-accepted strategic management models which form the basis for the conceptual framework used in this text. Keep in mind that all of these models have as part of their origins the same underlying paradigm, as depicted in Exhibit 1–6.

Exhibits 1–7 and 1–8 detail two of the dozens of published models of strategic management. Like most approaches, these similar models are divided into sections on strategy formulation and implementation. Although formulation and

---

Exhibit 1–7

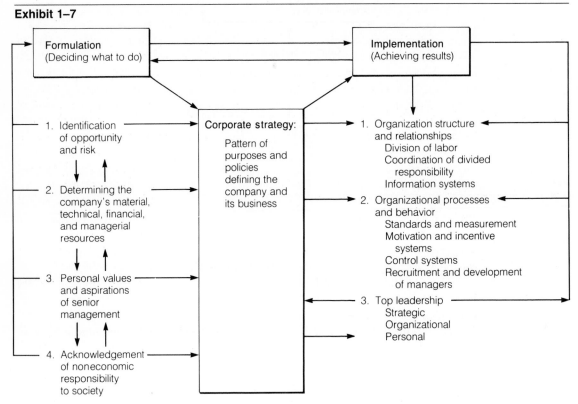

Source: Kenneth Andrews, *The Concept of Corporate Strategy*, rev ed. (Homewood, Ill.: Richard D. Irwin, 1980). Reprinted by permission.

Exhibit 1–8: Formulation and Implementation of Strategy

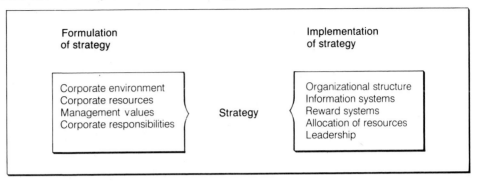

Source: Norman A. Berg, *General Management: An Analytical Approach* (Homewood, Ill.: Richard D. Irwin, 1984), p. 30. Reprinted by permission.

implementation are inextricably linked, for analytic purposes, they can be considered individually.

In both models, the major variables influencing strategy are (*a*) the preferences, personal values, and aspirations of top management, (*b*) the external environment, including competitive opportunities and risks, (*c*) the internal environment which focuses on the organization's managerial, financial, and technical resources and capabilities, and (*d*) organizational responsibility to society. The conceptual framework used in this text includes the first three of these variables. These will be examined in detail in Chapter 3. Acknowledgment of noneconomic responsibility to society is subsumed here under managerial preferences and values.

In Exhibit 1–7 there are a large number of arrows between the variables used to illustrate the interrelationships which exist. While in the general case, strategy influences structure, certainly in many instances the relationship can be in the other direction or, in fact, in both directions.

The strategy implementation half of the models in Exhibit 1–7 and 1–8 are composed of a separate group of variables. The major organization design variables are (*a*) information and control systems, (*b*) reward systems, (*c*) people, which includes leadership style, (*d*) organizational structure, and (*e*) resource allocation task. This last variable, task, is sometimes viewed as a bridge between formulation and implementation. In this text, all five of these variables are included as part of strategy implementation, although using a slightly different configuration. The role of these variables in the strategic management process will be discussed in detail in Chapters 4 and 5. An overview of the key variables used in the conceptual framework in this text is provided in Exhibit 1–9. As the arrows in this exhibit suggest, a constant review process takes place.

The case studies in this text were chosen to illustrate the impact/role of some or all of the variables in the conceptual framework. These case studies are all

Exhibit 1–9:   The Strategic Management Process: Basic Conceptual Framework

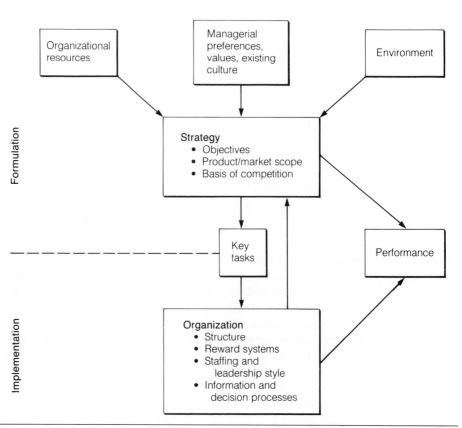

decision oriented, requiring students to make a decision as to a course of action for the organization. Achievement of a defensible overall strategy for the organization means that errors in tactics (the specific means of exercising the strategy) may not be fatal. In Chapter 2, a detailed framework for conducting a case study analysis—including the financial analysis—is provided. This material is included in order to provide some direction in developing "better" case analyses.

Notes to Chapter 1

1. From Charles W. Hofer, consulting ed., *West Series in Strategic Management* (St. Paul, Minn.: West Publishing, 1986), Common Foreword, p. xi.

2. Jay R. Galbraith and Robert K. Kazanjian, *Strategy Implementation: Structure, Systems and Process*, 2nd ed. (St. Paul, Minn.: West Publishing, 1986), p. 3.

3. Carl von Clausewitz, *On War*, originally published in 1832. Translation published

by Routledge and Kegan Paul, Ltd., 1908 (Middlesex, England: Pelican (Penguin) Books, 1968).

4. Michael Kamis, *Strategic Planning for Changing Times* (Dayton, Ohio: Cassette Recording Co., 1984).

5. William Curry, "A Condensed Version of Business Policy," mimeographed (Waterloo, Ont.: Wilfrid Laurier University, 1980).

6. J. N. Fry, note accompanying C.I.L. Inc. case, mimeographed (London, Ont.: University of Western Ontario, 1982).

7. For a more recent discussion, see Ian C. McMillan and Patricia E. Jones, *Strategy Formulation: Power and Politics*, 2nd ed. (St. Paul, Minn.: West Publishing, 1986).

8. Derek F. Abell, *Defining a Business: The Starting Point of Strategic Planning* (Englewood Cliffs, N.J.: Prentice-Hall, 1980), p. 169.

9. See also Michael E. Porter, *Competitive Strategy: Techniques for Analyzing Industries and Competitors* (New York: Free Press, 1980).

10. See Alfred D. Chandler, *Strategy and Structure* (Cambridge, Mass.: MIT Press, 1962).

CHAPTER 2

Case Analysis

Management is an action-oriented activity. It requires doing to achieve proficiency. Managers succeed or fail not so much because of what they know as because of what they do. A person cannot expect to succeed as a manager and become a "professional" simply by studying excellent books on management—no matter how thoroughly the text material is mastered nor how many A's are earned at exam time. Just like a skater needs to practice at being a better skater, a person who aspires to become a manager can benefit from practicing at being a manager.

Practicing Management via Case Analysis

In academic programs of management education, students practice at being managers via case analysis. A case sets forth, in a factual manner, the events and organizational circumstances surrounding a particular managerial situation. It puts the readers at the scene of the action and familiarizes them with the situation as it prevailed. A case can concern a whole industry, a single organization, or even just a part of an organization; the organization involved can be either profit seeking or not-for-profit. Cases about business organizations usually include descriptions of the industry and its competitive conditions, the organization's history and development, its products and markets, the backgrounds and personalities of the key people involved, the production facilities, the work climate, the organizational structure, the marketing methods, and the external environment, together with whatever pertinent financial, production, accounting, sales, and market information was available to management.

The essence of the student's role in the case method is to diagnose and size up the situation described in the case and to think through what, if any, actions

---

Reprinted by permission, with minor editorial changes, from Arthur A. Thompson and A. J. Strickland, *Strategic Management: Concepts and Cases* (Plano, Tex.: Business Publications, 1984), pp. 272–89.

need to be taken. The purpose is for the student, as analyst, to appraise the situation from a managerial perspective, asking: What factors have contributed to the situation? What problems are evident? How serious are they? What analysis is needed to probe for solutions? What actionable recommendations can be offered? What facts and figures support my position?

It should be emphasized that most cases are not intended to be examples of right and wrong, or good and bad management. The organizations concerned are selected neither because they are the best or the worst in their industry nor because they present an interesting and relevant analytical situation. The important thing about a case is that it represents an actual situation where managers were obligated to recognize and cope with the problems as they were.

Why Use Cases to Practice Management?

> A student of business with tact
> Absorbed many answers he lacked.
> But acquired a job,
> He said with a sob,
> "How *does* one fit answer to fact?"

The foregoing limerick was offered some years ago by Charles I. Gragg in a classic article, "Because Wisdom Can't Be Told," to illustrate what might happen to students of management without the benefit of cases.[1] Gragg observed that the mere act of listening to lectures and sound advice about management does little for anyone's management skills. He contended it was unlikely that accumulated managerial experience and wisdom could effectively be passed on by lectures and readings alone. Gragg suggested that if anything has been learned about the practice of management, it is that a storehouse of ready-made answers does not exist. Each managerial situation has unique aspects, requiring its own diagnosis and understanding as a prelude to judgment and action. In Gragg's view and in the view of other case method advocates, cases provide aspiring managers with an important and valid kind of daily practice in wrestling with management problems.

The case method is, indeed, *learning by doing*. The pedagogy of the case method of instruction is predicated on the benefits of acquiring managerial "experience" by means of simulated management exercises (cases). The best justification for cases is that few, if any, students during the course of their university education have an opportunity to come into direct personal contact with different kinds of companies and real-life managerial situations. Cases offer a viable substitute by bringing a variety of industries, organizations, and management problems into the classroom and permitting students to assume the manager's role. Management cases, therefore, provide students with a kind of experiential exercise in which to test their ability to apply their textbook knowledge about management.

Objectives of the Case Method

As the foregoing discussion suggests, using cases as an instructional technique is intended to produce four student-related results:[2]

1. Helping you to acquire the skills of putting textbook knowledge about management into practice.
2. Getting you out of the habit of being a receiver of facts; concepts, and techniques and into the habit of diagnosing problems, analyzing and evaluating alternatives, and formulating workable plans of action.
3. Training you to work out answers and solutions for yourself, as opposed to relying upon the authoritative crutch of the professor or a textbook.
4. Providing you with exposure to a range of firms and managerial situations (which might take a lifetime to experience personally), thus offering you a basis for comparison when you begin your own management career.

If you understand that these are the objectives of the case method of instruction, then you are less likely to be bothered by something that puzzles some students: "What is the answer to the case?" Being accustomed to textbook statements of fact and supposedly definitive lecture notes, students often find that discussions and analyses of managerial cases do not produce any hard answers. Instead, issues in the case are discussed pro and con. Various alternatives and approaches are evaluated. Usually, a good argument can be made for more than one course of action. If the class discussion concludes without a clear consensus on what to do and which way to go, some students may, at first, feel frustrated because they are not told "what the answer is" or "what the company actually did."

However, cases where answers are not clear-cut are quite realistic. Organizational problems whose analysis leads to a definite, single-pronged solution are likely to be so oversimplified and rare as to be trivial or devoid of practical value. In reality, several feasible courses of action may exist for dealing with the same set of circumstances. Moreover, in real-life management situations when one makes a decision or selects a particular course of action, there is no peeking at the back of a book to see if you have chosen the best thing to do. No book of provably correct answers exists; in fact, the first test of management action is *results*. The important thing for a student to understand in case analysis is that it is the managerial exercise of identifying, diagnosing, and recommending that counts rather than discovering the right answer or finding out what actually happened.

To put it another way, *the purpose of management cases is not to learn authoritative answers to specific managerial problems but to become skilled in the process of designing workable action plans through evaluation of the prevailing circumstances.* The aim of case analysis is not for you to try to guess what the instructor is thinking or what the organization did but, rather, to see whether you can support your views against the counterviews of the group or, failing to do so, join in the sense of discovery of different approaches and perspectives. Therefore, *in case analysis you are expected to bear the strains of thinking actively, of making managerial assessments which may be vigorously challenged, of offering your analysis, and of proposing action plans—this is how you are provided with meaningful practice at being a manager.*

Analyzing the case yourself is what initiates you in the ways of thinking ''managerially'' and exercising responsible judgment. At the same time, you can use cases to test the rigor and effectiveness of your own approach to the practice of management and to begin to evolve your own management philosophy and management style.

Use of the Socratic method of questioning-answering-questioning-answering, where there is no single correct answer but always another question, is at the heart of the case process. A good case can be used with student groups of varying qualifications. With the more highly experienced qualified groups, the other questions become tougher.

Preparing a Case for Class Discussion

Given that cases rest on the principle of learning by doing, their effectiveness hinges upon *you* making *your* analysis and reaching *your* own decisions and then in the classroom participating in a collective analysis and discussion of the issues. If this is your first experience with the case method, you may have to reorient your study habits. Since a case assignment emphasizes student participation, it is obvious that the effectiveness of the class discussion depends upon each student having studied the case *beforehand.* Consequently, unlike lecture courses where there is no imperative of specific preparation before each class and where assigned readings and reviews of lecture notes may be done at irregular intervals, *a case assignment requires conscientious preparation before class.* You cannot, after all, expect to get much out of hearing the class discuss a case with which you are totally unfamiliar.

Unfortunately, though, there is no nice, neat, proven procedure for conducting a case analysis. There is no formula, no fail-safe, step-by-step technique that we can recommend beyond emphasizing the sequence: *identify, evaluate, consider alternatives,* and *recommend.* Each case is a new situation and has its own set of issues, analytical requirements, and action alternatives.

A first step in understanding how the case method of teaching/learning works is to recognize that it represents a radical departure from the lecture/discussion/problem classroom technique. To begin with, members of the class do most of the talking. The instructor's role is to solicit student participation and guide the discussion. Expect the instructor to begin the class with such questions as: What is the organization's strategy? What are the strategic issues and problems confronting the company? What is your assessment of the company's situation? Is the industry an attractive one to be in? Is management doing a good job? Are the organization's objectives and strategies compatible with its skills and resources? Typically, members of the class will evaluate and test their opinions as much in discussions with each other as with the instructor. But irrespective of whether the discussion emphasis is instructor-student or student-student, members of the class carry the burden for analyzing the situation and for being prepared to present and defend their analysis in the classroom. Thus, you should expect an absence of professorial "here's how to do it," "right answers," and "hard knowledge for your notebook"; instead, be prepared for a discussion involving your size-up of the situation, what actions you would take, and why you would take them.[3]

Begin preparing for class by reading the case once for familiarity. An initial reading should give you the general flavor of the situation and make possible preliminary identification of issues. On the second reading, attempt to gain full command of the facts. Make some notes about apparent organizational objectives, strategies, policies, symptoms of problems, root problems, unresolved issues, and roles of key individuals. Be alert for issues or problems which are lurking beneath the surface. For instance, at first glance, it might appear that an issue in the case is whether a product has ample market potential at the current selling price; on closer examination, you may see the root problem is that the method being used to compensate salespeople fails to generate adequate incentive for achieving greater unit volume. Strive for a sharp, clear-cut size-up of the issues posed in the case situation.

To help diagnose the situation, put yourself in the position of some manager or managerial group portrayed in the case and get attuned to the overall environment facing management. Try to get a good feel for the condition of the company, the industry, and the economics of the business. Get a handle on how the market works and on the nature of competition. This is essential if you are to come up with solutions which will be both workable and acceptable in light of the prevailing external constraints and internal organizational realities. Do not be dismayed if you find it impractical to isolate the problems and issues into distinct categories which can be treated separately. Very few significant strategy management problems can be neatly sorted into mutually exclusive areas of concern. Furthermore, expect the cases (especially those in this book) to contain several problems and issues, rather than just one. Guard against making a single, simple statement of the problem unless the issue is very clear-cut. Admittedly, there will be cases where issues are well defined and the main problem is figuring out what to do; but in most cases you can expect a set of problems and issues to be present, some of which are related and some of which are not.

Next, you must move toward a solid evaluation of the case situation, based on the information given. Developing an ability to evaluate companies and size up their situations is the core of what strategic analysis is all about. The cases in this book, of course, are all strategy related, and they each require some form of strategic analysis, that is, analysis of how well the organization's strategy has been formulated (see Chapter 3) and implemented (see Chapter 4).

Uppermost in your efforts, strive for defensible arguments and positions. Do not rely upon just your opinion; support it with evidence! Analyze the available data and make whatever relevant accounting, financial, marketing, or operations calculations are necessary to support your assessment of the situation. Crunch the numbers! If your instructor has provided you with specific study questions for the case, by all means make some notes as to how you would answer them. Include in your notes all the reasons and evidence you can muster to support your diagnosis and evaluation.

Last, when information or data in the case is conflicting and/or various opinions are contradictory, decide which is more valid and why. Forcing you to make judgments about the validity of the data and information presented in the case is both deliberate and realistic. It is deliberate because one function of the case method is to help you develop your powers of judgment and inference. It is realistic because a great many managerial situations entail conflicting points of view.

Once you have thoroughly diagnosed the company's situation and weighed the pros and cons of various alternative courses of action, the final step of case analysis is to decide what you think the company needs to do to improve its performance. Draw up your set of recommendations on what to do and be prepared to give your action agenda. This is really the most crucial part of the process of case analysis; diagnosis divorced from corrective action is sterile. But bear in mind that proposing realistic, workable solutions and offering a hasty, ill-conceived "possibility" are not the same thing. Don't recommend anything you would not be prepared to do yourself if you were in the decision maker's shoes. Be sure you can give reasons why your recommendations are preferable to other options which exist.

On a few occasions, some desirable information may not be included in the case. In such instances, you may be inclined to complain about the lack of facts. A manager, however, uses more than facts upon which to base his or her decision. Moreover, it may be possible to make a number of inferences from the facts you do have. So be wary of rushing to include as part of your recommendations the need to get more information. From time to time, of course, a search for additional facts or information may be entirely appropriate, but you must also recognize that the organization's managers may not have had any more information available than that presented in the case. Before recommending that action be postponed until additional facts are uncovered, be sure that you think it will be worthwhile to get them and that the organization can afford to wait. In general, though, try to recommend a course of action based upon the evidence you have at hand.

Again, remember that rarely is there a "right" decision or just one "optimal" plan of action or an "approved" solution. Your goal should be to develop what you think is a pragmatic, defensible course of action which is based upon a serious analysis of the situation and which appears to you to be right in view of your assessment and weighing of the facts. Admittedly, someone else may evaluate the same facts in another way and thus have a different right solution, but since several good plans of action can normally be conceived, you should not be afraid to stick by your own analysis and judgment. One can make a strong argument for the view that the right answer for a manager is the one which he or she can propose, explain, defend, and make work when it is implemented. This is the middle ground we support between the ''no right answer'' and ''one right answer'' schools of thought. Clearly, there are better answers than others.

The Classroom Experience

In experiencing class discussion of management cases, you will, in all probability, notice very quickly that you will not have thought of everything in the case that your fellow students think of. While you will see things others did not, they will see things you did not. Do not be dismayed or alarmed by this. It is normal. As the old adage goes, ''Two heads are better than one.'' So it is to be expected that the class as a whole will do a more penetrating and searching job of case analysis than will any one person working alone. This is the power of group effort, and one of its virtues is that it will give you more insight into the variety of approaches and how to cope with differences of opinion. Second, you will see better why sometimes it is not managerially wise to assume a rigid position on an issue until a full range of views and information has been assembled. And, undoubtedly, somewhere along the way, you will begin to recognize that neither the instructor nor other students in the class have all the answers, and even if they think they do, you are still free to present and hold to your own views. The truth in the saying ''there's more than one way to skin a cat'' will be seen to apply nicely to most management situations.

For class discussion of cases to be useful and stimulating, you need to keep the following points in mind:

1. The case method enlists a maximum of individual participation in class discussion. It is not enough to be present as a silent observer; if every student took this approach, then there would be no discussion. (Thus, do not be surprised if a portion of your grade is based on your participation in case discussions.)

2. Although you should do your own independent work and independent thinking, don't hesitate to discuss the case with other students. Managers often discuss their problems with other key people.

3. During case discussions, expect and tolerate challenges to the views expressed. Be willing to submit your conclusions for scrutiny and rebuttal. State your views without fear of disapproval and overcome the hesitation of speaking out.

4. In orally presenting and defending your ideas, strive to be convincing and persuasive. Always give supporting evidence and reasons.

5. Expect the instructor to assume the role of extensive questioner and listener. Expect to be cross-examined for evidence and reasons by your instructor or by others in the class. Expect students to dominate the discussion and do most of the talking.

6. Although discussion of a case is a group process, this does not imply conformity to group opinion. Learning respect for the views and approaches of others is an integral part of case analysis exercises. But be willing to "swim against the tide" of majority opinion. In the practice of management, there is always room for originality, unorthodoxy, and unique personality.

7. In participating in the discussion, make a conscious effort to *contribute* rather than just talk. There *is* a big difference between saying something that builds the discussion and offering a long-winded, off-the-cuff remark that leaves the class wondering what the point was.

8. Effective case discussion can occur only if participants have the facts of the case well in hand; rehashing information in the case should be held to a minimum except as it provides documentation, comparisons, or support for your position. In making your point, assume that everyone has read the case and knows what "the case says."

9. During the discussion, new insights provided by the group's efforts are likely to emerge. Don't be alarmed or surprised if you and others in the class change your mind about some things as the discussion unfolds. Be alert for how these changes affect your analysis and recommendations (in case you are called on to speak).

10. Although there will always be situations in which more technical information is imperative to the making of an intelligent decision, try not to shirk from making decisions in the face of incomplete information. Wrestling with imperfect information is a normal condition managers face and is something you should get used to.

Preparing a Written Case Analysis

From time to time, your instructor may ask you to prepare a written analysis of the case assignment. Preparing a written case analysis is much like preparing a case for class discussion, except that your analysis, when completed, must be reduced to writing. Just as there was no set formula for preparing a case for oral discussion, there is no iron-clad procedure for doing a written case analysis. With a bit of experience, you will arrive at your own preferred method of attack in writing up a case, and you will learn to adjust your approach to the unique aspects that each case presents.

Your instructor may assign you a specific topic around which to prepare your written report. Common assignments include: (1) Identify and evaluate company X's corporate strategy. (2) In view of the opportunities and risks you see in the industry, what is your assessment of the company's position and strategy? (3) How would you size up the strategic situation of company Y? (4) What recommendation would you make to company Z's top management? (5) What specific functions and activities does the company have to perform especially well in order for its strategy to succeed?

Alternatively, you may be asked to do a comprehensive written case analysis. It is typical for a comprehensive written case analysis to emphasize four things:

1. Identification.
2. Analysis and evaluation.
3. Discussion of alternatives.
4. Presentation of recommendations.

You may wish to consider the following pointers in preparing a comprehensive written case analysis.[4]

Identification. It is essential that your paper reflect a sharply focused diagnosis of strategic issues and key problems and further, that you demonstrate good business judgment in sizing up the company's present situation. Make sure you understand and can identify the firm's strategy (see Chapters 1 and 3). You would probably be well advised to begin your paper by sizing up the company's situation, its strategy, and the significant problems and issues which confront management. State problems/issues as clearly and precisely as you can. Unless it is necessary to do so for emphasis, avoid recounting facts and history about the company (assume your professor has read the case and is familiar with the organization!).

Analysis and Evaluation. Very likely, you will find this section the hardest part of the report. Analysis is hard work! Study the tables, exhibits, and financial statements in the case carefully. Check out the firm's financial ratios, its profit margins and rates of return, and its capital structure and decide how strong the firm is financially. (Exhibit 2–1 contains a summary of various financial ratios and how they are calculated.) Similarly, look at marketing, production, managerial competences, and so on, and evaluate the factors underlying the organization's successes and failures. Decide whether it has a distinctive competence and, if so, whether it is capitalizing upon it. Check out the quality of the firm's business portfolio (see Appendix 3 in the Seagram case for a brief note on product portfolio management).

Check to see if the firm's strategy at all levels is working and determine the reasons why or why not. Appraise internal strengths and weaknesses and assess external opportunities and threats—to do a "SWOT analysis," see Exhibit 2–2 for suggestions of what to look for. Decide whether a competitor analysis is needed to clarify competitive forces (you may want to draw up a strategic group map as in Exhibit 2–3 and/or do an industry analysis as in Exhibit 3–1, in Chapter 3). Decide whether and why the firm's competitive position is getting stronger or weaker (see Exhibit 2–4 for suggestions of what to look for). Review the material in Chapters 3 and 4 to see if you have overlooked some aspect of strategy evaluation. Try to decide whether the main problems revolve around a need to revise strategy, a need to improve strategy implementation, or both. In appraising the quality of strategy implementation, you should review Chapter 4.

Exhibit 2–1: A Summary of Key Financial Ratios, How They Are Calculated, and What They Show

Ratio	*How Calculated*	*What It Shows*
Profitability ratios:		
1. Gross profit margin	$$\frac{\text{Sales} - \text{Cost of goods sold}}{\text{Sales}}$$	An indication of the total margin available to cover operating expenses and yield a profit.
2. Operating profit margin	$$\frac{\text{Profits before taxes and before interest}}{\text{Sales}}$$	An indication of the firm's profitability from current operations without regard to the interest charges accruing from the capital structure. (Helps to assess impact of different capital structures.)
3. Net profit margin (or return on sales)	$$\frac{\text{Profits after taxes}}{\text{Sales}}$$	Shows aftertax profits per dollar of sales. Subpar-profit margins indicate that the firm's sales prices are relatively low or that its costs are relatively high or both.
4. Return on total assets	$$\frac{\text{Profits after taxes}}{\text{Total assets}}$$ or $$\frac{\text{Profits after taxes} + \text{Interest}}{\text{Total assets}}$$	A measure of the return on total investment in the enterprise. It is sometimes desirable to add interest to aftertax profits to form the numerator of the ratio since total assets are financed by creditors as well as by stockholders; hence, it is accurate to measure the productivity of assets by the returns provided to both classes of investors.
5. Return on stockholders' equity (or return on net worth)	$$\frac{\text{Profits after taxes}}{\text{Total stockholders' equity}}$$	A measure of the rate of return on stockholders' investment in the enterprise.
6. Return on common equity	$$\frac{\text{Profits after taxes} - \text{Preferred stock dividends}}{\text{Total stockholders' equity} - \text{Par value of preferred stock}}$$	A measure of the rate of return on the investment which the owners of common stock have made in the enterprise.

Exhibit 2–1 *(continued)*

Ratio	How Calculated	What It Shows
7. Earnings per share	$$\frac{\text{Profits after taxes} - \text{Preferred stock dividends}}{\text{Number of shares of common stock outstanding}}$$	Shows the earnings available to the owners of common stock.
Liquidity ratios:		
1. Current ratio	$$\frac{\text{Current assets}}{\text{Current liabilities}}$$	Indicates the extent to which the claims of short-term creditors are covered by assets that are expected to be converted to cash in a period roughly corresponding to the maturity of the liabilities.
2. Quick ratio (or acid-test ratio)	$$\frac{\text{Current assets} - \text{Inventory}}{\text{Current liabilities}}$$	A measure of the firm's ability to pay off short-term obligations without relying upon the sale of its inventories.
3. Inventory to net working capital	$$\frac{\text{Inventory}}{\text{Current assets} - \text{Current liabilities}}$$	A measure of the extent to which the firm's working capital is tied up in inventory.
Leverage ratios:		
1. Debt-to-assets ratio	$$\frac{\text{Total debt}}{\text{Total assets}}$$	Measures the extent to which borrowed funds have been used to finance the firm's operations.
2. Debt-to-equity ratio	$$\frac{\text{Total debt}}{\text{Total stockholders' equity}}$$	Provides another measure of the funds provided by creditors versus the funds provided by owners.
3. Long-term debt-to-equity ratio	$$\frac{\text{Long-term debt}}{\text{Total stockholders' equity}}$$	A widely used measure of the balance between debt and equity in the firm's long-term capital structure.
4. Times-interest-earned (or coverage) ratios	$$\frac{\text{Profits before interest and taxes}}{\text{Total interest charges}}$$	Measures the extent to which earnings can decline without the firm becoming unable to meet its annual interest costs.

Exhibit 2–1 *(continued)*

Ratio	How Calculated	What It Shows
5. Fixed-charge coverage	$$\frac{\text{Profits before taxes and interest} + \text{Lease obligations}}{\text{Total interest charges} + \text{Lease obligations}}$$	A more inclusive indication of the firm's ability to meet all of its fixed-charge obligations.

Activity ratios:

Ratio	How Calculated	What It Shows
1. Inventory turnover	$$\frac{\text{Sales}}{\text{Inventory of finished goods}}$$	When compared to industry averages, it provides an indication of whether a company has excessive or perhaps inadequate finished-goods inventory.
2. Fixed-assets turnover	$$\frac{\text{Sales}}{\text{Fixed assets}}$$	A measure of the sales productivity and utilization of plant and equipment.
3. Total-assets turnover	$$\frac{\text{Sales}}{\text{Total assets}}$$	A measure of the utilization of all the firm's assets. A ratio below the industry average indicates the company is not generating a sufficient volume of business given the size of its asset investment.
4. Accounts-receivable turnover	$$\frac{\text{Annual credit sales}}{\text{Accounts receivable}}$$	A measure of the average length of time it takes the firm to collect the sales made on credit.
5. Average collection period	$$\frac{\text{Accounts receivable}}{\text{Total sales} \div 365}$$ or $$\frac{\text{Accounts receivable}}{\text{Average daily sales}}$$	Indicates the average length of time the firm must wait after making a sale before it receives payment.

Other ratios:

Ratio	How Calculated	What It Shows
1. Dividend yield on common stock	$$\frac{\text{Annual dividends per share}}{\text{Current market price per share}}$$	A measure of the return to owners received in the form of dividends.

Exhibit 2–1   *(concluded)*

Ratio	How Calculated	What It Shows
2. Price-earnings ratio	$\dfrac{\text{Current market price per share}}{\text{Aftertax earnings per share}}$	Faster growing or less risky firms tend to have higher price-earnings ratios than slower-growing or more-risky firms.
3. Dividend-payout ratio	$\dfrac{\text{Annual dividends per share}}{\text{Aftertax earnings per share}}$	Indicates the percentages of profits paid out as dividends.
4. Cash flow per share	$\dfrac{\text{Aftertax profits} + \text{Depreciation}}{\text{Number of common shares outstanding}}$	A measure of the discretionary funds over and above expenses available for use by the firm.
5. Break-even analysis	$\dfrac{\text{Fixed costs}}{\text{Contribution margin/unit (selling price/unit} - \text{variable cost/unit)}}$	A measure of how many units need to be sold to begin to make a profit; to demonstrate the relationship of revenue, expenses, and net income.

Note: Industry-average ratios against which a particular company's ratios may be judged are available in:
1. Statistics Canada, Corporation Financial Statistics (15 ratios for 182 industries).
2. *Key Business Ratios*, published by Dun and Bradstreet Canada (11 ratios for 166 lines of business).
3. *Market Research Handbook*, published by Statistics Canada (7 ratios for 17 industries).

In writing your analysis and evaluation, bear in mind:

1. You are obliged to offer supporting evidence for your views and judgments. Do not rely upon unsupported opinions, overgeneralizations, and platitudes as a substitute for tight, logical argument backed up with facts and figures.

2. If your analysis involves some important quantitative calculations, then you should use tables and charts to present the data clearly and efficiently. Don't just tack the exhibits on at the end of your report and let the reader figure out what they mean and why they were included. Instead, in the body of your report, cite some of the key numbers and summarize the conclusions to be drawn from the exhibits and refer the reader to your charts and exhibits for more details.

3. You should indicate you have command of the economics of the business and the key factors which are crucial to the organization's success or failure. Check to see that your analysis does not slight what the company needs to concentrate on in order to be a higher performer.

4. Your interpretation of the evidence should be reasonable and objective. Be wary of preparing a one-sided argument which omits all aspects not favourable to

Exhibit 2–2: The SWOT Analysis—with Suggestions of What to Look for

Internal

Strengths	*Weaknesses*
A distinctive competence?	No clear strategic direction?
Adequate financial resources?	A deteriorating competitive position?
Good competitive skills?	Obsolete facilities?
Well thought of by buyers?	Subpar profitability because . . .?
An acknowledged market leader?	Lack of managerial depth and talent?
Well-conceived functional area strategies?	Missing any key skills or competences?
Access to economies of scale?	Poor track record in implementing strategy?
Insulated (at least somewhat) from strong competitive pressures?	Plagued with internal operating problems?
Proprietary technology?	Vulnerable to competitive pressures?
Cost advantages?	Falling behind in R&D?
Competitive advantages?	Too narrow a product line?
Product innovation abilities?	Weak market image?
Proven management?	Competitive disadvantages?
Other?	Below-average marketing skills?
	Unable to finance needed changes in strategy?
	Other?

External

Opportunities	*Threats*
Serve additional customer groups?	Likely entry of new competitors?
Enter new markets or segments?	Rising sales of substitute products?
Expand product line to meet broader range of customer needs?	Slower market growth?
Diversify into related products?	Adverse government policies?
Add complementary products?	Growing competitive pressures?
Vertical integration?	Vulnerability to recession and business cycle?
Ability to move to better strategic group?	Growing bargaining power of customers or suppliers?
Complacency among rival firms?	Changing buyer needs and tastes?
Faster market growth?	Adverse demographic changes?
Other?	Other?

your conclusion. Likewise, try not to exaggerate or overdramatize. Endeavour to inject balance into your analysis and to avoid emotional rhetoric. Strive to display good business judgment.

Discussion of Alternatives.   There are typically many more alternatives available than a cursory study of the case reveals. A thorough case analysis should include a discussion of all major alternatives. It is important that meaningful differences exist between each alternative. In addition, the discussion of alternatives must go beyond the following:

- Do nothing
- Something obviously inappropriate
- The alternative to be recommended

Exhibit 2–3: Illustrative Strategic Group Map of Competitors in the Canadian Furniture Retail Business

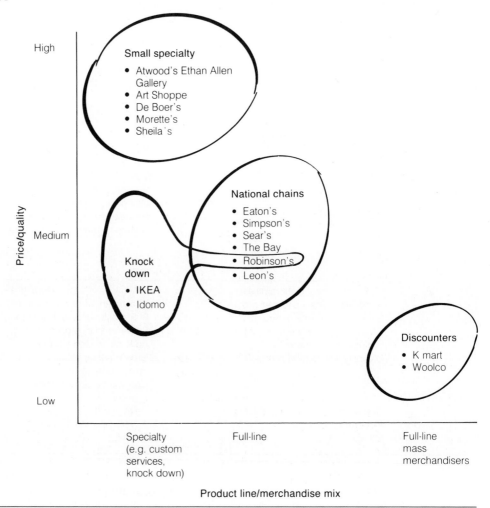

Each alternative discussed should be analyzed in terms of the associated pros and cons.

Recommendations. The final section of the written case analysis should consist of a set of definite recommendations and a plan of action. Your set of recommendations should address all of the problems/issues you identified and analyzed. If the recommendations come as a surprise or do not follow logically from the analysis, the effect is to weaken greatly your suggestions of what to do. Obviously, your recommendations for action should offer a reasonable prospect

---

Exhibit 2–4: Identifying the Pluses and Minuses in a Firm's Competitive Market Position

The Pluses	*The Minuses*
Strong in particular market segments?	Under attack from key rivals?
Rising market share?	Losing ground to rival firms because . . .?
A tough, proven competitor?	Below-average growth?
A pacesetting or distinctive strategy?	Lacks some key skills to compete effectively?
Growing customer base and customer loyalty?	Short on financial resources?
Above-average market visibility?	A slipping reputation with customers?
In a favorably situated strategic group?	Trailing in product development?
Concentrating on fastest-growing market segments?	In a strategic group that is destined to lose ground?
Strongly differentiated products?	Weak in areas where there is the most market potential?
Cost competitive?	Hard pressed to cope with competitive pressures?
Above-average profit margins?	Inadequate distribution?
Competitive advantages over leaders and key rivals?	A higher-cost producer?
Above-average marketing skills?	Too small to be a major factor in the marketplace?
Above-average technological and innovational capability?	No real distinctive competences?
A creative entrepreneurially alert management?	A relative newcomer with an unproven track record in this business?
Good market savvy?	A history of poorly timed or ill-chosen strategic moves?
Capable of capitalizing on opportunities?	Not in good position to deal with emerging threats?
Other?	Other?

---

of success. State what you think the consequences of your recommendations will be and indicate how your recommendations will solve the problems you identified. *Be sure that the company is financially able to carry out what you recommend.* Also check to see if your recommendations are workable in terms of acceptance by the persons involved, the organization's competence to implement them, and prevailing market and environmental constraints. Unless you feel justifiably *compelled* to do so, do not qualify, hedge, or weasel on the actions you believe should be taken.

Furthermore, state your recommendations in sufficient detail to be meaningful—get down to some definite nitty-gritty details. Avoid such unhelpful statements as "the organization should do more planning" or "the company should be more aggressive in marketing its product." State *specifically* what should be done and *make sure your recommendations are operational.* For instance, do not stop with saying, "The firm should improve its market position." Continue on with exactly *how* you think this should be done. And, finally, you should say something about how your plan should be implemented. Here you may wish to offer a definite agenda for action, stipulating a timetable and sequence for initiating actions, indicating priorities, and suggesting who should be responsible for doing what. For example, "Manager X should take the following steps: (1) _____, (2) _____, (3) _____, (4) _____." One way of organizing your recommendations is in a one-page summary according to the following chart:

	Do Nothing (Wait and See)	Immediate	Short Term (Specify Date)	Medium-Long Term (Specify)
Major Issues				
Minor Issues				

A key element in the recommendation summary is to assess the financial implications of each recommendation. Any proposed strategy must be feasible, which means, among other things, that the organization must be able to afford it. In addition, when there are major uncertainties, particularly in the medium to long term, contingency plans should be specified, that is, "If such and such transpires, then do X."

In preparing your plan of action, remember there is a great deal of difference between being responsible, on the one hand, for a decision which may be costly if it proves in error and, on the other hand, expressing a casual opinion as to some of the courses of action which might be taken when you do not have to bear the responsibility for any of the consequences. A good rule to follow in making your recommendations is to avoid recommending anything you would not yourself be willing to do if you were in management's shoes. The importance of learning to develop good judgment in a managerial situation is indicated by the fact that while the same information and operating data may be available to every manager or executive in an organization, the quality of the judgments about what the information means and what actions need to be taken do vary from person to person.[5] Developing good judgment is thus essential.

It should go without saying that your report should be organized and written in a manner that communicates well and is persuasive. Great ideas amount to little unless others can be convinced of their merit—this takes effective communication.

Keeping Tabs on Your Performance

Every instructor has his or her own procedure for evaluating student performance, so, with one exception, it is not possible to generalize about grades and the grading of case analyses. The one exception is that grades on case analyses (written or oral) almost never depend entirely on how you propose to solve the organization's difficulties. The important elements in evaluating student performance on case analyses consist of (*a*) the care with which facts and background knowledge are used, (*b*) demonstration of the ability to state problems and issues clearly, (*c*) the use of appropriate analytical techniques, (*d*) evidence of sound logic and argument, (*e*) consistency between analysis and recommendations, and (*f*) the ability to formulate reasonable and feasible recommendations for action. Remember, a hard-hitting, incisive, logical approach will almost always triumph over a seat-of-the-pants opinion, emotional rhetoric, and platitudes.

One final point. You may find it hard to keep a finger on the pulse of how much you are learning from cases. This contrasts with lecture/problem/discussion courses where experience has given you an intuitive feeling for how well you are acquiring substantive knowledge of theoretical concepts, problem-solving techniques, and institutional practices. But in a case course, where analytical ability and the skill of making sound judgments are less apparent, you may lack a sense of solid accomplishment, at least at first. Admittedly, additions to one's managerial skills and powers of diagnosis are not as noticeable or as tangible as a loose-leaf binder full of lecture notes. But this does not mean they are any less real or that you are making any less progress in learning how to be a manager.

To begin with, in the process of hunting around for solutions, very likely you will find that considerable knowledge about types of organizations, the nature of various businesses, the range of management practices, and so on has rubbed off. Moreover, you will be gaining a better grasp of how to evaluate risks and cope with the uncertainties of enterprise. Likewise, you will develop a sharper appreciation of both the common and the unique aspects of managerial encounters. You will become more comfortable with the processes whereby objectives are set, strategies are initiated, organizations are designed, methods of control are implemented and evaluated, performance is reappraised, and improvements are sought. Such processes are the essence of strategic management, and learning more about them through the case method is no less an achievement just because there is a dearth of finely calibrated measuring devices and authoritative crutches on which to lean.

Notes to Chapter 2

1. Charles I. Gragg, "Because Wisdom Can't Be Told," in *The Case Method at the Harvard Business School*, ed. M. P. McNair (New York: McGraw-Hill, 1954), p. 11.

2. Ibid., pp. 12–14; and D. R. Schoen and Philip A. Sprague, "What Is the Case Method?" in McNair, *The Case Method at the Harvard Business School*, pp. 78–79.

3. Schoen and Sprague, "What Is the Case Method?" p. 80.

4. For some additional ideas and viewpoints, you may wish to consult Thomas J. Raymond, "Written Analysis of Cases," in McNair, *The Case Method at the Harvard Business School*, pp. 139–63. In Raymond's article is an actual case, a sample analysis of the case, and a sample of a student's written report on the case.

5. Gragg, "Because Wisdom Can't Be Told," p. 10.

CHAPTER 3

Strategy Formulation

Making strategic decisions or choices is the critical function of the general manager. Strategic choices can be categorized in a number of ways. For example, they can relate to the extent of product line diversification, the extent of vertical integration, and the choice of cooperative strategy.

The process of making strategic decisions is known as strategy formulation. In formulating a strategy, the effective general manager makes strategic choices which are consistent with environmental threats and opportunities, organizational resources, and managerial preferences and values.

The first part of this chapter will outline in greater detail the variables of environment, resources, and preferences/values. The second part of the chapter will describe the various ways of categorizing strategic decisions.

The Influence on Strategy Formulation of Environment, Resources, and Managerial Preferences / Values

1. Environment

Six environments are of particular relevance in Canada to firms as they make strategic choices. The first is the industry environment. The key concerns in the industry environment are as follows:

   a. The elements of industry structure (see Exhibit 3–1).

   b. The stage in the life cycle of products in the industry (see Exhibit 3–2).

   c. The direction the industry is headed (for example, overcapacity, requiring rationalization).

   d. The forces (for example, political, social, economic, technological) driving the industry in a particular direction.

Exhibit 3–1: Elements of Industry Structure

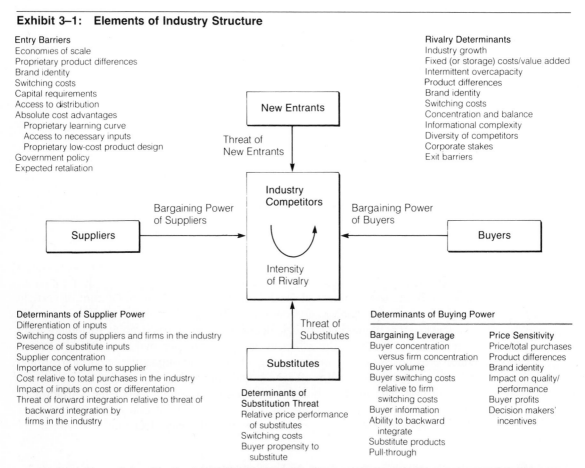

Entry Barriers
Economies of scale
Proprietary product differences
Brand identity
Switching costs
Capital requirements
Access to distribution
Absolute cost advantages
 Proprietary learning curve
 Access to necessary inputs
 Proprietary low-cost product design
Government policy
Expected retaliation

Rivalry Determinants
Industry growth
Fixed (or storage) costs/value added
Intermittent overcapacity
Product differences
Brand identity
Switching costs
Concentration and balance
Informational complexity
Diversity of competitors
Corporate stakes
Exit barriers

New Entrants

Threat of
New Entrants

Industry
Competitors

Bargaining Power
of Suppliers

Bargaining Power
of Buyers

Suppliers

Buyers

Intensity
of Rivalry

Determinants of Supplier Power
Differentiation of inputs
Switching costs of suppliers and firms in the industry
Presence of substitute inputs
Supplier concentration
Importance of volume to supplier
Cost relative to total purchases in the industry
Impact of inputs on cost or differentiation
Threat of forward integration relative to threat of
 backward integration by
 firms in the industry

Threat of
Substitutes

Substitutes

Determinants of
Substitution Threat
Relative price performance
 of substitutes
Switching costs
Buyer propensity to
 substitute

Determinants of Buying Power

Bargaining Leverage	Price Sensitivity
Buyer concentration versus firm concentration	Price/total purchases
	Product differences
Buyer volume	Brand identity
Buyer switching costs relative to firm switching costs	Impact on quality/performance
Buyer information	Buyer profits
Ability to backward integrate	Decision makers' incentives
Substitute products	
Pull-through	

 e. The underlying economics and performance of the business (for example, cost structures, profit levels).

 f. The key success factors (for example, cost, delivery).

 g. Demand segments and strategic groups (see Exhibit 2–3 for an example of strategic groups).

The first two concerns—industry structure and stage of the life cycle—require further explanation. As noted in Exhibit 3–1, each industry has a number of competitors, and their intensity of rivalry, which affects the potential for profitability, is determined by four major elements: (1) the threat of new entrants, (2) the threat of substitutes, (3) the bargaining power of buyers, (4) the bargaining power of suppliers. Each of these elements, in turn, is influenced by various

Exhibit 3–2: Product/Market Life-Cycle Stages

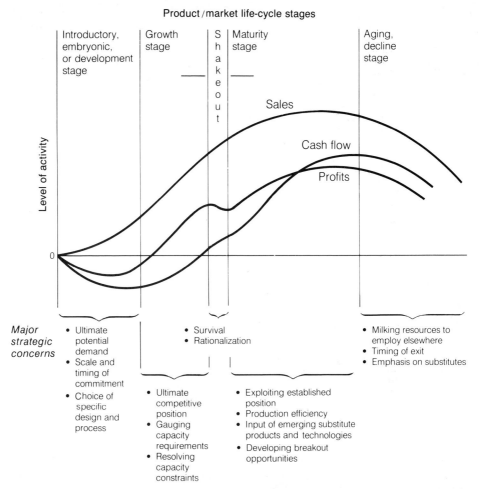

Source: Adapted with permission from L. A. Digman, *Strategic Management* (Plano, Tex.: Business Publications, 1986); and Joseph N. Fry and J. Peter Killing, *Strategic Analysis and Action* (Scarborough, Ont.: Prentice-Hall Canada, 1986).

factors as outlined in Exhibit 3–2. For example, entry barriers in the industry, which include such elements as economies of scale, determine the extent to which new entrants are a threat.

Another major element of the industry environment is the product/market life cycle which assumes that all products, and, therefore, industries, move through stages of a life cycle. The cycle begins at the development stage, moving to a growth stage, then shakeout, then maturity, and finally, the decline stage. It is important to note that while the sales of a particular product, and collectively the

Exhibit 3–3:   Some Global Canadian Firms and Their Competitors

Industry	Canadian Firm	Principal Competitors
Farm equipment	Massey-Ferguson	Deere, Komatsu, International Harvester
Telecommunications	Northern Telecom.	ITT, L. M. Ericsson, Siemens, AT&T
Mining	(1) Alcan	Alcoa, Kaiser, Alusuisse, Reynolds, Pechiney
	(2) Inco, Falconbridge	Hanna, AMAX, Western Mining Corp. Ltd.
Breweries	Labatt, Molson	Heineken, Philip Morris
Liquor	Seagram, Hiram Walker	Heublein, Brown-Forman

sales of similar products making up a particular industry, may follow these stages, the cash flow and profits are likely to follow somewhat different cycles. Furthermore, the major strategic concerns at each stage vary quite considerably. For example, at the introductory or embryonic stage, the concerns are the ultimate potential demand and the scale and timing of commitment, while at the decline stage, the concerns are milking resources to employ elsewhere, timing of a possible exit, and emphasis on substitutes.

In analyzing an industry, it is also useful to determine if the industry is a global industry, that is, an industry that requires global operations to compete effectively.[1] Firms in global industries must generally be true multinationals (that is, production and marketing in several foreign countries) in order to compete successfully. Some examples of global Canadian firms and their competitors appear in Exhibit 3–3. The firm-specific advantages of 20 large Canadian multinationals appear in Exhibit 3–4.

The second environment to consider is the competitive environment. The key concerns in the competitive environment are as follows:

a. The forces driving competition in the industry (which is a function of industry structure—see Exhibit 3–1).

b. The differences in the competitive approaches of rival firms (for example, price competition, advertising battles, increased customer service).

c. Strategies, positions, and competitive strength of market leaders and close rivals.

d. Why some rivals are doing better than others.

The third environment to consider, particularly in Canada where governments at all levels are so heavily involved in business, is the political/governmental environment.[2] This environment can have both positive and negative aspects because each of the various instruments used by government can represent an opportunity and/or threat to the firm. For example, taxes may have a negative impact when they increase input costs, whereas tax incentives may provide an opportunity when they are not available to competitors. A list of some of the various governing instruments and corresponding negative and beneficial aspects is contained in Exhibit 3–5.

Exhibit 3–4: Firm-Specific Advantages of Canadian MNEs

Firm	*Firm-Specific Advantage*
1. Abitibi-Price	World leader in newsprint sales; timberland leases; good and long-standing customer relationships.
2. Consolidated-Bathurst	Experience in the production, management, and marketing of diversified pulp and paper products; vertical integration; timberland leases.
3. Domtar	Product diversification; long-term leases and holdings of natural resources.
4. MacMillan Bloedel	Access to and control over high-quality coastal timber; vertical integration.
5. Alcan	Vertical integration; ownership of cheap hydroelectric power.
6. Inco	Quality, location, and size of proprietary mineral holdings; experience and market knowledge; cheap hydroelectric power.
7. Noranda	Ownership of mineral resources; product diversification; vertical integration; financial strength.
8. Cominco	Ownership of mineral resources; product diversification; vertical integration.
9. Seagram	Internationally recognized brand-name products; marketing; network of affiliated dealers.
10. Hiram Walker	Internationally recognized brand-name products; well-established marketing relationships with agents; ownership of oil and gas resources.
11. Molson	Brand names in beverage production; marketing expertise; product diversification into unrelated business.
12. Labatt	Brand-name beverages; marketing skills; diversification and integration into related agribusiness.
13. Northern Telecom	R&D technology in digital telephone switching equipment using semiconductors; aggressive worldwide marketing; efficient production; protected home market with Bell Canada.
14. Moore	Marketing network; innovative and adaptive to changing technology in office support systems; financial strength.
15. Massey-Ferguson	Worldwide distribution, sales and service network; well-known standardized products.
16. AMCA (Dominion Bridge)	Experience and expertise in the design, engineering, and marketing of resource-related equipment; product diversification; vertical integration.
17. Genstar	Vertical integration in construction; diversification.
18. NOVA	Provincial franchise for gas transmission; vertical integration; financial strength.
19. Bombardier	Management's ability to work with Canadian government in promoting exports; ability to obtain licenses; adoptive engineering.
20. National Sea	Leader in East Coast fishery; marketing knowledge; vertical integration.

Source: Alan M. Rugman and John McIlveen, *Mega-Firms: Profiles of Canada's 20 Most Successful Multinationals* (Toronto: Methuen Publications, 1985). Reprinted by permission.

Exhibit 3–5:   The Two Faces of Government Intervention

Governing Instrument	Negative Aspects ("Threats")	Beneficial Aspects ("Opportunities")
• Direct expenditures	• "Safety net" programs may reduce employees' incentive to work hard. • "Collective" decision making through the political process instead of decentralized decisions through markets.	• Government as a major customer (20 percent of GNP). • May obtain subsidies, grants, and other cash transfers.
• Taxes	• Depends on incidence, but likely to reduce return on capital, increase input costs, and reduce incentives to work.	• May obtain "loopholes" not available to competitors. • May obtain tariff protection.
• Regulation • Direct	• Can increase costs and restrict entry or restrict other forms of competition.	• Can benefit regulated firms by controlling competition and facilitating higher prices and returns to shareholders.
• Social	• Health, safety, and environmental regulation is likely to increase costs.	• May be exploited in a competitive context; benefits to the public may be made more apparent than real.
• Tax expenditures	• "Loopholes" will probably require higher nominal tax rates, hence require increased effort to avoid them.	• May sharply reduce effective tax rates; analogous to a subsidy.
• Loans and loan guarantees	• May not be able to obtain same benefits as competitors.	• May obtain capital below market rates (effectively a subsidy).
• Equity interests (mixed enterprises)	• May require firm to achieve social objectives that reduce profitability.	• May be passive investor interested only in financial returns. • Government board members may provide "inside information" on government plans/behaviour.
• Crown corporations	• May be an "unfair" competitor (almost infinite financial resources and access to inside information).	• Potential customer with a "deep pocket." • Sell out at a more favourable price (bail out).
• Suasion	• Need to alter economic behavior involuntarily in face of positive or negative inducements from government, yet no legislative action, that is, legitimate coercion.	• May forestall more-coercive, less-flexible forms of action; acquiescence may be based on a future quid pro quo.
• Chosen instruments*	• May not be able to obtain same benefits as competitors.	• Could obtain a variety of benefits such as sole source procurement by government, cheap loans/guarantees, R&D grants, special tax concessions, and so on. • A firm may be able to "choose the government" (for example, Dome Petroleum and Nova Corp.) and benefit greatly.

* See J. L. Howard and W. T. Stanbury, "Measuring Leviathan: The Size, Scope and Growth of Government in Canada," in *Probing Leviathan: An Investigation of Government in the Economy*, ed. George Lermer (Vancouver: The Fraser Institute, 1984), chap. 4 and appendix.

Source: W. T. Stanbury, *Business-Government Relations in Canada* (Toronto: Methuen Publications, 1986), pp. 78–79. Reprinted by permission.

Exhibit 3–6: Schematic Outline of Political Strategy Formulation

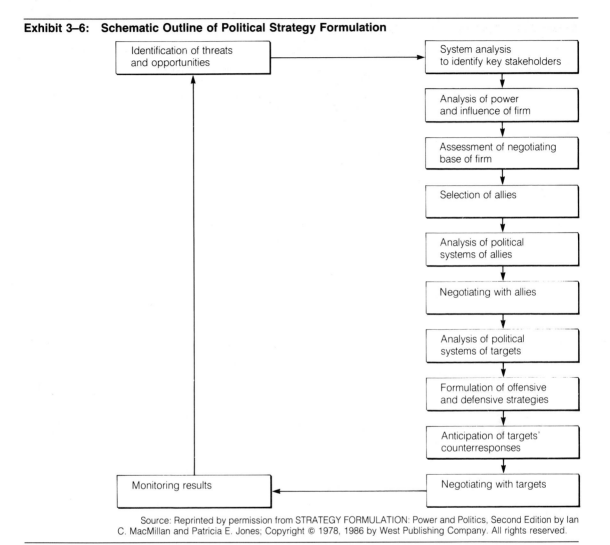

Because of the ongoing threats and opportunities in the Canadian political/governmental environment, it is important that Canadian general managers formulate a political strategy. The first step is to undertake a systems analysis to identify the key stakeholders influencing the various political/governmental threats and opportunities. The remaining steps are presented in Exhibit 3–6.

The fourth and fifth environments are the social and technological environments.[3] The social environment focuses on demographics (e.g., population growth rates), life-styles, and social values. The technological environment involves the institutions and activities related to the creation of new knowledge and the translation of new knowledge into products, processes, or materials.

Exhibit 3–7:   Differences between the Domestic and International Environments

Domestic	*International*
1. Single currency.	1. Currencies differing in stability and value.
2. Uniform financial and business climate.	2. Variety of economic climates.
3. Relatively homogeneous market.	3. Fragmented and diverse markets.
4. Uniform legal and accounting framework.	4. Diverse legal and accounting framework.
5. Relatively stable political climate.	5. Political change is often discontinuous.
6. Cultural mores and values are relatively well understood.	6. Cultural values and mores must be identified and understood.
7. Data are available and collection is relatively easy.	7. Collection of accurate data is a formidable task.

Source: Adapted from William W. Cain, "International Planning: Mission Impossible," *Columbia Journal of World Business* 5, no. 4 (July–August 1970), p. 58; and Steven Globerman, *Fundamentals of International Business Management* (Englewood Cliffs, N.J.: Prentice-Hall, 1986), p. 18. Reprinted by permission.

The sixth and final environment relevant to firms in Canada is the international environment. Given Canada's open economy, high levels of foreign ownership, and relatively small domestic market, Canadian firms, as seen in many of the cases in this book, are forced to be aware of the trends and market opportunities in countries outside Canada, particularly the United States. Some of the major differences between the environment in Canada and the international environment are presented in Exhibit 3–7.

There are, then, at least six environments which are important to strategic decision making in Canada: (1) industry, (2) competitive, (3) political/governmental, (4) social, (5) technological, and (6) international. Each of these must be considered in making strategic choices since analysis of these environments will indicate various opportunities and threats facing the organization. The objective in assessing the various environments is to formulate a strategy which best fits these environments. This is an ongoing challenge given that environments change continually.

2.   Resources

In identifying and assessing the resources of an organization, the first task is to determine if the organization has developed a distinctive competence, that is, something that it does particularly well. A distinctive competence might be greater proficiency in product development, an ability to respond quickly to changing customer requirements, or status as low-cost producer. Distinctive competences are typically consciously developed and may require special organization-building actions to nurture.

The second task concerning resources is to identify the nature of the resources in the organization, using the following categories:

a. Financial.

b. Manufacturing.

c. Marketing.

d. Technological.

e. Market position.

f. Managerial.

Once these resources are identified, various strategic possibilities can be assessed. The objective in this assessment is to achieve some harmony or "fit" between the resource requirements of the chosen strategy and the resources available. In attempting to achieve this fit, various strengths and weaknesses of the resource base of the firm in question can be identified *relative to* particular strategic alternatives. In other words, the resource base of a firm is a relative concept in strategic management. Resources can really be assessed only *in relation to* a particular strategy.

In assessing a resource base, a useful task is to determine if the firm's resource base is essentially narrow/specialized, that is, not easily transferred to other corporate situations (for example, specialized production skills) or is wide and easily transferred (for example, cash or sales staff with knowledge of many different products).

The key questions in examining a firm's resources are:

1. Is the firm successful because of some special resource or set of resources which can be described as the firm's distinctive competence?
2. What are the resource requirements of the firm's existing strategy, and are these currently available?
3. What are the resource requirements of various strategic alternatives, and how do these requirements compare to available resources?
4. Is the existing resource base narrow or wide?
5. How do the resources in the firm hinder or open up strategic possibilities?

3. Managerial Preference / Values

The final variable to consider in strategy formulation is managerial preferences and values. These preferences and values are derived from a manager's personal needs, beliefs, attitudes, and ethics. Because of differences in these personal attributes, different managers are likely to assess the same strategic alternative in different ways. For example, one manager who is particularly ambitious, with a strong need for power, is likely to support an expansionary move that another less-ambitious manager would not support. These differences in values and preferences can lead to major conflicts among key managers, so that the final strategic choice is frequently a negotiated compromise.

A variable related to managerial preferences and values is organizational "culture," sometimes called atmosphere. When a certain set of individual beliefs, attitudes, and expectations about company activities or guiding principles are shared widely in an organization, an identifiable organization culture or atmosphere has been established.

Because a culture, once set, is so pervasive and not easily changed, it is important that it be consistent with the organization's strategies. "A corporation's culture can be its major strength when it is consistent with its strategies."[4] The reverse is also true—a culture can be a major problem if it needs to be changed to conform to a new, more-appropriate strategy.

In summary, both managerial preferences and values, and culture should be consistent with an organization's strategy. When this is not the case, the general manager's job can be extremely difficult.

Categorizing Strategic Decisions

Having now described the key variables—environment, resources, managerial preferences, and values—that general managers must consider in making strategic choices, the next task is to describe the major ways of categorizing these strategic choices. The basic categories are as follows:

1. Product line diversification.

2. Extent of vertical integration.

3. Cooperative approaches.

4. Generic approaches.

5. Turnaround approaches.

Each of these categories will now be explained in greater detail.

1.   Product Line Diversification

Based on the extent of product line diversification, Wrigley identified the following four categories of firms: single product, dominant product, related product, and unrelated product. Each category represented a distinct corporate strategy, with measurable differences between each type in terms of their deviation from an original product technology or marketing emphasis.

In turn, the original product technology or marketing emphasis suggests an underlying skill base within the firm. This skill base or "core skill" was defined by Wrigley as "the collective knowledge, skills, habits of working together, as well as the collective experience of what the market will bear, that is required in the cadre of managerial and technical personnel if the firm is to survive and grow in a competitive market."[5]

Wrigley's four categories of firms were subsequently subdivided by Rumelt into a total of nine types (see Exhibit 3–8 for definitions of each and Exhibit 3–9

Exhibit 3–8: Definitions of Firm's Diversification Strategies

1. Single business: Firms that are basically committed to a single business in a single industry ($R_S > .95$).

2. Dominant business: Firms that have diversified to some extent but still obtain the preponderance of their revenues from a single business in a single industry ($.95 > R_S > .70$).

   a. Dominant-vertical: Vertically integrated dominant firms.

   b. Dominant-constrained: Nonvertical dominant firms that have diversified by building on some particular strength; their activities are strongly related.

   c. Dominant-linked: Nonvertical dominant firms that have diversified by building on several different strengths; activities are not closely related but are still linked to their dominant business.

   d. Dominant-unrelated: Nonvertical dominant firms whose diversified activities are not linked to their dominant business.

3. Related business:* Nonvertically integrated diversified firms operating in several industries but whose activities are linked ($R_S < .70$ and $R_r > .70$).

   a. Related-constrained: Related firms, all of whose activities are related to a central strength.

   b. Related-linked: Related firms that have diversified using several different strengths and hence are active in widely disparate businesses.

4. Unrelated business:† Nonvertical firms that have diversified without regard to the relationships between new business and current activities ($R_r < .70$ and $R_S > .70$).

   a. Unrelated passive: Unrelated business firms that do not qualify as active conglomerates (see definition below).

   b. Active conglomerates: Firms that have made at least five acquisitions in the past five years, of which at least three were unrelated to past activities.

Notes: R_S: Specialization ratio—proportion of a firm's revenues attributable to its largest single business in a given year.
R_r: Related ratio—proportion of a firm's revenues attributable to its largest group of related business.
* Related diversification has also been described as concentric diversification.
† Unrelated diversification has also been described as conglomerate diversification.
Source: Leonard Wrigley, "Divisional Autonomy and Diversification" (Doctoral dissertation, Harvard University, 1970).

for examples), each of which was then related to performance. Significantly, firms adopting a single-business, dominant-constrained, related-constrained or active-conglomerate strategy were observed to have above-average profitability. This held true in both a domestic (United States, Canada) and international (United States multinational, European multinational) context. These results are summarized in Exhibit 3–10.

The higher performance associated with firms having a single-product, dominant-constrained, or related-constrained product diversification is intuitively consistent with the "core skill" concept. It has been frequently emphasized that successful firms "stick to their knitting."[6] The above-average profitability associated with active conglomerates—the exception to the core skill concept—must

Exhibit 3–9: Examples of Different Product Diversification Strategies

Company	Diversification Strategy	Product Sales Breakdown in 1978		Percentage
1. Texaco	Single	Petroleum, natural gas		98%
		Petrochemicals		2
2. Exxon	Dominant vertical	Petroleum, natural gas		93
		Petroleum products	71%	
		Crude oil	16	
		Natural gas	3	
		Other	3	
		Chemical and other		7
3. IBM	Dominant constrained	Data processing		81
		Equipment	28	
		Retail and service	41	
		Service products	12	
		Office products		16
		Sales	9	
		Rentals	7	
		Other		3
4. Coca-Cola	Dominant linked	Soft drinks		76
		Other industries		24
5. Ford Motor	Dominant unrelated	Automotive		94
		Other industries		6
6. Honeywell	Related constrained	Information systems		37
		Environmental systems		25
		Industrial systems		20
		Aerospace		18
7. Du Pont	Related linked	CPS products		67
		Chemical	17	
		Plastic	22	
		Specialty	28	
		Fibers		33
8. Union Carbide	Unrelated passive	Chemicals		37
		Metals and carbon		18
		Batteries and auto products		17
		Gases and related products		16
		Specialty		12
9. Colgate-Palmolive	Active conglomerate	Household and personal care		68
		Food		14
		Health care		12
		Sports and other		6

be understood in their portfolio nature. Here, unrelated-product firms are actively bought and sold primarily on the basis of their short-term financial contribution to overall corporate profits. There are important implications for general managers of differences in the profitability levels associated with the degree of product diversification. Internally, whether a firm is considering an acquisition, a merger,

Exhibit 3–10: Comparison of Profitability by Diversification Strategy

Diversification Classification	Large U.S. Firms 1970			Top 200 Publicly Held Canadian Firms 1960–1975			Largest European MNEs 1970–1979			Largest U.S. MNEs 1970–1979		
	ROE*	Cases	Percent	ROE	Cases	Percent	ROE	Cases	Percent	ROE	Cases	Percent
Single product	13.20	11	6.2%	10.50	28	14%	—	0	0%	12.74	1	2%
Dominant (total)	11.34	54	29.2	8.44	82	41	8.74	10	20	13.37	21	42
Vertical	10.18	29	15.6	7.10	26	13	9.47	7	14	12.45	14	28
Constrained	14.91	13	7.1	11.20	16	8	—	0	0	14.58	5	10
Linked	10.28	10	5.6	8.90	20	10	7.05	3	6	21.47	1	2
Unrelated	10.28	2	0.9	7.50	20	10	—	0	0	12.21	1	2
Related (total)	13.16	83	45.2	8.13	56	28	8.09	27	54	11.96	20	40
Constrained	14.11	40	21.6	11.20	16	8	11.43	3	6	12.83	7	14
Linked	12.28	43	23.6	6.90	40	20	7.67	24	48	11.49	13	26
Unrelated (total)	11.94	35	19.4	7.10	34†	17	8.63	13	26	14.54	8	16
Passive	10.38	15	8.5	N/A	N/A	N/A	8.08	11	22	17.30‡	3	6
Active conglomerate	13.13	20	10.9	N/A	N/A	N/A	11.63	2	4	12.87	5	10
Total	12.38	183	100%	8.41	200	100%	8.36	50	100%	12.98	50	100%

* Return on equity (ROE) is defined as net income after taxes divided by the value of stockholders' equity.
† RCCC considered the unrelated category as one unit.
‡ This total is distorted by the inclusion of American Home Products which had an ROE of 28.02 percent, the highest of the 100 MNEs. Their previous classification would have been active conglomerate; however, for the past five years they have been consolidating their holdings.

Source: Paul W. Beamish and Richard C. DaCosta. "Factors Affecting the Comparative Performance of Multinational Enterprises" (European International Business Association Conference Proceedings, Rotterdam, Holland, 1984).

Data sources: Rumelt (1974) for 1970 U.S. sample. Richard Rumelt, *Strategy, Structure and Economic Performance* (Boston: Harvard University Press, 1974). Royal Commission on Corporate Concentration (RCCC) (1978) for Canadian sample. *Report of the Royal Commission on Corporate Concentration* (Hull, Quebec: Supply and Services Canada, 1978).

Stopford, Dunning, and Haberich (1981) for 1970–79 MNE samples. John M. Stopford, John H. Dunning, and Klaus D. Haberich, *The World Directory of Multinational Enterprises 1978–79* (Detroit: Gale Research Co., 1981).

or simply a change in product emphasis, the likely impact of the change upon profits can be now better assessed. External to the firm, product diversification strategy represents another tool which bankers, accountants, and investment dealers can use to assist them in assessing a firm's future profitability.

2. Extent of Vertical Integration

Each organization must choose the extent to which it (*a*) integrates backward to the original supplier of goods or services and (*b*) integrates forward to the ultimate customer. The greater the number of stages of integration an organization encompasses, the greater the number of strategic options it can subsequently develop or drop.

Some advantages of further vertical integration are typically to reduce vulnerability by securing supply and/or markets or to reduce transaction costs and absorb more of the value in the chain of stages of integration. In general, vertical integration helps a business to protect profit margins and market share by ensuring access to consumers or material inputs.

Some of the advantages and disadvantages of vertical integration are summarized in Exhibit 3–11.

3. Cooperative Strategies

One of the predominant trends in the past decade has been the increased use of cooperative strategies. Whether in the domestic or international market, more frequent use of joint ventures, licensing, countertrade, and technology/R&D collaboration has been observed. Characterizing these collaborative arrangements has been a willingness to either share, or split, managerial control in a particular undertaking.

A number of opportunities for sharing can come from a cooperative strategy. A detailed analysis of three of these opportunities—market related, operating, and management—is contained in Exhibit 3–12. As noted in this exhibit, a number of potential competitive advantages are associated with each type of opportunity for sharing, and a number of impediments can make the fit more illusory than real. Yet, a recent trend is the increase in cooperative arrangements between hitherto competing organizations.

A number of the cases in this book provide specific examples of cooperative strategies. These include cases on licensing (Note on Licensing, RM Industries, Patent Protection), countertrade (Raytheon), joint ventures (Redpath, Abbott, Magna), co-tenancy agreements (Canada Coke), cooperatives (Ontario Flower Growers), and technology sharing (IKEA).

The existence of so many potential cooperative strategies dramatically increases the opportunities available to Canadian businesses. Certainly there are conditions, however, which would suggest the use of one form over another.

Exhibit 3–11:   Some Advantages and Disadvantages of Vertical Integration

Advantages	*Disadvantages*
Internal benefits:	**Internal costs:**
Integration economies reduce costs by eliminating steps, reducing duplicate overhead, and cutting costs (technology dependent).	Need for overhead to coordinate vertical integration increases costs.
Improved coordination of activities reduces inventorying and other costs.	Burden of excess capacity from unevenly balanced minimum-efficient-scale plants (technology-dependent).
Avoid time-consuming tasks, such as price shopping, communicating design details, or negotiating contracts.	Poorly organized vertically integrated firms do not enjoy synergies that compensate for higher costs.
Competitive benefits:	**Competitive dangers:**
Avoid foreclosure to inputs, services, or markets.	Obsolete processes may be perpetuated.
Improved marketing or technological intelligence.	Creates mobility (or exit) barriers.
Opportunity to create product differentiation (increased value-added).	Links firm to sick adjacent businesses.
Superior control of firm's economic environment (market power).	Lose access to information from suppliers or distributors.
Create credibility for new products.	Synergies created through vertical integration may be overrated.
Synergies could be created by coordinating vertical activities skillfully.	Managers integrated before thinking through the most appropriate way to do so.

Source: Reprinted by permission of the publisher, from STRATEGIC FLEXIBILITY: A MANAGEMENT GUIDE FOR CHANGING TIMES by Kathryn Rudie Harrigan (Lexington, Mass.: Lexington Books, D. C. Heath and Company, Copyright 1985, D. C. Heath and Company).

Some of the considerations before deciding on the form of cooperation would include assessments of:

— Level of risk.
— Synergies/complementary skills to be gained (see Exhibit 3–12).
— Regulations influencing type of involvement.
— Managerial and financial resources available to go it alone.
— Speed of innovation required.

Exhibit 3–12: Opportunities for Adopting Cooperative Strategies

Types of Strategic Fit and Opportunities for Sharing	Potential Competitive Advantages	Impediments that Can Make Fit More Illusory than Real
Market-related strategic fits:		
Shared sales force activites and/or shared sales offices	• Lower selling costs. • Better market coverage. • Stronger technical advice to buyers. • Enhanced buyer convenience (can single source). • Improved access to buyers (have more products to sell).	• Buyers have different purchasing habits toward the products. • Different salespersons are more effective in representing the product. • Some products get more attention than others. • Buyers prefer to multiple source rather than single source their purchases.
Shared after-the-sale service and repair work	• Lower servicing costs. • Better utilization of service personnel (less idle time). • Faster servicing of customer calls.	• Different equipment and/or different labor skills are needed to handle repairs. • Buyers may do some in-house repairs.
Shared brand name	• Stronger brand image and company reputation. • Increased buyer confidence in the brand.	• Hurts reputation if quality of one product is lower.
Shared advertising and promotional activities	• Lower costs. • Greater clout in purchasing ads.	• Appropriate forms of messages are different. • Appropriate timing of promotions is different.
Common distribution channels	• Lower distribution costs. • Enhanced bargaining power with distributors and retailers to gain shelf space, shelf positioning, stronger push and more dealer attention, and better profit margins.	• Dealers resist being dominated by a single supplier and turn to multiple sources and lines. • Heavy use of the shared channel erodes willingness of other channels to carry or push the firm's products.
Shared order processing	• Lower order processing costs. • One-stop shopping for buyer enhances service and thus differentiation.	• Differences in ordering cycles disrupt order processing economies.
Operating fits:		
Joint procurement of purchased inputs	• Lower input costs. • Improved input quality. • Improved service from suppliers.	• Input needs are different in terms of quality or other specifications. • Inputs are needed at different plant locations, and centralized purchasing is not responsive to separate needs of each plant.

Exhibit 3–12 (*concluded*)

Types of Strategic Fit and Opportunities for Sharing	Potential Competitive Advantages	Impediments that Can Make Fit More Illusory than Real
Shared manufacturing and assembly facilities	• Lower manufacturing/assembly costs. • Better capacity utilization because peak demand for one product correlates with valley demand for other. • Bigger scale of operation improves access to better technology and results in better quality.	• Higher changeover costs in shifting from one product to another. • High cost special tooling or equipment is required to accommodate quality differences or design differences.
Shared inbound and/or outbound shipping and materials handling	• Lower freight and handling costs. • Better delivery reliability. • More frequent deliveries such that inventory costs are reduced.	• Input sources and/or plant locations are in different geographic areas. • Needs for frequency and reliability of inbound/outbound delivery differ among the business units.
Shared product and/or process technologies and/or technology development	• Lower product and/or process design costs because of shorter design times and transfers of knowledge from area to area. • More innovative ability, owing to scale of effort and attraction of better R&D personnel.	• Technologies are same, but the applications in different business units are different enough to prevent much sharing of real value.
Shared administrative support activities	• Lower administrative and operating overhead costs.	• Support activities are not a large proportion of cost, and sharing has little cost impact (and virtually no differentiation impact).
Management fits: Shared management know-how, operating skills, and proprietary information	• Efficient transfer of a distinctive competence—can create cost savings or enhance differentiation. • More-effective management as concerns strategy formulation, strategy implementation, and understanding of key success factors.	• Actual transfer of know-how is costly and/or stretches the key skill personnel too thinly. • Increased risks that proprietary information will leak out.

Source: Adapted with permission of The Free Press, a Division of Macmillan, Inc. from COMPETITIVE ADVANTAGE: Creating and Sustaining Superior Performance by Michael E. Porter. Copyright © 1985 by Michael E. Porter.

4. Generic Approaches

Following from the work of Michael Porter amongst others,[7] strategies can be viewed broadly as falling into one of the three following categories: (1) overall cost leadership, where the firm strives to be overall cost leader in the industry by using a range of functional policies compatible with industry economics; (2) differentiation, where the firm strives to be distinctive across the industry in some aspect of its products or services that is of value to the customer, such as quality or style; (3) focus, where a firm concentrates its efforts at serving a distinctively defined market segment, which may include some combination of a portion of a product line, particular customer segment, limited geographic area, or particular distribution channel. The firm choosing a focus or niche strategy may be able to achieve either or both of cost leadership or differentiation; however, it is unable to be the low cost producer or differentiated across the entire industry.

Each of the three generic strategies involves risks. Cost leadership is vulnerable to limitation by competitors or technology changes (for example, "technological leapfrogging"). Differentiation will not be sustained if the bases for differentiation become less important to buyers or competitors imitate. A focus strategy is vulnerable to imitation, or the target segment can become unattractive if demand disappears or if broadly targeted competitors overwhelm the segment.

5. Turnaround Approaches

When a business is in trouble—whether it be the result of such factors as strong competition, technological turbulence, or escalating interest rates—a different set of strategic choices faces the general manager. An attempt can be made to turn the business around, or the business can be immediately divested or liquidated. The business can also be "harvested," which involves optimizing cash flows through such tactics as curtailing all new investments, cutting advertising expenditures, or increasing prices, until the business is sold or liquidated.

The decision of whether to attempt a turnaround depends on the kind of turnaround strategy which is likely to be successful and then whether the firm is willing to bear the risks, devote the resources, and make the management commitment associated with this particular turnaround strategy.

Turnaround strategies can be classified as follows:[8]

A. Efficiency oriented

— Asset reduction (for example, disposal of assets).
— Cost cutting (for example, cutbacks in administrative R&D, marketing expenses).

B. Entrepreneurial oriented

— Revenue generation (for example, increase sales by product reintroduction, increased advertising, increased selling effort, lower prices).
— Product/market refocusing (for example, shift emphasis into defensible or lucrative niches).

Turnarounds can follow definite stages as follows: (1) change in management, (2) evaluation, (3) emergency, to "stop the bleeding" or "unload," (4) stabilization, emphasizing organization, that is, building, (5) return-to-normal growth.

Combining Strategic Categories

While there are a number of basic strategic choices facing general managers, some analysts have combined these choices. For example, strategic choices have been categorized according to the firm's competitive position and market growth to

Exhibit 3–13: Model of Grand Strategy Clusters

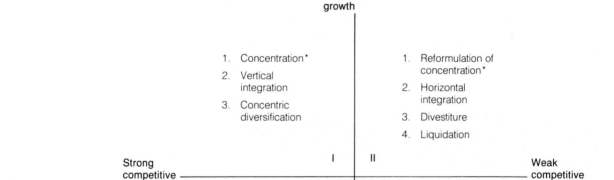

Rapid market growth

I
1. Concentration*
2. Vertical integration
3. Concentric diversification

II
1. Reformulation of concentration*
2. Horizontal integration
3. Divestiture
4. Liquidation

Strong competitive position — — — Weak competitive position

III
1. Concentric diversification
2. Conglomerate diversification
3. Joint ventures

IV
1. Turnaround or retrenchment
2. Concentric diversification
3. Conglomerate diversification
4. Divestiture
5. Liquidation

Slow market growth

Note: The grand strategy of innovation was omitted from this model. Grand strategies are listed in probable order of attractiveness.

*In this model, the grand strategy of concentration was meant to encompass market development and product development.

Source: Adapted from Arthur A. Thompson, Jr., and A. J. Strickland III, *Strategic Management: Concepts and Cases*, 3rd ed. (Plano, Tex.: Business Publications, 1984), p. 97; and John A. Pearce II and Richard B. Robinson, Jr., *Strategic Management: Strategy Formulation and Implementation*, 2nd ed. (Homewood, Ill.: Richard D. Irwin, 1985), p. 264. Reprinted by permission.

form "grand strategy clusters." One model of grand strategy clusters is presented in Exhibit 3–13.

Firms in quadrant I are in an excellent strategic position; their strategic alternatives are continued concentration on the existing business, vertical integration (particularly if there are excess resources), or a strategy known as concentric diversification, that is, adding businesses related to the firm in terms of technology, markets, or products.

Firms in quadrant II, that is, firms in a weak competitive position but in a rapid growth market, face four strategic alternatives: (1) formulation or reformulation of a concentration strategy, (2) horizontal integration, (3) divestiture, or (4) liquidation.

Firms in quadrant III, that is, firms in a weak competitive position and in a slow growth market, face the following strategic alternatives: (1) turnaround or minimal withdrawal through retrenchment, (2) concentric or conglomerate diversification, that is, adding related or unrelated businesses, (3) divestiture, or (4) liquidation.

Firms in quadrant IV, that is, firms in a strong competitive position in a slow-growth market, need to consider (1) diversification, either related or nonrelated, or (2) joint ventures.

In addition to classifying strategic choices into clusters, based on market growth and competitive position, strategic decisions have also been categorized by level, with the levels differentiated according to a wide variety of characteristics (see Exhibit 3–14). At least four levels of strategy can be identified: (1) societal, (2) corporate, (3) business, and (4) functional/operating. The characteristics which differentiate these levels vary widely as follows: (1) type of decision, (2) measurability of decision, (3) frequency of decision, (4) adaptability, (5) relation to present activities, (6) risk, (7) profit potential, (8) cost, (9) time horizon, (10) flexibility, (11) cooperation required, (12) applicability, and (13) focus.

In conclusion, there are many ways to categorize the strategic choices facing a general manager. The general manager's objective is to make choices which are most consistent with three variables: (1) environment, (2) resources, and (3) managerial preferences and values. This process can be extremely challenging given that the variables to be co-aligned are multifaceted and continually changing.

Notes to Chapter 3

1. Michael E. Porter, *Competitive Strategy: Techniques for Analyzing Industries and Competitors* (New York: Free Press, 1980), chap. 11.

2. See, for example, Mark C. Baetz and Donald H. Thain, *Canadian Cases in Business-Government Relations* (Toronto: Methuen Publications, 1985).

3. For more details on these and other dimensions of the environment, see Liam Fahey and V. K. Narayanan, *Macroenvironmental Analysis for Strategic Management* (St. Paul, Minn.: West Publishing, 1986).

Exhibit 3–14:   Characteristics of Strategic Management Decisions at Different Levels

	Level of Strategy			
Characteristic	*Societal*	*Corporate*	*Business*	*Functional/Operating*
Type of decision	Interpretive	Conceptual	Mixed	Operational
Measurability of decision	Value judgments	Value judgments dominant	Semiquantifiable	Usually quantifiable
Frequency of decision	Infrequent	Periodic or sporadic	Periodic or sporadic	Periodic
Adaptability	Low	Low	Medium	High
Relation to present activities	Wide range	Innovative	Mixed	Supplementary
Risk	Wide range	Wide range	Moderate	Low
Profit potential	Wide range	Large	Medium	Small
Cost	Major	Major	Medium	Modest
Time horizon	Long range	Long range	Medium range	Short range
Flexibility	High	High	Medium	Low
Cooperation required	High	Considerable	Moderate	Little
Applicability	All organizations	Multibusiness organizations	All organizations	All organizations
Focus	Mission, purpose, role in society	Which businesses and their interrelationships	How to compete most effectively	Functional and operational business-unit support
Examples	Which country to create employment in	Choice of business	Plant location	Inventory levels

Source: Adapted from John A. Pearce II and Richard B. Robinson, Jr., *Formulation and Implementation of Competitive Strategy*, 2nd ed. (Homewood, Ill.: Richard D. Irwin, 1985), fig. 1–2, p. 10; and Lester A. Digman, *Strategic Management* (Plano, Tex.: Business Publications, 1986), tab. 1–2, p. 27. Reprinted by permission.

4. ''Corporate Culture—The Hard-to-Change Values that Spell Success or Failure,'' *Business Week*, October 27, 1980.

5. Leonard Wrigley, ''Divisional Autonomy and Diversification'' (Doctoral dissertation, Harvard University, 1970).

6. See Thomas J. Peters and Robert H. Waterman, *In Search of Excellence* (New York: Harper & Row, 1982).

7. See Porter, *Competitive Strategy*.

8. For a more complete analysis of these turnaround strategies, see Donald C. Hambrick and Steven M. Schecter, ''Turnaround Strategies for Mature Industrial-Product Business Units,'' *Academy of Management Journal*, June 1983, pp. 231–48.

CHAPTER 4

Strategy Implementation

Once a strategy has been formulated, attention shifts to how that strategy will be implemented. As noted in Exhibit 1–9, before any strategy can be implemented, it is necessary to identify the key management tasks. But how can the key tasks be distinguished from those which are noncrucial?

Until recently, there has been little in the way of systematic means of determining key tasks. With the advent of the Value Chain as a basic tool for analyzing the sources of competitive advantage, a method is now available for determining what the key management tasks are and where in the organization those tasks must be exercised. Porter notes that:

> Competitive advantage grows fundamentally out of value a firm is able to create for its buyers that exceeds the firm's cost of creating it. . . . [The] two basic types of competitive advantage are cost leadership and differentiation. A firm can actually create and sustain a competitive advantage in its industry . . . and implement the broad generic strategies . . . by building a bridge between strategy and implementation.[1]

Identification of key management tasks through value-chain analysis is the bridge between formulation and implementation which students of strategic management can employ. In the next section, the basics of value-chain analysis are explained.

Value Chain

Value can be defined as attainable selling price and is measured by total revenue. Profits result when the attainable selling price exceeds product/service costs (that is, when a margin exists).

Not all firms strive for cost leadership in their quest for profits. Some firms emphasize differentiation as a means of achieving greater profitability. For example, automakers will deliberately add a vast array of "options" to the cars they produce in the hope that customers will pay for these high-margin items. These options will normally increase the attainable selling price (value). As a consequence, to analyze competitive position, value, not cost, must be used.

Having made this distinction between cost and value, the balance of this analysis will nonetheless focus primarily on cost since cost is the most tangible component of the value equation. Also, cost advantage is not only one of the two basic types of competitive advantage; it is also important to differentiation strategies because of the need for a differentiator to maintain cost proximity to competitors.

For a company to be competitively successful, its costs must be "in line with" those of rival producers, after taking into account, of course, that product differentiation creates justification for some cost differences. The need to be cost competitive is not so stringent as to *require* the costs of every firm in the industry to be *equal*, but as a rule, the more a firm's costs are above those of the low-cost producers, the more vulnerable its market position becomes. Given the numerous opportunities for there to be cost disparities among competing companies, it is incumbent upon firms to be alert to how their costs compare with rivals' costs and how they can remain cost competitive over the long run. This is where *strategic cost analysis* comes in.

Strategic cost analysis focuses on a firm's relative cost position vis-à-vis its rivals. The primary analytical tool of strategic cost analysis is the construction of a total industry value or *activity-cost chain* showing the makeup of costs all the way from the inception of raw materials and components production to the end price paid by ultimate customers.[2] The activity-cost chain thus includes more than just a firm's own internal cost structure; it includes the buildup of cost (and thus the "value" of the product) at each stage in the whole market chain of getting the product into the hands of the final user, as shown in Exhibit 4–1. Constructing an integrated activity-cost chain is more revealing than restricting attention to just a firm's own internal costs because a firm's overall ability to furnish end-users with its product at a competitive price can easily depend on cost factors originating either *backward* in the suppliers' portion of the activity-cost chain or *forward* in the distribution channel portion of the chain.

The task of constructing a complete cost chain is not easily accomplished. It requires breaking a firm's own historical cost accounting data out into several principle cost categories and developing cost estimates for the backward and forward channel portions of getting the product to the end-user as well. And it requires estimating the same cost elements for one's rivals and estimating their cost chains—an advanced art in competitive intelligence in itself. But despite the tedium of the task and the imprecision of some of the estimates, the payoff in exposing the cost competitiveness of one's position and the attendant strategic alternatives makes it a valuable analytical tool.

In Exhibit 4–1 observe that there are three main areas in the cost chain where important differences in the *relative* costs of competing firms can occur: in the suppliers' part of the cost chain, in their own respective activity segments, or in

Exhibit 4–1: Generic Activity—Cost Chain for a Representative Industry Situation

<--------------------------------- Total industry activity-cost chain --------------------------------->

Supplier-related activities	Manufacturing-related activities						Forward channel activities	
Collective costs attributable to supplier-related activities				Manufacturer's selling price				Price paid by/cost to the final user
Purchased materials, components, inputs, and inbound logistics	Production activities and operations	Marketing and sales activities	Customer service and outbound logistics activities	In-house staff support activities	General and administrative activities	Profit margin	Wholesale distributor and dealer network activities	Retailer activities

Specific activities and cost elements

Purchased materials, components, inputs, and inbound logistics	Production activities and operations	Marketing and sales activities	Customer service and outbound logistics activities	General and administrative activities (In-house staff support / G&A)	
Ingredient raw materials and component parts supplied by outsiders	Facilities and equipment	Sales force operations	Service reps	Payroll and benefits	Finance and accounting services
Energy	Processing	Advertising and promotion	Order processing	Recruiting and training	Legal services
Inbound shipping	Assembly and packaging	Market research	Service manuals and training	Internal communications	Public relations
Inbound materials handling	Labor	Technical literature	Spare parts	Computer services	General management
Inspection	Maintenance	Travel and entertainment	Transportation services	Procurement functions	Interest on borrowed funds
Warehousing	Process design	Dealer/distributor relations	Other outbound logistics costs	R&D	Tax-related costs
	Product design and testing		Scheduling	Safety and security	Regulatory compliance
	Quality and inspection			Supplies and equipment	
	Inventory management			Union relations	
	Internal materials handling				
	Manufacturing supervision				

Wholesale distributor and dealer network activities / Retailer activities: Includes all of the activities, associated costs, and markups of distributors, wholesale dealers, retailers, and any other forward channel allies whose efforts are utilized to get the product into the hands of end-users/customers the forward channel portion of the chain. To the extent that the reasons for a firm's lack of cost competitiveness lie either in the backward or forward sections of the cost chain, then its job of reestablishing cost competitiveness may well have to extend beyond its own in-house operations. When a firm has a cost disadvantage in the area of purchased inputs and inbound logistics, five strategic options quickly emerge for consideration:

- Negotiate more favorable prices with suppliers.
- Integrate backward to gain control over material costs.
- Try to use lower-priced substitute inputs.
- Search out sources of savings in inbound shipping and materials logistics costs.
- Try to make up the difference by initiating cost savings elsewhere in the overall cost chain.

When a firm's cost disadvantage occurs in the forward end of the cost chain, there are three corrective options:

- Push for more favorable terms with distributors and other forward channel allies.
- Change to a more-economical distribution strategy, including the possibility of forward integration.
- Try to make up the difference by initiating cost savings earlier in the cost chain.

It is likely, of course, that a substantial portion of any relative cost disadvantage lies within rival firms' own activity-cost structures. Here five options for restoring cost parity emerge:

- Initiate internal budget-tightening measures aimed at using fewer inputs to generate the desired output (cost-cutting retrenchment).
- Invest in cost-saving technological improvements.
- Innovate around the troublesome cost components as new investments are made in plant and equipment.
- Redesign the product to achieve cost reductions.
- Try to make up the internal cost disadvantage by achieving cost savings in the backward and forward portions of the cost chain.

The construction of activity-cost chains is a valuable tool for competitive diagnosis because of what it reveals about a firm's overall cost competitiveness and the relative cost positions of firms in the industry. Examining the makeup of one's own activity-cost chain and comparing it against the chains of important rival firms indicates who has how much of a cost advantage/disadvantage vis-à-vis major competitors and pinpoints which cost components in the cost chain are the source of the cost advantage or disadvantage. Strategic cost analysis adds much to the picture of the competitive environment, particularly concerning who the low-cost producers are, who is in the best position to compete on the basis of price, and who may be vulnerable to attack because of a poor relative cost position.

In summary, the specific activities and cost elements identified in Exhibit 4–1 provide much of the needed direction in determining the key tasks. In total, 46 specific items are noted. While not an all-inclusive list, it is sufficient to illustrate how key tasks can be viewed as the bridge between strategy formulation and implementation.

Organization Design Variables

With this background on how value chain analysis assists in determining the key management tasks, it is possible to move on to the major section in this chapter— organization design. As mentioned in Chapter 1, to implement any strategy, certain organizational actions must be taken. In this section, we review the major components for the design of organizations.

The major organization design variables to be used in implementing strategy are structure, information and decision processes, reward systems, and staffing and leadership style (see Exhibit 4–2).

Structure

Structure can be viewed as "the design of organization through which the enterprise is administered."[3] Structure is more than an organization chart. Here it is viewed as having three elements: division of labour (amount of role differentiation), shape (span of control and number of layers), and distribution of power (both vertical and horizontal, explicit and implicit).

Information and Decision Processes

"Across the structure, processes are overlaid to allocate resources and coordinate activities not handled by the department structure."[4] These information and decision processes include planning and control systems (for such things as budgets, schedules, and forecasts), integrating mechanisms (particularly necessary when the task context is one of high interdependence between the functional areas), and information systems (be they computerized, statistical, or informal).

Reward Systems

Perhaps the most easily understood element of organization design is reward systems. Decisions on compensation packages (however they are composed), on promotions (accompanied with any combination of such things as bigger offices, more status, a free parking space, increased holidays, a private secretary, and so forth), on ways of awarding outstanding performance, and on the design of jobs

Exhibit 4–2: Major Organization Design Variables

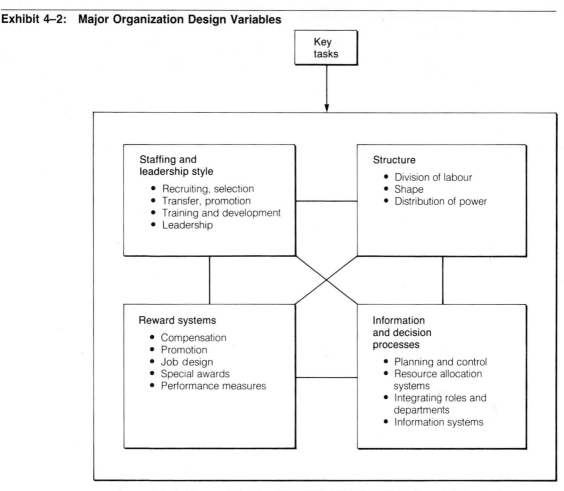

Source: Adapted by permission from STRATEGY IMPLEMENTATION, Second Edition by Galbraith and Kazanjian; Copyright © 1986 by West Publishing Company. All rights reserved. Page 115.

(and who gets the more-interesting or high-profile assignments), all can be designed in such a way as to reinforce desired behaviour.

Staffing and Leadership Style

People will make or break most organizations. Getting (recruiting, selection), grooming (training and development), and hanging on to (transfer, promotion) personnel is a critical part of every organization.

A key variable related to people is style. "Managers have personal styles of operation. They come to be identified as entrepreneurial, bureaucratic, hands on, authoritarian, or paternalistic.''[5] Since leadership styles are not easily changed, the choice of leader style is made with the choice of individual, and it is important to choose a style which fits the needs of the organization. Yet in some organizations, these style and ''people'' decisions are not given enough consideration.

Probably the greatest failing when organizations are designed is the lack of attempt at achieving consistency between (a) the organization design variables themselves and (b) those variables and the strategy as formulated. Also, if the strategy changes, all of the design variables may need to be adjusted to maintain the desired consistency and fit.

Specific examples of recommended configurations of strategy and organizational variables that constitute a fit are shown in Exhibit 4–3 for three broad strategies: single or dominant business, related diversified, and unrelated diversified.

How Structure Evolves as Strategy Evolves: The Stages Model[6]

In a number of respects, the strategist's approach to organization building is governed by the size and growth stage of the enterprise, as well as by the key success factors inherent in the organization's business. For instance, the type of organization structure that suits a small specialty steel firm relying upon a concentration strategy in a regional market is not likely to be suitable for a large, vertically integrated steel producer doing business in geographically diverse areas. The organization form that works best in a multiproduct, multitechnology, multibusiness corporation pursuing unrelated diversification is, understandably, likely to be different yet again. Recognition of this characteristic has prompted several attempts to formulate a model linking changes in organizational structure to stages in an organization's strategic development.[7]

The underpinning of the stages concept is that enterprises can be arrayed along a continuum running from very simple to very complex organizational forms and that there is a tendency for an organization to move along this continuum toward more complex forms as it grows in size, market coverage, and product-line scope and as the strategic aspects of its customer-technology-business portfolio become more intricate. Four distinct stages of strategy-related organization structure have been singled out.

Stage I. A Stage I organization is essentially a small, single-business enterprise managed by one person. The owner-entrepreneur has close daily contact with employees and each phase of operations. Most employees report directly to the owner, who makes all the pertinent decisions regarding objectives, strategy, daily operations, and so on. As a consequence, the organization's strengths, vulnerabilities, and resources are closely allied with the entrepreneur's personality, management ability and style, and personal financial situation. Not only is a Stage

Exhibit 4–3: Strategy-Organization Fit

Strategy	• Dominant business • Vertically integrated	• Unrelated diversified • Growth through acquisition	• Related diversified • Growth through internal development, some acquisition
Strategic focus and task focus	• Degree of integration • Market share • Product line breadth	• Degree of diversity • Types of business • Resource allocation across discrete businesses • Entry and exit businesses	• Realization of synergy from related products, process, technologies, markets • Resource allocation • Diversification opportunities
Structure and decision-making style	• Centralized functional • Top control of strategic decisions • Delegation of operations through plans and procedures	• Highly decentralized product divisions/profit centers • Small corporate office • No centralized line functions • Almost complete delegation of operations and strategy within existing businesses • Control through results, selection of management, and capital allocation	• Multidivisional/profit centers • Grouping of highly related business with some centralized functions within groups • Delegated responsibility for operations • Shared responsibility for strategy
Information and decision process	• Coordination and integration through structure, rules, planning, and budgeting • Use of integrating roles for project activity across functions	• No integration across businesses • Coordination and information flows between corporate and division levels around management information systems and budgets	• Coordinate and integrate across businesses and between levels with planning, integrating roles, integrating departments
Rewards	• Performance against functional objectives • Mix of objective and subjective performance measures	• Formula-based bonus on ROI or profitability of divisions • Equity rewards • Strict objective, impersonal evaluation	• Bonus based on divisional and corporate profit performance • Mix of objective and subjective performance measures
People and careers	• Primarily functional specialists • Some interfunctional movement to develop some general managers	• Aggressive, independent general managers of divisions • Career development opportunities are primarily intradivisional.	• Broad requirements for general managers and integrators • Career developments cross-functional, interdivisional, and corporate-divisional

I enterprise an extension of the interests, abilities, and limitations of its owner-entrepreneur but also its activities are typically concentrated in just one line of business. For the most part, Stage I enterprises are organized very simply with nearly all management decisions and functions being performed by the owner-entrepreneur.

Stage II. Stage II organizations differ from Stage I enterprises in one essential respect: An increased scale and scope of operations create a pervasive strategic need for management specialization and force a transition from one-person management to group management. However, a Stage II enterprise, although run by a team of managers with functionally specialized responsibilities, remains fundamentally a single-business operation. This is not to imply, though, that the categories of management specialization are uniform among large, single-business enterprises. In practice, there is wide variation. Some Stage II organizations prefer to divide strategic responsibilities along classic functional lines—marketing, production, finance, personnel, control, engineering, public relations, procurement, planning, and so on. In vertically integrated Stage II companies, the main organization units are sequenced according to the flow from one vertical stage to another. For example, the organizational building blocks of a large oil company usually consist of exploration, drilling, pipelines, refining, wholesale distribution, and retail sales. In a process-oriented Stage II company, the functional units are sequenced in order of the steps of the production process.

Stage III. Stage III embraces those organizations whose operations, though concentrated in a single field or product line, are large enough and scattered over a wide enough geographical area to justify having *geographically decentralized* operating units. These units all report to corporate headquarters and conform to corporate policies, but they are given the flexibility to tailor their unit's strategic plan to meet the specific needs of each respective geographic area. Ordinarily, each of the semiautonomous operating units of a Stage III organization is structured along functional lines.

The key difference between Stage II and Stage III, however, is that while the functional units of a Stage II organization stand or fall together (in that they are built around one business and one end market), the operating units of a Stage III firm can stand alone (or nearly so) in the sense that the operations in each geographic unit are not rigidly tied to or dependent on those in other areas. Characteristic firms in this category would be breweries, cement companies, and steel mills having production capacity and sales organizations in several geographically separate market areas.

Stage IV. Stage IV is typified by large, multiproduct, multiunit, multimarket enterprises decentralized by line of business. Their corporate strategies emphasize diversification, related and/or unrelated. As with Stage III companies, the semiautonomous operating units report to a corporate headquarters and conform to certain firmwide policies, but the divisional units pursue their own respective line-of-business strategies. Typically, each separate business unit is headed by a general manager who has profit-and-loss responsibility and whose authority extends across all of the unit's functional areas except, perhaps, accounting and capital investment (both of which are traditionally subject to corporate approval). Both business-strategy decisions and operating decisions are thus concentrated at the line-of-business level rather than at the corporate level. The organizational structure within the line-of-business unit may be along the lines of Stage I, II, or III types of organizations. A characteristic Stage IV company would be Canadian Pacific.

Movement through the Stages. The stages model provides useful insights into why organization structure tends to change in accordance with product-customer-technology relationships and new directions in corporate strategy. As firms have progressed from small, entrepreneurial enterprises following a basic concentration strategy to more complex strategic phases of volume expansion, vertical integration, geographic expansion, and line-of-business diversification, their organizational structures have evolved from unifunctional to functionally centralized to multidivisional decentralized organizational forms. Firms that remain single-line businesses almost always have some form of a centralized functional structure. Enterprises predominantly in one industry but slightly diversified typically have a hybrid structure; the dominant business is managed via a functional organization, and the diversified activities are handled through a decentralized divisionalized form. The more diversified an organization becomes, irrespective of whether the diversification is along related or unrelated lines, the more it moves toward some form of decentralized business units.

However, it is by no means imperative that organizations begin at Stage I and move in irreversible lockstep sequence toward Stage IV.[8] Some firms have moved from a Stage II organization to a Stage IV form without ever passing through Stage III. And some organizations exhibit characteristics of two or more stages simultaneously. Furthermore, some companies have found it desirable to revert to more centralized forms after decentralizing.

Still, it does appear that as the strategic emphasis shifts from a small, single-product business to large, dominant-product businesses and then on to broad diversification, a firm's organizational structure evolves, in turn, from one-person management to large group functional management to decentralized, line-of-business management. About 90 percent of the Fortune 500 firms (nearly all of which are diversified to one degree or another) have a divisionalized organizational structure with the primary basis for decentralization being line-of-business considerations.

Exhibit 4–4 summarizes some of the common organizational changes required in the transition from Stage I to Stage IV.

One final lesson that the stages model teaches is worth iterating. A reassessment of organization structure and authority is always useful whenever strategy is

Exhibit 4–4:   Common Organizational Changes Required in Transitions

	Entrepreneural Single Business Stage I	TO	Professional Single Business Stage II	TO	Professional Multibusiness Stages II and IV
Structure	Move from ill-defined functional specialization to well-articulated functions. Almost total centralization converted to substantial functional responsibility, authority. Integration by entrepreneur gives way to various integrating devices.		Move from functional to product/market (business unit) specialization. Development of corporate functions to manage business unit portfolio. Delegation of operating and some strategic discretion to units. Integration across units by corporate functions.		
Business-decision processes	Move planning and resource allocation from an extension of entrepreneurial preferences to more-objective processes. Increasing use of functional (sales, costs to budget) performance criteria.		Move planning and resource allocation focus from functional departments to business units. Strategic goals (market share, profits) used to assess and control businesses.		
Personnel-decision processes	Move to more-systematic procedures and objective criteria for staffing, training, and assessing individual performance. Rewards less subject to personal relationships, paternalism.		Further development of systematic procedures with broadening to emphasize the development of general managers. Rewards variable in relation to business unit performance.		
Leadership style	Move from a personally oriented, hands-on domination of operations to a less-obtrusive style emphasizing leadership and integration of functional units relative to strategic needs.		Senior management further distanced from operations. Symbolic and context setting aspects of style become more critical. Leadership in relation to corporate/business unit strategic needs.		

Source: Adapted from J. N. Fry and J. P. Killing, *Strategic Analysis and Action* (Scarborough, Ont.: Prentice-Hall Canada, 1986), fig. 10.8, p. 226. Used with permission.

changed.[9] A new strategy is likely to entail new or subtly different skills and key activities. If these changes go unrecognized, especially the subtle ones, the resulting mismatch between strategy and organization can pose implementation problems and curtail performance.

The Strategy-Related Pros and Cons of Alternative Organization Forms

There are essentially four strategy-related approaches to organization: (1) functional specialization, (2) geographic organization, (3) decentralized business/product divisions, and (4) matrix structures featuring *dual* lines of authority and strategic priority. Each form relates structure to strategy in a different way and, consequently, has its own set of strategy-related pros and cons.

The Functional Organization Structure

A functional organization structure tends to be effective in single-business units where key activities revolve around well-defined skills and areas of specialization. In such cases, in-depth specialization and focused concentration on performing functional area tasks and activities can enhance both operating efficiency and the development of a distinctive competence. Generally speaking, organizing by functional specialties promotes full utilization of the most up-to-date technical skills and helps a business capitalize on the efficiency gains to be had from using specialized manpower, facilities, and equipment. These are strategically important considerations for single-business organizations, dominant-product enterprises, and vertically integrated firms and account for why they usually have some kind of centralized, functionally specialized structure.

However, just what form the functional specialization will take varies according to customer-product-technology considerations. For instance, a technical instruments manufacturer may be organized around research and development, engineering, production, technical services, quality control, marketing, personnel, and finance and accounting. A municipal government may, on the other hand, be departmentalized according to purposeful function—fire, public safety, health services, water and sewer, streets, parks and recreation, and education. A university may divide up its organizational units into academic affairs, student services, alumni relations, athletics, buildings and grounds, institutional services, and budget control. Two types of functional organizational approaches are diagrammed in Exhibit 4–5.

The Achilles' heel of a functional structure is getting and keeping tight strategic coordination across the separated functional units. Functional specialists, partly because of how they were trained and the technical "mystique" of jobs, tend to develop their own mindset and ways of doing things. The more functional specialists differ in their perspectives and their approaches to task accomplishment, the more difficult it becomes to achieve both strategic and operating coordination between them. They neither "talk the same language" nor have an adequate understanding and appreciation for one another's strategic role, problems, and changed circumstances. Each functional group is more interested in its own "empire" and promoting its own strategic interest and importance (despite the lip service given to cooperation and "what's best for the company"). Tunnel vision and empire building in functional departments impose a time-consuming administrative burden on a general manager in terms of resolving cross-functional differences, enforcing joint cooperation, and opening lines of communication. In addition, a purely functional organization tends to be myopic when it comes to promoting entrepreneurial creativity, adapting quickly to major

Exhibit 4–5: Functional Organizational Structures

A. The building blocks of a "typical" functional organization structure

B. The building blocks of a process-oriented functional structure

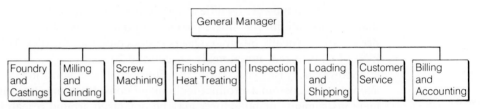

Advantages

- Enhances operating efficiency where tasks are routine and repetitive
- Preserves centralized control of strategic results
- Allows benefits of specialization and learning/experience curve effects to be fully exploited
- Simplifies training of management specialists
- Promotes high emphasis on craftsmanship and professional standards
- Well suited to developing distinctive competences in one or more functional areas
- Structure is tied to key activities within the business

Disadvantages

- Poses problems of functional coordination
- Can lead to interfunctional rivalry, conflict, and empire building
- May promote overspecialization and narrow management viewpoints
- Limited development of general managers
- Forces profit responsibility to the top
- Functional specialists often attach more importance to what is best for the functional area than to what is best for the whole business
- May lead to uneconomically small units or underutilization of specialized facilities and manpower
- Functional myopia often works against creative entrepreneurship, against adapting to change, and against attempts to restructure the activity-cost chain that threatens the status of one or more functional departments

customer-market-technological changes, and pursuing opportunities that go beyond the conventional boundaries of the industry.

Geographic Forms of Organization

Organizing according to geographic areas or territories is a rather common structural form for large-scale enterprises whose strategies need to be tailored to fit the particular needs and features of different geographical areas. As indicated in Exhibit 4–6, geographic organization has its advantages and disadvantages, but the chief reason for its popularity is that, for one reason or another, it promotes improved performance.

In the private sector, a territorial structure is typically utilized by chain store retailers, power companies, cement firms, railroads, airlines, the larger paper box and carton manufacturers, and large bakeries and dairy products enterprises. In the public sector, such organizations as the Canadian Red Cross and religious groups have adopted territorial structures in order to be directly accessible to geographically dispersed clienteles.

Decentralized Business Units

Grouping activities along business and product lines has been a clear-cut trend among diversified enterprises for the past half century, beginning with the pioneering efforts of Du Pont and General Motors in the 1920s. Separate business/product divisions emerged because diversification made a functionally specialized manager's job incredibly complex. Imagine the problems a manufacturing executive and his/her staff would have if put in charge of, say, 50 different plants using 20 different technologies to produce 30 different products in 8 different businesses/industries. In a multibusiness enterprise, the needs of strategy virtually dictate that the organizational sequence be corporate to line of business to functional area within a business rather than corporate to functional area (aggregated for all businesses). The latter produces a nightmare in making sense out of business strategy and achieving functional area coordination for a given business.

From a business strategy implementation standpoint, it is far more logical to group all the different activities that belong to the same business under one organizational roof, thereby creating line-of-business units (which, then, can be subdivided into whatever functional subunits that suit the key activities/critical tasks makeup of the business). The outcome not only is a structure which fits strategy but also a structure which makes the jobs of managers more doable. The creation of separate business units is then accomplished by decentralizing authority over the unit to the business-level manager. The approach, very simply, is to put entrepreneurially oriented general managers in charge of the business unit, giving them enough authority to formulate and implement the business

Exhibit 4–6: A Geographic Organizational Structure

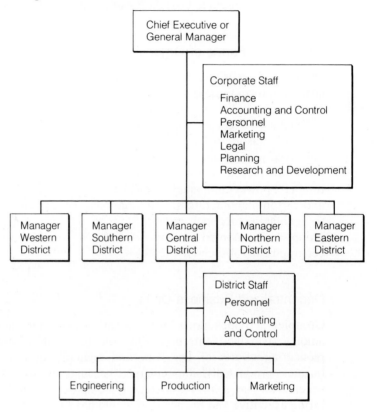

Advantages

- Allows tailoring of strategy to needs of each geographic market
- Delegates profit/loss responsibility to lowest strategic level
- Improves functional coordination within the target geographic market
- Takes advantage of economies of local operations
- Area units make an excellent training ground to higher-level general managers

Disadvantages

- Greater difficulty in maintaining consistent and uniform companywide practices
- Requires a larger management staff, especially general managers
- Leads to duplication of staff services
- Poses a problem of headquarters control over local operations

strategy that they deem appropriate, motivating them with incentives, and then holding them accountable for the results they produce. However, when strong strategic fit exists across related business units, it can be tough to get autonomy-conscious business-unit general managers to cooperate in coordinating and sharing related activities; each GM tends to want to argue long and hard about "turf" and about being held accountable for activities not totally under his/her control.

A typical line-of-business organizational structure is shown in Exhibit 4–7, along with the strategy-related pros and cons of this type of organizational form.

Matrix Forms of Organization

A matrix form of organization is a structure with two (or more) channels of command, two lines of budget authority, two sources of performance and reward, and so forth. The key feature of the matrix is that product (or business) and functional lines of authority are overlaid (to form a matrix or grid), and managerial authority over the activities in each unit/cell of the matrix is shared between the product manager and the functional manager—as shown in Exhibit 4–8. In a matrix structure, subordinates have a continuing dual assignment: to the business/product line/project and to their base function.[10] The outcome is a compromise between functional specialization (engineering, R&D, manufacturing, marketing, accounting) and product line or market segment or line-of-business specialization (where all of the specialized talents needed for the product line/market segment/line of business are assigned to the same divisional unit.)

A matrix-type organization is a genuinely different structural form and represents a "new way of life." One reason is that the unit-of-command principle is broken; two reporting channels, two bosses, and shared authority create a new kind of organizational climate. In essence, the matrix is a conflict resolution system through which strategic and operating priorities are negotiated, power is shared, and resources are allocated internally on a "strongest case for what is best overall for the unit" type basis.[11]

The impetus for matrix organizations stems from growing use of strategies that add new sources of diversity (products, customer groups, technology, lines of business) to a firm's range of activities. Out of this diversity are coming product managers, functional managers, geographic-area managers, new-venture managers, and business-level managers—all of whom have important *strategic* responsibilities. When at least two of several variables (product, customer, technology, geography, functional area, and market segment) have roughly equal strategic priorities, then a matrix theoretically can be an effective structural form. A matrix arrangement promotes internal checks and balances among competing viewpoints and perspectives, with separate managers for different dimensions of strategic initiative. A matrix approach thus allows *each* of several strategic considerations to be managed directly and to be formally represented in the organization structure. In this sense, it helps middle managers make trade-off decisions from an organizationwide perspective.[12]

Most applications of matrix organization are limited to a position of what the firm does (certain important functions) rather than spanning the whole of a large-scale diversified enterprise.

Exhibit 4–7: A Decentralized Business Division Type of Organization Structure

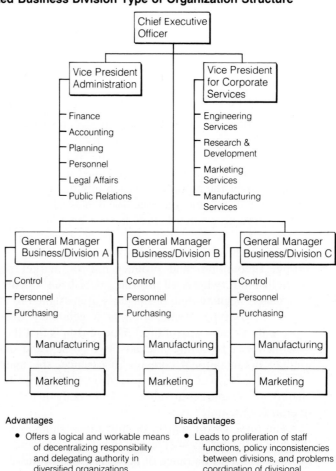

Advantages

- Offers a logical and workable means of decentralizing responsibility and delegating authority in diversified organizations

- Puts responsibility for business strategy in closer proximity to each business's unique environment

- Allows critical tasks and specialization to be organized to fit business strategy

- Frees CEO to handle corporate strategy issues

- Creates clear profit/loss accountability

Disadvantages

- Leads to proliferation of staff functions, policy inconsistencies between divisions, and problems of coordination of divisional operations

- Poses a problem of how much authority to centralize and how much to decentralize

- May lead to excessive divisional rivalry for corporate resources and attention

- Raises issue of how to allocate corporate-level overhead

- Business/division autonomy works against achieving coordination of related activities in different business units thus blocking to some extent the capture of strategic fit benefits

Exhibit 4–8: A Matrix Organization Structure

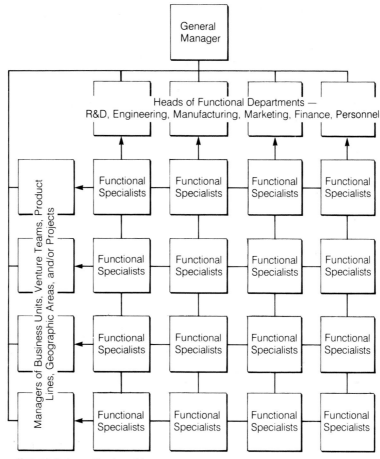

(Arrows indicate reporting channels)

Advantages	Disadvantages
• Permits more attention to each dimension of strategic priority	• Very complex to manage
• Creates checks and balances among competing viewpoints	• Hard to maintain "balance" between the two lines of authority
• Facilitates simultaneous pursuit of different types of strategic initiative	• So much shared authority can result in a transactions logjam and disproportionate amounts of time being spent on communications
• Promotes making trade-off decisions on the basis of "what's best for the organization as a whole"	• It is hard to move quickly and decisively without getting clearance from many other people
• Encourages cooperation, consensus-building, conflict resolution, and coordination of related activities	• Promotes an organizational bureaucracy and hamstrings creative entrepreneurship

A number of companies shun matrix organization because of its chief weaknesses.[13] It is a complex structure to manage; people often end up confused over to whom to report for what. Moreover, because the matrix signals that everything is important and, further, that everybody needs to communicate with everybody else, a "transactions logjam" can emerge. Actions turns into paralysis, since with shared authority, it is hard to move decisively without first considering many points of view and getting clearance from many other people. Sizable transactions costs and communications inefficiency can arise, as well as delays in responding. Even so, there are situations where the benefits of conflict resolution and consensus building outweigh these weaknesses.

Combination and Supplemental Methods of Organization

A single type of structural design is not always sufficient to meet the requirements of strategy. When this occurs, one option is to mix and blend the basic organization forms, matching structure to strategy, requirement by requirement, and unit by unit. Another is to supplement a basic organization design with special-situation devices such as project manager/project staff approaches, task force approaches, or venture teams.

Minicase: Illustration of Structure-Strategy Linkages

The following minicase can be used to assess alternative organizational structures. Suggested discussion questions follow this case.

T. G. Bright and Co., Limited—1986*

In 1977, T. G. Bright and Co., Limited (Brights) of Niagara Falls, Ontario, sold a wide range of wine products in Ontario in eight categories—sparkling, rosé, white table, port, sherry, appetizer, red table, and other (which included such diverse products as Muscatel, Mazel Tov, and sacramental wine). Through wholly owned subsidiaries, Brights also offered additional selections in many of these eight categories in other provinces.

* This case was prepared by Professor Paul W. Beamish of the School of Business and Economics, Wilfrid Laurier University, as a basis for classroom discussion. Copyright © 1986 by Paul W. Beamish.

Table 1: Percentage Share of Canadian Wine Market

	Ontario	Quebec	Rest of Country
Brights sales	55%	27%	18%
Total Canadian market	34	32	34

They were a small firm ($14 million in sales) with over half their sales volume in Ontario (see Table 1), most of their manufacturing in Ontario, and a product line which had not digressed from wine. Their 1977 organization is reflected in Figure 1.

By 1980, Brights' organization was modified to include a second regional operations manager (see Figure 2). A third production facility in Quebec had been acquired in 1979. With this acquisition, the proportion of sales in Quebec—27 percent in 1979—was expected to increase so that Brights would have the largest nongovernment operation in Quebec.

Several other organization changes were made:

1. Hatch became chairman and Arnold became president, with the position of executive vice president dropped.

2. The position of vice president, sales/marketing had been filled for a few months but of late had been vacant and was being managed by the president.

Figure 1: 1977 Organization

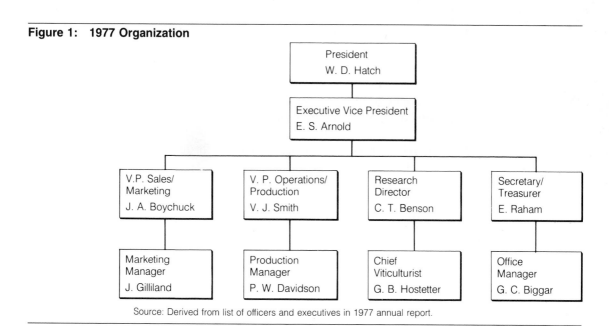

Source: Derived from list of officers and executives in 1977 annual report.

Figure 2:   1980 Organization

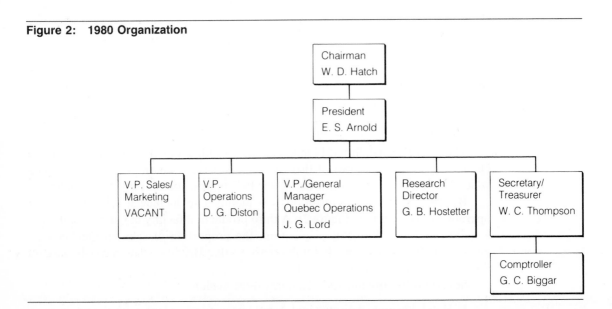

In late 1980, Brights formed a joint venture with the Inkameep Indian Band of Oliver, British Columbia, to establish a winery in B.C.'s Okanagan Valley. In 1984 and 1985, small winery operations were established in Manitoba and Nova Scotia, respectively. Sales in 1984 were nearly $38 million, net of excise and sales tax.

In 1985, a limited import operation in wines and spirits under the name of Wines of the Globe was established. (In 1984, the Province of Quebec modified its regulations to permit the bottling of imported wines by local wineries.)

Brights non-restaurant sales were through provincial government outlets, small grocery stores (in Quebec), and company-owned retail outlets. The company operated over 20 retail outlets in Ontario, with perhaps half being located in Toronto.

In order to keep pace with changing consumer tastes, Brights product mix had been steadily shifting away from fortified wines to those with lower alcohol levels. In addition, a greater proportion of sales was in white rather than red wines. With the purchase of a Quebec cider company in 1978, Brights acquired the ability and license to produce cider. Brights had also introduced a wine cooler, which combined specially fermented wine and pure spring water.

Grapes were supplied from three sources—company-owned vineyards, purchases from other grape growers, and concentrate and bulk purchases from other countries. Grapes purchased from local growers in Southern Ontario (and, to a lesser extent, the Okanagan region in B.C.) was the primary source of supply.

Figure 3: 1985 Organization

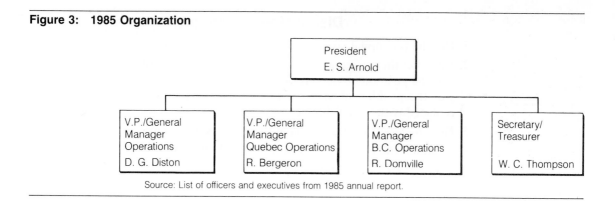

Source: List of officers and executives from 1985 annual report.

By 1985, Brights had once again modified their organization structure (see Figure 3).

The chairman, W. D. Hatch, died in 1985. The chairman's position was not reflected in the 1985 annual report list of officers and executives. In lieu of a vice president, sales/marketing, a staff director of marketing was appointed to work with the regional vice presidents. The previous vice president/general manager of Quebec Operations had left the company. His replacement held the title of vice president/general manager Eastern Division.

In 1986, W. C. Thompson resigned and G. C. Biggar became secretary. The designation for the three vice president/general managers changed from being in charge of Operations, Quebec Operations, and B. C. Operations to being in charge of the Central Division, Eastern Division, and Western Division, respectively.

Carling O'Keefe Limited, Toronto, Ontario, announced on June 26, 1986, that its wholly owned subsidiary, Jordan & Ste-Michelle Cellars Ltd., had been sold (including substantially all of its assets) to T. G. Bright and Co., Limited.

The purchase price was approximately $30 million. It was estimated that the transaction resulted in a loss to Carling O'Keefe Limited of approximately $7,750,000 after tax, or 36 cents per common share. The business had been unprofitable in 1986.

Jordan & Ste-Michelle Cellars Ltd. had wineries in St. Catharines, Ontario, and Surrey, British Columbia, and until September 1985, had operated a winery in Calgary, Alberta. Except for 33 company-operated retail stores in Ontario, all sales were made through outlets operated by provincial liquor boards. The company had recently entered into a joint venture to manufacture and distribute cider products for the U.S. market.

At the time of the sale, the gross income for Jordan & Ste-Michelle Cellars Ltd. was almost identical to that of Brights. The acquisition meant that Brights was now the largest winery in Canada by a large margin.

Discussion Questions

1. Did the functional structure make sense in 1977? If so, why?

2. Why was the position of executive vice president eliminated in 1980? Why was the position of vice president, marketing kept vacant in 1980/81? Why was the position of vice president, marketing ultimately eliminated and replaced with a staff director of marketing?

3. How big does a company have to be to justify a regional structure?

4. What alternatives are there to a regional structure in 1986? What are the pros and cons of each alternative?

5. Even with a regional structure, does this mean each regional vice president has a high degree of autonomy?

6. What kind of structure is Brights likely to have as a result of the acquisition? Subsequently?

Dealing with Significant Change

Organizations must constantly deal with change. On occasion, this change is of a significant nature; for example, a major shift in product or market emphasis, an acquisition or divestiture, or a fundamental difference in the competitive environment. Fortunately, the need for most significant change is to some extent predictable. As a result, abrupt realignments of a firm's strategy and organization are seldom required.

There is a view in some circles that change typically results primarily from a long-range planning process—a process in which a presumably omniscient strategic planner lays out precisely what is needed (see Exhibit 4–9).

Omniscience is in short supply in all organizations, and most managers will readily admit their knowledge is finite. Realistically then, planning tends to take place in a more incremental fashion.

Most good managers recognize the value of gaining practice with change through small, logical incremental steps rather than major one-time realignments. As one writer noted:

> An organization that is used to continuous small changes and that has balanced strategic expertise at the top with operating expertise and entrepreneurship at the bottom is probably better prepared for a big leap than is any organization that has gone for several years without any change at all.[14]

Further, these managers recognize that dealing with change will always create some level of stress in an organization, and too much stress all at once can be fatal. Exhibit 4–10 details some typical steps in the process of logical incrementalism. While at first glance this exhibit appears overly complicated, it is, in fact, quite straightforward. The process necessarily contains a large number of steps due to its contingent reinforcing behavioral nature. To understand the process,

Exhibit 4–9: Critical Steps in Long-Range Planning

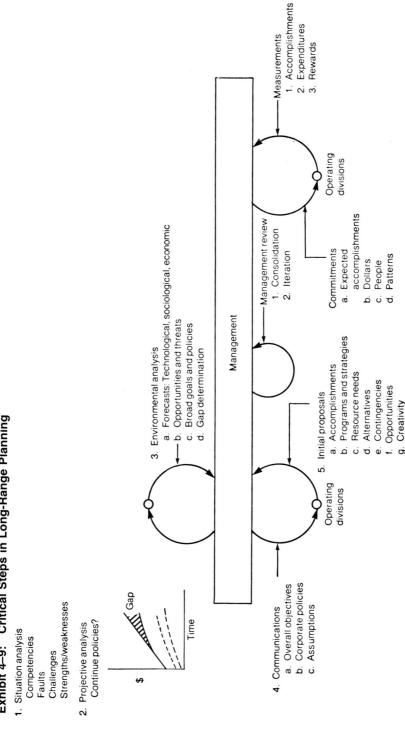

1. Situation analysis
   Competencies
   Faults
   Challenges
   Strengths/weaknesses

2. Projective analysis
   Continue policies?

3. Environmental analysis
   a. Forecasts: Technological, sociological, economic
   b. Opportunities and threats
   c. Broad goals and policies
   d. Gap determination

4. Communications
   a. Overall objectives
   b. Corporate policies
   c. Assumptions

5. Initial proposals
   a. Accomplishments
   b. Programs and strategies
   c. Resource needs
   d. Alternatives
   e. Contingencies
   f. Opportunities
   g. Creativity

Management

Management review
1. Consolidation
2. Iteration

Commitments
a. Expected accomplishments
b. Dollars
c. People
d. Patterns

Measurements
1. Accomplishments
2. Expenditures
3. Rewards

Operating divisions

Gap

Time

$

Source: James Brian Quinn, *Strategies for Change: Logical Incrementalism*, © 1980 by Richard D. Irwin, Inc. Reprinted by permission.

Exhibit 4–10: Some Typical Process Steps in Logical Incrementalism (highly simplified to help visualize a few basic relationships)

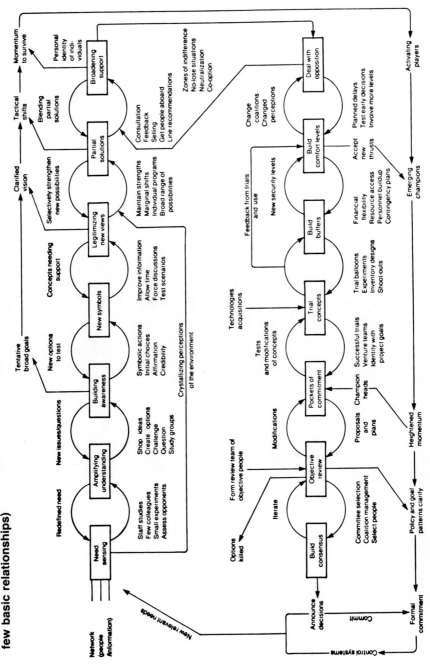

Source: James Brian Quinn, *Strategies for Change: Logical Incrementalism*, © 1980 by Richard D. Irwin, Inc. Reprinted by permission.

Exhibit 4–11: Achieving Readiness for and Implanting Strategic Change

Change Target Development	*Potential Obstacles*	*Common Management Tactics*
Awareness understanding: • Establishing a general appreciation of the need for and direction of change • Building a greater depth of knowledge of the situation, its consequences and potential remedies	• Ambiguous change requirements • Inertial resistance • Information bottlenecks • Limited capacity to understand	• Informal contact, lobbying • Loosening up exercises—target exposure, involvement • Short-term task forces
Capability: • Developing capacity to perform new tasks	• Personnel bottlenecks—inadequate training and experience • Support systems bottlenecks • Behavioral resistance	• Training programs • Support systems development • Personnel changes • Direct coaching
Commitment: • Developing genuine agreement about and support for the required changes	• Displacement of the problem • Behavioral resistance • Inadequacies, inconsistencies in support and incentive systems • Weak position of power	• Involvement activities • Partial solutions and demonstrations • Negotiations • Coalition building • Coercion • Personnel changes
Adoption: • Achieving change in behavior, effective performance	• Tangible risk • Lagging resistance, support factors • Poor readiness	• Close monitoring • Intensification and recycling of readiness efforts • Mop-up action
Reinforcement: • Sustaining effort and diligence in performing new tasks	• Loss of commitment • Resource and organizational inconsistencies	• Rewards for new behavior • Adjustment of resource and organizational factors
Recycling: • Defining and implementing improvements and new directions	• Problems in linking a series of changes • Complacency	• Training and structuring for flexibility • Continuous challenges for improvement

Source: J. N. Fry and J. P. Killing, *Strategic Analysis and Action* (Scarborough, Ont.: Prentice-Hall Canada, 1986), figs. 13.6 and 13.7. Reprinted by permission.

one need only work through it a proposed significant change such as entering a new market or entering a new business—when there is not complete agreement with the proposal initially.

Achieving readiness for strategic change requires an appreciation of the need for and direction of change, plus the development of capability and commitment.

To implant the change requires actual adoption, reinforcement, and refining. This process is usefully summarized in Exhibit 4–11, which also reviews the various obstacles at each stage and some common management tactics for dealing with the obstacles.

Notes to Chapter 4

1. Michael E. Porter, *Competitive Advantage* (New York: Free Press, 1985), p. 3.

2. The ins and outs of strategic cost analysis are discussed in greater length in Porter, *Competitive Advantage*, chap. 2. What follows is a distilled adaptation by Thompson and Strickland of the approach pioneered by Porter. See Arthur A. Thompson, Jr., and A. J. Strickland III, *Strategy Formulation and Implementation*, 3rd ed. (Plano, Tex.: Business Publications, 1986), pp. 135–37.

3. A. D. Chandler, *Strategy and Structure* (Cambridge, Mass.: MIT Press, 1962), p. 14.

4. Jay R. Galbraith and Robert K. Kazanjian, *Strategy Implementation*, 2nd ed. (St. Paul, Minn.: West Publishing, 1986), p. 114.

5. Joseph N. Fry and J. Peter Killing, *Strategic Analysis and Action* (Scarborough, Ont.: Prentice-Hall Canada, 1986), p. 202.

6. This section has been adapted from Thompson and Strickland, *Strategy Formulation and Implementation*, pp. 330–45.

7. See, for example, Malcolm S. Salter, "Stages of Corporate Development," *Journal of Business Policy* 1, no. 1 (Spring 1970), pp. 23–27; Donald H. Thain, "Stages of Corporate Development," *The Business Quarterly*, Winter 1969, pp. 32–45; Bruce R. Scott, "The Industrial State: Old Myths and New Realities," *Harvard Business Review* 51, no. 2 (March–April 1973), pp. 133–48; and Chandler, *Strategy and Structure*, chap. 1.

8. For a more thorough discussion of this point, see Salter, "Stages of Corporate Development," pp. 34–35.

9. For an excellent documentation of how a number of well-known corporations revised their organization structures to meet the needs of strategy changes and specific product/market developments, see Corey and Star, *Organization Strategy*, chap. 3. Boston: Division of Research, Harvard University Graduate School of Business Administration, 1971.

10. A more thorough treatment of matrix organizational forms can be found in Jay R. Galbraith, "Matrix Organizational Designs," *Business Horizons* 15, no. 1 (February 1971), pp. 29–40.

11. An excellent critique of matrix organizations is presented in Stanley M. Davis and Paul R. Lawrence, "Problems of Matrix Organizations," *Harvard Business Review* 56, no. 3 (May–June 1978), pp. 131–42.

12. Ibid., p. 132.

13. Thomas J. Peters and Robert H. Waterman, Jr., *In Search of Excellence* (New York: Harper & Row, 1982), pp. 306–7.

14. Robert A. Hayes, "Strategic Planning—Forward in Reverse?" *Harvard Business Review*, November–December 1985, p. 117.

CHAPTER 5

The General Manager's Role in the Implementation Process

The general manager (GM) is the person most responsible for leading and keynoting the tone, pace, and style of strategy implementation. There are many ways to proceed. The GM can opt for an active, visible role or a low-key, behind-the-scenes role. The GM can elect to make decisions authoritatively or on the basis of consensus, to delegate much or little, to be deeply involved in the details of implementation or to remain aloof from the day-to-day problems. The GM can choose whether to proceed swiftly (launching implementation initiatives on many fronts) or to move deliberately, content with gradual progress over a longer time frame. Moreover, the GM selects which of the central administrative tasks (see Exhibit 5–1) to concentrate on and why, which of the several administrative fits to work on first, and what steps to take to create the fits.

Choosing the Approach to Implementation

How the general manager goes about the implementation task is a function of his/her experience and accumulated knowledge about the business: whether the GM is new to the job or a secure incumbent; the GM's network of personal relationships with others in the organization; the GM's own diagnostic, administrative, interpersonal, and problem-solving skills; the authority that the GM has been given; and the GM's own leadership preferences for how to proceed. The remaining determinant of the GM's approach to strategy implementation is the context of the organization's situation—the seriousness of the firm's strategic difficulties, the nature and extent of the strategic change involved, the type of strategy being implemented, the strength of the ingrained behaviour patterns, the financial and organizational resources available to work with, the configuration of personal and organizational relationships that have permeated the firm's history, the pressures for short-term performance, and other such factors that make up the firm's "personality" and overall internal conditions.

Exhibit 5–1: The Administrative Aspects of Strategy Implementation

Building an Organization Capable of Carrying Out the Strategic Plan	+	*Allocating and Focusing Resources on Strategic Objectives*	+	*Galvanizing Organizationwide Commitment to the Chosen Strategic Plan*	+	*Installing Internal Administrative Support Systems*	+	*Exerting Strategic Leadership*
Key recurring issues: 1. How to match organization structure to the needs of strategy. 2. How to build and nurture a distinctive competence and to staff positions with the right talent and technical expertise. 3. What kind of core executive group is needed and whom to select for each slot.		*Key recurring issues:* 1. What budgets and programs are needed by each organizational unit to carry out its part of the strategic plan. 2. How to focus the performance of tasks on achieving organizational objectives rather than on just carrying out the assigned duties.		*Key recurring issues:* 1. How to motivate organizational units and individuals to accomplish strategy. 2. What kind of strategy-supportive work environment and corporate culture is called for. 3. How to create a results orientation and a spirit of high performance. 4. How to link the reward structure to strategic performance.		*Key recurring issues:* 1. What kinds of strategy-facilitating policies and procedures to establish. 2. How to get the right strategic information on a timely basis. 3. What "controls" are needed to keep the organization on its strategic course. 4. How to create all the helpful administrative fits.		*Key recurring issues:* 1. What leadership actions to take in shaping values, molding culture, and energizing strategy accomplishment. 2. How to keep the organization innovative, responsive, and opportunistic. 3. How to deal with the politics of strategy, cope with power struggles, and build consensus. 4. When and how to initiate corrective actions to improve strategy execution.

To some extent, therefore, each strategy implementation situation is unique enough to require the GM to custom-tailor an action agenda to fit the specific organizational environment at hand. This forces the GM to be conscious of all that strategy implementation involves and to diagnose carefully the action priorities and in what sequence things need to be done. The GM's role is thus all-important. The agenda for action and conclusions as to how hard and how fast to push for change are decisive in shaping the character of implementation and moving the process along.[1]

A strategy has not been implemented until the behavior has changed.[2] In most instances, the task of installing the new strategy and seeing the behavior of people in the organization changed is a formidable one for the GM. Yet with creativity and determination it is possible. In the balance of this chapter, we review the experiences of a Canadian management group faced with significant strategic change.

Of Boxes, Bubbles, and Effective Management*

Harvard Business Review
Soldiers Field Road
Boston, Massachusetts 02163

Dear Editors:

We are writing to tell you how events from 1979 on have forced us, a team of four general managers indistinguishable from thousands of others, to change our view of what managers should do. In 1979 we were working for Hugh Russel Inc., the 50th largest public company in Canada. Hugh Russel was an industrial distributor with some $535 million in sales and a net income of $14 million. The organization structure was conventional: 16 divisions in 4 groups, each with a group president reporting to the corporate office. Three volumes of corporate policy manuals spelled out detailed aspects of corporate life, including our corporate philosophy. In short, in 1979 our corporation was like thousands of other businesses in North America.

During 1980, however, through a series of unlikely turns, that situation changed drastically. Hugh Russel found itself acquired in a 100 percent leveraged buyout and then merged with a large, unprofitable (that's being kind!) steel fabricator, York Steel Construction, Ltd. The resulting entity was York Russel Inc., a privately held company except for the existence of some publicly owned preferred stock which obliged us to report to the public.

As members of the acquired company's corporate office, we waited nervously for the ax to fall. Nothing happened. Finally, after about six weeks, Wayne (now our president) asked the new owner if we could do anything to help the deal along. The new chairman was delighted and gave us complete access to information about the acquirer.

It soon became apparent that the acquiring organization had little management strength. The business had been run in an entrepreneurial style with hundreds of people reporting to a single autocrat. The business had, therefore, no comprehensive plan, and worse still, no money. The deal had been desperately conceived to shelter our profits from taxes and use the resulting cash flow to fund the excessive debt of the steel fabrication business.

Our first job was to hastily assemble a task force to put together a $300 million bank loan application and a credible turnaround plan. Our four-member management team (plus six others who formed a task force) did it in only six weeks. The merged business, York Russel, ended up with $10 million of equity and $275 million of debt on the eve of a recession that turned out to be the worst Canada had experienced since the Great Depression. It was our job then to save the new company, somehow.

Conceptual frameworks are important aids to managers' perceptions, and every team should have a member who can build them. Before the acquisition, the framework implicit in our organization was a "hard," rational model rather like those Thomas Peters and Robert Waterman describe.[1] Jay Galbraith's elaborate model is one of the purest examples of the structure-follows-strategy school.[2] The model clearly defines all elements and their relationships to each other, presumably so that they can be measured (see Exhibit 1).

Because circumstances changed after the acquisition, our framework fell apart almost immediately. Overnight we went from working for a growth company to working for one whose only objective was survival. Our old decentralized organization was cumbersome and expensive; our new organization needed cash, not profits. Bankers and suppliers swarmed all over us, and the quiet life of a management-controlled public company was gone.

Compounding our difficulties, the recession quickly revealed all sorts of problems in businesses that up to that time had given us no trouble. Even the core nuggets offered up only meager profits, while interest rates of up to 25 percent quickly destroyed what was left of the balance sheet.

In the heat of the crisis, the management team jelled quickly. At first each

---

[1] Thomas J. Peters and Robert H. Waterman, *In Search of Excellence* (New York: Harper & Row, 1982), p. 29.

[2] For the best of the hard box models we have come across, see Jay R. Galbraith, *Organization Design* (Reading, Mass.: Addison-Wesley, 1977).

Exhibit 1:   The Hard and Soft Model and How They Work Together

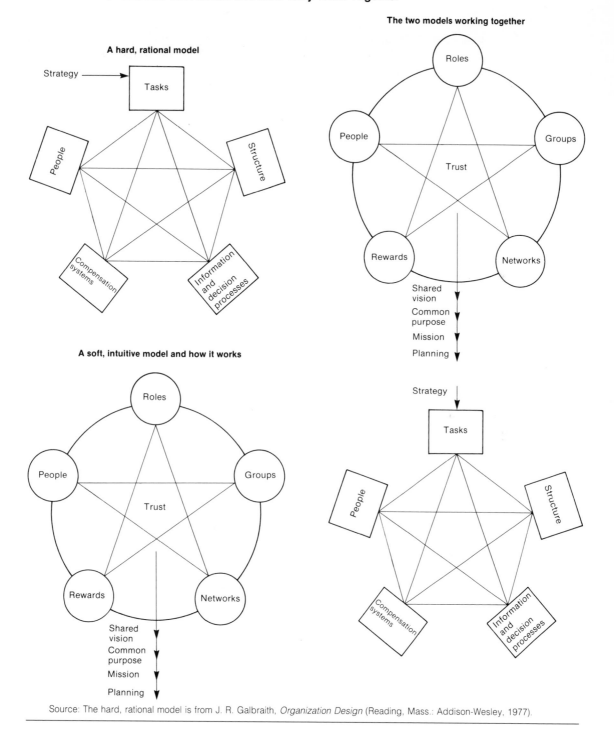

Source: The hard, rational model is from J. R. Galbraith, *Organization Design* (Reading, Mass.: Addison-Wesley, 1977).

member muddled in his own way, but as time went by, we started to gain a new understanding of how to be effective. Even now we do not completely understand the conceptual framework that has evolved, and maybe we never will. What follows is our best attempt to describe to you and your readers what guides us today.

Yours truly,
The management team

Two Models Are Better than One

The hard, rational model isn't wrong; it just isn't enough. There is something more. As it turns out, there is a great deal more.

At York Russel we have had to develop a "soft," intuitive framework that offers a counterpart to every element in the hard, rational framework. As Exhibit 1 shows and the following sections discuss, in the soft model, roles are the counterparts of tasks, groups replace structure, networks operate instead of information systems, the rewards are soft as opposed to hard, and people are viewed as social animals rather than as rational beings.

That may not sound very new. But we found that the key to effective management of not only our crisis but also the routine is to know whether we are in a hard "box" or a soft "bubble" context. By recognizing the dichotomy between the two, we can choose the appropriate framework.

☐ **Tasks . . .&. . .**	○ **Roles**
☐ *Static*	○ *Fluid*
☐ *Clarity*	○ *Ambiguity*
☐ *Content*	○ *Process*
☐ *Fact*	○ *Perception*
☐ *Science*	○ *Art*

These are some of our favorite words for contrasting these two aspects of management. Here's how we discovered them.

The merger changed our agenda completely. We had new shareholders, a new bank, a new business (the steel fabrication operations consisted of nine divisions), and a new relationship with the managers of our subsidiaries, who were used to being left alone to grow. The recession and high interest rates rendered the corporation insolvent. Bankruptcy loomed large. Further, our previously static way of operating became very fluid.

In general, few of us had clear tasks, and for the most part, we saw the future as ambiguous and fearful. We found ourselves describing what we had to do as roles rather than as tasks. At first our descriptions were crude. We talked of having an "inside man" who deals with administration, lawyers, and bankers versus an "outside man" who deals with operations, customers, and suppliers.

Some of us were "readers," others "writers," some "talkers," and others "listeners." As the readers studied the work of behavioral science researchers and talked to the listeners, we found some more useful classifications. Henry Mintzberg's description of managers' work in terms of three roles—interpersonal (figurehead, leader, liaison), informational (monitor, disseminator, spokesperson), and decisional—helped us see the variety of the job.[3] Edgar Schein's analysis of group roles helped us concentrate on the process of communication as well as on what was communicated.[4]

The most useful framework we used was the one Ichak Adize developed for decision-making roles.[5] In his view, a successful management team needs to play four distinct parts. The first is that of producer of results. A *producer* is action oriented and knowledgeable in his or her field; he or she helps compile plans with an eye to their implementability. The *administrator* supervises the system and manages the detail. The *entrepreneur* is a creative risk taker who initiates action, comes up with new ideas, and challenges existing policies. And the *integrator* brings people together socially and their ideas intellectually, and interprets the significance of events. The integrator gives the team a sense of direction and shared experience.

According to Adize, each member must have some appreciation of the others' roles (by having some facility in those areas), and it is essential that they get along socially. At York Russel, the producers (who typically come out of operations) and administrators (usually accountants) tend to be hard box players, while the entrepreneurs tend to live in the soft bubble. Integrators (friendly, unusually humble MBAs) move between the hard and the soft, and we've found a sense of humor is essential to being able to do that well.

The key to a functioning harmonious group, however, has been for members to understand that they might disagree with each other because they are in two different contexts. Different conceptual frameworks may lead people to different conclusions based on the same facts. Of the words describing tasks and roles, our favorite pair is *fact* versus *perception*. People in different boxes will argue with each other over facts, for facts in boxes are compelling—they seem so tangible. Only from the bubble can one see them for what they are: abstractions based on the logical frameworks, or boxes, being used.

☐ **Structure . . .&. . .**   ○ **Groups**
☐ *Cool*   ○ *Warm*
☐ *Formal*   ○ *Informal*
☐ *Closed*   ○ *Open*
☐ *Obedience*   ○ *Trust*
☐ *Independence*   ○ *Autonomy*

---

[3] Henry Mintzberg, "The Manager's Job: Folklore and Fact," *HBR*, July–August 1975, p. 49.

[4] Edgar H. Schein, *Process Consultation: Its Role in Organization Development* (Reading, Mass.: Addison-Wesley, 1969).

[5] Ichak Adize, *How to Solve the Mismanagement Crisis* (Los Angeles: MDOR Institute, 1979).

Our premerger corporation was a pretty cold place to work. Senior management kept control in a tight inner circle and then played hardball (in a hard box, of course) with the group presidents. Managers negotiated budgets and plans on a win-lose basis; action plans almost exclusively controlled what was done in the organization. Top managers kept a lot of information to themselves. People didn't trust each other very much.

The crises that struck the corporation in 1980 were so serious that we could not have concealed them even if we had wanted to. We were forced to put together a multitude of task forces consisting of people from all parts of the organization to address these urgent issues, and in the process, we had to reveal everything we knew, whether it was confidential or not.

We were amazed at the task forces' responses: instead of resigning en masse (the hard box players had said that people would leave the company when they found out that it was insolvent), the teams tackled their projects with passion. Warmth, a sense of belonging, and trust characterized the groups; the more we let them know what was going on, the more we received from them. Confidentiality is the enemy of trust. In the old days strategic plans were stamped "confidential." Now we know that paper plans mean nothing if they are not in the minds of the managers.

Division managers at first resented our intrusion into their formal, closed world. "What happened to independence?" they demanded. We described the soft counterpart—autonomy—to them. Unlike independence, autonomy cannot be granted once and for all. In our earlier life, division personnel told the corporate office what they thought it wanted to hear. "You've got to keep those guys at arm's length" was a typical division belief. An autonomous relationship depends on trust for its nourishment. "The more you level with us," we said, "the more we'll leave you alone." That took some getting used to.

But in the end autonomy worked. We gave division managers confidential information, shared our hopes and fears, and incorporated their views in our bubble. They needed to be helped out of their boxes, not to abandon them altogether but to gain a deeper appreciation of and insight into how they were running their businesses. Few could resist when we walked around showing a genuine interest in their views. Because easy access to each other and opportunities for communication determine how groups form and work together, we encouraged managers to keep their doors open. We called this creation of opportunities for communication by making senior management accessible "management by walking around." Chance encounters should not be left to chance.

Although the primary objective of all this communication is to produce trust among group members, an important by-product is that the integrators among us have started to "see" the communication process.[6] In other words, they are beginning to understand why people say what they say. This ability to "see"

---

[6] Edgar H. Schein's *Process Consultation*, p. 10, was very helpful in showing us how the process differs from the content.

communication is elusive at times, but when it is present, it enables us to "jump out of the box"—that is, to talk about the frameworks' supporting conclusions rather than the conclusion themselves. We have defused many potential confrontations and struck many deals by changing the context of the debate rather than the debate itself.[7]

Perhaps the best example of this process was our changing relationship with our lead banker. As the corporation's financial position deteriorated, our relationship with the bank became increasingly adversarial. The responsibility for our account rose steadily up the bank's hierarchy (we had eight different account managers in 18 months), and we received tougher and tougher "banker's speeches" from successively more senior executives. Although we worried a great deal that the bank might call the loan, the real risk was that our good businesses would be choked by overzealous efforts on the part of individual bankers to "hold the line."

Key to our ability to change the relationship was to understand why individuals were taking the positions they were. To achieve that understanding, we had to rely on a network of contacts both inside and outside the bank. We found that the bank had as many views as there were people we talked to. Fortunately, the severity of the recession and the proliferation of corporate loan problems had already blown everyone out of the old policy "boxes." It remained for us to gain the confidence of our contacts, exchange candid views of our positions, and present options that addressed the corporation's problems in the bank's context and deal with the bank's interests.

The "hard" vehicle for this was the renegotiation of our main financing agreement. During the more than six month negotiating process, our relationship with the bank swung 180 degrees from confrontation to collaboration. The corporation's problem became a joint bank-corporation problem. We had used the bubble to find a new box in which both the corporation and the bank could live.

☐ **Information**	
processes . . .&. . .	○ **Networks**
☐ *Hard*	○ *Soft*
☐ *Written*	○ *Oral*
☐ *Know*	○ *Feel*
☐ *Control*	○ *Influence*
☐ *Decision*	○ *Implementation*

Over the years, our corporation has developed some excellent information systems. Our EDP facility is second to none in our industry. Before the acquisition and merger, when people talked about or requested information, they

---

[7] Getting consensus among a group of managers poses the same challenge as negotiating a deal. *Getting to Yes* by Robert Fisher and William Ury (Boston: Houghton Mifflin, 1981) is a most helpful book for understanding the process.

meant hard, quantitative data and written reports that would be used for control and decision making. The crisis required that we make significant changes to these systems. Because, for example, we became more interested in cash flow than earnings per share, data had to be aggregated and presented in a new way.

The pivotal change, however, was our need to communicate with a slew of new audiences over which we had little control. For instance, although we still have preferred stock quoted in the public market, our principal new shareholders were family members with little experience in professional management of public companies. Our new bankers were in organizational turmoil themselves and took 18 months to realize the horror of what they had financed. Our suppliers, hitherto benign, faced a stream of bad financial news about us and other members of the industry. The rumor mill had us in receivership on a weekly basis.

Our plant closures and cutbacks across North America brought us into a new relationship with government, unions, and the press. And we had a new internal audience: our employees, who were understandably nervous about the "imminent" bankruptcy.

We had always had some relationship with these audiences, but now we saw what important sources of information they were and expanded these networks vastly.[8] Just as we had informed the division managers at the outset, we decided not to conceal from these other groups the fact that the corporation was insolvent but worthy of support. We made oral presentations supported by formal written material to cover the most important bases.

To our surprise, this candid approach totally disarmed potential antagonists. For instance, major suppliers could not understand why we had told them we were in trouble before the numbers revealed the fact. By the time the entire war story was news, there was no doubt that our suppliers' top managers, who tended not to live in the hard accounting box, were on our side. When their financial specialists concluded that we were insolvent, top management blithely responded, "We've known that for six months."

Sharing our view of the world with constituencies external to the corporation led to other unexpected benefits, such as working in each other's interests. Our reassurance to customers that we would be around to deliver on contracts strengthened the relationship. Adversity truly is opportunity!

Management by walking around was the key to communicating with employees in all parts of the company. As a result of the continual open communication, all employees appreciated the corporation's position. Their support has been most gratifying. One of our best talker-listeners (our president) tells of a meeting with a very nervous group of employees at one facility. After he had spent several hours explaining the company's situation, one blue-collar worker who had been with the company for years took him aside and told him that a group of employees

---

[8] For discussion of the importance of networks, see John P. Kotter, "What Effective General Managers Really Do," *HBR*, November–December 1982, p. 156.

would be prepared to take heavy pay cuts if it would save the business. It turns out that when others hear this story it reinforces *their* belief in the organization.

We have found that sharing our views and incorporating the views of others as appropriate has a curious effect on the making and the implementing of decisions. As we've said, in our previous existence the decisions we made were always backed up by hard information; management was decisive, and that was good. Unfortunately, too few of these "good" decisions ever got implemented. The simple process of making the decision the way we did often set up resistance down the line. As the decision was handed down to consecutive organizational levels, it lost impetus until eventually it was unclear whether the decision was right in the first place.

Now we worry a good deal less about making decisions; they arise as fairly obvious conclusions drawn from a mass of shared assumptions. It's the assumptions that we spend our time working on. One of our "producers" (an executive vice president) calls it "conditioning," and indeed it is. Of course, making decisions this way requires that senior management build networks with people many layers down in the organization. This kind of communication is directly at odds with the communication policy laid down in the premerger corporation, which emphasized direct-line reporting.

A consequence of this network information process is that we often have to wait for the right time to make a decision. We call the wait a creative stall. In the old organization it would have been called procrastination, but what we're doing is waiting for some important players to come "on-side" before making an announcement.[9] In our terms, you "prepare in the box and wait in the bubble."

Once the time is right, however, implementation is rapid. Everyone is totally involved and has given thought to what has to be done. Not only is the time it takes for the decision to be made and implemented shorter than in the past but also the whole process strengthens the organization rather than weakening it through bitterness about how the decision was made.

☐ **People . . .&. . .**	○ **People**
☐ *Rational*	○ *Social*
☐ *Produce*	○ *Create*
☐ *Think*	○ *Imagine*
☐ *Tell*	○ *Inspire*
☐ *Work*	○ *Play*

In the old, premerger days, it was convenient to regard employees as rational, welfare-maximizing beings; it made motivating them so much easier and planning less messy.

But because the crisis made it necessary to close many operations and terminate thousands of employees, we had to deal with people's social nature. We

---

[9] For discussion of a "creative stall" being applied in practice, see Stratford P. Sherman, "Muddling to Victory at Geico," *Fortune*, September 5, 1983, p. 66.

could prepare people intellectually by sharing our opinions and, to some extent, protect them physically with severance packages, but we struggled with how to handle the emotional aspects. Especially for long-service employees, severing the bond with the company was the emotional equivalent of death.

Humor is what rescued us. Laughter allows people to jump out of their emotional boxes or rigid belief structures. None of us can remember having laughed as much as we have over the past three years. Although much of the humor has inevitably been of the gallows variety, it has been an important ingredient in releasing tension and building trust.

Now everyone knows that people are social as well as rational animals. Indeed, we knew it back in the premerger days, but somehow back then we never came to grips with the social aspect, maybe because the rational view of people has an appealing simplicity and clarity. Lombard's Law applied to us—routine, structured tasks drove out nonroutine, unstructured activities.[10]

☐ **Compensation**	
systems . . .&. . .	○ **Rewards**
☐ *Direct*	○ *Indirect*
☐ *Objective*	○ *Subjective*
☐ *Profit*	○ *Fun*
☐ *Failure*	○ *Mistake*
☐ *Hygiene*	○ *Motivator*
☐ *Managing*	○ *Caring*

In our premerger organization, the "total compensation policy" meant you could take your money any way you liked—salary, loans, fringes, and so forth. Management thought this policy catered to individual needs and was, therefore, motivating. Similarly, the "Personal Development Program" required managers to make formal annual reviews of their employees' performances. For some reason, management thought that this also had something to do with motivation. The annual reviews, however, had become a meaningless routine, with managers constrained to be nice to the review subject because they had to work with him or her the next day.

The 1981 recession put a stop to all this by spurring us to freeze all direct compensation. Profit-based compensation disappeared; morale went up.

The management team discussed this decision for hours. As the savings from the freeze would pay for a few weeks' interest only, the numbers made no sense at all. Some of us prophesied doom. "We will lose the best people," we argued. Instead, the symbolic freeze brought the crisis home to everyone. We had all made a sacrifice, a contribution that senior management could recognize at a future time.

---

[10] Louis B. Barnes, "Managing the Paradox of Organizational Trust," *HBR*, March–April 1981, p. 107.

Even though the academics say they aren't scientifically valid, we still like Frederick Herzberg's definition of motivators (our interpretations of them are in parentheses).[11]

Achievement (what you believe you did).
Recognition (what others think you did).
Work itself (what you really do).
Responsibility (what you help others do).
Advancement (what you think you can do).
Growth (what you believe you might do).

The New Framework at Work

The diagram of the soft model in the exhibit shows our view of how our management process seems to work. When the motivating rewards are applied to people playing the necessary roles and working together in groups that are characterized by open communication and are linked to networks throughout the organization, the immediate product is a high degree of mutual trust. This trust allows groups to develop a shared vision that in turn enhances a sense of common purpose. From this process people develop a feeling of having a mission of their own. The mission is spiritual in the sense of being an important effort much larger than oneself. This kind of involvement is highly motivating. Mission is the soft counterpart of strategy.

☐ **Strategy . . .&. . .**	○ **Mission**
☐ *Objectives*	○ *Values*
☐ *Policies*	○ *Norms*
☐ *Forecast*	○ *Vision*
☐ *Clockworks*	○ *Frameworks*
☐ *Right*	○ *Useful*
☐ *Target*	○ *Direction*
☐ *Precise*	○ *Vague*
☐ *Necessary*	○ *Sufficient*

Listed are some of our favorite words for contrasting these two polarities. We find them useful for understanding why clear definition of objectives is not essential for motivating people. Hard box planners advocate the hard box elements and tend to be overinvested in using their various models, or "clockworks" as we call them. Whether it's a Boston Consulting Group matrix or an Arthur D. Little life-cycle curve, too often planners wind them up and managers act according to what they dictate without looking at the assumptions, many of which may be invalid, implicit in the frameworks.

We use the models only as take-off points for discussion. They do not have to

---

[11] In "One More Time: How Do You Motivate Employees?" *HBR*, January–February 1968, p. 53.

be right, only useful. If they don't yield genuine insights we put them aside. The hard box cannot be dispensed with. On the contrary, it is essential—but not sufficient.

The key element in developing a shared purpose is mutual trust. Without trust, people will engage in all kinds of self-centered behavior to assert their own identities and influence co-workers to their own ends. Under these circumstances, they just won't hear others, and efforts to develop a shared vision are doomed. Nothing destroys trust faster than hard box attitudes toward problems that don't require such treatment.

Trust is self-reproductive. When trust is present in a situation, chain reactions occur as people share frameworks and exchange unshielded views. The closer and more tightly knit the group is, the more likely it is that these reactions will spread, generating a shared vision and common purpose.

Once the sense of common purpose and mission is established, the managing group is ready to enter the hard box of strategy (see the right-hand side of Exhibit 1). Now the specifics of task, structure , information, and decision processes are no longer likely to be controversial or threatening. Implementation becomes astonishingly simple. Action plans are necessary to control hard box implementation, but once the participants in the soft bubble share the picture, things seem to happen by themselves as team members play their roles and fill the gaps as they see them. Since efforts to seize control of bubble activity are likely to prove disastrous, it is most fortunate that people act spontaneously without being "organized." Paradoxically, one can achieve control in the bubble only by letting go—which gets right back to trust.

☐ **Boxes . . .&. . .**	○ **Bubbles**
☐ *Solve*	○ *Dissolve*
☐ *Sequential*	○ *Lateral*
☐ *Left brain*	○ *Right brain*
☐ *Serious*	○ *Humorous*
☐ *Explain*	○ *Explore*
☐ *Rational*	○ *Intuitive*
☐ *Conscious*	○ *Unconscious*
☐ *Learn*	○ *Remember*
☐ *Knowledge*	○ *Wisdom*
☐ *Lens*	○ *Mirror*
☐ *Full*	○ *Empty*
☐ *Words*	○ *Pictures*
☐ *Objects*	○ *Symbols*
☐ *Description*	○ *Parable*

In the hard box, the leadership model is that of the general who gives crisp, precise instructions as to who is to do what and when. In the soft bubble, the leadership model is that of the shepherd, who follows his flock watchfully as it meanders along the natural contours of the land. He carries the weak and collects the strays, for they all have a contribution to make. This style may be inefficient, but it is effective. The whole flock reaches its destination at more or less the same time.[12]

Thought and language are keys to changing perceptions. Boxes and bubbles describe the hard and soft thought structures, respectively. Boxes have rigid, opaque sides; walls have to be broken down to join boxes, although if the lid is off, one can jump out. Bubbles have flexible, transparent sides that can easily expand and join with other bubbles. Bubbles float but can easily burst. In boxes problems are to be solved; in bubbles they are dissolved. The trick is to change the context of the problem, that is, to jump out of the box. This technique has many applications.

We have noticed a number of articles in your publication that concern values and ethics in business, and some people have suggested that business students be required to attend classes in ethics. From our view of the world, sending students to specific courses is a hard box solution and would be ineffective. Ethical behavior is absent from some businesses not because the managers have no ethics (or have the wrong ones) but because the hard "strategy box" does not emphasize them as being valuable. The hard box deals in objectives, and anyone who raises value issues in that context will not survive long.

In contrast, in the "mission bubble" people feel free to talk about values and ethics because there is trust. The problem of the lack of ethical behavior is dissolved.

We have found bubble thinking to be the intellectual equivalent of judo; a person does not resist an attacker but goes with the flow, thereby adding his strength to the other's momentum. Thus when suppliers demanded that their financial exposure to our lack of creditworthiness be reduced, we agreed and suggested that they protect themselves by supplying goods to us on consignment. After all, their own financial analysis showed we couldn't pay them any money! In some cases we actually got consignment deals, and where we didn't the scheme failed because of nervous lawyers (also hard box players) rather than reluctance on the part of the supplier.

Bubble thought structures are characterized by what Edward de Bono calls lateral thinking.[13] The sequential or vertical thought structure is logical and rational; it proceeds through logical stages and depends on a yes-no test at each step. De Bono suggests that in lateral thinking the yes-no test must be suspended, for the purpose is to explore not explain, to test assumptions not conclusions.

We do the same kind of questioning when we do what we call "humming a lot." When confronted with what initially appears to be an unpalatable idea, an

---

[12] For another view of the shepherd role, see the poem by Nancy Esposito, "The Good Shepherd," *HBR*, July–August 1983, p. 121.

[13] See Edward de Bono, *The Use of Lateral Thinking* (London: Jonathan Cape, 1967), and *PO: Beyond Yes and No* (New York: Simon & Schuster, 1972).

effective manager will say "hmm" and wait until the idea has been developed and its implications considered. Quite often, even when an initial idea is out of the question, the fact that we have considered it seriously will lead to a different, innovative solution.

We have found it useful to think of the action opposite to the one we intend taking. When selling businesses we found it helpful to think about acquiring purchasers. This led to deeper research into purchasers' backgrounds and motives and to a more effective packaging and presentation of the businesses to be sold. This approach encourages novel ideas and makes the people who generate them (the entrepreneurs) feel that their ideas, however "dumb," will not be rejected out of hand.

In hard box thought structures, one tends to use conceptual frameworks as lenses, to sit on one side and examine an object on the other. In bubble structures, the frameworks are mirrors reflecting one's own nature and its effect on one's perceptions; object and subject are on the same side. In the hard box, knowledge is facts, from learning; in the bubble, knowledge is wisdom, from experience.

Bubble thought structures are not easily described in words. Language itself is a box reflecting our cultural heritage and emphasizing some features of reality at the expense of others. Part of our struggle during the past three years has been to unlearn many scientific management concepts and develop a new vocabulary. We have come up with some new phrases and words: management by walking around, creative stall, asking dumb questions, jumping out of the box, creating a crisis, humming a lot, and muddling. We have also attached new meanings to old words such as fact and perception, independence and autonomy, hard and soft, solve and dissolve, and so forth.

Three Years Later

What we have told you about works in a crisis. And we can well understand your asking whether this approach can work when the business is stable and people lapse back into boxes. We have developed two methods of preventing this lapse.

1. If There Isn't a Crisis, We Create One. One way to stir things up is familiar to anyone who has ever worked in a hard box organization. Intimidation, terror, and the use of raw power will produce all the stress you need. But eventually people run out of adrenalin and the organization is drained, not invigorated.

In a bubble organization, managers dig for opportunities in a much more relaxed manner. During the last three years, for instance, many of our divisions that were profitable and liquid were still in need of strategic overhaul. During the course of walking around, we unearthed many important issues by asking dumb questions.

The more important of the issues that surface this way offer an opportunity to put a champion (someone who believes in the importance of the issue) in charge of a team of people who can play all the roles required to handle the issue. The champion then sets out with his or her group to go through the incremental development process—developing trust, building both a hard box picture and a shared vision, and, finally, establishing strategy. By the time the strategy is arrived at, the task force disciples have such zeal and sense of mission that they are ready to take the issue to larger groups, using the same process.

Two by-products of asking dumb questions deserve mention. First, when senior management talks to people at all levels, people at all levels start talking to each other. Second, things tend to get fixed before they break. In answering a senior manager's casual question, a welder on the shop floor of a steel fabrication plant revealed that some critical welds had failed quality tests and the customer's inspector was threatening to reject an entire bridge. A small ad hoc task force, which included the inspector (with the customer's permission), got everyone off the hook and alerted top management to a potential weakness in the quality control function.

Applying the principles in other areas takes years to bear fruit. We are now using the process to listen to customers and suppliers. We never knew how to do this before. Now it is clear that it is necessary to create an excuse (crisis) for going to see them, share "secrets," build trust, share a vision, and capture them in your bubble. It's very simple, and early results have been excellent. We call it a soft revolution.

2. Infuse Activities that Some Might Think Prosaic with Real Significance. The focus should be on people first, and always on caring rather than managing. The following approach works in good times as well as bad:

> Use a graphic vocabulary that describes what you do.

> Share confidential information, personal hopes and fears to create a common vision and promote trust.

> Seize every opportunity (open doors, management by walking around, networks) to make a point, emphasize a value, disseminate information, share an experience, express interest, and show you care.

> Recognize performance and contribution of as many people as possible. Rituals and ceremonies—retirements, promotions, birthdays—present great opportunities.

> Use incentive programs whose main objective is not compensation but recognition.

We have tried to approach things this way, and for us the results have been significant. Now three years after the crisis first struck our corporation, we are a very different organization. Of our 25 divisions, we have closed 7 and sold 16. Five of the latter were bought by Federal Industries, Ltd. of Winnipeg. Some 860 employees including us, the four members of the management team, have gone to Federal. These divisions are healthy and raring to go. Two divisions remain at York Russel, which has changed its name to YRI-YORK, Ltd.

Now we face new questions, such as how one recruits into a management team. We know that we have to help people grow into the team, and fortunately we find that they flourish in our warm climate. But trust takes time to develop, and the bubble is fragile. The risk is greatest when we have to transplant a senior person from outside, because time pressures may not allow us to be sure we are compatible. The danger is not only to the team itself but also to the person joining it.

Our new framework has given us a much deeper appreciation of the management process and the roles effective general managers play. For example, it is clear that while managers can delegate tasks in the hard box rather easily—perhaps because they can define them—it's impossible to delegate soft bubble activities. The latter are difficult to isolate from each other because their integration takes place in one brain.

Similarly, the hard box general management roles of producer and administrator can be formally taught, and business schools do a fine job of it. The soft roles of entrepreneur and integrator can probably not be taught formally. Instead, managers must learn from mentors. Over time they will adopt behavior patterns that allow them to play the required roles. It would seem, however, that natural ability and an individual's upbringing probably play a much larger part in determining effectiveness in the soft roles than in the hard roles; it is easier to teach a soft bubble player the hard box roles than it is to teach the soft roles to a hard box player.

In the three-year period when we had to do things so differently, we created our own culture, with its own language, symbols, norms, and customs. As with other groups, the acculturation process began when people got together in groups and trusted and cared about each other.[14]

In contrast with our premerger culture, the new culture is much more sympathetic toward and supportive of the use of teams and consensus decision making. In this respect, it would seem to be similar to oriental ways of thinking that place a premium on the same processes. Taoists, for instance, would have no trouble recognizing the polarities of the hard box and the soft bubble and the need to keep a balance between the two.[15]

☐ **Heaven . . .&. . .**   ◯ **Earth**
☐ *Yang*   ◯ *Yin*
☐ *Father*   ◯ *Mother*
☐ *Man*   ◯ *Woman*

---

[14] To explore the current concern with creating strong organizational cultures in North American corporations, see Terrence E. Deal and Alan A. Kennedy, *Corporate Cultures* (Reading, Mass.: Addison-Wesley, 1982).

[15] For discussion of Tao and some applications, we highly recommend Benjamin Hoff, *The Tao of Pooh* (New York: E. P. Dutton, 1982), p. 67; also Allen Watts, *Tao: The Watercourse Way* (New York: Pantheon Books, 1975).

These symbols are instructive. After all, most of us grew up with two bosses: father usually played the hard box parts, while mother played the soft, intuitive, and entrepreneurial roles. The family is the original team, formed to handle the most complex management task ever faced. Of late, we seem to have fired too many of its members—a mistake we can learn from.

Toward a Managerial Theory of Relativity

The traditional hard box view of management, like the traditional orientation of physics, is valid (and very useful) only within a narrow range of phenomena. Once one gets outside the range, one needs new principles. In physics, cosmologists at the macro level as well as students of subatomic particles at the micro level use Einstein's theory of relativity as an explanatory principle and set Newton's physics aside.[16] For us, the theory in the bubble is our managerial theory of relativity. At the macro level it reminds us that how management phenomena appear depends on one's perspective and biases. At the micro level we remember that all jobs have both hard and soft components.

This latter point is of particular importance to people like us in the service industry. The steel we distribute is indistinguishable from anyone else's. We insist on rigid standards regarding how steel is handled, what reporting systems are used, and so forth. But hard box standards alone won't be enough to set us apart from our competitors. That takes service, a soft concept. And everyone has to be involved. Switchboard operators are in the front line; every contact is an opportunity to share the bubble. Truck drivers and warehouse workers make their own special contribution—by taking pride in the cleanliness of their equipment or by keeping the inventory neat and accessible.

With the box and bubble concept, managers can unlock many of the paradoxes of management and handle the inherent ambiguities. You don't do one or the other absolutely; you do what is appropriate. For instance, the other day in one of our operations the biweekly payroll run deducted what appeared to be random amounts from the sales representatives' pay packets. The branch affected was in an uproar. After taking some hard box steps to remedy the situation, our vice president of human resources seized the opportunity to go out to the branch and talk to the sales team. He was delighted with the response. The sales force saw that he understood the situation and cared about them, and he got to meet them all, which will make future contacts easier. But neither the hard box nor soft bubble approach on its own would have been appropriate. We need both. As one team member put it, "You have to find the bubble in the box and put the box in the bubble." Exactly.

The amazing thing is that the process works so well. The spirit of cooperation among senior managers is intense, and we seem to be getting "luckier" as we go

---

[16] Fritjof Capra, *The Tao of Physics* (London: Fontana Paperbacks, 1983).

along. When a "magic" event takes place it means that somehow we got the timing just right.[17] And there is great joy in that.

Notes to Chapter 5

[1] The material to this point in the chapter has been reprinted by permission, with minor editorial changes, from Arthur A. Thompson, Jr., and A. J. Strickland III, *Strategy Formulation and Implementation*, 3rd ed. (Plano Tex.: Business Publications, 1986), pp. 322–24.

[2] Derek Abell and John Hammond, presentation at Strategic Management Conference, Barcelona, Spain, October 1985.

---

[17] Carl Jung developed the concept of synchronicity to explain such events. See, for example, Ira Progoff, *Jung, Synchronicity and Human Destiny—Non-Causal Dimensions of Human Experience* (New York: Julian Press, 1973). For an excellent discussion of Jung's work and its relevance to our times, see Laurens van de Post, *Jung and the Story of Our Time* (New York: Random House, 1975).

SECTION TWO

CASES

Abbott Consultants Limited

In January 1980, Mr. Brian Kelly, president of Abbott Consultants Ltd. of London, Ontario, was reflecting on what he could have done in terms of organization design and control to have avoided the ongoing criminal investigations concerning the activities of two recent Abbott employees. Issues relating to fraud, conspiracy, and secret commissions had arisen around the methods of operation of Abbott managers while acting as purchasing agents for a Canadian aid program with Nigeria.

Background

The Nigerian Civil War began in June 1967 after the Eastern Region of Nigeria declared itself an independent republic called Biafra. The war lasted until January 1970, when Biafra surrendered and accepted Nigeria's leader, Colonel Yakubu Gowon, as the head of state.

Following this disastrous civil war, Nigeria's leaders began work to repair war damages through programs for rehabilitation and reconstruction. Two of the Nigerian states which formed part of the Eastern Region (Biafra) were South East State and East Central State. These states were very badly damaged during the war, and the Federal Government of Nigeria was particularly concerned with providing attention there as quickly as possible.

As part of the rehabilitation program, the Federal Government of Nigeria applied to the Government of Canada for loans through the Canadian International Development Agency (CIDA). One of these loans was in the amount of $3 million of which $1.4 million was to be used to acquire tools and machinery for trade schools located in East Central State and agricultural training equipment for the South East State.

The $3 million rehabilitation loan to Nigeria was granted by agreement dated December 8, 1972. This loan was, in fact, aid in that it was interest free and repayment was not to commence for 10 years. Payments beginning in March 1982 were to be paid semiannually for 40 years. (See Exhibit 1 for extracts from loan agreement.) In most cases, loans such as these are forgiven by Canada.

The agreement noted that funds would not leave Canada; instead Nigeria would be given a $3 million credit from CIDA which would be drawn upon as

This case was prepared by Randy Hoffman, York University, and researched by James Szarka. Copyright © 1986 by Randy Hoffman. This version was edited by Paul W. Beamish.

Exhibit 1

EXCERPTS FROM THE 1972 AGREEMENT

BETWEEN

THE GOVERNMENT OF CANADA

- AND -

THE GOVERNMENT OF THE FEDERAL REPUBLIC OF NIGERIA

(hereinafter called "Nigeria")

ARTICLE III
Withdrawals of Proceeds of Loan

Section 3.03
   Nigeria or its designated agent shall provide Canada with a copy of each invitation to tender, calls for proposals, bids, contracts under purchase orders for the procurement of goods and services in receipt of which any withdrawal is to be made.

Section 3.05
   Nigeria or its designated agent shall furnish, or cause to be furnished, to Canada such documents and other evidence in support of its application.

ANNEX "B"

Procurement Procedures

4. The companies invited to tender, or submit proposals shall:
   a. Send copies of all tenders and proposals to the Canadian International Development Agency at the same time as they are forwarded to the recipient procurement authority. (The copies of these documents received by the Canadian International Development Agency will be treated as confidential and not opened until the dates established by the recipient.)
6. The purchaser shall provide copies of all orders and contracts to Canada and Canada shall issue a confirming purchase order to the supplier.
7. Suppliers shall be instructed to send three copies of their invoices covering the C.I.F. Nigerian Port cost to the Government of Nigeria or its designated agents.
8. The Nigerian buyer will certify the invoices stating that the equipment, material or services have been received in good order, and forward two copies to the authorized agent of the Federal Government. Nigeria shall also certify that the invoice is accepted and may be charged against loan funds.
9. One copy of each of the certified invoices will be returned by the authorized agent to Canada where payment will be made to the supplier.

goods and services were received. Also of significance were the requirements that the goods be purchased in Canada and were to have not less than 66⅔ percent Canadian content. Following the loan agreement, Nigeria was to provide a "shopping list" of material required by the two states and provide this list to CIDA for approval.

Some delays occurred in Nigeria, and the final commitment date for utilization of the $3 million rehabilitation loan was extended from December 31, 1973, to June 30, 1975, by mutual agreement of Canada and Nigeria.

The requirement for Nigeria to fill its "shopping list" with primarily Canadian goods meant that shopping had to be done in Canada. Canadian manufacturers and suppliers would have to be contacted for necessary quotes and assistance in determining what was actually needed by Nigeria for their schools. Preliminary lists prepared by the two Nigerian states were very crude, that is, describing machines, generally without detailed description of horsepower, electrics, and so forth. It was, therefore, necessary to refine the shopping lists and contact numerous manufacturers in Canada, receive quotes, select those who would supply the goods, and submit the final shopping list with all quotes to CIDA for approval.

On similar loans to Third World countries, this procurement function was provided for the borrowing nation by a Canadian crown agency acting on behalf of CIDA. At this time, the agency was elsewhere committed and could not perform this for Nigeria. This contributed to the delay in fulfilling the material requirements of the agreement and necessitated the extensions mentioned earlier.

In October 1973, Mike McPherson, vice president of Abbott Consultants Ltd. of London, Ontario, was in Lagos, Nigeria, on a marketing trip investigating the possibility of becoming a consultant to a World Bank project in Nigeria. McPherson was to visit six states in Nigeria regarding this project. (This never materialized.) While in Lagos, McPherson met Canadian officials and learned of the $3 million rehabilitation loan. He was advised that normally a Canadian crown agency performed the procurement of goods, but in this case, Abbott might be able to obtain a contract for that service. Although Abbott was not experienced in the sourcing and procurement field, the offer seemed interesting to McPherson, who thought it could lead to more international business for Abbott.

Also, while in Lagos, McPherson met Donald Osubu, managing director at Goldcoast Inc., a Nigerian company which acted as equipment agent for a number of foreign firms, including American and Canadian companies. Osubu's firm provided after-sales service as well as liaison for and between the foreign companies and their Nigerian customers.

McPherson visited the Nigerian states in connection with the World Bank project, and while in East Central State, he questioned state officials about Abbott acting as their equipment procurement coordinator in Canada on the CIDA rehabilitation loan. The officials were quite receptive to this proposal but stressed they would be responsible for handling equipment from the port of entry in Nigeria to their final destination. McPherson was unable to visit South East State, but later developments proved they would want a similar arrangement to that of the East Central State. Although the $3 million loan was between Canada and the Federal Government of Nigeria, McPherson learned the $1.4 million equipment component was to be directed by the two states involved which were entitled to $700,000 each.

McPherson returned to Canada and discussed the CIDA project with Abbott President Brian Kelly, who became very enthused about the potential of this project. In November 1973, Abbott officials McPherson and Kelly visited Ottawa and approached CIDA officials and advised them they were interested in providing the equipment coordination for the two Nigerian states. Abbott indicated it would prepare a proposal for the Nigerians, and CIDA officials agreed to review this and make necessary suggestions for improvement, if necessary.

In December 1973, McPherson returned to Nigeria on business relating to the World Bank project and while there, again met with a CIDA official. The official agreed to submit the Abbott proposal to the Federal Ministry of Finance–Nigeria on Abbott's behalf when same was received. McPherson returned to Canada, and a draft proposal of services was prepared and submitted to CIDA in Ottawa for review.

During Christmas holiday 1973, Donald Osubu visited Canada and met with Abbott officials, including McPherson and Kelly to discuss the possibility that Goldcoast Inc. of Nigeria could act as Abbott's local associate in Nigeria. The advantages to Abbott of having a local firm with some influence (McPherson had learned this on his earlier trips) was that it would help Abbott get the contract and also expedite further negotiations with federal and state officials in Nigeria. Also discussed during this visit was the type of return to be expected by each company. It was agreed Abbott would get 60 percent of all commissions or service allowances and Goldcoast, 40 percent. Neither CIDA nor the Nigerian governments were aware of this agreement. (CIDA and the Nigerian governments were later made aware that Goldcoast and Abbott were sharing the equipment procurement fees which were to be paid by the Nigerian states directly.)

In February 1974, Abbott submitted a proposal for the East Central State portion of the CIDA project to the CIDA official in Lagos, Nigeria, who was to submit it to the Federal Ministry of Finance in Nigeria and to East Central State. In March 1974, the proposal was reviewed by CIDA Ottawa, and a revised proposal containing changes recommended by a CIDA Ottawa official was sent to Lagos. This revision was acknowledged by Lagos shortly thereafter.

Abbott mentioned Goldcoast Inc. as their potential Nigerian associate in the proposal, and shortly thereafter Goldcoast Inc. began negotiations on behalf of Abbott with the government of East Central State and Federal Finance authorities. In May 1974, Osubu wrote to McPherson telling him of these meetings and also of the refusal of both federal and state authorities to pay Abbott and Goldcoast an after-sales service fee, as such agents' fees are usually paid by the manufacturer. Osubu hinted that all would have been well if they could have hidden their fees in the equipment prices.

Negotiations continued between Abbott/Goldcoast and East Central State between May 1974 and August 1974. In September of 1974, East Central State wrote to Abbott and advised them to commence work on the project. Donald Osubu visited London, Ontario, during September 1974 to discuss the project with McPherson and Kelly. McPherson appointed Charles Lee, a salaried employee of Abbott who also received a bonus each year based on the profitability of Abbott, to be in charge of the Nigerian project. Lee was given the title, director of International Division. Philip Rugger, another Abbott employee with some sales and engineering experience, was assigned to be Lee's assistant in the project. Lee and Osubu, through several meetings, organized the plan to carry out the project, and it was later alleged this concept was discussed openly with CIDA officials in Ottawa by Kelly, Lee, and Osubu. CIDA apparently supported Abbott's plan but cautioned Abbott to ensure contracts were duly signed before commencing any work on the project. (See below.)

The implementation plan for the project was as follows:

1. Abbott, on receipt of the preliminary equipment lists from the respective states in Nigeria would source equipment suppliers and obtain quotes from which a final equipment list would be prepared for approval of all parties (CIDA, Nigeria, states).

2. Abbott personnel would visit manufacturers/suppliers to ensure goods fulfilled requirements of the Nigerian states.

3. Abbott would forward invoices received from suppliers on receipt of goods at Abbott shipping facilities to CIDA Ottawa.

4. CIDA would examine invoices and ensure goods met requirements of final equipment list. On verifying this, CIDA would authorize payment of invoices by cheque payable to Abbott.

5. Abbott would pay suppliers for goods within 30 days of receiving payment from CIDA.

6. Abbott was to be responsible for packaging, warehousing, inspection, and handling of equipment to be shipped to Nigeria. Abbott hired its subsidiary Able Systems to perform this function. A fee of approximately 5 percent of the $1.4 million ($70,000) was charged by Able Systems to Abbott Consultants for this service. This was subsequently invoiced to CIDA and paid from the loan proceeds.

7. Abbott organized overseas shipping of goods and also insurance. These costs were to be paid on receipt of invoices and bills of lading by CIDA from the loan proceeds.

8. Abbott and their Nigerian agent Goldcoast Inc. would receive 3 percent ($42,000) of the total cost of equipment as a fee for providing the purchasing agent services. This fee was to be paid directly by the two Nigerian states and not from CIDA loan proceeds.

Enquiries made at a later time established that both Abbott and CIDA were aware of the provisions of items 1 through 8 above.

Another source of revenue in this project for Abbott/Goldcoast related to "after-sales service" fees purported by Abbott to have been discussed with CIDA officials during early meetings. This was flatly denied by CIDA personnel, and it was later found that there was an obvious attempt to hide those fees in the invoiced price of goods.

Charles Lee, in a later memo to file, described the after-sales services as follows:

> A large number of the equipment purchased had included in the purchase price a component for "after-sales service." This "after-sales service" consists of handling enquiries on equipment sold on behalf of the manufacturer or supplier, processing the re-order of parts, accessories, or repair parts during the warranty period. This service allowance was generally around 10 percent of the price of the equipment. As Goldcoast Inc. was also involved in this service, it was agreed that they would receive 40 percent of this service allowance, while Abbott would receive 60 percent.

Some suppliers paid after-sales service on materials such as small tools, that is, hammers, saws, files. Many suppliers recorded this service as merely commissions. It was later learned the total of after-sales service allowance received from suppliers and manufacturers was approximately $100,000. ($60,000 for Abbott and $40,000 for Goldcoast.)

In September 1974, Abbott sent copies of agreements to Goldcoast Inc. and to the East Central State. (See Exhibit 2.) Goldcoast returned the signed agreement almost immediately. East Central State signed their agreement January 21, 1975.

In November 1974, Osubu approached officials in South East State to get them to agree to Abbott/Goldcoast acting as their equipment managers in Canada under similar conditions proposed to the East Central State. In December 1974, Abbott received an official request from South East State for submission of proposal similar to East Central State which they subsequently forwarded in April 1975.

In February 1975, Abbott received a contract from East Central State which had been signed January 21, 1975. Abbott commenced immediately to prepare equipment lists and quotations. In May 1975, Abbott received a signed contract from the South East State and commenced preparation of lists/quotations.

In June 1975, the equipment lists, including prices, were completed. Charles Lee proceeded to Nigeria to discuss the lists and obtain approval from the states to start procurement. Osubu of Goldcoast Inc. accompanied Lee to Enugu and Calabar, the provincial capitals of the two states, to meet the officials responsible for approval.

In July 1975, authorization was received by Abbott from the East Central State to begin procurement of equipment as per the approved final list or "shopping list." CIDA was provided copies of this list by Nigeria. CIDA notified Abbott of this by letter and provided Abbott with a letter of introduction for suppliers.

Able Systems Ltd. was formally commissioned through Abbott to coordinate all crating, labeling, and shipping of goods. In August 1975, Abbott received

Exhibit 2

ABBOTT CONSULTANTS LTD.
LONDON, ONTARIO

Re: Agreement between Abbott Consulting and Goldcoast Inc.

Based on the agreement reached during our recent discussions on the above noted project, Abbott Consultants Ltd. (Abbott) hereby authorize Goldcoast Inc. (GCI) to act as its agent in Nigeria according to the terms set out herein.

1.0   Scope of Work and Allocation of Responsibilities

We confirm that Abbott will be responsible for all work within Canada and that GCI will coordinate all activity in Nigeria. The procedure as recommended by the Canadian High Commission will be followed on this project according to the following separation of responsibilities.

2.0   Abbott Responsibilities

2.1   Identification of suitable and available Canadian and (if necessary and approved by CIDA) foreign equipment.

2.2   Preparation of full Equipment List Proposal giving CIF prices, Port Harcourt.

2.3   Submission of Equipment List Proposal to CIDA, Ottawa, for approval.

2.4   Arrangements for CIDA to forward Equipment List Proposal to the Canadian High Commission/Lagos for forwarding to the Federal Ministry of Finance, Nigeria.

2.5   (Upon formal approval of Equipment List Proposal), placing of all orders for equipments as per approved list.

2.6   Arranging for all guarantees, spare parts, servicing etc.

2.7   Arranging for all inland transportation, packaging and insurance to port of departure.

2.8   Arranging for all crating, insurance and shipping CIF Port Harcourt from port of departure.

2.9   Delivery of Bill of Lading to CIDA, Ottawa.

2.10 Processing of all accounts in Canada upon receipt of payment by CIDA.

3.0   GCI Responsibilities

3.1   Closing of contractual arrangements with East Central State on behalf of Abbott.

3.2   Finalization of all outstanding equipment specification questions.

3.3   Expediting the processing of approval of the final equipment list proposal by the East Central State Government.

3.4   Checking equipment packages for damage, completeness, etc. and reporting any deficiencies for insurance claims purposes and for replacement of equipment.

Exhibit 2 (*concluded*)

3.5 Arranging for delivery of equipment to the State Government on arrival at Port Harcourt.

3.6 On receipt of the copy of Bill of Lading to expedite the release of payment to Abbott.

3.7 Act on Abbott's behalf to provide service during guarantee period and after sales service.

3.8 Making arrangements for remittance to Abbott of its share of fee in foreign exchange.

3.9 To act on Abbott's behalf on all matters pertaining to this project.

The consulting fee as per initial arrangements will be three percent (3%) of the CIF cost of all equipment approved for purchase by the East Central State paid to Abbott/GCI by the East Central State Government.

As per our discussions, we confirm that the fee on this project will be shared according to a 60/40 ratio with the larger percentage to Abbott to cover start-up costs. The actual portion to be shared will be the net profit after expenses. As per our arrangement the East Central State Government will be advised to remit the fee to Abbott through GCI. (Understood to refer to total gross fees/commission that has accrued from the contract.)

4.0 Agreement

If you accept the terms of this agreement as set out above, please indicate acceptance by signing a copy of this letter in the appropriate place and return at your earliest convenience.

---

authorization from CIDA to begin procurement of equipment. Able Systems then rented a warehouse to handle the receipt of equipment from the many suppliers and used this warehouse for approximately three months to crate equipment for export shipping, and so forth. Two shipments were made from New York during October and December 1975. Some delays occurred at the Nigerian destinations, and the shipments finally arrived in Calabar, Nigeria, in February and March of 1976. Reports from Goldcoast Inc. to Able indicated some crates were broken and contents exposed, and there were difficulties experienced by state officials in arranging inland transportation.

During April and May 1976, Abbott continued procurement for the third and final shipment of goods for this project. This shipment was crated and prepared for shipping in the warehouse of one of Abbott's suppliers, who charged Able Systems for rent and use of lift trucks, and so forth. In June 1976, the third shipment left new York and arrived in Calabar, Nigeria, in August 1976.

Further claims of missing and damaged goods and equipment were received by Abbott from the state governments. In one situation, several crates destined for one state arrived in another, and it was not until December 1977 that it was acknowledged. Insurance claims were registered and problems arose here as well, as it was difficult to verify goods shipped to packing lists and bills of lading. Abbott found it necessary to contact suppliers in Canada again to verify what goods they had supplied, and in many cases they received no cooperation at all. These problems continued into 1979, when the final shipment of miscellaneous items was made to East Central State. During this period of difficulty, Goldcoast Inc. did little to assist Abbott in their problems. Letters went unanswered or when answered were very vague and general. During April and May 1977, Charles Lee and his assistant Phil Rugger both left Abbott—Rugger being laid off due to lack of work and Lee fired for cause (incompetence).

In the latter part of 1978 when Abbott was contacting various suppliers/manufacturers, they learned from one such supplier that he felt there was "something fishy" about the project and had relayed these feelings to a Canadian government official. Abbott, concerned about its position vis-à-vis CIDA, intensified its examination of the project. The supplier who tipped off Abbott indicated that Lee and Rugger had attempted to get the supplier and an associate to pay them personally a substantial kickback.

As the analysis of the project continued, it became more evident that documentation was missing, and it was possible there had been theft or fraudulent diversions of equipment that should have gone to Nigeria. Abbott met with its solicitor, who was aware of the contents of the Criminal Code (see the Appendix for excerpts), and it was decided to report the matter to the Ontario Provincial Police. This occurred in early 1979 and an investigation was commenced.

Investigation

The investigation into this matter was complicated by the following issues:

1. The government of Nigeria both at the state and federal level changed, and government officials who may have had dealings in this transaction were no longer available. Later on, South East State changed its name to Anambra, and East Central State changed to Cross River State.

2. Goldcoast Inc. would not cooperate as they were a party to any wrong doing that *may* have occurred.

3. Thefts and losses actually occurred in Nigeria, and it would be extremely difficult, if not impossible, to precisely determine what goods actually arrived in Nigeria.

4. The time element. Many persons involved forgot or chose to forget relevant discussions, and so forth, and blamed this on the lapse of time. Required records may also have been destroyed.

5. Questions remained as to what offenses, if any, occurred and whether they were enforceable in Canada.

6. Questions also remained as to who, if anyone, was the aggrieved party or the victim? CIDA? Nigeria? State governments? Abbott? Canadian public?

Procurement of Equipment

On receiving authorization from CIDA in August 1975 to begin procurement of equipment for the two Nigerian states, Charles Lee and Phil Rugger began visiting various suppliers and manufacturers. Appproximately 42 separate firms did business directly with Abbott. Of these, 22 firms agreed to pay service allowances totalling nearly $100,000. Lee and Rugger convinced those suppliers that the service allowance was necessary to ensure that goods reached their final destination in Nigeria and indicated the money was to be paid to Goldcoast Inc., a Nigerian firm who would pay all bribes. Briefly, they told suppliers that "this is the way they do business over there." Suppliers were not told that Abbott would receive 60 percent of the service allowance back from Goldcoast Inc.

Lee and Rugger were left basically to themselves during this project with Lee responsible for reporting progress to Abbott President Brian Kelly. (See Exhibits 3 and 4 for samples of reports.) It became obvious to Lee and Rugger that they could also profit from this matter personally, and they formed a separate company of their own called Transworld Marketing. Some suppliers were told to pay Transworld for the service allowance. In some cases, Lee and Rugger invoiced suppliers for assistance services provided them, such as vehicle design. The supplier would pay Transworld directly and include these costs as part of his invoice to Abbott. Lee and Rugger had also claimed their hours worked on the particular projects through Able Systems. All Abbott personnel submitted time sheets for hours utilized on this project. CIDA was billed for these hours through Able Systems under the category of Professional Inspection and Direction. The final result was that CIDA (Nigeria) paid twice for certain services performed by Lee and Rugger. Lee and Rugger, according to President Brian Kelly, were not entitled or authorized to engage privately in any work in connection with this project. In all, Lee and Rugger personally received approximately $25,000 in money and goods through their involvement. They also managed to obtain various types of tools and equipment for themselves which were paid for by CIDA funds. In total, therefore, "service allowance" or other payments to Abbott/Goldcoast and Lee/Rugger was $125,000.

It does not appear that CIDA, the Federal Government of Nigeria, or the two states in Nigeria were aware of these payments to Abbott/Goldcoast or to Lee/Rugger. The method used to hide these payments was simple. The firm would invoice Nigeria through Abbott for a purchase price which included the allowance for service. The service allowance was *not* itemized or isolated on the invoice. In a couple of cases where it was, the invoices were returned for correction. Abbott would submit the invoice to CIDA for payment. CIDA would examine the invoices, verifying them to the final "shopping list" and to the quotations, and then authorize payment to Abbott. Abbott would then pay the supplier the full amount, and the supplier would issue a cheque to Goldcoast Inc. or Transworld Marketing depending on the arrangement made by Lee/Rugger. Payments made to

Exhibit 3

ABBOTT CONSULTANTS LTD.
LONDON, ONTARIO

Date: April 30, 1977
Prepared by: Charles Lee
Project: $3 million rehabilitation loan, Nigeria
Client: East Central State Government
               South East State Government
Subject: Status report

Present copies to: N/A
Date of event: April 30, 1977
Location: Toronto

1.0 General

Abbott Consultants Ltd. (Abbott), on the 17th September 1974 entered into an agreement with East Central State Government of Nigeria to act as their purchasing agent in Canada under the $3.0 million rehabilitation loan from Canada through the Canadian International Development Agency (CIDA).

Similarly, on 30th April 1975, Abbott entered into another agreement with the South East State Government of Nigeria under the same loan project.

These states have since changed their names respectively to Anambra State and Cross River State.

Abbott's fee for services under the project was negotiated and agreed at 3 percent of the CIF value of equipment purchased and delivered. This fee was to be shared on a 60-40 basis with Goldcoast Inc., the bigger portion going to Abbott.

2.0 Status of Project

Over 97 percent of the total amount of $1.4 million was spent leaving approximately $38,061.07 yet to be committed to the purchase of further equipment and services.

All three shipments of equipment have arrived in Nigeria, and ensuing insurance claims are being pursued for damage and loss with the insurance company on the first two shipments.

3.0 Prepayment of After-Sales Services

A large number of the equipment purchased had included in the purchase price a component for "after-sales service." This "after-sales service" consists of handling of inquiries on equipment sold on behalf of the manufacturer or suppliers, and processing the reorder of parts, accessories, and repair parts during the warranty period.

Exhibit 3 (*concluded*)

This service allowance was generally around 10 percent of the price of the equipment. As Goldcoast Inc. was also involved in this service, it was agreed that they would receive 40 percent of this service allowance whilst Abbott would receive 60 percent.

4.0 Packaging, Warehousing, Inspection, Handling

Able Systems Ltd. was engaged by Abbott to process all the crating, warehousing, inspection, and handling of all equipment purchases.

Able Systems Ltd. was also charged with the responsibility of processing all matters relating to taxes, customs duties, and duty drawback claims on this project.

Able Systems Ltd. billed Abbott Ltd. a total of $68,719.54 for these services.

Insurance claims currently underway are being handled by Able Systems.

Exhibit 4

ABLE SYSTEMS INC.

Date: May 31, 1977
Prepared by: Charles Lee, Abbott Consultants Ltd.
Project: CIDA rehabilitation loan, Nigeria
Client: Anambra State (East Central)
               Cross River State (South East)
Subject: Service allowances

Present copies to: Goldcoast Inc.

A large number of the equipment purchased had included in the purchase price a component for "after-sales service." This "after-sales service" consists of handling of inquiries on equipment sold on behalf of the manufacturer or suppliers, processing the re-order of parts, accessories, and repair parts during the warranty period.

This service allowance was generally around 10 percent of the price of the equipment and was provided by those suppliers who did not have representation in Nigeria to service this project.

As Goldcoast Inc. is also involved in this project, it was agreed that they would receive 40 percent of this service allowance whilst Able Systems would receive 60 percent.

Of the $83,963.85 received from the suppliers, as per the attached, Able Systems is to receive $50,378.31 (60 percent) with Goldcoast Inc. the balance.

Amount paid to date GCI	$17,374.84
Balance owing	16,210.70
Total (40% of $83,963.85)	$33,585.54

Goldcoast were reported by Lee to Abbott, but, of course, Abbott knew nothing of payments to Transworld Marketing (Lee/Rugger).

In any event, it didn't cost the suppliers anything to comply with these requests as the fee was merely "added on." On subsequent questioning, many suppliers stated they would not have even considered this type of arrangement in domestic dealings, but since it was a foreign transaction and they were told "that's the way they do business over there," they agreed to make the payments.

Controls

Brian Kelly and Mike McPherson had left the actual operational activities totally to Lee and his assistant Philip Rugger. James Dougan, another vice president of Abbott who had a minimal input in negotiations and planning for this project, suddenly found the International Division of Abbott to be his responsibility. The result of this adjustment in Abbott's organizational structure caused Dougan some concern and bitterness, and he responded by adopting a "hands-off" policy allowing Lee and Rugger a free rein with the procurement activities. Lee would prepare status reports during the procurement process, and those would be submitted directly to Abbott President Kelly, who wrongly assumed Dougan was fully apprised of the progress. When the problems surfaced at a much later date, it was found that the record-keeping system was totally inadequate and it was impossible for Kelly's staff to learn what had actually occurred. As stated earlier, Abbott staff then had to contact various suppliers asking for copies of invoices, and so forth, and the response was generally quite negative. Kelly blamed Dougan for failing to ensure that Lee and Rugger were functioning correctly and, in early 1978, asked for his resignation which was submitted.

The implementation of the procurement plan had the following paper flow requirement:

1. Lee and Rugger visited the various suppliers and received quotes on the needed equipment (per the "shopping lists"). After "negotiations" with those companies selected to supply the equipment, orders were made and the equipment was delivered to a warehouse rented by Lee for crating same. Invoices (two copies) were sent directly to Abbott by the suppliers for Lee's attention. On receiving these invoices and other related correspondence and payment cheques from suppliers, CIDA, Goldcoast Inc., or the Nigerian states, an Abbott receptionist would date stamp the material and provide all copies to Lee. No separate record was made of amounts of cheques and invoices by any other Abbott staff.

2. Lee would forward supplier invoices by "batch" to CIDA for payment. On checking invoices to their copy of the "shopping lists," CIDA would approve payment to Abbott and cheques would be sent out. On receipt of these cheques, Lee would deposit them into a bank account set up specifically for the project and later make payment to suppliers (much later in many cases. Some suppliers complained Abbott was holding funds as

long as possible and using them for unrelated Abbott expenses). Lee would provide Abbott's bookkeeping staff with amounts of deposits and disbursements.

With respect to the crating and shipping function, Lee and Rugger were totally in charge of this activity as well, operating on behalf of Able Systems Ltd. All man-hours expended on the project were recorded on Able Systems time sheets, and these were included in the "batches" of invoices sent to CIDA.

Lee and Rugger would personally visit (in most cases) those suppliers who had agreed to pay the "service allowance" or commission to Goldcoast Inc. (or Transworld Marketing) with the Abbott payment cheques for goods supplied. There would then be an exchange of cheques, Lee leaving with the "service allowance" cheque. Those cheques made payable to Goldcoast were accumulated by Lee and would be deposited into Goldcoast's account in Ottawa. Osubu had a relative in Ottawa who would be contacted and would make the required 60 percent payment to Abbott at the time of the deposits. Lee would return with these cheques and deposit them into the Abbott Nigeria project bank account.

Abbott, at the time, was also involved in numerous projects involving their usual type of business activity, and Kelly paid little attention to the progress of the Nigerian project other than asking the very general type of questions such as "How are things going?" to which Lee would respond, "Just great, we're making a lot of money," to which Kelly would respond, "Super."

Appendix: Excerpts from the Criminal Code of Canada

PARTIES TO OFFENSES
SECTION 21 (1) AND (2)

(1) Everyone is a party to an offence who
   a. Actually commits it,
   b. Does or omits to do anything for the purpose of aiding any person to commit it, or
   c. Abets any person in committing it,

(2) Where two or more persons form an intention in common to carry out an unlawful purpose and to assist each other therein and any of them, in carrying out the common purpose, commits an offence, each of them who knew or ought to have known that the commission of the offence would be a probable consequence of carrying out the common purpose is a party to that offence.

THEFT
SECTION 283(1)

(1) Everyone commits theft who fraudulently and without colour of right takes, or

fraudulently and without colour of right converts to his use or to the use of another person, anything whether animate or inanimate, with intent,

a. To deprive, temporarily or absolutely, the owner of it or a person who has a special property or interest in it, of the thing or of his property or interest in it,

b. To pledge it or deposit it as security,

c. To part with it under a condition with respect to this return that the person who parts with it may be unable to perform, or

d. To deal with it in such a manner that it cannot be restored in the condition in which it was at the time it was taken or converted.

CRIMINAL BREACH OF TRUST
SECTION 296

Everyone who, being a trustee of anything for the use or benefit, whether in whole or in part, of another person, or for a public or charitable purpose, converts, with intent to defraud and in violation of his trust, that thing or any part of it to a use that is not authorized by the trust is guilty of an indictable offence and is liable to imprisonment for fourteen years. 1953–54, c.51, s.282.

FRAUD
SECTION 338 (1) (2)

(1) Everyone who, by deceit, falsehood or other fraudulent means, whether or not it is a false pretence within the meaning of this Act, defrauds the public or any person, whether ascertained or not, of any property, money or valuable security,

a. Is guilty of an indictable offence and is liable to imprisonment for ten years, where the subject matter of the fraud is a testamentary instrument or where the value thereof exceeds two hundred dollars; or

b. Is guilty
   i. of an indictable offence and is liable to imprisonment for two years, or
   ii. of an offence punishable on summary conviction, where the value of the property of which the public or any person is defrauded does not exceed two hundred dollars.

(2) Everyone who, by deceit, falsehood or other fraudulent means, whether or not it is a false pretence within the meaning of this Act, with intent to defraud, affects the public market price of stocks, shares, merchandise or anything that is offered for sale to the public, is guilty of an indictable offence and is liable to imprisonment for ten years.

SECRET COMMISSION
SECTION 383 (1) (2) (3) (4)

(1) Everyone commits an offence who

a. Corruptly
   i. gives, offers or agrees to give or offer to an agent, or
   ii. being an agent, demands, accepts or offers or agrees to accept from any person,

   a reward, advantage or benefit of any kind as consideration for doing or forbearing to do, or for having done or forborne to do, any act relating to the affairs or business of his principal or for showing or forbearing to show favour or disfavour to any person with relation to the affairs or business of his principal; or

b. With intent to deceive a principal gives to an agent of that principal, or being an agent, uses with intent to deceive his principal, a receipt, account, or other writing

    i. in which the principal has an interest,

    ii. that contains any statement that is false or erroneous or defective in any material particular, and

    iii. that it is intended to mislead the principal.

(2) Everyone commits an offence who is knowingly privy to the commission of an offence under Subsection (1).

(3) A person who commits an offence under this section is guilty of an indictable offence and is liable to imprisonment for two years.

(4) In this section "Agent" included an employee, and "Principal" includes an employer.

CONSPIRACY
SECTION 423 (1) (2) (3)

(1) Except where otherwise expressly provided by law, the following provisions apply in respect of conspiracy, namely

a. Everyone who conspired with any one to commit murder or to cause another person to be murdered, whether in Canada or not, is guilty of an indictable offence and is liable to imprisonment for fourteen years;

b. Everyone who conspires with any one to prosecute a person for an alleged offence, knowing that he did not commit that offence, is guilty of an indictable offence and is liable

    i. to imprisonment for ten years, if the alleged offence is one for which, upon conviction, that person would be liable to be sentenced to death or to imprisonment for life or for fourteen years, or

    ii. to imprisonment for five years, if the alleged offence is one for which, upon conviction, that person would be liable to imprisonment for less than fourteen years;

c. Everyone who conspires with any one to induce, by false pretenses, false representations or other fraudulent means, a woman to commit adultery or fornication, is guilty of an indictable offence and is liable to imprisonment for two years; and

d. Everyone who conspires with any one to commit an indictable offence not provided for in paragraph (a), (b), or (c) is guilty of an indictable offence and is liable to the same punishment as that to which an accused who is guilty of that offence would, upon conviction, be liable.

(2) Everyone who conspires with any one

a. To effect an unlawful purpose, or

b. To effect a lawful purpose by unlawful means, is guilty of an indictable offence and is liable to imprisonment for two years.

(3) Everyone who, while in Canada, conspires with any one to do anything referred to in Subsection (1) or (2) in a place outside Canada that is an offence under the laws of that place shall be deemed to have conspired to do in Canada that thing.

(4) Everyone who, while in a place outside Canada, conspires with any one to do anything referred to in Subsection (1) or (2) in Canada shall be deemed to have conspired in Canada to do that thing.

Case 2

ABC Ltd. (Revised)

In early 1980, Mr. A. Simon, president of ABC Ltd., a small company located in Montreal, talked about the problems of his firm and its future direction. Of particular concern was defining the nature of ABC's business and developing a product-market strategy.

The History of ABC

ABC was incorporated in late 1970 by Mr. A. Ross, a self-employed engineer; Mr. B. Carter, a sales representative for G-Enterprises; and Mr. A. Simon, also self-employed in research and development subcontracting. The company was formed to produce load stabilizers, a product designed to reduce electricity costs during periods of high usage. This new type of load stabilizer competed with the mechanical load stabilizers then in existence. In 1970, ABC produced the first electronic load stabilizer in Canada.

The electronic load stabilizer was supported by the provincial hydroelectric company (Hydro Quebec) and users. The market need for this product can be illustrated by a short description of the problems it was designed to solve.

In the 1960s, electric energy was cheap and abundant in the Province of Quebec. Companies often installed larger-capacity electric motors than required in order to reduce capital replacement costs. Although the initial cost was higher, longer life and less wear provided smaller total life cost. Sawmills, especially, found it cheaper to use electric energy for their heating and power needs. Hydro Quebec responded by supplying service to sawmills even when they were isolated. In building the service lines, the capacity of the line would be designed for the peak usage of the sawmill. Although the peak usage would occur infrequently, any smaller service line would burn out. Companies were encouraged by discounts to become totally electric. Faced with variations in demand in users and finding its returns reduced by heavy capital investment and discounts, Hydro Quebec introduced a tariff schedule which billed peak electrical usage at a substantially higher rate than regular demand.

The concept of a load stabilizer to smooth out electrical power usage became obvious. A load stabilizer would cut off nonessential energy demand in the plant when peaks became apparent. Firms which were totally electrically dependent found that paybacks from load stabilizers were very short.

The application of load stabilizers was particularly desirable in firms which had or were installing concrete wire mesh heating systems. The stabilizer would provide electricity for heat at times other than when the plant was producing or the sawmill was operating.

The major competitor of ABC was G-Enterprises, which had developed a mechanical unit. G-Enterprises also sold wire mesh heating systems. Since it was to the mutual advantage of Hydro Quebec and other power companies to have a load stabilizer installed on new construction, an electric company representative and a salesman for G-Enterprises would visit a new construction site together. The electric company representative would promote a 100 percent electrical system. A G-Enterprises representative would illustrate the feasibility of a total electrical system by using their products. Favours were often exchanged between representatives.

ABC Ltd. evolved from the association of Carter, working with Simon, and Ross, who was then going under the name of Ross and Associates, Engineering Consultants. Ross learned of the development in the field of load stabilizers from a friend in the electric company. His major interest was in the field of wire mesh heating. Ross became friendly with Carter, a representative for G-Enterprises. The arrangement initially was that Carter sold the load stabilizer and wire mesh heating systems of his company, and Ross performed the engineering services required for installation of the products. Together, they could give the customer a complete package, including installation.

The size and bulkiness of the electromechanical load stabilizer produced by G-Enterprises presented certain difficulties. Carter and Ross subsequently proposed to G-Enterprises that the electromechanical unit be converted to solid-state electronics. The idea was rejected on the grounds that the company had made a substantial investment in electromechanical technology, there was no effective competitor, and the unit worked well.

Carter and Ross began to pursue the possibility of the development of an electronic load stabilizer with Simon, a self-employed engineer in research and development. Simon believed that the unit could be developed for $40,000. Simon agreed to invest $20,000 and Ross, $20,000. Carter agreed to invest $20,000 at a later date. The development took one year, and by August 1970, the first prototype was ready. ABC was incorporated by Ross, Carter, and Simon in the summer of 1970.

The unit was approved by the Canadian Standards Association in the fall of 1970, and the first sale was made to a sheet metal firm. The product was not patented because the partners feared other companies would copy the product. In January 1971, the partners decided to devote the majority of their time to the new business. G-Enterprises within a few years abandoned the load stabilizer field and moved into laser technology.

The Early Years, 1972–1973

The partners operated the company from a rented office, where the units were also assembled. Mr. C. E. Sen, a salesman, was hired away from G-Enterprises. Carter and Sen built sales upon their previous contacts, which were made while working for G-Enterprises. Electronic load stabilizers and wire mesh heating systems were the only products offered by ABC Ltd. Sales increased rapidly, and by August 1971, a technician was added to the staff. Simon gave up his research and development activities and devoted himself full-time to ABC Ltd.

One of the problem areas which surfaced and which would recur in the future related to installation of the units. An electrician was now required to connect the load stabilizer. Also, an entirely new main panel board and a control switch were required which had to be incorporated in a cubicle and installed together.

Sales in 1971 amounted to $214,000. Mr. Sen was made a partner, with an ownership of 10 percent.

The partners decided to pay no dividends but to use all their funds for research and development. They also assumed that they could, by innovation, build a solid firm and perhaps sell out at an attractive capital gain. Their expectations about a sellout were not unrealistic. Westinghouse approached them about a buyout, but the terms were not attractive.

The Development of New Products

In 1972, ABC developed its second product—a pool heater. The development of the pool heater and the firm's entry into the consumer market was partly accidental. Carter and his neighbour had installed swimming pools in their back yards. Heating the pool became a necessity because of the cool summer nights. Carter's neighbour began to investigate the purchase of a pool heater and found that because he heated with electricity, the addition of an electric pool heater required expensive modifications to his present electrical system. Carter shared the identical problem. Carter took the problem to Simon, who found that by applying the electronic load control mechanism to a pool heater, a unit could be operated without expensive changes in the house's present electrical systems. Two units were produced and installed—one in Carter's pool and the other in the neighbour's pool. The results were excellent.

ABC began to produce pool heaters and to market them through electricians. The results were very poor. Although the electricians were impressed with the units, they were more anxious to sell units which were already on the market, since they required expensive changes to the existing house electrical systems at a price between $1,000 and $2,000. The cost of installation of an ABC heater was $50–$100.

ABC conducted a market survey and concluded that the proper channel was through pool retailers such as Val-Mar, Dauphin, and so on. Pool dealers had found that the expensive heating units were obstacles to sales. The retailers of pools found that the low-cost ABC unit solved some of the sales problems.

ABC first produced a 10 kw unit, made of stainless steel. Pool dealers soon began to suggest other models since the 10 kw was too large for smaller pools and too small for big pools. By 1973, ABC began to produce four models—P-5; P-10; P-15; P-20. The company began to have problems with inventories of the various models.

During visits to sawmill operators, Ross, who had retained his consulting business, sold ABC products and also a new hydraulic water jet system for debarking logs. Mill operators shared with Ross their problems in keeping track of inventory and transformation costs. Ross shared these concerns with Simon, who proposed that an analog computer, sensors, and the use of microprocessors would solve the mill owners' problems. Work was begun on a working model called the MS-1000, and the first unit was completed in 1973. Four units were produced. Problems resulted from dust in the mills which clogged the sensor. Servicing costs were high because of the location of the mills. At the end of 1973, ABC discovered that a Swedish firm also produced similar units at substantially lower costs.

The MS-1000 cost approximately $200,000 to develop. Only one additional unit was sold in 1974. The product was discontinued in 1974, although servicing costs would continue for several years.

In 1973, Hyrdo Quebec moved from a position of active marketing of electricity to a passive marketing position. A punitive tariff schedule began to be strictly applied. ABC decided to concentrate on the energy conservation sector.

At the same time, the decision to discontinue the MS-1000 left development costs unpaid. In view of the switch in Hydro Quebec's concern for energy conservation, the company decided to make use of its microprocessors, which had represented the major cost of the development of the MS-1000. Hydro Quebec had decided to apply the penalty tariffication to KVARs. (KVARs measure the wastage when volts and amps are out of phase.) Hydro firms install two meters in a plant—one is for watts (volts x amps), the other is for KVARs. Some industries had an operator control the flow of electricity to eliminate KVARs. ABC decided to enter this market with its microprocessors and to develop an automatic power factor.

In 1974, the first global oil crisis was making itself felt. In view of the escalating costs of oil, many residential oil users were switching to electricity. ABC entered the market with an H-15 air duct heater. The technology was to attach a load stabilizer to an electric heating element which was installed in the air duct system of the existing oil furnace. After a market survey, they decided that the market could absorb at least 1,000 units annually. ABC immediately produced 500 units. The units were promoted through electricians. Four hundred units were sold, and the market disappeared. From 1974 to 1979, ABC would hold an inventory of 100 units, with no market for the product.

In 1975, ABC saw an opportunity to enter the U.S. market by bidding on a project for a proposed energy control system through Niagara-Mohawk. Although ABC believed they would have the lowest bid and were encouraged to bid on the project, they lost the bid. They believed the reason was their Canadian identity.

The lack of sales of the power factor, the cost of bidding on the Niagara-Mohawk (New York State Power Company) study, and the lack of sales of the electric heaters made the company short of cash. Although the company believed entry into the U.S. market required the formation of a U.S. subsidiary, no action was taken.

In 1976, the company received a contract from the Regie des Installations Olympiques who were having trouble with the ice on the cables at the Olympic stadium in Montreal. The cash generated from the R.I.O. permitted ABC to build a new plant. A site was chosen in Laval, Quebec, and in mid-1976, the company moved into a new plant.

The Power Factor

The power factor to automatically regulate KVARs was fully developed by mid-1976. The major problem was marketing. Users did not understand KVARs, the penalty rate, nor the system. It took an average of three days to make a sales presentation. Sixty thousand dollars worth of the power factors were sold in 1976. Consequently, the company decided to push this aspect of their business.

The market for the power factor increased dramatically when Hydro Quebec announced that effective January 1, 1979, efficiency ratings of 95 percent would be required to avoid penalty rates. In 1977, sales reached $350,000. The company anticipated that other companies such as IBM, Honeywell, and Johnson Controls would enter the Canadian market. Honeywell had developed a similar product earlier and was marketing it in the United States as a "total energy management system." Johnson Controls were also in the business. ABC added a sales agent in Vancouver for the power factor and other products in 1977.

The power factor designed to regulate KVARs was combined with the microprocessors and sensing systems to create a total energy management system labelled the 10-series. The total energy system permitted the automatic control of lights, heat, and power utilization of elevators, escalators, doors, and so forth. The system also provided warnings about open doors, over-utilization of electricity, and so on.

In early 1978, the company received a major boost for its 10-series total energy system when it was awarded a contract for a post office. A large food chain purchased one of their energy control systems. Sales were extended to the Western market, where a distributor was instrumental in selling $200,000 of power factors to major British Columbia lumber operators.

By late 1978, ABC Ltd. operated three assembly plants (5,400 square feet, 1,000 square feet, and 2,500 square feet). A 3,200 square-feet expansion was planned for the 5,400 square-feet plant. These plants were under the supervision of a production manager, who along with a sales manager and a vice president, were the three senior executives reporting to the president.

The Year 1979

In 1979, the company began to face different types of problems. The plant was unable to handle incoming orders, and backlogs developed. The air duct heaters (50 in stock in early 1979) which had been sitting on the shelf since 1975 were sold out in June. Orders for this product increased in September and again in December. The president was unsure of the source of the demand and tried to estimate how many more to produce.

Mr. Ross sold his engineering firm and joined ABC on a full-time basis. A 10-series model was sold to a major real estate investment company. The company began to push the 10-series through promotions at trade fairs and advertising in trade journals. The sales manager, Mr. Sen, expressed the new orientation of the company. "Now we are shifting our efforts from the power factor, our present breadwinner, to the 10-series. We feel it's the product of the future."

However, Mr. Simon recognized that ABC still had many different kinds of problems and pondered which was the wisest direction to go. He noted that:

In our type of business, complexity can kill your market. People either don't understand or just don't care. In the future, we will have to change. Our products will have to come from the market. Take the pool heaters—we are in the business just by luck. We had the load stabilizers, and they wouldn't sell. There was a conflict of interest with the electricians. We attached the load stabilizers to a pool heater, and our promotion has been to the pool dealers, not the electricians. Now, we're in the pool heater market. Just luck.

Take the air duct heaters. How do you find clients? It seemed like the perfect product. For five years, we couldn't sell a single one. Now, all of a sudden, orders are pouring in. How come? We're not sure. Do we produce, do we stock? Seventy percent of heating systems are oil/air in Quebec. There's potential, but then?

You know we are a small firm. Sometimes it's good, sometimes it's bad. Large firms are slow to react. They've got so much paperwork. When I developed the paging device,[1] I think I had more paperwork to prepare for them than I spent time developing the thing. Paperwork costs are astronomical for them. On the other hand, we might have only a tenth or less of the expense there. But we suffer in another area: back-up.

Being small has another drawback. It's hard to get in the door. People don't trust us.

You know, large companies can invest in pure R&D; that's fine. But they lack a "feeling." Companies such as the food chain like us. We have the technical ability. They don't. They're sales only. So they know that since we are small, we'll take care of them. But then if we were back at $250,000 (sales), no, they wouldn't want us.

The big companies usually come to us when they have a problem. We are sort of a last resort. You know, large companies like Alcan, for example, have set specifications (rules) for purchasing. We've got to try to change those specifications;

---

[1] A separate product, unrelated to those previously discussed.

it's costly. I understand. They don't want to take the risk on small guys like us. But that's hard on us.

The pool-heater market is great. It's the right size for us, and it's too small to attract the big guys. We try to look for markets that are highly variable and technical with few buyers. We use the strategy: buy Canadian, buy Quebec—and it works.

We are better than Honeywell technologywise. We are faster, less costly, and more advanced. They said it. But then the risk is greater with ABC. We're small.

We are trying the bigger jobs. We underprice the big companies. They burn themselves out on technical jobs.

We are successful locally. We have got opportunities to go across Canada. But how do you train salesmen? Then there is service. I must answer all the technical questions. We are looking for standard products to go national. We have got to change from R&D innovation to marketing innovation. Our products are the best in the world, but they don't sell. We are getting too diversified, and that's dangerous. We will stay with buildings, and we will quote high on the other jobs.

Take the new government complex, for example. It's a three-to-six-man-month proposal. We can bid 40 percent lower than the competition. But then they will think that we are jokers and not serious. They are probably including us in there just because they need a third bid. And you know that, on the government jobs, we must absorb the consulting costs.

We have got to get to know the marketing side. We are concentrating on shaping up our present products. We are already too diversified. We are not looking for new products right now. Nobody is sure in this field, not even us.

We're too weak on the marketing side. We must look up customers. Maybe rental of our products is a solution?

There are many new products in energy conservation. Evaluation of them is hard. What are the proper ones? Firms (R&D-wise) are in front of the market. That's where you get burned. Especially small firms.

Appendix 1:   Extracts from the Financial Statements of ABC Ltd.

ABC LTD.
Balance Sheet Data
(in thousands)

	1970	1971	1972	1973	1974	1975	1976	1977	1978	1979
Assets										
Current assets:										
Cash	$3	$ 5	—	—	$ 10	$ 11	$ 13	—	—	$ 5
Accounts receivable (net) . .	—	77	$ 75	$ 84	166	104	238	$258	$375	300
Inventory (cost)	1	16	68	103	85	161	199	253	277	460
Other	—	—	—	1	—	4	4	6	14	2
Total current assets	4	98	143	188	261	280	454	517	666	767
Fixed assets	—	3	3	3	4	8	164	171	180	205
Other	—	—	—	—	—	—	1	2	4	7
Total assets	$4	$101	$146	$191	$265	$288	$619	$690	$850	$979

Appendix 1   (*concluded*)

Liabilities and Equity

Current liabilities:

Accounts payable accrued		$ 29	$ 24	$ 28	$ 46	$ 69	$115	$128	$185	$166
Overdraft and bank loan		22	62	77	97	60	148	222	318	340
Other	$1	7	2	10	8	19	33	18	20	47
Total current liabilities	1	58	88	115	151	148	296	368	523	553
Long-term debt		18	33	39	35	34	157	156	154	157
Other								4	2	3	5
Total liabilities	1	76	121	154	186	182	457	526	680	715
Equity										
Capital stock						10	10	10	10	10	10
Retained earnings	3	25	25	37	69	96	152	154	160	254
Total equity	3	25	25	37	79	106	162	164	170	264
Total liabilities and equity	$4	$101	$146	$191	$265	$288	$619	$690	$850	$979

Appendix 2:   Sales Summary (dollars in thousands)

Year	Pool Heater	Service	Air Duct Heater	Load Stabilizers	Trellis*	Power Factors	10-Series	Total
Sales:								
1979	$398	$22	$59	$133	$ 96	$1,086	$108	$1,902
1978	284	16	10	118	171	584	44	1,227
1977	305		20	146	166	249	140	1,026
1976	210			280	140	70		700
Sales by percentage ($):								
1979	21%	1%	3%	7%	5%	57%	6%	100%
1978	23	1	1	9	14	47	5	100
1977	30		2	14	16	24	14	100
1976	30			40	20	10		100

Sales by territory:	Quebec	Canada	USA	Total
1979	$1,148	$702	$52	$1,902
1978	976	129	48	1,155

* Part of a load stabilizing system.

Case 3

Air Canada

Introduction

In mid-1986, senior executives at Air Canada were confronted with two of the most dramatic events ever to hit both the federally owned airline and the industry: privatization and deregulation. Top management was preparing its response to a federal government white paper, "Freedom to Move," containing proposals to change radically the regulatory environment. At the same time, it was reported in the media that a memorandum signed by Transport Minister Donald Mazankowski contained a recommendation to sell up to 40 percent of the stock of Air Canada with the remainder to be sold at a future date. It was now up to Air Canada's managers to respond to the various issues it faced.

The next section sets out the changes in regulatory policy taking place in mid-1986. Next a brief history of the industry, together with a summary of the effects of regulatory reform in the United States and a summary of the changing attitudes of other carriers, provides perspective to the issues faced by the management of Air Canada.

Current Changes in Regulatory Policy

In February of 1984, Lloyd Axworthy, then Canada's minister of transport, announced plans to substantially liberalize and ultimately deregulate the Canadian airline industry. On May 10th of the same year, Axworthy introduced a "New Canadian Air Policy" which brought about a substantive change in the approach to regulation in the airline industry. Prior to May 10th, regulatory policy encompassed the following:

- Complete entry regulation for firms and routes.
- Complete regulation of airfares.
- Selective service quality regulation including frequency of service, capacity, aircraft type, and intermediate stop requirements.
- Regulation of conditions surrounding airfares.
- Regulation of exit from markets.

This case was prepared by David W. Gillen, Wilfrid Laurier University, and Tae H. Oum and Michael W. Tretheway of the University of British Columbia. Information was gathered from carrier's annual reports, Statistics Canada, and books and articles written by the authors, in particular, D. W. Gillen, T. H. Oum, and M. W. Tretheway (1985), *Canadian Airline Deregulation and Privatization: Assessing Effects and Prospects*, Centre for Transportation Studies, University of British Columbia. This case was copyrighted © 1986 by Wilfrid Laurier University.

- Regulation of the geographic region in which a carrier might fly and the level and type of service it could provide.
- The use of PCN (public convenience and necessity) criteria for entry and exit with the benefits of competition given little weight.

In this status quo policy, Air Canada was charged with maintaining a profitable operation and was subject to the same regulation as other carriers. In the May 10th policy, Canada was divided into two areas, north and south, with the "old" rules applying to the north and a wholesale change in the rules governing the south as follows:

- Unlimited entry into round-trip charter market.
- Freedom of exit from market when faced with new entry.
- Consolidation of licenses and removal of the conditions of service on airline routes.
- Freedom to reduce prices.
- Price increases allowed up to the inflation rate of air input price index excluding labour.
- PCN remained the basis for regulatory decision making.
- Air Canada was restricted from engaging in competitive pricing and scheduling practices unless it was responding to similar actions by private carriers. Air Canada could also not receive funds from the government unless it met "acceptable financial tests."

The thrust of the May 10th policy was to introduce significant elements of competition into the airline industry but was not intended to be deregulation. Rather, it contained "made in Canada" provisions designed to allow adjustment and strategic planning among incumbent carriers. It soon became apparent that the policy was increasing service and competition, with greatest expansion in the industry at the regional and commuter levels. In fact, Air Canada and CP Air gave up a few routes to smaller airlines with whom they had interline agreements. Unlike the United States, few new carriers emerged, but the United States had undergone complete deregulation, and Canada was only liberalizing.

The May 10th changes in the regulatory structure were the first changes to policy despite the gradual liberalization of the industry begun in the mid-to-late 1970s. In 1985, Don Mazankowski, then the federal minister of transport, issued a white paper entitled "Freedom to Move" which essentially outlined the changes to transport policy the government was intent on making; specifically to deregulate. In particular, the white paper suggested elimination of price and entry controls and a change in the basis of decision making by the regulators from PCN to an emphasis on "fit, willing, and able."

Air Canada faced significant changes in the political and economic environment in which it operated. However, the May 10, 1984, policy change said nothing about what *to do* with the crown carrier, only what the airline could not do. In particular, the 1978 Air Canada Act seemed to have established a relative ranking of objectives—the airline was, like private carriers, first to be profit oriented and was placed in the same position before regulation as other *private* carriers. The change in regulatory policy, in effect, removed any remaining basis for maintaining a crown air carrier; it seemed the natural course of events would lead to a wholly or partially privatized Air Canada.

Brief History

Air Canada (called Trans Canada Airlines until 1963) was created in 1932 to provide a transcontinental air network linking all regions of Canada and to provide service to areas private carriers would not. The crown carrier and the regulation of the industry went hand in hand. Air Canada was given preferred treatment, was treated differently before regulatory agencies (until 1978), and was the focal point with regard to regulatory decisions involving other carriers to ensure they complemented, not competed with, the crown carrier. In essence, a crown carrier had been selected as the appropriate instrument to ensure national linkages and also a continuous and high level of service.

Since the mid-1970s, regulatory policy had been gradually liberalized. Restrictions on charter operations (both domestic and international) were reduced, and charter-class fares were permitted albeit with fences such as advanced booking, minimum stay, and cancellation conditions on scheduled flights. There was also a gradual easing and eventual elimination (in 1979) of all restrictions on CP Air's capacity on transcontinental routes which increased the carrier's ability to compete with Air Canada. A significant event in this period was the passage of the New Air Canada Act which placed Air Canada on an equal footing with other carriers under regulatory control. Furthermore, the act instructed the crown carrier to be market oriented and profit seeking.

In the past, the management of Air Canada believed regulatory reform had proceeded far enough and argued together with senior executives at CP Air and Pacific Western Airlines (PWA) for a "middle ground." Wardair wanted a more rapid move to deregulation, while the Canadian Transport Commission stated that an evolutionary not revolutionary change to greater reliance on market forces was needed. Even after the Air Transport Committee hearings held in 1982, the positions of the participants cited above had not changed.

It was not until 1984 when Lloyd Axworthy introduced reforms to the regulatory environment that some changes in the position of managements took place. CP Air in particular responded to the new direction in regulatory policy by bringing in senior management from the United States (where the airline industry was deregulated in 1978) and becoming very aggressive with mergers to take over EPA (Eastern Provincial Airways) and Nordair. PWA similarly changed its management personnel and structure in the face of seemingly inevitable change. Air Canada was against the reform, and senior management voiced their opposition at every opportunity. This response led the minister of transport, who represented the equity shareholder the Canadian taxpayers, to tell them to stop and align themselves with government policy. The airline grudgingly capitulated.

Deregulation in the United States

Although the 1978 U.S. Airline Deregulation Act provided for a phased implementation of reform, the U.S. Civil Aeronautics Board, under the chairmanship of Dr. Alfred Kahn, effectively moved to complete deregulation immediately after its passage. Because entry was made totally free, the U.S. industry witnessed the emergence of new carriers within two to three years after its passage. Most of these could be characterized as low cost, nonunion, and without restrictive work rules. As these carriers entered markets, severe pressure was put on incumbent carriers.

Before an appearance of the new carriers (it takes a year or two to organize an airline from scratch), carriers which had been confined to specific city-pair markets began to branch out, entering other markets when they saw some synergy with current operations or lucrative profit potential. Several charter carriers, such as World and Capital, commenced scheduled services. Intrastate carriers crossed former regulatory boundaries. Local service carriers started to add transcontinental routes suited to their networks.

With deregulation, both incumbent and new-entrant carriers were faced with various strategic choices. In terms of pricing, incumbent carriers generally selected from one of three alternatives: (1) capacity-controlled discount fares (i.e., "fences" around various discount fares so that price-insensitive passengers would not shift out of higher fare to lower fare classes); (2) peak and off-peak pricing (i.e., higher prices at peak times and lower prices at off-peak or low-load factor times); (3) predatory pricing to meet the competitive response of low fare new-entrant carriers.

New-entrant carriers, who were mostly nonunionized with cost structures lower than the incumbent or major carriers chose from one of four pricing categories: (1) less for less (i.e., low fare and no-frills service targeted at price-sensitive travellers); (2) more for less (i.e., full service at less than standard coach fares to steal market share); (3) more for more (i.e., higher fares but first class service); (4) same for same (i.e., same service as incumbents at same price but aggressive marketing and/or scheduling to steal market share). Studies on the U.S. experience found that the least successful choice was "more for less."

Both incumbent and entrant carriers were also faced with another set of strategic choices as follows: (1) wide-market full service (i.e., full service to many destinations and multiple hubs); (2) wide-market no-frills service; (3) focused-market full service (i.e., a geographic niche with a defensible hub city); (4) focused-market no-frills service (usually combined with "less for less" pricing in high-density markets). Studies found that the two most successful strategies were wide-market full service and focused-market full service. The focused-market full service strategy was successfully combined with a "more for more" pricing strategy to focus on the price-insensitive but service-sensitive traveller.

The main technical and analytical aspects of the impact of deregulation in the United States up to 1985 were as follows:

- U.S. load factors increased on average since deregulation. (They fell off with the recession (1979–82) but were still greater than those of previous recessions.) As the local service carriers added long-stage and higher-density routes, their load factors rose toward those of the larger trunk airlines.
- Former U.S. charter airlines became scheduled airlines.
- Freight decreased in importance for passenger carriers (from 9 percent to 6 percent of revenues). Specialized air express carriers, such as Federal Express, UPS, and Purolator emerged.
- There appears to have been some synergy between regional/feeder and transcontinental routes. Similarly, there may have been synergy between transcontinental and international routes.
- The feed from third-level carriers became important to the trunk and local-service carriers. Nevertheless, no attempt was made to merge a third-level carrier into a large carrier. This suggests there must have been some cost saving in keeping the two types of services separate.
- Since deregulation, almost all air carriers adopted hub-and-spoke route networks. There were two types of hubs. The "complexing" type of hub coordinated batches of arrivals and departures to provide passengers with good service. Since resources could be idle for long periods, it was expensive to operate. A point-to-point hub operated at low cost on a continuous basis. It was suitable only for markets where service levels were not as important as price.
- Annual productivity growth increased from 2.8 to 5.1 percent, thereby outperforming the U.S. business sector.

The number of employees in the U.S. airline industry, in December 1985, was 31,500 *greater* than in December 1978. However, there were significant structural changes within the industry, with the major carriers losing over 9,000 employees since 1978, the nationals gaining 15,000, and new entrants and commuter airliners gaining 25,000. The use of part-time labour increased. While more than 100 airlines were formed after deregulation, 36 carriers sought bankruptcy court protection, and 26 were bought by others.

Wage rates in the U.S. industry had increased at the rate of inflation since the early 1980s, and average compensation per employee increased every year since deregulation.

Aggregate operating profits recovered from the 1979–82 recession to establish two record highs in 1984 and 1985.

Alternative Policies with Respect to Air Canada

The move from a regulated environment to competition between firms represented a fundamental structural change. Management decisions were no longer insulated and inefficiency no longer protected by the artificial administrative rules characteristic of regulation.

Table 1A: Air Canada

	1980	1981	1982	1983	1984
Financial data ($ millions):					
Operating revenues:					
Passenger	$1,642.9	$1,857.0	$1,860.9	$1,844.5	$1,989.0
Cargo	219.1	255.3	264.6	269.7	298.5
Other	119.8	145.9	180.4	199.4	230.0
Total operating revenues	1,981.8	2,258.2	2,305.9	2,313.6	2,517.5
Operating expenses:					
Salaries, wages, and benefits	694.7	773.5	842.1	831.3	873.2*
Aircraft fuel	418.6	567.2	566.4	538.5	542.2
Depreciation, amortization, and obsolescence	130.2	131.1	152.7	144.4	164.7
Other (e.g., maintenance, administration, operation)	647.9	712.8	770.5	771.0	894.6
Total operating expenses	1,891.4	2,184.6	2,331.7	2,285.2	2,474.7
Net income (loss)	$ 57.0	$ 40.1	$ (32.6)	$ 3.8	$ 27.0
Total assets	$1,688.3	$1,869.9	$2,040.6	$2,190.6	$2,512.6
Long-term debt and capital leases (including current portion)	633.5	710.0	891.6	1,092.5	1,315.2
Shareholder's equity	501.2	528.2	482.3	486.1	513.1
Debt/equity	56%	57%	65%	69%	72%
Operating statistics:					
Revenue passenger miles (RPM)† (millions)	15,176	14,351	13.590	12,728	13,905
Available seat miles (ASM)‡ (millions)	22,521	22,008	21,524	19,588	20,396
Passenger load factor (percent)	67.4%	65.2%	63.1%	65.0%	68.2%
Yield per RPM (in cents)	10.8	12.9	13.7	14.4	14.3
Fleet size	122	122	113	115	108
Average number of employees	23,700	23,500	23,300	21,600	21,800

```
      * Statistics Canada figures for 1984 are as follows:
         1. Salaries and wages       =      769.5
         2. Fuel and oil             =      541.5
         3. Depreciation             =      151.9
         4. Maintenance, operation,
            and administration       =      828.5
                                          2,291.4
```

† RPM = Number of passengers flown times length of flight.
‡ ASM = Total number of passenger seats available times the number of miles flown.
Source: Air Canada Annual Reports.

The management of Air Canada faced a more difficult task than other carriers since it entered the competitive marketplace with the shackles of crown owner-ship and it was unclear what course the government would follow. Air Canada's major competitor had traditionally been CP Air, but this could change with deregulation. (The operating and financial statistics of Air Canada and CP Air for the past four years are contained in Tables 1A and 1B). A set of alternative policies which the government could pursue follows.

Table 1B: CP Air

	1980	*1981*	*1982*	*1983*	*1984*
Financial data ($ millions):					
Operating revenues:					
Passenger	$ 521.7	$ 639.9	$ 642.5	$ 661.9	N/A*
Cargo	61.2	62.9	77.0	82.2	N/A
Other	100.9	111.5	143.3	121.5	N/A
Total operating revenues	683.8	814.3	862.8	865.6	932.9
Operating expenses:					
Flying	234.9	308.1	305.1	301.8	N/A†
Aircraft and servicing	92.3	106.3	119.8	118.2	N/A
Sales	115.9	136.9	163.3	171.6	N/A
Other	219.2	265.8	288.7	275.6	N/A
Total operating expenses	662.3	817.1	876.9	867.2	879.9
Net income (loss)	$ 6.8	$ (17.5)	$ (34.7)	$ (13.1)	$ 17.2
Interest on long-term debt	$ (22.4)	$ (37.8)	$ (57.0)	$ (38.8)	$ (41.6)
Long-term debt	292.3	453.2	585.0	414.7	523.3
Debt/equity	86.4%	91.3%	95.8%	53.8%	N/A
Current assets	$ 147.0	$ 148.8	$ 105.0	$ 129.6	$ 248.1
Properties	484.0	670.0	818.4	738.0	859.8
Operating statistics:					
Revenue passenger miles (millions)	5,797	5,992	5,531	5,735	10,233‡
Available seat miles (millions)	8,265	8,727	8,446	8,196	14,614‡
Passenger load factor (percent)	70.1%	68.7%	65.5%	70.0%	70.0%
Yield per RPM (in cents)	9.0	10.7	11.8	11.5	N/A
Fleet size	30	32	31	31	31
Average number of employees	8,291	8,860	7,994	7,370	7,555

* N/A—information was not available.
† Statistics Canada figures for 1984 are as follows:
   1. Salaries and wages   = 253.5
   2. Fuel and oil   = 215.3
   3. Depreciation   =   55.9
   4. Management, operations,
      and administration   = 355.2
                              879.9
‡ Revenue passenger miles and available seat miles are expressed in kilometers in 1984.
Source: CP Annual Reports.

Option I: Pre-May 10, 1984, Air Canada Policy. This is a status quo policy in which Air Canada is 100 percent federally owned. The carrier has reasonable access to public funds without achieving a rigorous private-sector investment test and is expected to establish and provide a service standard for all of Canada.

Option II: Post-May 10, 1984, Air Canada Policy. The carrier must achieve a private-sector test for access to additional funds. The carrier is constrained somewhat in its ability to initiate competitive moves in domestic markets. Federal government ownership of 100 percent of Air Canada continues.

Option III: Privatization without Breakup. Air Canada is sold to the private sector in entirety. There is no breakup of Air Canada, nor are any of its divisions or routes spun off.

There are three alternative ways to privatize Air Canada. The first of these is sale of Air Canada to the highest bidder. Under this alternative, Air Canada is most likely to be sold to a single entity (unlikely another airline). The new owner will exercise complete control over Air Canada, and by all rights the carrier should rapidly become a very effective competitor especially in a deregulated environment.

A second method for the sale of Air Canada would be a general sale or placement of stock. This, for example, is the method that was used for the sale of Pacific Western Airlines in late 1983. Under this scenario, the ownership of Air Canada is likely to be dispersed among a fairly large number of investors. In this case, there is no assurance that the new owners of Air Canada will exercise effective control over the carrier.

A third alternative for the privatization is to sell shares to the company's employees. Air Canada's management have previously recommended this option, at least in part. There is a precedent for this, given that several airlines in the United States such as Eastern Airlines and Pan American have sold stock to their employees as a means to provide productivity incentives and to achieve wage and work-rule concessions from labour. Some of the new upstart airlines in the United States also had employee stock ownership. People Express required a substantial ownership of its stock before one could become an employee of the airline.

Option IV: Privatization with Breakup. Under this policy, there is a dismemberment of the carrier into one or more pieces. Each of the pieces in turn is sold to the private sector.

Methods of Breakup

There are a number of different ways in which Air Canada could be broken up.

One potential breakup is to divide Air Canada into a domestic airline and an international airline. While this would significantly reduce the size of Air Canada in an absolute sense, it does little to reduce the dominance of Air Canada in domestic markets.

There is some evidence suggesting that there are some synergies (or as economists would say, economies of scope) between domestic and international operations. For example, prior to U.S. deregulation, Pan American Airlines operated essentially no domestic routes within the United States (other than a few routes from the West Coast to Hawaii). One of Pan Am's first moves in the deregulated U.S. environment was to open several domestic routes. It was also successful in obtaining control of a domestic carrier, National Airlines. Pan Am, however, soon found that simply having a domestic route system did nothing to improve its overall position. It discovered that for a good synergy between domestic and international operations, the domestic operations must feed the international operations. As a result, from 1980 to 1986 the former National Airlines network essentially disappeared. Pan Am transferred the employees and the airplanes to different domestic routes which better feed Pan Am's major international hubs in New York, Miami, Los Angeles, and San Francisco. By careful planning of schedules and routes, Pan Am was able to carry international passengers for a much longer trip length. The passenger could now travel on the domestic system to the international gateway and from there overseas.

A second alternative being considered was to have Air Canada broken into two or three pieces. Each of these smaller carriers would have a set of regional routes. Each of these regional carriers in turn would receive rights and the necessary equipment and personnel to operate in transcontinental markets. This would give each of the regional carriers an intelligent route structure in the sense that the regional carrier would be able to gather feed and take it on the long hauls. The two (or three) carriers would compete with each other and with CP Air and Wardair on transcontinental routes. Each of the new regional carriers would also be in competition with one or more of the existing regional carriers.

Air Canada as Dominant Player in the Industry

Air Canada's management faced the legacy of being a crown corporation and having been a favoured firm in the industry. As a result of this favoured status, other carriers and interested groups such as the Consumers' Association of Canada expressed concern with respect to Air Canada's dominance of the market and the effect it would have on the performance of a deregulated airline industry. In 1986 Air Canada had a 60 percent share of the domestic Canadian market. This large market share was a concern if it represented a substantial number of markets in which the carrier was a monopoly. It could also be a concern if it indicated that Air Canada had deeper financial pockets than its competitors and thus was able to survive a long and protracted battle to achieve monopoly power.

Some observers of the Canadian airline industry suggested that Air Canada's dominance of the domestic market per se was no need for concern. Some claimed that the threat of entry into markets would force Air Canada to behave properly.

Others, such as former Minister of Transport Lloyd Axworthy, suggested that Air Canada's relatively high cost structure would give it a disadvantage in markets. Axworthy claimed that potential competitors could quickly drive Air Canada out from a market due to its high fares.

From 1984 to 1986, CP Air and others moved more quickly than Air Canada to lower cost structures. In particular, CP Air was much more aggressive and successful than Air Canada in reducing work forces and in asking labour for wage cutbacks and work rule concessions.

Simulation of Alternative Scenarios

Experts on airline cost and demand analysis performed simulations of each of the following scenarios:

1. *Pre-May 10th Air Canada policy:* Air Canada has reasonable access to public funds for its capital needs without going through a rigorous private-sector investment test.

2. *May 10th policy:* There is continued 100 percent public ownership with access to additional public funds only when the private sector's criterion is met. Air Canada is constrained in its ability to act competitively in domestic markets.

3. *Privatization without breakup:* It is assumed the new owners exercise control over the carrier.

4. *a. Privatization in two pieces:* Each piece has a regional network and transcontinental rights.

   b. Privatization in three pieces: Each piece has a regional network and transcontinental rights.

Results of Cost Simulations

The results of the simulations of alternative policies toward Air Canada are summarized in Table 2.

As compared with the pre-May 10th Air Canada policy, the May 10th Air Canada policy resulted in a cost efficiency improvement of 3.1 percent, a total saving of $108 million. This occurred principally through reducing the excess capital stock of Air Canada by applying a more rigid financial test for accessing public funds.

Privatization without breakup would result in Air Canada improving its cost efficiency by 10.6 percent. This in turn provided incentives for CP Air and the regionals to improve their cost efficiency by 1.3 percent and 1.6 percent, respectively, amounting to a total saving of $239 million. Air Canada's cost saving comes from a significant reduction in capital stock (25 percent reduction), dropping 10 percent of its points (which increase average traffic density of its network by 10 percent), and reduction of labour input prices by 5 percent. Since Air Canada's labour input prices have served as an industry standard, the

Table 2: Cost Simulation Results for Alternative Air Canada Policies (regulatory policy fixed at the May 10th, 1984, policy)

	Industry	Air Canada	CP Air	Regionals
(a) Pre-May 10th Air Canada policy (status quo):				
Output* (in millions)	4,443	2,680	1,236	527
Passenger	74.3%	76.2%	73.3%	66.4%
Freight	19.2%	21.2%	18.7%	10.6%
Charter	6.5%	2.6%	8.0%	23.0%
Capital cost ($ millions)	$445	$280	$110	$55
Total cost ($ millions)	$3,468	$2,069	$783	$616
(b) May 10th Air Canada policy:				
Changes:				
Capital stock[†]	Only Air Canada changes	10% reduction	No change	No change
Results:				
Total cost ($ millions)	$3,404	$2,004	$783	$616
Percent change	−1.8%	−3.1%	0%	0%
(c) Privatization without breakup:				
Changes:				
Output	No change	No change	No change	No change
Points served[‡]	Only Air Canada changes	10% reduction	No change	No change
Stage length[§]	Only Air Canada changes	10% increase	No change	No change
Labour prices	5% reduction	5% reduction	5% reduction	5% reduction
Capital stock	Only Air Canada changes	25% reduction	No change	No change
Results:				
Total cost ($ millions)	$3,229	$1,850	$773	$606
Percent change	−6.9%	−10.6%	−1.3%	−1.6%
(d.1) Privatization in two pieces:				
Changes:				
Output	No change	50% each piece	No change	No change
Points served	Only Air Canada changes	60% each piece	No change	No change
Stage length	No change	No change	No change	No change
Labour prices	5% reduction	5% reduction	5% reduction	5% reduction
Capital stock	Only Air Canada changes	37.5% of total	No change	No change
Results:				
Total cost ($ millions)	$3,299	$1,920	$773	$606
Percent change	−4.9%	−7.2%	−1.3%	−1.6%
(d.2) Privatization in three pieces:				
Changes:				
Output	No change	33.3% each piece	No change	No change
Points served	Only Air Canada changes	46% each piece	No change	No change
Stage length	No change	No change	No change	No change
Labour prices	5% reduction	5% reduction	5% reduction	5% reduction
Capital stock	Only Air Canada changes	25% each piece	No change	No change
Results:				
Total cost ($ millions)	$3,287	$1,908	$773	$606
Percent change	−5.3%	−7.8%	−1.3%	−1.6%

* Output is expressed in terms of revenue tonne kilometers. It is measured in these units because passengers and cargo have been aggregated. To translate this measure into revenue passenger miles, each passenger is assumed to weigh 200 pounds.

[†] Capital stock refers to the total dollar value of all capital employed, including aircraft, engines, buildings, properties, and inventory.

[‡] The number of cities served by a carrier.

[§] Stage length refers to average distance flown between cities in the carrier's route network.

reduction of Air Canada's labour prices is likely to trigger other carriers' labour prices by the same factor.

Privatization in two pieces reduces Air Canada's total cost by only 7.2 percent because the two new carriers must separately serve some identical points on their transcontinental routes. This reduces benefits of density economies. Total cost saving of the industry would be about $169 million.

Privatization in three pieces would reduce Air Canada's cost by 7.8 percent and the industry's cost by 5.3 percent. Total saving would be about $181 million. Note there is very little difference in cost savings between a two- and three-way breakup.

In analyzing public policy toward Air Canada, two issues need to be considered: (1) whether to change its ownership (that is, privatization) and (2) whether to break it up to reduce its market dominance. The issue of policy toward Air Canada is inextricably intertwined with that of regulatory policy. Outcomes of regulatory reform depend critically on how Air Canada functions in Canadian markets. Similarly, outcomes of policy changes toward Air Canada depend on the regulatory environment.

If Air Canada were to be privatized, the sale price the government could realize would depend on whether a privatized Air Canada was free to roam in a protected regulated environment or had to face the discipline of a free market. In the free market case, Air Canada's sale price will depend on whether it can use its current market dominance to its advantage or be restrained or perhaps broken up.

Privatization could take one of three forms:

1. *Sale on the open market to the highest bidder.* The price received would reflect expectations of changes in regulatory policy. The new shareholders could force efficiency improvements by the airline.

2. *General stock sale.* This would be an open market operation which could disperse ownership widely among individuals and institutions. In contrast to number one, dispersed shareholders might not be able to force management to improve efficiency.

3. *Sale to employees.* This could represent a majority or minority interest. Efficiency gains would presumably be easier to obtain since labour would have an equity incentive.

There were various combinations of the above that could be considered. In addition, the government could hold minority or majority interests in the air carrier.

A privatized Air Canada, even in a liberalized policy environment, is likely to achieve some significant cost savings. These savings are conditional on the assumption that a privatized Air Canada will have no objective other than maximizing profits subject to the same regulatory constraints other carriers face. It is also assumed that Air Canada is no longer required to establish a level of service to be maintained everywhere in Canada. It will further be free to drop some points not as well suited to its fleet of jet aircraft. Finally, it will no longer be required to establish and maintain a high level of wages to be copied by all other Canadian air carriers.

Costs were simulated for this scenario and found to fall by 6.9 percent. The sources of these gains are reducing excess capital (it will no longer be required to set a high service standard in all markets), dropping some short stage routes better suited to regional or third-level carriers, and a modest (5 percent) reduction in real wages.

Research on airline cost functions has demonstrated that Air Canada has no economies of firm size to exploit (there may be diseconomies) and has exhausted most economies of traffic density. This suggests that it is unlikely to add any new Canadian cities to its network. It also suggests that it would not attempt to increase density of service in existing markets. This would result in no net increase in Air Canada's traffic, although the dropping of some short stage routes would increase its stage length. In other words, existing carriers should not fear Air Canada attempting to gobble up the 40 percent of domestic traffic it does not already have, since doing so would not give it any cost advantage. There is a qualification to this: Air Canada has presently achieved all available economies of traffic density, and costs may be relatively flat (that is, constant) even with increases in density; so while Air Canada would not lower costs by going after a greater share of its existing markets, it would not be faced with cost increases either.

Much of the cost savings predicted to come from privatization are attributable to removing Air Canada's requirement of maintaining the service standard for Canada. This requirement results in higher service levels than some markets warrant and maintenance of service on some short stage length routes. Eliminating Air Canada's use as a policy instrument, not privatization per se, results in savings.

Privatization with Breakup

In the simulation, Air Canada was broken up into one or two pieces, and each piece was sold to the private sector. Each consisted of a set of regional routes coupled with some transcontinental routes. The pieces were allowed to compete with each other, particularly in transcontinental markets.

The simulations indicated that a two-way breakup would result in cost savings of 4.9 percent, while a three-way breakup would result in cost savings of 5.3 percent. The reduction in excess capital was the major contributor to cost savings, as in the case of privatization without breakup.

Since there would be some duplication of points by the new carriers, traffic density (output per point) would fall 17 percent for a two-way breakup and 28 percent for a three-way breakup relative to a single large carrier. Returns to traffic density were roughly constant in this range, so there should be no cost advantage or disadvantage of this. Nevertheless, the smaller broken-up pieces of Air Canada could seek to improve their market shares. If both carriers were aggressive and successful, this could be at the expense of existing private carriers such as CP Air.

There was some evidence that there is an S-curve effect of market share versus capacity offered. That is, up to a 50 percent market share, a carrier could add a given percentage to the number of seats it offered per week in a market and gain a *greater* increase in its market share. After a 50 percent market share, there are decreasing market-share returns to capacity additions. This means that CP Air and others should have less to fear from a dominant (60 percent market share) Air Canada than from a set of smaller broken-up carriers. The latter are more apt to set off a capacity war.

Changes in Both Crown Carrier and Regulatory Policy

Impacts become increasingly speculative with both regulatory and crown carrier policy changes. There is a common thread, however, A privatization policy (with or without breakup), just like a move toward advanced liberalization or deregulation, involves an increase in competitive behaviour in airline markets. Both policies combined would lead to more of the benefits of competition (such as reduced costs leading to lower fares leading to greater traffic) and more of the costs of competition (dropping jet service at small communities, greater profit variability, asking labour for wage or work rule concessions).

The main points of simultaneous changes in these policies were as follows:

- Both privatization (with or without breakup) and regulatory reform lower costs.
- If both occur at the same time, the speed at which markets adjust to new cost levels may be faster.
- Cost reductions should be greatest with deregulation and a breakup of Air Canada, particularly if part of Air Canada is transferred to existing carriers allowing them to reap traffic density economies.
- A privatized Air Canada may be more apt to drop short stage routes under the freedoms of advanced liberalization or deregulation. This could result in even stronger (or at least faster) growth for small carriers than without privatization.
- The pieces of a broken-up Air Canada could attempt to increase each of their market shares under greater regulatory freedom, possibly at the expense of existing carriers.
- The pieces of a broken-up Air Canada, due to their stronger regional affiliations, may be less inclined to drop small regional points from their networks.

Impact on the Organization

In assessing the various scenarios described above, the senior management of Air Canada also had to consider the impacts on their own internal organization as well as on their competitors, particularly CP Air.

Air Canada had significantly more employees than anyone else in the industry. They were not only tied to work rules established through union contracts of the past but also suffered from the politicization of changes to meet competition, due to their crown status. Their competition did not face this significant constraint in adjusting to the new market conditions. CP Air was reported to have had traditionally somewhat higher salaries for pilots and co-pilots, but Air Canada had significantly higher salaries for general management—about 50 percent higher.[1] In summary, on the labour front, Air Canada faced formidable problems. It had more employees, the unions were powerful and could politicize the process of negotiation, average wages were traditionally higher[2] and thus to remain competitive, greater concessions were needed.

In the short term, not only was the airline faced with a need to lower input costs but also to increase productivity. From the experience of U.S. airlines with deregulation, a significant change would have to occur in Air Canada's route network, specifically to move to a hub-and-spoke system, and this would mean dropping some cities and perhaps adding others. As a crown corporation, it had been difficult to drop any city from its route structure because of the political consequences.

In the longer term, to maintain its status as 10th largest carrier in the world, Air Canada planned to purchase new aircraft, a decision which was probably the most important a carrier had to make. The type of aircraft selected was contingent upon the network structure as well as market size. Air Canada's fleet of DC-9 and Boeing 727 aircraft was ready to be replaced—representing a major capital outlay—and the type selected would determine the carrier's success in a given market setting. The key factors were to avoid the overcapacity of the past and have the flexibility to shift between markets. Air Canada was aiming to grow on its intercontinental routes.

A final compounding factor was the decision-making structure of Air Canada. As in many large corporations, there was a large bureaucracy. Any decision not only went through a number of layers but was also being decided by managers who had a ''regulatory psychology.'' Both of these factors had to change if the airline was going to be competitive. CP Air had not only streamlined its management and vested decision-making power in fewer top managers but had also brought in a new president from the United States where the industry had been deregulated for several years.

Some observers felt that Air Canada suffered the malaise of similar state-owned firms: inefficiency from overcapitalization, inefficient pricing principles, and managers who had long periods of tenure and who had little incentive to adopt the most efficient input combinations because they could not realize the gains from their efforts.

---

[1] See Statistics Canada Catalogue No. 51-206, 5 1-101.

[2] For example, from 1975 to 1981, average wages for Air Canada employees were approximately $4,000 greater than the next closest competitor, CP Air. In 1981, Air Canada paid an average salary of approximately $39,000.

Privatization of Air Canada

In 1984, a Toronto-based group of Air Canada employees created the Air Canada Employee Ownership Committee. The Committee surveyed Air Canada employees and found that about a quarter of the airline's employees were interested in purchasing stock. The group developed and presented to the federal government an employee buyout plan for up to 40 percent of the airline, but in early 1985 Prime Minister Mulroney stated publicly:

> Air Canada is not for sale. There may be some persuasive arguments in the case of Air Canada that some people can make in regard to the disposition of equity. I'll take a look at it. But Canada needs a national airline.[3]

Various observers of the prospects for privatizing Air Canada pointed out that one of the difficulties would be setting an appropriate price for an equity issue. The federal government would want to obtain a good return on its ever increasing investment; for example, in the 1978 Air Canada Act, Ottawa assumed approximately $329 million of the airline debt in exchange for 329,000 shares. At the same time, an equity issue would have to be priced to overcome concerns that the airline was facing a possibly tougher environment with deregulation.

Another issue was the percentage of equity to be privatized. If Air Canada was partially privatized, it might suffer from the continuing "shackles of Crown ownership," yet if only partially privatized, a continuing status as Canada's national airline might ensure preferential treatment in international bilateral airline agreements, thereby providing continued access to the more profitable overseas flights. (All international routes were negotiated on a bilateral basis).

Another issue was the potential ownership of the airline. Given that Air Canada had acquired a good international reputation, there might be investor interest outside Canada. However, the federal government might not allow even a significant majority of Air Canada shares to be held outside Canada.

By mid-1986, the government had given no indication of its intentions on the privatization issue, only that the federal cabinet's privatization committee was studying a document related to the issue. The press noted in June, 1986 that "executives of Air Canada have been pushing the government to sell off at least part of the company for some time. The company needs an injection of cash to go ahead with future plans to revitalize its fleet."[4]

Position of Air Canada's Management

The issues of deregulation and privatization had been examined and discussed by various players (see the Appendix). It was now time for Air Canada's manage-

---

[3] *The Globe and Mail*, January 15, 1985, p. 1.

[4] *Kitchener-Waterloo Record*, June 18, 1986, p. B7.

ment to take a position. Should they push for both privatization and deregulation? If so, what would be the strategic and organizational consequences?

Appendix: Position of Key Stakeholders, 1981–1986

Air Canada

In 1981 both top managers of Air Canada, Claude Taylor and Pierre Jeannoit, responded to the Economic Council of Canada's call for deregulation by claiming competition was already fierce. Both argued that the recent introductions of discount fares and liberalized entry regulations gave the Canadian consumer most of the benefits of deregulation. Both stated a move away from government protection toward free competition would ruin the industry. It was not until 1984 and only after strong arguments from Lloyd Axworthy, then minister of transport, that Air Canada executives supported the moves to deregulation. The support was cautious and called for a plan of regular reviews. By 1986 both executives were calling for privatization so they could better meet competition from CP Air.

CP Air

Gerald Manning, a vice president of CP Air, concurred with Air Canada executives claiming that deregulation would create market chaos. CP generally wanted the industry regulations to remain intact but to have CP given greater freedom to compete equally with Air Canada. By 1984 CP recognized regulation had created inefficiencies and welcomed the changes introduced by Lloyd Axworthy. The company was being restructured for the forthcoming changes in the competitive environment although there was concern about the market dominance of Air Canada and its favoured position as the crown-owned carrier.

Other Airlines

A major voice lobbying for regulatory changes was Max Ward of Wardair, a major charter airline. He continually argued for greater freedom for Wardair in the domestic market.

Regional carriers such as Eastern Provincial and Pacific Western favoured moves to a more liberalized environment.

Government

Officials at both Transport Canada, the policy-making body, and the Air Transport Board of the Canadian Transport Commission sided with Air Canada and CP Air. They continually frustrated all efforts to introduce greater competition, and it was only after Lloyd Axworthy circumvented their actions that any signs of competition and lower fares were introduced.

Other Groups

Labour unions lobbied heavily to stop any moves to deregulation or any freer competition. Labour has been the biggest gainer from regulation both in terms of higher wages and greater employment because of work rules.

Academics and the Consumers Association of Canada had always called for freer competition so that firms in the industry were subject to the rigours of the marketplace. Both groups argued such competition would provide a broader range of price-quality fare combinations.

Case 4

American Skate Corporation

Introduction

In August 1979 Mr. Alan Adams, general manager of American Skate Corporation, and Mr. C. Herbert Charlton, president of American Skate's Canadian parent, Dominion Skate and, incidentally, Mr. Adam's father-in-law, were reviewing the $2 million financial package put together during the summer of 1979 for the opening of a roller skate plant in Berlin, New Hampshire. The New Hampshire plant was viewed by both men as being a critical element in the Canadian parent's plan for a major U.S. expansion to take advantage of the tremendous roller skating boom in North America. Nonetheless, Alan Adams and Herb Charlton wanted to reconsider all the relevant aspects of the plan before making a final decision to proceed with the Berlin plant. The proposed package involved $1,650,000 long-term debt from various U.S. and New Hampshire development groups, a lease-purchase agreement totalling $500,000 for a 44,000-square-foot plant capable of initially adding 20 percent and, within a year, 200 percent to Dominion's production capacity. All of the debt issued to the subsidiary American Skate was to be guaranteed by both Dominion Skate, which owned all of American Skate's stock, and by Herb Charlton personally.

"Alan, I don't mind going out on the limb if the deal is a good one," Herb told his son-in-law, "but I want you to help me double-check this New Hampshire project in all its aspects. I know I've called the shots pretty much so far, but this will be your baby."

The following paragraphs describe the roller skate industry, the background of both Dominion and American Skate and of their top managements, and the financial package that had been put together during the spring and summer of 1979.

The Roller Skating Industry

Roller skates were first introduced in Holland during the 18th century, and consisted of wooden spools strung on a wooden frame, which was in turn nailed onto the bottom of wooden shoes. These skates were difficult to turn, but this problem was overcome by an American inventor, James Leonard Plympton of

This case has been prepared by Jonathan Foster, London School of Economics, and John Barnett, University of New Hampshire. Copyright © 1984 by J. Foster and J. Barnett.

New York. In 1863 Mr. Plympton put four independent wooden wheels on a shoe, making the skate easier to turn. This original pair of Plympton's skates is now housed in the National Museum of Roller Skating in Lincoln, Nebraska, along with pictures of the first roller skating arena, which Mr. Plympton opened in New York a few years later.

The modern roller skate consists of the boot, a base plate, wheels and ball bearings, and the toe stop. The manufacturing process of a complete roller skate includes the following steps: (1) using sets of dies to cut the various parts of the boot from leather or other boot material; (2) machine stitching the various parts of the boot including adding "counters" of reinforcing material in the heel and adding eyelets; (3) stitching the boot together around a mold of a foot, called a last; (4) buffing or "roughing" the leather so that it would accept glue; (5) using a combination of glue and staples and a series of machine steps to complete the toe and heel; (6) removing the last; (7) attaching the base plate; (8) securing the wheels and toe stops to the base plate; and (9) inspecting and packing.

Very few manufacturers performed all these steps. Many bought the finished boot from others and attached the base plate, wheels, and toe stop. The manufacturers sold completed skates to sporting goods retailers, distributors, and wholesalers, to chain stores, and to roller skating rinks.

The stimulus for growth in the roller skating industry came from skateboard technology. During the skateboard craze in the mid-1970s, wide polyurethane wheels and precision bearings were perfected that allowed for a quiet ride on pavement. Further, the polyurethane wheels were much more absorbent than earlier metal or hard rubber wheels. As the roller skate manufacturers adopted these wheels and bearings in the late 1970s, the roller skate explosion began as skates moved out of rinks and into the streets and parks.

The roller skating industry just prior to the 1978–79 explosion consisted of a few privately held companies of which Dominion Skate was the only fully integrated major manufacturer. *Time* magazine reported that total industry sales were about a million pairs of skates per year.[1] The major firms included Roller Derby Skate, Chicago Roller Skate, Dominion Skate, and Sure-Grip International, and total dollar sales for the industry were estimated by the casewriters as $25 to $30 million. Roller Derby Skate of Litchfield, Illinois, *Business Week* observed, "dominated U.S. roller skate manufacturing with aggressive pricing of its low-end models."[2]

The roller skate explosion had North American and international repercussions. Table 1 shows *Business Week*'s estimate of 1979 sales by the U.S. leaders:

Keith Parker, the marketing vice president of Nash Manufacturing, described how his company, a major skateboard manufacturer, converted to roller skates in a 60-day period in the fall of 1978. Producing 8,000 pairs a day by the summer of 1979, Mr. Parker commented:

---

[1] *Time*, August 6, 1979, p. 66.

[2] *Business Week*, August 27, 1979, p. 120.

Table 1:   Estimated 1979 Sales

Company	Estimated 1979 Sales in Millions of Dollars
Roller Derby Skate (Litchfield, Illinois)	$ 50–60
Nash Manufacturing (Fort Worth, Texas)	25
Sure-Grip International/RC Sports (California)	20–25
Chicago Roller Skate (Chicago, Illinois)	15–20
Mattel (California)	7–10
Total top five U.S. companies	$117–140
Estimated total U.S. sales	$200

Source: *Business Week*, August 27, 1979, p. 120.

The key to our success is that we've expanded much quicker than others. But demand has to hold for another year if we're going to make much profit. . . . The skate business is in such an uproar that we could ship a million pairs tomorrow and still have back orders.[3]

New U.S. manufacturers joined the industry, including Nash and Mattel, the $500 million toy manufacturer that invested over $1 million to begin producing roller skates in March 1979. Further, foreign manufacturers expanded into the North American market. Imports rose from $2 million in 1978 to $30 million in 1979, led by Taiwanese imports. Over 90 factories produced skates in Taiwan, and that nation soon had 85 percent of the U.S. imported market.[4]

The top-of-the-line, premium-priced skates continued to be manufactured in the United States. While children's and low-priced skates might retail from $20 to $50, with adult prices averaging $60, the well-regarded competition skates produced by the Dayton-based Snyder Skate Company were selling from $110 to $175 a pair. Snyder reports 1979 sales up 30 percent from 1978.

Articles on roller skating appeared in almost every major periodical during 1979, including *Changing Times, The Saturday Evening Post, Popular Mechanics, People, McCalls, Redbook,* and *Glamour*. Skates were endorsed by O. J. Simpson and were worn by Linda Ronstadt on a phonograph album cover. The number of roller skating rinks doubled to over 6,000 during the 1970–78 period—500 new rinks were being added in 1979—and roller disco became a major leisure activity.

Bill Butler, the "Godfather of Roller Disco," looked forward to the opening in the fall of 1979 of his chic New York nightspot, the Roller Ballroom. Butler, who had skated for 38 of his 45 years, had a perspective on skating including a "whole philosophy of life" based on the sport. Nonetheless, *Popular Mechanics* commented:

---

[3] Ibid.

[4] *The Wall Street Journal*, April 6, 1981, p. 25.

New products come on the market so fast nowadays that even the Godfather of Roller Disco has trouble keeping up. Consider, for example, the two cycle, 1.2 HP engine that Motoboard International of Sunnyvale, California, suggests you slip on the back of your skate. For $289 you can zip down the highway at 40 MPH with the wind blowing through your hair and your whole life passing before your eyes.[5]

Sports Illustrated devoted several pages to a guide on buying skates in its October 15, 1979, issue and specifically recommended Reidell and Oberhamer tops for boots ($40 to $90 retail), Chicago or Sure-Grip for the plates and wheels ($20 to $100 retail), and Snyder as the top of the line, with custom skates as high as $400 a pair. Butler commented that his ideal choice was a plate by Snyder, a Reidell boot, and Krypto wheels.

Positive signs for the roller skating industry included a Gallup Poll in early 1979 that showed roller skating fifth in popularity among teenagers, ahead of both tennis and skiing and following basketball, baseball, swimming, and bowling. Both the Girl Scouts and the Boy Scouts gave merit badges for roller skating proficiency.

Fifty percent of the U.S. teenage market would represent about 25 million pairs of skates. The total of North American skaters was estimated at between 30 and 40 million individuals, most of whom skated at rinks where rental skates were available. Chicago Roller Skate was particularly aggressive in skating rink sales.

Many commentators were optimistic. A vice president of Herman's World of Sporting Goods reported a 400 percent increase in skate sales during the first half of 1979 at its 90 stores and noted that "the only thing that is slowing growth is product availability.[6] Mattel's Louis Miraula stated:

> The universe of potential skaters is enormous. Because of the new wheel, people discovered roller skating was an outdoor sport, à la jogging, but a lot more fun. The growth of this industry has a fad quality right now, but there is still that hard-core business that is not going to change substantially.[7]

The optimistic manufacturers predicted $400 million in annual skate sales would be achieved by the early 1980s.

Somewhat more cautious views were expressed in the August 27, 1979, issue of *Business Week* by Chicago Skate, which had concentrated on rink sales:

> An idiot could make money in today's market. I'm walking on tiptoe, trying to gauge whether this is just another fad or has several years of life.
>
> Joseph Sheuelson
Vice President, Sales
Chicago Skate

by Roller Derby's national sales manager:

---

[5] *Popular Mechanics* 151 (June 1979).

[6] *Business Week*, August 27, 1979, p. 120.

[7] Ibid.

The demand is tremendous, but we don't know exactly where it is going. In many ways, what is happening is as new to us as to anybody, although we're the leader in the business.

> Kenneth Neidl
> *National Sales Manager*
> *Roller Derby Skate*

and by Sure-Grip/RC Sports:

This is an extremely fast-growing industry, paralleling the sustained demand for bicycles that began 10 years ago. Most manufacturers are now living in a fairy-tale world where demand exceeds supply. In such an atmosphere, those that don't keep their heads could get hurt very badly.

> Dennis Lane
> *International Marketing Director*
> *RC Sports*

A more negative view was expressed by a financial analyst:

By its very definition, the "in thing" gets stale after a while. When everyone who is interested in roller skates has a couple of pairs, that's going to be it.

> Harold Vogel
> *Leisure Industries Analyst*
> *Merrill Lynch*

Brunswick Corp., the national sporting goods company, sold its small skate division. A skateboard manufacturer, whose 1979 sales were one fifth of 1978's, said he couldn't tell if "roller skates might be like skateboards—here today, gone tomorrow."

Dominion and American Skate

Dominion Skate's Early Years

Herb Charlton had gone to work for his uncle, owner of Dunn's Skate, Ltd., when he was very young. By the time his uncle died in 1946, Herb, then 32, had had substantial experience in all aspects of roller skate manufacture. Not wishing to continue working for his aunt, Herb left Dunn's and began Dominion Skate in the basement of his house near Mississauga, Ontario. Within a few years, Dominion and its three employees overflowed Herb's basement and garage and moved into a vacant school a few doors from the house. In 1958 an older plant facility in Mississauga, a short drive from Herb's house, was leased, giving Dominion a 3,000-square-foot, two-storied building. Additions were made to this plant in 1962, 1970, and 1972. A second plant was leased 15 miles away in Toronto in 1973 and an assembly plant in Mississauga in January 1979. By August 1979 Dominion employed 120 people at three rented locations:

Location	Year Opened	Activity	Square Feet
Mississauga	1958	Manufacturing, assembly	20,000
Toronto	1973	Manufacturing, assembly	20,000
Mississauga	1979	Assembly	10,000

Each plant had a salaried plant manager, each of whom had worked with Herb for some time. Herb Charlton's policy of no layoffs and competitive wages resulted in a hard-working labour force that also had a low turnover rate.

Management

Herb Charlton, 65 years old in 1979, was president and chief financial officer of Dominion Skate and president of American Skate. While Herb made all important decisions, he was assisted by his son Paul, 33, director of plant engineering, his daughter Naomi, 31, office manager, and his son-in-law Alan Adams, 37, production manager and, more recently, general manager of the American subsidiary, American Skate Corporation.

Like Herb Charlton, Alan had dropped out of school and had held several positions as a factory worker and as a printer's apprentice. In 1958 Alan, then 17, went to work for Dominion Skate at the suggestion of Herb's daughter whom Alan was then dating and to whom he was subsequently married.

Dominion sold roller skates, ice skates, and children's double-runner bob skates through a distributor to a small group of retail accounts throughout Canada, ice skates helping to offset the seasonality of roller skates. Paul and Alan would occasionally call on these retail accounts, or Herb would infrequently show customers around the Ontario plants. Dominion had a reputation with its customers for a high-quality, medium-priced skate. Dominion had kept pace with industry technology, and its advertisements referred to its "space age skates" with models called "All American Dream" and "Inertia."

U.S. sales were handled by a marketing firm, King R. Lee and Associates, Santa Ana, California. King Lee in turn called on 10 specialty distributors in the United States.

Operations were financed by small working capital loans from local banks, by advances from Herb Charlton, and by trade credit.

Total production capacity was about 285,000 pairs a year. This capacity was based upon one-shift operations. Alan Adams noted that Herb Charlton didn't like to have more than one shift.

> I guess it was partially due to his wanting to be on top of things. Herb relied on personal inspection rather than formal production control systems. This philosophy of personal control extended to stock ownership as well. I had asked him about my owning some stock, so that I could have some security, but even after 20 plus years of working for him, I never got any stock.

Financial Results

Exhibits 1, 2, and 3 present balance sheets, income statements, and related financial statistics for the years of 1976, 1977, and 1978, and the six months ending June 1979.

Exhibit 1

DOMINION SKATE CO., LTD.
Balance Sheets
(Canadian $)

	For Six Months Ended June 30, 1979	For the Year Ended December 31		
		1978	1977	1976
Assets				
Current assets:				
Cash, certificates of deposit	$ 109,100	$ 239,700	$ 173,800	$ 22,400
Accounts receivable	1,081,300	682,600	464,000	286,300
Net inventory	486,000	461,700	218,300	211,500
Total current assets	1,676,400	1,384,000	856,100	520,200
Fixed assets—net:				
Machinery, equipment	93,100	103,400	78,100	50,400
Vehicles, leasehold improvements	23,400	26,700	13,300	4,400
Total fixed assets	116,500	130,100	91,400	54,800
Other assets:				
Goodwill	15,000	15,000	15,000	15,000
Land deposits	211,200	211,200	—	—
Total other assets	226,200	226,200	15,000	15,000
Total assets	$2,019,100	$1,740,300	$ 962,500	$ 590,000
Liabilities				
Accounts payable, accruals	$ 636,800	$ 706,100	$ 497,400	$ 257,600
Taxes payable	173,700	170,200	38,600	12,200
Bank loan	–0–	50,000	–0–	95,000
Shareholder advances	246,600	219,900	101,200	54,800
Total liabilities	1,057,100	1,146,200	637,200	419,600
Equity				
Preferred stock	100	100	100	100
Retained earnings	961,900	594,000	325,200	170,300
Total equity	962,000	594,100	325,300	170,400
Total liabilities, equity	$2,019,100	$1,740,300	$ 962,500	$ 590,000

Exhibit 2

DOMINION SKATE CO., LTD.
Income Statement
(Canadian $)

	For Six Months Ended June 30, 1979	For the Year Ended December 31		
		1978	1977	1976
Sales	$2,655,800	$4,267,100	$3,182,600	$1,518,600
Less: Cost of sales	1,581,900	2,540,500	2,099,900	889,200
Gross profit	1,073,900	1,725,600	1,082,700	629,400
Operating expenses:				
Administrative payroll, sales commissions	410,500	811,800	649,800	445,800
Supplies, freight	65,500	137,500	69,300	51,300
Advertising	1,100	10,600	3,400	2,400
Insurance	12,200	15,800	9,700	6,800
Professional fees	1,800	2,200	1,200	900
Office expenses	4,500	10,500	6,700	4,600
Repairs	3,300	2,700	2,100	500
Rent	34,300	52,800	42,000	33,800
Telephone, Utilities	13,400	20,000	15,400	11,100
Travel	1,300	1,300	500	200
Vehicle	2,400	2,200	4,100	2,800
Miscellaneous*	27,500	54,400	30,200	16,400
Depreciation	13,600	34,400	24,800	15,000
Bad debt	12,700	21,500	1,000	(5,300)
Total operating expenses	604,100	1,177,700	860,200	586,300
Operating profit	469,800	547,900	222,500	43,100
Interest expense	5,900	5,100	9,200	6,800
Taxes	180,500	189,300	58,500	17,400
Total	186,400	194,400	67,700	24,200
Profit after tax	$ 283,400	$ 353,500	$ 154,800	$ 18,900

*Donations (Baptist Church) 1978, 1979 at annual rate of $22,000. Pensions at annual rate of $11,000 (1978), $15,000 (1979). Balance is discounts.

The Financial Package

Berlin, New Hampshire, was considered as a site for U.S. expansion because a Canadian supplier had recently expanded into New Hampshire and had told Mr. Charlton that he "got a good deal" in New Hampshire. Northern New Hampshire was less than a day's drive from Toronto and less than half a day's drive from Montreal, where Dominion's Canadian distributor was located. Finally, Berlin development groups had actively pursued Dominion, once its expansion interests were known.

Exhibit 3: Dominion Skate Co, Ltd. (selected financial statistics)

	1979 (6 months)	1978	1977	1976
Solvency:				
Debt/equity	1.1	1.9	2.0	2.5
Times interest earned	79.6	107.4	24.2	6.3
Liquidity:				
Net working capital	$619,300	$237,800	$218,900	$100,600
Current ratio	1.6	1.2	1.3	1.2
Funds management:				
Days sales in receivables	$ 74	$ 58	$ 53	$ 68
Days cost goods in payables	72	101	87	107
Inventory turnover	5.6	12.6	14.8	
Profitability:				
Return on sales	11%	8%	5%	1%
Return on assets	14	20	16	3
Return on equity	29	60	48	11

The financial plan put together as of August 1979 included: (1) a working capital loan of $1,150,000 from the Economic Development Administration (EDA), a branch of the U.S. Department of Commerce; (2) a loan of $100,000 from a New Hampshire venture capital group; (3) a loan of $400,000 from the Berlin (New Hampshire) Economic Development Council (BEDCO); and (4) a lease-purchase agreement with the Berlin Industrial Development and Park Authority (BIDPA).

Berlin, New Hampshire, about 175 miles north of Boston, had a serious unemployment problem among its population of 13,000. The Converse Rubber Company, a manufacturer of athletic shoes, had closed in early 1979, laying off 400. The only significant employers in Berlin were the James River paper company, employing 1,200 to 1,500, and Bass Shoe, employing 250 to 350. Thus BEDCO and BIDPA were anxiously encouraging American Skate to locate in Berlin. BEDCO, directed by a board of business and labour officials and city government representatives, usually lent $5,000 for every job created by a new employer. BEDCO offered American Skate $400,000 at 6 percent annual interest, due in quarterly installments of $10,000, provided that American match its $400,000 with equity.

BIDPA, the developer/administrator of a small industrial park, had a board of directors similar to BEDCO. BIDPA had already built a 44,000-square-foot building, which was vacant and incurring interest charges. BIDPA offered American a 22-year lease-purchase agreement totalling $500,000, with gradually increasing monthly payments. Real estate taxes were waived.

In addition to the Berlin debt, a New Hampshire venture capital group also offered a $100,000 loan at prime (then about 12 percent) plus 1 percent. The State of New Hampshire was, of course, attractive to Charlton and Adams as it had no

Exhibit 4: Estimated Total Skate Orders by Lee's 10 Distributors for All Skates of All Manufacturers

Firm	Annual Volume in Pairs
Gordon & Smith, San Diego, California	93,500
L. Cohen, Los Angeles, California	20,500
Smoothill, San Rafael, California	65,000
West Coast Cycle, Culver City, California	156,000
Bike Factory, Bellevue, Washington	31,000
Donel Distributors, Garland, Texas	31,000
Southeastern Sales, Florence, Alabama	15,500
Tuflex, Ft. Lauderdale, Florida	78,000
A.W.H. Sales, Evanston, Illinois	65,000
Lubins, Watertown, Massachusetts	31,000
Total	586,500

personal state income, sales, or use taxes and was replacing inventory and similar taxes with a flat 8 percent of net profits tax on businesses.

The EDA, offered a 10½ percent $1,150,000 loan, payable over seven years, with gradually increasing monthly payments. Thus, pressure for economic support expressed itself not only from local and state groups but at the federal level as well.

Equipment for the Berlin plant location was available to American Skate for $130,000 from Tiera Footwear of Dover, New Hampshire, which was in liquidation. Tiera's equipment would be sufficient for American's needs.

In trying to determine sales and costs, Herb Charlton and Alan Adams asked King Lee for an estimate of the potential total skate orders from Lee's 10 U.S. distributors for all skate manufacturers. This estimate, totalling 586,500 pairs a year, is reproduced in Exhibit 4. Lee was unsure what percentage of these total orders American Skate might expect to receive.

Dominion Skate estimated its own Canadian sales potential as 312,000 pairs a year. As mentioned above, Dominion's current productive capacity was 286,000 pairs a year. Dominion estimated that the total North American industry sales for all manufacturers would climb from the pre-1979 level of $30 million to over $200 million in the early 1980s, falling to $100 million by 1984.

The Berlin plant would initially produce at an annual level of 65,000 pairs and within one year could be producing as many as 520,000 pairs on a two-shift basis. Initial employment of 100 should be 300 in two years, if the company's predictions were accurate.

The differential cost of producing a pair of skates was estimated by the company as shown in Exhibit 5. This cost is for an average pair and would be equally true for Ontario or New Hampshire production. New Hampshire administrative salaries would be about $200,000 a year, half of which would be the general manager's salary, and other overhead costs might be an additional $100,000.

Exhibit 5: Cost Estimates for Average Pair of Skates

Selling price		$12.95
Materials:		
Boot	$2.85	
Plate	.77	
Wheels	1.28	
Bearings	1.04	
Toe stop	.14	
Hardware	.35	
Axle	.20	
Box	.19	
Other	.16	
Total materials		6.98
Labour		.75
Selling commission		1.56
Total		9.29
Gross profit		$ 3.66

Summary

Both Herb Charlton and Alan Adams believed that the financial package available to them now could not be modified further. At a meeting to reach a decision on the Berlin plant, the following dialogue occurred:

Adams: In addition to liens on all the equipment, you will have to personally guarantee all these loans. But how can you beat $400,000 at 6 percent and $1,500,000 at 1½ percent below prime?

Charlton: Alan, I believe in growth. Every two or three years we've leased new space or bought new equipment. That cycle means 1979 is a year for more growth. Still, it will be your project to live with. What do you think?

Case 5

Arcop ("Architects in Co-Partnership")

By 1966 Arcop ("Architects in Co-Partnership") had experienced a period of dramatic growth. The firm evolved from a working relationship of three architects in a basement in Montreal in 1953 to a renowned designer of major buildings involving six partners with billings of over $3 million and a staff of almost 150 people.

With rapid growth also came a fundamental conflict among the Arcop partners concerning the need for formal organization and structure. In particular, Guy Desbarats, one of the partners who tended to assume responsibility for the administrative work, favoured a clearer and tighter organization structure for the firm, while Ray Affleck, another partner, preferred a loose structure that would not restrict his work. One of Ray's allies on the issue, Fred Lebensold, summarized his position as follows:

> Once we get institutionalized, organized, categorized, that's when we are dead. . . . The most important considerations for us are the preservation of our spirit . . . and the preservation of our quality.

The Arcop partners wondered how their fundamental conflicts about the formalization and control of the firm should be resolved.

The Origins of Arcop

The origins of Arcop can be traced to 1953, when Ray Affleck, Guy Desbarats, and Jean Michaud pooled their resources to start their own independent architectural practice in a basement office. They were joined shortly afterward by Hasen Size. All of them, with the exception of Jean, had met while teaching architecture on a part-time basis at McGill University. The group hired a secretary and a student draftsman to assist them in their work.

In these early years, they each obtained and conducted their own work, most of which was in the form of small residential or commercial jobs. However, the start of collaborative effort began when Jean and Ray worked together on the Town of Mount Royal Post Office and Hasen and Guy worked on the Beaver Lake

This case is taken directly, with minor editing, from H. Mintzberg, J. Shamsie, S. Otis, and J. A. Waters, "Strategy of Design: A Study of 'Architects in Co-Partnership,' " to appear in J. Grant, ed. *Significant Development in Strategic Management*, forthcoming. Permission to reproduce has been granted by H. Mintzberg.

Pavillion. These were generally regarded as the first modern buildings in Montreal. In general, this work reflected a shared commitment among the partners to innovation and excellence. The Town of Mount Royal Post Office became the first public building to receive a Canadian national award for architecture.

The development of Arcop was encouraged by the many architectural competitions being organized all across the country to support the development of domestic talent. In late 1954 the group joined forces with another colleague at McGill, Fred Lebensold, and one of Fred's students, Dimitri Dimakopoulos, to prepare a submission for a performing arts centre in Vancouver. Their joint entry was awarded first place in the competition, and the group, now six architects, had its first large job: the Queen Elizabeth Theatre.

The award necessitated a firm partnership agreement. As Fred noted, "We suddenly realized . . . that it wasn't just a competition . . . it was a real job . . . . We had never done a job of that size before . . . never." The theatre became the first job shared among all the partners. However, the partners continued to work more or less on their own on other small residential and commercial jobs, occasionally splitting the work. In 1956 they all moved into a two-storey house in Montreal and hired several architects and draftsmen primarily to assist with the work for the theatre. The total staff approached 15 people by early 1958. An office manager was hired to oversee the nontechnical office functions, including billing and record maintenance.

Around this time, the emerging organization was further crystallized as a result of a visit from I. M. Pei and Associates, a large U.S. firm in need of a local group to supervise production of a major commercial complex planned for Montreal. Commenting on the partners' response to I. M. Pei, Ray noted, "They were very New York, offices right on Madison Avenue . . . asked to see our brochures, C.V.s . . . we did not have any, of course, so we had to put something together."

Dimitri described the initial meeting with I. M. Pei as follows: "They came up to see us in our building. . . . We had quickly fixed the office up, put pictures on the walls, we all tried to look proper. . . . While we were sitting around the conference table, I. M. Pei leaned back and one of the pictures we had stuck on the wall fell off and landed on his head. . . . There was a grim silence for a moment or two, then we all burst out laughing spontaneously. . . . It seemed to clinch the job."

Thus Arcop was selected to work with I. M. Pei on the complex called Place Ville Marie, which was the first skyscraper in Canada and involved extensive aboveground and underground levels, mostly oriented to commercial and retail activities. Arcop was hired to manage the later stages of work leading to construction and provided only limited input to the design. As a result, Arcop's involvement began only late in this period, after completion of the design work and procurement of the rights for the site.

As the Place Ville Marie job developed, the partners decided to expand their partnership to cover all their jobs. Being radical in their outlook, the firm adopted the name Arcop, standing for "architects in co-partnership" and emphasizing the values of equality and collaboration. However, the laws governing professional practice required use of the names of the partners, so these were placed in alphabetical order to denote lack of hierarchy.

Despite the egalitarian intentions, the partners discovered that, with so many partners, someone had to take formal charge of the execution of each project, whether or not the work was shared. Moreover, they found that clients preferred dealing with a single partner as primary contact. Hence there was an understanding that a partner would take charge of each job, and this was usually worked out between them on an informal basis.

The group was also learning to work in affiliation with other architectural firms. As a mirror image of its work in Montreal with I. M. Pei, Arcop associated with a firm in Vancouver to supervise the construction work on the Queen Elizabeth Theatre.

In summary, the originating period of Arcop saw the six partners being drawn into a closer and closer relationship. They banded together informally to enter a competition, and winning it forced them to band together formally. They scrambled to create the appearance of a more tightly knit group to get the Place Ville Marie job, and getting it knitted them more tightly together in all their work. From a collection of individuals largely doing their own work, by 1958 the group had coalesced into a full-fledged partnership with feelings about a strong architectural mission.

Growth and Coping with Growth: A Period of Expansion and Growing Tension (1958–1966)

With the partnership firmly established, Arcop experienced a period of dramatic growth and professional achievement. From 1958 to 1961 the firm entered seven competitions and won five of them. The quality of their winning designs was felt to reflect the intense collaboration among the partners. In addition, the group engaged in moderate promotion and speculative work through the early part of this period to solicit other new business.

In 1958 the group moved to a large office in downtown Montreal, and soon after, some of the partners began working on the design of an office building to house Arcop's own practice. The overall staff grew from 15 in 1958 to 43 at the beginning of 1961, largely as a response to the construction work on Place Ville Marie. The firm was hiring bright young architects and giving them major responsibilities on various jobs. It also appointed two associates by 1961. With the addition of another performing arts centre, Place des Arts in Montreal, the work centered largely in Quebec, at least early in the period (93 percent by 1961).

Most of the collaboration among the partners occurred in the early stages of conceptual design work. Once work got underway, collaboration was usually limited to meetings to review the progress on different jobs. Individual partners generally controlled their own jobs, working closely with their clients.

The partners were also learning to manage bigger jobs. Staff was organized into teams headed by job captains, who were responsible for different sections based upon the actual physical parts of the structure as well as certain functional divisions of the work. Later, project managers were appointed to assume overall charge of jobs, working under a partner. With the increased workload, tensions arose around the participation of one of the partners, who was perceived by some of his colleagues as less involved in the architectural work. He left the partnership in 1960.

The rapid growth also required increased attention to the management of the overall practice. Guy Desbarats tended to assume responsibility for most of the administrative work, assisted by Susan Ellis, the office manager. The partners discovered, however, that they differed fundamentally in their emphasis on formal organization and structure. In particular, Ray Affleck preferred a loose structure, while Guy favoured a clearer and tighter organization structure. Ray commented, "In the early days, it was a healthy difference." But it remained an ongoing tension. Another source of tension was the selection of partner-in-charge on desirable projects. In this and other cases, conflicts were generally sorted out informally among the partners, but underlying stresses remained in the group.

In 1961 Arcop hired a firm of management consultants to consider some of these issues. The consultants concluded that the partners had to decide upon a desirable balance between design achievement and profitability, since most jobs, excepting Place Ville Marie, were not generating sufficient profits. The partners were also urged to reach consensus on a desired size for the firm, on the services to be offered, and on the types of work to pursue. It was also suggested that a senior management person be hired to handle business affairs and that other roles be established to schedule and plan the work.

Around the same time, the work volume grew and became more diverse. With work winding down on Place Ville Marie and Place des Arts in Montreal, new work included another performing arts centre and a set of provincial government buildings, both in Prince Edward Island. These resulted in a surge of work in Eastern Canada that represented close to 25 percent of total volume in 1963 and 1964. Other jobs continued in or around Montreal on the Laval Civic Centre and on a few educational buildings, mostly for McGill University.

With continued growth of work, certain of the suggestions made by the management consultants were gradually implemented. Expertise was built up in the areas of design, drafting, graphics, specifications, field supervision, and interior design. In something of a matrix-management approach, individuals from these various functional areas worked closely with each other on job teams, coordinated by a project manager. Ray Affleck described one clear example of the resulting departmentalization: "We got some young ladies . . . they had a little corner. . . . They were not architects, they were specialists in furnishings, colours. . . . We formed them into a little department." Other changes included the appointment of a production manager, with responsibility for scheduling and supervising the staff on the various jobs, and the hiring of business managers to manage finances. Finally, a construction manager was appointed to assist the technical and field supervision staff with the contruction phase of the jobs.

In 1963, the firm—with 52 staff members at this point—moved into the office building that some of the partners had begun to design in 1958. This move also put the firm into the realty business in a small way in order to rent the excess office space. A modified profit-sharing plan was also introduced for the associates and the senior staff in 1963.

But as the mid-1960s approached, the firm was about to experience a great spurt of growth as a result of the simultaneous occurrence of several very large jobs. Work on Expo 67, the world's fair held in Montreal in conjunction with Canada's Centennial of 1967, involved a grouping of exhibition buildings. The performing arts centre stream continued with the National Arts Centre in Ottawa and the Arts and Culture centre in St. John's, Newfoundland. Commercial work continued with Place Bonaventure, a combination exhibition hall, office building, shopping concourse, and hotel. Although Ray Affleck took this job somewhat reluctantly, it eventually had a major impact on his and Arcop's reputation. Another commercial job consisted of subsequent additions to the ongoing Place Ville Marie complex. As such, the work of the firm began to return to Quebec, which together with Ottawa accounted for over 85 percent of volume by 1966.

As might be expected, the firm also experienced a dramatic growth of staff, increasing from 52 in 1963 to 146 in early 1966. The number of associates also grew from two in 1963 to six in 1965.

Staff were added to fill in the various functional areas. The interior design department, in particular, began to lobby for a more independent practice. Its members wanted to take steps, including a possible change of location, to solicit independent work. The partners rejected the idea, however, because most viewed the department's role as serving the architectural function.

Administrative demands paralleled the growth in work, with the result that a number of senior office positions, including one to handle public relations, were created. Nevertheless, there was a growing concern among the various administrative managers that the firm was making insufficient profits and even losing money on the big jobs. Ray commented, "There was a feeling that we were inefficient . . . we should be making more money . . . everything should be going like clockwork."

Another management consultant was hired in 1964 and recommended more standardized accounting techniques and more systematic performance control reports. The partners subsequently asked the other senior staff, mostly associates, to form a management committee to deal with the administration of the firm. This committee was headed by Roger Marshall, who, in 1965, was appointed executive director and given extensive powers to manage the daily operations. Under

Marshall's direction, formal committees were established to deal with specific management challenges—for example, to create job descriptions and clarify responsibilities, to review job contracts and administer budgets, and to review salaries and recommend employment or dismissal of staff.

Further, two separate subsidiaries were registered in 1966, largely as a result of Guy Desbarat's initiatives. Each employing a different part of the staff, they were intended to control the operations of the practice (as well as to minimize taxes) and to give more control to the senior staff, who were appointed directors and executives. These subsidiaries billed the partnership for services rendered.

However, all these efforts at formalization and control received little support from the other partners, who insisted on being consulted on almost all decisions and would tolerate no changes that infringed on their personal control of their jobs, regardless of cost or profit considerations. One partner assessed Marshall as executive director in the following way: "It was a terrible disfavour we did to him since he was trying to coordinate the uncoordinatable."

While all this was going on, the partners were working increasingly on their own jobs, even during the initial design phase and even to the point where partners were deliberately excluding other parties from their own projects. An early indication of breakdown in the collaborative ethic had occurred in 1963 when a plaque appeared at the completed Place des Arts building specifically mentioning one partner as the architect. This ran contrary to the agreement that the firm as a whole would be credited with all work. Although the plaque was subsequently removed, the incident was a harbinger of future conflicts. These conflicts showed up particularly in the distribution of the larger jobs. Guy had developed criteria for appointment of partners-in-charge on new jobs, emphasizing rotation among the partners depending on their current workloads. Nevertheless, this did not prevent them from lobbying for prestigious jobs in a manner that undermined the cooperative spirit of the firm.

The declining collaboration among the partners brought increasing polarization among the rest of the staff as each partner began working more exclusively with certain individuals. In one instance, a job was lost because one partner would not release a particular staff member requested by a potential client.

The continuing rapid growth put the unresolved conflicts into sharp perspective. Guy described the problems facing the firm as follows: "The more successful we were, the more tensions we created." The core conflict revolved around the growth and formalization of the firm. Again, the different orientations were represented particularly by Guy, who pushed for a larger and more tightly organized firm, and Ray, who preferred a smaller and looser practice that would not curb his freedom. The breakdown in collaboration became a breakdown in communication. Dimitri remarked, "Guy and Ray found themselves in boxes . . . with no windows or doors open."

In 1966 the partners attempted to recreate the earlier atmosphere through weekend retreats away from the office, but these were unsuccessful. Reflecting on the situation, Guy commented, "Our spirit had lost its dynamism . . . because of the individual thrust." Dimitri recalled, "There was a feeling of a lost touch."

Where to from Here?

As of 1966, Arcop, along with the industry, had experienced great growth and success (see Figures 1, 2 and 3). However, the success of Arcop seemed to be driving the partners away from the very collaboration which produced the success. This in turn was forcing a choice among the Arcop partners about the type of organization that could best carry out the basic mission of the firm.

Figure 1:   Arcop and Industry Billings (1958–1966)

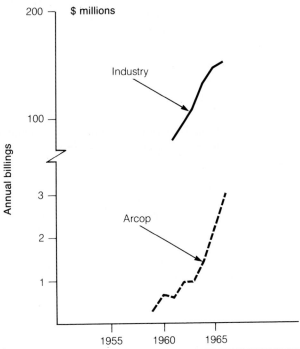

Figure 2:   Distribution of Work Volume in Jobs over $500,000 (to 1966)

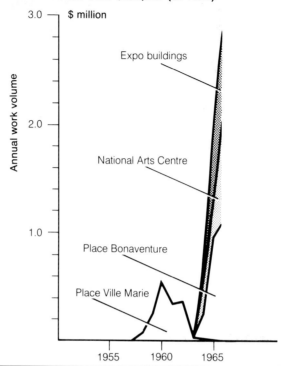

Figure 3:   Arcop Net Profits as a Percentage of Billings

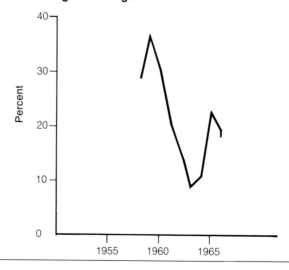

Appendix: Background on Architectural Firms in Canada

Architects must be registered by provincial boards to be able to practice on their own in Canada, although they can work in firms under registered architects without obtaining registration. Most Canadian architectural firms exist as individual proprietorships or partnerships because most provinces do not allow incorporation. However, some firms have incorporated service companies which employ nonregistered architects. The majority of staff in architectural firms are architects and drafting or technical people, with a smaller number of people employed to carry out administrative and office tasks.

Like most professional service firms, architectural firms gain new business largely on the basis of established reputation. Nevertheless, this reputation can be supported by a variety of marketing efforts, such as the development of personal contacts, doing promotion in the form of brochures, entering competitions, or even doing speculative work at little or no cost to the potential client.

Case 6

Blue Mountain Resorts Limited

In July 1975 Mr. George Weider, president of Blue Mountain Resorts Limited, was preparing to meet with his board of directors and present plans for the future direction of the company.

Various projects were being considered in an effort to provide maximum utilization of the resort area. The construction of additional hotel accommodations, another triple chairlift, other recreational facilities, real estate development for chalets and condominiums, and the development of convention facilities were among the possibilities that could be considered.

Management differed on the relative value of some of the projects but recognized that the time had come for a careful analysis to determine priorities for the planned undertakings. Two projects—the added hotel accommodations and new triple chairlift—appeared to have the highest degree of priority, but each would require an investment of such magnitude that the company could only undertake one or the other, not both, within the time horizon currently being considered by Weider. Gross revenues of the company had risen from just under half a million dollars in 1969 to about $1.2 million in 1974 with net profit of $41,000 and $56,000, respectively.

Background

Blue Mountain came into being as a ski resort in 1938 when a small group of club-oriented, relatively wealthy ski enthusiasts from Toronto, Ontario, founded the Toronto and Collingwood Ski Clubs. In 1941 Mr. Jozo Weider became the manager of the Toronto Ski Club and for the next 30 years directly controlled the growth and development of the whole Blue Mountain region.

Jozo Weider had left his job of managing a ski resort in Czechoslovakia in 1939 to come to Canada. While teaching skiing in Quebec, he heard about the Collingwood region and subsequently moved there, convinced that Blue Mountain had great potential for skiing. It was within easy driving distance of metropolitan Toronto (95 miles) and it had the second highest vertical drop (700 feet) in the region.

The difficulty of securing funds for the installation of lifts and the purchase of land hampered the growth of Blue Mountain in its early years. However, Weider did eventually manage to acquire 200 acres on the north area of the region and

This case was prepared by Professor W. H. Ellis of McGill University. Copyright © 1980 by W. H. Ellis.

later obtained an additional 400 acres to the south. Most people thought the land was worthless. It was, in fact, totally inadequate for farming, and, consequently, few people could conceive of it as a potential ski market.

Weider always had an interest in the arts. In keeping with his philosophy that ski resort operators had to diversify and make use of their hills and facilities the year round, he brought national ballet companies to Blue Mountain in the early years. To provide suitable facilities for them, he built a stage on the hill and a concert shell at the base. However, the market was apparently not ready for this class of performance, the projects weren't planned too carefully, the resort was insufficiently well known, and "they were a failure."

The crafts were also an interest of Weider, and he began a ceramic school with the assistance of a mold maker who had been a dishwasher in the kitchen clubhouses. Courses in the arts and crafts were given in the basement of one of the old buildings. At the same time, Weider broadened his own knowledge by reading books on the subjects and built the pottery operation into a major business—Blue Mountain Pottery Limited. The local availability of a durable flexible clay suitable for the pottery was, of course, an important ingredient to the success of the business. But pottery was, in fact, only a means to an end in that the sale of the pottery business in 1967 enabled Weider to devote his full energies and enthusiasm to the ski business.

Operations

Only in the decade since 1964 had skiing in the Collingwood region attained the mass marketing level requiring extensive investment in tows, snowmaking equipment, and accommodations.

The first uphill improvement from the tow rope was a Poma lift, installed at the north area in 1956. Between 1968 and 1971, three $150,000 chairlifts were installed and the Base Lodge constructed at a cost of $200,000. Snowmaking facilities became a necessity in order to provide the maximum utilization of the lifts day in and day out throughout the skiing season. Accordingly, snowmaking began in the mid-1960s, and the system, completed in 1973 at a cost of approximately $600,000, represented the company's largest single investment. The snowmaking system was further expanded in the summer of 1975 with the aid of a $515,000 Ontario Development Corporation loan. Part of the loan was also used for a new triple chairlift and expansion of cafeteria facilities at the hotel. The chairlift was in operation during the winter of 1974–75 and was capable of carrying 1,800 skiers per hour.

In mid-year 1975, there was a total of 16 uphill facilities—six chairlifts, two T-bars, four Pomas, and four rope tows (see Exhibit 1). Nearly 10 miles of steel pipe were buried beneath the frost line to carry water from the 25-million-gallon lake feeding 12 snow guns, capable of firing over 100 gallons of water per minute. The system had the capacity to cover 120 acres, 60 percent of all trails, with one foot of snow in less than a week or one acre with one foot of snow every two

Exhibit 1: Ski Facilities

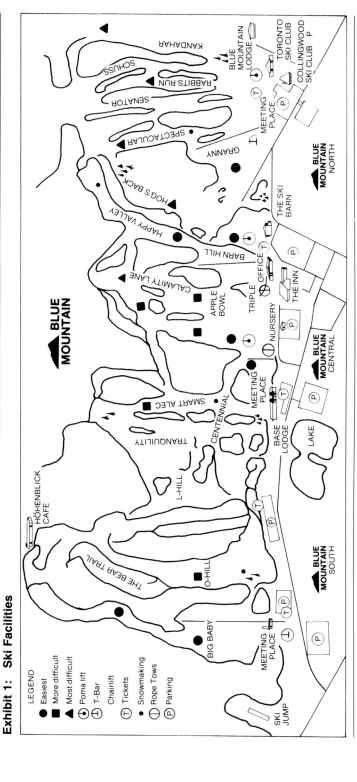

hours. The 20 trails were groomed by 30 pieces of equipment, including six $20,000 tracked Snocats.

Five restaurants were located on the property—the Base Lodge, the Hohenblick Cafe on top of the mountain, the Ski Barn, the Inn, and the Toronto Ski Club—with a total seating capacity of over 1,000 people. The first four restaurants were operated through an arrangement with an outside caterer, while the Toronto Ski Club conducted its own food operations. The Blue Mountain Inn, with 20 units and located at the foot of the mountain, registered over 90 percent occupancy in the summertime. It featured an indoor heated pool, color TV, licensed dining room, and four tennis courts.

The Blue Mountain complex required approximately 150 people in the winter excluding the 50 ski instructors and 60 volunteer ski patrollers who were employed in the Ernie McCulloch Ski School. The Blue Mountain people were engaged on the lifts, in grooming the hills, in operating the snowmaking equipment, in the restaurants and the inn, in the nursery, in the ski shop, in administration, and for general maintenance and construction. All the repairs and installation of equipment were handled by Blue Mountain's own full-time staff. Included among the workers were two welders, two carpenters, and two grooming operators who served as bulldozer operators in the summer.

Marketing

The slopes at Blue Mountain, like other facilities and accommodations, tended to be underutilized during weekdays but crowded on weekends causing queues at the chairlift loading points.

The installation of a triple chairlift, for the 1974–75 season, had done much to alleviate the waiting. On busy weekends the wait was currently seldom more than 15 minutes. The resort, however, still had the reputation of "being crowded."

Management now basically felt that in the winter they needed a little more cooperation from the weatherman and more midweek business. The snowmaking, begun in the 1960s, had gone a long way toward working with the weatherman. According to Mr. Gordon Canning, vice president and general manager, snowmaking probably added $200,000 in revenue for the 1974–75 season. With regard to the midweek business, a trend had begun to become apparent with a greater use of facilities. "The midweek business has gone really well and we are concentrating on it," Canning reported. Blue Mountain served seven segments of the ski market, identified in Table 1 in order of magnitude of revenue production in 1975.

Weekend Individuals

Market studies showed that the skiers in this largest segment (41 percent) tended to be young, relatively affluent, single individuals and young couples, without families, under 35 years of age. Approximately 20 percent of these could be

Table 1: Relative Importance of Market Segments

Segment	Percent
Weekend individuals	41%
Season pass holders	18
Midweek individuals	16
Special seasonal markets	15
Weekend groups	6
Midweek groups	3
Ski week packages	1
	100%

beginners or novices at any one time. A large number of the weekend individual skiers were said to be professional personnel or holding management-level positions. To these skiers, services were considered to be as important as the hills. This meant, therefore, continued pressure on Blue Mountain management for more and better facilities, rental equipment, and entertainment.

An increased demand was being experienced for rentals and lessons which, in turn, reflected a further need for more beginner facilities and services.

A major problem encountered with this and other segments of the market was related to snow reports. If there happened to be little or no snow in the southern part of the province and the U.S. border points, the assumption was frequently made that there was no snow at Blue Mountain. It was crucial, therefore, to dispense up-to-the-minute information on the real ski conditions. This information also had to reach into the United States since "much of the business comes from Ohio, Michigan, Illinois, and Indiana. They are starting on three-day weekends," stated Canning. (See Exhibit 2.) It was equally important to provide "first class" facilities all around such as for food, washrooms, bars, lift operations, and entertainment.

Management considered that its immediate objectives for this weekend market segment were to present the image of a "first class" resort, modern, swinging, to get the most accurate information to the skiing public, and to improve the on-site facilities. A total of 75,600 weekend tickets were sold in 1970, dropping down to 36,500 in 1973 and rising to 72,300 in 1975. (See Exhibit 3.) A weekend ticket cost $8.00 per day in 1974–75 and was expected to rise to $9.00 for the 1975–76 season (see Exhibit 4).

Season Pass Holders

This second largest market segment (18 percent) represented essentially the "hard core" of family skiers who committed from $300 to $500 annually before the season started. Although the family aspect of the season pass represented over 70 percent of the total season pass tickets sold, a significant growth was experienced in the sale of the single season passes as the figures in Table 2 indicate.

Exhibit 2:   Geographic Location and Distances

Distance (by car) from:

Toronto	2 hours				
Buffalo	4 hours	Chicago	10 hours	Cleveland	7 hours
Detroit	5 hours	Rochester	5 hours	Toledo	6 hours

The uphill capacity of Blue Mountain had been determined as 6,000, and according to an agreement with the Toronto Ski Club, whose members were all season pass holders, not to presell more than one third of the capacity, the limit for season passes would be 2,000.

While management fully recognized the importance of the weekend individuals, the season pass holder, as primarily the family skier, had to be regarded as the ambassador for the resort. To the extent that the resort wished to maintain this clientele, the feeling that a special-privilege class ought to accrue to this segment was the view expressed in one market study.

Midweek Individuals

"The midweek market is very important. It has done very well. We are concentrating on it and are going to take advantage of it through marketing. We

Exhibit 3:   Blue Mountain Resorts Limited, Comparative Statement of Tickets Sold (six month periods ending April 30th)

	1975	1974	1973	1972	1971	1970
Weekend:						
Day ticket	59,790	41,351	31,336	54,412	62,241	69,173
Half day	8,708	6,589	3,675	—	—	—
Red lift	3,844	3,188	1,536	2,400	4,397	6,501
Total weekend	72,342	51,128	36,547	56,812	66,638	75,674
Weekday:						
Day ticket	35,225	20,994	19,748	19,007	19,427	15,129
Half day	6,785	4,217	2,291	1,385	1,123	823
Red lift	1,177	822	—	—	—	—
Rope tow	3,244	2,625	2,504	3,475	4,507	3,755
Single rides	—	—	—	10,140	13,240	11,301
Total weekday	46,431	28,658	24,543	34,007	38,297	31,008
Weekly	468	379	242	490	737	472
Groups	21,842	16,062	8,410	15,008	11,857	9,677
Mini ski weeks	2,259	978	—	—	—	—
Total tickets sold	143,342	97,205	69,742	106,317	117,529	116,831
Members	7,144	8,907	9,247	15,606	13,724	12,131
Nonmembers	136,198	88,298	60,495	90,711	103,805	104,700

have looked at our weekends, and it is going to be very difficult to squeeze anything more out of the weekends,'' commented Canning.

Although ranked third in terms of lift revenue, this category showed an 85 percent increase for the 1975 season compared with 1974 (see Exhibit 5).

Market studies showed that a large proportion, probably 60 percent, of the midweek individual skiers were professional people and university students. "'Goof-off' students appeared to have comprised the largest proportion of these skiers, primarily from Ontario points because 90 percent of the visits were of the single-day variety.''

Since these skiers were "one-day" trippers, the greatest single attraction was the snow conditions. Hence the importance of both the snowmaking equipment and also the accurate radio reporting in the major centers of population in southern Ontario mentioned previously.

It had been determined that many of these individuals listened to the rock stations, primarily CHUM-FM and CFTR-AM, so that snow conditions and other promotional information could be made available through these outlets.

Management held hopes that this market segment would continue to grow, and opportunities seen for midweek skiers were to capitalize on midweek holidays for high school students and university students with flexible schedules. The "mini ski week," whereby individuals skiing for three consecutive days get one dollar per day reduction on their lift tickets, was introduced in 1974 and had been well received by this market (see Exhibit 4).

Exhibit 4(A): Ski Rates for 1974–1975 Seasons

COLLINGWOOD, ONTARIO

RATES FOR 1974-1975 SEASONS

LIFTS

Weekends & SCHOOL HOLIDAYS
All Lifts...$ 8.00
Red Lifts...$ 6.00
Rope Tow (any day).................................$ 2.00
All Lifts Afternoon, after 1:30 p.m...............$ 5.00

Regular Weekdays
All Lifts, 3 or more operating....................$ 6.00
Red Lifts...$ 4.00
All Lifts Afternoon, after 1:30 p.m...............$ 4.00
All Lifts Monday to Friday........................$25.00

Mini Ski Week
Any three or more consecutive days, $1.00 off regular rate per day. e.g. Monday, Tuesday, Wednesday & Thursday....$20.00

INSTRUCTION
Group Lessons (1 hour)............................$ 4.00
Group Lessons (2 hours)..........................$ 6.00
Children 12 and under (1 hour)...................$ 3.00
Book of four 1 hour lessons.......................$12.00
Private Lesson (1 hour)..........................$10.00
  with two people..........................each $ 7.50
  with three people........................each $ 6.00
  with Assistant Director..................$12.00
  with Director............................$24.00
Ski Week (12 hours)..............................$25.00

Cross Country
Group Lesson (1 hour) minimum of 5 people.........$ 4.00
Group Lesson (2 hours) minimum of 5 people.........$ 6.00

RENTALS
Skis, Boots & Poles
Per day...$7.00
Afternoon, after 1:00 p.m........................$ 3.50
Per Week (5 days)................................$24.50
Cross Country per day............................$ 5.50
Cross Country Afternoon, after 1:00 p.m..........$ 3.50
N.B. Rental rates include breakage insurance but do not include 7% Provincial Sales Tax.

NURSERY
Full Day..$ 4.00
Half Day..$ 2.00
Only trained children 2 years and over accepted.
Open 9:00 a.m. to 12:00 noon and 1:00 p.m. to 4:30 p.m.

WEEKDAY SEASON PASS
Monday to Friday including Christmas & Spring Break....$80.00

For information call 705-445-0231

ACCOMMODATION

BLUE MOUNTAIN INN - Winter

CAA & AAA approved, heated pool, 2 double beds, 4 piece bath and balcony in each unit. Licensed dining room.

WEEKENDS, CHRISTMAS & SPRING BREAK - PER DAY

Breakfast, Dinner & Lodging

Single..$ 26.00
Two per room..............................each $ 22.00
Three per room............................each $ 18.00
Four per room.............................each $ 15.00
Children two years and under.......................Free

SPECIAL MINI SKI WEEK PACKAGE - January 1st to 5th

Includes 4 nights accommodation, all meals, all lifts and 8 hours of lessons

Single...$126.00
Two per room.............................each $116.40
Three per room...........................each $108.20
Four per room............................each $106.00
Children 12 years and under when sharing room
with parent..............................each $ 86.00

MINI SKI WEEKS

Mini Ski Weeks are available at several local motels throughout the 1974-1975 season (except Christmas). These packages include accommodation, lifts and breakfast. More information on request.

Accommodation rates do not include 7% Accommodation Tax or 10% Food Tax on dinners.

ALL RATES SUBJECT TO CHANGE WITHOUT NOTICE

SKI WEEKS:

		DECEMBER 1974				
Sun	Mon	Tue	Wed	Thu	Fri	Sat
	1	2	3	4	5	6	7
A 8	9	10	11	12	13	14
B 15	16	17	18	19	20	21
22	23	24	25	26	27	28
29	30	31				

		JANUARY 1975				
Sun	Mon	Tue	Wed	Thu	Fri	Sat
			1	2	3	4
C 5	6	7	8	9	10	11
D 12	13	14	15	16	17	18
E 19	20	21	22	23	24	25
F 26	27	28	29	30	31	

		FEBRUARY 1975				
Sun	Mon	Tue	Wed	Thu	Fri	Sat
						1
G 2	3	4	5	6	7	8
H 9	10	11	12	13	14	15
I 16	17	18	19	20	21	22
J 23	24	25	26	27	28	

		MARCH 1975				
Sun	Mon	Tue	Wed	Thu	Fri	Sat
						1
K 2	3	4	5	6	7	8
L 9	10	11	12	13	14	15
16	17	18	19	20	21	22
M 23/ 24/		25	26	27	28	29
N 30	31					

Exhibit 4(B): Ski Rates for 1974–1975

SKI WEEK PACKAGES - Not available Christmas or Spring Break

#1 Includes 5 nights accommodation, all meals, all lifts and 12 hours of lessons. Awards night banquet, gluhwein and movie nights.

Single	$157.50
Two per room	each $147.50
Three per room	each $137.50
Four per room	each $132.50
Children 12 years and under when sharing room with parents	each $112.50

#2 Includes 5 nights accommodation, all meals, all lifts. Awards night banquet, gluhwein and movie nights.

Single	$135.00
Two per room	each $125.00
Three per room	each $115.00
Four per room	each $110.00
Children 12 years and under when sharing room with parents	each $ 90.00

#3 Includes 5 nights accommodation, 5 breakfasts, 1 dinner all lifts and 12 hours of lessons. Awards night banquet, gluhwein movie nights.

Single	$123.50
Two per room	each $113.50
Three per room	each $103.50
Four per room	each $ 98.50
Children 12 years and under when sharing room with parents	each $ 90.50

#4 Includes 5 nights accommodation, 5 breakfasts, 1 dinner, all lifts. Awards night banquet, gluhwein and movie nights.

Single	$101.00
Two per room	each $ 91.00
Three per room	each $ 81.00
Four per room	each $ 76.00
Children 12 years and under when sharing room with parents	each $ 68.30

N.B. Ski Weeks begin with dinner on Sunday evening between 6:00 and 8:00 p.m., check in time is 2:00 p.m. Ski Weeks end Friday after lunch, check out time 12:00 noon.

Accommodation rates do not include 7% Accommodation Tax or 10% Food Tax on dinners.

ALL RATES ARE SUBJECT TO CHANGE WITHOUT NOTICE

GROUP RATES FOR 1974-1975 SEASON

Blue Mountain offers special group lift, lesson and rental rates provided that:

(a)   There are 20 or more in the group.
(b)   You let us know in advance, in writing, the number of lift tickets, rentals and lessons required and when you will be here. In cases where rentals are required a list of height, weight, street shoe size, sex, age and name must be received by our office at least 10 days prior to the trip.
(c)   One person comes in to the Administration Office to purchase all the tickets at once. Charges will not be accepted.

REGULAR GROUPS WEEKDAYS (Not School Holidays)

	Group Rate	Regular Rate
Lift	$5.00	$6.00
Alpine 1 hr. lesson (minimum 5 people)	$2.00	$4.00
Alpine 2 hr. lesson (minimum 5 people)	$3.00	$6.00
C.C. 1 hr. lesson (minimum 5 people)	$2.00	$4.00
C.C. 2 hr. lesson (minimum 5 people)	$3.00	$6.00
Alpine Rental (complete set)	$5.00	$7.00
C.C. Rental (complete set)	$4.00	$5.50

STUDENT GROUPS WEEKDAYS (Not School Holidays)

	Group Rate	Regular Rate
Lift	$3.50	$6.00
Alpine 1 hr. lesson (minimum 5 people)	$2.00	$4.00
Alpine 2 hr. lesson (minimum 5 people)	$3.00	$6.00
C.C. 1 hr. lesson (minimum 5 people)	$2.00	$4.00
C.C. 2 hr. lesson (minimum 5 people)	$3.00	$6.00
Alpine Rental (complete set)	$3.75	$7.00
C.C. Rental (complete set)	$3.00	$5.50

REGULAR OR STUDENT GROUPS WEEKENDS & HOLIDAYS

	Group Rate	Regular Rate
Lift	$7.20	$8.00

No reduction on rentals or lessons.

N.B. Above rental rates include .50c breakage insurance but do not include 7% Provincial Sales Tax.

GROUP ACCOMMODATION

The Blue Mountain Inn offers a maximum of 10 rooms to any one group on a weekend, based on at least four persons per room. The weekend package includes two nights accommodation, two breakfasts, lunch Saturday or Sunday, dinner Saturday evening and two days all lift tickets. The following per person rate is based on four or more persons per room. Weekend Package - $46.52 per person, tax included.

Table 2: Season Ticket Sales

	1975	1974	1973	1972	1971	1970
Family number	1,054	1,097	737	751	746	621
Single number	581	420	213	267	277	260
Total	1,635	1,517	950	1,018	1,023	881
Average season ticket per day, 20 skiing days	$6.07	6.12	5.27	4.42	4.26	3.95
Average season ticket price	$121.40	122.40	105.37	88.41	85.11	79.00

Special Seasonal Markets

These markets have traditionally been the pre-season period (that is, early December), Christmas, and the spring break in the Ontario school system in mid-March.

Pre-season skiing activities have been subject to the availability of snow and therefore could not be depended upon. With added snowmaking facilities, an earlier start would be feasible with a corresponding added degree of dependability.

Special packages and groups sales in these three special market categories were envisaged as potential incentives to increasing the volume in forthcoming seasons.

Daily snow reports and saturation radio could be embarked upon if snow conditions warranted.

Weekend Groups

Group activities in Ontario centered on the various types of the numerous ski clubs, that is, vagabond, university, high school, or service clubs. Although the existence of these clubs was well known, management expressed the view that a problem existed with getting ski clubs to come to Blue Mountain more frequently than once a season which studies showed was generally the case. Opportunities were believed to be available for increasing revenue from this segment of the market by improving the frequency of visits by the existing groups and contacting new ones.

Nearby U.S. areas were heavily populated and had numerous ski clubs, but by the same token, the distance to Blue Mountain was great. Reaching these widespread groups in an efficient manner presented a major difficulty.

The organization of sales agents and travel agents with appropriate commission structure, generally 5 percent to 10 percent, was considered to be a means of reaching this market, together with promotional material.

Groups of 20 or more individuals were entitled to a 10 percent reduction in the price of lift tickets.

Exhibit 5: Comparative Lift Ticket and Catering Sales Analysis (six month periods ending April 30th)

	1975		1974		1973		1972		1971		1970	
	Amount	Percent	Amount	Percent	Amount	Percent	Amount	Percent	Amount	Percent	Amount	Percent
Weekend tickets	$ 455,143	40.5%	$333,533	43.0%	$191,297	38.3%	$415,925	57.6%	$442,172	55.1%	$493,215	61.3%
Weekend groups	67,621	6.0	35,871	4.7	16,514	3.3	36,985	5.1	37,973	4.7	35,211	4.4
Weekday tickets	176,907	15.7	95,597	12.3	53,996	10.7	73,956	10.3	76,138	9.4	82,637	10.3
Weekday groups	34,591	3.1	25,853	3.3	15,883	3.2	28,398	3.9	19,760	2.5	16,678	2.0
Ski weeks—inn guests	5,342	0.5	4,147	0.5	3,960	0.8	5,940	0.8	7,280	0.1	4,670	0.6
Ski weeks—outsiders	5,918	0.5	3,706	0.5	1,795	0.0	4,825	0.1	5,580	0.1	4,895	0.6
Season passes	198,500	17.6	189,605	24.4	104,230	20.9	90,006	12.6	87,064	10.8	69,602	8.7
Christmas holiday	83,030	7.4	66,002	8.5	105,068	21.0	48,500	6.7	91,128	11.4	77,829	9.7
Spring holiday	84,023	7.5	12,923	1.7	9,129	1.8	20,784	2.9	33,476	4.2	19,440	2.4
Ski scene	—	—	—	—	—	—	—	—	—	—	—	—
Mini ski weeks	13,198	1.2	8,594	1.1	—	—	—	—	2,214	0.3	—	—
Total lift sales	$1,124,273	100.0%	$775,831	100.0%	$501,872	100.0%	$725,319	100.0%	$802,785	100.0%	$804,147	100.0%
Overall average daily ticket sale	$ 6.33		$ 5.94		$ 5.53		$ 5.64		$ 5.70		$ 5.90	
Average daily ticket sale, excluding season tickets	6.50		6.06		5.70		5.97		6.08		6.28	
Average daily season pass ticket	6.07		6.12		5.27		4.42		4.26		3.95	
Average daily weekday season ticket	5.63		4.00		4.01		—		—		—	
Total catering sales	330,581		221,272		106,350		156,287		149,514		N.A.	
Average food and beverage consumption per daily skier visit	1.85		1.69		1.17		1.21		0.94		N.A.	

Source: Company records.

Midweek Groups

Because of the one-day feature, the skiers in this market segment were mainly from elementary and high schools, colleges and universities.

Among the major concerns encountered with servicing this group was the distance to Blue Mountain compared with competitive areas such as Barrie, Ontario, and Mansfield, Ontario, between 50 to 60 miles from Toronto (see Exhibit 2). Other difficulties were in setting up a sales organization to reach this widespread market on an individual basis as well as providing adequate compensation for so doing while at the same time keeping the cost of the trip below $10.

Management believed this market could be increased with closer attention being paid to it by appointed sales agents concentrating on the schools, ski clubs, and social clubs. For example, in Toronto, there was an increase in 1975–76 to 12 (school) professional development days compared with 9 in previous years. Canning reported, "We have had 1,200 students from North York by bus on February 14th and at least another 1,200 who came up on their own on a Friday. That meant 2,400 to 2,500 from one school board." Efforts had been made also to get students to Blue Mountain for educational visits through their physical education departments.

Ski Week Packages

The principal market for this smallest lift-revenue-producing segment was thought to be the U.S. border cities.

One significant reason for this relatively small size was believed to be that if the experienced skier had a ski week planned, he would prefer to go to the resorts in the Province of Quebec, the western regions of Canada, or the United States or even to Europe.

The lack of promotional effort in the past directed to this market may have been a major factor contributing to the status of this market segment.

Summing up the marketing aspects of Blue Mountain ski operations, Canning said:

> We know that we have rainouts and we know that we have days that are just not good for skiing, windy and cold, and we can advertise all we want, but we know we just aren't going to get those 6,000 skiers here. So we dropped back our advertising budget to about $50,000 this year [1975] compared with nearly $80,000 in 1974.
>
> Another opportunity for us is pre-Christmas, if the snow comes. Last year it didn't come, but we still had $9,000 revenue through to January 1, 1975. If it does come, though, we want to be there with some kind of promotion. We will begin making snow at the earliest opportunity, probably in November. We have to find a way to be ready in December. That is our number two opportunity.
>
> Our number one opportunity is our midweek. As for weekends, we have just got to try and maintain what we have got. It is better for us if we can lengthen the season at the beginning rather than at the end because people's interest begins to wane about the end of March.
>
> The "over-crowded" image is indelibly imprinted on people's minds, and we are

trying to get over that by putting up a new cafeteria and improving the base facilities. We will take every opportunity we get to make them feel it is not so crowded. We have always tried to sell ski weeks, but we don't have a hotel that holds 300 people which would justify having a band every night and a recreational director as some resorts do like Grey Rocks, in the Province of Quebec. Then you could put together a complete package that makes the ski school spin.

Snow also does not stay as long naturally here as in some areas, but we believe that with the snowmaking plant we now have, except for one or two weeks, they will be able to say that a good holiday is available at Blue Mountain. People are taking long weekends, and that is something we are going to exploit. Accommodation is not really the problem; the right package is. The short midweek package and the long weekends will help us through. Accommodations built up one midweek lift revenue, and we have already seen how it has come along.

Our American market will continue to grow weekend and midweek. We have never spent very much money down there, but we know the market is there. It would particularly help our midweek revenue. The Americans have a five- to seven-hour drive which means that they would be more likely to take three or four days off to come midweek. People do have the time off, if a person really wants to get away even with his family.

An integral facet of the ski marketing program was the Ernie McCulloch Ski School. Invited by the late Jozo Weider to provide ski instruction, McCulloch was a renowned Canadian skier, coach, and instructor. His ski school in turn employed approximately 50 full-time instructors during the winter season. Originally called the Blue Mountain Ski School, the name was changed in 1969 to its present format in order to capitalize on his name.

Competitive Facilities

Blue Mountain was the biggest resort in terms of ski facilities in the central Ontario ski region. Its appeal was directed more to single individual skiers rather than to families and more so than any other resort in the area. "We don't even push for families." Accordingly, skiing at Blue Mountain was geared 65 percent to intermediate, 25 percent to beginners, and 10 percent to expert skiers. It did face competition for skier patronage from other resorts.

The Talisman Ski Resort and Georgian Peaks Resort were approximately the same distance from the southern Ontario market. Facilities like Mansfield Skiways, Medonte Mountain, Moonstone Ski Resort, Snow Valley Resort, Horseshoe Valley, and Hockley Hills were all situated close to Barrie, Ontario, or at comparable distances from Toronto, Ontario. These latter areas could be reached by car from Toronto in approximately one hour, while it took nearly two hours to drive to the Blue Mountain region.

The Talisman Ski Resort, 97 miles northeast of Toronto at Kimberley, Ontario, offered three chairlifts, one T-bar, and one rope tow, a 600-foot vertical rise, daily fees of $5–$8, and a Resort Hotel and Beaver Lodge with dining-dancing and licensed lounge at the hill.

Georgian Peaks Resort, located two miles west of Blue Mountain and 92 miles north of Toronto at Thornbury, Ontario, had the same lift facilities as the Talisman, a vertical rise of 820 feet, and daily fees of $4–$8. The accommodation listed a day lodge with cafeteria and bar at the hill, dancing every Saturday evening, and ski weeks in conjunction with a motel eight miles away. Motel and hotel accommodation was located in nearby Collingwood or Meaford, and dormitory facilities were available for groups of 20 or more.

A press release in the summer of 1975 stated that Georgian Peaks was up for sale having suffered losses of about $180,000 in 1974–75, $100,000 in 1973–74, and $200,000 in the 1972–73 season.

The ski facilities offered by the resorts to the south had slopes somewhat less, ranging from about 330-feet to 400-feet vertical drop, with daily rates varying from $5 to $8, and most had snowmaking equipment. Their greatest advantage, however, lay in their proximity to the southern Ontario populace, a fact well known and recognized by the management of Blue Mountain.

Affiliated Activities

Greater utilization of the extensive and expensive facilities once the skiing season was over had presented serious problems for the management of Blue Mountain for many years. Every effort had been made to use as many as possible of the employees in the summer months to upgrade the facilities. For example, craftsmen made all the chairs for the triple lift as well as the lift terminals; machinery and other equipment was overhauled, painted, repaired, and general maintenance work undertaken. However, these activities did little to maximize the utilization of the physical plant. It was to this end and in keeping with the philosophy expressed earlier by the late Mr. Weider that saw the start of the summer music and also the real estate programs as an integral part of the resort area development.

Blue Mountain Summer School of the Arts

This school was founded in 1972 and was operated in conjunction with Georgian College in Barrie, Ontario. Enrollment in the summer of 1974 was 300 with participation in some 20 courses ranging from batik and ceramics, yoga, and horsemanship to tennis and winemaking. The courses ran through June, July, and August with fees from $10 to $45 per course.

Blue Mountain Summer School of Music and Dance

Georgian College, Barrie, and George Brown College, Toronto, participated in the opening of this school in 1974. Programs included orchestral and keyboard, band, vocal and music theatre, guitar, and dance. Two hundred students enrolled in the period July 6 to August 16, 1975. Tuition with room and board ranged from $135 to $160 per week.

Blue Mountain Summer School of Contemporary Music

Oriented toward a music festival, the program started in the summer of 1974, attracting 125 students ranging in ages from 11 to 65 years. The schedule for the 10 days, June 22 to July 2, 1975, was designed to present most aspects of contemporary music—rock and roll, jazz, and folk. Tuition with room and board cost $225 per student.

Blue Mountain Summer Chairlift

Opened initially in the summer of 1974 as a further means of utilizing facilities that would otherwise be idle in the summer, the chairlift carried 18,000 people at a rate of $1.50 for adults and $1.00 for children. Snacks were available at the top from the Skyline Cafe, known as the Hohenblick Cafe during the winter months.

Blue Mountain Central Reservation Service

This service connected 21 hotels and lodges in that region providing accommodation reservations to a total of 600 rooms. Deluxe hotel to dormitory facilities were available by telephone or writing to the central service.

Craigleith Development Limited

Over 400 acres of developmental land had been acquired by this company, owned by the Weider family interests. Lot sales had begun in 1969 at around $4,000, and by 1975 the latest sales were in the neighborhood of $20,000 each. The company expected to build 38 condominiums, sell some of them, rent others, and rent still others when the owners went away. By renting some of the accommodations, problems would be solved without requiring a large capital investment. There was a shopping centre and a restaurant nearby that would be expanded by Craigleith until it covered a 10-acre site.

Personnel

Following the death of Jozo Weider in October 1971, his son George Weider became chairman of the board of directors and president of Blue Mountain Resorts Limited at the age of 31 (see Exhibit 6). Under his direction, nearly $1.5 million was invested in plant and facilities in the expansion program undertaken within the next four years (1971–75). Holding a doctor of philosophy degree, Weider was also a professor at an Ontario University.

Exhibit 6: Organization Chart, 1975

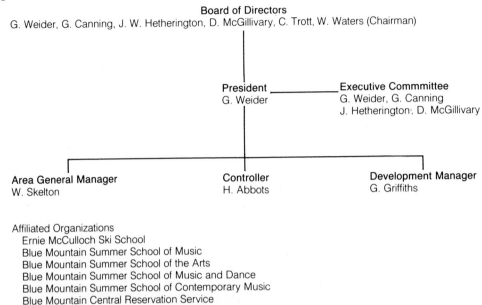

Board of Directors
G. Weider, G. Canning, J. W. Hetherington, D. McGillivary, C. Trott, W. Waters (Chairman)

President _____ **Executive Commmittee**
G. Weider   G. Weider, G. Canning
                                J. Hetherington, D. McGillivary

Area General Manager	Controller	Development Manager
W. Skelton	H. Abbots	G. Griffiths

Affiliated Organizations
  Ernie McCulloch Ski School
  Blue Mountain Summer School of Music
  Blue Mountain Summer School of the Arts
  Blue Mountain Summer School of Music and Dance
  Blue Mountain Summer School of Contemporary Music
  Blue Mountain Central Reservation Service

Gordon Canning, (32), executive vice president and general manager, engineered much of the expansion and development that had taken place since 1971. He obtained a bachelor of science degree from Queen's University, a master's degree in mathematics from the University of Waterloo, and a master of business administration degree from York University. He had worked previously with Imperial Oil Limited in the computer services department and in 1970 with the wholesale distributor of cross-country skis during which time his association began with Weider and Blue Mountain Resorts Limited. Canning was a brother-in-law of George Weider.

The other members of the board of directors were:

Dr. D. McGillivary   A physician and brother-in-law of George Weider.

Mr. J. W. Hetherington   President, Venturecan Limited, a marketing firm.

Mr. C. Trott   Business, Collingwood, Ontario.

Mr. W. Waters   Business, Collingwood, Ontario.

Finance

With the assistance of a number of friends, including the late Senator Peter Campbell, who became a partner, Jozo Weider gradually obtained control over the ski operation and built up Blue Mountain Resorts Limited. The sale in 1967 of

Blue Mountain Pottery Limited provided much needed financial resources. These enabled Weider to concentrate on developing the ski facilities which had been his principal interest for a long time. Funds from the pottery business also enabled Weider to purchase the shares of the partnership held by Senator Campbell and to acquire 200 acres of land at the foot of the mountain. By 1975 the Weider family held 75 percent of the shares of Blue Mountain Limited, 8 percent were held by the Toronto Ski Club, with the remaining 17 percent held by individuals, some of whom were employees of the company.

Since 1965 skiing capacity had tripled and revenues had grown from $445,000 in 1969 to $1,137,000 at fiscal year-end in October 1974. (Exhibits 7 to 11 contain the financial data.) Nearly 70 percent of the revenue in that year came from lift and season tickets compared with about 90 percent in 1969. This change reflected the broadened base of the operations that management had been planning in order to lessen its dependence on any one function. Further evidence of broadening activity can be seen by an examination of lift ticket sales in terms of revenue and numbers sold. In 1970 weekend and weekday tickets accounted for 61 percent and 10 percent, respectively, of tickets sold compared with 40 percent and 16 percent, respectively, by 1975 (see Exhibits 3 and 5).

The bane of most ski resorts had always been the concentration of skiers on weekends, with lifts and accommodation relatively quiet during the week. The trend observed in the analysis of figures showed a greater proportion of midweek activity and was the basis of the comment by Canning that midweek business was "doing well now; we are concentrating on it and we know more about it."

Ski rates were competitive with surrounding locations at $8 per day for weekends and $6 per day for midweeks during the 1974–75 season. They were expected to increase to $9 and $7 per day, respectively, for the 1975–76 winter skiing. Reduced rates were available for half-day skiing. The introduction in the 1973–74 season of the mini ski week where for three consecutive days midweek tickets were reduced one dollar per day proved to have been popular and showed signs of growing. Season ticket sales contributed nearly 9 percent of the lift revenues in 1970, compared with about 18 percent in 1975, reaching a peak at 24 percent during the 1974 season. There had been a steady growth in the actual number of these tickets sold in the past three years from 950 to 1,635 in the past season, mainly in terms of single tickets rather than for family usage.

While total revenues for the fiscal years 1969 to 1974 rose two and a half times, operating costs rose approximately threefold (see Exhibit 8). "Construction costs are heavy and the season is relatively short, but we did have a good year last year [1975] mostly because of snowmaking," reported Canning.

Over $1 million had been spent for a snowmaking system, the first part of which was completed in 1973 and expanded further for the 1974–75 season. Lift revenues had grown substantially on a comparable six month basis (see Exhibit 11) and so had the sales of beverages, nearly doubling from $33,900 in 1974 to $63,000 in 1975.

Exhibit 7

BLUE MOUNTAIN RESORTS LIMITED
Balance Sheet at October 31
(in thousands)

	1974	1973	1972	1971	1970	1969
Assets						
Current assets:						
Cash	$ 0	$ 9,397	$ 1,930	$ 9,403	$ 10,962	$ 1,039
Deposit receipts	12,179	0	0	0	0	0
Accounts receivable	11,603	8,660	63,262	52,924	36,108	20,692
Life insurance proceeds receivable	0	0	0	200,000	0	0
Amount receivable from employees re: share purchase	0	0	0	941	0	0
Notes receivable	0	0	0	1,172	16,440	3,661
Income taxes receivable	32,290	54,200	0	0	0	0
Inventories, at cost which is not in excess of net realization value	32,138	18,225	14,938	15,754	13,942	0
Prepaid expenses	14,404	12,854	5,041	5,291	2,256	5,862
Total current assets	102,614	103,336	85,171	285,485	79,708	31,254
Investments, at cost:						
Mortgage receivable	2,200	2,700	9,200	10,200	0	0
Shares in golf club	6,375	6,375	6,375	0	0	0
Total investments	8,575	9,075	15,575	10,200	0	0
Fixed assets, at cost	2,761,257	2,423,709	1,950,017	1,508,709	1,320,585	1,119,128
Less: Accumulated depreciation	928,335	808,120	695,644	601,137	518,111	439,493
Total fixed assets	1,832,922	1,615,589	1,254,373	907,572	802,474	679,635
Other assets:						
Deferred financing expenses	0	0	0	0	1,232	2,463
Total assets	$1,944,111	$1,728,000	$1,355,119	$1,203,257	$883,414	$713,352
Liabilities						
Current liabilities:						
Bank overdraft	$ 38,087	$ 0	$ 0	$ 14,067	$ 0	$ 4,142
Bank loan	50,000	110,000	150,000	125,000	0	50,000
Accounts payable and accrued liabilities	99,443	60,799	70,554	63,085	61,351	80,223
Note payable to affiliated company	0	0	67,046	0	0	75,000
Loans payable to shareholders	0	0	0	0	21,640	5,000
Mortgage payable to Industrial Development Bank	0	0	0	44,000	0	0
8% debentures, due June 30, 1971	0	0	0	0	100,000	0
Conditional sales agreement payable to Pomo-lift Industries Ltd.	0	0	0	9,000	0	0
Customers' deposits	5,165	9,926	325	0	0	0
Income taxes payable	0	0	40,208	57,250	139,334	5,450
Current portion of long-term liabilities	70,509	63,540	12,135	0	62,000	62,000
Total current liabilities	263,204	244,265	340,268	312,402	384,325	281,815

Exhibit 7 *(concluded)*

	1974	1973	1972	1971	1970	1969
Deferred income taxes	151,566	131,866	91,756	82,092	68,510	55,600
Long-term exclusive of current portion	605,300	484,410	47,950	0	53,000	215,000
Total liabilities	420,070	860,541	479,974	394,494	495,845	552,415

Shareholders' Equity

Capital stock
Authorized—5% noncumulative
redeemable (at $26.25)
preference shares, par value
$25 each convertible into 25   (See note below)
common shares—common
shares, no par value
Issued:

	1974	1973	1972	1971	1970	1969
Preference shares	$ 350	$ 350	$ 1,575	$ 1,725	$ 10,325	$ 68,875
Common shares	295,774	295,774	294,399	294,399	201,064	53,750
	296,124	296,124	296,124	296,124	211,389	122,625
Retained income	627,917	571,335	579,021	512,639	166,190	38,312
Total shareholders' equity .	924,041	867,459	875,145	808,763	377,579	160,937
Total liabilities and shareholders' equity	$1,944,111	$1,728,000	$1,355,119	$1,203,257	$ 883,414	$ 713,352

Note: Number of shares authorized

	1974	1973	1972	1971	1970	1969
Preference	1,219	1,219	1,268	1,274	1,618	3,960
Common	239,525	239,525	238,300	238,150	229,550	171,000
Number of shares issued						
Preference	14	14	63	69	413	2,755
Common	156,550	156,550	155,325	155,175	129,660	53,050

Source: Company records.

Since 1973, the music school had provided a contribution to overhead through the rental of buildings, food operations, and accommodation facilities in the summer months. In 1975, Canning stated, "We get some income from the rental of our properties, and we rent to George Brown College which finances the summer school. We run the accommodation and food and should have $5,000 out of our share plus $8,000 rental fee for the use of our facilities as studios. That makes $13,000, and we will have spent $3,000 making the facilities suitable. This doesn't leave us very much, but it could grow."

In addition to the summer school operations, the company had an arrangement with a food organization to manage and operate its four restaurants and also an arrangement with the Ernie McCulloch Ski School. (See Exhibit 12 for a description of summer activities in the Blue Mountain area.)

Exhibit 8

BLUE MOUNTAIN RESORTS LIMITED
Income and Retained Income Statement
For the Year Ended October 31
(in thousands)

	1974	1973	1972	1971	1970	1969
Revenue:						
Lift and tow tickets	$ 600,399	$397,642	$648,899	$738,515	$755,635	$360,922
Season tickets	189,605	104,230	90,006	87,064	69,602	39,529
Accommodation	41,809	35,744	0	32,412	44,906	27,331
Catering	238,775	113,656	0	0	0	0
Interest	7,039	3,137	6,673	5,240	7,748	5,389
Rentals	10,105	7,084	17,131	9,420	0	0
Tucker Snocat	8,138	9,055	31,703	4,121	0	0
Music school	21,124	0	0	0	0	0
Miscellaneous	20,159	3,700	1,349	15,846	3,725	11,868
Total revenue	1,137,153	674,248	795,761	892,618	881,616	445,039
Expenses:						
Administrative and general	328,389	239,251	203,090	201,422	227,945	111,078
Lifts, hills, roads, and snowmaking	225,494	169,689	246,271	221,329	220,503	133,116
Accommodation	26,639	19,652	0	18,552	31,043	28,288
Catering	211,728	102,088	0	0	0	0
Interest:—Short-term debt	1,545	10,331	5,526	5,840	11,613	12,502
Long-term debt	64,621	26,872	4,727	5,333	8,000	8,000
Rentals	1,172	1,686	8,316	0	0	1,931
Tucker Snocat	6,797	7,280	26,819	0	0	0
Ski instruction	0	0	0	0	0	9,070
Music school	32,338	0	0	0	0	0
Amortization of financial expense	0	0	0	1,232	1,232	1,232
Total expenses	898,723	576,849	494,749	453,708	500,336	305,217
Income before depreciation and income taxes	238,430	97,399	301,012	438,910	381,280	139,822
Depreciation	154,768	112,475	94,508	84,037	80,126	63,902
Income (loss) before income taxes	83,662	(15,076)	206,504	354,873	301,154	75,920
Income taxes:						
Current payable (recoverable)	7,380	(47,500)	83,782	155,328	142,938	16,117
Deferred	19,700	40,110	9,644	13,582	12,910	18,450
	27,080	(7,390)	93,446	168,910	155,848	34,567
(A) Income before extraordinary item						
Extraordinary item:						
Life insurance proceeds	0	0	0	200,000	0	0
(B) Income before extraordinary item	0	0	0	185,963	145,306	0
Net income (loss) for the year	56,582	(7,686)	113,058	385,963	145,306	41,353
Balance of retained income at beginning of year	571,335	568,734	512,639	166,190	38,312	5,658
Adjustment of prior year's income taxes	0	10,287	0	0	0	0
As restated	571,335	579,021	512,639	166,190	38,312	5,658
Dividend on preference shares	0	0	(79)	(496)	(516)	(3,494)
Dividend on common shares	0	0	(46,597)	(39,018)	(16,912)	(5,205)
Balance of retained income at end of year	$ 627,917	$571,335	$579,021	$512,639	$166,190	$38,312
Earnings (loss) per share ($ per share)	0.36	(0.05)	(0.73)	0	0	0
Before extraordinary item	0	0	0	1.19	1.12	0.74
After extraordinary item	0	0	0	2.49	1.12	0

Exhibit 9

BLUE MOUNTAIN RESORTS LIMITED
Statement of Changes in Financial Position
For the Year Ended October 31
(in thousands)

	1974	1973	1972	1971	1970	1969
Source of working capital:						
Operations:						
Net income (loss) for the year	$ 56,582	$ (7,686)	$ 113,058	$ 385,963	$ 145,306	$ 41,353
Add expenses not requiring use of working capital:						
Depreciation	154,768	112,475	94,508	84,037	80,126	63,902
Amortization of deferred financing expenses	0	0	0	1,232	1,232	1,232
Increase in deferred income taxes	19,700	40,110	9,664	13,582	12,910	18,450
Common shares issued in payment of expense	0	0	0	560	5,151	1,000
Loss on disposal of fixed assets	322	0	0	0	0	0
	231,372	144,899	217,230	485,374	244,725	125,937
Long-term debt assumed, net of current portion	186,000	450,000	50,787	0	0	0
Sales of fixed assets—proceeds	90	950	0	8,435	2,121	4,548
Sale of common shares for cash	0	0	0	84,175	83,613	0
Reduction of mortgages receivable	500	6,500	1,000	0	0	0
Total sources	417,962	602,349	269,017	577,984	330,459	130,485
Use of working capital:						
Assumption of mortgages receivable	0	0	0	10,200	0	0
Purchase of fixed assets	372,513	474,641	441,308	197,570	205,087	288,349
Purchase of Golf Club shares	0	0	6,375	0	0	0
Dividend on preference shares	0	0	79	496	516	3,494
Dividend on common shares	0	0	46,597	39,018	16,912	5,205
Reduction in long-term liabilities	65,110	13,540	2,838	53,000	162,000	17,000
Total uses	437,623	488,181	497,197	300,284	384,515	314,048
Net increase (decrease) in working capital	(19,661)	114,168	(228,180)	277,700	(54,056)	(183,563)
Working capital (deficiency) at beginning of year	(140,929)	(255,097)	(26,917)	(304,617)	(250,561)	(66,998)
Working capital (deficiency) at end of year	(160,590)	(140,929)	(255,097)	(26,917)	(304,617)	(250,561)
Current assets	102,614	103,336	85,171	285,485	79,708	31,254
Current liabilities	263,204	244,265	340,268	312,402	384,325	281,815
Working capital (deficiency) at end of year	$(160,590)	$(140,929)	$(255,097)	$(26,917)	$(304,617)	$(250,561)

Exhibit 10

BLUE MOUNTAIN RESORTS LIMITED
Comparative Balance Sheet—Prepared without Audit
Six Month Periods Ending April 30th
(in thousands)

	1975	1974	1973	1972	1971	1970
Assets						
Current assets:						
Cash on hand	$ 516,470	$ 147,838	$ (117,800)	$ 1,408	$ 50,432	$ 8,480
Accounts receivable	33,055	53,507	7,155	43,823	45,173	41,010
Other receivables	231	223	11,895	86,968	226,308	226,630
Inventories	15,915	21,676	19,802	18,579	15,264	540
Prepaid accounts	13,547	10,703	8,168	9,953	2,541	8,750
Work in progress	429,016	29,992	200,353	27,330	40,438	22,250
Refundable corp. tax						1,790
Mortgage receivable	2,200	2,700	3,200			
Accruals	152		339			
Total current assets	1,010,586	266,639	113,112	188,061	380,156	309,450
Fixed (net)	1,489,928	1,594,771	1,154,019	931,092	760,539	683,120
Other investments	6,375	6,375	6,375			
Total assets	$2,506,889	$1,867,785	$1,293,507	$1,119,963	$1,140,695	$992,570
Liabilities						
Current	$ 51,762	$ 7,706	$ 118,031	$ 44,511	$ 56,117	$111,360
Long term	676,401*	484,410	44,939		184,000	246,000
Deferred income tax	151,566	131,866	91,756	82,092		
Shareholders equity	1,627,160	1,243,803	1,038,781	993,360	900,518	635,210
Total liabilities	$2,506,889	$1,867,785	$1,293,507	$1,119,963	$1,140,695	$992,570

* Note: Approximately $350,000 of the long-term debt represented part of a loan from the Ontario Development Corporation (15 years at low interest). The remaining $165,000 of the loan had not yet been drawn.

The Future

From 1970 to 1975, in particular, a number of steps had been taken by management in the development of Blue Mountain Resorts. The directors, however, held different opinions about the desirability of proceeding toward one or another of the alternatives that were available, recognizing that the financial resources of the company precluded their undertaking more than one major commitment at a time, certainly within the immediate future.

In the summer of 1975 Weider and Canning summed up their views about the future operations of the company and the alternatives they had to deal with in the statements that follow:

We are considering other means of increasing revenue and profits without necessarily

Exhibit 11

BLUE MOUNTAIN RESORTS LIMITED
Comparative Income Statement—Prepared without Audit
Period Ending April 30th
(in thousands)

	1975	1974	1973	1972	1971	1970
Gross margin:						
Accommodations	$ 20,051	$ 17,180	$ 12,378	—	$ 15,995	$ 16,875
Lifts	902,119	598,988	335,421	557,612	628,545	646,605
Tennis club	417	1,230	1,135	—	5	—
Machine shop	999	23,256	(970)	(2,584)	236	—
Tucker Snocat	4,746	800	3,403	5,542	3,589	—
Rentals	769	7,584	5,326	4,966	1,706	—
Food	23,594	(7,675)	11,583	—	—	—
Beverages	63,008	33,902	3,773	—	—	—
Other income	14,278	10,486	906	—	—	—
Total gross margin	1,029,981	685,751	372,955	565,536	650,076	663,480
Indirect expense:						
Commission	126	—	—	—	—	—
Advertising	53,023	77,085	41,879	30,855	35,548	28,413
Automobile	3,714	1,894	2,232	2,109	2,687	666
Bank charges	183	(26)	368	192	597	652
Cash short-over	572	—	—	189	163	2,891
Depreciation	101,250	92,850	72,000	72,000	72,000	67,200
Directors fees	325	125	425	225	419	1,250
Donations	775	1,150	1,860	2,245	585	3,980
Insurances	13,525	10,648	9,000	11,489	9,490	5,560
Interest bank	26,570	28,049	4,378	2,013	82	606
Interest debenture/loan	—	—	1,256	—	4,000	4,000
Interest mortgage	1,684	2,433	3,119	2,451	3,519	7,182
Licenses and fees	1,430	436	35	1,042	41	554
Municipal taxes	17,728	10,120	6,258	3,600	4,665	7,675
Membership fees	1,855	1,516	1,941	373	545	—
Payroll-office expense	69,070	56,183	48,344	34,596	35,241	40,128
Postage	1,514	770	832	1,099	1,134	812
Professional services	4,575	13,732	5,400	5,400	4,762	5,741
Repair and maintenance	2,675	2,418	31	538	2	22
Sundry	5,977	2,855	9,523	3,986	2,481	3,771
Telephone	9,194	6,132	4,207	4,108	3,609	3,413
Travel	2,862	3,520	3,651	2,589	5,463	7,422
Utilities	2,582	2,672	974	1,335	1,498	153
Unallocated payroll	—	(7,600)	1,317	(997)	(8,590)	(16,032)
Music department	—	2,415	—	—	—	—
Interest O.D.C.	7,000	—	—	—	—	—
Total indirect expense	328,209	309,377	219,030	181,437	179,941	176,059
Net income before taxes	$ 701,772	$376,374	$153,925	$384,099	$470,135	$487,421

Exhibit 12: Summary Attractions in the Blue Mountain Area

ATTRACTIONS IN THE BLUE MOUNTAIN AREA

1. SUMMER CHAIRLIFT: Get a lift this summer! Ride to the top of the mountain and enjoy a panoramic view of beautiful Georgian Bay.

2. SKYLINE CAFE: Once at the top of the mountain enjoy a delicious lunch in our rustic little cafe.

3. CONCERT SHELL: On most summer evenings students and faculty of the Blue Mountain Summer School of Music and Dance perform in public concerts at the outdoor Concert Shell or in the adjoining Base Lodge. There is no charge and everyone is welcome to attend. For concert schedule call 445-0231.

4. BRUCE TRAIL: This famous hiking trail runs from Niagara Falls to Tobermory.

5. BLUE MOUNTAIN INN: This summer the Inn will be closed for the addition of a 200 seat dining facility.

6. ARTIST'S STUDIO: Robert G. Kemp, resident artist since 1961, invites you to view his many paintings done in the surrounding district. He's open every day from 9:00 a.m. to 9:00 p.m. and displays work in many media from oil to water colour. 445-2577

7. TYROLEAN VILLAGE: Deluxe swiss chalets for rent weekly, monthly or seasonally. Ten tennis courts, tennis bubble, an outdoor heated pool, horses for hire, riding lessons, trail rides. Year round country comfort. Inquire locally at

8. 445-1467 or in Toronto 534-8452
ARROWHEAD RANCH: In July and August this is primarily a boy's and girl's camp with extremely high standards of riding, camping and swimming. Spring and Fall the ranch caters to organizations and individuals. Skiing groups are welcome in the Winter. 445-3987

9. CRAIGLEITH PARK: All facilities for renting Camper trucks, trailers etc. Beach and playgrounds. 445-4467

10. PINE POTTERY: This is one of the first potteries in the area and displays many traditional pieces as well as the more modern creations. 445-0497

11. CANADIAN PINE SHOP: See an excellent selection of Canadian antiques, hand wovens and gifts. 445-5080

12. KAUFMAN HOUSE: Here at Kaufman House you'll see twenty beautifully furnished and decorated rooms in Kaufman's lines of superb furniture. Traditional period and modern. 445-6000

13. BLUE MOUNTAIN POTTERY: There's a factory sales outlet and an observation studio where you can watch skilled craftsmen making pottery. Open every day of the year. Plant tours for groups can be arranged by appointment. 445-3000

AVILA WOOL & NEEDLECRAFT: Featuring Appleton's Crewel Needlepoint. Let your imagination and creativity run wild in this unique little shop. Blend your colour schemes or create yarns inexpensively or create high fashioned designs from beautiful European Yarns. 445-5801

CANADA GOOSE: Here you will find an art selection of authentic Canadian Eskimo and Indian crafts, gifts and souvenirs. 445-1761

COLLINGWOOD NATURAL HEALTH FOODS: Health is our business. We offer natural, wholesome foods, including organically grown grains, dried fruit, balkan yogurt, unpasteurized honey and herbal teas. In addition, we carry cosmetics, books and vitamins. 445-5566 e.j.'s gifts. Come and browse among a pot pourri of tempting things. Gifts for all seasons and occasions. A wide selection of paper goods, copper, brass, jewellery and many other pleasing items. 445-3845

GATEWAY TAVERN: A modern licensed dining room featuring luncheon specials and a dinner menu that appeals to both hearty eaters and those with lighter appetites. Open Monday to Saturday 11:30 to 9:00. Sunday 12:00 to 7:00. 445-6282

GINGERBREAD HOUSE: Children's fashions designed with creative imagination, perfect fit and great value for your little wonders. A broad selection for both boys and girls, from casual to dressy in infant to size 14. 445-5650

HEN & CHICKENS: A fashion boutique catering to the contemporary woman. Lingerie, daytime and evening wear featuring Leonard, Ann Klein and Katja of Sweden in sizes 6 to 18. Please come in and browse. 445-3642

LESSELS REAL ESTATE LIMITED: A local company fully qualified in all departments of real estate, employing only qualified personnel and specializing in the Township of Collingwood. 445-1991

NOR MOS ARTS: Peruvian arts and crafts. Various special pieces of fine hand painted ceramics, wall hangings, leather and suede goods.

ROCQUE'S CARPET & COLOUR T.V.: A unique retailer of broadloom, stereo and colour T.V. Excellent selection of well displayed quality lines. Zenith authorized sales and service. Bargains on carpet remnants and cuttings. 445-5059

14

undergoing a major feat of expansion. For instance, the midweek business had been increasing, and this is a major factor of our marketing strategy. We are exploring other means in line with the resort's off-season activities.

We have calculated the return on investment for a new cafeteria that we are just installing right now at a cost of $300,000. We need this in terms of sport facilities for the ski traffic. So if we double our capacity, there is a great danger of overdependence on the one sport, and we could face a diminishing return on our investment.

We haven't made the decision whether we should build another triple chairlift—we have already chosen the location—and add to the snowmaking or build a hotel and go into a 12-month operation. The hotel would probably do quite well in the wintertime especially with the support facilities we have, the snowmaking especially, and the growth of the area. More people would come in midweek so there would be more fun. We would have a bar here, and it would probably do quite well. Throughout the week, we would have a house band. Now that's the winter situation.

The next question is the summer. It is really easy to say, "Why don't you do something in the summer?" So many people have said this to us in the past. It is also easy to say we should have the music school, but maybe we should not have it. Maybe we should have had something else.

We do see a lot of opportunities. We have created traffic around here now through the music school, and it is generating a little bit of income for us. It is making a little contribution and not really draining our resources.

The music school might be regarded as the basis from which a festival program could be developed similar to Stratford, Ontario. We see the Stratford and Kitchener hotels full as a result of the business going on at Stratford. If we could fill up the hotels in Collingwood and hold people overnight, then we would benefit by this whole thing. Our hotel would be filled now [July], and we would be able to say that we had a strong second season which we don't have now.

So we have the winter which is reasonably solid for a hotel operation and summer which is coming along because we have created a business and something to hold people over with. Now we have to go into the other seasons with convention or conference business. We are in a good location for it, but we would be taking on a risk.

We could build a large hotel with an investment of about $500,000. This is something that would have to be sold. The new triple chairlift has already paid for itself. If we install another chairlift, we know we would get a return on our investment, although we could get a poor winter at anytime. But a good convention hotel will keep going, weather or not. But we would be going into a field that we know less well than running a chairlift. We know how to install chairlifts and how to run them. When we get into the hotel operation, we are going to need a brand new sales effort and different thinking.

For example, Talisman Ski Resort at first would not rent out to conventions in the wintertime, but then they got hit by bad winters and said, "Why not get in on a sure thing—let's take a convention if someone wants to come.'' You take a chance on not getting lift revenue. You get less lift revenue from a convention goer than you would from a person coming for a ski week because the latter is here to ski. But we would decide on how we could operate that when it happens. Probably if we added 30 or 40 rooms (including meeting rooms), it would be at least $500,000 in added investment. We could then make a go of it in conventions.

Take the music school. If George Brown stays with us we will succeed in establishing our festival. That will require added accommodation. In the convention business, we are getting into a field we know less well. This is the decision we have to make.

Case 7

Bridgeview General Hospital

In November 1984 the administration of the Bridgeview General Hospital had to make some major decisions regarding the future of its computer software development program. A management consulting firm had recommended forming a venture company to market the program. This posed a number of issues such as the following: Could the company be formed in such a way so as to be integrated with the existing organizational structure of the hospital? What should the new management team look like? What should be the goals and objectives of the new company? What would be the probable fiscal impact?

The Hospital

Bridgeview General was a large metropolitan teaching hospital affiliated with a university. The hospital employed 5,500 people and had an annual budget of $160 million. The hospital had a board of directors that was responsible for overseeing its operations.

The hospital was financed by the provincial government which provided funds for operating as well as capital expenditures. Until 1984 the provincial government did not insist on strict fiscal control from hospital administrators; it routinely picked up any operating deficits. This practice had been discontinued in order to make hospitals more efficient and accountable. Administrators were encouraged to be as efficient as possible and were now allowed to keep surplus funds out of their operating budgets that resulted from in-house cost cutting. These "discretionary" funds could be spent as the hospital wished. The size of the discretionary funds was limited to 1 percent of the annual operating budget to a maximum of 10 percent over 10 years.

The Product

Bridgeview General had been developing computer software systems for its own use since 1964. It had developed a hospital information system with unique features including flexibility, proven Canadian track record, nonstop processing,

This case has been prepared by Denise Walters under the supervision of Dr. William A. Preshing, Department of Marketing and Economic Analysis, University of Alberta, Canada. While factual, all names, dates, and location have been disguised. This case is based on a business plan written by Joan Barichello, Keith Reister, and Kevin Chin.

Copyright © 1985 by Wm. A. Preshing. Revised by Paul W. Beamish, 1986. Preparation of this case was made possible by a grant from the Department of Regional and Industrial Expansion, Canada.

Exhibit 1:   Simplified Model of Hospital Information Flows

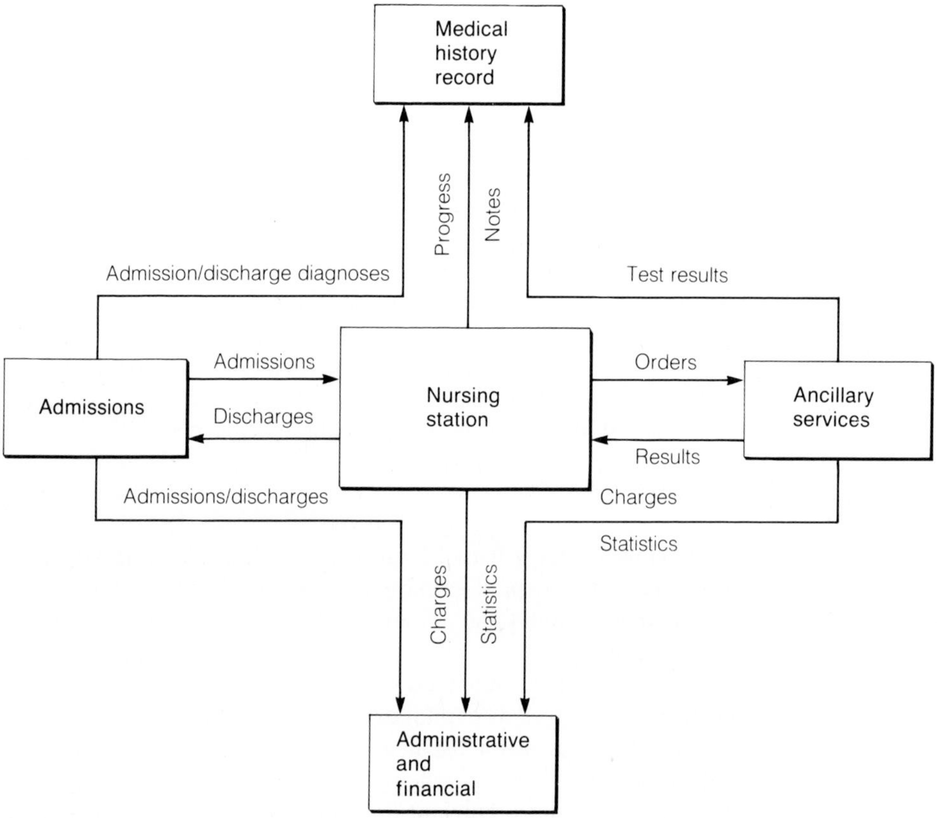

From G. Kolenaty, "Hospital Information Systems Planning," in *Systems Science in Health Care*, ed. C. Tilquin (Willowdale, Ont.: Pergamon Press, © 1981). Reprinted by permission.

ease of use, and tight security. Bridgeview's interactive system was an integrated hospitalwide information system. Its state-of-the-art design enabled it to better organize and coordinate hospital procedures, transmit information quickly to where it was needed, and dramatically reduce manual recording of data.

The key to the flexibility of the system was expandability. The hospital could start with the patient administration module, which tracked patients from admission to discharge, and add other modules including material management, radiology, pharmacy, and general administration modules when funds were available. Each of the system's modules was compatible with the others. See Exhibit 1 for a simplified model of hospital information flows.

The system could grow by adding processors rather than replacing existing equipment. The system could expand from 2 to 16 processors. If more were needed, up to 14 systems with 16 processors each could be added using high-speed

Exhibit 2: Staff Requirements: Different Systems

	Bridgeview	Delta	Duet	Cabot
Number of operators	4	20	20	15
Salary cost at $35,000 each	$140,000	$700,000	$700,000	$525,000

fibre optics (a total of 224 processors). The system was currently in use at five Canadian hospitals. Users of the system had found it most satisfactory.

The hospital's system had a continuous processing capacity and was unique in that it virtually eliminated the risk of system failure. Unlike other computer systems, if one processor failed, the system did not go down, but the workload was instantly redistributed among other processors, allowing the malfunctioning unit to be repaired without interfering with use. In addition, the Bridgeview system required only four operators, at significant cost savings (see Exhibit 2).

The system was "user-friendly" and could be learned by all types of hospital personnel. Confidential data was protected by assigning entry codes to personnel that allowed access only to authorized information.

Research concerning competitors' pricing and hospitals' views on Bridgeview's Hospital Information Systems (HIS) indicated that at $250,000 the product would be competitive and attractive. For an 800-bed hospital, a year's operating cost saving would more than cover the cost of this software.

The Market

In Canada there were 1,250 general care hospitals with an average bedsize of 140. The potential customers for this system were general hospitals of more than 200 beds. There were 300 such hospitals in Canada, with the majority located in Ontario and Quebec. Very few hospitals currently owned computer systems, and those that did generally had a financial system, but not a complete patient care system like Bridgeview's. All of these hospitals were expected to have systems within the next 10 years.

Approximately 3 percent of hospital budgets were allocated to computerized information processing. As salaries and workloads increased, there was pressure on the hospitals to automate their systems. A survey done by the management consulting firm showed that nearly three quarters of the respondents planned to either update their system or acquire a new one altogether within the next three years.

The same survey showed that the three most important features of a hospital computer system were: (1) service and technical support, (2) integrated, modular software, and (3) hardware reliability. It is noteworthy that price was not one of the three most important considerations.

The Canadian hospital computer market in 1984 was estimated at $190 million

Exhibit 3: Canadian Market Forecast: Hospital Computer Expenditures (dollars in millions)

Primary Product	1984	1985	1986	1987	1988	1989
Computer hardware (15 percent growth)	$117	$135	$155	$178	$205	$235
Shared services (23 percent annual growth)	45	55	68	84	103	127
Software and management services (31 percent annual growth)	28	37	48	63	82	108
Total (20 percent annual growth)	$190	$227	$271	$325	$390	$470

(3.5 percent of the total Canadian computer industry) with an anticipated growth of 20 percent annually (see Exhibit 3). Bridgeview's market share and sales forecasts are shown in Exhibit 4. Based on American statistics, there were expected to be approximately 30 buying decisions each year in Canada, and this rate was expected to accelerate.

The Competition

In Canada the market leaders in hospital information systems were Delta Corporation, The Duet Company, and Cabot Computers. Delta Corporation serviced 30 percent of all hospitals over 25 beds with their financial management system. They encouraged hospitals to group together on a time-sharing basis to have access to computer facilities.

The Duet Company was a large American firm with a well-established reputation for reliability and service. They offered both financial and patient care systems, but despite the fact that they were very well known, they had failed to penetrate the Canadian market.

Cabot Computers, also American, marketed both financial and patient care systems. They were currently testing a "Canadianized" patient care system in an

Exhibit 4: Market Share and Sales Forecast

	1985	1986	1987	1988	1989
Total software services market (units)	37	48	63	82	108
Bridgeview system: units sold	2	4	6	8	10
Bridgeview system (average cost $1.5 million)	3	6	10	13	17
Bridgeview software component sales revenue ($ million)	.25	.5	.75	1.0	1.25

eastern hospital but had not yet ironed out all of the bugs. The primary difference between the Canadian and the American systems was in the costing structure, which was much more intricate in American hospitals (that is, every aspirin was added to the bill).

In addition to these major suppliers of hospital information systems (HIS) in Canada, several different metropolitan hospitals marketed the financial and patient care systems they had developed for their own use. Neither had seen their systems introduced to large numbers of other hospitals.

In summary, Bridgeview's competitors were all in the early stages of product and market development. The high development costs presented a significant barrier to entry of new firms. Bridgeview General had a competitive advantage in that its product was well developed and ready to be introduced.

The Venture Company

Bridgeview General obtained legal advice that marketing the computer software system should be separate from the hospital's day-to-day operations. This would limit the hospital's liability to the subsidiary organization. The hospital's board of directors would function as the board of directors for the venture company, and the hospital would provide overall direction and technical development of the system. The senior administrative organization is shown in Exhibit 5.

Exhibit 5: Bridgeview General Hospital Organizational Structure

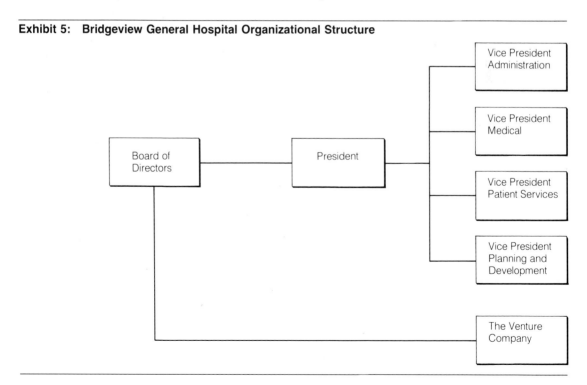

Exhibit 6:   Organization Chart, Department of Information Systems

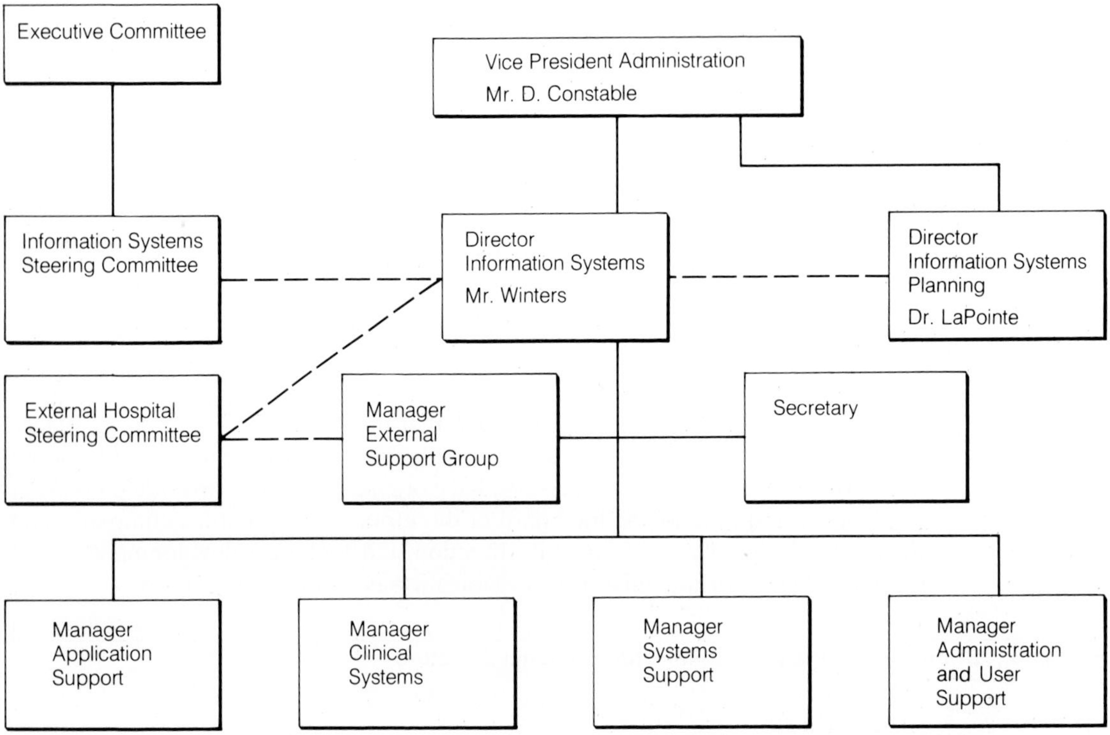

```
┌─────────────────────┐                    ┌────────────────────────────────┐
│ Executive Committee │                    │ Vice President Administration  │
│                     │                    │ Mr. D. Constable               │
└─────────────────────┘                    └────────────────────────────────┘

┌─────────────────────┐   ┌──────────────────────┐   ┌──────────────────────┐
│ Information Systems │   │ Director             │   │ Director             │
│ Steering Committee  │---│ Information Systems  │---│ Information Systems   │
│                     │   │ Mr. Winters          │   │ Planning             │
│                     │   │                      │   │ Dr. LaPointe         │
└─────────────────────┘   └──────────────────────┘   └──────────────────────┘

┌─────────────────────┐   ┌──────────────────┐   ┌──────────────┐
│ External Hospital   │   │ Manager          │   │ Secretary    │
│ Steering Committee  │---│ External         │   │              │
│                     │   │ Support Group    │   │              │
└─────────────────────┘   └──────────────────┘   └──────────────┘

┌────────────┐  ┌────────────┐  ┌────────────┐  ┌────────────────┐
│ Manager    │  │ Manager    │  │ Manager    │  │ Manager        │
│ Application│  │ Clinical   │  │ Systems    │  │ Administration │
│ Support    │  │ Systems    │  │ Support    │  │ and User       │
│            │  │            │  │            │  │ Support        │
└────────────┘  └────────────┘  └────────────┘  └────────────────┘
```

Two employees of the hospital, Mr. Winters (director of informational systems) and Dr. LaPointe (director of information system planning—see Exhibit 6), would be involved in the initial set-up of the venture company. Dr. LaPointe was the inventor of the system, and both men were very familiar with it. Nevertheless, they would not be a permanent part of the venture company but would donate only about 10 percent of their time to assist the new management.

The venture company was to be run by businessmen who had experience in the computer industry. It was believed they should be entrepreneurs, dedicated to making a success of the venture. Although they would be formally responsible to the board of directors, they would liaise daily with Don Constable, VP adminis-tration, for Bridgeview. (See Exhibit 7 for the proposed qualifications and compensation of the individual to be hired to manage the venture company.)

The hospital was willing to provide $100,000 in seed capital to the venture company and would become the sole owner of it. In addition, legal assistance in regard to copyright, liability, and contract design could be provided by the hospital's lawyers.

The consulting firm recommended that, in view of Bridgeview's lack of sales

Exhibit 7: Director of Information Systems Venture

Successful Applicant:
Qualifications:
— Highly motivated.
— Independent.
— Strong entrepreneurial spirit.
— Total personal involvement in all aspects of operations.
— Strong leadership.
— Results oriented.
— Solid background in new venture development.
— Experiences in negotiation and customer relations.
— Good knowledge of public administration and complex organizations.
— Excellent presentation and communication skills.
— Knowledge of medical system.
— Degree in Business Administration.
— Reports to the University Hospital's board but liaises with the vice president, administration on a day-to-day basis.

Compensation:
— Manager of the new company if successfully created.
— Salary of $50,000 per year, plus 10 percent commission (on profit before tax).

force, marketing expertise, or access to distribution channels, the hospital should license a software representative for distribution of its system. The representative would be responsible for all aspects of marketing and after-sales service, and, in return, would receive 50 percent of all software sales revenues (that is, .5 × $250,000/unit) in addition to a commission on hardware sales (from the hardware manufacturer) and an implementation fee. This remuneration structure (standard in the industry) would be very attractive to potential software representatives.

In addition to the $125,000 sales revenue, the venture company would charge an ongoing yearly maintenance fee of 10 percent of the sales revenue. It then would regularly keep the software representative up-to-date with new developments in the system.

Since the development of the Bridgeview system was funded by one of the provincial governments in Western Canada, any hospitals within that province could request the use of the software without charge. The venture company would not be able to charge these hospitals for using the Bridgeview system.

Originally, the product would be marketed within Canada. This was because the system would have to undergo significant changes in order to be accepted in foreign markets. Nevertheless, international opportunities existed—Australia had already expressed interest.

Income earned by the venture company would be subject to 25 percent tax. It was expected that the company would be profitable from the first year of operation (see Exhibit 8).

The profit-making nature of the company presented some problems for the

Exhibit 8

THE VENTURE COMPANY
Pro Forma Income Statement
1985–1989
(dollars in thousands)

	1985	1986	1987	1988	1989
Number of units sold	2	4	6	8	10
Revenue/unit	$125	$125	$125	$125	$125
(after marketing representative compensation)					
Sales revenue	250	500	750	1,000	1,250
Maintenance revenue					
(10 percent of sales revenue):					
From year 1985	25	25	25	25	25
From year 1986	0	50	50	50	50
From year 1987	0	0	75	75	75
From year 1988	0	0	0	100	100
From year 1989	0	0	0	0	125
Total revenue	275	575	900	1,250	1,625
Royalty fee (3 percent of sales revenue payable to Bridgeview)	8	15	23	30	38
Salary ($50,000 and 25 percent burden)	63	63	63	63	63
Secretarial service	10	20	20	20	20
Rent of furnished office	6	6	6	9	9
Travel expense	10	10	12	12	15
Advertising expense	20	20	15	15	15
Phone calls	3	5	6	6	9
Miscellaneous expense	10	5	5	5	5
Total expense before commission	130	144	150	160	174
Profit before commission and tax	145	431	750	1,090	1,451
Manager's 10 percent commission (profit sharing)	15	43	75	109	145
Profit before tax	$130	$388	$675	$981	$1,306

hospital. First of all, the objectives of the venture company could be in conflict with those of the hospital: Bridgeview was, at best, a cost minimizer, not a profit maximizer. This conflict might not be important at first, but there could be a philosophical difference in business decision making between the venture company management and the board of directors. The board would be made up of members of the community who may or may not have business backgrounds. They were used to presiding over a nonprofit organization and would have to make some adjustments to the venture company's profit-making status. The venture company would have other objectives including raising Bridgeview

General's profile within the industry and making a contribution to a more-sophisticated health care system. These objectives, along with that of profit generation, would have to be assessed and prioritized.

The final consideration was of a political and financial nature. As was previously outlined, the provincial government was encouraging fiscal restraint on the part of hospitals. On the other hand, it did not support profit-making activities by these institutions. There were at least two possible government reactions if the venture company was formed: The hospital's operating budget could be cut by the amount of money the company generated, or the province might allow Bridgeview to operate the venture company without reducing its funding. The latter action would require a special policy statement from the government. There was precedent for this action: Another provincial government had allowed two other hospitals in the province to market computer software without having their budget allocations reduced. However, both of the other hospitals in the province had failed to generate a significant amount of money through their business ventures. If Bridgeview was financially successful, it was expected that the provincial government would likely intervene.

The company would have to develop a strategy to influence government policymakers in the hospital's favour. While it was expected that working through political channels might take some time and have uncertain results, Bridgeview ran a risk if they waited—even six months—before launching the venture company. If, in the interim, one of their competitors was successful in "Canadianizing" and selling their software, the hospital might find it much more difficult to break into the market. The competition had established distribution channels and sales forces that could effectively sew up the market.

The provincial government was under considerable pressure to reduce health care expenditures wherever possible. These constituted the largest and fastest-growing expenditures in the provincial budget. Operation of health care facilities in 1984–85 would cost $1.5 billion, an increase of $98 million over the previous year. In view of this, Bridgeview could not be overly confident that the government would allow them to operate the venture company unimpeded.

Case 8

Brookfield Bros. (1968) Ltd. (A)

In April 1981 George and Bob Blunden were once again discussing the future of Brookfield Bros. (1968) Ltd., a $3 million retailer of building materials owned by George and managed by his son Bob. This conversation was part of a regular monthly reevaluation of the firm, necessitated by mounting losses and the uncertain future of the building material industry in Halifax, Nova Scotia.

George argued, "We both know that we can't go on forever with Brookfield losing money like this. Blunden Construction can't continue to support Brookfield, and even more important, Blunden Construction cannot be jeopardized in an effort to save an unprofitable company. We have to decide what we are going to do with this business, and if we're going to get out, we are going to do it on our terms and in our way, paying all of our creditors 100 cents on the dollar, before someone puts Brookfield in bankruptcy and I lose everything."

"Bob, either you're going to have to come up with a viable business plan to turn things around, or we're going to have to get out of the business before things get much worse."

As Bob returned to his office, he was considering once again the basic alternatives as he saw them: (1) continue operations, reduce expenses as much as possible and wait for the eventual industry turnaround; (2) retrench with a major reduction in staff, inventories, and receivables to weather the storm; (3) sell the business; or (4) liquidate the business.

The firm's sales and net income after taxes for the period 1968–80 are presented in Exhibit 1. Year-to-date sales and net income as of March 31, 1981, were $598,065 and ($54,638), respectively. Sales were down 2.6 percent from March 1980, while the loss was $11,579 greater than March 1980. The firm used the calendar year for financial purposes.

The primary cause of the current losses was high interest rates (the rate the firm was paying the bank had risen from 9 percent in March 1978 to 24 percent in June 1981). This affected the firm in two ways. First, it significantly increased the firm's costs of financing inventory and receivables. Second, by increasing mortgage rates, it reduced the level of residential construction activity, which seriously reduced the demand for building materials.

This case was prepared by Professors Robert Blunden and Philip Rosson of Dalhousie University. The authors gratefully acknowledge the financial support of the Department of Regional Industrial Expansion, Small Business Secretariat in the development of the case. Copyright © 1985 by Robert Blunden and Philip Rosson.

Exhibit 1: Brookfield Bros. (1968) Ltd. Sales and Net Income, 1968–1980 (dollars in thousands)

	Sales	Net Income
1968	$1,034*	$ 9.5
1969	712	.1
1970	688	(52.1)
1971	906	(9.0)
1972	1,166	8.3
1973	1,398	21.3
1974	1,855	28.0
1975	1,752	9.3
1976	1,611	(74.1)
1977	1,798	13.3
1978	2,559	47.9
1979	2,886	(35.4)
1980	3,156	(73.5)

* Includes approximately $448,000 of construction revenues.

Company Background

Brookfield Bros. was founded in 1863, making it the oldest operating building supply dealer in Halifax. Its fortunes grew with the city, and as a result it was well known to most builders and many do-it-yourselfers in the Halifax-Dartmouth area. The firm was owned by the Brookfield family until 1968, when its property on the Halifax waterfront was expropriated to allow highway improvements.

At that time its inventory and name were sold to George Blunden, who operated a successful construction and millwork firm in Spryfield called Blunden Supplies Limited. This included a small retail showroom from which building materials were sold in the local area.

George Blunden was a successful, self-made contractor. He had left high school in 1949 to start Blunden Supplies with his father who was a master millwright, carpenter, and cabinetmaker. He was responsible for leading the firm into larger construction projects and new markets and, in the process, built Blunden Supplies to the point where 1967 sales and net income were $1,240,695 and $24,594, respectively. In that year retail sales represented about $200,000 of total sales. In 1968 the inventory and name of Brookfield Bros. was acquired and the name changed to Brookfield Bros. (1968) Ltd.

For three reasons, George saw the acquisition of Brookfield Bros. as an opportunity to expand building material sales. First, rising labour costs were expected to fuel major increases in sales to do-it-yourselfers. Second, it was felt that other Halifax contractors were reluctant to buy from Blunden Supplies because it was seen as a competitor and that the separate and respected Brookfield name would facilitate increased sales to them. Future construction activity would be carried out under the name of Blunden Construction and retail sales under the Brookfield banner. Third, Brookfield Bros.' existing customer base and reputation would enable the Blunden group of companies to expand its revenues.

In the process of changing ownership, Brookfield was moved from its city core location to Spryfield, a suburb of Halifax, where it shared premises with Blunden Construction.

As in most small businesses, the personal values and leadership style of the owner permeated the organization. In particular, George Blunden had a strong sense of personal integrity and business ethics inherited from his father. These attitudes guided the businesses. His authoritarian and task-oriented management style had served him well in the construction industry, but he recognized that the retail business required a more people-oriented approach, and Brookfield's managers reflected that.

George's first love was the construction industry, and he ran Blunden Construction himself. Brookfield Bros. was run by a series of managers from its acquisition until early 1977 when his son Bob assumed full operating responsibility. During this nine-year period, the firm's financial performance was erratic although sales did grow (see Exhibit 1). The variability in annual performance was partly due to the large turnover in management—four managers in nine years. They left for a variety of reasons—from poor performance to being hired away by the competition. In 1971 the retail floor space was greatly increased from the previous 1,600 square feet to 6,500 square feet.

Bob had grown up in the family business although he had never intended to enter it on a full-time basis. He had started shovelling shavings in the mill at the age of 14 and worked in shipping, invoicing, inside sales, and as assistant manager by 1974. In the same year, he completed his bachelor of commerce degree at Dalhousie University at Halifax, then attended Northwestern University in Illinois where he was awarded his master of management degree in 1976. He joined the firm that year as marketing manager and eight months later assumed full operating responsibility. He also taught marketing at Dalhousie University on a part-time basis.

When he joined the firm in mid-1976, it was in serious financial difficulty. Bob was responsible for the major cost cutting and staff reduction that turned the business around. After assuming operating responsibility in early 1977, he began to rebuild the organization and, as can be seen from the financial statements (Appendixes 1 and 2), was successful.

After his initial success in turning the business around, Bob started planning to build Brookfield into a chain of stores through Nova Scotia. However, by 1980 the company was in trouble again, and thoughts of expansion had to be set aside. Bob also thought that his career was no longer progressing as it should.

Products, Markets, and Sales

Brookfield Bros. was a full-line building material retailer. A partial list of products sold would include lumber, plywood, roofing, insulation, drywall, hardware, paint, mouldings, doors, windows, floorcovering, and decorator products for the home.

Brookfield's customers could be segmented into the following six different markets:

1. *Consumer*—made up essentially of do-it-yourselfers, hobbyists, and home-owners who repaired and maintained their homes. Primarily cash sales (80 percent), made either by coming into the retail store or phoning in orders for delivery. This segment was the primary target of most of the advertising budget.

2. *Individual builders*—made up of individuals who built their own homes (not for sale). These sales were predominantly charged to allow the individual to work within their mortgage draws.[1] These customers were serviced both by the inside sales staff and outside sales representatives, the latter calling on the individuals at their construction site or home. They bought a large amount of building materials in a short period, and after completing their home, reverted to the ''consumer'' market segment. They became aware of Brookfield by word of mouth or the spill-over effect of consumer advertising.

3. *Package homes*—made up of individuals who built their own homes. Similar to the previous segment except that in this case a complete home package was purchased rather than simply buying the materials necessary to construct the home. Package homes were not restricted to Brookfield designs and were offered designed to customer's own plans. Usually a package included prebuilt interior and exterior wall panels and all of the material (in its normal unassembled form) necessary to complete the house. The primary advantage to a buyer was that he knew exactly what the materials to build the house would cost, whereas the advantage to the firm was that the builder would buy everything from the one supplier rather than shopping at several building supply dealers. Package homes were generally sold on a charge basis.

4. *Contractor/institutional*—made up of contractors, from large general contractors building office towers to smaller residential contractors who built two or three houses a year. This segment also included institutions such as universities, hospitals, schools, and so forth, which purchased for their own use. This market was primarily serviced by outside sales representatives who called on the builder's purchasing agent. Advertising had little effect other than to possibly create awareness. Sales were made on a charge basis.

---

[1] Mortgage draws are the customary method by which mortgage firms disburse funds to builders. They usually take place at specific stages in the construction process, such as when the structure has its roof on and is water tight and when the insulation is installed. There are usually three to five draws to a construction mortgage, and therefore, the builder requires interim financing. Such financing is often supplied as trade credit by the building material suppliers and subcontractors.

5. *Government*—made up of all three levels of government—federal, provincial, and municipal. Business from this segment was won through a closed tender process and serviced by the manager.

6. *Affiliated companies*—made up of all sales to Blunden Construction and other construction operations owned by George Blunden. All sales were charged.

Sales and gross margins by market segment for the period 1976 through March 1981 are provided in Exhibit 2.

A major concern of management was credit sales and their subsequent bad-debt losses. The building industry was dominated by small independent builders who were poorly financed; as a result, losses on credit sales could be substantial. Credit sales had historically represented about 60 percent of total sales but by 1980 had risen to 70 percent. Of further concern was the increased concentration of receivables in one or two large accounts (recently a single account had accounted for almost one quarter of the receivable balance). The bankruptcy or financial difficulty of such an account could easily bankrupt Brookfield Bros. as well. This problem was being exacerbated by the increased concentration on the contractor and builder markets.

Exhibit 2

Sales by Markets, 1976–1981 (dollars in thousands)

	1976	1977	1978	1979	1980	1981 (January– March)
Consumer	$735	$900	$969	$1,040	$1,180	$167
Individual builders	214	198	201	265	220	30
Package homes	38	210	236	296	112	24
Contractor/institutional	474	415	892	818	1,251	232
Government	(Included	above	in	258	220	119
		institutional)				
Affiliated companies	151	81	297	198	172	26
Total	1,609	1,803	2,595	2,875	3,156	598

Gross Margins by Markets, 1977–1981 (percent of sales)

			1977	1978	1979	1980	1981
Consumer			24.1%	23.8%	24.0%	24.0%	25.1%
Individual builders			23.3	22.9	22.2	20.8	19.5
Package homes			25.0	24.5	26.0	23.7	17.1
Contractor/institutional			21.1	19.6	18.8	18.1	14.3
Government			(Included	above	in	16.9	13.3
				institutional)			
Affiliated companies			14.9	14.3	13.9	14.7	15.7
Total			23.0	21.2	21.0	20.4	17.6

Location

Brookfield Bros. was located in Spryfield—essentially a lower-class residential area made up of apartments and single-family dwellings. It lies across an arm of water from the main peninsula of Halifax and is about five miles from the city centre. The map (Appendix 3) shows the location of Brookfield and its competitors. For the past several years, most of the residential construction had been in the Bedford, Sackville, Forest Hills, and Colby Village areas of the Halifax-Dartmouth metropolitan area.

Brookfield's location was a key factor in its business strategy. It was a poor location—in a low-income residential area of Halifax, 3 to 10 miles from present areas of residential construction and requiring customers to navigate a traffic circle to shop there. As a result, Bob Blunden essentially took the approach that the firm's marketing strategy must compensate for its locational disadvantage. This involved primarily focusing on contractor, builder, and government markets, telephone business, and strong price competition in the consumer market segment so as to provide the incentive to travel to the Brookfield store.

For expansion purposes, the firm held a prime retail location on the main artery in Bedford, but they had been hesitant to develop it until Brookfield was financially stable. Moving the Brookfield operation to this or another site had been considered in the past, but such actions had always been deferred because of the financial uncertainty of the business and the desire not to endanger the construction company.

Corporate Ownership and Structure

Brookfield Bros. (1968) Ltd. was one of the Blunden group of companies that also included Blunden Construction, Bluco Construction, Bluco Holdings, and Brookfield Bros. Brookfield Bros. Ltd. was simply an incorporated shell which had been prepared for a second branch; it had never operated. Bluco Holdings was only a holding company. Blunden and Bluco Construction companies were George's primary interest and the historical profit makers in the group.

From a financial perspective, the firms operated as a unit. Money was loaned between the firms to minimize total borrowings, although it was only in recent years that interest expense had properly been allocated to reflect this practice. The group of companies shared some staff, principally the comptroller and some office staff. The construction companies were expected to buy from Brookfield if the terms were similar and it was not inconvenient. Banking agreements treated the companies as a group by including cross guarantees[2] between all of the firms as well as a personal guarantee from George Blunden. Exhibit 3 shows details of the net income of the construction companies.

George Blunden, either directly or indirectly through other firms, owned 80.7

---

[2] A cross guarantee is a legal agreement whereby each of the parties jointly and individually guarantees the liabilities of each of the others.

Exhibit 3: Consolidated Net Income, Blunden and Bluco Construction (dollars in thousands)

1968	$20.0
1969	27.0
1970	1.6
1971	(.5)
1972	21.0
1973	37.0
1974	72.6
1975	34.5
1976	15.4
1977	6.5
1978	22.5
1979	58.0
1980	89.8

percent and controlled 95 percent of the outstanding common shares of Brookfield Bros.

The firm was organized along functional lines with the sales force organized around market segments. (See Exhibit 4.)

Competition

Brookfield Bros. was an intermediate-sized player in the metropolitan building materials market. Its competitors included other full-line building material dealers, building material departments of mass retailers such as K mart and Woolco (and, it was rumoured, soon Canadian Tire), expanded hardware stores, and lumber mills and wholesalers selling direct to contractors or institutional users.

The largest single building material retailer in the trading area was *Piercey Supplies Ltd.*, which had been founded in 1915. It was ideally located, the only competitor in the heart of peninsular Halifax, and had created a name synonymous with building materials in Halifax. Piercey's enjoyed a large contractor and consumer trade based primarily on its location and depth of stock. The consensus in the industry was, "If Piercey's didn't have it, no one would." It also had a reputation for being the most expensive in town. With higher prices and large volume, its margins were substantial for the industry, and the firm was believed to be very sound financially. (For a comparison of the prices of metro-area building supply dealers, see Exhibit 7.)

Nova Scotia Building Supplies was a chain of approximately 10 outlets in Nova Scotia and one in New Brunswick that had grown over the previous 15 years through acquisition. Two of the chain branches competed with Brookfield. Its main branch and head office was located in Waverley (outside of Halifax) and primarily served the contractor and institutional markets because of its poor location for retail operations. In contrast, NSBS's Cole Harbour branch primarily served consumers and local contractors from an excellent location. NSBS was

Exhibit 4: Brookfield Bros. Organizational Structure, April 1, 1981

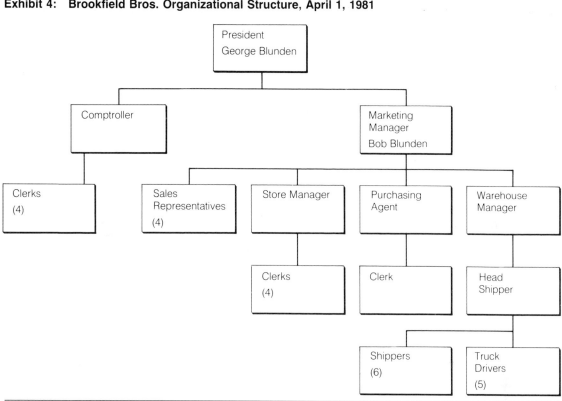

aggressive in pursuing all of its markets and was a major force in the industry. However, it was constantly rumoured to be in financial difficulties.

Halliday Craftsman was a chain of approximately eight full-line building material outlets in Nova Scotia and New Brunswick. It was headquartered in Truro, a town 60 miles from Halifax. The company had two stores in the greater Halifax area which primarily targeted the consumer segment. As a division of a larger Canadian firm, it was considered financially sound. However, it was not a significant force in the market because of its unaggressive management.

MacCulloch Buildall was also a Nova Scotian chain made up of about 10 outlets, 3 of which were located in the metro area. Until recently, there had been four Halifax-area branches, but one store had been closed. The three remaining stores were in good locations but were being overshadowed in each case by nearby competitor stores. MacCulloch was also rumoured to be in financial difficulty.

Payzant Building Products was an independent operation owned and managed by John Payzant. It was well located in Lower Sackville and enjoyed a very loyal clientele. It was considered financially sound.

Exhibit 5: Metropolitan Halifax Building Materials Retailers

Rank	Firm	Location	Sales Estimate
1	Piercey Supplies Ltd.	Halifax	$6–$8 million
2	Nova Scotia Building Supplies	Waverley	$5–$6 million
3	Nova Scotia Building Supplies	Cole Harbour	$2 million
4	Halliday Craftsman	Halifax	$2 million
5	Halliday Craftsman	Dartmouth	$2 million
6	Brookfield Bros.	Spryfield	$3 million
7	MacCulloch's Buildall	Halifax	$2 million
8	MacCulloch's Buildall	Cole Harbour	$1.5 million
9	MacCulloch's Buildall	Sackville	$1.5 million
10	Payzant Building Products	Sackville	$3 million
11	Dartmouth Building Supplies	Lawrencetown	$2 million
12	Alfa Building Supplies	Dartmouth	$.5 million
13	Woolco	Dartmouth	$.5 million
14	K mart	Dartmouth	$.5 million

Dartmouth Building Supplies was the "maverick" in the local industry. It had a poor location some distance from its markets and concentrated on large contractors and commercial and institutional accounts. It was the most aggressive force in the bulk building material business in town. Because of its low prices, more-traditional building supply dealers in the area felt it must be losing money.

Alfa Building Supplies was a small and stagnant operation which served a very local area and a few longstanding customers.

In recent years, *K mart* and *Woolco* had both opened significant building material departments in their local stores. They were aggressive price advertisers to the consumer market and were expected to further penetrate the local market. For some time it had been rumoured that *Canadian Tire* would expand its hardware lines into building materials. This was a matter of concern to the existing

Exhibit 6: Building Material Retailers and Their Primary Target Markets

	Consumer	Individual Builders	Package Homes	Contractor/ Institutional	Government
Piercey	X	X	X	X	X
NSBS (2, 3)	X	X		X	X
Halliday (4, 5)	X	X	X	X	X
Brookfield	X	X	X	X	X
MacCulloch (7, 8, 9)	X	X	X	X	X
Payzant	X	X		X	X
Dartmouth		X		X	X
Alfa	X			X	
Woolco	X				
K mart	X				

Exhibit 7: Price of a Basket of Goods at Selected Building Material Dealers

Rank	Firm	Price	Percent of Average
1	Piercey Supplies	$913.20	129%
2	Halliday Craftsman	742.51	105
3	MacCulloch's Buildall	720.38	102
4	Alfa Building Supplies	719.53	102
5	Payzant Building Products	652.02	92
6	Nova Scotia Building Supplies	603.71	85
7	Brookfield Bros.	602.45	85
	Average	$707.69	100%

building material dealers. The sophisticated marketing activities of K mart, Woolco, and, perhaps, Canadian Tire could radically upset the consumer segment of the market.

Selected data on Brookfield's principal competitors are shown in Exhibits 5, 6, 7, and 8.

In 1980, a group of local university students conducted a market basket survey, by telephone, to determine the relative prices of area building material dealers. The basket was composed of 25 items covering paint, electrical, plumbing, lumber, hardware, and building material lines. The students also assessed the quality of telephone service. The results are included in Exhibits 7 and 8.

Exhibit 8: Rating of Telephone Service of Selected Building Material Dealers

	Poor						Excellent
Brookfield Bros.	1	2	3	4	5	6	(7)
MacCulloch's Buildall	1	2	3	4	5	(6)	7
Piercey Supplies	1	2	3	4	5	(6)	7
Alfa Building Supplies	1	2	3	4	5	(6)	7
Nova Scotia Building Supplies	1	2	3	4	5	(6)	7
Payzant Building Products	1	2	3	4	(5)	6	7
Halliday Craftsman	1	2	(3)	4	5	6	7

Industry Trends

The building material industry in Nova Scotia was characterized by firms with relatively low marketing skills. They were generally family-owned merchants rather than professionally managed businesses. Barriers to entry were few and small. As such, the industry was particularly susceptible to inroads by mass retailers or larger, more sophisticated retailers from other markets; especially since the consumer segment is of growing importance to sales and consumer marketing is a strength of these newer competitors.

Buying groups played an important role in the industry. By joining a buying group, independent firms could largely offset the lower costs which chain store operators had enjoyed through their greater buying power. Buying groups were national or regional firms (usually owned by its members) which bought the goods from the manufacturer or wholesaler and resold them to the retailer-member. Sometimes called voluntary chains, they came about in Canada and had retained a place in the distribution channel because of the large year-end rebates available from most suppliers based on annual purchasing volume. A large group would in most cases achieve maximum rebates whereas an independent dealer might receive none or very small rebates on its own. Rebates for most products were in the 3 percent to 10 percent range. In some cases, members of buying groups received lower prices on goods as well, but the chief benefit of group membership was the rebate levels attainable. All of the full-line building retailers in Halifax (Numbers 1–11 in Exhibit 5) were members of groups.

Regarding buying groups, Bob Blunden commented, "If it weren't for Bold Lumber, our buying group, we would have been forced out of the business long ago by the chains. In fact, our rebates are usually far in excess of our net profits."

The Economic Environment and Residential Construction

Like others in the industry, Bob recognized that the Canadian economy was going through a recessionary period in 1981. Real GNP declined in 1980 and was expected to increase only marginally in 1981. The construction industry was tied closely to the economic fortunes of the country—construction activity being largely determined by the general level of economic activity and interest rates. The bulk of the construction industry's current problems was a direct result of the economy. One local bright spot, however, was the promise of offshore oil and gas development which could bring an attendant boom for Halifax. This could be the salvation of the local economy.

In their deliberations, the decision makers at Brookfield were not helped much by conflicting economic projections. For example, whereas housing starts for Nova Scotia for the period 1968–80 were a matter of record (see Exhibit 9), forecasts for 1981–84 varied widely. Projections of the Labour Research Division of the Provincial Department of Labour, and of Clayton Research Associates Ltd., a respected housing forecaster, are shown in Exhibits 10 and 11.

In early 1980, the Labour Research Division of the Provincial Department of Labour reported the following in their *Construction Forecasts 1980–84*.

> Housing in the 1980s is not expected to provide the levels of activity which were seen during the middle 70s. The underlying demand for housing in the 80s will not be as strong, due mainly to demographic changes in the Canadian population. Currently, factors such as high interest rates, lack of serviced land, housing costs, and changing government policy have depressed the housing industry.
>
> Housing starts in 1980 are expected to reach 4,200 units. This is in sharp contrast to 1977 when 7,495 units were started. While the number of units started will rise

Exhibit 9: Nova Scotia Housing Starts, 1968–1980

	Single and Duplex	Apartments and Other	Total	Percent Change	Metro Percent of Provincial Total
1968	2,919	1,494	4,413		
1969	3,685	3,157	6,842	+55%	
1970	3,495	2,383	5,878	−14	
1971	4,804	2,504	7,308	+24	35%
1972	3,486	1,678	5,164	−29	49
1973	4,082	3,652	7,734	+50	54
1974	3,750	2,258	6,008	−22	52
1975	4,185	2,181	6,366	+ 6	43
1976	4,670	2,800	7,470	+17	47
1977	3,917	3,578	7,495	0	44
1978	3,291	1,562	4,853	−35	44
1979	3,195	1,343	4,538	− 6	38
1980	2,771	1,124	3,895	−14	24

Source: Statistics Canada.

annually during the first half of the 80s, the peak will only be in the area of 5,400 starts in 1984.

In the same report, the Department of Labour projected the following housing starts for the province (see Exhibit 10).

In January 1981 Clayton Research Associates Ltd., in a comprehensive report prepared for the Housing and Urban Development Association of Canada, made the following projections:

Housing starts are projected to increase moderately in 1981 to a level of about 184,000 units [nationally]—this is still well below the projected average annual requirement for the third year in a row. The tight markets and pent-up demand resulting from this underbuilding in the 1979–1981 period are projected to result in high activity levels in 1982–1984 before settling back towards more normal levels in 1985.

In the same report, housing starts were projected by province for the period 1981–85. The relevant data for Nova Scotia is included in Exhibit 11.

Exhibit 10: Projected Number of Nova Scotia Housing Starts, 1980–1984

1980	4,200
1981	4,410
1982	4,675
1983	5,002
1984	5,352

Source: *Construction Forecasts 1980–84*, Labour Research Division, Department of Labour, Province of Nova Scotia, 1980.

Exhibit 11:   Projected Total Housing Starts For Nova Scotia, 1981–1985

1981	5,000
1982	7,000
1983	7,000
1984	8,000
1985	8,000

Source: Clayton Research Associates Ltd.

Bob had also collected some other economic data which he felt might be useful in forecasting the future of the Nova Scotian building material industry. It is presented in Exhibit 12.

Exhibit 12:   Selected Economic Data, 1968–1980

	GNP*	Mortgage Rates†	CPI Housing‡
1968	72,586		
1969	79,815		
1970	85,685		
1971	94,450		100.0
1972	105,234		n/a
1973	123,560		112.6
1974	147,528		122.3
1975	165,343		132.4
1976	191,031	11.78%	149.0
1977	208,806	10.36	163.6
1978	229,698	10.60	175.1
1979	260,305	11.98	185.7
1980	288,136	14.32	201.5

* Gross national product of Canada in millions of dollars.
† Average of prime conventional mortgage interest rates.
‡ Consumer price index for housing components in Halifax.
Source: Statistics Canada.

Brookfield Bros. (1968) Ltd. Strategy 1977–1981

Bob Blunden was the chief architect of Brookfield's strategy from 1977 to 1981. To a great extent, it reflected his concerns about the firm's location and his desire to grow the firm into a major player in the provincial market.

In February 1977 Bob assumed operating control of the business and was able to quickly turn it around by cutting costs, targeting new markets, and infecting the organization with a renewed enthusiasm and mission. The cost cutting had begun the month before with the layoff of one third of the staff in early January and the institution of tight controls on purchasing and expenses. The consumer market was targeted with more aggressive pricing and advertising to encourage do-it-yourselfers to drive the extra two or three miles to shop at Brookfield or to shop by phone and save. The general theme was one of value—good products and service at reasonable prices. The other major market thrust was complete home packages for individuals building their own homes. This market was less competitive, offered substantial growth opportunities and better margins, and was approached with aggressive advertising and competitive prices. The employees were easily inspired to perform because the firm's mission was now clear: survival. The earlier layoff of the poor performers also served to motivate those remaining.

Plans for further growth and the locational problem of Brookfield led to the targeting of contractor markets in 1978–79. The sales force was reorganized around its markets with one salesman dealing with individual builders and another concentrating on contractors, rather than geographically as had been the case before. In 1979 another salesman was added to lead the efforts to capture part of the large general contractor market. These contractors were engaged in larger projects and commercial construction rather than residential wood frame building.

Things had gone well for a time, but 1979 and 1980 results were disappointing, and Bob sensed the next few years would be difficult for Brookfield. He thought about the four alternatives facing the firm and decided to review each in turn.

Appendix 1

BROOKFIELD BROS. (1968) LTD.
Statement of Income and Retained Earnings
1974–1981
(in thousands)

	1974	1975	1976	1977	1978	1979	1980	January–March 1981
Sales	$1,855	$1,752	$1,611	$1,798	$2,559	$2,886	$3,156	$ 598
Cost of sales:								
Beginning inventory	300	369	430	373	395	649	645	491
Purchases	1,419	1,272	1,113	1,324	2,158	2,221	2,297	618
Freight in	15	21	11	8	20	5	16	1
	1,735	1,662	1,554	1,706	2,573	2,875	2,957	1,110
Ending inventory	369	430	373	395	649	645	491	639
	1,366	1,232	1,181	1,311	1,924	2,229	2,466	471
Gross profit	489	520	430	487	635	657	690	127
Expenses	460	537	536	515	605	731	809	190
	29	(18)	(106)	(28)	29	(75)	(120)	(63)
Other income	37	63	59	63	43	62	68	16
Profit BD&T	65	45	(47)	35	72	(13)	(51)	(47)
Depreciation	28	33	27	22	24	22	22	6
Income taxes	9	3	(3)	—	—	—	—	—
Net profit (loss)	$ 28	$ 9	$ (71)	$ 13	$ 48	$ (35)	$ (74)	$ (53)
Retained earnings, beginning	$ 187	$ 215	$ 224	$ 153	$ 166	$ 214	$ 178	$ 105
Retained earnings, end	215	224	153	166	214	178	105	52

Appendix 2

BROOKFIELD BROS. (1968) LTD.
Balance Sheets
1974–1981
(in thousands)

	1974	1975	1976	1977	1978	1979	1980	January–March 1981
Assets								
Current assets:								
Cash	$ 1	$ 1	$ 1	$ 1	$ 1	—	$ 4	$ 2
Receivables	452	526	327	369	410	$ 482	423	396
Inventories	369	430	373	395	649	645	491	639
Property held for resale	—	—	44	—	—	—	—	—
Prepaid expenses	12	23	22	17	18	19	22	32
Investments	8	9	9	11	11	25	29	25
Land, buildings, and equipment	221	227	209	191	192	185	190	186*
Goodwill	5	5	5	5	5	5	5	5
Total assets	$1,068	$1,219	$ 988	$ 988	$1,286	$1,360	$1,164	$1,285
Liabilities								
Current liabilities:								
Bank loan and overdraft	$ 340	$ 448	$ 420	$ 264	$ 395	$ 400	—	$ 348
Payables and accruals								
Trade	139	190	84	178	271	169	$ 270	233
Affiliated company	139	103	132	64	114	127	374	191
Long-term debt payable within one year	15	35	32	23	40	68	68	71
Income taxes payable	5	1	—	—	—	—	—	—
Total current liabilities	637	776	668	529	821	763	712	843
Long-term liabilities	197	200	148	274	231	399	327	353
Total liabilities	834	975	816	803	1,052	1,162	1,039	1,196
Shareholders' Equity								
Capital stock	20	20	20	20	20	20	20	20
Retained earnings	215	224	153	166	214	178	105	69
Total shareholders' equities	235	244	173	186	234	198	125	89
Total liabilities and shareholders' equity	$1,068	$1,219	$ 988	$ 988	$1,286	$1,360	$1,164	$1,285

* Off balance sheet assets representing Spryfield land and buildings are worth about $500,000.

Appendix 3: Map of Halifax–Dartmouth Metro Area

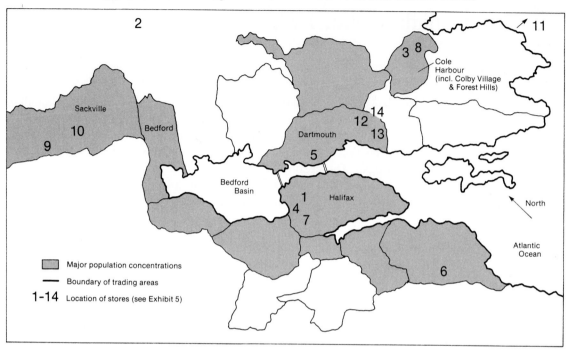

Case 9

Canada Coke, Ltd.

On July 30, 1974, Charles M. Hall, a recent graduate from a leading Canadian business school, had been on his first assignment with the Canadian subsidiary of the American Aluminum Corporation (AMAL) for only two weeks when he found himself facing the first important set of decisions of his career. Hall's Seattle-based boss, Edgar Thompson, had assigned him the responsibility for the petroleum coke aspects of the primary aluminum production process, and with this responsibility came two immediate decisions of important long-run consequences.

The first decision was whether or not to accept an offer from British Columbia Aluminum, Ltd., a Canadian company, to supply 50,000 tons of petroleum coke to Seattle, Washington, at a delivered price of 10 percent less than the delivered price of the best alternative source of petroleum coke from U.S. sources. AMAL used large quantities of petroleum coke and needed to purchase 50,000 tons in order to tide it over the next six months.

The second decision was to determine and recommend with justification a price at which a new long-run source of petroleum coke should be transferred from a newly formed Canadian subsidiary to AMAL's U.S. smelting operation.

Before making these decisions, Hall reviewed what he knew about AMAL operations.

AMAL Structure

American Aluminum Corporation, a U.S. corporation located in Seattle, Washington, on the West Coast of the Pacific Northwest, refined high-quality aluminum ingot from aluminum oxide (alumina) which was transported in bulk ocean carriers from bauxite mines in Western Australia to AMAL's smelter. The aluminum smelting process combined a few basic raw materials (alumina, cryolite, aluminum flouride, pitch, and petroleum coke) with large quantities of electric power to produce aluminum ingot. AMAL's smelter was located so that it had access to a deep-water harbour for unloading the alumina as well as convenient rail service and relatively inexpensive hydroelectric power.

This case was prepared by J. Frederick Truitt, Associate Professor of International Business, School of Business Administration, University of Washington, and Paul W. Beamish of the School of Business and Economics, Wilfrid Laurier University. Copyright © 1986 by J. Frederick Truitt and Paul W. Beamish. It is partially derived from the American Aluminum Corporation Case © J. Frederick Truitt, the Graduate School of Business Administration, University of Washington, 1980. Names, dates, and places have been disguised. All monetary figures in the case are expressed in U.S. dollars.

Exhibit 1:   Corporate Ownership Structure: American Aluminum Corporation

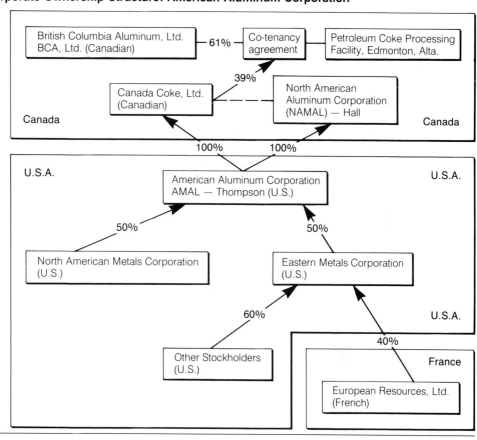

AMAL was owned by two U.S. corporations, Eastern Metals Corporation and North American Metals Corporation. Each owned 50 percent of AMAL. Eastern Metals Corporation was, in turn, 40 percent owned by European Resources, Ltd., a French corporation, and 60 percent owned by U.S. stockholders. (See Exhibit 1.)

The Petroleum Coke Supply Problem

During the two years immediately preceding Hall's assignment, AMAL had been experiencing problems securing dependable supplies of petroleum coke[1] at a

---

[1] Petroleum coke is the last product resulting from the petroleum refining process after all the higher-grade fuels and chemicals are taken off. Before the coke is suitable for use in the aluminum smelting process, it must go through a calcining process which removes the impurities in the coke.

stable and reasonable price. AMAL used a maximum of 110,000 tons of petroleum coke per year, and between late 1973 and July 1974, the delivered price of petroleum coke had increased from $45 per ton to $90. This dramatic increase in price along with interruptions in supply and decrease in the quality of petroleum coke available from U.S. West Coast refineries led AMAL to seek an alternative source of supply for a substantial portion of its petroleum coke requirements.

Canada Coke, Ltd.

AMAL management decided in late 1973 to procure their petroleum coke from Canada and had entered into a joint venture with British Columbia Aluminum, Ltd., (BCA, Ltd.) to construct a petroleum coke processing facility near the petroleum refineries in Edmonton, Alberta. Canada Coke, Ltd., was formed as a wholly-owned Canadian subsidiary to carry out the details of the venture with BCA, Ltd.

Canada Coke was a corporate facade or "non-firm" in the sense that it employed no management personnel. All managerial decisions involving Canada Coke, Ltd., were made by AMAL personnel such as Edgar Thompson in the United States. Nevertheless, while decisions involving Canada Coke, Ltd., were ultimately made in the United States, they could be heavily influenced by Hall's recommendations.

Hall was physically based in an office in Edmonton, Alberta, and was the sole employee of AMAL's wholly-owned umbrella Canadian subsidiary, North American Aluminum or NAMAL. Hall's position had been created for three reasons. The first reason was to provide assistance on issues relating to Canada Coke. The second reason was related to the ambiguous attitude of many Canadians to foreign ownership of their nonrenewable resources. While the foreign investment and job creation was welcomed, many Canadians were uncomfortable with what they viewed as excessive foreign control. AMAL's parent companies, having experienced negative public opinion with their investments in other countries (and in one instance, expropriation), were sensitive to these attitudes and so created Hall's position to keep them abreast of public opinion and to ensure that decisions regarding such things as transfer prices were consistent with the letter and spirit of Canadian regulations. (See the appendix for the 1975 set of Canadian rules for foreign corporate behaviour.) AMAL did not wish to engage in any drawn-out battles with the Canadian Department of Revenue, and Hall had been instructed to avoid these.

The third reason for the creation of Hall's position was to investigate other investment opportunities in Canada for AMAL. Although there were currently no specific proposals, Hall recognized that much of his time would ultimately be spent on this activity.

Hall found the nature of the agreement between AMAL's Canada Coke, Ltd.,

Exhibit 2: Flow of Petroleum Coke from Edmonton

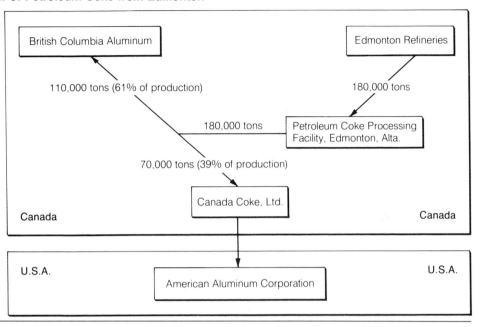

and BCA, Ltd., interesting because it did not seem to fit into any of the familiar categories (wholly owned subsidiary, joint venture, licensing arrangement, and so forth) he had studied in his business program. AMAL (through Canada Coke, Ltd.) and BCA, Ltd., shared the output of the newly constructed petroleum coke processing facility proportional to the contribution each partner made to financing the construction of the facility. The arrangement was in many ways similar to a joint venture between AMAL and BCA, Ltd., but was, in fact, termed a *co-tenancy agreement*. The petroleum coke producing facility had no separate legal identity, and the co-tenancy form allowed each of the participating companies to write down their respective shares in the asset at different depreciation schedules. AMAL had decided to write down its share in the new facility using the straight line method of depreciation over a 20-year period.

BCA, Ltd., contributed 61 percent of the cost of constructing the petroleum coke processing facility and was scheduled to take 61 percent of its annual 180,000-ton production. AMAL, through Canada Coke, Ltd., contributed 39 percent of the construction cost and was scheduled to take 39 percent of the annual 180,000-ton production when the facility came on stream some time in the next six months. (See Exhibits 1 and 2.) BCA, Ltd., was the operating partner in the co-tenancy arrangement and was to provide coke to AMAL through Canada Coke, Ltd., at a cost determined by the following schedule:

Actual operating cost of calcining process (does not include depreciation)	$5.00 per ton
Management fee	.50 per ton
Coke purchasing commission	.40 per ton
	5.90 per ton
Cost of green coke from refineries	40.00 per ton
Total cost charged by BCA, Ltd., the operating company of the co-tenancy arrangement, to Canada Coke, Ltd.	45.90 per ton

Transporting the refined Canadian coke from the Edmonton facility to the AMAL's smelter was estimated to cost $13 per ton. The U.S. tariff on petroleum coke imports was 7.5 percent ad valorem.

Canada Coke, Ltd., was financed with $850,000 in capital stock and $2 million in loans at the prime rate of 12 percent from a major Canadian bank. That is, AMAL's 39 percent participation in the Edmonton coke facility was through Canada Coke, Ltd., in the amount of $2.85 million.

The Transfer Pricing Decision

The decision to go to Canada in this particular arrangement had been put into motion before Hall had joined AMAL. What remained for Hall to recommend was the price at which Canada Coke, Ltd., sold its 39 percent share of the petroleum coke output from the calcining facility to AMAL. Since Canada Coke, Ltd.'s profits, and hence Canadian income tax liability, were dependent almost entirely on this transfer price, Hall saw the need to proceed carefully, lest AMAL run afoul of Canadian (let alone U.S.) income tax authorities. Whatever price was determined, Hall knew he would be called to defend it to Revenue Canada officials. Therefore, he sought the assistance of tax lawyers on the corporate staff who noted the following:

A. Since AMAL was owned by two large, complex U.S. corporations, the tax rates of these parent corporations had to be taken into account when calculating AMAL's effective tax rate. The effective rate of U.S. income tax turned out to be in the 30 to 35 percent range.

B. The effective tax rate for Canada Coke, Ltd., was 41 percent.

C. The judgment of Canadian tax authorities on the propriety transfer pricing decision would be based on the "arm's-length" guideline, that is, the transfer price had to be close to the price that would be used by two unrelated organizations. The two basic methods for determining an "arm's-length" transfer price favoured by Canadian authorities were:

(1) A market price between unrelated organizations.

(2) If a market price was not available as a guideline, a comparison of rates of return on the total assets of similar independent operations with the

expectation that a foreign-owned subsidiary in transfer pricing relationships with its parent company would earn a return on total assets (RTA) comparable to independent firms. (RTA equals net profit before interest and tax/total assets.)

Earlier in the week Hall took a day away from his office and drove over to a large university library in order to look up some more information on the petroleum coke industry in Canada. He found that the RTA for petroleum coke operations in Canada averaged a surprisingly low 5 percent. Later he verified this figure by telephone with the Canadian consulate nearest AMAL's smelter. He also found that to the best of his and the consulate's knowledge, there was no market price for petroleum coke in Western Canada because there were no sales of petroleum coke between independent companies in Western Canada.

It was Friday morning, the weather was promising, and Hall was looking forward to a relaxing weekend. But the weekend would be all the more relaxing if in the next couple of hours he could determine the range of potential transfer prices, make the decisions on the BCA, Ltd., offer and Canada Coke, Ltd., transfer price, and write the two-page justification for his recommendations.

Appendix: New Principles of International Business Conduct

Foreign-controlled businesses in Canada are expected to operate in ways that will bring significant benefit to Canada. To this end, they should pursue policies that will foster their independence in decision making, their innovative and other entrepreneurial capabilities, their efficiency, and their identification with Canada and the aspirations of the Canadian people.

Within these general objectives, the following principles of good corporate behaviour are recommended by the Canadian government. Foreign-controlled firms in Canada should:

1. Pursue a high degree of autonomy in the exercise of decision-making and risk-taking functions, including innovative activity and the marketing of any resulting new products.
2. Develop as an integral part of the Canadian operation an autonomous capability for technological innovation, including research, development, engineering, industrial design, and preproduction activities, and for production, marketing, purchasing, and accounting.
3. Retain in Canada a sufficient share of earnings to give strong financial support to the growth and entrepreneurial potential of the Canadian operation, having in mind a fair return to shareholders on capital invested.
4. Strive for a full international mandate for innovation and market development when it will enable the Canadian company to improve its efficiency by specialization of productive operations.

5. Aggressively pursue and develop market opportunities throughout international markets as well as in Canada.

6. Extend the processing in Canada of natural resource products to the maximum extent feasible on an economic basis.

7. Search out and develop economic sources of supply in Canada for domestically produced goods and for professional and other services.

8. Foster a Canadian outlook within management, as well as enlarged career opportunities within Canada, by promoting Canadians to senior- and middle-management positions, by assisting this process with an effective management training program, and by including a majority of Canadians on boards of directors of all Canadian companies, in accordance with the spirit of federal legislative initiatives.

Case 10

Canadian Casting Company
Limited

In July 1980 Peter Johnston, 45, president of the Canadian Casting Company Limited (CCC), Ancaster, Ontario, was deeply involved with a review of his current operations and plans for expanding the company's facilities and personnel. CCC had grown rapidly in the four years since he had taken it over, for the second time, so that now all aspects seemed to be "bursting at the seams."

Canadian Casting Company, as its name implies, was engaged in the casting of a wide variety of intricate parts, requiring a high degree of precision and quality for an equally diverse number of industries. Johnston regained control of the company in 1976. Sales for the fiscal year ending on March 31, 1980, had risen to over $2.8 million with a net profit of approximately $334,000. (See Tables 1 to 4.)

The Casting Process

Investment casting, the process utilized by CCC, was also known as the "lost-wax" process or "precision" casting. The concept was said to have been developed initially in China some 4,000 to 5,000 years ago, and trade literature described it thus:

> The term *investment* refers to a cloak, or special covering, in this case, a refractory mold, surrounding a refractory-covered wax pattern. In this process, a wax pattern must be made for every casting and gating system; that is, the pattern is expendable.

A number of variants of the process existed, but they had the following points in common: (See the appendix for further explanation.)

- Disposable or expendable patterns are used.
- Molding is done with a fluid aggregate or slurry.
- The aggregate is hardened in contact with the pattern, providing precise reproduction of the pattern.
- The aggregate is bonded with an inorganic ceramic binder.
- The mold is heated to drive off all wax.
- Pouring is performed with the mold preheated to a controlled temperature in order to pour thin sections that would not otherwise fill out.

This case was prepared by Professor W. H. Ellis of McGill University. All names have been disguised. Copyright © 1981 by Professor W. H. Ellis. Edited by Mark C. Baetz, 1986.

Company Background

Following his graduation as an electrical engineer from a well-known Canadian university, Johnston joined a large firm specializing in electronics. "Electronics were my life at the time," remarked Johnston, who added that having seen a radio at an earlier age, "by the time I was 11, I started working night and day studying it." By 1971 Johnston had risen to the position of chief engineer of the company's communications division. Johnston described his situation as follows:

> At that point, I had studied on my own, had my engineering degree, and had worked on electronics all my life. Having achieved the position of chief engineer, I said, "Where do I go from here at the age of 36?" My main goal all through life was to do some kind of innovation, to do experiments, and if I wanted to do that in the future, I had to have a foundation that I could control, that I could utilize, like having the people, the facilities, and the resources. I said, "This is where my electronics career ends. There isn't much further I can go in this company."

The electronics firm had a division that made investment castings but had been operating at a loss of about $250,000 annually for five or six years. The company had decided to cease the casting operation and to dispose of it. Johnston described subsequent events as follows: "Just at that time, I started thinking of my own career. I had heard about the investment casting plant, so I thought I would take a chance on it and subsequently made arrangements for its purchase in November 1971."

Production

Coming from an electronics background, investment casting was indeed a "foreign field" to Johnston. However, with an engineering degree and a desire to innovate, Johnston "went in there and worked on the process, first in department number one, then number two, and so on until I understood the whole process. I did everything in the whole plant."

CCC faced a difficult introductory period of approximately eight months with "no orders and seven people to pay." Finally, after approximately eight months of calling on former customers, orders started to come in. By August 1972, some 10 months after taking over CCC from the electronics parent, Johnston had received "so many orders, I didn't know what to do with them—about $300,000 worth without the money to produce them." The situation was alleviated somewhat when orders and production increased rapidly. By mid-1975 CCC purchased a machine shop that machined castings and custom-produced parts for aircraft. By that time, there were 85 employees.

In discussing the production process, Johnston stated that precision investment casting has been around for 4,000 or 5,000 years but had not been controlled until recently by scientific means:

> Having been in the electronics business, being used to the progress in technology, I may be able to push more than other people in the industry. I am going to find a better

way of doing it. So this is one of the reasons CCC is keeping ahead of others in production. We would like to mechanize the processes a bit more and obtain more consistency.

Pursuing production and his product philosophy further, it was Johnston's view that the day of simple products was gone and it was necessary to go with high technology products. For example, he argued:

> If you go out and make a pair of shoes for people, which everybody can do, then the chance of survival is very, very small. Besides, there are developing countries that can take over at any time they want to. Look at textiles; there is no way that you can compete. Within the Western Hemisphere, we have to stay with high technology to be able to survive and be profitable. The first thing you should say when you look at a product is "Can we survive with it?"

To emphasize this point further, Johnston added that he looked at precision casting products and believed there was a definite market for them. "I can survive knowing that this kind of process cannot be replaced in the near future. There are no replacements, even now, and I don't see any in the immediate future. Therefore, there is an excellent chance for CCC."

Financing

"Of course, I didn't have the money in 1971 to buy the investment castings operation," remarked Johnston in talking about the financial aspects of CCC, "but I looked for a partner and found one in the person of Lester Greenfield. Together, with all my savings, we bought it with a very small amount of cash."

The initial financing of CCC consisted of $5,000 from Johnston's personal savings and an equal amount from Greenfield. With this pool of $10,000, they negotiated a price of $160,000 for the plant, the balance payable over a period of 10 years.

A $20,000 line of credit was negotiated with the banks but disappeared very quickly with no production underway. Even with orders to $300,000 and receivables at $60,000, the banking fraternity was reluctant to provide any additional backing. Finally, one bank agreed to give CCC 75 percent of the value of the accounts receivable on the basis of a personal guarantee to be equally signed by both Johnston and Greenfield. When Greenfield refused to sign, the bank's retort to Johnston was, "If your partner has no confidence, why should we lend you the money?"

Faced with this critical situation, Johnston's only recourse was to friends, who ultimately contributed a total of $120,000, all on the basis of Johnston's personal guarantee. With this backing, together with a continued growth in orders and accounts receivable, a commercial bank finally agreed to lend CCC up to the value of 60 percent of the receivables. However, increased orders created a corresponding demand for inventory, which in turn required more cash than Johnston had raised through personal loans and regular commercial banking facilities. The Federal Business Development Bank (FBDB), which had previously refused to provide funding, was approached again and this time, mid-1975, saw the way clear to grant additional financing, with sales of the company reaching $1.2 million. In fact, by 1976 the FBDB approached Johnston to invest 30 percent, but Johnston said he was not interested.

A Change of Ownership

In early 1976 Greenfield concluded he would like to change his role from being a passive, silent partner to one of running CCC and said to Johnston, "Let me take over; you run the production part, and I will look after management."

Johnston pointed out that the business and customers were built upon a close relationship which required comprehensive technical knowledge beyond the pure casting technology. He commented to Greenfield, "To run a business like ours is not a matter of mass producing the components. Pure administration alone is not really the normal way of operating this business. For example, you can't sit down and do time studies; these are all jobbers—each part is different." Following further discussion, a meeting of the board of directors was held at which time Johnston was out-voted by the combination of Mr. and Mrs. Greenfield, both of whom were directors. Johnston was promptly told to step aside as president of the company.

The dialogue that ensued went along these lines: "Fine, I'm fired," said Johnston. "I am going to leave the company, but let's make a decision right now at this meeting. We are going to have a sell-out agreement set here and now. You have the option. You can buy me out or sell it to me, at whatever price you come up with. I don't care." Greenfield replied, "We'll have a buy-out agreement, and I will buy you out. I will give you $75,000 cash in 90 days, and I'll buy you out." Johnston answered, "Right! I'll take it, and I'll leave the company, but with one stipulation. I am free to do whatever I want to do."

The stipulation was received with something less than enthusiasm by Greenfield. A compromise was finally reached granting Johnston's decree but on the added condition that Johnston guarantee the $220,000 in loans outstanding at the time. Johnston believed that he had no choice.

Johnston commented on the situation that developed over the ensuing six months:

> In a very short time, by the beginning of 1977, Greenfield and the company were in deep financial trouble. I found out why. Once I left, my partner didn't really know the processes and yet insisted on controlling everything. He took a stopwatch, went inside and started timing everybody, and insisted that everyone work faster. He insisted on it because he thought that if the current production methods could make so much money for the company, by pushing the workers a little bit more, he could increase the output correspondingly. Well, the operators disagreed. They disliked someone standing behind them and timing them. He didn't go through the foremen, the supervisors, or the production managers. He went directly down to the

production level and said, "You can go faster than that." The workers replied, "Sure we can go faster, but it may not be good." "Do it anyway!" The workers did as they were told with the result that the rejection rate soared to 85 percent compared with the normal rate of 12 percent. Greenfield, himself, would put the castings in the box, even if they were of doubtful quality.

After about six months of this, Greenfield asked the accountant to contact me, to see if I would buy the company back. Following a third refusal, we agreed to terms and arranged a joint meeting with a lawyer and an accountant to complete the transaction.

On arriving at the meeting, Greenfield announced that he was not going to sell and turned around and walked out. By August 1977 the bank took over and liquidated the company.

In the six-month interval after leaving the company, Johnston had started to build up a related casting business. By the time the liquidation proceedings had been completed on CCC, Johnston's new operation was underway, serving different customers and markets. Now Johnston was able to merge the two functions and again took over CCC's complete facilities. When word of CCC's demise reached many long-standing customers, "They flocked to my office—from Florida, Hughes Aircraft in Tucson, Lockheed, Pratt and Whitney, Boeing—they all came in here. They sat here and said, 'Now, Peter, what are you going to do? We need castings.'"

It is the custom in the investment casting industry that the customer retains ownership of the tools required for the production of the specific products it orders. With the liquidation under Greenfield, customers had to obtain a release from the creditors in order to transfer the material to Johnston's new operation. Customers then came to Johnston, saying, "Peter, we need the castings now. Can you get them fast?"

Johnston explained subsequent events as follows:

> They sat here for weeks until we could get the process started again. We worked here day and night, trying to get things done. We had a hard time in that period because these big customers cannot stop their production. Often they might have as many as 5,000 people waiting on a production or assembly line for one small casting piece.
>
> Companies like Boeing are so big and yet they couldn't do much about it. Whenever they can, they take a tool to somebody else in the States, but a lot of them cannot do this type of casting. We finally got it going. For four and a half years, I worked 16 hours a day, day in and day out, but we got the volume up to about $1.2 million in our first year.

Management Philosophy

In reflecting on his corporate experience to date, Johnston described some of his management philosophies in the following way:

> I have found out one thing that perhaps management people haven't thought much about, and that is the internal atmosphere you try to generate in your company. This

is all the responsibility of the president since nobody else can set it. If I want a certain atmosphere in the company, I'll make sure I set it up myself.

In Johnston's view, one of the most important ways that a certain atmosphere was set was in the way managers dealt with people. Johnston explained his approach to people as follows:

In a small company, it is possible to know everybody and care about what they are doing. If I saw something not being done correctly, I would pick up the casting, call the individual aside, and say, "You can do better than that. I will show you how to do it." I would then demonstrate the correct procedure to the employee and repeat it until the employee attained perfection. They knew that I didn't crucify them. They were learning something. If you do enough of this, people will respect you and care about their work. Once a person makes a mistake, they know it. All I say is, "That's a mistake, and now let's do it properly."

It was Johnston's philosophy never to "put a person down," and he insisted that all his managers followed a similar philosophy. Teamwork was also regarded highly. "People have to work together, and I insist on it in the company," he commented.

Although the managers in CCC had their titles and clearly defined responsibilities, this did not preclude Johnston from imparting to them, "Every job in the company is your job. If I am shorthanded in here, you come and help me; if you are shorthanded, then I go on the line. Every problem is yours. Once you have that atmosphere, the people know it is crucial that we have to work together as a team. More than that, they all know each other's job well enough that they can step in if anything happens."

Through the medium of regular formal and informal meetings, attempts were made to guarantee that this "teamwork atmosphere" prevailed and moved down the line to the direct labour, ensuring that they were happy with the company. This, in Johnston's view, avoided a lot of problems, including union problems. "You treat people like human beings. We make a point of never pushing people around. If one does 10 pieces a day and another does 2, we leave the latter alone, knowing that these are their individual speeds. We want it that way because in this business quality is everything, not the speed of production."

In addition to creating the team atmosphere, bonuses were awarded every six months, "depending on the whole company's performance, not the individual—the whole company's. At the end of every six months, I worked out the figures, sales against the number of employees, and determined what the bonus would be."

Johnston recognized that this was easy to do with 100 to 120 employees and expressed the opinion that some other criteria would have to be developed when CCC became substantially larger. At this point in time, "It works out fine, maybe one of the reasons being that all the people know and trust me."

As an illustration of the team atmosphere that was apparent in the early stages of the company's operation and continued throughout, Johnston recalled the production of the first castings. "Because customers were waiting for their orders, we had worked into the evening, and at 9:00 P.M., we poured the first casting. The production manager said, 'Fine, now let's stop and call it a day.' The men got cleaned up and walked into my office where I was still working, carrying two bottles of whiskey. I didn't know it, but they had had these bottles hiding inside for a week, waiting for this particular moment. We drank until midnight. So they do sort of care for the company."

A Look to the Future

In keeping with his product philosophy, Johnston believed that there was virtually no end to the demand for CCC's investment precision castings. With expected improvements in technology, Johnston was forecasting nearly $6 million by 1983 and expected sales up to $30 million to $40 million a year before too many years passed by.

Part of the reason for Johnston's optimism for increased sales was the lack of competition. In Canada, a total of 10 companies were reported to be engaged in CCC's type of "lost-wax" process, compared to 235 in the United States. Johnston further assessed the competition in the following way:

> There aren't that many good companies who can produce premium quality products. So, really, the competition is not that great. For example, there are parts that we make now that can only be produced by six companies in the world, not just in North America.
>
> When you get that kind of technology, people will buy from you, and they push you to produce it. That is the kind of industry we are in and the kind of company we operate. But you have to keep up with recent developments. You have to have new ideas. You have to produce technology that other people don't have so that you are always in the forefront. If you stay in the top 10, you are O.K. In fact, I would like to stay in the first 2 if I can, but that takes time. It's not too bad though. After starting production again in 1977, we were able to get into the top 10.

In addition to the expansion of the casting part of the business, Johnston was considering that the next area of development might be machining. "Certain castings have to be machined before being used. Right now, the customer asks us to do it, but we don't have the means."

In looking to the future, Johnston was also concerned about the plant's physical location should continued expansion take place, particularly outside Canada. CCC sales were currently in the United States, the United Kingdom, Germany, and France, with contacts in Hong Kong, Israel, and Spain—"whoever deals in aeroplanes or electronic equipment."

Not the least of Johnston's concerns about the future growth of CCC was the role he should play. "I worry about that a lot. Although I have 10 management people under me running the company [see Exhibit 1], I have yet to find one who can run the whole show. Finding people is very difficult. I am looking for good people all the time. I'll be glad to take every day off and let somebody run the show for me."

Table 1

CANADIAN CASTING COMPANY LIMITED
Balance Sheet
At March 31

	1980	1979	1978	1977 (5 Months Ending March 31)
Assets				
Current assets:				
Accounts receivable	$ 646,209	$ 406,205	$260,469	$ 11,654
Loans receivable	4,505	13,871	—	1,313
Inventories	760,997	383,595	228,643	39,740
Prepaid expenses	14,619	25,671	14,082	—
Rent deposit/subscriptions receivable	—	—	—	4,500
Total current assets	1,426,330	829,342	503,194	57,207
Fixed assets	1,736,355	458,633	344,037	230,081
Other	5,186	7,527	9,869	13,469
Total assets	$3,167,851	$1,295,502	$857,100	$ 300,757
Liabilities				
Current liabilities:				
Bank indebtedness	$ 557,435	$ 254,539	$162,712	$ 87,735
Accounts payable and accrued charges	409,567	219,832	155,733	41,134
Income taxes payable	40,172	4,620	14,840	—
Long-term debt due within one year	81,692	61,130	21,250	6,250
Deferred income taxes	3,163	6,900	—	—
Total current liabilities	1,092,029	547,021	354,535	135,119
Long-term debt	1,225,221	316,792	284,152	159,560
Deferred income taxes	135,927	51,780	30,138	127
Total liabilities	2,453,177	915,593	668,825	294,806
Shareholders' Equity				
Capital stock	5,500	5,500	5,500	5,500
Retained earnings	709,174	374,409	182,775	451
Total shareholders' equity	714,674	379,909	188,275	5,951
Total liabilities and shareholders' equity	$3,167,851	$1,295,502	$857,100	$ 300,757

Table 2

CANADIAN CASTING COMPANY LIMITED
Statement of Earnings and Retained Earnings
For the Years Ended March 31

	1980	1979	1978	1977 (5 Months Ending March 31)
Sales	$2,824,637	$1,980,304	$1,280,843	$11,668
Cost of goods sold (schedule) inventory, end of period	1,989,162	1,482,677	833,163	5,614
Gross profit	835,475	497,627	447,680	6,054
Expenses:				
Advertising and sales promotion	25,997	16,151	16,075	683
Amortization—deferred expenses	2,342	2,342	3,600	220
Amortization—leasehold improvements	—	—	—	298
Automobile	15,294	11,597	13,427	—
Bad debts (recovery)	(1,453)	10,442	2,000	—
Commissions	88,142	59,973	25,026	—
Delivery and freight out	5,494	12,226	5,297	—
Depreciation—automobile	1,808	2,584	—	—
Depreciation—machinery and equipment	—	—	—	1,550
Depreciation—office furniture and equipment	2,987	2,243	1,342	75
Directors' fees	—	700	12,500	—
Donations	50	500	100	—
Dues and subscriptions	1,695	617	379	—
Equipment rental	—	—	10,362	—
Factory expense	—	—	—	175
Interest and bank charges	27,481	9,937	20,437	—
Interest on long-term debt	52,609	20,040	14,757	—
Loss on disposal of fixed asset	—	832	—	—
Management fees	2,890	3,175	39,652	—
Office salaries	113,002	74,076	21,845	—
Office supplies and postage	8,827	7,588	4,097	—
Professional fees	21,661	22,212	11,838	1,000
Rent	—	—	—	1,123
Sales discounts	11,278	10,704	6,472	—
Telephone	10,471	8,301	7,675	—
Travel	7,710	3,265	3,624	352
Total expenses	398,285	279,505	220,505	5,476
Earnings from operations	437,190	218,122	227,175	578
Other earnings				
Rental income	18,238	—	—	—
Earnings before income taxes	455,428	218,122	227,175	578
Income taxes	120,663	26,488	44,851	127
Net earnings	334,765	191,634	182,324	451
Retained earnings, beginning of year	374,409	182,775	451	—
Retained earnings, end of year	$ 709,174	$ 374,409	$ 182,775	$ 451

Table 3

CANADIAN CASTING COMPANY LIMITED
Statement of Changes in Financial Position
For the Years Ended March 31

	1980	1979	1978	1977 (5 Months Ending March 31)
Source of working capital:				
From operations:				
Net earnings	$ 334,765	$191,634	$182,324	$ 451
Items not requiring an outlay of working capital:				
Depreciation	134,238	61,318	42,056	1,625
Deferred income taxes	84,147	21,642	30,011	127
Amortization—deferred expenses	2,342	2,342	3,600	—
Amortization of leasehold improvements	—	—	—	298
Loss on disposal of fixed asset	—	832	—	—
	555,492	277,768	257,991	2,501
Increase in long-term debt	908,429	32,640	124,592	—
Issue of common shares	—	—	—	5,500
Loan payable—shareholder	—	—	—	115,810
Loan payable	—	—	—	43,750
Sale of fixed asset	—	1,285	—	—
	1,463,921	311,693	382,583	167,561
Use of working capital:				
Additions to fixed assets	1,411,941	178,031	156,012	—
Purchase of fixed assets	—	—	—	232,004
Purchase of other assets	—	—	—	13,469
Increase in working capital	51,980	133,662	226,571	(77,912)
Working capital, beginning of year	282,321	148,659	(77,912)	—
Working capital, end of year	$ 334,301	$282,321	$148,659	$(77,912)
Represented by:				
Current assets	$1,426,330	$829,342	$503,194	$ 57,207
Current liabilities	1,092,029	547,021	354,535	135,119
Working capital	$ 334,301	$282,321	$148,659	$(77,912)

Table 4

CANADIAN CASTING COMPANY LIMITED
Schedule
For the Years Ended March 31

	1980	1979	1978
Cost of goods sold:			
Raw materials:			
Inventory, beginning of year	$ 232,105	$ 102,972	$ 25,598
Purchases	533,327	435,598	286,746
Freight and duty	15,132	19,197	7,954
	780,564	557,767	320,298
Inventory, end of year	481,544	232,105	102,972
	299,020	325,662	217,326
Direct costs:			
Direct labour	803,938	594,918	404,589
Payroll levies	85,345	57,923	37,016
Contract labour	62,691	49,074	16,210
Tools and dies	525,413	261,271	138,082
	1,477,387	963,186	595,897
Manufacturing expenses:			
Amortization—leasehold improvements	5,579	5,077	4,535
Amortization—jigs and fixtures	4,650	4,650	4,650
Depreciation—machinery and equipment	72,312	46,764	31,529
Depreciation—building	46,902	—	—
Electricity and heating	79,493	66,432	33,094
Insurance	4,042	8,989	1,338
Plant maintenance and repairs	22,933	20,011	2,998
Production costs	—	—	5,889
Rent	37,371	26,744	15,933
Shop supplies	45,270	23,753	13,474
Taxes	22,166	17,228	18,029
	340,718	219,648	131,469
	2,117,125	1,508,496	944,692
Work in process			
Inventory, beginning of year	118,411	113,875	14,142
	2,235,536	1,622,371	958,834
Inventory, end of year	227,428	118,411	113,875
Cost of goods manufactured	2,008,108	1,503,960	844,959
Finished goods			
Inventory, beginning of year	33,079	11,796	—
	2,041,187	1,515,756	844,959
Inventory, end of year	52,025	33,079	11,796
Cost of goods sold	$1,989,162	$1,482,677	$833,163

Exhibit 1: Organization Chart (1980)

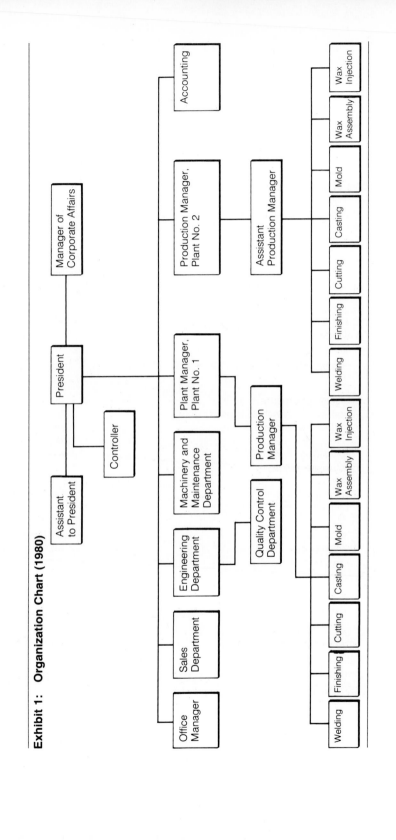

Appendix

With many years of experience in manufacturing precision investment castings, Canadian Casting Co. is able to meet the most demanding requirements, to transform designs into actual components, and to meet tight delivery dates. The Foundry produces castings in ferrous & non-ferrous castable alloys by the lost wax method of investment castings. This method produces castings of a high level of precision, complexity and quality and can save many costly machining operations.

Meticulous quality control and the most modern equipment ensure close conformity with drawings and specifications and a high degree of consistency between the individual castings. Careful selection of raw materials and the use of a well proven investment shell process in addition to our own process patents, produce castings of excellent definition, surface finish and metallurgical quality.

FACTS YOU SHOULD KNOW ABOUT CASTINGS

PRECISION INVESTMENT CASTINGS require one wax pattern for each casting to be made. For this a die (tooling) is required. This is followed by mold making, removal of the wax pattern from the mold cavity and, finally, filling of the mold cavity with metal. The casting is produced by breaking the mold apart and cutting it away from its gating arrangement.

SAND CASTINGS are less precise as a general rule, and require a great deal of machining so that the final component cost is high, usually with one additional disadvantage of lower quality.

PERMANENT MOLD CASTINGS compare with Investment Castings in quality. However, the process does not allow for the same precision and complexity. More machining operations are needed, usually resulting in a higher final cost.

DIE CASTINGS are mass-produced and Investment Castings normally cannot compete with them. However, die prices are usually 10 times greater, so that the price per casting may go up considerably on limited runs. In such cases, properly designed investment castings can offer a high quality product at a competitive, and even lower, price.

Investment Casting Process

How it works...

1 WAX INJECTION	2 WAX PATTERN REMOVAL	3 WAX ASSEMBLY

4 SLURRY DIP	5 SHELL MOLDING	6 DEWAX	7 PRE HEAT MOLD

8 POURING OF METAL	9 SHELL REMOVAL	10 GATE REMOVAL	11 CASTING

Canadian Tire Corporation

In November 1981 Dean Muncaster, president and CEO of the Canadian Tire Corporation (CTC), was assessing the position he should take with respect to the takeover of White Stores, Inc., which was headquartered in Wichita Falls, Texas. Since 1977 CTC had been looking for an opportunity to expand to the United States and preferably into the Sunbelt states. For a price that was not to exceed $45 million (U.S.) pending a year-end audit, CTC would acquire White's 81 retail stores, 4 warehouses, trucking fleet, and access to more than 425 independent dealer-owned stores centred in Texas, Louisiana, Oklahoma, and 11 other states. It was now up to Dean Muncaster to decide if he should recommend to the board that Canadian Tire proceed with the purchase.

In order to place Muncaster's decision in context, this case will outline the following: (1) history of Canadian Tire, (2) the Canadian Tire success formula, (3) American/Sunbelt retail market considerations, (4) White Stores, Inc., and (5) other options available.

History of Canadian Tire

In 1922, two brothers, Alfred and John Billes, invested $1,900 and formed Hamilton Tire and Garage Ltd. in Hamilton, Ontario. They dealt primarily in automobile parts and servicing. The firm, renamed Canadian Tire, grew quickly and in 1927 had three stores in Toronto. During the 1930s, the company started supplying other automobile parts and service centres in Ontario. Prior to World War II, six stores existed in Ontario.

The Billes family demonstrated significant innovation during their early years, a trademark that remained as one of the cornerstones to the firm's success. For instance, the first CTC store on Yonge Street in Toronto in 1937 had stockroom clerks on roller skates moving parts to the sales counter for increased customer service time. CTC adopted computer-aided accounting and inventory control procedures as early as 1963. Throughout the 1970s, CTC built one of the most modern distribution networks in the country, utilizing the latest technology in warehousing and inventory control.

By the end of 1981 the firm had grown to 348 retail stores and 83 gasoline stations. The product line had been expanded to include hardware products,

This case was written primarily from published sources by Mark C. Baetz and Ralph Troschke, School of Business and Economics, Wilfrid Laurier University. Copyright © 1986 by Wilfrid Laurier University.

lawn-care products, sporting goods, and small household appliances. Internationally, CTC had purchased a 36 percent controlling interest in McEwan's Ltd. of Australia in 1979.

Much of the success of CTC was attributed by some observers to the leadership of Dean Muncaster, age 48, who had been involved with CTC since he was 12 years old. Muncaster had worked in his father's store in Sudbury during summers while attending the University of Western Ontario and Northwestern. In 1957 he was hired by Canadian Tire as a financial analyst. Approximately two years later, he left Canadian Tire in Toronto and returned to Sudbury to be the manager of the Sudbury dealership held by his father. He returned to Toronto in 1961 as a vice president and became president in 1966. Muncaster's accomplishments were astounding. During his presidency, CTC's sales rose from $100 million (1966) to over $1.3 billion (1981), and after-tax net income reached $51.4 million or $4.05 per share. He was well liked and respected by CTC's dealer network and by Canadian financial experts.

Muncaster was faced with managing three divergent groups while steering CTC. The three groups were, first, Alfred Billes and his family, second, the heirs of John Billes headed by John's son, Dick, and, third, the dealer network. The two factions of the Billes family collectively controlled 60.8 percent of the voting shares in the corporation (representing only 8.5 percent of all outstanding shares) and were not always in agreement with one another. For example, Muncaster's decision to enter the Australian market was heavily contested between the two family groups, with Dick Billes in favour and Alfred Billes in opposition. The decision left its scars.

The Billes family was active in the corporation. They managed several stores and held directorships on the board. Their influence was not always evident to the general public as they shunned the limelight and the media.

The Canadian Tire Success Formula

CTC was extremely successful due to the corporation's emphasis on the dealer-run network, advantages incurred from its highly modernized distribution system, and a marketing program which clearly established its desired image in the minds of the consumers. The dealer-manager network was the cornerstone to CTC's success and essential in an understanding of corporate values and strategies.

The dealer-run stores were a type of franchise operation. CTC usually owned the building (87 percent of the time) and acted as the central buyer, distributor, national advertiser, and dealer recruiter. The dealer ran the store as his own business. He would buy all of his goods from CTC (approximately 6,000 of 32,000 products were mandatory), and most operational decisions (for example, personnel, local advertising, and so forth) were his to make. CTC wanted to blend the entrepreneurial spirit with that of a corporate manager. It was hoped that this arrangement would provide individual dealers with enough incentive to turn their stores into a success. The dealers did not have to pay franchise fees but had to invest a minimum of $50,000 into their locations. They were free to reap as much profit as they could from their stores.

The corporation was very careful in its selection of prospective dealers. The ability to invest at least $50,000 was not the only criterion. Exhaustive examinations and interviews were utilized to trim the 1,000–1,200 applicants down to the final 50 trainees. The trainees spent three months of in-class training followed by six months of in-store training before posting to a store. Corporate support was always available after the training period on any retailing issue, and dealer-support group meetings were numerous. The system worked so well, in fact, that virtually no dealer failure was encountered by CTC.

The desire for revenues and profits was instilled through the dealer-run network. The advanced distribution system ensured that the parent corporation managed its costs to make its own profit. As well, by having the right merchandise in the right store at the right time, the system ensured customer satisfaction. The key ingredients in this distribution system were three fully automated one-storied warehouses (one in Edmonton and two in Toronto) which utilized robotics, conveyor belts, and computerized cataloguing of parts. The inventory levels of the warehouses, as well as those of individual retail operators, were monitored by computers. Re-order points of the retail and wholesale levels were automatically triggered on a nightly basis. This ensured a maximum delivery time of two days to retail outlets.

The result of CTC's advanced distribution system, from a customer's point of view, was constant availability and selection of thousands of products that CTC carried. This became a trademark of the firm. Inventories were also reduced, increasing CTC's inventory turnover and decreasing its carrying charges. This made profitability easier to attain for CTC and its retailers.

The constant availability and broad selection of numerous products were part of an image that CTC had built for itself through an effective marketing campaign. Consumers also came to know Canadian Tire as a retail outlet offering value with a reputation for low price. This was especially important during 1981 as inflation, interest rates, and unemployment all rose. The value–low price appeal attracted a lot of people who had turned into "do-it-yourselfers" during this period. The average purchase at a Canadian Tire store was $15, and these purchases were said to be interest-rate-proof as they were small "must" expenditures. While the average purchase seemed low, CTC would see approximately 2 million customers per week according to Muncaster.

The typical customer found it difficult to enter the store and buy just one item. Due to the firm's low prices and broad product lines, it was not uncommon to witness the typical customer filling up a shopping basket with various products.

Muncaster identified several additional key factors to CTC's success: (1) CTC became known as a place for "more than just tires," a theme employed in its advertising. Traditionally, 80 percent of CTC's customers had been male, but by 1981, the split was almost even. (2) To lure customers back to the store, the firm employed "Canadian Tire money" which was a form of discount coupons given to customers after each cash purchase. (3) Twice per year, 7 million catalogues listing the entire CTC product line were published and distributed to households across Canada.

These factors led to unusually high growth rates and startling financial successes for CTC. Exhibits 1 and 2 highlight the performance of the corporation during this period of high growth and image development. Walter Hachborn, general manager of Home Hardware Stores Ltd., CTC's major Canadian competitor, explained the success of CTC in the following way: "Canadian Tire has succeeded because of excellent marketing and superior merchandising combined with the fact that they were the first to fill a void in the Canadian retailing market. They happened to come along at the right time and place."

Suppliers to CTC were also impressed with CTC operations. One supplier

Exhibit 1: Four-Year Review of Performance (dollars in thousands except per share amounts)

	1980	1979	1978	1977
Comparative Income Statement				
Gross operating revenue	$1,057,536	$935,753	$798,717	$718,114
Pre-tax income	72,240	69,583	53,938	52,240
Taxes on income	34,513	33,070	25,163	23,750
Income before extraordinary gain	37,727	36,513	28,775	28,490
Extraordinary gain	901	2,195	694	1,000
Net income	38,628	38,708	29,469	29,490
Cash dividends	8,487	7,017	10,435	5,800
Income retained and reinvested	30,141	31,691	19,034	23,690
Comparative Balance Sheet				
Current assets	435,183	343,372	312,831	277,894
Investments	44,151	49,371	1,823	1,014
Net property and equipment	266,854	244,496	235,989	218,209
Other assets	2,213	2,582	3,620	4,026
Total assets	748,401	639,821	554,263	501,143
Current liabilities	279,451	211,903	165,040	134,511
Long-term debt	136,387	136,361	138,377	142,317
Deferred income taxes	3,599	3,822	3,382	1,512
Shareholders' equity	328,964	287,735	247,464	222,803
Per Share Data				
Income before extraordinary gain	3.07	3.07	2.49	2.50
Net income	3.14	3.26	2.55	2.59
Dividends	.69	.59	.90	.51
Shareholders' equity	26.75	24.20	21.40	19.59
Statistics at Year-End				
Number of associate stores	333	319	314	314
Number of gasoline stations	71	64	62	61
Number of Class A shareholders	8,665	9,310	10,435	10,035
Number of common shareholders	1,252	1,315	1,450	1,417

Source: Canadian Tire annual report, 1980.

Exhibit 2:   Canadian Tire Performance Comparison (dollars in thousands except per share amounts)

	1981 (52 Weeks)*	1980 (53 Weeks)	Annual Change
Gross operating revenue	$1,340,764	$1,057,536	26.8%
Pre-tax income	100,432	72,240	39.0
Income taxes	48,966	34,513	41.9
Income before extraordinary gain	51,466	37,727	36.4
Net income	53,678	38,628	39.0
Dividends	9,936	8,487	17.1
Income retained and reinvested	43,742	30,141	45.1
Per share:			
Income before extraordinary gain	4.05	3.07	31.9
Net income	4.22	3.14	34.4
Dividends	0.78	0.69	13.0
Shareholders' equity	30.44	26.75	13.8

* Estimated.

noted; ''We've been impressed by the energy levels exhibited by the CTC head office when negotiating contracts, and although they have pushed the cost of advertising our product in their catalogue on to us, we consider their organization as top-notch.''

Despite the phenomenal growth, it was apparent to Muncaster and other senior CTC executives that CTC growth could not be sustained indefinitely. Since 1977 CTC had been following a master plan prepared by Muncaster for future growth. The strategy in 1977 was to blanket the Canadian market by expanding into British Columbia, as yet untapped, and by establishing retail outlets in any community or suburban area that could support a successful regular-sized CTC store. It was estimated in 1980 that 65 percent of Canadians lived within 15 minutes of a Canadian Tire store, and it was felt that by 1985, the maximum penetration of 400 stores would be reached.

The strategy also called for growth into other countries and markets with an English language/cultural component as well as a similar economic base. The Australian entry had taken place in 1979, and the United States was earmarked for entry in 1981. Carrying the CTC concept into these countries was not expected to be difficult, and consumer acceptance was anticipated to be high.

The need to expand was foremost in the mind of Muncaster. As CTC approached 400 stores, the firm was expected to reach its physical limit, and without further expansion, an adverse impact on operating performance was anticipated. Expansion in British Columbia was well underway by 1981, and CTC had attempted to diversify somewhat by getting into gasoline stations and a small automobile engine remanufacturing plant for resale of the engines at its stores. These developments merely held off the inevitable total market saturation by CTC.

The Australian venture into McEwan's, a hardware chain, was intended to allow CTC to enter Australia to gain a foothold, then to expand its operations and to conquer Australia as Canada was conquered. The Australian venture was a small one, involving only a $2.2 million investment for a 36 percent interest. However, McEwan's suffered losses of $1,837,000 (Canadian) in 1980 and $548,000 in 1981. While performance was improving, CTC was disappointed. The Foreign Investment Review Board of Australia had also made it clear that it would prohibit CTC from acquiring a greater than 50 percent share in the Australian firm. CTC decided to sell off the investment in 1982 and use the funds of the sale toward the costs of an entry into the United States.

The Australian experience put some pressure on the president of CTC to seek out a successful expansion opportunity whereby the firm could parachute its Canadian success formula and reap large rewards. The original timetable called for an expansion to the U.S. market. Muncaster had favoured the Sunbelt states as they had exhibited the fastest growth in populations and incomes. Demographic trends from 1973 to 1981 definitely pointed to this area of the United States as a ripening market. Some disagreement existed in CTC management as some favoured expansion to the northeast, where climatic conditions and automobile models tended to parallel those of the Canadian market more closely.

American/Sunbelt Retail Market Considerations

In its analysis of the Sunbelt area, CTC managers felt that no competitors had a stranglehold on the things that CTC did well. Given the successes in Canada which CTC had enjoyed even when the retailing industry was on a decline, the general consensus amongst the management of CTC in Toronto was that the Sunbelt market was a "sure-fired success." Long-term demographic studies were undertaken, and a heavy reliance was placed on their favourable findings (see Exhibit 3).

It was noted that only six major competitors existed for Canadian Tire in the Texas and Sunbelt markets: Sears Roebuck, Montgomery Ward, K mart, Builder's Square, Home Depo, and Handy Dan. The first three competitors did,

---

Exhibit 3: Sample Demographics for Texas

1. Texas was the second-largest state in retail sales.
2. Houston was eighth and Dallas was ninth in terms of ranking the size of metropolitan statistical areas.
3. Dallas was expected to increase by 12.9 percent in population from 1980 to 1984; Houston, by 14.2 percent; the U.S. average was only 5.2 percent.
4. Mean income (1977):

Dallas	$19,443
Houston	18,340
New York	16,714
U.S. average	17,137

however, carry a lot of clout within the market. For example, Sears was heavily involved in auto parts and services, and it was not unusual for Sears to have 16 or more auto bays as opposed to 5–6 at White's. Wal-Mart, a potential entrant to this market and a major U.S. retailing force, had chosen at this point in time to forego expansion into the major metropolitan areas in the state of Texas.

On a television documentary, one prominent retail market analyst in Houston described the market characteristics of the United States and, in particular, the Sunbelt states, as follows:

1. In any U.S. market, three markets were at work: a national one, a regional one, and one based on local climate.

2. Retailing in the United States, and more so in the Sunbelt, was highly competitive and highly dynamic (that is, the rate of change was far greater in the United States than in Canada).

3. The Sunbelt market was witnessing an ever-increasing number of retail entrants who were scrambling to get into very specific market niches.

4. Corporate image and advertising had to be slanted to two very different groups: the English- and the Spanish-speaking populations.

5. Promotional campaigns should take into account a high degree of illiteracy and a variety of racial problems (for example, white versus black, white versus Mexican, Mexican versus black).

6. The impact of revenues flowing from oil after 1973 had created a "gold rush" in the area where even poorly run businesses could make money and new people were arriving everyday (making the overall population's average age 26).

7. Every neighbourhood in this area varied due to its ethnic composition.

8. Shopping malls predominated since most consumers preferred one-stop shopping.

9. Sunbelt consumers were sophisticated, however, and would visit a variety of shops (usually specialty stores) within one mall to accomplish their shopping needs.

10. Compared to Canada, stores in the United States tended to be far larger, especially department stores, where 25,000 square feet would be considered a small area.

11. The U.S. consumer enjoyed a wide option of shopping choices (for example, it would have been typical to see 40 brands of an automotive product available on one shelf).

12. Older downtown areas were considered marginal and these "strip centres" tended to cater to neighbourhood traffic.

13. Hardware and sporting goods stores in Texas were a rarity as every major store sold this kind of merchandise.

14. Some observers considered the Houston area as the toughest market in the United States.

15. Consumers needed to identify with a firm's message (that is, a reason for its existence) in order for it to survive and prosper.

White Stores, Inc.

The White Stores were held by Household International Ltd. of Chicago, which was one of the largest retailers in the United States. At approximately $150 million (U.S.) in annual sales, White's represented only 4 percent of Household's revenues. It was an insignificant holding to this large firm and thus received very little attention from its owners.

Although White's was losing money, CTC felt that if the price was low enough, it could refurbish the units and have them take on a CTC philosophy and market appeal. It was felt that a time frame of two to three years would be necessary before White's could break even and start to contribute to corporate profits. It was felt that the added top management attention and CTC's successful Canadian strategy could turn this firm around and represent a springboard for further U.S. expansion.

With White's, CTC would be acquiring 81 retail outlets, access to supply 425 independent dealer-owned stores, and 4 warehouses. The chain of stores covered Texas (the majority), Louisiana, New Mexico, and Oklahoma as well as 10 other states. Approximately half of the White-owned outlets were on leased properties, while all of the real estate (that is, land and buildings) of the other half were owned by White Stores. The price tag of a maximum of $45 million (U.S.) seemed reasonable to CTC executives when compared to recent costs of $2.5 million per store to establish new outlets in British Columbia. Exhibit 4 shows a proposed financing scheme for the acquisition.

CTC saw other positive factors in the purchase option. The White Stores name was long established, and therefore CTC assumed the name would be a source of loyalty and brand recognition. White's had a store size (approximately 25,000 square feet), which was similar to that of the typical CTC store. As well, like CTC, White's had only a few brands for their products. In general, White Stores did many of the same things that CTC did: automotive service and parts sales; and other broad product lines were available which were similar to CTC except that White's carried furniture as well. This probably would be dropped if the purchase was made. Plenty of warehouse capacity existed. It was estimated that the four warehouses could conduct two to three times their existing volumes without any further capital. The current warehouse utilization rate varied between 30 and 50 percent. The infrastructure for expansion, therefore, was in place.

There were some concerns with an acquisition of White Stores. The locations of many of the stores were not in prime commercial or retail areas but, rather, in local neighbourhoods. In some of these neighbourhoods, the people were Mexican and could not read or understand English. CTC proposed to gradually relocate

Exhibit 4: Purchase of White Stores—Financing (Canadian dollars in thousands)

Net working capital to be acquired . . .		$12,134
Property and equipment,		
including capitalized leases		
and leasehold interests	$35,658	
Long-term portion of capital		
lease obligations	(287)	35,371
Other assets		208
Net assets to be acquired		$47,713
The effect on consolidated working capital is:		
Use of working capital:		
Payment on closing		$15,904
Promissory note due		
December 31, 1982		10,603
		26,507
Working capital to be acquired		(12,134)
Net use of working capital		$14,373

these by establishing a greater concentration of stores in prime retail space in the lucrative Dallas-Fort Worth market. Further, the 81 stores owned by White Stores were not dealer operated but company owned and operated. CTC felt that this would have to change and become a number one priority in terms of introducing its philosophy and corporate objectives. Although CTC would prefer a dealer network to replicate the strategy in Canada, some of the states containing White Stores locations prohibited exclusive distributor-dealer relationships because of antitrust legislation. Finally, most of the stores were in desperate need of refurbishing. A lot of the outlets were 20 to 30 years old and looked it. CTC did not feel that this would be a problem as it had anticipated having to pour up to an additional $100 million (U.S.) over the following 2½ years into the project.

Other Options

Other growth options had been tossed around CTC's corporate office in Toronto. One option being considered was to access the U.S. market by building a new chain from the ground up and, therefore, not be confined by an existing organization's limitations and problems. However, costs and the time commitment to establish a major foothold made this a difficult option to pursue. Another option was to search out an acquisition in the nearby northeastern U.S. states. One CTC executive who favoured this option noted: "We should expand to a market that is similar to our own—with the same climate, the same autos, and the same kind of products. A place that is close enough, that if there is a problem we can do something about it." But this meant ignoring the fastest-growing segment of the United States, namely, the Sunbelt. A third option involved oil and gas opportunities in Canada. The existing Liberal government in Ottawa heavily favoured Canadian involvement in this industrial sector. The difficulty here was a lack of expertise on the part of CTC's management in this field. A fourth option was vertical integration. The manufacture of CTC products would require a massive capital investment into a field where CTC again had little expertise, and production runs for only CTC dealers would not always prove economical. Furthermore, due to CTC's large size, it already controlled a fair amount of power in distribution channels and could, therefore, already influence prices to some extent. Finally, CTC could turn to real estate sales. The firm had already engaged in some of this type of business and had made a small amount of money at it. Interest rates, however, were unsettlingly high and unstable. Furthermore, the risk involved in a massive venture of this nature might not have been acceptable to CTC shareholders.

Muncaster had a difficult decision ahead of him. Growth in Canada for CTC would peak in approximately three to four years, so the groundwork for a new growth spurt would have to be laid down shortly. Shareholders would not react favourably to a flattening out of earnings per share after 1985. The White Stores acquisition would involve a major refurbishing program to bring the White Stores up to par, and this would create a temporary short-term drain on CTC's earnings. Nevertheless, it was felt that the highly successful Canadian Tire formula could be applied to White Stores in the United States and yield the same kind of performance as that experienced in Canada.

The Turnaround Strategy

As the president and executive vice president of CTC more closely examined White Stores, they agreed on the following turnaround strategy if they were to acquire White's:

- There would be an aggressive renovation schedule at a cost of $100 million (U.S.) to be completed by the end of 1983. Up to 22 stores would be closed at any one time for up to two months for the renovation.
- CTC dealers would be brought in to run some of the stores with a goal of 81 dealer-run stores by the end of 1983.
- The merchandise mix (currently at 23,000 items) would be phased in gradually. (See Exhibit 5 for existing mix and other information on the typical store.)
- More money would be spent on advertising than spent by the average U.S. retailer in order to develop a clear image. The predominant form of advertising would be flyers.
- The White Stores name would be retained to take advantage of existing customer loyalty.
- In order to gain market share and increase store traffic, White's would use loss leaders.

Exhibit 5:   Typical White's Store/White's Auto Centre

Typical store size in square feet (excluding auto bays):	
Gross area	24,000 sq. ft.
Selling area	14,000
Percent selling area to gross area	58%
Number of auto service bays	5–6
Store focus and sales mix:	
Auto	10–50%
Hardware	15–20
Lawn and garden	15
Sporting goods	15
Housewares	10
Electronics, miscellaneous	5
Promotion mix of sales*	50
Typical inventory (at cost)	U.S. $900,000
Number of products carried	22,000
Final retail gross margin	16–22%
Store sales per year (breakeven point)	U.S. $2.5 million

* Percentage of products under promotion discounts.

- In order to help dealers finance their inventories, credit would be given quite freely, although at the prevailing interest rates. If a dealer could not afford a shipment of goods, the price to the dealer would be lowered and the difference added to the notes payable to White's.
- No additional capital would be required to upgrade warehousing facilities since the four warehouses were remaining at 30–35 percent capacity.
- The independent dealer network would be reduced from the existing 425 to 300 stores by cutting off the outlying dealers.

Muncaster summarized the strategy; "We plan to change their [White's] merchandise offering substantially. . . . We believe the appeal will be in a merchandise offering which you see in a Canadian Tire Store." With this strategy, CTC expected White's to break even by the third year.

Case 12

Clear-Vue Plastic Packaging Ltd.

I want to use Clear-Vue as the money-making machine which fuels the product development, initial production, and marketing of all the tremendously exciting products we now have in the pipeline, such as our super magnets, nuclear-radiated garlic, and solar heaters.

Thus enthused Mr. Kenneth Arrow in the late summer of 1976. Arrow, president of Clear-Vue Plastic Packaging Ltd., a Vancouver custom blister and skin packaging firm, was examining several expansion options in order to maintain the current growth rate in sales and to improve the financial condition of the company. Arrow was an engineer who had managed two high-technology, research-oriented companies and had carried out a variety of engineering consulting projects before founding his plastic packaging firm in 1962. Although he possessed a broad array of technology skills and had attended a highly regarded, three-month advanced management program, he was uncertain which of his many ideas for expansion would succeed best.

Arrow faced all the problems of an entrepreneur with only 20 employees who must soon make the quantum leap to a formal organization with functional managers. At the same time, the choice of product line constantly badgered him in his day-to-day operations. The difficulty of this choice was accentuated by his personal preference for developing proprietary, high-technology products with their excitement and promise of high rewards although he knew well enough the significant development costs and risks of failure which were coupled with these potential benefits. Pending resolution of these product uncertainties, the specific production capabilities, which should be outstandingly competitive, remained undetermined. Also, although Arrow believed a hungry market existed for most of the products he was considering, he wondered whether more formal market information might not be helpful. While trying to make these strategic decisions, his attention was constantly diverted to the hour-by-hour operational demands of the company and to meetings of numerous professional and civic associations in which he was involved. But because of cash constraints which hampered current operations and an expiring lease which forced Clear-Vue to move in a few months, he knew that a decision was urgently needed.

This case was prepared by Ross Henderson and Richard Knudson, University of Manitoba. Copyright © 1977 by the Department of Business Administration, The University of Manitoba.

In an effort to get to the heart of the situation and formulate an explicit corporate strategy, Arrow assembled the following information.

The Industry

Custom blister and skin plastic packaging was a new, small, and ill-defined industry. Consumer goods were delivered to the packager's plant by the whole-saler or retailer who retained title to the goods. Using an extensive amount of hand labour, the individual items were mounted on preprinted cards behind a transparent, semi-rigid plastic blister or a clinging, flexible plastic skin. The packaged items, much bulkier after packaging, were then returned to the owner for distribution. A hole in the cardboard permitted displaying the item on a peg board, the printed cardboard provided brand name, instructions, and colour, while the clear plastic permitted visual inspection of the goods without damage or pilferage. The cost of this packaging was found justified in facilitating retail sales during the late 1950s, and by 1976 it was common to see many mass-produced items displayed for sale in this manner. Manufacturers often packaged their own goods this way at the factory. But because of the added bulk, the operation was frequently done for wholesalers and retailers by custom packagers near their central warehouse. Accordingly, a number of small firms had been established to serve this market in the 1960s and 1970s.

Locally, Clear-Vue was the oldest and largest company in this business. However, three competitors shared the local market, which was estimated at $750,000 annually in 1976. In Canada, 125 firms were listed as engaged in blister and skin packaging. Several of these had volumes substantially over $1 million per year, but it was believed that much of their volume came from other products and services. However, the total market for custom blister and skin packaging in Canada was estimated at $10 million to $15 million annually in 1976. Additionally, many long-run items were packaged "in-house" by manufacturers. This captive production possibly equalled the custom market. Most of the competitors for the custom market also offered other products or services for sale along with their custom packaging service. Typical of these additional products were vacuum formed (or thermo-formed) plastic products made from sheet. These used the same process which produced the blisters.

No formal estimate of past growth trend or forecast of future sales was available, but expenditures on such packaging were generally believed to be increasing. The small firms were all struggling to survive at present with the expectation that sales growth would make them profitable and financially stable.

Company History

Clear-Vue Plastic Packaging Ltd. was founded in 1962 by Arrow and another engineer, Jock Campbell, to provide a skin packaging service to local retailers using a new machine which had been discarded by a large consumer goods manufacturer as inoperable. Ingenuity of the two partners succeeded in getting the machine to operate satisfactorily, and, subsequently, Campbell went on to establish his own metal fabricating business. Arrow possessed an outstanding flair for innovation, an engaging, easy selling manner, and exceptional ability to solve three or four operating problems at a time with unruffled equanimity. He had used these abilities to bring Clear-Vue through many a crisis due to lack of equity, adding customers, equipment, and products at each opportunity. Gradually, with persistent sales effort, he gained as customers two dozen distributors and retailers who had local head offices or central warehouses. Equipment was usually bought nearly new, at distress prices, after being rejected as inoperable by the original owner. Added products usually possessed high-technology characteristics, which delighted Arrow's sense of innovation. Arrow successfully developed a wide range of products: plastic food trays, plastic greenhouses which could grow tomatoes without sunlight, nuclear-radiated foods, high-intensity magnets, and a

Exhibit 1

CLEAR-VUE PLASTIC PACKAGING LTD.
Profit and Loss Statement
Years Ending December 31st

	1971	1972	1973	1974	1975
Sales:					
Net sales	$58,411	$121,281	$149,331	$180,161	$189,830
Cost of sales:					
Inventory, January 1	2,000	7,500	10,000	19,219	40,159
Materials and subcontracts	18,359	45,540	51,505	104,225	59,233
Wages	24,563	30,224	53,020	43,707	56,536
Total cost of sales	44,922	83,264	114,525	167,151	155,928
Less: Inventory, December 31	7,500	10,000	19,219	40,159	25,644
Material and wages for capital cost	2,000	—	—	—	—
Net cost of sales	35,422	73,264	95,306	126,992	130,284
Gross margin	22,989	48,017	54,025	53,169	59,546
Expenses:					
Bank charges and interest	2,321	2,624	2,914	4,027	3,152
Depreciation	2,826	1,900	2,175	—	3,123
Salaries	8,000	11,500	13,378	—	12,000
Heat and utilities	893	388	—	—	6,724
Rent	2,330	6,379	14,256	11,838	11,238
Maintenance and supervision (allocated from associated company)	—	9,800	10,700	14,700	11,802
Other expenses	6,305	3,493	9,185	10,814	12,675
Total operating expense	22,675	38,708	52,608	41,379	60,714
Net before tax	314	9,309	1,417	11,790	(1,168)
Income tax	—	2,292	384	885	(390)
Net after tax	$ 314	$ 7,017	$ 1,033	$ 10,905	$ (778)

device for sewing human veins automatically. Sales slowly climbed to the quarter million dollar level by 1976. (See Exhibits 1 and 2 for financial information.) Profits, however, were elusive. The lack of profits seemed due partly to the broad product line and partly to product development costs. But Arrow was convinced that exceptional opportunities existed for exploitation of his new products if more of his time could be freed from day-to-day operations and if cash from profits or new equity were to be made available. He felt that he must move from the present one-man management situation to a structure where responsibility for important

Exhibit 2

CLEAR-VUE PLASTIC PACKAGING LTD.
Balance Sheet
At December 31st

	1971	1972	1973	1974	1975
Assets					
Current assets:					
Accounts receivable	$ 5,818.34	$14,454	$13,299	$ 18,671	$12,456
Inventory (estimated)	7,500.00	10,000	19,219	40,159	25,644
Due from associated company	8,018.14	8,687	7,905	5,401	3,346
Due from director	976.57	10,385	13,067	13,693	
Income taxes recoverable	—	—	158	—	869
Total current assets	22,313.05	43,506	53,648	77,924	42,315
Machinery and equipment	23,101.44	34,265	37,697	47,626	49,326
Less: Depreciation	11,793.68	9,543	11,718	11,718	14,841
Net equipment	11,307.76	24,722	25,979	35,908	34,485
Incorporation costs	32.00	32	32	32	32
Leasehold improvement—net	—	4,212	3,744	5,157	4,642
Total assets	$33,652.81	$72,472	$83,403	$119,021	$81,474
Liabilities and Equity					
Current liabilities:					
Bank indebtedness	$13,713.73	$17,597	$17,357	$ 8,164	$13,097
Accounts payable	11,612.71	32,955	43,099	62,646	44,118
Income and other taxes	—	3,436	4,367	5,559	4,693
Current part of long-term debt	—	2,400	2,400	2,200	—
Payable to shareholder	—	—	—	—	463
Total current liabilities	25,326.44	56,388	67,223	78,569	62,371
Long-term debt, equipment liens	8,364.71	4,415	2,936	1,303	—
Deferred income tax	—	1,494	2,036	2,036	3,789
Total liabilities	33,691.15	62,297	72,195	81,908	66,160
Capital stock—3 shares issued	3.00	3	3	15,003	15,003
Retained earnings (deficit)	38.34	10,172	11,205	22,110	311
Total liabilities and equity	$33,652.81	$72,472	$83,403	$119,021	$81,474

functions such as production, control, and marketing was delegated to individual managers reporting to him. At the same time, he wanted to secure adequate profits from existing operations to fund a rapid expansion. He examined the existing operations to see how this might be accomplished.

Product Line

During the first nine months of 1976, sales revenue of $137,356 could be divided among 10 categories as shown in Exhibit 3. A regular retail, seasonal surge in volume was expected to boost sales to $250,000 by December 31st. Most of this revenue came from blister packaging, vacuum forming, skin packaging, plus the preprinted cards and die work for these categories. Blisters were typically formed from rolls of clear, polyvinyl chloride plastic sheet; vacuum formed products were produced from a clear or opaque white, high-impact polystyrene; while skin packaging utilized clear, polyethylene film. A total of 351 jobs was completed to the end of September 1976. Price lists detailed 78 different packages and products, but this number was greatly increased by a common price for packaging a wide variety of hardware items. Probably 150 different packages and products had been produced. Each package or product had specifications which Arrow obtained by telephone, mail, or personal visit, a task which took from one hour to one day of his time for each specification. Quantities on a job ranged from 16 to 95,000 cards, but the average was 3,000, and the median quantity, about 1,400. A setup of varying difficulty and cost was required at least once at each stage in the process for each job. A request for prompt delivery of part of an order sometimes required extra setups. Proprietary product items were included in this volume, although so far their dollar volume was small except for an injection moulded electric wiring clip. This product was wholly specified by Clear-Vue, based on a patent. In contrast, customer packaging specifications were determined entirely by the customer.

Usually, Arrow completed negotiations for a job several days or weeks before the arrival of the goods to be packaged. Cards were printed on Clear-Vue stock by a commercial printer, and these cards, the goods, plus any special plastic arrived in the plant at separate times. Subsequently, the goods were packaged and shipped; sometimes in a few days but more commonly in two to three weeks and, more frequently than desired, not for two or three months. Almost every job required special instructions, material, or process, and these Arrow handled calmly, usually carrying on two or three conversations or calculations at any one time during his business day.

Manufacturing

Equipment and Layout

Packaging and production operations were currently carried on in 16,000 square feet of rented basement in an old, but solid, industrial building. Clear-Vue would

Exhibit 3: Sales Analysis by Process

Process	January Qty.	January $	February Qty.	February $	March Qty.	March $	April Qty.	April $	May Qty.	May $	June Qty.	June $	July Qty.	July $	August Qty.	August $	September Qty.	September $	Total Qty.	Total $
Blister packaging or blister manufacturing	71,946	$5,113	52,286	$3,832	90,735	$5,500	52,169	$3,230	28,575	$2,850	86,259	$6,227	53,697	$5,337	20,387	$1,193	26,546	$2,286	482,600	$35,568
Skin packaging	20,629	1,416	10,550	728	10,704	738	15,644	1,074	13,487	949	18,179	1,410	10,024	734	8,041	567	15,114	1,547	122,372	9,163
Vacuum forming	6,062	561	7,348	6,284	12,810	5,098	150	525	11,214	1,524	4,000	229	4,200	241	43,280	6,442	26,700	4,001	119,964	24,905
Manufacturing hollow-core plugs	1,230	369	6,142	1,843									4,170	1,251	2,629	789				4,252
Shrink wrapping					1,218	319									800	160				479
Injection moulding									26,343	2,507			51,000	944			258,624	12,572	335,967	16,023
Attach aluminum foil to pharmacy cards	2,473	346	6,693	937	8,132	1,139	4,900	686	7,800	1,092	5,150	595	15,400	1,294	31,000	260	2,100	176		6,525
Folding plastic, laminating, and packaging in plastic bags	2,440	403	4,370	734	4,200	693			600	63					28	21	140	91		2,005
Labour and material charge on various jobs		864		263		1,268		976		288		64		263		2,586		76		6,648
Prepayment on dies, backing cards		527		1,575		2,000				6,710		4,950		1,445		2,467		1,200		20,874
Packaging revenue		9,599		16,196		16,755		6,491		15,983		13,475		11,509		14,485		21,949		126,443
Other revenue		550		98		1,113		2,359		562		243		5,515		345		129		10,914
Total		$10,149		$16,294		$17,868		$8,850		$16,545		$13,718		$17,024		$14,830		$22,078		$137,356

have to move from this location in February 1977, and Arrow was looking for a suitable plant and considering how to lay it out. The existing layout is shown in Exhibit 4A. The extensive variety of equipment is detailed in Exhibit 4B with the location of each indicated in Exhibit 4A. The western portion of the plant was occupied by an inventory of raw materials, finished packaged goods, and finished

Exhibit 4A

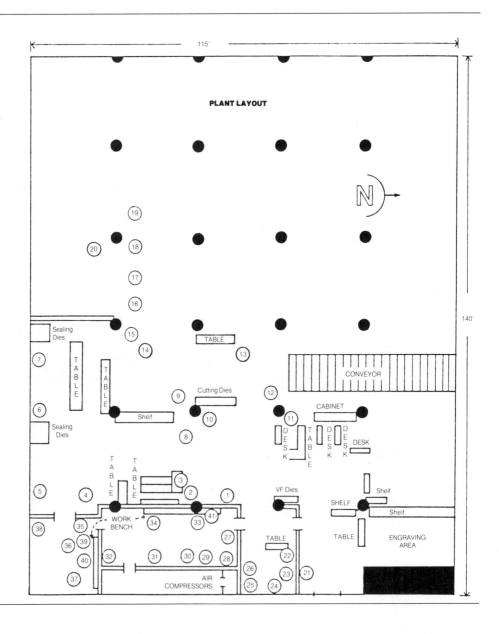

Exhibit 4B: Plant Layout Machine Index

Machine
Number

1	Vacuum forming machine
2	Skin packaging machine
3	Hand shear (32″) blade
4	Foot shear (37″) blade
5	Semi-automatic vacuum forming machine ("The Automatic")
6	Blister sealer
7	Blister sealer
8	Box stapler
9	Power shear (43″) blade
10	Blister cutter
11	Catalog wrapper
12	Hand jack
13	Foot shear (28″) blade
14	Plastic folding machine
15	Automatic blister packaging machine
16	Blister cutter (Press-O-Matic)
17	Plastic shrinker
18	Heat sealer—(Weldotron)—pharmacy cards foil
19	Electronic palstic engraver
20	Plastic chopper
21	Adhesive card coater
22	Time clock
23	Small metal lathe
24	Knife-making machine
25	Injection moulding machine
26	Extruder
27	Arc welder
28	Big drill press (18″)
29	Small drill press (10″)
30	Milling machine
31	Big metal lathe
32	Turret lathe
33	Power hacksaw
34	Acetylene torch
35	Band saw (1′ throat)
36	Table saw
37	Table sander
38	Jig saw (2′ throat)
39	Bench grinder—wire wheel
40	Abrasive belt grinder
41	Bench grinder—grinding wheel

injection moulded parts made on speculation. Possibly 300 different items were included in total. All the various kinds of inventory were heaped in helter-skelter fashion, mostly without access aisles, much of it covered with dust and difficult to see because light was very dim. Arrow's desk was in the unpartitioned production area, and the general impression for a newcomer was one of busy, cheerful chaos.

Work Force

Usually 10 to 20 employees were moving material, packaging goods, making tools, or hunting for something mislaid. Exhibit 5 outlines some characteristics of 10 of the more regular employees. Additionally, Arrow had 10 or more other people come in to work in the evenings or on Saturdays. Hours for these were flexible. On one occasion, he had temporarily boosted the work force to 100 for a rush job. Most of these people were paid at or just above the minimum wage of $2.95 per hour except Jack, the toolmaker and equipment-repair man, who was paid significantly more.

Marg and Jane commonly worked on the vacuum forming and skin packaging machines, respectively. Intense, speedy workers, they were exceedingly loyal to Arrow and took responsibility as lead hands to select work, instruct, and set the pace. In one financial crisis, Jane had offered to get a second mortgage on her house to help Arrow and keep the firm afloat. Marg talked often of her married children but never let it slow her work, or that of others on whom she kept an eye. She would run to the phone when necessary and conduct some business for the firm, trying not to miss the rhythm of her work while she did so.

Marji, Rachel, Nancy, and Chris formed the nucleus of a bevy of smiling women who had recently immigrated to Canada from the Philippines. They worked with great alacrity at blister sealing, helping with skin packaging, handling goods, and doing the other manual tasks at which they were exceedingly dextrous. Jack repaired and adjusted machines, made tools and dies, and helped the women when he could. Asked by Anita, one of the Filipinos, what colour she should paint her high-powered new car, he had replied, "Yellow, because you say it's a lemon." A week later, Anita, with a huge grin, invited him for a spin in her yellow car. All had a good time joking back and forth about such matters. An assortment of part-time male helpers assisted Jack in his work. Instructions were given by Mr. Arrow, Mrs. Arrow (who was secretary, accountant, and clerk), Jack, Marg, Jane, or Marji.

Generally everyone had an idea what should be done and worked cheerfully and industriously. Coffee breaks in the morning and afternoon were social events which Arrow joined when he could, with pleasant chatter and, often, a common bowl of food supplied by one of the women being enjoyed around a big table. Informality, trust, and goodwill were evident. Arrow was invariably smiling, unfailingly courteous, and exceedingly tolerant in allowing workers to achieve speed in their work in the way they thought best. The Filipino women were always

Exhibit 5:   Employee Description

Jack   53 years old
        9 years with company
        Grade 4 education
        Pay: $5.00/hour

— Considered to be a foreman but does not actually manage anyone.
— Seems to be a "jack-of-all-trades."
— Usually works wherever he is needed.
— Typical jobs include:
     Machinery dies.   Fixing machines.
     Setting up machines.   Unloading trucks.
     Changing rolls of plastic.
— First one in the plant in the morning.
— A sheet that lists the production orders and jobs in process was seen on Jack's desk; however, there seemed to be no indication of the work following this schedule.
— He is a "kidder;" likes to joke around with the other staff.

Marg   43 years old
        7 years with company
        Grade 9 education
        Pay: $3.00/hour
        Married

— Very talkative: "It's difficult to stop her."
— Enjoys working with machines—used to work in a box factory.
— She feels that it takes a certain kind of person to be able to do her type of work.
— She mentioned that university students could never do her kind of work—she felt that they were incapable.
— Loves to talk about her grown daughter.
— She feels that the pressure is on her and Jane to get the work out.
— She is a steady worker.

Jane   65 years old
        6 years with company
        Grade 10 education
        Pay: $3.00/hour

— Seems to be almost hyperactive when it comes to work.
— She works like a machine—very fast.
— Always the first employee to start work after a break or lunch.
— Considering retirement.
— Seems to work well with the Filipinos—there is usually one there to help her with the skin packaging (Chris).

Pam   21 years old
        4 months with company
        Grade 9 education
        Pay: $2.95/hour
        Married

— Married young—three children.
— Takes off a lot of time (kids sick, and so forth).
— Works on the "automatic" or helps Jane.
— Worked as an assembly line worker before this job.
— Sells do-it-yourself painting kits during her spare time.

Marji   26 years old
        3 years with company
        High school education
          (in the Philippines)
        Pay: $2.95/hour

— Short, dark complexion, black hair.
— Supervises the other Filipino women.
— Usually looks after the evening work.
— Seems quite versatile—works everywhere.
— Loads and unloads stock.
— Other Filipinos seem to come to her when they have difficulties.
— Smiles often.

Rachel   33 years old
        3 years with company
        High school education
          (in the Philippines)
        Pay: $2.95/hour

— Quiet.
— Works on the blister sealer.

Nancy   20 years old
        2 years with company
        High school education
          (in the Philippines)
        Pay: $2.95/hour

— Happy, likes to talk.
— Works on the blister sealers.
— Cousin to Marji.

Chris   20 years old
        5 months with company
        High school education
          (in the Philippines)

— Tall, quite attractive, big smile.
— Moves to wherever they need help.
— Usually works with Jane.

smiling broadly, and most of the workers indicated that they enjoyed working for Clear-Vue, in spite of the tedious routines and often tense efforts to make deliveries. No formal time standards or incentive wages were used. New tasks were described by word of mouth. Job methods were not recorded. But the democratic, informal manner of conducting business along with the naturally happy outlook of many of the employees seemed to have established an esprit de corps that caused everyone to work their best. Still, the processes with many steps and the great variety of packaging jobs frequently caused hesitation, uncertainty, and a significant waste of time due to stopping, inquiring for information or materials, and starting again.

Processes

Three manufacturing processes accounted for the majority of the sales: (1) vacuum forming and blister packaging, (2) skin packaging, and (3) injection moulding. The first two processes are detailed in Exhibits 6 and 7, and both show a long sequence of operations. Injection moulding was carried out on one fully automatic machine which produced two pieces at a time, or about 700 pieces an hour, once very close tolerance dies were installed and the hopper was filled with ground-up, scrap polyethylene. Most of the 258,000 pieces made on this machine in 1976 were a patented electric wiring clip for which substantial orders were on hand. If the machine was operating at all, this process was unattended and under control. The other two processes required many variations from job to job.

Vacuum formed blisters and products might or might not use the full die-making process. Card printing might be done or not depending upon stock on hand. A new card might require several consultations on artwork and printing. New dies might have to be altered after trial, or the plastic specifications occasionally might be changed because it did not form correctly. Skin packaging required few variations, but the arrangement of merchandise on the card was different for each order. The women usually took a number of cards to discover how to place screws, pieces of wire, or other awkward-shaped merchandise prior to establishing a good method and rhythm for a skin packaging job. It was always tricky to balance a large panel of multiple cards, each with its merchandise in place, while sliding it into the skin packaging machine. If the goods slipped, the panel had to be put down until they were rearranged. The high manual-labour content of the processes gave them a high variability from job to job. The machine-controlled processes of making blisters and heat sealing or skin sealing the plastic represented a much smaller portion of the processes. Even these portions varied, but to a lesser degree.

This variability caused Arrow difficulty in estimating and controlling costs, delivery, and sometimes quality of the job. He did much of his cost estimating and pricing based on material costs, using a rule of thumb that price should be three to five times the material cost. He also used a standard processing cost per thousand at times, and occasionally did a quick stopwatch study to check labour input. Often these calculations did not take into account differences in material

Exhibit 6:   Blister Packaging and Vacuum Forming Processes

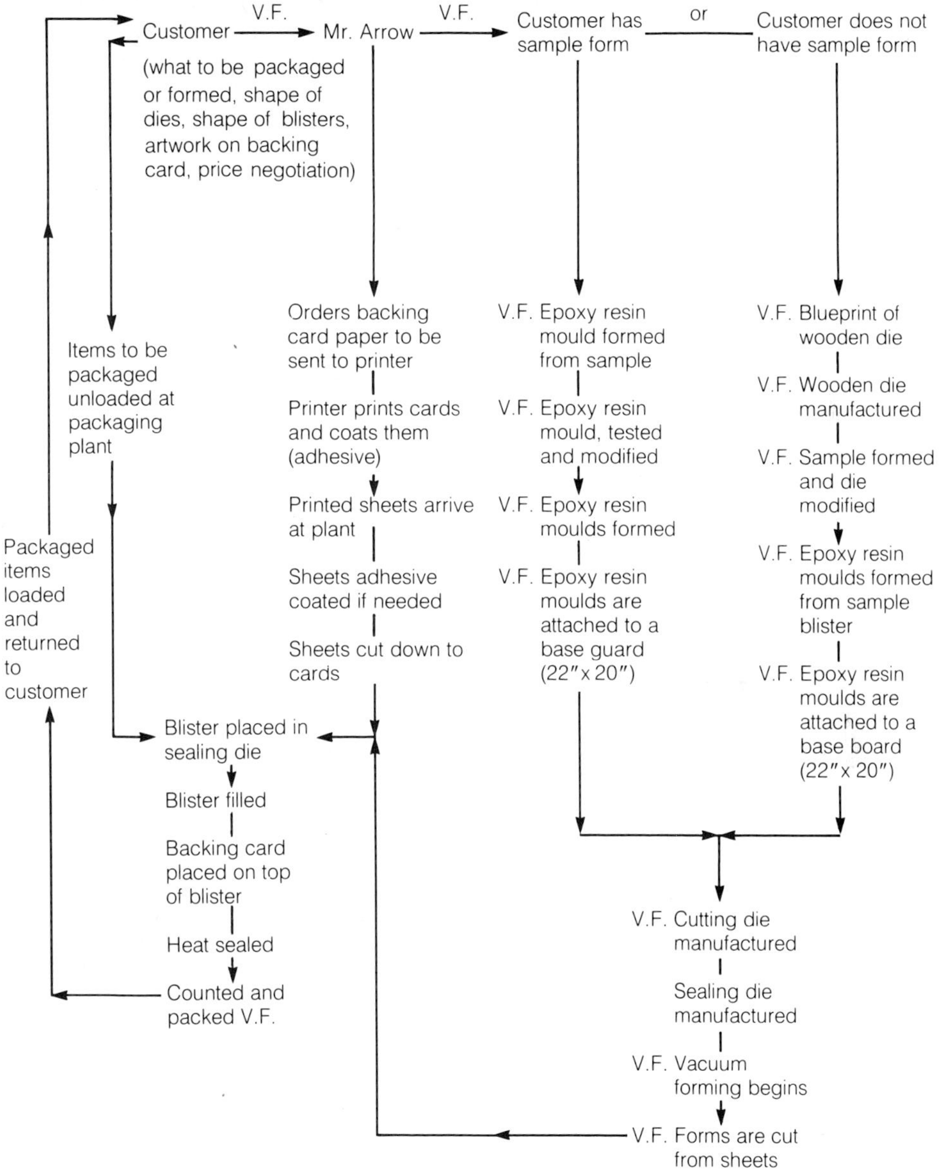

Customer —V.F.→ Mr. Arrow —V.F.→ Customer has sample form   or   Customer does not have sample form

(what to be packaged or formed, shape of dies, shape of blisters, artwork on backing card, price negotiation)

Items to be packaged unloaded at packaging plant

Orders backing card paper to be sent to printer

Printer prints cards and coats them (adhesive)

Printed sheets arrive at plant

Sheets adhesive coated if needed

Sheets cut down to cards

Packaged items loaded and returned to customer

V.F. Epoxy resin mould formed from sample

V.F. Epoxy resin mould, tested and modified

V.F. Epoxy resin moulds formed

V.F. Epoxy resin moulds are attached to a base guard (22" x 20")

V.F. Blueprint of wooden die

V.F. Wooden die manufactured

V.F. Sample formed and die modified

V.F. Epoxy resin moulds formed from sample blister

V.F. Epoxy resin moulds are attached to a base board (22" x 20")

Blister placed in sealing die

Blister filled

Backing card placed on top of blister

Heat sealed

Counted and packed V.F.

V.F. Cutting die manufactured

Sealing die manufactured

V.F. Vacuum forming begins

V.F. Forms are cut from sheets

V.F. — Representing the vacuum forming process which has fewer steps than the process for blister packaging.

Exhibit 7: Skin Packaging Process

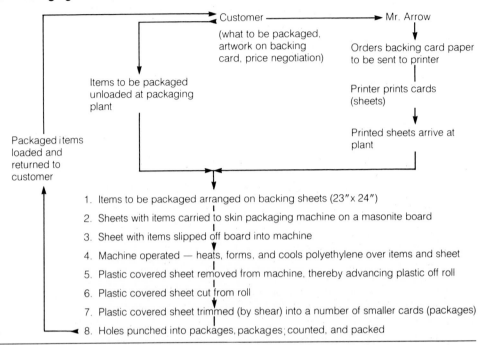

1. Items to be packaged arranged on backing sheets (23" x 24")
2. Sheets with items carried to skin packaging machine on a masonite board
3. Sheet with items slipped off board into machine
4. Machine operated — heats, forms, and cools polyethylene over items and sheet
5. Plastic covered sheet removed from machine, thereby advancing plastic off roll
6. Plastic covered sheet cut from roll
7. Plastic covered sheet trimmed (by shear) into a number of smaller cards (packages)
8. Holes punched into packages, packages counted, and packed

handling or other manual labour tasks. However, no actual job costs were collected, and so he was not certain what cost differences might exist from job to job in the same process.

Cost Analyses

In an attempt to understand how costs varied from job to job, Arrow arranged for a recent graduate in business administration to observe activities in the plant and prepare cost analyses for several jobs, going through each process. These analyses are shown in Exhibits 8 and 9. Additionally, some raw material costs were assembled as shown in Exhibit 10. He was anxious to examine these costs more closely because the analyst had told him that a number of items seemed to exhibit much less than the 33 percent gross margin, as a percent of selling price, which he desired. Some jobs showed apparent losses. In any case, it seemed certain that margins varied considerably from job to job. He thought that this might be part of the reason for the lack of profits.

Organization and Control

Arrow was not certain whether Clear-Vue had made a profit, loss, or broke even in the nine months to date in 1976, because a profit-and-loss statement and

Exhibit 8: Cost Analysis I

	Skin Packaging			
Product	Microphones (M)	Glue—tubes	Hinges (M)	Solder sample cards
Machine	Skin package (per sheet)	Skin package (per sheet)	Skin package (per sheet)	Skin package (per sheet)
Backing sheet size*	23″ × 24″	23″ × 23.75″	22.75″ × 23″	23″ × 23.5″
Number of cards/ sheet	15	15	24	12
Printing cost/sheet*	.185¢	.165¢	.178¢	.018¢
Type of plastic	Poly	Poly	Poly	Poly
Amount of plastic/ backing sheet	25″–26″	25″–26″	25″–26″	25″–26″
Align items on sheet and carry sheet to machine	8 minutes	6 minutes	13–30 minutes	1.57 minutes
Heat, form, cool, remove	1.15 minutes	1.15 minutes	1.15 minutes	1.15 minutes
Trim sheets into cards	2.7 minutes	1.5 minutes	2.5 minutes	1.0 minute
Punch holes	1.7 minutes	1.7 minutes	1.7 minutes	
Selling price	$72.00/1,000 cards	$75.00/1,000 cards	$68.00/1,000 cards	$175.00/1,000 cards

* Backing sheets invoiced separately at double the cost of printing.

accompanying balance sheet were prepared by the auditors only once a year, usually in February. Monthly he obtained a list of accounts receivable which he followed closely, often phoning customers to expedite payment or to ascertain whether a cheque was in the mail. Cash was always in short supply and was often urgently needed for the payroll, to satisfy the bank or trade creditors, or for sales and payroll taxes. A statement of accounts payable was also prepared each month to assist Arrow in explaining to suppliers and in buying where credit accommodation might still be available. No job costs were compiled, nor were any process or work-center costs recorded. Likewise, no inventory control records were kept, nor was there any formal production control or scheduling procedure. Arrow kept an impressive array of facts and figures in his mind which he could quote rapidly and accurately, but usually he was too busy to assemble them into some useful order through which they could be better examined. He hoped that the job cost analysis would be a start to such cost examination and improved control. To date, control had been handled with his excellent memory and on-the-spot supervision.

The existing control system would have to change if responsibility was delegated to functional managers. Currently, Arrow gave nearly all the direct orders himself, although in his absence, Jack, Mrs. Arrow, Marg, Jane or Marji would give such orders as seemed suitable. He was anxious to hire a production

Exhibit 9: Cost Analysis II

	Blister Packs			Vacuum Forming				
Customer	Clear-Vue	Swedka	Swedka	World Airways	World Airways	National Hotels Ltd.	Mister Donut	Druggist Services
Product	#100 wiring clip blisters	FNF-6 knives	DP-306 knives	Dinner tray tops/ 9" × 12"	Dinner tray bottoms/ 9" × 12"	Square dishes 3-1/2" × 3-1/2"	Donut trays 8" × 9"	Phar. blisters 5" × 6-1/2"
Machine	Manual vacuum form	Manual vacuum form	Manual vacuum form	Automatic vacuum form	Manual vacuum form	Manual vacuum form	Automatic vacuum form	Automatic vacuum form
Backing sheet size	24.5" × 27"	Supplied	Supplied					
Number of cards/ sheet	12	by	by					
Printing cost/ sheet	.158¢	customer	customer					
Fold and assemble cards (sec./ card)			18 seconds					
Type of plastic	PVC 22" × .010"	PVC 22" × .010"	PVC 22" × .010"	HIPS 12-1/4" × .020"	HIPS 12-1/4" × .010"	HIPS 11" × .010"	OPS 12" × .010"	PVC 12" × .008"
Weight of plastic roll	100 lbs.	100 lbs.	100 lbs.	160 lbs.	128 lbs.	101 lbs._	124 lbs.	100 lbs.

Number of items formed/die	9 blisters	4 blisters	4 blisters	1 tray	2 trays	12 dishes	1 tray	2 blisters
Sheet size of plastic/die	19.5"	15.5"	15.5"	13"	26"	26"	9.6"	8.5"
Sheets of plastic/roll	442	556	556	1,500	1,083	907	3,000	2,515
Machine setup time	3/4 to 1 hour	3/4 to 1 hour	3/4 to 1 hour	1 to 1-1/2 hours	3/4 to 1 hour	3/4 to 1-1/2 hours	1 to 1-1/2 hours	1 to 1-1/2 hours
Operation time (heat, form, cool, pile)/sheet	88 seconds	88 seconds	88 seconds		54 seconds	41 seconds		
Cut-out formed items/sheet	100 seconds	48 seconds	48 seconds		45 seconds	96 seconds		
Operation time (heat, form, cool, cut, pile)/sheet				18 seconds			19.3 seconds	13.2 seconds
Filling and sealing blister/package	81.1 seconds	15.6 seconds	30 seconds					
Packing	144 seconds 36 pkgs./box	48 seconds 12 pkgs./box	48 seconds 12 pkgs./box	450 seconds 140/box	450 seconds 140/box	550 seconds 1,200/box	250 seconds 400/box	300 seconds 720/box
Counting and packaging nails	118 sec./pkg.							
Selling price	$150/1,000 pkgs.	$100/1,000 pkgs.	$135.50/1,000 pkgs.	$240/1,000	$220/1,000	$80/1,000	$57.30/1,000	$60/1,000

Exhibit 10: Raw Material Costs

Material	Colour	Gauge	Width	Length	Weight	Yield	Base Cost	Transportation	Duty	Total Cost
High impact polystyrene (HIPS)	White	.010	11 in.		101 lbs.	2,618 sq. in./lb.	.605¢ lb.	.06¢ lb.		66.5¢ lb.
HIPS	Cream	.010	12.25 in.		128 lbs.	2,618 sq. in./lb.	.605¢ lb.	.06¢ lb.		66.5¢ lb.
HIPS	Cream	.020	12.25 in.		160 lbs.	1,309 sq. in./lb.	.605¢ lb.	.06¢ lb.		66.5¢ lb.
Oriented polystyrene (OPS)	Clear	.010	12 in.	2,398 ft.	124 lbs.	2,630 sq. in./lb.	.60¢ lb.	.06¢ lb.		75¢ lb.
Polyvinyl chloride (PVC)	Clear	.008	12 in.	1,781.5 ft.	100 lbs.	2,740 sq. in./lb.	.54¢ lb.	.06¢ lb.	.175¢ lb.	77.5¢ lb.
PVC	Clear	.010	22 in.	718.5 ft.	100 lbs.	2,050 sq. in./lb.	.54¢ lb.	.06¢ lb.	.175¢ lb.	77.5¢ lb.
Polyethylene (POLY)	Clear	.005	27.5 in.	984.24 ft.		2,880 sq. in./lb.	.60¢ lb.	.06¢ lb.	.175¢ lb.	83.5¢ lb.

	Caliper	Basis Weight	Square Feet per Ton	Price per 1,000 Square Feet		
				1 Full Roll	Over 5 Tons	Over 15 Tons
#1 News back sheets	.024 in.	99	20,202	$21.15	$20.64	$20.14

manager and a controller to change this situation. He realized that authority as well as responsibility would have to be delegated to these new people.

During 1975, a graduate M.B.A. had been hired to take such responsibility, but since he spent most of his time talking to his girlfriend on the telephone and writing on papers which seemed to have little to do with the immediate business at hand, his resignation had been accepted after six months. Clearly, the process of establishing good managers in the new positions while still carrying on the urgent day-to-day operations would be a tricky transition.

Marketing

Further attention would likely have to be given to marketing activities. These were limited to occasional sales calls by Arrow on about two dozen regular customers and half a dozen prospects. He had made sales forays into other cities several times, making cold calls to gain new customers. Although he enjoyed doing this, time was lacking to carry on such activities consistently, and only small continuing revenues were received as a result of these calls.

Arrow's extensive involvement in many professional and civic organizations, often as an officer, provided many daily contacts which generated sales. Frequently, these were for new products which required expensive development, and although Arrow knew what to do technically, lack of time and money usually prevented completion of such development and sales within a reasonable period. Actual orders usually came by telephone and required further numerous phone calls before complete specifications and order terms were agreed upon. These phone calls represented the major productive marketing activity, and little advertising or formal market research was done.

Expansion of Clear-Vue seemed to require that the current marketing procedure be much refined and that the new marketing attack be executed far more aggressively. Meanwhile, during 1976, unfilled orders ranged from $50,000 to $70,000.

New Product Development

The question of which products to produce and sell always seemed to be popping up. Preponderant among Mr. Arrow's personal preferences was an unalloyed joy in making a technologically new product or process work. No technology was too difficult or esoteric for him to become enthused over, to explore, and then to solve. Faced with packaging imported garlic, he had developed a process of nuclear radiation which preserved it; he supervised plant breeding and genetic research to choose the best variety for local growing and was contracting to have such a crop grown. High-density magnets, equal in power to the existing state of the art but additionally possessing this magnetic power at high and low temperatures, were under development at the patent stage. Shortly, Arrow hoped to enter the small electric motor business with these magnets, then follow this up with electric bicycles and electric cars. Later, he hoped to sell a premium gyroscope for high-speed aircraft and space ships which would not require expensive, weighty heating equipment. He was also considering setting up a process to make the copper plated plastic for printed circuit boards and couple that with a circuit board manufacturing operation. Solar heaters were another key interest. Clear-Vue had just recently signed an agreement to sell a new, U.S. manufactured solar heater in Canada and later to manufacture it. Closer at hand was the machinery in the plant to make a serrated-blade bread knife, along with the stainless steel raw material from which it could be made. Although nothing was seriously wrong with this equipment, everyone was too busy to get it going. A market for the knife was believed to exist in large quantities. Also under consideration were plastic drinking cups for vending machines, clear plastic drinking glasses for airlines, and clear plastic vials for pharmaceutical manufacturers.

A large, but unmeasured, amount of money had gone into development of previous products. For example, a plastic display sign had eaten up about $10,000 during the past year but had come on the market behind a competitor, so the final development steps were not completed. Earlier, the automatic suturing device for human veins had cost about $5,000, most of which had been recovered but without a payback. It was clear that some better method for choosing and developing new products would have to be agreed upon. Arrow knew that his tremendous enthusiasm for new products made it difficult to be objective, but he was uncertain how to use his undoubted talents in the area without stifling them through rigid procedures.

Corporate Strategy

Arrow knew that a formal and clear decision on product policy was the cornerstone of a successful corporate strategy. At the same time, he knew he must develop his organization structure and some controls to allow Clear-Vue to survive and grow. He was also concerned about retaining the cheerful, loyal, democratic esprit de corps which existed among his employees since he felt this was both productive and suited his personal attitudes. Meanwhile, the urgent need for cash and the need to move to another building would force him to do something very soon. As Arrow waited with a telephone in each hand or drove his new, fire-engine red luxury Volvo to a professional meeting, he tried to decide how to formulate an integrated strategy in order to let Clear-Vue successfully seize all the opportunities he saw ahead without falling prey to the bankruptcy trustee due to miscalculations.

Case 13

Cooper Canada Limited: A Bid for CCM

"We will have to act fast if we want to acquire CCM's skate and hockey equipment business," said John Cooper, vice chairman of Cooper Canada Ltd., on Friday, November 26, 1982.

> CCM has been insolvent for several weeks. An interim receiver, appointed October 14, has been authorized by the creditors to give management until January 23 to arrange new financing. If nothing can be worked out, CCM will be declared bankrupt. Last week our people visited their St. Jean plant and Toronto offices to take a look. Right after they got back, the receiver called me wanting to know how soon we could make a bid. He said speed is critical because he expects other bids at any moment. He warned me that these bids will have tight time limits—they'll be good for 24 or 48 hours—and he might get a quick decision from the Royal Bank and the Enterprise Development Board, the two main creditors. That could be at any time with anybody's bid. They are not waiting for January 23 because CCM's situation worsens every day. The quicker they can settle this, the better for all concerned.

John Cooper continued,

> This morning I had a visit from Raymond Dutil, vice president of Pro Cycle, a large Quebec bicycle company, who is going to submit a bid early next week, subject to making a deal with someone else to buy CCM's winter goods business. Dutil, who is a sincere and able guy, is interested in acquiring the CCM bicycle business, mainly for the name and parts inventory. He came to us first because he knows we are in the strongest position to do something with CCM's winter goods. A joint bid with him would be attractive because there is no way we want to get involved in the bicycle business. However, CCM skates are still up there with the best, and this is a unique opportunity to complete our hockey line. I have agreed to meet with Dutil, his key people, and their lawyer next Monday afternoon to make an offer. That gives us only the weekend to make up our minds. It's too bad we are under such time pressure, but that's the way this deal is.

Some elements of the fit between Cooper and CCM's winter goods business were obvious. Cooper could completely outfit a hockey player except for sweater and skates. CCM's skate line was still one of the most respected in the business. However, the value of, and how Cooper would handle, CCM's competing lines of hockey sticks and protective equipment were less clear.

This case was prepared by Professor Donald H. Thain. Copyright © 1985 by the University of Western Ontario.

For several years CCM's competitors had noted its problems with a certain sense of satisfaction and relief. However, the prospect of CCM on the auction block was a major concern for several companies, including Cooper, that could be significantly affected. Because many of its assets were valuable and enduring, someone was certain to pick up some or all of the business. Since this would have a major impact on the structure and competitive balance of the industry, there was much speculation as to who would buy what, for how much, when, and how, and what their turnaround strategy would be. The rivalry among several potential buyers promised to be intense. Furthermore, the St. Jean plant represented up to 200 politically sensitive, vulnerable jobs. Industry executives feared that the Quebec government might become involved either directly or indirectly.

To describe the context in which Cooper's top managers had to decide what, if anything, to do, this case presents information about the industry, the Cooper company, and CCM.

The Sporting Goods Industry

Canadian-produced sporting goods covered a wide and varied range of sport and recreational activities. The major products are listed in Table 1. Athletic apparel and footwear were not included in the industry statistics. A rough estimate of the total retail market for 1981 was $1.5 billion,[1] and it had been growing steadily at a rate of 17 percent annually since 1971. The value of shipments[2] increased from $82 to $400 million from 1970 to 1980. Compared to the average of all manufacturing industries during the 1970s, the sporting goods industry had a higher increase in both value of shipments and number of employees. However, productivity per employee did not increase at the same pace as the average of all manufacturing industries. Of the 196 establishments in Canada in 1980, only 7 percent had more than 100 employees, but they accounted for 53 percent of shipments and employment.

One consulting report listed major factors on the Canadian market as follows:

1. While the sporting goods market may be regarded as essentially mature, it is by no means static. Increased levels of disposable income, leisure time, and the perceived beneficial effects of an active lifestyle predispose consumers to increased participation in sports. This trend should continue as the population ages.

2. Consumer requirements for sporting equipment are performance, protection, safety, and durability (they will accept innovation with respect to these

---

[1] Casewriter's estimate for total sporting goods.

[2] Value of shipments was based on the manufacturer's reported value.

Table 1:   Major Industry Product Categories

	1980 Value of Shipments ($000)	Percent
Ice skates	$ 61,459	16.3%
Hockey equipment	23,423	6.2
Hockey sticks	22,888	6.1
Bicycles	70,415	18.7
Swimming pools, accessories	45,076	11.9
Gymnasium equipment	16,502	4.4
Golf clubs	15,407	4.1
Baseball equipment, supplies	9,799	2.6
Snow skis	7,957	2.1
Fishing equipment	7,005	1.9
Playground equipment	4,395	1.2
Football equipment, supplies	2,052	0.5
Skiing equipment	1,939	0.5
All others	88,977	23.5
Total	$377,294	100.0%

Source: Statistics Canada.

factors). Brand awareness will continue to be an important product attribute. As the cost of equipment rises, consumers will increasingly rely on brands with which they are familiar rather than new or "no-name" (house brand) products.

3. Team sports (especially the "big ticket" activities of football and hockey) can be expected to continue to decline as the birthrate increases. Should a mini-baby boom materialize in the mid-1980s, this trend will be interrupted in the 1990s. Therefore, to increase sales in these markets, manufacturers will have to take share from other competitors through superior products, intermittent price wars, and/or industry rationalization. Manufacturers could focus on the growing adult market and its activities, which are primarily non-team sports.

4. Profit margins should increase as the adult market is less price sensitive than that for children. The decline in the number of children per family will lower unit sales but should increase available dollars for equipment expenditures per child.

5. The largest Canadian markets are in Quebec and points west. Alberta and British Columbia are particularly important as these areas have a somewhat more youthful population and spend a higher proportion of their income on recreational equipment.

6. The "soft goods" market is a high potential area for growth. It will be difficult, however, to protect this area from imports.

7. The main location for sporting good sales will continue to be specialty stores. These specialized sporting goods stores will probably increase their market share at the expense of department and home and auto supply stores.

Hockey Equipment Industry

There were three basic product lines: protective equipment (for example, helmets, gloves, pants, shin pads, elbow pads, shoulder pads), skates, and sticks. Often apparel completed a company's line—primarily sweaters, socks, and underwear (not covered in Statistics Canada figures for industry shipments). The most growth was seen in helmets and pads. Total growth from 1971 to 1980 was positive for all products. However, from 1979 to 1980 the production of hockey equipment and skates declined. At the same time, exports of hockey sticks decreased, and exports of hockey equipment and pads increased. Products and rough market shares of the major competitors are shown in Exhibit 1.

Because product excellence established a positive reputation for Canadian brands, exports of hockey equipment increased from $20 million in 1971 to $41.5

Exhibit 1: Products and Estimated Market Shares of Major Competitors in the Canadian Hockey Equipment Market, 1981

Company	Skates	Hockey Equipment	Sticks	Apparel
Cooper		69%	7%	31%
Canadien		7	12	
CCM	25%	7	6	
D & R		7		
Jofa		3		
Koho		2.5	10.5	
Sherwood			25	
Victoriaville			11	
Louisville			6.5	
Titan			11	
Maska				42
Bernard				11
Sandow				10
Bauer	33			
Lange	5			
Micron	13			
Daoust	17			
Orbit	5			
Roos	1			
Ridell	1			
Others		4.5	11	4
	100%	100%	100%	100%
($ millions)	$78	$31.5	$29	$27

Source: Rough estimates by Cooper product managers.

million in 1980. Skates represented the largest export product. The United States was the largest market with Scandinavia and Western Europe also being strong markets. Japan and Australia were developing new markets.

Hockey Equipment—Protective

As indicated in Table 2, hockey players needed to purchase a great deal of protective equipment. Prices varied considerably depending on quality. Equipment costs per player ranged from $100–$200 for beginners to $1,500 for professionals. Significant research and development efforts were devoted to these products to ensure maximum protection and comfort. Companies needed to be strong in development to maintain and gain market share. Cooper dominated this market with a 69 percent share.

The hockey player also needed nonprotective items such as pucks and tape. These items had not changed over the years and were relatively low in cost.

The rapidly changing technology of hockey equipment was described in

Table 2:   Standard Hockey Equipment

	Men's	Boy's
Hockey equipment:		
Protective:		
Pants	$40–$130	$30–$60
Gloves	50–140	25–70
Helmets	27–45	27–45
Cooperall	115–125	98
Shin pads	20–75	20–75
Elbow pads	19–50	7–25
Shoulder pads	25–70	14–40
Pants	40–130	30–60
Gloves	50–140	25–70
Helmets	27–45	27–45
Nonprotective:		
Hockey nets	Frame–946/net–225	
Puck	.50	.50
Tape	2–8	2–8
Skates:		
Leather	89–229	40–129
Moulded	69–175	39–89
Sticks:		
Wood, fiberglass	11–22	10–14
Aluminum	30–50	20–40
Apparel:		
Sweaters	20–100	20–100
Socks	10	10
Underwear	10–15	5–10

excerpts from an article in the Toronto Maple Leaf Gardens Program in early 1982:

> Space-age hockey equipment is speeding up the game and cutting down on injuries. Technological breakthroughs are sending the NHL where it has never gone before— to lighter, cooler, stronger, tighter-fitting one-piece body protection; aluminum or fiberglass and plastic laminated sticks; and zicron-guarded, carbon-bladed skates encased in ballistic, and nylon-wrapped boots.
>
> This space-age equipment has speeded up the game and cut down on injuries. And it's made the felt and fibre shin, shoulder, elbow, and pant pads, one-piece ash sticks, and leather tube skates so popular only a decade ago obsolete. . . .
>
> The evolution turned revolution in NHL gear is the by-product of by-products. New foams, plastics, nylon, and fiberglass (many invented in Korea during the 50s to keep fighting forces warm and protected) have made things "lighter and stronger," says one long-time equipment manufacturer. "All these new inventions have been developed to conform to the game of hockey." . . .
>
> Leaf trainer Danny Lemelin thinks skates have "changed most dramatically" in the past few years. He points out that most are four ounces lighter because of the plastic blade holder and nylon boot.
>
> NHL players have three different widths (narrow, medium, wide) to choose from, and lengths measured down by quarter sizes. Wally McLeod, Ontario sales representative for Daoust Skates Canada, adds another twist to custom fitting skates and uses his best-known client, Wayne Gretzky, as an example.
>
> "Wayne has an 8¾ left skate and an 8 right," he says. "No two human feet are the same size. We do it for all NHLers." . . .
>
> What's the most dramatic change in hockey equipment over the years? Some would argue helmets—up to 80 percent of NHLers use them now.
>
> Ostrander disagrees. "It's the new foams," he says. "The one-piece suits," argues Parsons. "The lightness," says Stanley. "Management's concern," adds Gardner. "Sticks," says Leader. "Skates," agrees McLeod and Lemelin.
>
> "The most dramatic change?" ponders practical Hanna. "The price!"
>
> However, all are convinced that equipment will get even lighter and better throughout the 1980s.

Designing a skate to give outstanding performance and protection required extensive research and development. Leather had been the first material used in boots and was still used in most high-quality, high-priced skates. Over 90 percent of NHL players wore leather skates. However, in the 70s moulded boots had entered the market and were competitive in price and performance with a leather-booted skate, especially in the low-priced market.

Skate blades were available from three sources in Canada. The largest manufacturer, the St. Lawrence company of Montreal, sold mainly to CCM and Daoust. Canpro Ltd. owned by Warrington, the parent company of Bauer, sold mainly to Bauer, Micron, and Lange as well as other skate manufacturers. CCM manufactured their own Tuuk blades and sold some to other skatemakers. While blade technology had changed significantly in the late 70s with the introduction of plastic mounts to replace tubes, the major current change was the trend back to carbon steel from the newer stainless steel.

Information on the total Canadian hockey skate market and the skates of major competitors segmented into sewn and moulded hockey and figure skates is presented in Exhibit 2.

Hockey skates were also segmented by price point as follows:

Range	Price	1982 Estimated Share (Units)
High	More than $200	15%
Medium	$120–$180	20
Low	Less than $90	65

Industry observers noted that the high- and low-end market shares were increasing and the medium range decreasing. The breakdown of CCM's total unit skate sales in the high-, medium-, and low-price ranges was approximately 60

Exhibit 2
Canadian Hockey Skate Production (thousands of pairs)

Year	Sewn	Moulded	Total
1977	1,050	50	1,100
1978	775	150	925
1979	1,050	250	1,300
1980	850	300	1,150
1981	970	400	1,370
1982 (forecast)	750	300	1,050
1983 (forecast)	900	350	1,250

1982 Factory Sales and Market Shares of Leading Competitors (thousands of pairs)

	Sewn	Percent	Moulded	Percent	Total	Percent	Amount (in thousands)	Percent	Dollar Average of Total
Bauer	305	42.9%	50	13.7%	355	32.9%	$20,265	35.4%	57.08
Micron	—	—	185	50.5	185	17.2	8,690	15.2	46.97
Lange	—	—	100	27.3	100	9.3	3,280	5.8	32.80
Daoust	205	28.7	—	—	205	19.0	9,780	17.0	47.70
CCM	147	20.6	6	1.6	153	14.2	12,050	21.0	78.76
Orbit	55	7.8	25	6.8	80	7.4	3,205	5.6	40.06
Total	712	100%	366	100%	1078	100%	$57,270	100%	$53.13

1982 Hockey Skate Sales by Geographic Market (thousands of pairs)

Manufacturer	Canada	United States	Europe	Far East	Total
Canadian	785	238	67	15	1,105
Non-Canadian	—	312	233	25	570
Totals	785	550	300	40	1,675

Source: Estimates based on industry information and case writer's estimates.

percent, 25 percent, and 15 percent, respectively, and that of Bauer, the largest company, was thought to be 20 percent, 30 percent, and 50 percent, respectively.

Sticks

Changes in the composition of sticks were continually occurring. What had started out as a one-piece blade and handle developed into a two-piece solid wood handle and blade, and, later, a three-piece wooden stick, laminated handle, curved blade, and fiberglass handle and/or blade. The most recent development was an aluminum handle with a replaceable wooden blade. Changes were intended to improve strength and passing and shooting accuracy. These changes required a medium amount of research and development work. Sherwood-Drolet led in this market with a 25 percent share.

Apparel

Differences in prices of sweaters and socks were due basically to the material used in the product. The most popular sweater materials were polyester and cotton knits because of their strength and lightness. Designs of sweaters were fairly standard, with lettering and cresting done separately. Socks were a standard product with little differentiation. Sport Maska controlled 42 percent of this market because of its quality product, excellent distribution, and good rapport with dealers.

Distribution

Sporting goods were sold in retail outlets which included specialty, independent, department, discount, chain, and catalogue stores. Manufacturers used four sales channels to reach the retailer:

1. Distributors with their own sales force.
2. Distributors who used sales agents.
3. Distributors who sold to wholesalers.
4. Retail stores directly through their own sales force.

In Canada, the most common route was through distributors who used sales agents. Manufacturers wanted agents who would represent their product aggressively, seek out new orders, and provide them with market feedback. Usually these agents either were, or had been, actively involved in sports. However, since the agents sold multiple lines, it was difficult to control their activities and level and mix of sales. Most companies used a sales force of 10 to 12 to cover most of Canada. A few small companies utilized wholesalers to supplement their sales force.

Retail outlets had experienced little real growth in sales and were finding themselves with increasing inventories. Therefore, retailers started carrying shallower stocks, ordering more frequently, and relying on manufacturers or distributors to provide backup inventories. This trend meant that bargaining power had shifted from the manufacturers to the retailers who were trying to gain volume discounts and delivery advantages by reducing the number of suppliers. In general, large national and regional chain and discount stores had become mass merchandisers whose aim was to supply the consumer with a complete range of products and one-stop shopping convenience.

Specialty stores became more important because the higher prices and special new features of many products increased the need for salespersons with strong product knowledge to deal with rising consumer needs for purchase assistance. These stores were usually small operations that served a specialized market niche. Many of their owners and/or managers first became involved in the business because of interests and associations they developed as former players. In fact, many managers at all levels of the sporting goods industry were old players who had pursued their favourite sports and hobbies as a business activity.

In some cases, this interest was coupled with a keen business sense, but in many cases, their operations were based on an emotional attachment to the business, gut-feel judgments, and extensive reliance on teammates, friends, and acquaintances from erstwhile playing days.

Promotion

Three types of promotion were used: company and product promotion, direct advertising, and trade-show participation. Product and image promotion was the most-effective form of advertising. Because professional players set industry trends, it was important to get popular players to use and/or endorse products. To recruit these players, pro detail men from sports equipment manufacturers were assigned to players to make sure their equipment fit perfectly and that the player was loyal to the brand. It was also important to get as many players as possible wearing the products so that the brand name would enjoy good exposure during televised games. Therefore, the detail men also tried to work through team trainers to supply most of the team with their brand. One industry expert reported that these transactions were not always highly ethical, and incentives like money and cars were used to push a product. Many competitors used these sales methods, and although it appeared to be the way to do business, Cooper relied on high quality, fast service in fitting and repairs, and intensive sales efforts and was not involved with special deals or endorsement contracts with any players. Promotion was also achieved through the sponsorship of tournaments and camps, use of branded sports bags, and extensive shelf and display space at retail.

Direct advertising through the media was generally used only by the larger firms. Print advertising was more extensively used and was directed at a more concentrated population.

Trade shows significantly influenced retail buyers. Many sales took place at the shows, bookings were made for orders, and sales were made on follow-up calls by sales forces. The Canadian Sporting Goods Association organized two shows annually.

Cooper Canada

The company began in 1905 as General Leather Goods Ltd. producing small leather goods. In 1946 Jack Cooper left Eaton's to join the company as its first and, until 1951, only salesperson. In 1946 Jack Cooper and Cecil Weeks bought out the company's original owner and changed the name to Cooper-Weeks. In 1954 Jack Cooper acquired Cecil Weeks's interests; the company became the exclusive Canadian manufacturer of Buxton Leathergoods through a special licensing contract and opened a leather finishing division. In 1963 manufacturing rights for Atlantic golf bags and casual luggage were obtained. Cooper Barbados opened in 1969 and closed in 1982 as a result of several problems. In 1970 the company changed its name to Cooper Canada Ltd. and went public. In 1972 a new 380,000-square-foot head office and factory was opened in west Toronto; Hespeler-St. Mary's Wood Specialities, a hockey stick and baseball bat manufacturer, was purchased; and the first Cooper sports camp opened in Oakville. The camp had been sold out and was profitable every year. In 1974 Cooper International Inc., a U.S. subsidiary, bought a 55,000-square-foot building in Lewiston, New York. In 1977 Toronto area warehousing and distribution facilities were consolidated in a 252,000-square-foot building at Airport Park in Mississauga. In 1979 Winnwell Ltd., producers of knitted and sewn athletic apparel and hockey and baseball equipment and balls, was purchased. In 1982, J. B. Foam, manufacturers of plastic foam pads and products, was purchased and moved from Gananoque, Ontario, into the Toronto plant.

Management

Jack Cooper, "the chief," and his two sons, John and Don,[3] owned 82 percent of the company's outstanding common stock. Jack Cooper, who retained voting control, was chairman and chief executive officer, and Henry Nolting was president and chief operating officer. John Cooper was vice chairman and deputy chief executive officer. They worked closely together, meeting for frequent discussions daily. The company's organization is shown in Exhibit 3. Management's immediate concerns were to increase sales and margins; to implement a badly needed information system to strengthen control activities in marketing, production, and finance (with one hoped-for benefit being a reduction in inventory carrying costs); to reduce short-term bank debt and high interest expenses; to bring the leather goods division from a loss into a profitable position while

---

[3] Don, who had managed the leather goods division for several years, left the company in 1980 and started a women's sportswear retailing company. He remained a director.

Exhibit 3: Organization Chart

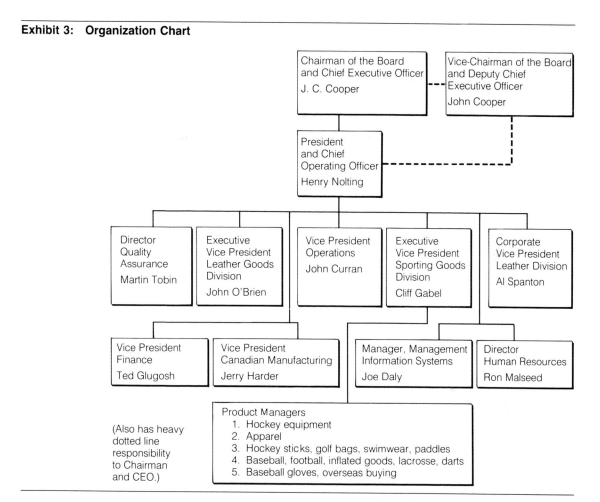

retaining its market leadership; and to iron out troublesome technical and production problems in J. B. Foam.

Long-term goals called for further development of the sporting goods division to increase growth and utilize the great strengths of the Cooper name. Additions to the product line were sought through new-product development and/or acquisition. Cooper was also developing more export markets for its sporting goods products.

Performance

From 1971 to 1981 the performance of Cooper had been variable. Growth had always been foremost among Jack Cooper's prime goals. Sales had increased continually since 1969, except in 1975. However, earnings had fluctuated widely over the same period. Earnings dropped in 1979 because of problems absorbing

Exhibit 4

COOPER CANADA LTD.
Consolidated Balance Sheet
As at December 31
(in thousands)

	1981	1980	1979	1978	1977	1976	1975
Assets							
Current assets:							
Short-term bank deposit	—	$ 1,790	—	$ 22	$ 95	$ 103	$ 2,465
Accounts receivable	$ 9,726	10,625	$10,315	9,185	8,340	8,513	7,789
Inventories*:							
Raw materials	6,177	8,792	13,064	5,675	5,535	4,539	4,186
Work in process	1,593	1,758	1,817	1,006	1,379	1,181	1,000
Finished goods	15,954	11,669	10,530	10,937	10,839	7,275	6,876
Prepaid expenses, etc.	580	691	545	886	706	757	408
Total current assets	34,030	35,325	39,271	27,714	26,897	22,371	22,727
Fixed assets at cost:							
Buildings	6,179	6,145	6,145	6,117	6,078	5,968	5,888
Mach., equip., etc.	4,191	4,521	4,171	3,354	3,174	2,743	2,523
Dies, moulds, etc.	235	567	619	435	284	159	217
Land	91	91	91	90	90	90	90
Less: Accum. deprec.	5,351	5,104	4,518	4,000	3,712	3,194	2,773
Total fixed assets	5,345	6,220	6,508	5,998	5,914	5,767	5,946
Def. financing exp.	—	—	—	—	76	87	97
Invest. non-consol. subsids.	1,122	—	—	—	—	—	—
Deferred income taxes	373	581	533	—	—	—	—
Total assets	$40,870	$42,126	$46,312	$33,713	$32,889	$28,227	$28,771
Liabilities							
Current liabilities:							
Bank indebtedness	$10,373	$15,853	$17,423	$ 8,283	$ 6,955	$ 6,160	$12,420
Accts. payable	3,463	3,380	6,380	3,153	3,576	3,093	1,927
Income and other taxes payable	1,002	695	641	352	314	1,126	592
Long-term debt due	16	233	603	1,134	1,059	1,309	1,109
Total current liabilities	14,854	20,161	25,047	12,924	11,905	11,690	16,049
Long-term debt:							
Bank loans	9,000	4,000	5,375	5,875	6,900	4,000	1,500
10% sinking fund debentures, due 1990	1,582	1,892	1,920	2,053	2,148	2,276	2,362
6.5% mortgage, due 1992	248	265	273	291	280	268	275
Notes payable to shareholders	—	125	437	504	—	—	—
Less: Amt. due 1 yr.	16	233	603	1,134	1,059	1,309	1,109
Deferred taxes	—	—	—	418	397	455	408

* At lower of cost (determined on a first-in, first-out basis) and net realizable value.

Exhibit 4 *(concluded)*

	1981	1980	1979	1978	1977	1976	1975
Shareholders' Equity							
Capital stock:							
Preference	—	—	—	—	—	171	173
Common	3,403	3,392	3,392	2,764	2,716	2,710	2,696
Retained earnings	11,799	12,524	10,471	10,016	9,600	7,963	6,414
Total liabilities and shareholders' equity	$40,870	$42,126	$46,312	$33,713	$32,889	$28,227	$28,771

Note: Due to truncating, sums may not equal totals in 1978 and prior years.

Pension costs—As at December 31, 1981, unfunded past service benefits were estimated at approximately $272,500, which the company intends to fund and charge to earnings over the next nine years.

Lease agreements—Annual rentals (excluding certain occupancy charges) under lease agreements for warehouse premises amount to approximately $450,000 annually to 1992. Outstanding letters of credit at December 31, 1981, amounted to approximately $1,978,000.

Contingent liabilities—Company is contesting an income tax assessment plus interest thereon totaling $480,000.

	1981	1980	1979	1978	1977	1976	1975
Working capital ($000s):							
Current assets	$34,030	$35,325	$39,271	$27,714	$26,897	$22,371	$22,727
Current liabilities	14,854	20,161	25,047	12,924	11,905	11,690	16,049
Working capital	$19,176	$15,164	$14,224	$14,790	$14,991	$10,680	$6,677
Ratio	2.29–1	1.75–1	1.57–1	2.14–1	2.26–1	1.91–1	1.42–1
Equities:							
Net worth* ($000s)	$15,202	$15,916	$13,863	$12,780	$12,240	$10,758	$9,187
Debentures, per $1,000	10,609	9,412	8,220	7,225	6,698	5,727	4,890
Common	10.23	10.73	9.35	9.10	8.81	7.64	6.53

* Available for capital stock. Based on shareholders' equity. Debentures taken in at par before calculating their equity.

	1981	1980	1979	1978	1977	1976	1975
Shares outstanding:							
Preference	—	—	—	—	—	3,425	3,465
Common	1,486,270	1,483,270	1,483,270	1,404,654	1,388,504	1,386,444	1,380,244

Source: Company financial reports.

the purchase of Winnwell Sports, and in 1981 high interest rates, the recession, and disposal of the Barbados operations all hurt the bottom line. However, in 1982 interim figures indicated much stronger performance. Although little growth was seen in sales, tight inventory and cost controls heavily emphasized by Henry Nolting helped to increase earnings. Return on equity, which had decreased from 16 percent in 1978 to a loss in 1981, was expected to improve in 1982 despite the recession. Cooper financial statements are presented in Exhibits 4 and 5.

Finance

Incorporated as a public company on April 30, 1970, Cooper issued 275,000 shares at a price of $8.25 which netted $2,268,750. A $2.5 million debenture at 10 percent interest was also issued in 1970. The sinking fund covenant of these debentures required the company to redeem $100,000 in principal annually to 1989. The 121

Exhibit 5

COOPER CANADA LTD.
Consolidated Statement of Income and Retained Earnings
Years Ended December 31
(in thousands)

	1981	1980	1979	1978	1977	1976	1975
Gross sales	$66,988	$65,531	$58,712	$52,656	$46,023	$41,846	$36,317
Less: Disc., tax & freight	4,161	3,348	2,902	3,227	3,219	2,795	2,413
Net sales	62,827	62,183	55,810	49,429	42,803	39,051	33,904
Less: Oper. costs	57,049	55,901	51,844	44,364	38,538	34,556	29,790
Net before deprec., etc.	5,778	6,282	3,966	5,064	4,265	4,494	4,113
Less:							
Deprec. & amort.	724	746	748	626	609	561	561
L.-term debt interest	1,905	934	1,022	929	778	991	438
Other interest	2,933	2,866	2,068	1,138	941	707	1,708
Add:							
Foreign exch. gain	(105)	369	(107)	216	173	—	—
Earns. discont. opers.	929	—	—	—	—	—	—
Less: Income taxes:							
Current	14	176	20	525	518	624	199
Deferred	208	►48	►454	21	►58	47	274
Net income, operations	818	1,977	455	2,039	1,650	1,562	931
Add: Extraord. item□	(1,543)	76	—	—	—	—	128
Net income	(725)	2,053	455	2,039	1,650	1,562	1,059
Add: Previous ret. earns.	12,524	10,471	10,016	9,600	7,963	6,414	5,370
Less:							
Dividends	—	—	—	1,403	13	13	15
Tax paid	—	—	—	▲221	—	—	—
Retained earnings	$11,799	$12,524	$10,471	$10,016	$ 9,600	$ 7,963	$ 6,414

Note:—Due to truncating, sums may not equal totals in 1978 and prior years.
▲15% taxes paid on a portion of 1971 undistributed surplus on hand.
►Credit.
□ In 1981, provision for loss on discontinuance of Barbados operations; in 1980, reduction of income taxes on application of prior years' losses; in 1975, net profit on the sale of fixed assets.

Remuneration—Of directors and officers has been as follows: $395,548 in 1980; $281,041 in 1979; $435,962 in 1978; $400,582 in 1977; $350,822 in 1976; and $351.812 in 1975.

	1981	1980	1979	1978	1977	1976	1975
Times all interest earned:							
Before deprec. & amort.	1.19	1.65	1.28	2.45	2.48	2.65	1.92
After deprec. & amort.	1.04	1.46	1.04	2.15	2.13	2.32	1.65
Earnings per share:							
(A) Based on net income, operations							
Pref.: Times earned	—	—	—	—	121.06	112.87	61.40
Common: Earned	$0.55	$1.33	$0.31	$1.45	$1.18	$1.12	$0.66
(B) Based on net income							
Pref.: Times earned	—	—	—	—	121.06	112.87	69.84
Common: Earned	$0.49	$1.38	$0.31	$1.45	$1.18	$1.12	$0.76
Dividends paid or declared:							
Preference	—	—	—	—	$4.00	$4.00	$4.00
Common	—	—	—	►$1.00	—	—	—

►Tax-deferred. Includes 25 cents extraordinary dividend and 25 cents prepayment of 1979 dividend.

Exhibit 5 (*continued*)

Historical Summary (as originally stated in company's annual reports for the respective years—dollars in thousands)

Year Ended Dec. 31	Total Assets	Working Capital	Long-Term Debt	Shareholders' Equity	Net Sales	Net Income, Operations	Earnings per Common Share	Common Stock Price Range High	Common Stock Price Range Low
1969	$ 5,536	$ 1,914	$ 410	$ 2,147	$10,214	$ 521			
1970	10,081	4,973	2,557	5,185	12,850	815	$0.58		
1971	12,466	5,828	2,552	6,232	17,469	1,121	0.82	$15.50*	$ 8.88*
1972	18,639	6,406	4,547	7,565	21,760	1,004	0.75	19.00	14.63
1973	29,516	6,207	4,284	8,116	30,638	534	0.37	16.75	8.00
1974	31,125	5,554	3,676	8,267	35,658	267	0.18	9.88	1.90
1975	28,772	6,678	4,138	9,285	33,904	932	0.66	3.85	2.00
1976	28,227	10,681	6,545	10,846	39,051	1,563	1.12	5.63	2.30
1977	32,889	14,991	8,269	12,316	42,804	1,650	1.18	5.50	4.10
1978	33,713	14,791	8,725	12,780	49,429	2,040	1.45	9.00	4.40
1979	46,312	14,224	8,005	13,863	55,810	455	0.31	8.75	6.50
1980	42,126	15,164	6,282	15,916	62,183	1,977	1.33	7.25	4.30
1981	40,870	19,176	10,830	15,202	62,827	818	0.55	8.25	5.00

* Listed February 19, 1971.
Source: Company financial reports.

Industry Segments for Cooper Canada (dollars in thousands)

	Sporting Goods 1981	Sporting Goods 1980	Leather Goods and Leather Finishing 1981	Leather Goods and Leather Finishing 1980	Consolidated 1981	Consolidated 1980
Net sales to outside customers	$46,913	$45,873	$15,914	$16,236	$62,827	$62,109
Intersegment sales			162	374		
Revenue	46,913	45,873	16,076	16,610	62,827	62,109
Operating profit (i)	7,434	6,211	1,678	1,687	8,939	7,849
Deduct:						
General corporate expenses					3,990	3,497
Interest expense					4,838	3,798
Income taxes					222	39
					9,050	7,334
Earnings (loss) from continuing operations					(111)	515
Net earnings of non-consolidated subsidiaries (discontinued operations)					929	1,462
Earnings before extraordinary items					818	1,977
Extraordinary items					(1,543)	76
Earnings for the year					(725)	2,053

Exhibit 5 (*concluded*)

	Sporting Goods		Leather Goods and Leather Finishing		Consolidated	
	1981	1980	1981	1980	1981	1980
Identifiable assets (i)	28,703	26,873	8,001	9,862	36,321	36,525
Corporate assets					4,549	5,669
Total assets					$40,870	$42,194
Capital expenditures	254	325	110	70	364	395
Depreciation and amortization	457	406	171	155	628	561

Geographic Segments for Cooper Canada (dollars in thousands)

	Canada		United States		Consolidated	
	1981	1980	1981	1980	1981	1980
Net sales to outside customers (ii)	$51,506	$51,590	$11,321	$10,519	$62,827	$62,109
Intersegment sales	5,616	5,604				
Revenue	57,122	57,194	11,321	10,519	62,827	62,109
Operating profit (i)	7,823	7,275	1,289	623	8,939	7,849
Deduct:						
General corporate expenses					3,990	3,497
Interest expense					4,838	3,798
Income taxes					222	39
					9,050	7,334
Earnings (loss) from continuing operations					(111)	515
Net earnings of non-consolidated subsidiaries (discontinued operations)					929	1,462
Earnings before extraordinary items					818	1,977
Extraordinary items					(1,543)	76
Earnings (loss) for the year					(725)	2,053
Identifiable assets (i)	30,403	29,319	6,301	7,416	36,321	36,525
Corporate assets					4,549	5,669
Total assets					$40,870	$42,194

(i) Consolidated operating profit and identifiable assets are shown net of intercompany eliminations of $173 ($49 in 1980) and $383 ($210 in 1980), respectively.

(ii) Canadian sales include $6,190 ($7,227 in 1980) of export sales.

percent sales growth from 1970 to a new record of $30.6 million in 1973 was made possible by the 1970 capital infusion. Shares were listed on the Toronto Stock Exchange on February 19, 1971, and opened trading at $8⅞. The shares showed remarkable market strength and traded as high as $19 in 1972. The company policy, reflected in the price-earnings (P/E) ratio of about 20 to 1, was to reinvest all earnings. The high P/E ratio was maintained until 1974 when earnings were barely adequate to cover interest on a $16 million term loan. The stock fell to its lowest price of $1.90 in 1974 and had since fluctuated below $10 per share.

The first dividend payment of 25 cents per share was made on May 23, 1978. On December 15, 1978, a special dividend payment of 75 cents per share was composed of a 25-cent regular dividend, a 25-cent extraordinary dividend, and a 25-cent prepayment of 1979 dividends. Company officials indicated that dividends had not been paid since, due to high financing costs and the uncertainty of future earnings.

Debt Financing

A bank operating loan and other term loans were the company's major sources of financing. Cooper had not issued any debentures since 1970. Banking services for Canada were provided by the Canadian Imperial Bank of Commerce (CIBC) and for Cooper International by Marine Midland Bank of Buffalo, New York. The CIBC provided an operating loan to a maximum line of $16 million at ¼ percent above prime and a term loan at ¾ percent above prime to be paid in $1 million per year installments in the first five years and $2 million per year thereafter. The bank prime rate was currently 12 percent but had been as high as 18 percent in mid-1982.

Working Capital

The objective of Cooper in the recession of the early 1980s was to minimize capital expenditures without adversely affecting manufacturing or productivity. The payback requirement approval of capital expenditures was 2.5 years or better. Typical annual capital expenditures were additions of new dies and moulds and the purchase of manufacturing equipment.

Speedy filling of customer orders was a major factor in maintaining customer loyalty. Cooper had a policy of providing a fill rate of 90 percent in nonpeak seasons and 80 percent in peak seasons. This required a large working capital as Cooper carried over 12,000 stockkeeping units (SKUs). The inventory as of December 31, 1981, was $23.7 million, which consisted of $6.2 million in raw materials, $1.6 million in work in process, and $15.9 million in finished goods. A company objective was to reduce total inventory to a more manageable $18 million by the end of 1982. One manager indicated that the past company policy of producing 120 percent of forecast sales to satisfy unforecast customer demand was changed to producing to a level of 100 percent of forecast sales, a major factor in reducing inventory.

The sporting goods division carried 65 percent to 80 percent of the total company inventory. The raw material inventory carried by the sporting goods division was expected to fluctuate between $2.2 and $4.7 million. A work-in-process inventory of $1.8 million was maintained. Sporting goods finished goods inventory reached as high as $18 million each April for deliveries of fall goods. An inventory turnover of 2.7 was expected for the division.

Information Systems

A monthly report of sales and gross profit for each SKU and product line was available to each product manager. Quarterly reports provided by cost accounting attempted to determine actual margins realized by each division on each product line. Product managers were also provided a report on the inventory for each SKU. Product managers were expected to make decisions on pricing and provide input on production levels based on the information provided by these reports.

Product managers were evaluated on the basis of sales, market share, and product margins. The market share was expected to be maintained or increased to achieve sales growth. Product line margins were compared to the company average. However, a major argument of the department and product managers, particularly for leather goods, was that allocated overheads were not fair or accurate. The cost accounting department had struggled with this problem for years.

Marketing

In sporting goods, Cooper produced and/or distributed more than 7,500 SKUs. Its products covered a wide range of categories including hockey sticks, hockey equipment, apparel (hockey, baseball, and soccer action wear), sports bags, baseball/softball accessories (bats, softballs, baseballs, equipment, and accessories), ball gloves, inflated goods (balls), footballs, golf bags, darts, swim goods, and paddles. All these products except baseball gloves, inflated goods, darts, and swim goods were manufactured by Cooper.

Hockey equipment was the company's major line and future growth area. Hockey equipment sales had been growing steadily. Cooper expected increased growth with its new Cooperall, an elasticized body garment which held all protective pads in place. This product was a major innovation designed, developed, and introduced by Cooper and copied by several competitors. Cooper's market shares in hockey equipment were strong in the United States.

Cooper products covered a wide range of quality and price points. For example, in hockey equipment, the Cooper line ranged from the highest, used by top professional teams around the world, to medium-low for the beginning player.

In baseball equipment and supplies, the quality and price covered a medium high to low range, appealing from younger to more experienced players but not professionals.

Distribution of Cooper goods was through its 25-man sales force that provided the most extensive national coverage of any company in the industry. The total customer base was around 1,600. Because Cooper and CCM had been competitive across a wide product line and Cooper accounts usually sold Bauer skates, significant overlap of Cooper and CCM accounts was not extensive. Sales were distributed equally among the East, Ontario, and West. National coverage by its own sales force gave Cooper an advantage over its competitors, few of whom had such coverage. However, a concern was that 90 percent of sales were made to 20 percent of accounts, and almost 40 percent of sales were made to only 20 major customers.

Salesmen were organized on a geographic basis and were paid on a salary plus bonus minus expenses system, with no upper limit on bonuses. Salesmen monitored consumer preferences and trends, feeding such information to the research and new-product development group. Most competitors sold through distributors and agents, a method that traded off company loyalty and management control for the lower costs of 5–7 percent commission.

Cliff Gabel, executive vice president, sporting goods, reported that the sales force was enthusiastic about adding skates to their line. No one in the Cooper organization had any in-depth experience in the skate business. Mr. Gabel, who was widely known and highly respected in the industry, had maintained a good relationship with several key marketing managers at CCM, some of whom were now retired. He believed that one man in particular who had an outstanding reputation as perhaps the "best skate man around" would welcome the opportunity to help Cooper take over and manage CCM should the opportunity arise. A key retired manager from the Bauer Company, who was a good friend of John Cooper, was also thought to be available.

Cooper was the largest national advertiser in the sporting goods industry and had won awards for the quality of its TV and print ads. The latest campaign had featured the Cooperall and was aired during the 1982 Stanley Cup telecasts.

Manufacturing

Cooper had two manufacturing facilities. The plant in west Toronto did the bulk of the work, and the older Hespeler woodworking plant in Cambridge produced hockey sticks, baseball bats, and canoe paddles. Manufacturing departments were primarily stand-alone operations. Each department manufactured hundreds of separate products that involved thousands of parts, requiring control procedures that were complex and numerous.

There was an excess of relatively expensive manufacturing space in the Toronto plant because it was built larger than necessary in 1976. In addition, several products, previously produced in Canada, had since been contracted to off-shore manufacturers at lower costs. These manufacturers were primarily in the Orient and did contract work for most of Cooper's competitors. As a result, Cooper's designs were widely and easily copied by the other companies.

In order to keep its competitive edge, Cooper worked hard to improve its product lines with top priority given to hockey equipment. Eight research people worked full-time on product development. They were also available to customize products for professional players. Through its extensive research and development, Cooper was able to design products that were at the leading edge of technology and design, ensuring that athletes would receive the best possible action and protection from Cooper equipment. This product leadership in hockey equipment had earned a leading worldwide reputation for quality.

Cooper chose to act as a "stockhouse," filling as many orders as possible on request. However, after-deadline requests were treated on an individual basis, with major customers usually receiving products from an extra production run, depending on the time of year. In approximately 10 percent to 20 percent of such cases, it was more cost effective to miss the sale rather than set up production and be faced with possible inventory costs.

CCM

Incorporated in 1899 as the Canadian Cycle and Motor Company, CCM was Canada's oldest sporting goods manufacturer. Over its history, CCM had been engaged in three separate businesses: bicycles, automobiles, and sporting goods including skates, hockey sticks, and equipment.

Its early years were described as follows:

> At its founding, CCM held out the promise of beating foreign competitors and building a name for Canada in manufacturing.
>
> It came into being at a time when U.S. and British bicycle makers were flooding the market with leisure vehicles. The answer, as Ontario industrialists conceived it, was for five domestic companies to amalgamate and form a single company. . . .
>
> CCM eventually grew to become Canada's single dominant manufacturer of bicycles and sporting goods, with plants in Toronto and St. Jean, Quebec, and exports worldwide.[4]

Bicycles

CCM produced good quality, reasonably priced bicycles and related products such as children's tricycles and wagons and, later, exercise cycles. As the most completely integrated bicycle manufacturer in Canada, CCM made all components except tires, handlegrips, and leather seats. The company soon gained a reputation at home and abroad for a solid product sold by a large independent dealer network that provided excellent market coverage and customer service.

---

[4] *The Globe and Mail*, Monday, February 28, 1983, p. B4.

CCM's success in bicycles began to fade in the early 1950s. Competition from low-priced imports increased. As sales, margins, and cash flow suffered, expenditures for retooling and modernizing the old Toronto plant were slashed. Labour relations deteriorated. However, in the long run, it was a poor marketing strategy and departure from the company's well-established culture that were most detrimental to CCM. For years the company's operating philosophy had been summarized as follows: "We believe that quality comes before price, that the dealer is entitled to a fair profit, and that prices should be maintained."

Departing from this policy during the 1970s, CCM sold increasingly to major department stores at volume discount prices that didn't fully cover overhead. This upset independent dealers who found themselves at a disadvantage to volume retailers who were able to buy and sell for less. Gradually the dealership network eroded until CCM found itself largely dependent on a few major outlets. When the bicycle boom faded, the majors no longer sold large volumes of bicycles. Since CCM had allowed many of its relationships with independent, specialty retailers to lapse, severe distribution problems accelerated the company's decline.

From 1979 to 1982 sales from the cycle division had increased from $33 million to $35 million. However, with concurrent double-digit inflation, unit sales declined. Although the cycle division contributed over 55 percent of sales from 1979 to 1981, its gross margins declined from 51 percent to 46 percent of total gross margin.

Skate and Hockey Equipment

CCM's other major products were skates, hockey sticks, and equipment. These operations were begun in 1905 to even out the seasonal sales and production of bicycles. Originally CCM manufactured high-quality blades and riveted them to the best available boots purchased from George Tackaberry of Brandon, Manitoba, to make the top skates used by virtually all professional and high-level amateur hockey players. Later, to fill out the line, it purchased lower-quality boots from two small shoe companies in Quebec and its hockey equipment from other manufacturers. By 1967 all winter goods were manufactured by the company in what was then a large, modern, efficient plant in St. Jean, Quebec.

Through industry-leading research and development and product innovation, CCM became the world's premier hockey skate manufacturer. For years, many people in Europe equated Canada with hockey and hockey with CCM.

Ownership

Up to 1960, CCM was part of Russell Industries, a publicly held company. For decades a solid, old-fashioned management team, under authoritative leadership, was unified in its belief in quality and service.

In 1961 Levy Industries Ltd., an auto parts firm, bought Russell Industries.

As new owners, the Levy brothers became actively involved in the business. According to widely circulated industry reports, immediate profitability dominated thinking, and underlying problems were given little attention. Historical concern for quality, service, dealers, customers, and employees was displaced by management fire fighting. Several experienced managers left the company. Serious labour trouble ensued. As a result of its tough leadership and management's weakness, the militant United Auto Workers union demanded and got higher wages and benefits.

A past top manager of CCM commented:

> The Levys acquired the company from wealth accumulated in buying and selling used automobile parts, where they were masters. But when it came to owning and running a manufacturing company, they were catastrophic. They didn't understand anything about analysing basic problems and coming up with long-term solutions. They couldn't keep their fingers off anything, and everything they touched turned into a disaster. Customer service, dealer support, and employee relations suffered particularly.

In 1968 the Levys sold to Seaway Multicorp, a company reorganized by Norton Cooper, described as a "36-year-old Canadian boy wonder who, in about a year, built a conglomerate empire with sales of $100 million after making a fortune in the stock market several years ago." With his gains he purchased controlling interest in Seaway Hotels, a chain of unprofitable hotels. Through this vehicle he was able to raise $29 million to purchase control of Levy Industries. Within a year Norton Cooper had diversified into areas such as wood products, auto and industrial equipment, aircraft parts, food processing, sports products, and bicycles. The internal struggles that developed between Cooper and the Levys were said to be disastrous for CCM.

In 1978 Seaway sold CCM to Maxwell Cummings and Sons Holdings Ltd., a Montreal automobile dealer. The Levys, who had retained ownership of the real estate, charged Cummings excessive rents which increased yearly. Under Cummings ownership, CCM continued to decline.

Performance

Company performance from 1976 to 1981 showed the results of the mismanagement since its first takeover in 1961. Industry observers reported that the company would have failed without a pre-election federal government bail-out loan to save 700 jobs. Despite sales growth from 1978 to 1981, the only profitable year was 1980 when earnings were $1.1 million on sales of $60 million. Sales in 1982 were expected to decline, and CCM expected to lose $4.3 million, due partly to a long summer strike at the bicycle plant in Weston.

The company's financial position, as at September 30, 1982, was summarized by the interim receiver as follows:

> CCM owes two secured creditors $33 million—the Royal Bank, $28 million, and the

Enterprise Development Board, $5 million—while the liquidation value of the company is $11.6 million less than its total debts of $41 million.

Preferred creditors are owed $1.2 million, and product liability claims amount to almost $13 million—$12 million of which rests on the resolution of a New York civil suit lodged by a hockey player who suffered an injury while wearing a CCM helmet.

The CCM financial statements available to Cooper are presented in Exhibits 6 to 9.

Marketing

While CCM's world-class strength was in leather skates, it also produced and sold hockey equipment and sticks. Like other leading skate manufacturers, CCM concentrated heavily on supplying skates to professional players because they were the trendsetters. Three special "pro detail men" were employed to sell and service these players who were often given custom-fitted skates free of charge.

Up to the mid-70s, when it began to slide, CCM's share of the Canadian and worldwide hockey skate markets had been approximately 60 percent, 30 percent, and 20 percent of the high-, medium-, and low-priced markets, respectively. Because of its domination of the top end of the market, "Super Tack," its long-established premium brand name, was better known around the world than CCM. It concentrated on sewn leather boots but produced some moulded skates. Although the largest contributor to fixed costs, skate sales declined from 68 percent of winter goods sales in 1980 to 58 percent in 1982. At the same time, protective equipment sales roughly doubled from 14 percent to 26 percent, with gross margins of 24 percent. Total gross margin as a percent of sales decreased from 27.8 percent in 1980 to 26.6 percent in 1982.

Distribution

From 1945 to 1982, CCM's dealer network had shrunk form 2,500 to 1,500 and its sales force from 21 to 12. All sold the total CCM line but spent most of their time on winter goods. Up to 1970 the salesmen had been paid salary plus car and expenses and had been encouraged to service the dealer and customers. However, by 1982 industry sources reported that the salesmen were strictly on a commission basis and, pressured to get orders through as many dealers as possible, spent little time on service.

Although CCM's reputation for service was slipping, its reputation for quality had been maintained fairly well. A quick survey of a few present or past CCM dealers, in November 1982, indicated that approximately one third said they would never carry CCM again; one third would consider carrying CCM again if they could be assured of delivery and service; and one third would stick with CCM through thick and thin because they were enthusiastic about the product and the name.

Exhibit 6

CCM
Consolidated Balance Sheet
At September 30
(in thousands)

	Forecast 1982	1981	1980	1979	1978
Assets					
Current assets:					
Cash		$ 30	$ 46	$ 130	$ 1,259
Accounts receivable	$ 17,290	18,355	17,364	15,179	11,081
Inventories:					
Raw materials		8,281	9,087	8,046	4,933
Work in process		2,371	1,942	1,412	1,349
Finished goods		11,814	10,105	7,681	6,967
Total inventories	17,536	22,466	21,134	17,140	13,249
Prepaid expenses		276	173	172	278
Total current assets	34,826	41,127	38,719	32,621	25,867
Fixed assets:					
Building		2,277	2,128	2,152	2,136
Machinery and equipment*		4,866	4,208	3,500	2,916
Total fixed assets at cost		7,143	6,337	5,652	5,052
Accumulated depreciation		(3,868)	(2,983)	(2,322)	(1,675)
Total fixed assets	2,887	3,275	3,354	3,330	3,377
Deferred charges		258	82	135	284
Goodwill	2,760	2,220	2,280	2,340	—
Total long-term assets	5,647	5,753	5,715	5,805	3,661
Total assets	$ 40,473	$46,880	$44,434	$38,426	$29,528
Liabilities					
Current liabilities:					
Bank	$ 22,402	$19,934	$16,164	$12,955	$ 8,602
Accounts payable and accrued liabilities	5,678	10,572	9,511	7,383	3,586
Long-term debt—due current year		423	422	993	985
Total current liabilities	28,080	30,929	26,097	21,331	13,173
Long-term debt	14,967	15,379	15,782	16,328	17,317
Deferred gain		52	262	471	681
Total liabilities	43,047	46,360	42,141	38,131	31,171
Shareholders' Equity					
Capital stock		4,800	4,800	3,800	1,400
Contributed surplus		5,000	5,000	5,000	5,000
Deficit		(9,280)	(7,505)	(8,505)	(8,043)
Shareholder equity (deficit)	(2,574)	520	2,295	295	(1,643)
Total liabilities and shareholders' equity	$ 40,473	$46,880	$44,434	$38,426	$29,528

* Does not include land, manufacturing, and warehousing space and machinery and equipment for which rent was to be $839,000 (1982) and $859,000 (1983). Most land and buildings owned by the Levys.

Source: 1978–1981 auditor reports. 1982 estimates by CCM management.

Exhibit 7

CCM
Consolidated Statement of Earnings
At September 30
(in thousands)

	Estimate 1982	1981	Percent	1980	Percent	1979	Percent	1978	Percent
Net sales	$59,622	$60,979	100.0%	$57,922	100.0%	$47,805	100.0%	$25,194	100.0%
Cost of sales		47,540		43,505		36,483		23,044	
Gross margin		13,439	22.0	14,417	24.9	11,322	23.7	2,150	8.5
Expenses:									
Selling and administration		8,810	14.4	8,250	14.2	7,947	16.6	5,266	20.9
Interest:									
Long-term debt		1,881		1,774		2,026		713	
Other interest		3,733		2,581		1,240		987	
Total interest cost		5,614	9.2	4,355	7.5	3,266	6.8	1,700	6.7
Depreciation of fixed assets		891	1.5	724	1.3	652	1.4	311	1.2
Amortization of deferred charges		49		63		69		373	
Amortization of goodwill		60		60		60			
Amortization of deferred gain		(210)		(210)		(210)		(64)	
Total selling and administration and other		15,214	24.9	13,243	22.9	11,785	24.7	7,587	30.1
Operating earnings (loss)	(4,300)	(1,775)	(2.9)	1,174	2.0	(462)	(1.0)	(5,437)	(21.6)
Provision for income taxes		—		527		—		—	
Earnings (loss) before extraordinary item		(1,775)		647		(462)		(5,437)	
Extraordinary item		—		—		—		3,882	
Income tax reduction (loss carry forward)				527					
Net profit (loss)		$ (1,775)	(2.9)	$ 1,174	2.0	$ (462)	(1.0)	$ (1,555)	(6.2)

Source: Statements for 1978–1981, auditor reports. Estimate for 1982 calculated by CCM management.

Exhibit 8

CCM
Winter Goods Operations
(in thousands)

| | Actual Year Ended | | | | | | Projected Year Ending | |
	September 30, 1980	Percent	September 30, 1981	Percent	September 30, 1982	Percent	December 31, 1983	Percent
Sales:								
Skates	$17,148		$16,530		$14,304		$16,500	
Sticks	1,413		2,307		1,445		2,000	
Helmets	1,774		1,814		1,714		2,000	
Protective	3,681		5,047		6,455		6,000	
Sundries	1,250		838		787		1,000	
	25,266		26,536		24,705		27,500	
Gross margins:								
Skates	5,985	35.0%	5,604	34.0%	4,577	32.0%	5,940	36.0%
Sticks	(230)	(16.3)	(30)	(1.3)	(267)	(18.5)	—	—
Helmets	415	23.4	424	23.4	492	28.7	600	30.0
Protective	482	13.1	934	18.5	1,556	24.1	1,350	22.5
Sundries	381	30.5	262	31.3	215	27.3	300	30.0
	7,033	27.8%	7,194	27.1%	6,573	26.6%	8,190	29.8%
Expenses:								
Selling			(Not available)				1,291	
Administration							661	
Warehouse and distribution							1,086	
Financial							618	
							3,656	
Net before income taxes							$ 4,534	

Source: 1980–1982 from audited financial statements. 1983 projections estimated by CCM management.

Exhibit 9: Summary of CCM Winter Goods Assets (At Cost) October 29, 1982 (dollars in thousands)

Inventories:			
Finished goods:			
Skates	$1,861		
Sticks	407		
Helmets	264		
Protective	1,476		
Sundries	349		
		$ 4,357	
Raw material:			
Skates	1,264		
Protective	798		
Blades	1,604		
		3,666	
Work in process:			
Skates	216		
Sticks	250		
Protective	234		
Blades	25		
		725	
		8,748	
Fixed assets:			
St. Jean	1,200		
Hudson	70		
Nylite	867		
		2,137	
		$10,885	

Source: CCM management estimates.

CCM leased a 10,000-square-foot warehouse in Hudson, New Hampshire, which carried an average of $1.5 million in finished goods inventory and was responsible for U.S. sales of approximately $6 to $7 million in 1982.

Of the 16 people employed, 5 were salesmen who carried only the CCM line and received 3½ percent commission, a very low rate for the industry. The lease expired in December 1986. European sales of approximately $3.2 million in 1982 were generated through distributors only, as CCM had no permanent salesmen in Europe.

Manufacturing

Early in November Henry Nolting, president, and Jerry Harder, vice president, manufacturing, of Cooper Canada Ltd. visited CCM's winter goods plant in St. Jean. Following are excerpts from their reports on the visit:

To: John Cooper

From: Henry Nolting

Date: November 26, 1982

The facility is divided into three parts: (1) woodworking, (2) protective equipment manufacturing, and (3) skate manufacturing.

The woodworking facility is not modern, looks somewhat like ours as far as equipment and machinery are concerned, and it is not surprising that they do not turn a profit in that part of their operation.

The protective equipment manufacturing has nothing in it which we do not know, there is nothing innovative being done, and as far as I am concerned, it is worth very little.

Raw material storage is all computerized with regard to quantities and location of materials. It works, and they have no major problems in this area.

Not very much raw material on hand, and based on their manufacturing activity level, that is not surprising. They have been running down all inventories for several years.

The existing machine shop is old and dirty, and there is nothing in it which I would like to buy. They have, at present, approximately 100 people working, but cleaning up work in process. The people are very slow; they seem to be puzzled, unenthusiastic, and listless.

There seems to be a lot of old stock in the finished goods warehouse.

I saw SG40 shinguards which, as far as construction is concerned, looked better than ours.

The skate manufacturing operation seems reasonable despite the fact that there are no great innovations. The bootmaking part is something which is easily transferable to our location. Jerry feels he would like to have it and can run it. The whole layout seems relatively simple but modern enough and efficient. The equipment is not new but in good repair.

Boot manufacturing: The cement lasting operations seem very efficient indeed. Fancy stitching done with patterns marked properly on the fabric before the machine starts stitching. Very well done. Super Tacks, custom Tacks, all mixed up in the same production line. It doesn't seem good to me. All people on piece work.

There are approximately 40 sewing and related machines in the bootmaking operation. The layout is simple and efficient.

There are "no smoking" signs in the factory and warehouse, and everybody smokes.

The finished goods warehouse has a big stock of Propacs (copies of Cooperall)!

Only one shipping dock is being used. The other two are piled high with skids— no activity.

All raw materials are issued in the precise quantities required to complete orders. This is extremely well done.

The R&D department has two employees. They have had tremendous problems with their Propacs and are constantly trying to improve the product. They are working very closely with the Quebec Nordiques in perfecting this product. They have never done any helmet-related work at that facility.

The roof in the stick-making facility is leaking, and that part of their plant is badly maintained.

CCM helmets are produced by Disco Injection Moulding Company, which is a division of Magna, the automotive people. CCM owns the tooling but have no contract with Disco. The transactions are on a purchase order basis. They receive the helmets fully packaged and packed. They also obtain moulded skates from Disco.

The CCM design people are working on a new helmet mould; cost of the tool, $82,000, of which they have paid $27,000 so far.

They expect to have the mould producing shells by the end of March, and there has been no disruption in finishing the tooling. They are also working on two versions of face guards for the new helmets.

An injection moulder in St. Jean, Quebec, owns the moulds for the plastic parts which are being consumed in their operations since CCM did not want to lay out the capital. The moulder is charging an appropriate amount on the parts so that he gets paid for the tooling that way.

The Nylite Company, a wholly owned subsidiary of CCM, owns the moulds for the skates.

We think their sporting goods division lost approximately half a million dollars each year in 1980 and 1981, sharing equally in the total company loss of $4.3 million at end of September 1982!

Eighty percent of all their hockey gloves are now coming from the Far East.

They have an outmoded IBM 370 computer in operation to which are hooked the terminals from their Canadian offices and from the United States.

The offices are in terrible condition. They are old and in an unbelievable mess.

The president's assessment of the situation is that somebody will buy the assets, and he feels that they might go for book value. His opinion is that nobody could pick it up for less.

To: Henry Nolting

From: Jerry Harder

Date: November 28, 1982

My observations of the manufacturing operation:

The cutting room offered no new or different ideas—the equipment is standard and tends to be old. The cutting operation contains the leather sole prep machinery needed for the skate line. This equipment looked adequate and in fairly good repair. Stick operation: there is little here and nothing new. We could use some of the equipment to augment ours in Hespeler, especially some bending equipment for the Pro Shop. This operation is well behind Hespeler in methods and quality and, I suspect, in quantity.

The skate sewing line has good basic shoemaking equipment. It appeared adequate and properly maintained. While this machinery is different from ours, it is needed to produce footwear and does not involve any major different skills or mechanics required by our operators.

The major lasting machines are leased from United Shoe Machinery, which is normal in this trade. They do own some machinery on these lines which tended to be old. However, the machines apparently work. They say they have 3,000 plus pairs of lasts (many are specials for individual players) at about $25 per pair. The lasts I saw were in very good repair.

The machine shop was well equipped—much more than ours. We could use some of this machinery.

The skatemaking is a basic flat-lasting, thermo-cement operation with which I am very familiar. It is the most common shoemaking procedure where a separate unit sole is applied. I saw no secrets or tricks in skatemaking, and I had thought there would be. There are just normal shoemaking skills required, and we would only need to have an experienced lasting room foreman to carry on.

I was told that the lasting line was designed for 2,400 pair per day. They have made 1,800 pair a day on it. Specials or factory orders are 5 percent of their production.

Most people are on incentive—even some of the indirect employees such as conveyor operators and material movers. The lasting lines are on a group incentive paid by line output. This is good. Labour rates are set at a levelled 100 percent but are guaranteed at 125 percent efficiency. However, the general manager told me that the rates are loose on purpose, and most earn 140 percent or more. He said it was difficult to keep people at 125 percent of their base. This is a classic case of lying to yourself on your costing and variable overhead system.

Not counting raw material storage, I think we would need at least 25,000 square feet, which excludes cutting, to accommodate the skatemaking operation. This is equal to 42 of our present 600-square-foot bays. To give you another perspective, this area would be slightly larger than the whole area now devoted to apparel. Because of the size, we would have to do major relocations of our existing floors. Also, we must be careful of the existing electrical supplies—I would make a cautious estimate of a $25,000 rewiring charge.

Organization

As a result of natural attrition and dim prospects, the CCM organization had been shrunk to skeleton status. While it was reportedly limping along, many of the best and most experienced managers had either retired or moved on to better opportunities.

Competitors

There were many manufacturers of hockey equipment, helmets, skates, and sticks in Canada. Some were Canadian owned, others were foreign owned with manufacturing facilities in Canada, while others were foreign owned with only a marketing organization in Canada. Not all of the companies produced and/or marketed a full line of hockey equipment but chose to specialize in two or three product lines. Several of the Canadian companies were small and privately owned, especially those which produced hockey sticks and skates.

In considering which companies were in a good position to purchase CCM, financial strength and management capability were important. Of the many competitors, the following eight were logical contenders:

(1) Canadian Hockey Industries. Canadian Hockey Industries was a small company that made high-quality hockey sticks. Its use of fibreglass technology and other materials such as graphite, plastics, laminates, and aluminum had resulted in producing the most unique stick line in the market. It also marketed a full line of hockey equipment, including a helmet, but no skates or apparel.

Located in Drummondville, Quebec, it had sales of $10 million in 1981, which had been growing rapidly for the past five years. In the factory it employed approximately 120 workers. It was owned by AMER industries, a Finnish company which also owned Koho.

(2) Koho.   Owned by AMER industries of Finland, Koho shared marketing, distribution, and some hockey stick manufacturing with Canadian Hockey Industries. It was thought to be the largest hockey stick manufacturer in the world. It also manufactured and marketed hockey equipment and helmets but no skates or apparel.

Koho had sales of approximately $14 million from about 800 or 900 dealers serviced by six or seven commission agents who primarily sold Koho and Canadian. Major accounts included large department stores such as Eatons, Simpsons, and Sears, sporting goods chains such as Collegiate Sports, and other stores such as Canadian Tire.

Sticks were manufactured in the Canadian plant in Quebec; sticks and some hockey equipment were manufactured in Finland, and some hockey equipment was purchased in the Orient.

Its organization in Canada was headed by a sales manager who reported to a president for North America. The United States also had a sales manager who reported to the North American president. This president reported to the head office of AMER, a very large and profitable corporation that was involved with shipbuilding, steel, food, and tobacco.

(3) Jofa.   Jofa was a Volvo-owned company that manufactured and marketed hockey equipment, hockey sticks, and skates but not apparel. It had one factory in Sherbrooke, Quebec, and others in Sweden. The rest of its products were purchased in the Orient.

Sales of $10 million were achieved through 700 to 800 dealers and approximately seven commissioned sales agents. Major accounts included large department stores and sporting goods stores and Canadian Tire.

The organization of the company was thin, with one director of marketing responsible for all of North America. Supporting him were a sales manager and a small number of commissioned sales agents.

(4) Sherwood-Drolet.   This Quebec company, Canadian owned until 1969, was 80 percent owned by an American firm, ATO Inc. ATO was the world's largest integrated producer of fire protection equipment and also owned Rawlings and Adirondack sporting goods in the United States.

Sherwood, a producer of high-quality hockey sticks, had been an industry leader in sales and in the introduction of new materials and production processes. It had one of the most automated plants in the industry, enabling it to produce large volumes of sticks of consistent quality. In 1981 its share of the Canadian market was 25 percent.

Sales of approximately $15 million came from approximately 600 dealers. The company's direct sales were aided by 10 sales agents who sold to 300 dealers.

(5)   Hillerich and Bradsby.   With head office and manufacturing facility located in Wallaceburg, Ontario, it was a wholly owned subsidiary of H & B, Louisville, Kentucky, the world's top baseball bat manufacturer. Besides producing the Louisville hockey stick and being a market leader in brightly coloured goalie sticks, it was making aggressive inroads into the baseball glove and accessory markets. It had also earned a good name for itself in manufacturing golf clubs that were sold primarily through club professionals. The plant employed 62 people.

Sales in 1981 were about $6 million. H & B's distribution system included warehouses in Richmond, British Columbia; Dorval, Quebec; Winnipeg, Manitoba; and Concord, Ontario. The sales were achieved primarily through commissioned sales agents to approximately 400 dealers. Management was reportedly very strong.

(6)   Warrington Industries (Bauer, Micron, and Lange).   Bauer had been in the skate business for many years and was CCM's major competitor. This Canadian-owned company was located in Kitchener, Ontario, and produced only skates and shoes. It employed 400 in the skate business and 150 in the shoe business.

Sales of approximately $30 million were generated by 12 to 15 agents through a dealership of 1,200 stores. Warrington was in turn owned by Cemp Investments, a firm representing the interest of the Bronfman family that was involved in Seagram.

(7)   Sport Maska.   A high-quality hockey jersey and good distribution system resulted in Maska hockey jerseys being exclusive suppliers to the NHL and worn by 42 percent of Canadian hockey players. Besides hockey jerseys and apparel, its business consisted of spring and summer ball uniforms and apparel, soccer jerseys, and leisure wear. The plant in St. Hyacinthe, Quebec, employed approximately 175 people.

Sales in Canada were achieved by approximately nine commissioned agents through 1,200 to 1,500 dealers across Canada. The agents did not carry Maska exclusively. Its distribution was coast to coast across the United States through the use of commission agents. Recently, Maska had purchased Sandow, another Canadian athletic apparel company, and had consolidated the manufacturing into its own plant.

Sport Maska was a private company that appeared to be profitable and have a strong equity base. Industry sources felt that the management team, directed by President Denny Coter, was strong and had good depth.

(8)   Irwin Toy Company.   Another possible buyer could have been a summer goods company that saw the winter goods division of CCM as a way to even out sales and production. If such a company purchased CCM, it might be able to build CCM's market share through improved distribution and better service. However, the positions of the competitors would remain relatively stable, at least in the short term. Although Cooper managers did not feel that there were any summer goods manufacturers who were in a good position to make a serious bid, they had heard that Irwin Toy Company, the Canadian marketer for Rawlings, was interested in CCM. The Rawlings product lines carried by Irwin were primarily baseball and football equipment and apparel. This large company had sufficient financial strength to purchase CCM. Its product lines included toys, electronic equipment, home leisure specialties, and sporting goods and apparel. It had two manufacturing facilities; however, the manufacturing was very simple, with very little research and development required.

Irwin's top strengths were in marketing and distributing consumer goods, skills which were much needed in CCM. However, Irwin's established distribution system was in summer goods, and different contacts would be necessary for winter goods.

In reviewing this list of possible bidders for CCM, John Cooper felt that the strongest competitive threats would be Warrington's and Sport Maska. Both companies had strong management teams, well-established distribution systems, and adequate financial strength. In addition, both companies were Canadian owned and would not face possible delay and veto of their offer by the Foreign Investment Review Agency. Immediate decisions and action were essential if Cooper wanted to acquire CCM. Two questions puzzled John Cooper: If we don't buy CCM, who will? How will it affect our business?

Dafoe and Dafoe, Inc. (A)

On September 12, 1984, Ken Dafoe, president of Dafoe and Dafoe, Inc., a Canadian-owned manufacturer of various consumer products, was visiting his California plant when he received the following message from Henkel Corporation, a large German chemical corporation:

> We need a decision from you in one week. We will sell our factory in France for one franc plus the existing stocks of raw materials and finished goods for cash. There are now only 25 people in the factory. Contact Mr. Jacobi by the 19th.

Ken Dafoe's initial reaction to the message was that the offer from Henkel to sell Cypris (pronounced "Sepree"), a manufacturing company in France, sounded like a marvelous deal, but he wondered about the sudden change in terms of the proposal. Earlier in the year Henkel wanted $1.5 million (U.S.) for Cypris, and after thinking about it for a couple of months, Ken decided he was not interested. Now, however, one franc was tempting.

Ken Dafoe's Background

Ken Dafoe was born and raised in Hamilton, Ontario. He attended Michigan State University on a track scholarship. As he put it:

> The scholarship was my only chance at a formal education. My parents couldn't afford to send me, and I couldn't afford to send myself.

In his second year at Michigan State, he married his high-school sweetheart, Heather. He graduated with a bachelor of arts degree in Business Administration in 1958.

After graduation he sold insurance for a few months. He then worked as a salesman for Procter & Gamble in London, Ontario, for about a year. Ken recalled moving his sales territory from 21st to 2nd place in sales volume. He left the company when they wouldn't give him the promotion he requested.

His next job proved to have a particularly significant impact on Ken as a manager. In 1960 he accepted a sales manager position with Johnson & Johnson of New Brunswick, New Jersey, and was sent to the Caribbean. He travelled the islands for several years and was then put in charge of a new plant in Trinidad that manufactured sanitary napkins. He had heard stories about how lazy the people

This case was prepared by Mark C. Baetz with Paul W. Beamish, Wilfrid Laurier University. Copyright © 1986 by Wilfrid Laurier University.

there were, how they would not work for a "white man," and all the trouble he would encounter running the Trinidad plant. Ken encountered no difficulties. He attributed this to treating his workers with respect. He said:

> I don't care what colour people are. As long as you treat them with respect and show them why something has to be done, they will respond. I worked right along side them. When they saw me climbing over bales of paper, they figured if I was willing to work and I was the boss, they certainly could work hard as well.

Ken was determined to make the plant a success. He wanted his workers to show the head office in New Jersey that they could be profitable right from the start. The workers volunteered to work Saturdays for no pay during the initial start-up to make the plant profitable. In the first year the plant showed a minimal $1,000 deficit.

Trinidad was where Ken acquired certain philosophies about how to manage and motivate people. It was also where he learned about putting a sanitary napkin plant together from scratch. Ken attributed some of his success in Trinidad to his boss. He explained as follows:

> My boss at Johnson & Johnson only saw me twice a year. This gave me the independence to use my common sense in starting up and managing the new plant. I like to use the same philosophy with the start-up and ongoing management of my various plants. I like to give my plant managers the same sort of independence I had at Johnson & Johnson.

In 1966 Ken was transferred to Jamaica. He spent four years there. When civil strife broke out in 1970, Ken asked to be transferred. He was sent to Mexico, which was another place where Ken was supposed to find himself a social outcast. Apparently no Johnson & Johnson manager had ever been able to break into the Mexican social scene, but Ken claimed he had no difficulties with the Mexican people. The Dafoes were always invited to parties. At these parties the Dafoes were the only ones who could not speak Spanish. Their effort to communicate was appreciated, and they were able to transcend the language barrier.

By this time Ken had two children, and Heather wanted them educated in Canada. Ken could not get Johnson & Johnson to transfer him, so he resigned. He found a job as a general manager of the Texpack plant in Brantford, Ontario. Texpack, later called McGaw Manufacturing, was a division of American Hospital Supply Corporation of Chicago. Six weeks after Ken joined Texpack, the employees went on strike. The strike turned out to be one of the most bitter in Brantford's history, and Ken Dafoe was in the centre of it.

Ken loathed the way the union "used" its people, and as a result, he was determined to break the strike. After 96 days, head office gave in. Ken commented on the situation:

> It broke my heart. We were winning. I have nothing against unions and fair negotiations, but when the union turns a bunch of people into an angry mob then uses

them for its own purpose, I'll fight back. I'm a fighter! If I think you're playing unfair or trying to use me, I'll fight you 'til the end.

Ken left Texpack in 1973 to become vice president and general manager of Stearns & Foster Canada Limited, a Cincinnati-based company with plants in Brantford, Toronto, and Montreal. The company manufactured material used in sanitary napkins and disposable diapers.

Company Origins and History

At Stearns & Foster, Ken sensed that an opportunity existed in the Canadian sanitary napkin market. At the time, private label and generic products were becoming more and more prevalent in the consumer goods industry, but no one in Canada was manufacturing sanitary napkins for that market. In 1975 Ken Dafoe decided to exploit the market opportunity, and he set up a company called Safex Ltd., to be run by his wife. He located the company in 10,000 square feet of leased space in Brantford and soon began manufacturing sanitary napkins. The original financing of $250,000 for Safex came from the bank, a mortgage on the Dafoe house, a $138,000 loan from the Federal Business Development Bank (FBDB), and $2,000 in equity financing from FBDB. (On December 23, 1977, FBDB sold its equity interest back to the company for $40,000.) Later financing came from the Ontario Development Corporation ($1 million: half in the form of a five-year interest-free loan and half as a bank guarantee) and venture capital of $300,000 from International Nickel Company (Inco) which became major shareholders. Ken described the episode with Inco as follows:

> Inco hired Venture Founders of Boston for a handsome fee to find entrepreneurs with sound ideas. After Venture Founders located what they considered to be suitable entrepreneurs, they would recommend them to Inco who in turn would put up seed money to get these entrepreneurs off the ground in return for a minority interest.
>
> After we had been rejected by five more-traditional venture capital firms, I wrote to Venture Founders in Boston, and they did not reply to my letter. When I called them, they said that they were not interested in sanitary napkins. I kept talking on the phone long enough to get a personal interview the next day in Toronto. In this interview, they told me they had received 600 applications and were picking 25 for their weekend seminars. They said that I would probably not get into the seminar but that they would try and see if it was possible.
>
> Before I arrived back home back home in Brantford, they phoned to say I had been accepted. After attending these weekend seminars, Heather and I travelled to Boston and put on a 4½ hour presentation to seven members of the Venture Founders firm. At this presentation, I was told that while I might be successful in Canada, I would have a tougher time convincing U.S. chains to jump into private label sanitary napkins. I got mad with them and told them they were crazy; the day before I'd signed up K mart in the United States to sell our products! They were convinced and agreed to recommend that Inco provide us with some capital. After that, Venture Founders used us as an example of the kind of firm they can find for those with venture capital!

The original two employees in Safex were Heather Dafoe and Don Brennan. Ken Dafoe worked in the company part-time, planning to join full-time once business reached a certain level. Before this level was reached, Stearns & Foster fired him in 1976 for conflict of interest. Ken commented: "I got caught six months early."

In May 1978 Safex was renamed Dafoe and Dafoe, Inc. (hereafter D & D), and the plant space was increased to 20,000 square feet at the same location. By this time the company was manufacturing sanitary napkins, tampons, and diapers. In September 1979 the company purchased and moved to a modern 87,000-square-foot plant on the outskirts of Brantford. Several acres of land were purchased with the plant which allowed for possible future expansion.

In December 1979 in a joint venture with one of its suppliers, the company opened a plant in Milton Keynes, England, in 11,000 square feet of leased space. The plant employed 24 people.

Within two years D & D opened three new plants in the United States as wholly owned subsidiaries. In April 1980 a 40,000-square-foot plant of leased space was opened in Atlanta, Georgia, with 56 people. In September 1981 a 42,000-square-foot plant of leased space with 31 employees was opened in San Diego, California. In July 1982 a 71,000-square-foot plant of leased space with 56 employees was opened in Philadelphia, Pennsylvania.

Once the Pennsylvania plant was fully operational, the company had enough productive capacity to support approximately $80 million in sales. The company had a total of 19 sanitary napkin machines, 11 cotton swab machines, 5 diaper machines, and 1 tampon machine in a total of 5 plants in 3 countries.

In mid-1984 D & D signed a lease to expand its plant in the United Kingdom to 40,000 square feet, effective November 1, 1984.

Corporate Objectives

Ken Dafoe described the objectives for D & D as follows:

> One of our objectives is to be the best company in Brantford for people to work for. Johnson Wax (S. C. Johnson & Son Ltd.) has the best name now, and I told them I'm after them.
>
> Another objective is to have a $100 million company by 1985. If all goes as planned, 1990 sales should be $248 million. In fact, I see no reason why we can't be a billion-dollar company!

In terms of his personal objectives, Ken Dafoe commented:

> Even though I have been approached a number of times to sell the business, I'm not interested in selling now. I want to keep my options open. I may go public, if all goes well, but Heather and I will still keep 51 percent of the business [see Exhibit 1 for current share ownership]. If I sold the company, I'd have a lot of money in the bank and I'd go nuts! You don't just work for the money; it's working for the sake of accomplishment. At the same time, I aim to hire people who want to work hard to get rich.

Exhibit 1:   Percentage Ownership of Dafoe and Dafoe, Inc., 1984

Kenneth F. Dafoe	34.001%
Heather M. Dafoe	32.999
Inco Ltd.	24.300
Venture Founders	2.700
Don Brennan	2.000
Stock options	4.000
	100.000%

Notes: 1. Inco had one seat on the company's six-person board of directors.
2. Venture Founders Corp. of Boston was a consulting firm which recommended that Inco invest in D & D. The consulting firm investigated several hundred businesses before recommending D & D. As a finder's fee, Venture Founders received 2.7 percent equity interest in D & D.

Another of my objectives is to run this company as though my employees are family. I want to know all their birthdays, anniversaries, and so forth. I want to make them feel proud to work here. I already have 11 people with a company car. Also I make sure my employees know what things cost, and I talk in percentages; otherwise they'll think I'm rich and take things for granted. I have acquired an airplane and a limousine. Not wanting to hide these acquisitions from my employees, I showed them off at a company party.

Marketing Strategy

D & D had to initially overcome four major problems in successfully marketing a private label sanitary napkin: (1) customer loyalty to two brands—Modess (made by Johnson & Johnson) and Kotex (made by Kimberly-Clark), (2) store buyer bias, that is, the buyers felt women would not change their brand loyalty, (3) lack of advertising, that is, D & D did not advertise since this would compete with the private label products; this lack of advertising meant the woman customer was unaware of D & D's product, (4) large company discount buying; Johnson & Johnson and Kimberly-Clark offered greater "package" discounts the larger the total purchase, and, therefore, any purchase from D & D would reduce the size of the "package" discounts received from these other firms.

Ken Dafoe and Jason Taggart, vice president of marketing, developed a strategy to overcome the above barriers. This strategy had the following components:

1. Forty percent lower price for similar quality product. (According to Ken Dafoe, D & D was able to offer the lower price because of more effective overhead utilization through increased volume, virtually no advertising, selling only to major chains, and taking lower profit margins from the name brand manufacturers.)

2. Unique packaging—a resealable flip-top box and four- and five-colour artwork.

3. Emphasis on the greater profit potential for the retailer of a private label program (the retailer could expect to receive a margin of 30 percent versus the 10 percent margin offered in comparable national brands).

4. Fast service, that is, one-week turnaround, so that one week after the order was placed, it was on its way to the customer.

With this strategy, D & D captured several major accounts, including Shoppers Drug Mart, Woolco, The Bay, and Sears. In the United States some of the firm's major accounts were Revco (1,560 drug stores) K mart (2,400 stores), and Kroger (1,750 stores). By 1984 no one customer accounted for more than 5 percent of total company sales. The company manufactured its products under 100 brand names including their own controlled brands.

Most of the company's dollar volume of sales came from sanitary napkins, which were sold to the consumer/retail segment of the market in Canada, the United States, and the United Kingdom from the plants in those countries, as well as being exported to Australia, the Caribbean, and Africa. D & D also competed in the Canadian industrial/institutional and hospital segments but on a smaller scale. The second largest component of company sales was diapers. Tampons and cotton swabs accounted for a very small percentage of company sales.

D & D Corporate Environment

It was estimated that the total North American market (including generics) for product categories in which D & D competed in 1980 was as follows (dollars in millions):

Sanitary napkins and tampons	$ 770
Disposable baby diapers	1,000
Adult diapers	25
Cotton swabs	15

As noted earlier, sanitary napkins represented by far the greatest single component of D & D sales, and, furthermore, Ken Dafoe expected this to remain the case in the future. For these reasons, the description of D & D's corporate environment will focus on the sanitary napkin industry.

The North American sanitary napkin market was dominated by Johnson & Johnson (J&J) and Kimberly-Clark (K-C). These two companies captured, respectively, about 50 percent and 30 percent of the market in 1984. Other competitors were Scott Paper and Playtex. The market had grown about 113 percent from 1970 to 1980, partly because of product improvements. In addition a ban on television and radio advertising was lifted in 1972. As a result most companies began major TV advertising campaigns which increased consumer awareness and encouraged greater use of the product. Both product innovation and advertising established brand loyalty.

None of the major companies were selling to generic or private label markets in 1984. Ken Dafoe explained why as follows:

> The multinational name brand companies can't sell generics or private label of the same quality or they will kill their own brand, and they can't compete on price.

Before 1975 some private labelling had been done by K-C and J&J which supplied such Canadian customers as Zellers and The Bay. However, these companies put private labels only on the irregular products which at the time were beginning to lose market share to the newer versions. Furthermore, these private label products were eventually phased out—they were merely cheaper versions of K-C's and J&J's name brands, they were no real bargain for the customer, and they were resented by the store because they were inferior.

In 1981, Ken Dafoe described the competitive threat in the sanitary napkin market as follows:

> Kimberly-Clark have said specifically that they were coming after us. They recently copied our packaging. This is the first I've ever heard of a major manufacturer stealing a packaging design from the little guy.

One of the most recent trends in the menstrual care industry was a shift away from tampons (internal protection) to feminine napkins (external protection). This shift occurred partly because of the popularity of the minipad, partly because increased absorbency permitted the need for fewer tampons, and partly because of a suspected link between tampon use and toxic shock syndrome, a rare but sometimes fatal illness primarily affecting young women during their menstrual period. A number of companies producing tampons removed their products from the market in 1980 because of the suspected link to toxic shock syndrome. Up to 1977 tampons had been capturing an ever-increasing percentage of the menstrual care market. In 1980 napkins had about 53 percent of this market, while tampons had 47 percent, up from 35 percent 10 years earlier. Not all companies competed in both the tampon and napkin markets. For example, Tampax and Procter & Gamble (P&G) produced only tampon products. After P&G had to remove its tampon product from the market because of a suspected link with toxic shock syndrome, the company indicated it would attempt to break into the napkin market with a new type of napkin.

Ken Dafoe summarized his company's approach to the sanitary napkin market as follows:

> I am not interested in being a leader in research and development in sanitary napkins. Let someone else spend the money. Besides, the feminine protection business is a growth business. Although it has changed dramatically over the past decade to more convenient and smaller products, our market will remain fairly steady. Our product is a needed product and could not be "outdated" overnight. Furthermore, from our travels around the world, we are sufficiently aware of market trends and developments to change with the market.

Production Strategy

D & D's production strategy embodied the following:

- D & D plants employed no more than 200 employees. In 1981 Ken Dafoe noted: "A company of 1,000 employees cannot run as efficiently as a company of 100 or 200. We are not running as efficiently now as we were when we only had 60 employees because people start taking the telephone and photocopying machine for granted . . . the bigger we get, the more the waste."
- All products in the D & D line were manufactured at world headquarters in Brantford (about 65 percent of Brantford production was shipped to the United States).
- All new products and their corresponding machines were first tested in Brantford before ordering new machines for other plants.
- D & D aimed to make plants as attractive as possible; Ken Dafoe noted: "The competition has schlocky plants. A clean plant impresses our customers. After all, we are in a sanitary business."
- D & D employed mainly females in the plants.
- All plants operated 24 hours per day, 5 days a week; preventative maintenance was supposed to be one shift per month per machine but did not occur this often.
- D & D paid higher-than-average wages and provided better-than-average fringe benefits.
- D & D used two suppliers for every raw material.

Despite its well-defined production policies, D & D had experienced some problems in the production area. From 1979 to 1981 Ken fired three plant managers in two different plants. There seemed to be many reasons for the firings —inability to get machines operating at capacity, not paying enough attention to quality control resulting in customer dissatisfaction, not getting to know the employees, little interest in learning about accounting. Ken seemed to sense a slight weakness in the production function of D & D when he commented as follows:

> I am not really a manufacturing person. One of the few people in the company who *has* manufacturing and engineering expertise is Don Brennan. When some of our equipment arrived eight months late from Sweden, Don completely assembled it and got it running in about one month. He also contributed immensely to the success of the company, and we could not have grown so quickly without him. However, I think we need to supplement his expertise by hiring some engineering graduates.

Instead of hiring engineering graduates, Ken and Heather decided to hire a number of young, inexperienced business graduates, and within a short period of time, these recent graduates were given various key assignments including the plant manager positions for the company's newly opened plants (see Exhibit 2 for a profile of the D & D management group in 1984). In general, Ken was quite

---

Exhibit 2: Profile of Dafoe and Dafoe Management Group, 1984

Name	Age	Present Position	Previous Position	Education/Full-Time Experience with Other Companies
Ken Dafoe	49	Chairman/CEO	President	B.A., Michigan State University. Salesman: Procter & Gamble; salesmanager: Johnson & Johnson; managing director: Johnson & Johnson; director of marketing: J & J Mexico; general manager: Texpack; vice president and general manager: Stearns & Foster.
Heather Dafoe	48	President	VP/GM	High School: Delta Secondary. Worked in one-girl office doing everything. Unable to work in West Indies or Mexico. Started own company when children started school.
Jason Taggart	39	Senior Vice President	VP/Marketing	B.A., Mount Allison University. Worked for Uniroyal in private label tires. Director of marketing at Victor Compometer in Cambridge, Ontario. Part owner of Hamilton-Taggart, making truck cabs for camping. Joined D & D when sales were below $1 million annually.
Jim Harrison	39	Corporate Quality Control Manager	General Manager Canada	Joined Dafoe and Dafoe, Inc. in 1983 as general manager of Canada. Harding Carpets: 14 years holding various positions in the plant and quality control areas. Prior to joining Dafoe was plant manager of the Brantford Harding plant.
Blair McEwen*	24	Plant Manager Pennsylvania	Product Manager Canada	Joined Dafoe immediately following graduation from University of Western Ontario (UWO) undergraduate business program in 1981. No full-time work experience, only various summer jobs during school.
Kevin McGraw*	24	General Manager California	Summer employment Dafoe	Joined Dafoe immediately following graduation from undergrad business program at UWO in 1981. Worked for Dafoe during summers and various school breaks. Immediately upon joining Dafoe full time was sent to start the company in California.
Eric Johnson*	24	General Manager Pennsylvania	Personnel Manager Dafoe Canada	Joined Dafoe following graduation from undergrad business program at UWO in 1981. Worked in various positions such as product manager, personnel manager, and sales coordinator in Canada prior to going to Pennsylvania.

Note: In addition to those above, there were also plant managers in each plant under the general managers. There were also salespeople both as reps., and sales managers.
* While at UWO, all three of these managers had worked together on a business policy field project to study Dafoe and Dafoe.

---

pleased with the performance of these new managers, and in turn these new managers were excited and enthusiastic about their jobs.

Strategy-Making Process and Corporate Organization

Ken was clearly the key figure in the strategy-making process of D & D. For example, Ken described how Atlanta was chosen as the location of the first U.S. plant for the company:

For several reasons, we had decided to manufacture in the United States. The market potential for generic and private label products seemed to be greater in the United States than in Canada. I knew we could not service many of the large and rapidly growing U.S. markets from our Brantford plant because of transportation costs and because we needed to give good service to build up our customer base. Inco carried out a study of population density and growth for us and told us that after the Eastern Seaboard, the U.S. Southeast was projected to be the fastest growing U.S market. The next issue was to choose a specific location. I had a lead on a site in Kentucky. The local government was going to give us some assistance. However, it took several plane connections and a long car ride to reach the potential plant site. I decided that Atlanta seemed far more suitable since it was easy to reach by plane, and was clearly the hub of the U.S. Southeast.

While Heather admitted that Ken typically made the final decisions on strategy for the company, she usually played the role of devil's advocate "to question the assumptions in Ken's dreams for the company." Ken commented on the management relationship with his wife in the following way:

We have our problems at times. I've made decisions, and she has changed them. She has made decisions, and I've changed them. But in general we work together. Nevertheless, our people know who to go to for whatever they want. Some of them will come to me for certain things, and some will go to Heather for things. Basically, Heather is the tough one. I'm the easy guy. If you want something, come to me.

The D & D corporate structure was quite informal. For example, Jason Taggart, the vice president of marketing, often called the shipper directly to see if an order had been shipped. Ken Dafoe sometimes spoke to one of the shift supervisors directly rather than going through the vice president of manufacturing. Further, Ken and Heather maintained an "open door" policy. They urged any employee to come directly to them for any problem they felt was not being resolved. Ken handled the external side of the business—marketing, arranging financing, finding suppliers, and so forth, and Heather handled the internal side of the business—production, accounting, and so on.

When new plants were established, Ken Dafoe and Jason Taggart usually did the initial selling themselves rather than give that job to the local vice president and general manager. All selling for D & D was done out of Brantford, but it was the responsibility of each plant manager to become acquainted with their local customers.

In terms of information and control systems, all plant managers prepared monthly production budgets and sent monthly cost and production output reports to headquarters in Brantford. Standard costs were established for each product group. These standard costs were used in pricing decisions. D & D monitored costs by comparing current and previous months' material costs as a percentage of sales. To facilitate financing with the banks, Ken Dafoe prepared monthly production budgets for each plant based on projected sales levels.

D & D's inventory control system consisted of perpetual inventory records which kept track of incoming and outgoing stock, whether it was new materials or finished goods. D & D had been experiencing out-of-stock situations in its Brantford plant that resulted in shutting down the line. These problems seemed to be a result of the fact that minimum-maximum stock levels and order quantities for new materials had not yet been adjusted for the increased production capacity at Brantford.

As part of its reward and punishment system, D & D rewarded various managers with company cars, bonuses, and stock options (for example, Don Brennan, vice president of engineering, had 2 percent ownership). Both factory and office workers were eligible for a share of D & D profits. In 1979 the profit-sharing plan paid each employee $1,000, and in 1980 the plan paid $1,500 for each employee. The company also added fringe benefits as they could afford them. Many of these benefits were given without the workers knowing about it until they were in effect. The company had no unions in any of its plants. When a union did try to organize the firm early in 1980, the employees voted against it.

In April 1981, 130 D & D employees gathered for a champagne luncheon at the Brantford Golf and Country Club. Ken promised the party to his employees when D & D reached $1 million in sales in one month, a milestone passed in March 1981. In addition to drinks and meals, the employees received an interim profit-sharing cheque for $750. Several also received gold pins under D & D's service award program.

In general, the D & D president, Ken Dafoe, was highly motivated, enthusiastic, energetic, and seemed to have captured both the loyalty and energy of other company managers. For example, his vice president of marketing, who once managed his own company, commented as follows:

> I didn't think I could work for someone else again, but Ken is different. He offers you the avenue to rise to your own potential. He is the keenest businessman I have ever worked for and does not hesitate to share his knowledge. He'll tell you anything you want to know if he is able.

Corporate Performance

At the end of October 1981, D & D received an Industrial Achievement Award from the Ontario government. This award was given to 10 Ontario businesses every year for superlative performance over a three-year period. More specifically, the award publicly recognized companies which created new jobs, increased production, improved sales, broke into new markets, increased exports, replaced imported goods, and showed technological or product innovation. A release from the Ministry of Industry and Tourism stated that from 1978 to 1980, D & D met all of these criteria.

For competitive reasons, Ken Dafoe did not want to be too specific about his sales and profit levels. He was willing to say the following in mid-1984:

> After a loss in the first year of our operations, we have had our ups and downs; one of our plants which had been experiencing losses is now showing a profit. There has

been quite a variation in the profits among the plants. Generally, the profits have been reasonable. In 1983, we turned the company around in terms of profits and expect a much larger profit in 1984 with a range of $1–$2 million net after tax. We have capacity now for just over $100 million in sales, and our actual sales this year will likely be about $50 million.

Cypris

Ken Dafoe was first told about the Cypris company in the fall of 1983. Ken was having lunch one day in Dusseldorf, West Germany, with Arno Jacobi, vice president marketing of Henkel Corp., a large chemical company manufacturing and retailing such products as soaps, hair dyes, and perfumes. Henkel had been supplying Dafoe and Dafoe with tampons for the U.K. market. Ken described the conversation with Jacobi that day:

> Jacobi told me that Henkel had bought a large cosmetics company in France. This company, given the name Henkel Bonetti, owned a small cotton manufacturer in France known as Cypris. According to Jacobi, the Cypris products did not fit into the strategy of Henkel, so they wanted to get rid of Cypris and wondered if I was interested. I said I am interested so send me more information on the company.

In March 1984 Jacobi sent a package of details about Cypris with the message that Henkel intended to close the Cypris deal as soon as possible. Ken reviewed the materials and summarized the pertinent details (see Exhibit 3).

Soon after receiving the information on Cypris, Ken went to France to tour the plant and was impressed on a number of counts. The plant was quite modern and well situated, given that 85 percent of the European market was located within 500 kilometres, and excellent transportation was nearby. Because the plant was located near the German border, many of the employees were of the work-oriented German background. Although the machinery in the plant was old, there had not been much technological change in the kinds of machines involved in the production process.

Arno Jacobi indicated to Ken Dafoe that the asking price for Cypris was $1.5 million (U.S.). After two months of thinking about it, Ken decided to write back to say he was not interested. He explained why as follows: "I did not want to put $1.5 million into France and I did not really have anyone in our management group who was fluent in French. Only two of our people had any experience with French: Eric Johnson, who grew up in Ottawa and spoke very little French, and Jason Taggart, who grew up in Montreal and could converse in French but was not actually fluent."

After receiving the negative response from Dafoe, Henkel continued to keep the issue of the Cypris plant on the agenda in all meetings with D & D. This was because there were two major problems facing Henkel if it could find no buyer and it simply shut down Cypris. First, Henkel Bonetti had been the recipient of extensive government assistance in France, and Henkel was concerned about a backlash if the plant was shut down. Second, French labour laws were quite

Exhibit 3:   Summary of Cypris Operations

(A)   *Sales and profitability, 1983 (millions francs—7FF = $1CDN):*

		Number of Machines
Cotton swabs	FF 10.5	5
Zigzag cotton*	10.0	2
Cosmetic pads/discs	6.3	4
Cotton balls	6.0	5
	FF 32.8	16

Volume rebates	4.6
Bonuses (salesmen)	3.5
Net sales	24.7
Freight/warehousing	2.5
Production cost (full costing)	17.2
Contribution to overhead and profit	5.0
Overhead	3.5
Profit before tax	1.5
Profit after tax	.8 × 10 price/earning ratio
	= 8.0 profitability value

* Zigzag cotton was either 100 or 200 grams of cotton folded in a zigzag or accordian style and either perforated or not. When perforated, a definite amount could be removed. Zigzag cotton was similar to one pound cotton sold in pharmacies in Canada and was used for medical reasons and for a variety of other uses including removing make-up and removing nail polish, etc.

(B)   *Book value of Cypris (as of December 31, 1983):*

	(millions francs)
1. Down payments and interest fees on leasing/purchase of land and buildings	FF 1.6
2. Capital investments as installations (air filter, and so forth)	3.1
3. Book value of production machines	3.1
Total	FF 7.8

(C)   *Other key facts:*

1. As of March 14, 1984, there was FF 4.1 (million) of finished goods and packaging materials in stock.
2. The leasing/purchasing contract will be fulfilled in 1993; remaining payments total FF 5.8 (million).
3. Fifty-nine people are involved directly in the production process (49 workers, mostly young women).
4. Three clients represented one half of Cypris's business in the Cypris brand sales.
5. One third of Cypris sales were private label products, and the remaining two thirds were the Cypris brand; about one third of the Cypris brand sales were contracted centrally, without the intervention of salesmen.
6. Cypris had a capacity of 1,200 tons and produced 678 tons in 1983. According to the Cotton Association, French production capacity in 1983 was 20,000 tons, actual production was 14,000 tons, and French consumption was 13,000 tons. This market included foods, pharmacies, and hospitals.
7. The largest single competitor to Cypris was Tempo Sanys with 4,200 tons of capacity and actual production of 3,500 tons.

Exhibit 3 *(concluded)*

8. The volumes (in tons), trends, and value (in millions of French francs) in the food market only in 1983 were estimated as follows:

	Volume	Value	Trends
Cotton swabs	1,200	132	Strong increase
Zigzag cotton	5,668	281	Slow decline
Cosmetic pads/discs	713	68	Strong increase
Cotton balls	570	60	Slow increase
	8,151	541	(increased 11.5 percent)

restrictive, and Henkel would face significant severance costs to employees in the event of a plant shutdown. These concerns led Henkel to make the offer to Ken Dafoe to sell Cypris for one French franc.

A Decision

When Ken received the message that Henkel would sell Cypris for one French franc, he was delighted. He felt Cypris could give D & D a big boost to sales and profit. He expected he would export all the production from France to the United States for the first 6 to 12 months while rebuilding the business in Europe, and he felt additional machines could be ordered to increase the productive capacity. In general, he felt the Cypris product line could fit in well with the D & D product line.

On the plane back from California, Ken thought about the response he might give to Jacobi. He drafted the following telex:

> We are pleased to purchase Cypris for 1 French franc. We will purchase subject to the following conditions:
>
> 1. We are given 30 days to arrange financing with a French bank.
> 2. Inventory amounts and costs will be approved by outside auditors.
> 3. You will give us three months to pay for the inventory following closing.

Ken wondered if he should add any further conditions. He suspected that Cypris was in receivership and wondered how that might affect things.

Case 15

Dominion Engineering Works

During the summer of 1980, Walter Fell, newly appointed general manager of the Canadian firm, Dominion Engineering Works (DEW), considered the prospects of his company's paper machine operation. Accounting for 16 percent of DEW's sales, paper machinery was one of DEW's major businesses. Although he was impressed by the revival of DEW's paper machine business over the last couple of years, Mr. Fell was aware that DEW faced some serious competition from a number of larger firms that were expanding rapidly worldwide.

Historically, the company's paper machinery efforts had been limited to the Canadian market, but DEW's parent company, Canadian General Electric, was now pressuring DEW to reevaluate its international competitiveness. Canadian General Electric was no longer content to be a "mini-GE" serving only the Canadian market, and unless a business within the corporation could demonstrate its international competitive ability, it could cease to expect long-term support. For the managers at DEW, and for Walter Fell in particular, the task was to determine whether DEW's paper machinery business could establish itself and hold its own against worldwide competitors.

DEW Company Background

During World War I when European manufacturers were unable to provide service or parts to Canada's paper mills and power companies, Dominion Bridge Company was urged to set up a paper machinery operation on Canadian soil. The company established Dominion Engineering Works as a new subsidiary, and in its first decade of operation DEW built 43 paper machines and established itself as the major supplier to the Canadian paper industry. As the new company grew, it added mining equipment and steel rolling mills to its original product line of hydroturbines and paper machines, in each case becoming the first Canadian manufacturer of such equipment.

In 1962 DEW was acquired by Canadian General Electric (CGE), the rationale for acquisition being that DEW and CGE had several complementary businesses with numerous customers in common. Combining the companies would serve these customers better. It would also provide CGE and its parent company, the

U.S. giant, General Electric, with entry into some completely new areas, including paper machinery.

In 1979 CGE was GE's largest foreign affiliate, with sales in excess of $1.3 billion (see Exhibit 1). Organizationally, DEW was part of CGE's Apparatus and Heavy Machinery Division (see Exhibit 2). The plant was a 1.2 million-square-foot general engineering shop occupying 85 acres outside Montreal and employing almost 2,000 people. It boasted some of the largest capacity equipment in the country and was able to handle everything from gigantic turbines to small machine parts.

Although paper machinery had been one of DEW's more profitable product lines in earlier decades, and again as late as the mid-1970s, in recent years return on sales for the Pulp and Paper Section had been well below DEW's average. (For a comparison of DEW's paper machinery with other lines see Exhibit 3.)

GE is a results-oriented company, and below-budget performance was not taken lightly. As one manager in the DEW operation explained:

> GE has been running at around 6 percent return on sales while CGE has been struggling to stay at half that level. That means they have been taking a lot of heat in Toronto (CGE headquarters), and we feel it here in DEW. Dominion is running under budget again this year, and even though paper machinery is doing OK, it will be tough for all of us. Strategic plans and long-term investments are still important in GE, but you have to live in the real world of current results as well.

Canadian General Electric in 1980 was placing a good deal of pressure on its businesses to improve their short-term operating performance through various cost control and productivity programs. More important, the company was urging its subsidiaries to broaden their horizons, to look beyond Canada, and to recognize the global dimensions of their industry structure. CGE was determined to change its original mission and become an internationally focused company with a growing range of products unique in the GE system. "World-class technical and cost competitiveness" was the goal.

It was against this background that Walter Fell was assessing DEW's paper machinery business. Before outlining DEW's position, however, it is important to take a look at the industry served by DEW's paper machinery and to examine in brief the strategies of DEW's competitors in the field.

The Paper Machine Industry

The fate of the paper machine manufacturers was inextricably linked to the health of their customers, the paper manufacturers. Unfortunately, the 1970s had been a difficult decade in the paper industry. Demand growth was not only slowing but was also becoming increasingly cyclical. Paper-making capacity which was expanded in good times, lay idle during downturns in the demand cycle such as the period from the mid-to-late 1970s. In such times, prices weakened and profitability fell.

Exhibit 1

General Electric Company (dollars in millions; per-share amounts in dollars)

Summary of operations:	1979	1978	1977	1976	1975	1974	1973	1972	1971	1970
Sales of products and services to customers	$ 22,460.6	$ 19,653.8	$ 17,518.6	$15,697.3	$14,105.1	$13,918.2	$11,944.6	$10,473.7	$ 9,556.7	$ 8,833.8
Net earnings	1,408.8	1,229.7	1,088.2	930.6	688.5	705.3	661.4	572.6	509.5	363.0
Earnings per common share	6.20	5.39	4.79	4.12	3.07	3.16	2.97	2.57	2.30	1.66
Dividends declared per common share	2.75	2.50	2.10	1.70	1.60	1.60	1.50	1.40	1.38	1.30
Earnings as a percentage of sales	6.3%	6.3%	6.2%	5.9%	4.9%	5.1%	5.5%	5.5%	5.3%	4.1%
Earned on average shareowners' equity	20.2%	19.6%	19.4%	18.9%	15.7%	17.8%	18.4%	17.5%	17.2%	13.4%
Current assets	9,384.5	8,755.0	7,865.2	6,685.0	5,750.4	5,334.4	4,597.4	4,056.8	3,700.0	3,383.1
Current liabilities	6,871.8	6,175.2	5,417.0	4,604.9	4,163.0	4,032.4	3,588.2	2,920.8	2,893.8	2,689.4
Working capital	$ 2,512.7	$ 2,579.8	$ 2,448.2	$ 2,080.1	$ 1,587.4	$ 1,302.0	$ 1,009.2	$ 1,136.0	$ 806.2	$ 693.7
Short-term borrowings	$ 871.0	$ 960.3	$ 772.1	$ 611.1	$ 667.2	$ 655.9	$ 675.6	$ 453.3	$ 581.7	$ 670.2
Long-term borrowings	946.8	993.8	1,284.3	1,322.3	1,239.5	1,402.9	1,166.2	1,191.2	1,016.2	691.3
Minority interest in equity of consolidated affiliates	151.7	150.8	131.4	119.0	104.6	86.4	62.4	53.4	50.4	45.0
Shareowners' equity	7,362.3	6,586.7	5,942.9	5,252.9	4,617.0	4,172.2	3,774.3	3,420.2	3,105.4	2,819.1
Total capital invested	$ 9,331.8	$ 8,691.6	$ 8,130.7	$ 7,305.3	$ 6,628.3	$ 6,317.4	$ 5,678.5	$ 5,118.1	$ 4,753.7	$ 4,225.6
Earned on average total capital invested	17.6%	16.3%	15.8%	15.1%	12.5%	13.4%	13.7%	12.7%	12.3%	10.2%

Canadian General Electric Company, Ltd. (dollars in thousands, except per share amounts)

	1979	1978	1977	1976	1975	1974	1973	1972	1971	1970
Sales of products and services	$1,338,730	$1,103,965	$1,079,727	$ 879,427	$ 822,134	$ 709,913	$ 583,414	$ 530,174	$ 495,755	$ 489,992
Net earnings (before extraordinary items)	38,330	33,612	30,534	32,699	36,075	23,893	18,680	16,504	13,212	11,359
Net earnings per share	4.69	4.11	3.73	4.00	4.41	2.92	2.28	2.02	1.62	1.39
Earnings as a percentage of sales	3.0%	3.2%	2.9%	3.7%	4.4%	3.4%	3.2%	3.1%	2.7%	2.3%
Current assets	$ 681,216	$ 532,129	$ 496,860	$ 406,778	$ 441,296	$ 382,615	$ 256,300	$ 233,667	$ 240,943	$ 253,379
Current liabilities	432,993	310,076	312,651	239,219	288,830	246,996	131,572	126,543	141,864	149,819
Total assets	904,148	730,274	666,024	571,187	602,435	563,754	429,720	409,951	412,918	409,922
Average number of employees	19,767	18,662	18,823	17,512	18,789	19,193	17,890	17,583	17,950	19,789

Exhibit 2:   Partial Organization Chart

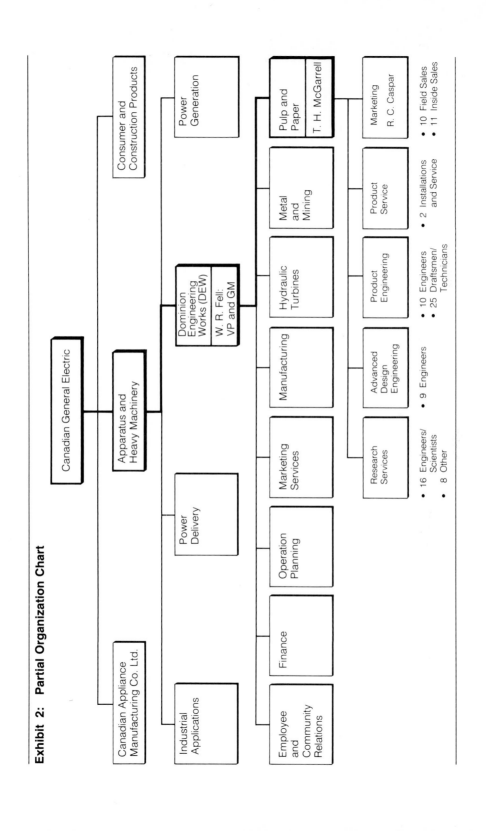

Exhibit 3: Summary of Operations by Product: 1979 (dollars in thousands)

	Pulp and Paper	Hydraulic	Metal and Mining	Manu-facturing	Field Instal-lations	Adjustments/ Eliminations	Total
Orders received	$27,391	$ 22,788	$100,771	$723	$ 3,253	$ (788)	$154,138
Unfilled orders							
(at end of period)	24,188	117,604	97,358	664	27,074	(727)	266,161
Sales	11,202	35,887	16,728	719	5,455	(823)	69,168
Inventory costs:							
Material	5,158	9,432	6,258	36	3,620	(1,110)	23,394
Conversion cost	3,121	15,516	7,931	633	745	8	27,954
Cont. engineering	679	1,170	596	—	—	—	2,445
Total inventory costs	8,958	26,118	14,785	669	4,365	(1,102)	53,793
Inventory margin	2,244	9,769	1,943	50	1,090	279	15,375
Period costs:							
Manufacturing:							
(Over)/underabsorbed expenses	467	817	692	178	—	—	2,154
Depreciation	341	1,206	647	55	—	—	2,249
Engineering and marketing:							
Direct expense	782	1,645	1,879	—	—	—	4,306
Allocated expenses (research, marketing, service)	138	265	142	3	39	—	509
Warranty expense	116	267	265	18	—	—	666
Finance and administration:							
Allocated finance and corporate charges	811	2,249	1,633	70	266	(200)	4,829
Other	—	—	—	—	—	690	690
Total period cost	2,655	6,449	5,258	324	227	490	15,403
Income from sales	(411)	3,320	(3,315)	(274)	863	(211)	(28)
Other income	244	220	(28)	—	15	(7)	444
Total income	(167)	3,540	(3,343)	(274)	878	(218)	416
Income tax	(97)	1,402	(1,517)	(123)	381	(474)	(428)
Net operating income	(70)	2,138	(1,826)	(151)	497	256	844
Net interest (on progress payments)	277	495	433	43	12	—	1,174
Net income	207	2,633	(1,393)	(194)	509	256	2,018
Percent inventory margins	20.0%	27.2%	11.6%	7.0%	20.0%	—	22.2%
Percent net increase to sales	1.8%	7.3%	(8.3)%	(27.0)%	9.3%	—	2.9%

These problems were exacerbated by three important economic and political developments of the 1970s. Increasing oil prices, soaring interest rates, and tightening environmental regulations all had direct and severe impacts on the paper industry and led to rapidly escalating operating costs. In this environment, it was not surprising that the global demand for new paper machines dropped from an annual average of 160 machines in the late 1960s to less than half that level a decade later.

To add to the turbulence, some well-entrenched papermaking practices were being challenged. Technologically, the newly developed "twin-wire" machines began to replace the traditional fourdrinier equipment, based on technology 150 years old. Furthermore, a trend to using different raw materials in paper manufacture was also affecting machine builders. In developing countries, nonwood fibers were becoming increasingly important, while in the industrial world, recycled paper was seen as a defense against escalating pulp costs.

Faced with declining demand for new machines in their home markets, several of the major paper machine builders began to expand abroad in the late 1960s. In particular, the U.S. company Beloit, German-based Voith, and the Finnish consortium TVW established sales offices and manufacturing operations in industrialized and developing countries worldwide. Their objectives were not only to tap these additional markets but also to gain access to various incentive programs offered by host country governments, to achieve sourcing flexibility and perhaps lower labour costs, and to develop their technology in response to the new materials being used as papermaking stock.

The shares of the paper machinery market accounted for by these three large companies increased substantially. By 1974 they had already captured a combined worldwide market share of 40 percent on a tonnage installed basis, and by 1979 that figure had increased to 52 percent. As of the end of 1979 the "Big Three" held a 68 percent share of all new orders placed for the period 1980 and beyond. It seemed as if small- and medium-sized companies like DEW risked being trampled as the three dominant companies jostled for position as the leading global paper machine company.

DEW's Position and Strategy

Changing conditions in the world paper industry during the late 1960s represented an obvious challenge to DEW's traditional strategy. Protected by a tariff on machinery imports, Dominion had successfully pursued its "national champion" role from the 1920s, when the company was founded, until the 1960s. In 1964, however, the major U.S. company, Beloit, established a Canadian subsidiary; before the decade was out, Beloit dominated the national market in tissue, linerboard, and fine-paper machines. Dominion retained its pre-eminence in the newsprint machine market, but it was clear to the company that Beloit was a force to be reckoned with.

Dominion reacted to the new competitive challenge in two ways. First, like its competitors, DEW looked abroad for other market opportunities and soon established licensees in Italy and Japan. Second, the company innovated techno-logically. DEW's research engineers had cooperated with the Pulp and Paper Research Institute of Canada (a body organized by the Canadian paper industry and financed to a large extent by government research grants) in the development of the first twin-wire former. The invention was quickly recognized as a major advance in papermaking technology, the first in over 150 years. It seemed particularly suited to the newsprint segment but subsequently was adapted for tissue and printing and writing paper manufacture.

DEW hoped that the Papriformer (PPRIC's trade name for its twin-wire machine) would give the company a significant edge on its competitors and, indeed, for some time it did. Armed with its new product, DEW moved into the U.S. market and won a major contract in 1972. DEW now employed a U.S salesman and based him in Texas to take advantage of the rapid expansion of the paper industry in the American South. In five years, DEW had taken orders for seven machines—an impressive performance with a new invention in a conser-vative industry.

To keep up with the new surge in demand, DEW decided to restrict design changes and customization of the Papriformer to a minimum. The idea was to standardize the machine as much as possible. Unfortunately, however, a number of DEW's customers were experimenting at this time with new materials like de-inked recycled newsprint and thermo-mechanical pulp. When the companies called on DEW for help, some felt that the response was disappointing. The product engineering manager who joined Dominion during this period recalled:

> We were convinced that the problems we were experiencing were due to the various elements being changed by the customer. However, in retrospect, I would have to say that DEW did not follow up quickly enough with sufficient engineering capability to help the customer correct some of the problems which emerged. We simply did not have the available personnel resources. The reaction of the customer was to blame the Papriformer rather than the changes in process they were trying to make. Our reputation suffered a little.

The lack of personnel resources was tied to the economic downturn of 1975 and to DEW's parent company's response to that situation. When DEW's major businesses reported a decline in orders during the recession, CGE pressured operating management to cut costs in order to protect profits. The paper machinery section of DEW cut its sales force from 25 to 9, its advance design staff from 8 to 3, and its product engineers and draftsmen from 35 to 14.

Following the company's initial success with the Papriformer, not a single paper machine was sold in the four years from 1975 to 1979. The only business booked by the Pulp and Paper Section was for spare parts, components, and small or partial rebuilds. DEW's paper machinery business was operating around breakeven, with no relief in sight.

At the end of 1977, DEW recruited Tom McGarrell, an engineer and manager who had spent eight years with Beloit, the world's largest paper machine manufacturer, and seven years with Abitibi-Price, the world's largest newsprint manufacturer. When McGarrell became manager of the Pulp and Paper Section, sales were running at 40 percent of their 1974 peak, and new orders booked over the previous three years were less than half that of the three years prior to that.

With no new machine order received in two and half years, McGarrell knew that morale in the Pulp and Paper Section was low and that support by senior DEW management was, at best, tentative. There was talk of acquiring a manufacturing and marketing base in the United States but McGarrell felt that the company's priorities lay elsewhere:

> I felt we had an urgent task to face in rebuilding our internal pulp and paper organization. Furthermore, we had done little to improve our technology in seven or eight years while competitors like Beloit, Voith, and TVW had used the mid-70s as a time to upgrade their products. We suddenly woke up when the market picked up in 1978–79, and we found we were losing orders. Our machine technology was out of date, and our market share was slipping.

McGarrell acknowledged the seriousness of the threat from abroad, with Beloit, Black Clawson, Voith, and particularly TVW making themselves felt in Canada. The foreign onslaught, he believed, had reduced DEW's share of the large and attractive Canadian market from 50 percent in 1972–74 to 10–12 percent in 1977–79. DEW's defense of the Canadian newsprint market segment on which it had focused was slipping.

However, the battle McGarrell faced within the company was almost as challenging as the one taking place externally. As he put it:

> Within the company there was a strong belief that nothing had changed apart from a cyclical downturn. People had a hard time accepting the fact that DEW did not have a 50 percent market share and that we were not the technological leaders. They had assumed that when the cycle turned up we would be carried with it. That wasn't the case. We were being left behind.

McGarrell spent his first three years with DEW rebuilding his organization and improving performance of the existing product lines. The following paragraphs detail the situation in each of DEW's major functional areas.

Manufacturing

DEW's 1.2 million-square-foot plant, though large, was a general engineering shop, and as such, it suffered certain cost disadvantages in comparison with plants specializing in paper machine production. Management believed, however, that the differential was no more than 5 percent or 10 percent and that the disadvantage was more than compensated for when downturns in the very cyclical paper industry left specialist plants idle. (See Exhibit 4 for an illustration of the time lag between receiving and shipping an order.) But the general shop had its problems, especially in hard times, as a DEW manufacturing manager explained:

Exhibit 4: Orders Received and Sales Billed (dollars in thousands)

	1967	1968	1969	1970	1971	1972	1973	1974	1975	1976	1977	1978
Paper Section:												
Orders	$11,025	$12,300	$10,100	$ 7,144	$ 7,600	$13,046	$14,623	$20,022	$ 5,919	$ 9,310	$ 9,056	$11,092
Sales	17,984	13,967	12,795	11,223	5,951	5,885	8,274	19,960	16,804	11,982	8,751	8,588
Hydraulic Section:												
Orders	30,136	12,603	4,215	13,997	15,965	11,105	30,129	42,133	15,083	6,464	67,586	36,378
Sales	8,630	7,669	9,286	12,052	15,460	13,287	16,871	18,084	19,571	23,599	19,215	30,319
Metal and Mining Section:												
Orders	20,253	14,464	20,332	17,439	24,249	17,196	35,704	72,344	38,761	14,086	15,424	19,350
Sales	20,529	22,319	18,826	23,960	19,567	21,973	15,446	19,276	45,351	53,185	24,630	14,562
Total DEW:												
Orders	61,414	39,367	34,647	38,580	47,814	41,347	80,456	134,499	59,763	29,860	92,066	66,820
Sales	47,143	43,955	30,907	47,235	40,978	41,145	40,591	57,320	81,726	88,766	52,596	53,469

First, because we run a general engineering shop we tend to have general-purpose tools rather than specialized equipment. Tools have been grouped by function, and the production flow for a particular machine may be somewhat inefficient.

Second, in competition for capacity with our other product lines, paper machinery orders may suffer. In general, the equipment necessary for making paper machines is smaller and more common than that required, say, for a turbine. In a crunch, the paper machinery work is most easily subcontracted, and that raises costs.

Finally, there is a more subtle problem that paper machines face in a plant such as ours. The manufacturing area is evaluated on its dollar volume. If it is near the end of a period and there is a need to try to meet budget, the larger, more-expensive units are pushed through the system. It is easier to get a turbine through the plant than a lot of small components for a paper machine.

DEW's manufacturing suffered, of course, from the threefold increase in the cost of materials that afflicted the industry in the 1970s. Environmental problems with the traditional equipment, as mentioned earlier, forced up the costs of materials—and materials accounted for almost half of machine cost—as stainless steel replaced the less-expensive materials used formerly.

At the same time, labor costs rose to a point where they were accounting for 30 percent to 40 percent of the cost of a new machine. Companies such as Voith and Beloit were quick to take advantage of cheaper labor costs in Spain, Brazil, and other countries, but DEW was reluctant to use foreign sources. Despite savings it could obtain by sourcing from its Italian licensee, Over Meccanica, DEW felt that customers were displeased to learn of the foreign manufacture of their multimillion-dollar machines. Then, too, DEW was pressing the Canadian government to support local manufacturers and could hardly supply its home market with foreign-made machines. DEW felt it was able, nonetheless, to quote prices in the United States comparable with Beloit's although, as one manager pointed out, the slightest strengthening of the Canadian dollar would make this difficult to continue.

Dew's manufacturing manager believed, in any case, that internal problems were the key to DEW's high labor costs. Uneven work flow and the loss of experienced personnel had cut into the company's efficiency.

> When the market fell away in the mid-1970s, we had to cut back people at all levels. In the plant that meant the loss of critical skills and expertise that had been developed over the years. Without building a complete machine in four years, we lost the ability to manage the product flow through the plant, and we lost efficiency in our operations. For example, to machine a dryer head used to take us six or seven hours in 1973 and 1974. But in 1979, after the personnel cutbacks and the new-order drought, the same operation was taking over 35 hours. We're now down to 20 hours, but we're still trying to relearn our old efficient methods, and it's really costing us.

With the market upturn of the late 1970s, the Pulp and Paper Section was able to convince management to expand and upgrade its paper machine manufacturing capability. By 1980 more than $3 million worth of new plant and equipment was being installed, and overall capacity was expected to increase from 1.5 to 2.5 complete paper machines a year.

Marketing

The Canadian market for paper machinery took off in 1978 and 1979 following an upturn in the economy and the announcement of a new five-year government program to finance up to 11 percent of the cost of upgrading plant and equipment. DEW saw in this program not only a capital investment stimulus "that should help us get through the next valley in the investment cycle" but also a barrier to foreign competitors. As one senior manager explained, "When, for example, TVW won a contract that was 11 percent funded by the Canadian government, we were able to raise a hell of a fuss. Essentially, these projects have to be supplied by Canadian manufacturers now."

The government also offered an export financing program that provided 10- to 15-year loans to overseas buyers at 9½ percent interest in an era when the prime rate was approaching 20 percent. Despite this assistance from the government, DEW's sales force continued to face tough competition both at home and abroad. The Finnish consortium TVW, in particular, was pricing aggressively to gain a share of the Canadian market. And to make matters worse, recent tariff reductions on paper machinery from 15 percent to 13¼ percent were only the beginning of a series of reductions agreed to under GATT negotiations.

One of Tom McGarrell's first moves when he took over DEW's Pulp and Paper Section was to appoint Roman Caspar, then manager of the company's Advanced Design Engineering, as marketing manager. Caspar, in turn, set about rebuilding the company's depleted sales force, which had gone from 25 to 9 in the cutbacks of the mid-1970s. By 1980 he had the staff back up to 23, with 9 field personnel: 7 covering Canada, 1 responsible for the United States, and 1 for export markets.

Caspar felt that DEW had concentrated too heavily on the newsprint segment of the Canadian market, turning overseas only in slack times. He pointed to the success of DEW's Italian licensee, Over Meccanica, in selling five Papriformers during the company's last slack period, 1974–78. Some of these had been for fine-paper and tissue applications. And he noted, too, that DEW's Japanese licensee had entirely missed the Japanese boom of 1968–74, largely because DEW had not made an aggressive effort to adapt its headbox design to local needs. Caspar commented:

> These are the kinds of problems and opportunities I feel I should be working on now, but there seems to be an internal resistance to letting me do so. The message seems to be to focus on the Canadian market.

Research and Development

When he took over DEW's Pulp and Paper Section, Tom McGarrell found three groups of engineers, scientists, and technologists under his control. Research

Services did basic research relating to any of DEW's businesses and was funded to a large extent by federal research grants. One of McGarrell's early efforts was to focus their efforts on issues that were less abstract and more directly related to the company's products and markets.

Advanced Design Engineering was responsible for basic paper machine design. In Tom McGarrell's view, they had been too focused on internal experiments that interested them and were not at all aware of the design breakthroughs being made on competitive machines. His objective was to shift their attention outward to respond more to changing market and competitive realities.

Product Engineering was responsible for drawing specifications and adapting basic machine designs to specific customer needs. However, when McGarrell inherited the group, it was so understaffed it was unable to handle major design changes. Even operating manuals could not be prepared, with the result that customers were calling for assistance more frequently.

In keeping with his stated policy of rebuilding the organization, Tom McGarrell brought in new managers from other top companies and pushed to expand each group while narrowing its focus to meet the immediate needs of the company. His greatest frustration was that DEW had no pilot plant of its own and had to rely on the facilities of Over Meccanica, PPRIC, or even customers' plants to do its testing. By 1979, however, McGarrell felt that DEW had caught up with most of the technological advances made by its competitors in the mid-1970s. He explained:

> The work we've done over the last few years should help us broaden our product line from our present newsprint dominance. We have a new former in development that should give us the uniform fiber distribution needed to sell machines for printing and writing paper. Over Meccanica's experience with tissue machines should help us make the changes needed in headbox and drainage configuration to get into that segment. It won't be easy to break into these markets, but now that we have the basics right, at least we can begin to work on it.
>
> Technological changes come in waves which correspond to new industry priorities. Several years ago, when the major concern was pollution control, the forming process became critical. When energy costs rose, pressing and drying technology was key. We've been catching up in these areas, but I believe we can now begin work in the critical concern of the future—productivity. We are working on a major project jointly with a customer and the Pulp and Paper Institute that I'm very excited about.

Tom McGarrell was very optimistic about DEW's ability to regain the technological leadership it had lost in the early 1970s.

> I think we have learned a great deal in the last few years. Even though DEW is under budget pressure this year, we are not being forced to cut key personnel as we were in the past. In fact, we will add two or three people to our Advanced Engineering Group next year, and our overall R&D budget should exceed $1 million compared to

Exhibit 5: Paper Machines by Dominion Engineering Works Limited, Montreal, Canada

Year	Purchaser	Location	New or Rebuild	Wire Width	Product	Design Speed (FPM)
1968	Facelle Company	United States	New (2)	214"	Tissue	4,000
1968	MacMillan Bloedel Ltd.	Canada	New	238"	Newsprint	2,500
1969	M. P. Industrial Mills (Man. Forestry Resources, Ltd.)	Canada	New	280"	Pulp and bag	2,500
1970	B. C. Forest Products Ltd.	Canada	New	178"	Pulp	500
1972	St. Regis Paper (Southland)	United States	New (Papriformer*)	326"	Newsprint	3,500
1972	Kruger Inc.	Canada	Rebuild (Papriformer*)	174"	Newsprint	2,500
1973	Kruger Inc.	Canada	New (Papriformer*)	261"	Newsprint	3,000
1973	Consolidated-Bathurst	Canada	Rebuild (Papriformer*)	238"	Newsprint	2,500
1974	F. F. Soucy Inc.	Canada	New (Papriformer*)	261"	Newsprint	3,000
1974	Garden State Paper Co.	United States	Rebuild (Papriformer*)	261"	Newsprint	3,000
1974	Consolidated-Bathurst	Canada	Rebuild (2 Papriformers*)	238"	Newsprint	3,000
1979	Kruger Inc.	Canada	Rebuild	160"	Newsprint	3,000
1979	MacMillan Bloedel	Canada	Rebuild	186"	Linerboard	2,300
1979	Midtec Paper Corp.	United States	New	249"	Newsprint	3,000
1980	Quebec North Shore	Canada	Rebuild	262"	Newsprint	3,000
1980	Consolidated-Bathurst	Canada	Rebuild (Papriformer*)	238"	Newsprint	3,000
1980	Donohue-Normick Inc.	Canada	New (Papriformer*)	326"	Newsprint	4,000

* Papriformer is DEW's trade name for its twin-wire former.

less than $100,000 when I first arrived. In my view, that should give us the chance to regain our leadership position.

As of mid-1980, DEW had added a second new machine order to the one received in 1979, breaking the order drought that had continued since 1974 (see Exhibit 5). McGarrell felt he had the momentum to launch a major new offensive in the paper machine business. The only cloud on the horizon was his belief that the paper industry was headed into a cyclical downturn in 1981.

Senior Management's Decision

As Dominion Engineering's new general manager, Walter Fell knew that his evaluation of the paper machine business would be critical. He also realized that he had to take into account not only the external competitive situation but also CGE's goal of shedding its "mini-GE" image and achieving international competitiveness.

Walter Fell saw some clear advantages for DEW's paper machine business. The company had certainly been a world technological leader with the twin-wire Papriformer, and CGE was the only part of the GE system that had paper machine technology and manufacturing capability. He commented:

> There is a lot about this business that makes sense for us strategically. The critical question is whether we can become a world-scale competitor. Now you can't make a business world class in two weeks, or even in a year. We need to think about what we can do by 1985. For the paper machine business, the question is what route to follow. Is an acquisition more feasible than an internal growth program? Do we have to become a full-line company or can we stay with our specialized newsprint line? Do we have to conquer the world in one fell swoop or can we take a more focused and gradual approach?
>
> These are the questions I'm looking to Tom McGarrell, Roman Caspar, and the others to answer. I've told them they have an AAA credit rating and that we're not stopped from doing anything. In fact, the chairman has been floating ideas about acquisitions for awhile. But before we do anything, we have to know what it is we're trying to become and justify the way to get there.

What to do with the paper machinery business had become a hot topic at DEW in the summer of 1980. Not only was Walter Fell eager to have the topic analyzed by the time he sent DEW's strategic plan to CGE in Toronto, but there was a competitive development that concerned Tom McGarrell. Rumors were circulating in the industry that the industry leader, Beloit, had been showing an interest in KMW, the Swedish manufacturer that dominated the tissue machine market. Apparently, KMW's financial performance had been poor in recent years, and some industry observers were convinced that its parent company was willing to discuss the sale of the business.

Dysys Inc.

As spring began to show itself in April 1984, Peter Gregson and Ted Mussett were wondering about the future direction of Dysys Inc., a two-year-old company in which they each had a 50 percent shareholding. The company, while profitable, was not performing at the level desired, and the co-owners were concerned about this situation.

The Current Situation

By 1984 Dysys had a number of market offerings. It acted as a dealer for a computerized restaurant information system and for a line of microcomputers and peripheral devices. Dysys also produced custom computer hardware and software in response to individual orders from customers. It provided consulting assistance to microcomputer users in the local area and, finally, was developing two products that it felt would have relatively wide application. These were the Production Information Network and the Brick. (Financial data are presented in Exhibit 1.)

Dysys currently employed seven individuals, although only four of these were full-timers. The firm's management was: Peter Gregson—the founder of the business and president; Ted Mussett—vice president and general manager; and Chris Zinck—chief technologist and systems engineer.

The four full-time persons were Ted Mussett, Chris Zinck, Tom Cooper, and David Lane. David was an engineering technologist, hired to complete one of the R&D projects. Tom was a customer service representative trainee and looked after sales of the restaurant system and computer supplies. Ted was nominally in charge of marketing but found that he was involved in every facet of the company's operations from project scheduling to payables and receivables. Chris had become the firm's production man and was also involved in price quotes. (See Exhibit 2 for an organization chart.)

Matt Silver was employed part-time on a contract basis in his capacity as a business systems analyst. Fay Pape acted as a consultant, working on implementation and training in restaurants that adopted the computerized information systems. Peter Gregson was the final part-timer. Although president of the

This case was prepared by Professors Philip Rosson and Robert Blunden of Dalhousie University. The authors gratefully acknowledge the financial support of the Department of Regional Industrial Expansion, Small Business Secretariat in the development of the case. Some of the case information was collected by MBA students Tom Boudreau, Mellany Hellstern, Alan McGee, Douglas Munn, and Roberta Thomson.

Exhibit 1: Financial Data (eight months' financial information, 1983–1984, by business activity)

Activity	Revenue	Percent of Total	Cost of Goods Sold	Percent Margin
Remanco Restaurant Information System	$ 30,000	18.5%	n.b.a.	?
Computer systems (Chameleon, peripherals, software)	67,000	41.4	$51,375	23%
Computer supplies	9,300	5.7	8,300	11
System maintenance	8,500	5.3	3,800	55
Custom products (the Brick, Bar Code Reader, etc.)	24,600	15.2	13,197	46
Custom software	8,400	5.2	n.b.a.	?
Industrial Research Assistance Program grant	14,000	8.7	n.a.	n.a.
Total	$161,800			

Notes: 1. Remanco revenues are commissions earned by company.
2. n.b.a. = No breakdown available.
3. n.a. = Not applicable.
4. Total salaries for the period were $45,000.
5. Total overhead for the period (including salaries) was $75,000.

---

company, Peter had many "irons in the fire." He had a part-time teaching position at the Technical University of Nova Scotia as well as being a Ph.D. student at the same institution. When Peter was around, he got involved with all kinds of activities, such as contacting customers, dreaming up new product ideas, and constructing hardware.

Dysys History

When Peter Gregson founded Dysys, he was 30 years old. He was an electrical engineer by training, with a diploma in engineering (St. Mary's University, Halifax), and bachelor and master degrees in electrical engineering (Technical University of Nova Scotia) earned between 1969 and 1977. Following schooling, Peter worked in a local electronics firm and as a scientist at a government research establishment. During the school and employee period, Peter had run his own small businesses on the side. He found moonlighting enjoyable because it provided him with an extra challenge as well as additional income.

In 1977 he had formed his most serious business venture, along with a partner. This company, called Micronet Limited, grew quickly, from sales of $10,000 in its first year to almost $1 million in 1980–81. The principal product the company developed was an automatic meter reader for use in an experiment into electrical consumption patterns conducted by the Nova Scotia Power Corporation. Other products revolved around the use of microprocessors to control energy. Peter joined the company full-time as vice president of R&D in 1980, but Micronet

Exhibit 2: Organization Chart

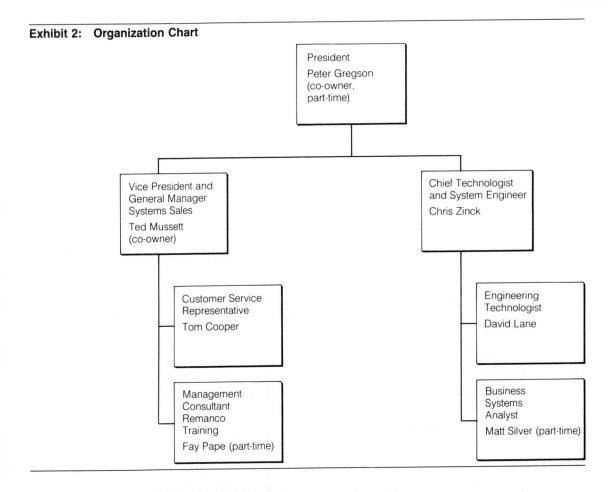

found it hard to sustain sales, so that by the end of 1981, a cash infusion was needed. This was secured from a venture capital company in Boston. One of the agreements worked out by this firm and his partner was that Peter should no longer be an equal shareholder.

Angered by this decision, Peter decided to sell most of his shares and to leave the company six months later. In the meantime, with his adrenaline pumping hard, he strode off to the office of the Registar of Joint Stock Companies in Halifax, Nova Scotia, determined to register a new company. On the way, he decided on the name Dysys—a contraction of dynamic systems. This reflected his skill and experience designing microprocessors for dynamic situations. Once the company was registered, his thoughts turned to the matter of what exactly the company would do. Peter considered this during his last months with Micronet. One very real constraint was finance. With no capital behind him, there was considerable pressure to produce an immediate cash flow. Apart from anything else, there would be a mortgage payment due on his home a month after he left Micronet. This would be the first hurdle to be surmounted.

Given this situation, Peter realized that he had no time for any development work. Any computer-based product that he sold had to be built and ready to go. His first few days in business (in May 1982) involved a furious round of telephone calls to both potential customers and dealers. Eventually, a likely customer was located at the Technical University of Nova Scotia (TUNS). With this customer in mind, he decided to buy a system with his credit card. Since he was able to collect the price of the system from TUNS quickly, Peter used the 45-day credit period (from the purchase) to provide initial financing for his firm.

Next, a research contract was entered into with the provincially owned Nova Scotia Research Foundation, and some modems (a peripheral device that lets the computer transmit or receive information over a telephone line) were sold to Dalhousie University, both in Halifax. He also lined up a part-time teaching position at TUNS. Business developed over the ensuing months. However, things did not move as quickly as expected—for whereas Peter felt he could acquire a year's worth of income in about 7 months, it ended up taking 18 months.

Ted Mussett (whom Peter had known for about 10 years) joined Dysys as an equal partner with Peter in July 1982. Ted was a biologist by training who, since graduating from Dalhousie University in 1977, had taken further courses in mathematics, statistics, computer science, accounting, and data processing. Ted had also worked for the ill-fated Micronet as a representative responsible for sales of a computerized restaurant management system. He brought this line of products across to Dysys when Micronet went out of business in the summer of 1982.

In April 1983 Chris Zinck joined the company. Chris had earned bachelor degrees in computer science (Dalhousie, 1981) and in engineering (TUNS, 1983). In his last three years as a student, Chris had worked with local computing firms during summer vacations, developing his software skills in a business context. Chris's name was recommended to Peter and Ted when they were looking for an additional staff member, and he joined Dysys on a summer student employment grant. Chris originally worked at developing an interface between the restaurant information system and a liquor dispensing system. Later he was kept on to work on the Production Information Network (PIN), a plant automation project Dysys was developing for small- and medium-sized manufacturers.

The Dysys Mission

In establishing Dysys, Peter Gregson was cognizant of the huge potential for any competent firm in the computer field. Initially Peter realized that he had to run his business so that his family's bills might be paid. With time, however, he saw a viable role for a company that acted in a technically sophisticated *consulting* capacity and as a *designer* and *manufacturer* of innovative microelectric products.

In the consulting capacity, Peter's experience told him that small- and medium-sized local businesses needed advice on the computer hardware and software best suited to their own particular applications and requirements. At the same time, Peter wanted to continue development of the PIN, which he had initiated while at Micronet, as well as other industrial control devices.

Dysys Activities in 1984

By the spring of 1984 Dysys was operating in a number of different areas. Dysys acted as a dealer for the Remanco Restaurant Information System, for Seequa's Chameleon line of microcomputers, and for various computer peripheral devices.

Dealer Business

The Remanco Restaurant Information System. Remanco Systems Inc. was a Canadian company headquartered in Toronto that developed a computer-based management tool for the restaurant industry. The company was founded by a restaurateur looking for a solution to improving the productivity of his operation with technology. Established in 1977, it made its first volume shipments in 1981. In 1983 it expected to sell about 1,500 systems, 65 percent in the United States, 15 percent in Canada, and 20 percent in other world markets.

The Remanco system covered three areas of restaurant operation: service, payment, and management. Users of the system talked about it as bringing the restaurant into the 1980s. A typical system included a microprocessor, a terminal with keyboard, and two disk drives located near the kitchen or another central place, plus an array of terminal/printers or printers with preset menu instructions scattered around the serving stations. One adopter describes the system as follows:

> The server's terminal relays a clearly printed order to the kitchen or the bar, so there's no misunderstanding there. And at the end the guest is given a clear, complete, legible bill. It puts the finishing touch to the gracious service, the elegant presentation of the food.
>
> For the servers, the terminal unclutters their minds, frees them from pencils and paper, gives them a calmer, unruffled approach to serving guests. In the kitchen, orders are placed in sequence, clearly, and the chefs don't feel harassed. The system cuts down on the confusion all round.
>
> For reports and data gathering, we use information on what has been ordered to help us establish trends and demands. We like to satisfy our guests—who tend to be discriminating about their food—so we change the menu every three months or so. With the data we can get from the Remanco system, we can take popular offerings and let our chefs create new and imaginative things from them.

The comprehensive record of all sales helps us exercise tight cash control and also speeds up the process of determining our food and liquor costs—and inventory—on a daily basis. [See Exhibit 3.]

Dysys was the agent for this system in Nova Scotia, receiving a 21 percent commission on sales and fees for installation, training, and implementation. It had sold the Remanco system to a number of restaurants in Halifax, including The Henry House, Le Bistro, and Clipper II. These were fine-quality restaurants, which seated 100 diners or more and had their own definable "ambience." The price of a typical Remanco system was in the order of $25,000 plus service contract fees. However, price could vary from $20,000 to $200,000 depending on the number of terminals required.

Systems like the Remanco were felt to be too costly for small establishments, owner-operated businesses, and beverage rooms with limited food offerings. Since the Halifax market was restricted to about 20 more sales, Dysys management was planning to move outside the metropolitan area, hoping to secure orders from other eating establishments. As well, they expected to capitalize on a verbal agreement with Remanco giving them the line for the Maritime provinces of New Brunswick, Nova Scotia, and Prince Edward Island. However, the company could not even entertain such expansion with its present staffing and commitments.

In the opinion of the Dysys personnel, the Remanco system was the best currently available. It was a simple, proven system and competitive with competing offerings such as NCR, Sweda, and Data General. Competition in the local market was provided by five manufacturers.

The Chameleon Line of Microcomputers. Microcomputers were a phenomenal growth industry in the early 1980s. As well as the computers themselves, computer peripherals (such as printers), software, and publications all experienced large sales increases. Numerous entries were made by companies hoping to achieve their financial dreams. In the Halifax area alone—which lagged behind other parts of the country—there were more than 50 computer consultants, distributors, dealers, and franchise stores. There was also a small number of hardware and software producers.

By 1983 it was estimated that more than 150 computer manufacturers were competing in the microcomputer market. Two companies—Apple Computer, Inc., and Tandy Corporation (with its Radio Shack brand and retail stores)—had made much of the early running and in 1981 were the leading and second companies, respectively. Then in August 1981 IBM launched its Personal Computer (PC) and within two years developed a 26 percent share of the critical United States market.

The success of the PC meant that IBM was unable to fill all its orders quickly. In fact, it was reported that demand for PCs was six times in excess of IBM's

---

Exhibit 3: Remanco Restaurant Information System—Benefits and Competition

A. Service benefits:

1. Increase in server efficiency eliminating trips to bar and kitchen.

2. Reduces overhead by eliminating prenumbered guest checks:
   No purchase cost.
   No distribution cost.
   No auditing cost.
   No storage cost.

3. Increase kitchen efficiency:
   Orders in sequence.
   Orders readable.
   No errors.

4. Out-of-stock items displayed immediately.

RESULT: Improved customer service, larger sections, higher table turns, reduced labour cost . . .
   higher profit.

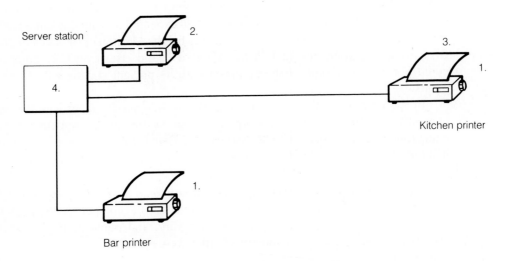

B. Payment benefits:

1. All information regarding a guest check is available at any terminal.

2. All transaction data recorded.

3. Permits server payment with security through accountability.

4. Front desk posting in hotel.

RESULT: Quick and simple function requiring *no* cashier leading to:
   Labour savings.
   Greater control of cash.

Exhibit 3 (*concluded*)

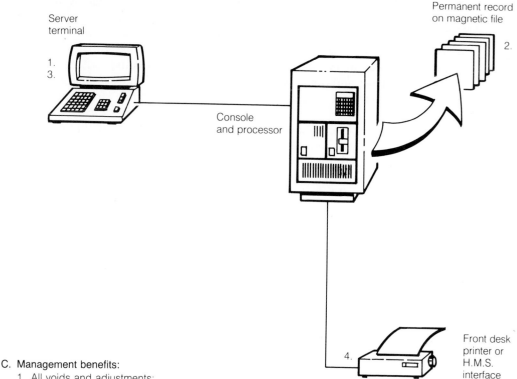

C. Management benefits:
1. All voids and adjustments:
   Reported concisely.
   Accounted for by reason, guest check, and server/manager.
2. Organizes and reports by category, sales of each item:
   Per shift.
   Per day.
   Per week, per month, quarterly, yearly.
3. Automatically updates perpetual inventory daily. Receipts and other adjustments are easily accepted by system. Daily ordering needs printed.
4. Logs all employees' time (serving and kitchen staff) enabling daily labour cost reporting as percent of sales:
   Group.
   Category.
   Individually.

D. Dysys competition—as viewed by Dysys management:
   Data Terminal System: Comparable benefits to Remanco, limited market penetration due to restricted marketing efforts.
   NCR: Similar benefits to Remanco; servicing not satisfactory in Halifax.
   Sweda: Limited report generating and storage capabilities but popular with buyers not requiring advanced management benefits; expanding product offerings; good local reputation.
   Micro Systems and Victor: Limited capabilities in current systems but potential to expand offerings; presently not a serious competitor to Remanco.

building capacity.[1] This situation spawned an entirely new industry—the production of IBM-compatible computers by companies such as Eagle, Corona, and Compaq. These firms and others were able to produce PC clones because IBM had published the computer's technical specifications, showing how the machine was built and how it operated. This decision—an unusual one for IBM—had been consciously taken in 1981 so that other manufacturers could write applications software and make additional products for the PC. IBM management considered this a vital component in a strategy to quickly establish a strong presence in microcomputers.

Whether a long-term future existed for IBM-compatible computers was not certain. Some analysts felt that once IBM was able to make up the production shortfall of 1982 and 1983, problems would exist for the PC clones. Others, however, saw a good future for these firms, predicting that United States retail sales of IBM-compatible computers would hit $7 billion (equal to estimated IBM PC sales) in 1988.[2]

In view of the apparent opportunities in microcomputers in December 1983, Dysys management was able—at Matt Silver's suggestion—to secure the Atlantic Provinces dealership for the Chameleon microcomputer line manufactured by the Seequa Computer Corporation of Annapolis, Maryland. Seequa was a privately owned corporation that had been in existence since 1979. Growth had recently forced the company to move to larger premises and expand its work force. An IBM or Apple dealership would have been preferred, but both companies were already well represented in the Halifax/Dartmouth area. Given this situation, Dysys considered the Chameleon to be the next-best choice, for Seequa claimed real benefits for its computer. Its advertising noted that

> The Chameleon by Seequa does everything an IBM PC does, for about $2,000 less than an IBM.
>
> The Chameleon lets you run popular IBM software like Lotus 1-2-3 and Wordstar. It has a full 83-key keyboard just like an IBM, disk drives like an IBM, and a bright 80 × 25 character screen just like an IBM.
>
> But it's not just the Chameleon's similarities to the IBM that should interest you. Its advantages should, too.
>
> The Chameleon also has an 8-bit microprocessor that lets you run any of the thousands of CPM-80 programs available. It comes complete with two of the best programs around, Perfect Writer and Perfect Calc. It's portable, and you can plug it in and start computing the moment you unwrap it.
>
> So if you've been interested in an IBM personal computer, now you know where you can get one for $2,650. Wherever they sell Chameleons.

An independent review in a leading computer magazine found the Chameleon Plus to be reliable (running most IBM software) and to offer more features and a lower price than its IBM equivalent. Some drawbacks noted included: faults with

---

[1] "Personal Computers: And the Winner Is IBM," *Business Week,* October 3, 1983, p. 78.

[2] "IBM's Personal Computer Spawns an Industry," *Business Week,* August 15, 1983, p. 88.

casing and latch, the unavailability of certain software supposed to be included in the basic price of the machine, and the 28-pound weight of the computer. On this latter point, however, the Chameleon fared no worse than other "portables."

Dysys saw three market segments which offered potential for the Chameleon product line: (1) business, (2) students, and (3) personal usage. They operated on a mark-up of about 25 percent and offered a service contract to adopters in return for a fee of $300 each year. Dysys also handled repairs—either in-house or through return to the manufacturer. Seequa extended Dysys 15 days' credit.

In addition to the Chameleon computers, a line of computer peripherals was also carried so that Dysys could offer customers a complete range from which to buy.

Custom Hardware and Software Business

Several pieces of custom hardware and software had been developed by Dysys. One recent development was the Bar Code Reader—others are highlighted in Exhibit 4.

The Bar Code Reader. It was believed that many applications existed for this piece of applied technology, although Dysys had only filled one contract to date. This was at the Dalhousie University athletic complex, where two bar coded readers were part of an entrance and security sytem. Users of the facility slid their ID card through the slot on top of the reader. If the bar code shown on the ID card was "cleared" by the main-frame university computer (to which the reader was connected), a green light shone and the turnstile would permit entry.

Other bar code reader system applications were envisaged in manufacturing,

---

Exhibit 4: Custom Hardware and Software Projects Completed by Dysys

Among the projects Dysys has completed are:

Hardware

1. Bar Code Reader.
2. Emergency Intercom Controller—a contract with the Victoria General Hospital in Halifax. This device, designed by Peter Gregson, included a computer board which was set in an intercom. By activating one switch, such as a buzzer in a bathroom, a number of stations could be contacted simultaneously, including a base station (nurses) and the appropriate emergency unit.
3. Eye Movement System—two units sold, one each to McMaster University Medical School (Hamilton) and Dalhousie University Medical School. Developed by Peter prior to founding of Dysys, the system was used for studying the motion of eyes in humans and animals.

Software

1. Membership systems for Maritime Commercial Travellers Association and Halifax Board of Trade.
2. Accounting system for Halifax Board of Trade.

---

where the ID card would be replaced by a work ticket, material control card, or voucher. Such applications included: employee timekeeping, inventory and shipping control, and security. It was also planned to use the Bar Code Reader in PIN.

The other hardware developments Dysys was involved with could be customized but had general application and so were believed to have wide sales potential.

The Brick.   This was a fully functional, single-board computer that had been developed for in-house use at Dysys. It had been in Peter Gregson's mind for a couple of years, and he had used a three-week break between projects at the end of the summer in 1983 to push it along. The key element of the Brick was the board's design which permitted a great deal of flexibility in use. All parts of the Brick would be bought-in, assembly involving the soldering of off-the-shelf chips to the Dysys-designed boards. It was anticipated that a Brick could be assembled in about 45 minutes. The Brick was to be an integral part of the PIN, but other applications were envisaged.

This cleverly designed computer would sell for between $300 and $600, depending on the precise features demanded by the customer. Some $200 had recently been spent to produce photos and a specification sheet for promotion purposes. Copies of each had been sent to a number of publications requesting that the Brick be described in their new product sections. These included such magazines as *Byte* (computers) and *Industrial Engineering*. It was hoped that a good level of interest would result from this initiative.

The Production Information Network.   PIN was the brainchild of Peter Gregson, and he had begun to work on this project back in his Micronet days. A PIN prototype had been installed by Crossley Karastan—a carpet manufacturer located in Truro, Nova Scotia. Details of this installation had generated a lot of excitement at a production show in Toronto in 1981, but Micronet never followed up on the enquiries made.

Peter and Chris talked about factory productivity as follows:

> In these days of increasing labour costs and reduced selling prices, manufacturers must make their profits from increased automation and plant optimization. Tools that assist them to do this are necessary. Only the largest corporations are able to finance complete automation, and as a result there are an enormous number of firms that are still labour intensive or at least require significant amounts of labour to run the production line.
>
> The needs of the smaller firm have only recently started to attract the attention of system suppliers. A 1983 report in *Fortune* magazine described the market as "new and relatively naive . . . a little mystery and a lot of promises go a long way." At Dysys we have a tool for the smaller producer concerned about productivity.

Dysys had in mind a system that would allow manufacturers to exert control over the production line as well as to collect information on production. Production control might include: (1) tracking, controlling, and providing alarms

Exhibit 5:   The Production Information Network

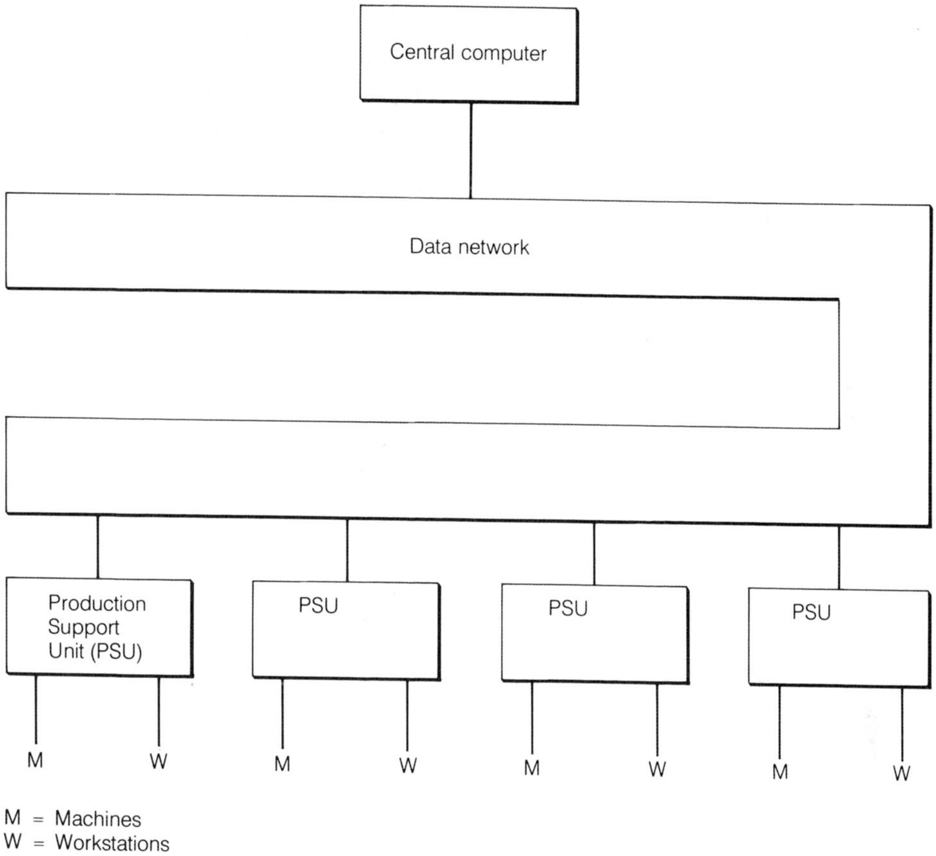

M = Machines
W = Workstations

on small changes in process parameters such as temperatures and pressures, thereby reducing wastage of materials, and (2) tracking work in process to anticipate bottlenecks and raw materials shortages. Production information collected might be: (1) machine down-time data including reasons, so as to improve plant productivity, and (2) data on line for materials resource planning systems. It was estimated that a manufacturer could recover 3 to 5 percent of gross sales if these and other tasks were performed.

This would be achieved as shown in Exhibit 5. The three main components of the system were the *production support units* (PSU), connected through a *data network* to a *central computer*. The PSUs would be installed on key machines and at other workstations, providing some control capability, and have an operator interface to assist the worker at the station. Summary data and alarm conditions would be passed to the central computer for further processing.

Peter and Chris continued:

When completed the PIN will be a general purpose, flexible, low-cost means to obtain detailed and up-to-date information on every major aspect of a factory's operation. It allows management to improve quality, productivity, and profitability by keeping them informed about the factory *now* instead of a week from now.

Development of PIN and the Brick

Although Dysys management anticipated that the PIN and the Brick would contribute significantly to future revenue, both projects had slipped behind schedule in recent months. Chris Zinck headed up the research and development on PIN, but with the need for business to sustain Dysys operations, he found himself working on a variety of projects. As a result, PIN deadlines had been hard to meet. This was not a significant problem at this stage as no other company offered a similar production information system.

Dysys planned to focus its PIN development efforts mostly on the PSU and on the network linking the PSUs and the central computer. The central computers would be a bought-in item whose cost was estimated at around $75,000. Each PSU was anticipated to cost about $3,000. The intention of the company's management was to develop PIN in two stages. The first item to be produced was a stand-alone PSU, sold to customers as an introduction to the PIN system. This would connect to a maximum of 16 lines on the machinery it was to monitor. At various times during the day, a manager might get reports from the PSU dumped to a connected printer. The second stage involved developing the multiple-station PSU and its linkage to the central computer.

Four technical problems had to be overcome before PIN would be fully operational: (1) a suitable method of communicating between the central computer and numerous PSUs had to be developed; (2) a microprocessor high-level language in which the operating software for the PSU will be written had to be selected, modified, or written from scratch; (3) the software to implement the PSU had to be designed and developed; and (4) the required hardware to implement the PSU had to be developed. The second problem was considered the most critical and innovative part of the system.

Dysys management felt that the PIN project had a reasonably successful chance of completion. Dysys experience in developing prior hardware and software would aid them with the PIN. Because of this experience, management regarded Dysys as ahead of most companies in the area of production monitoring at the present time.

Some 40 companies in the metropolitan Halifax area were thought to be potential customers. At some stage Dysys would have to line up one company for test purposes. Crossley Karastan was the obvious candidate—having had four years of useful life from the previous prototype, but Peter's main contact there was no longer with the firm.

If the Dysys development worked out, the market for the system could be very large. The management of Dysys occasionally speculated how the PIN would be marketed. For the most part, however, their attention was focused on solving the technical problems the system faced and in keeping the firm's "head above water." In part, work on the PIN was financed by a $30,000 grant from the National Research Council under its Industrial Research Assistance Program. A second payment in the same amount was expected in September 1984. By the spring of 1984 Dysys was about six months behind the schedule they had in mind for the PIN. As one component of the PIN, the Brick was also experiencing some slippage in development.

The Dysys Management

Peter Gregson was regarded by other members of the Dysys organization as something of a visionary. He was quite eager to take on any technically interesting job for one customer if it had the potential for later, broader sales. Although devoted to the development of the PIN, he was favourably disposed to considering other innovative product areas as long as these offered the possibility of long-run profitability.

Ted Mussett was generally considered to be strong in the areas of consulting with small- and medium-sized businesses on the applicability of microprocessors and associated software to office applications and in marketing the products for which Dysys held dealerships. Where Ted felt he could use more expertise, however, was in the custom end of the business, for he felt ill-equipped to prepare price quotations and to schedule work involving in-house development of hardware or software. This problem had shown itself when a Board of Trade contract took longer than expected and, consequently, ran over budget.

Because of this sort of difficulty, Chris Zinck was consulted prior to many projects being accepted. In fact, Chris ended up working in a number of areas which made it hard to push the PIN project ahead quickly. Chris partly covered for Peter Gregson's absence from the firm. He shared many of Peter's characteristics, being technically competent and liking involvement in new and interesting projects.

One idea the management team was toying with was the recruitment of a technical salesperson to compensate for Ted's lack of experience in bidding on and developing technical proposals. Such an appointment would also help Ted by freeing up some time for general administration. Dysys had no office personnel, so it was Ted who looked after payables, receivables, payroll, paper flow, and telephone reception. This meant that he spent a lot of time dealing with office concerns when he felt his skills were in the selling function.

The Future

Peter, Ted, and Chris were all a little concerned about the future of Dysys. The need to generate cash flows to ensure survival had pulled the firm in some directions that were not initially planned. Furthermore, due to project conflicts, some of the areas where the company believed it had a real edge had not been developed as quickly as they might. Although neither of the two co-owners had invested much money in the firm, both were anxious to see it succeed. Ted enjoyed being his own boss and was prepared to settle for a ''reasonable'' income to ensure the firm's survival and future prosperity. Peter continued to enjoy having his own company.

Working capital requirements had increased quite a bit recently with the adoption of the Chameleon line. Considerable inventory had to be carried, and Dysys acquired a bank loan of $10,000 for this purpose in January 1984. Management hoped to limit future bank financing to that needed to cover purchase orders on a short-term basis. However, they were beginning to recognize that more substantial funding might be necessary. Both of the owners were really against the idea of increased debt. Having been ''burned'' with Micronet, Peter was hesitant to become too financially exposed with Dysys. As well, the newness of Dysys and its lack of really tangible assets did not predispose bankers too favourably to the firm.

However, further capitalization appeared necessary if the dealer activities, development of the PIN and the Brick, and custom work were all to go ahead.

Exhibit 6: Project Assessments

Projects Dysys had undertaken to date were assessed by Peter Gregson, Ted Mussett, Chris Zinck, Tom Cooper, and David Lane. Assessments were made of each project's financial return to Dysys as well as the project's success as perceived by the customer.

	Assessment	
	Dysys	*Customer*
Remanco Restaurant Information System:		
A number of installations for a Halifax restaurant owner	Good	Good
Clipper II (Autobar—see below)	Fair	Good
Computer systems:		
The predecessor to Chameleon	Poor	Fair
Chameleon	Good	Good
Custom hardware and software:		
Shipboard Rules of Road Training Device	Good	Good
Two consulting projects carried out by Peter Gregson	Good(2)	Good(1)/Fair(1)
Maritime Commercial Travellers Association	Poor	Good
Autobar—development of automatic liquor dispenser to tie		
into Remanco system	Poor	Poor
Bar Code Reader	Poor	Poor
The Brick	Good	Good
Eye Movement system	Poor	Good
Production Support Unit	Good	Not completed
Board of Trade/Emergency Intercom Controller	Poor	Not completed

More government money was one option. Although not to be overlooked, government funding had certain associated drawbacks. First, they required extensive record keeping and the generation of considerable paperwork—all expensive activities. Second, too much reliance on government could also lead to insularity from the rigorous competition of the marketplace. All things considered, the Dysys management team had to decide what to do—both in the near future as well as in the longer term. To aid them in their deliberations, the four full-timers and Peter Gregson had come up with an assessment of the various projects Dysys had been involved in since its formation in 1982 (see Exhibit 6).

Case 17

Falconbridge Nickel Mines, Ltd.

In January 1978 Gord Slade, the recently appointed vice president and general manager of the Canadian Nickel Division (Sudbury Operations) of Falconbridge Nickel Mines, Ltd., was preparing for a planning meeting with his senior management team. The consolidated earnings reports for 1977 showed that the company had suffered a consolidated loss of $29 million. The Integrated Nickel Operations, of which the Canadian Nickel Division was part, had recorded a loss of over $21 million. Forecast reports indicated that the slack in world nickel demand that had begun in 1975 would not abate in 1978, and the company had already announced reductions in both production levels and personnel levels. Employee morale, union-management relations, and community-company relations were at an all-time low. In the midst of all these problems, an immediate issue facing Slade was whether he should continue an organization development program which had been initiated by his recently deceased predecessor.

The Nickel Industry: Historical Perspective

Nickel is a hard, lustrous metal with properties that make it suitable for use in the manufacture of a wide range of alloys. When mixed with other metals, it provides the resultant alloy with durability, strength, hardness, and resistance to corrosion and tarnish. The demand for nickel is a derived demand, dependent to a large extent on the fortunes of the steel industry. The steel industry consumes nickel principally as an alloying ingredient in the production of stainless steel.[1] In terms of end uses, significant segments include consumer products, machinery and transportation, automotive items, electronics, chemicals, and the petroleum industry. While nickel has many uses for peacetime industrial purposes, it is also viewed as a strategic metal in the manufacture of military goods.

Nickel occurs in the form of nickel silicate in both simple and complex ores in many parts of the world, but most deposits are either too small or too low in grade to permit economic exploitation. Further, new mine complexes evolve over extended periods of time, and there can be a time lag of anywhere from 2 to 15 years between the discovery of ore reserves and the actual production of a

This case is adapted, by Mark C. Baetz, from Stella M. Nkomo, "Falconbridge Nickel Mines, Ltd.," in Comerford and Callaghan, STRATEGIC MANAGEMENT: TEXT, TOOLS, AND CASES FOR BUSINESS POLICY (Boston: Kent Publishing Company, 1985), pp. 768–802. Copyright © 1985 by Wadsworth, Inc. Reprinted by permission of Kent Publishing Company, a division of Wadsworth, Inc.

[1] Standard and Poor's Industry Surveys, no. 2 (January 1981), p. M188.

Exhibit 1: World Smelter-Refinery Production of Nickel (in metric tons)

Year	United States	Canada	Greece	New Caledonia	Dominican Republic	Cuba	USSR*	World Total
R1977	34,400	168,700	9,600	28,300	24,900	18,500	165,000	723,700
1976	30,600	176,400	16,500	38,200	24,400	18,400	151,000	736,400
1975	19,900	178,000	14,800	52,800	26,900	18,500	143,000	703,900
1974	12,700	190,900	15,100	48,500	31,200	15,000	134,600	717,500
1973	12,600	174,200	13,900	35,800	30,100	17,000	130,000	653,900
1972	14,300	147,200	11,300	37,300	17,400	17,600	124,000	591,400
1971	15,452	206,619	10,000	32,200	25,500	36,281	115,000	600,000
1970	15,500	204,000	8,600	28,000	28,000	36,000	110,000	604,800
1969	15,800	124,000	5,600	23,900	23,900	37,000	105,000	473,200

* Estimated, R—Revised.
Source: World Bureau of Metal Statistics.

saleable product. The large nickel-copper deposits discovered in 1883 in the Sudbury Basin in Ontario made it possible for Canadian producers to benefit from decreasing costs in extracting the ore as the scale of mining expanded. For almost a century, Canada has been the dominant nickel-producing country in the world, but that dominance has been challenged by a large expansion in production in other countries, such as the USSR. (See Exhibit 1.)

The early leadership of Canada in the nickel industry was matched by the dominance of one company in the basin. The Canadian Copper Company (which later became part of International Nickel Company) was able to secure the largest and highest grade of ore in the area and to become at times the only producer there.[2] The small number of economically feasible refining processes helped to limit the number of producers. Control over both mines and a refining process that enabled a company to produce refined nickel was the key to success in the industry. When International Nickel was formed in April 1902, it became the sole producer of nickel in the Sudbury district. This monopoly was short-lived with the emergence of Falconbridge Nickel Mines in 1928. In 1953 a third, smaller company, Sherritt Gordon Mines, began producing at Lynn Lake, Manitoba. For the next 20 years, these firms competed in an environment of growing demand with only short periods of reduced demand (see Exhibit 2).

The major problem confronting the nickel industry has been the disparity between peace and war requirements. During both world wars, it was the Canadian nickel producers who not only successfully supplied the Allies with the nickel required for military purposes but also met essential civilian needs. Defense needs forced producers to accelerate and expand production to increase the supply of nickel. During peacetime, however, the problem became one of developing a volume of commercial demand commensurate with the excess

---

[2] O. W. Main, *The Canadian Nickel Industry* (Toronto: The University of Toronto Press, 1955), p. 111.

Exhibit 2:   World Nickel Shipments—World, Less People's Republic of China, Comecon Countries, and Cuba

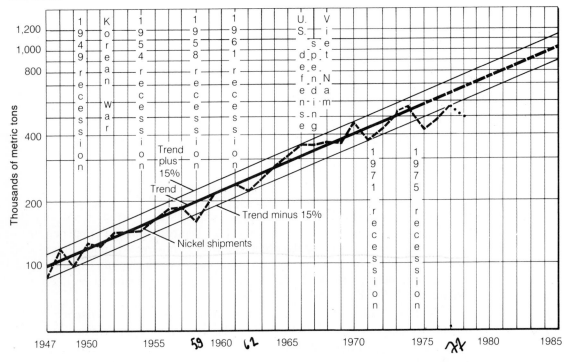

Historical figures 1947–1974
Metallgesellschaft A.G.
1975-Falconbridge International Limited

Long-term forecast
Falconbridge International Limited

Short-term forecast
Falconbridge International Limited

Source: Company documents.

production capacity. The familiar pattern for the industry has been the need to gear up production to meet wartime requirements and then to revert to the task of trying to build up peacetime markets at the end of the war.

The Significance and Operations of Falconbridge

The rise of Falconbridge Nickel Mines to the position of a major nickel producer came from an aggressive exploratory program and from contracts signed with the U.S. government. Under these long-term contracts, the company delivered over 200 million pounds of nickel to the United States. Through the 1952–1962 decade, these sales made it possible for Falconbridge to secure the necessary funds for expansion and provided a stability of production that was unusual in an industry known for the cyclical nature of its demand.

From its beginning until around 1962, Falconbridge Nickel Mines concentrated upon the mining, milling, and smelting operations located in the Sudbury Basin. A refinery in Norway was the only operation outside of the Sudbury area. The purchase of this refinery in 1930 had given Falconbridge access to important trade secrets and the patent rights to the electrolytic nickel refining process. In 1962 the company merged with its corporate parent, Ventures, Ltd. Through this merger, Falconbridge acquired the holdings of several wholly owned subsidiary and associated companies spread across four continents that had previously been under the control of Ventures. With this merger Falconbridge entered a new phase in its development as a corporation.

In 1977 Falconbridge was a large, multinational company engaged in the exploration, mining, smelting, and refining of mineral ores and the marketing of mineral products, on a worldwide basis, directly and through subsidiary and associated companies. (See Exhibit 3.) The primary products of the company were nickel and copper, although many other mineral products, such as cobalt, gold, and silver were also produced (see Exhibit 4). In response to changes in customer needs and technical developments in the stainless steel industry, Falconbridge diversified its basic nickel product to include: (1) nickel 98—a granular form of pure nickel for high alloy melting applications, (2) nickel crowns,

Exhibit 3: Falconbridge Nickel Mines, Ltd.

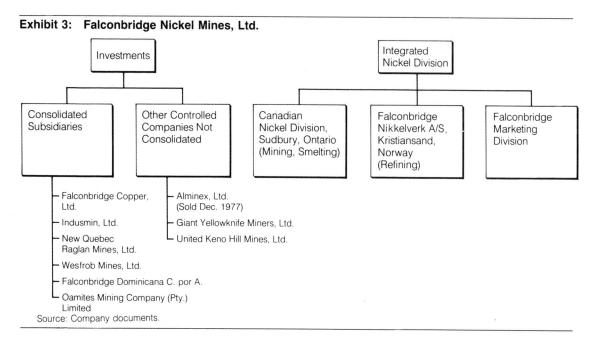

Source: Company documents.

Exhibit 4: Products and Locations of Major Divisions and Subsidiaries

Business	Principal Products	Principal Location of Assets
Intergrated Nickel Operations	Nickel, copper, cobalt	Ontario, Manitoba, Norway
Alminex, Ltd. (sold 1977)	Oil and gas	Alberta
Falconbridge Copper, Ltd.	Copper, zinc, and precious metals	Ontario, Quebec
Falconbridge Dominicana	Ferronickel	Dominican Republic
Indusmin, Ltd.	Industrial minerals and castings	Ontario, Quebec
Oamites Mining Company (Proprietary Ltd.)	Copper	Southwest Africa
Wesfrob Mines, Ltd.	Iron and copper	British Columbia

Source: Falconbridge Nickel Mines, Ltd., annual report, 1978.

and (3) ferronickel—an ingot product for steel making.[3] The volumes of the various Falconbridge metal products and sales prices for these products are shown in Exhibits 5 and 6.

Integrated Nickel Operations

The Integrated Nickel Operations of Falconbridge consisted of the Nickel Division, Sudbury Operations; Falconbridge Nikkelverk; and the Falconbridge Marketing Division. These divisions were engaged in the integrated operations of mining, milling, smelting, refining, and marketing of nickel mainly derived from Canadian ores. These operations constituted the core business of Falconbridge.

The marketing function was structured to serve worldwide customers. In addition to marketing nickel, ferronickel, copper, and various by-products, they also negotiated sales and purchase contracts covering a variety of ferrous and nonferrous metal concentrates, refined precious metals, and other raw materials.[4] Shipments of Falconbridge's products were made to all major world markets, including Europe, Japan, and North America. In recent years, as part of a long-range plan to restructure its worldwide marketing activities, Falconbridge strategically located commercial operations in Bermuda, the United States, and Europe. This decentralization gave Falconbridge the capability to develop a stronger marketing presence and a closer involvement with its customers' needs.

The production operations of the Integrated Nickel Division were interdependent with mining and reduction of ore to a substance known as matte done at Sudbury, and the matte refining was handled by the Norwegian refinery. The matte produced at Sudbury was sent by rail to Quebec, where it was then shipped

[3] Falconbridge Nickel Mines, Ltd. (Presentation to a Select Committee of the Ontario Legislature, January 4, 1978), pp. 16–17.

[4] Falconbridge Nickel Mines, Ltd., annual report, 1976, p. 33.

Exhibit 5:   Metal Deliveries (pounds) by the Integrated Nickel Operations and the Ferronickel Division of Falconbridge

	1974	1975	1976	1977
Refined nickel in all forms*	93,595,000	65,177,000	83,615,000	34,887,000
Ferronickel	73,828,000	50,270,000	59,781,000	43,394,000
	167,423,000	115,447,000	143,396,000	78,281,000
Copper*	56,133,000	42,978,000	36,081,000	44,949,000
Cobalt	2,468,000	1,365,000	2,079,000	1,494,000

* Includes nickel and copper refined and sold on a commission basis.
Source: 1975 and 1977 annual reports.

Exhibit 6:   Metal Sales Prices, 1974–1977

	1974	1975	1976	1977
Metal sales prices (per pound—U.S. currency):				
Electrolytic nickel (at December 31)	$1.85	$2.20	$2.41	$2.08
Ferronickel (at December 31)	1.46	2.18	2.36	2.00
Copper (per London Metal Exchange)				
January 1	0.89	0.55	0.53	0.61
High	1.47	0.64	0.77	0.70
December 31	0.56	0.53	0.61	0.57

Source: 1975 and 1977 annual reports.

to Norway for refining. The refinery produced refined nickel cathodes, nickel 98 granules, and nickel crowns, as well as copper cathodes, cobalt cathodes, and liquid SO_2.[5] Additional metals recovered include gold, silver, platinum, palladium, iridium, ruthenium, rhodium, and selenium.

Nickel Division—Sudbury Operations

Sudbury Operations produced over 90 percent of the nickel treated at the refinery. Copper and cobalt were secondary products of the division. Sudbury Operations was by far the largest group in the company, employing over 4,000 workers in 1975 (see Exhibit 7) and was the second largest employer in the Sudbury community. Inco Metals, with approximately 15,000 employees, was the largest employer and the major competitor for labour in the area. Sudbury, with a population of over 150,000, was the largest nickel-mining community in the world. As mining communities go, Sudbury was quite typical. Its prosperity and survival were closely intertwined with the profitability and operations of Falconbridge and Inco.

Employees of Sudbury Operations were represented by three unions. Local 598 of the Sudbury Mine, Mill, and Smelter Workers' Union represented the

---

[5] Select Committee Report, p. 5.

Exhibit 7: Nickel Division—Sudbury Operations: Manpower, 1974–1977

	1974	1975	1976	1977
Production and maintenance	3,405	2,937	2,943	2,699
Office, clerical, and technical	538	519	475	400
Staff	571	564	551	478
Other	60	68	30	29
Total	4,574	4,088	3,999	3,606

Source: Company documents.

---

production and maintenance workers. This was the last remaining independent local of the old Mine, Mill, and Smelter Workers' Union that was taken over across North America by the United Steelworkers in the late 1950s. The local had a reputation of being a strong union capable of tough bargaining on behalf of its membership. Since 1967 the office, clerical, and technical employees were represented by the United Steelworkers of America. A small third union represented the security guards. Unlike Falconbridge, Inco's production workers were represented by the United Steelworkers of America.

The production facilities of the Sudbury operations included 10 mines, 3 concentrators, and 1 smelter in 1975. Two of the mines were under development, three of the mines were temporarily closed in 1975, and one of the concentrators was temporarily closed. A project to build new smelting facilities at an estimated cost of $85 million to reduce the emission of SO_2 and particulates to the atmosphere was started in 1974 with a scheduled completion date of April 1978.

Organization Structure at Falconbridge

Falconbridge's corporate organization structure was designed to operate a widely divergent group of companies. In 1975 the company consisted of four major divisions: Nickel Division, Ferronickel Division, Minerals Division, and Eastern Minerals Division (see Exhibit 8). Corporate headquarters were located in downtown Toronto, and research facilities were located at Thornhill, Ontario, and Kristiansand, Norway.

At the Sudbury Operations, the managers of technical services, mine development, production, metallurgy, and administrative services all reported directly to the assistant general manager (see Exhibit 9). The position of shift boss was equivalent to that of a first-line supervisor.

Given the nature of the mining business, the production function was seen as the critical unit in the achievement of performance goals and objectives. Hierarchical authority relationships, detailed rules and regulations, and a tight military style of organization so typical of firms in the mining industry had served Falconbridge well.

Exhibit 8:   Corporate Organization Structure, 1975

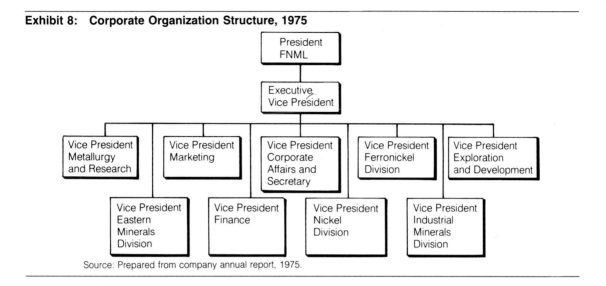

Source: Prepared from company annual report, 1975.

Reorganization

In 1976 as part of a major reorganization at the corporate level, John Mather was appointed president of a newly formed Canadian Nickel Division. His mandate was to improve the overall effectiveness of Sudbury Operations. Mather had been president and managing director of Indusmin, Ltd., a subsidiary company that produced industrial minerals and metal castings.[6] The reorganization resulted in greater autonomy for Sudbury Operations, which was made part of the Canadian Nickel Division. The positions of executive vice president, vice president— Nickel Division, and assistant vice president—Nickel Division were eliminated, and a four-person senior management team was established with Mather reporting directly to the president of Falconbridge. Under the realignment, the vice president and general manager of Sudbury Operations reported directly to Mather. A functional structure was established at the operational level. Under the new structure, the levels of management were reduced from 13 to 7 (see Exhibit 10). The new structure was intended to shorten lines of communication, to decentralize authority and responsibility, to improve participative decision making, and to help build the long-term strength of the company. Mather established five key objectives for organization development for the division:[7]

1. To reduce the number of levels of supervision.

2. To select the best possible candidates for managerial positions.

[6] Falconbridge Nickel Mines, Ltd., annual report, 1976, p. 10.

[7] G. R. Buckland, "What's Happening at Falconbridge?" (Speech to Sudbury Council of the Institute of Canadian Bankers, May 14, 1980).

Exhibit 9:   Corporate Organization and Sudbury Operations Organization, Early 1970s

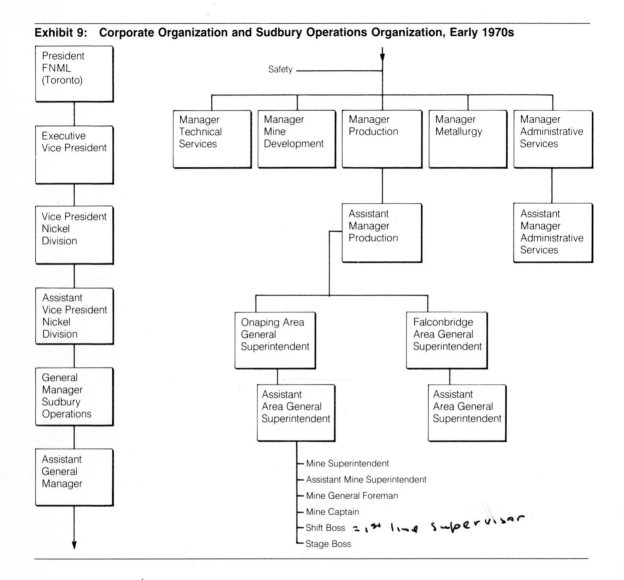

3. To push authority down in the organization.

4. To emphasize performance, related to costs and profits consciousness.

5. To adopt a team approach to problem solving and decision making.

The new organization structure at Sudbury Operations was implemented all at once to minimize disruption. Mather firmly believed that the change process could be successful if it was carried out quickly. Under Mather's leadership the management team and other supervisory employees attended intensive organization development seminars. At these seminars, issues and concerns were

Exhibit 10: Structure after Reorganization in 1976 and 1977

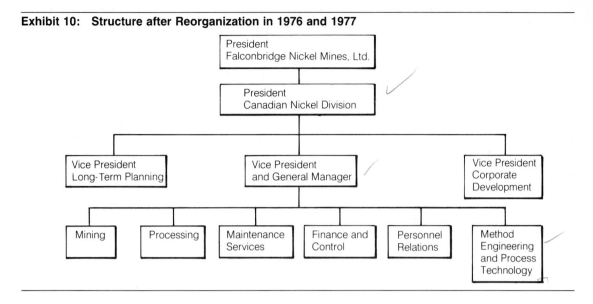

discussed in an open and candid manner. This process was designed to have individuals evaluate their own management styles, to learn team-style management, to understand the requisites of effective management behavior, and to make individuals receptive to change. Mather's goal was to build a strong management team capable of working together in achieving organizational goals and objectives. Mather was an advocate of participative management, and he was determined to implement that style of management in the division. Effectiveness areas with measurement criteria were developed for each functional group. Areas of responsibilities were developed for each functional group. Areas of responsibilities were developed through a team process. (Exhibit 11 gives examples of the effectiveness areas and measurement criteria for two managers—the general manager and the manager of mines.) By mid-1977 the organization development program was in full gear, and the gradual process of improving the effectiveness of Sudbury Operations had begun. While receptivity to change was high, the implementation of the new process was not without strain.

Ups and Downs of the Nickel Market

Through the late 1960s Falconbridge, Inco, and Sherritt accounted for about two thirds of the total supply of nickel. During this period production levels could not keep up with demand, and a world shortage developed. The nickel shortage was so chronic that additional supplies were made available from U.S. government stockpiles and by increased imports from communist countries, especially the USSR.

Projections of future nickel market demand in 1970 were quite optimistic, and

---

Exhibit 11: Management Team Effectiveness Areas

Effectiveness Areas	*Measurement Criteria*
General manager:	
1. Subordinate effectiveness	Subordinate objectives achieved
2. Allocation of capital	Relative ROI
3. Health and safety policy	Policy implemented
4. Production level: present and long-term Sudbury Operations	Production level set in time
Manager—mines:	
1. Mining production strategy	$/lb. NiCu hoisted*
2. Capital allocation	ROI
3. Mine development	In time and at cost

  * NiCu = Abbreviations for nickel and copper respectively.
  Source: Company documents.

---

an annual growth rate of 6 percent was predicted with only temporary periods of over- and undersupply. Nickel producer prices rose from U.S. 77¾ cents a pound in 1965 to $1.28 a pound in November 1969. Price was expected to climb to $3 a pound during the 1970s.[8] These predictions of steady demand and increasing prices made it prudent for existing producers to develop new supply sources and for new firms to enter the market. In 1970 Falconbridge and other producers announced major new investments in lateritic operations in the tropics.[9] New firms entering both the sulfuric and lateritic nickel market included Western Mining Corporation, Amax, and Freeport, Queensland Nickel. By-product nickel derived from the expanding mining industry in South Africa also increased supplies of nickel. The cumulative impact of all these developments was a huge increase in nickel production between 1971 and 1974.

During 1975 a substantial oversupply of nickel developed, mainly as the result of reductions in specialty steel production, which had dropped as low as 60 percent of 1974 output in important international markets.[10] Much of the nickel sold in 1974 had simply accumulated as excessive user inventory because many consumers had purchased metal as a hedge against inflationary commodity prices. Industry shipments fell 35 percent in 1975.

Unlike earlier downturns, a simultaneous weakness developed in both capital and consumer goods demand. However, many industry watchers expected that market improvement would occur in 1976 and 1977. After a brief upsurge in the early part of 1976, the anticipated stabilization did not occur, and industry shipments continued their downward trend while producer inventory levels rose (see Exhibit 12). This situation had an adverse impact on the performance of the Integrated Nickel Operations of Falconbridge. (See Exhibit 13.) By 1977 the

---

  [8] Guy Stanley and John Eichmanis, "The Great Inco Layoff Dilemma," *The Financial Post,* November 4, 1978, p. 40.

  [9] Ibid., p. 4.

  [10] Falconbridge Nickel Mines, Ltd., annual report, 1975, p. 25.

Exhibit 12:   Noncommunist World: Nickel Production/Nickel Shipments, 1967–1976

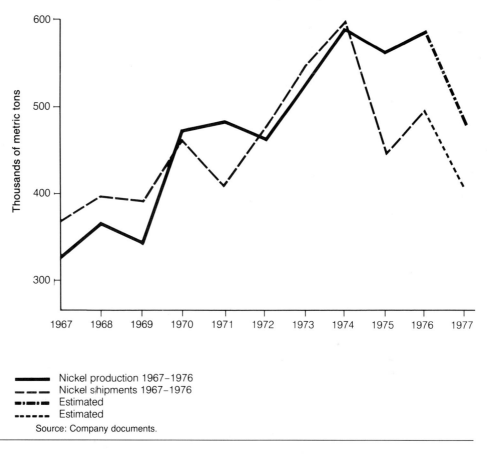

Nickel production 1967–1976
Nickel sihipments 1967–1976
Estimated
Estimated
Source: Company documents.

inventories of metals at Falconbridge had reached $135 million, increasing steadily from $30 million in 1974.

Labour Relations at Falconbridge, 1975–1977

During 1975 both Falconbridge and International Nickel were engaged in contract negotiations with their production workers, and the traditional model was for Inco to set the "district pattern." Russ Buckland, manager of human resources and public affairs, described the process this way:

> Tactically it's to our advantage to go second (in terms of negotiations) because our viability depends on being able to be cost competitive with Inco. Certainly, this does not allow us to pay signficantly more than a miner receives at Inco. The objective is to pay the same as Inco with a few additional things that make us more attractive in order to attract and retain good employees.

Exhibit 13: Overview of Performance of Falconbridge, 1973–1977 (dollars in thousands)

	1977	1976	1975	1974	1973
Earnings (loss):					
Revenues	$381,684	$483,480	$409,888	$443,508	$426,834
Earnings (loss)—contributions after consolidation adjustments before extraordinary item:					
Unallocated corporate[a]	(16,303)	(5,717)	(4,352)	(2,688)	(2,711)
Alminex Limited	3,776	3,424	2,952	2,922	2,040
Falconbridge Copper Limited	2,913	1,637	198	3,981	12,295
Falconbridge Dominicana, C. por A	2,788	8,834	5,689	3,309	9,933
Indusmin Limited[b]	1,251	2,019	2,821	1,307	1,287
Integrated nickel operations	(21,629)	4,727	(5,390)	16,395	19,425
Oamites Mining Company (Prop.) Limited	(336)	128	739	1,433	2,406
United Keno Hill Mines Limited	1,168	841	1,442	2,946	1,159
Wesfrob Mines Limited	(2,211)	(337)	(1,361)	539	2,753
Others[b]	(640)	(853)	503	451	756
Earnings (loss) (before extraordinary item)	(29,223)	14,703	3,221	30,595	49,343
Property, plant, and equipment (net):					
Producing	304,768	255,217	283,611	282,803	303,767
Nonproducing	150,356	167,654	143,178	137,504	105,021
Long-term debt	291,394	223,715	255,121	274,616	288,493
Shareholders' data:					
Shareholders' equity	383,127	321,249	311,433	312,437	291,887
Exploration, research and development:					
Exploration	$ 9,726	$ 8,325	$ 7,826	$ 11,432	$ 8,895
Research and development	3,844	3,769	4,100	4,382	3,304
Capital expenditures:					
Expenditures (net) on property, plant equipment, development and preproduction:					
Integrated nickel operations[c]	62,267	27,954	38,161	30,442	21,156
Falconbridge Dominicana, C. por A RD	2,908	1,490	1,934	5,571	2,123
Falconbridge Copper, Ltd.[d]	5,415	8,903	7,400	14,968	9,076
Consolidated total	78,848	44,188	56,367	59,315	40,632
Metal sales (000 pounds):					
Integrated nickel operations:					
Nickel	32,047	80,176	61,524	89,464	99,408
Copper	42,677	34,076	40,713	53,981	53,725
Falconbridge Nickel Mines, Ltd..					
Nickel in ferronickel[e]	43,394	59,781	50,270	73,828	67,644
Falconbridge Copper, Ltd.[d]					
Copper	92,369	82,939	77,503	56,911	80,935
Zinc	89,032	73,430	73,767	30,838	37,950

Exhibit 13 (*concluded*)

	1977	1976	1975	1974	1973
Ore Reserves (000 tons):					
Falconbridge Nickel Mines, Ltd.	80,670	83,405	89,099	90,578	92,798
Falconbridge Dominicana, C. por A	70,000	72,500	63,700	66,000	68,500
Falconbridge Copper, Ltd.*d*	8,653	7,187	9,234	11,004	11,287

Notes: a. Before interest in earnings of Alminex Limited and United Keno Hill Mines Limited which are shown separately.
  b. For comparative purposes the 1973 to 1975 figures have been restated to combine the contribution of Indusmin and Fahralloy Canada, Ltd. In 1976, Fahramet, Ltd., a subsidiary of Indusmin, Ltd., acquired the operating assets of Fahralloy Canada, Ltd.
  c. Includes both the integrated nickel operations and company's corporate operations.
  d. This company was formed through an amalgamation of a number of companies in 1971. For comparative purposes the figures have been presented as if the amalgamation had been in effect thoughout 1968 to 1971.
  e. Ferronickel sales to customers.
Source: Company annual report, 1977.

After Inco successfully concluded its collective bargaining in July 1975, Falconbridge management fully expected production and maintenance workers to settle on the district pattern. However, on August 21, 1975, production and maintenance workers decided to test the district pattern and went out on a 10-week strike. The last strike at Sudbury Operations was in 1969.

After the strike began, the Canadian government announced that it would be instituting wage and price controls to curb inflation. This announcement led to a great deal of concern over the progress of negotiations aimed at settling the strike. Under the Wage and Price Guidelines instituted by the Federal Anti-Inflation Review Board, employers were allowed to pay only up to the same rate paid to employees working in the same community who performed similar jobs. This meant that the Falconbridge workers could receive under these new government regulations only what the Inco workers were receiving. The three-year contract, which was approved by the Review Board, while providing substantial increase in both wages and benefits, conformed with the district pattern. Many union members were not pleased with the way things had developed and felt that they had in essence not gained anything from their strike. The strike and production curtailment costs amounted to over $8 million to the company.[11]

In early November, shortly after the strike was over, management announced a temporary cutback in production due to the continued effects of a depressed nickel market. In a two-phase program, the Fecunis Lake Mill; the East, Fecunis Lake, and Onaping Mines; and one furnace in the smelter were temporarily closed down. Notice of termination required by Ontario's Labour Laws was posted on November 21, November 28, and December 5.[12] The layoff procedure was implemented in accordance with terms established in the collective agreements.

[11] Ibid.

[12] Falconbridge Nickel Mines, Ltd., company press release, November 14, 1975.

The curtailment of operations, coming shortly after the settlement of a long strike, imposed an additional strain on union-management relations.

The steelworkers union claimed that the procedures used by Falconbridge to lay off employees were illegal under the Ontario Provincial Employment Standards Act[13] and filed a complaint with the Ontario Ministry of Labour. They claimed that employees should have received a longer 12-week notice period as there was a permanent discontinuance of part of Falconbridge's business in the Sudbury area, and in the absence of this notice each employee was now entitled to 12 weeks of severance pay. The Steelworkers were later joined by the Mine, Mill Union in this challenge to the company's actions. Company officials maintained that they were in full compliance with the Ontario Labour Act because there was not to be a permanent discontinuance of all or any part of the company's business; rather, these plants were closed on a temporary basis only. On October 6, 1976, Falconbridge was ordered by an Ontario Ministry of Labour–appointed referee to pay almost $1 million in severance pay to the 407 employees who had been laid off.[14] This matter was subsequently appealed successfully by the company at a higher court.

The decrease in production of nickel, cobalt, and copper at Sudbury also affected the operating rate of the refinery in Norway. Capacity was maintained at about two thirds of its normal rate, and the labour force was adjusted accordingly. Weak nickel demand also necessitated the temporary suspension of the $85 million Smelter Environment Improvement Program at Sudbury on which a substantial amount of construction work had already been completed.

Layoffs

As 1977 unfolded there were some indications that the nickel market, which had made a brief recovery in 1976, was again deteriorating. Although management was concerned, production plans remained unchanged into August of that year. When the nickel market did not improve, management officials of Sudbury Operations met with the representatives of the Mine, Mill, and Smelter Workers' Union and the United Steelworkers of America on August 10, 1977, to notify them of a revised production plan for the remainder of the year.

Mather assembled his new management team to determine the best way in which to handle the necessary reduction in the work force. The key objectives in reducing personnel were to minimize the impact on people and at the same time to reduce personnel costs. A first decision was to shut down Sudbury Operations completely for a four-week period from September 11 to October 9, 1977, then to shut down for a four-day weekend over the Remembrance Day Holiday and over the week from Christmas to New Year's Day. These total shutdowns were an

---

[13] Section 40 of the Employment Standards Act permits an employer to terminate large numbers of employees with regular notice requirements provided the number does not exceed 10 percent of the total work force and provided the terminations are not caused by permanent discontinuance of all or part of that business.

[14] *The Sudbury Star*, October 5, 1976.

alternative to layoffs.[15] G. A. Allen, vice president and general manager of Sudbury Operations, said the company's decision to curtail production was deferred as long as possible "in the hope that production curtailments could be avoided." It was also announced at that time that additional measures would be taken if nickel sales did not improve.

At the end of August, following a full review of personnel requirements by the management team at the reduced 1977 production level, it was decided that the total work force would have to be reduced by an additional 350 employees by the end of 1977. This reduction included 80 salaried positions, 70 office, clerical, and technical positions, and 200 production and maintenance positions. Additionally, it was decided that the North Mine would be temporarily closed and placed on standby. Expenditures in the Sudbury area for new projects, development, exploration, and research were postponed or delayed. To reduce the impact of the layoffs on younger service employees, the company introduced a number of programs; a special early retirement program was offered on a voluntary basis to all union employees 60 years of age and over. It was also expected that normal attrition would help to reduce the number of employees to be laid off. Discussions with union officials resulted in the early retirement program being extended to workers 55 and over, and a special extended-leave-of-absence policy was also adopted so that highly skilled workers could take leaves rather than be laid off. All of these efforts were undertaken to lessen the impact of layoffs on employees.

Decreased production at Sudbury affected production plans at the Norwegian refinery, and plans were made to reduce the working hours of all employees by 20 percent with a corresponding reduction in pay. Similar programs were planned for the Metallurgical Laboratories at Thornhill, Ontario, and a staff reduction was made at corporate headquarters.

An Unexpected Change in Management

On September 7, 1977, John Mather, president of the Canadian Nickel Division; Gordon A. Allen, vice president, Canadian Nickel Division, and general manager, Sudbury Operations; and Roy A. Cleland, manager, engineering and process technology, Sudbury Operations, together with the company's controller and its chief pilot were killed in an air crash while travelling on a business flight from Sudbury to Toronto. The loss of these top management people combined with the earlier trauma of the shutdown of operations and layoffs sent morale at Sudbury Operations even lower. Gord Slade, who had been vice president of corporate development of the Canadian Nickel Division, took over operations and was appointed vice president and general manager of the Canadian Nickel Division. Slade had been fully committed to the organization development program that had been begun by Mather.

Slade had barely been in his new position for two months when the continuing

[15] Falconbridge Nickel Mines, Ltd., company press release.

weakness in the nickel market necessitated a further revision of production plans. In late 1977 management again met with the union representatives to advise them of 1978 production plans. Union representatives were advised that 1978 production requirements had been set at 45–50 million pounds of nickel in order to avoid additional buildup of inventory and to conserve cash. These plans were expected to result in the elimination of approximately 750 additional jobs, and a seven-week total shutdown of Sudbury Operations was scheduled in 1978.

By the end of 1977 the total reduction in the work force at year end was greater than the planned 350 that had been announced back in August. In fact, a total of 434 jobs had been eliminated through a combination of retirements, layoffs, and extended leaves of absence. Despite these measures, inventories of finished nickel in all forms amounted to 78,262,000 pounds at the end of 1977 compared with an inventory of 18,277,000 pounds at the end of 1976.

These layoffs were not unique to Falconbridge. Inco had also been forced to announce the layoff of 3,450 employees due to a 15 percent reduction in production. Civic, union, and political representatives were deeply concerned about the effect of the layoffs on the economic well-being of the Sudbury community.[16] Local community leaders felt that the layoffs would be extremely difficult for the community to absorb and that the negative social and economic impact would be tremendous. In response to these concerns, the Ontario legislature appointed a select committee to look into the layoffs in the nickel industry. Both Falconbridge and Inco were asked to appear before this committee in January 1978.

The Organization Development Program

While Slade was considering the various problems he faced, he knew he would soon have to make a decision about the organization development program which had been initiated in 1976 under John Mather. There were a number of initiatives which Slade was considering as part of this program.

The first initiative Slade considered was the use of team role labs (TRL). A TRL is an intensive three-day training session designed to focus attention on the development of each member of the team. At these sessions the emphasis is on analyzing individual roles, effectiveness, and responsibilities. The purpose of these sessions is to sharpen areas of responsibility and authority and to build commitment to both individual and team objectives. Openness and frankness would be encouraged during these sessions.

Teams could be organized around all management levels and departments. The senior management team, which consisted of Gord Slade and the five managers reporting directly to him, would be responsible for setting long-range planning objectives. During their TRL sessions, objectives would be set in the

---

[16] Norm Tollinsky, *Northern Life*, December 14, 1977.

areas of company policy, production, human resource utilization, and so forth. In turn, each of the five managers with the department heads could be involved in the TRL process to define the roles of the team and each individual member of the team. Responsibilities and objectives would be determined through consensus. All would participate in decisions affecting the entire team. In a like fashion, department heads, with their supervisors, would define their departments' responsibilities and objectives. In essence, the team leaders would function as "linking pins"—that is, they would be members of groups in which they were the managers or supervisors, and second, they would be members of groups in which they were one of the subordinates. Through this process long-range and strategic objectives would be integrated with departmental objectives, unit objectives, and the objectives of each individual in the organization. As a result, performance objectives and effectiveness areas would be clearly delineated, and each individual would have a clear understanding of the relationship of his or her responsibilities to the overall objectives of the company. The TRL exercise could be repeated each year and be an integral part of an overall organization development program for the division.

A second initiative being considered by Slade was a yearly attitude survey of all employees to find out their concerns in such areas as management style, leadership, organization structure, and company policies. Some of the questions on the survey being considered were as follows: "Supervisors are trusted around here—agree or disagree?" and "My job is important in this organization—agree or disagree?" The results of these annual surveys could be communicated in detail to all employees. Survey findings could provide information not only on companywide attitudes but also on attitudes within each department. Departmental teams could discuss the results of these surveys for their particular departments, and all department members could participate in developing action plans to solve any problems that might exist.

A third initiative being considered by Slade was a series of meetings to improve overall company communications. One type of meeting being considered was a "President's Annual Meeting." At such a meeting, employees in groups of 100 could meet during regular work hours with Gord Slade and other members of the senior management team to discuss company performance, long-term plans, and any problems or issues facing the company. The President's Annual Meeting could also take place in the evening so that employees' spouses and friends could be invited. Quarterly meetings could also be held with union executives of the three unions in the company to discuss production plans and any concerns or issues that existed. Additionally, meetings could be held with various groups of employees to discuss major changes in policy and programs before changes were made. Slade was also considering issuing to all employees a "Statement of Policy and Aims of the Management Team at Sudbury Operations." One draft of such a statement read as follows:

It is the aim of the Management of Sudbury Operations to:

1. Utilize available mineral resources to provide maximum long-term benefits for the shareholders, the employees, and the community.
2. Foster greater understanding of the company's activities by employees and the public.
3. Provide wages, benefits, and a quality of working life that will attract, motivate, and retain competent employees.
4. Encourage creativity and innovation so that we will occupy a position of leadership in the industry.
5. Give equal consideration to safety, health, and production in the design and operation of the company's facilities.
6. Minimize the effect of the company's operations on the natural environment.
7. Support education, cultural, and other community service organizations.

Other program and policies considered by Slade included:

- Ski days for families and friends of employees.
- Plant tours for families.
- Talk nights for major organization units.
- Christmas get-togethers for all employees.
- Replacement of number tags for underground employees by name tags.
- Removal of time clocks.
- Increased support to cultural groups and activities throughout the Sudbury area.

Slade wondered if he should wait to make a decision concerning the organization development program until the company's operating conditions improved.

Case 18

Federal Bermuda Line (A)

In March 1975 Mr. Lawrence G. Pathy, president of Federal Commerce and Navigation (1974) Ltd. was assessing a consultants report regarding the potential of a proposed shipping service for his company. At issue was whether to establish a new service from Halifax, Nova Scotia, to Hamilton, Bermuda.

The Federal Commerce and Navigation (1974) Ltd. was a Canadian company with its head office in Montreal, Quebec. As a subsidiary of Fednav Limited, a holding company, Federal Commerce and Navigation (1974) Ltd. offered various transportation services. In 1974 Mr. Pathy had commissioned a shipping consultant, Mr. John Grice of Analytic Services Limited, Halifax, to perform a feasibility study of the proposed service. The study report was completed by March 1975 and presented to Mr. Pathy. A summary of the most important points for Mr. Pathy to consider follows.

A Halifax-Bermuda Container Service—Feasibility Study

Bermuda is a British colony with responsible internal self-government. It has an area of 20.59 square miles and is located 756 miles (1217 kilometres) south-southwest of Halifax and 697 miles (1122 kilometres) south-southeast of New York. It lies astride the trade routes between Europe and the Gulf of Mexico and those routes linking Europe to the Far East via the Panama Canal. Furthermore, it is located on the trade route between Eastern Canada and the Caribbean. Historically, it has been serviced by ships plying those trade routes.

Bermuda has a resident population of 60,000, including 3,000 U.S. Air Force personnel and their dependents. Bermuda's trade flows are virtually all one-way, imports dominating almost nonexistent exports.

Industry and Trade

The principal local industry is tourism, which is the mainstay of the economy. Ranked second is the "exempted company" business, namely the use of Bermuda as an offshore financial centre and corporate base by international business organizations. These pay moderate annual license fees, employ large numbers of local staff, and purchase or rent considerable office space and private accommodation, but their activities are *outside* Bermuda.

This case was prepared by Professor Philip Rosson of Dalhousie University. Copyright © 1977 by Philip Rosson.

Exhibit 1: Total Bermuda Imports and Exports

	Value in Million U.S. Dollars (F.O.B.)*	
Year	Imports	Exports
1938	$ 9	$ 1
1948	29	4
1958	48	22
1963	55	39
1967	68	60
1968	73	65
1969	83	77
1970	87	81
1971	108	92
1972	114	36
1973	123	30
1974	155	34

* F.O.B. = Free on Board. The seller or supplier of goods is responsible for the cost of delivering them to the ship.
Source: *Yearbook of International Trade Statistics,* 1975, vol. 1, United Nations.

The relatively high cost of local labour—in a community where there are many more local jobs generated than there are Bermudians to fill them—has tended to reduce the effort to create local manufacturing industry in Bermuda (see Exhibits 1 and 2). Nevertheless, certain key industries do flourish—for example, the preparation of airline meals for all carriers serving Bermuda; the manufacture of paints; local arts and crafts including pottery, silkscreening, and woodworking; the distillation of various perfumes, toiletries, and a liquor made from loquat juice; ship repairs and servicing; printing and publishing. Service trades are also important and include banking and financial services; accountancy/audit preparation; wholesale and retail dealing in a wide range of goods and services. These all take advantage of Bermuda's stable political climate, absence of direct taxation, favourable geographical site close to the principal tourist and financial markets, and extremely well-developed communications.

Imports

The 10 leading nations supplying products to Bermuda in 1973 were as follows: United States (45 percent share), United Kingdom (20 percent), Canada (10 percent), Aruba/Curacao and France (3 percent each), New Zealand, Venezuela, West Germany, Netherlands, and Denmark (2 percent each). The Aruba/Curacao and Venezuela imports are largely of petroleum products. Thus 91 percent of Bermuda's imports are from 10 countries, and 75 percent are from 3 countries. The imports are almost totally of consumer goods that readily lend themselves to containerization. The U.S. trade is almost fully containerized, but this is not the case with U.K. and European cargoes; 80 percent of this trade moves on a

Exhibit 2:   Bermuda Imports and Exports for Selected Countries (U.S. dollars in thousands)

Year	General Imports F.O.B.				General Exports F.O.B.			
	1971	1972	1973	1974	1971	1972	1973	1974
EEC (Nine)	$34,589	$34,147	$37,373	$37,450	$47,040	$17,135	$6,179	$8,816
EFTA	2,127	1,903	1,826	2,059	3,623	307	2,169	1,003
United Kingdom	24,192	22,820	24,665	23,003	20,546	4,114	788	1,072
United States/								
Puerto Rico	48,747	54,666	55,372	68,696	1,535	2,080	4,172	4,865
Canada	13,063	13,323	12,082	13,394	586	508	808	968
New Zealand	1,911	2,975	2,924	3,664	307	1,190	2,025	473
Australia	51	67	100	66	14,673	2,332	1,014	1,140
Japan	1,522	2,464	1,947	2,721	5,413	2,147	946	122
Hong Kong	963	1,134	1,291	1,544	9	18	71	59

Source: *Yearbook of International Trade Statistics,* 1975, vol. 1, United Nations.

break-bulk basis. However, Bermuda importers are now demanding a container-ized service from European ports.

There are 34 product categories that are important for Canadian exporters to Bermuda. In each of these categories, Canada shipped $100,000 or more of goods and held the leading, second, or third highest share of imports. In two other categories—perfumes and cosmetics, and telecommunications equipment—the $100,000 or more imports criterion was met, but import share rank placed Canada fifth and fourth, respectively.

Hamilton is the port of entry through which all shipments are handled. The port has some 150,000 square feet of wharf area and 70,000 square feet of shed space. The Bermuda Government has granted a monopoly to Stevedoring Services Ltd., which handles all ships at Hamilton. This company has two mobile cranes, each of which is capable of working a small container ship to a finish. In consort they can complete the discharge and loading of a 100-TEU[1] capacity ship in 12 hours. Yard equipment includes two Silent Hoist top lift trucks.

Some current port practices at Hamilton are of interest to the prospective operator. All reefer and chilled containers are immediately stripped at the dock and are loaded for the same ship. This avoids having a $25,000 container out of circulation until the next ship arrives. Also, 40-foot containers are not allowed on the road at all, are allowed on the dock only with special permission, and must be stripped to be returned to the same ship. In addition, a customs ruling requiring that all containers with more than one consignee must be stripped at the dock results in some 45 percent of the containers being stripped on the dock, with only 55 percent currently moving over the road on a house-to-house basis. All inland transportation is by road.

---

[1] TEU = Twenty-foot container equivalent units.

Existing Shipping Services to Bermuda

A. European Cargoes to Bermuda. At present there are five shipping lines offering a service to Bermuda:

1. Ozean/Stinnes Linien: Loading at Hamburg, Bremen, Antwerp, Rotterdam, and London—service to Bermuda and Mexico's east coast—every three to four weeks.
2. Deutsche Seereederei of Rostock: Loading at Hamburg, Antwerp, and London—service to Bermuda, Nassau, and Mexico's east coast—every two weeks.
3. Intercontinental Transport: Loading at Hamburg, Bremen, Rotterdam, Antwerp, and London—service to Bermuda and Mexico's east coast—every two weeks.
4. Pacific Steam Navigation: Loading at Liverpool—service to Bermuda, Nassau, and South America's west coast—every three weeks.

The incremental break-bulk nature of the Bermuda trade for these lines creates certain problems. The first concerns service frequency; no line offers the weekly service that Bermuda importers desire, sailings ranging from every two to four weeks. This means that importers are unable to pipeline supplies in the way they would prefer. Instead, they have to make do with larger, less-frequent consignments. The second problem centres on the lack of containerization. This leads to higher rates of pilferage and damage than the importers find acceptable.

Partly in response to these problems, United States Lines now offers weekly containerized shipments to Bermuda through a feeder service connection—the Bermuda Express Service. In this way, cargoes are transshipped from United States Lines ships in New York and loaded for the shuttle service to Hamilton, Bermuda.

5. United States Lines: Loading at LeHavre, Antwerp, Hamburg, Rotterdam, Felixstowe, Liverpool—service to New York, Philadelphia, Baltimore, Jacksonville, Savannah, Los Angeles, San Francisco, Hawaii, and Japan with a feeder ship connection (Bermuda Express Service) to Bermuda from New York—weekly.

The reaction of Bermuda importers to United States Line's containerized service out of New York is very positive, emphasizing the advantages of containers in reducing pilferage and damage and permitting goods to be pipelined and shipped in smaller consignments from the U.K./Continent. Equally important is the weekly frequency of the service.

B. U.S. Cargoes to Bermuda. Two shipping lines offer shipping services from the U.S. East Coast to Bermuda:

1. Bermuda Express Service: Weekly shuttle service from New York to

Bermuda—characterized by a high degree of reliability, fully containerized, with substantial reefer capacity (18–20 reefer or chilled containers per sailing).

2. Pan Atlantic Shipping Ltd.: Fortnightly service from Miami and Jacksonville to Bermuda—also provides reefer containers.

C. Canadian Cargoes to Bermuda. Only one shipping line—Saguenay Shipping Ltd. (a subsidiary of Alcan)—offers a service for Canadian cargoes Bermuda-bound. It serves the ports of Montreal and Halifax, Bermuda, the Caribbean Islands, and Venezuela/Guyana. On the return trip to Canada, Saguenay carries bauxite that is loaded in Jamaica. Service frequency is monthly. In 1974–1975 the first winter sailing out of Montreal began. Before this, winter operations were run out of Halifax. The ship used is a large bulk carrier that carries containers in the holds southbound and bauxite northbound. While it can carry containers as deck cargo, this ship is not ideally suited for the nonbauxite cargoes it carries. Saguenay competes for Canadian business with the Bermuda Express Service out of New York. Importers interviewed in Bermuda were unanimous in their severe criticism of Saguenay's service, characterizing it as irregular, unreliable, infrequent, and arrogant. They cited these as reasons for shipping Canadian cargo via the Port of New York and also for sourcing supplies (especially food products) in the United States that would otherwise be sourced in Canada (much of it in the Maritimes). Rates on the Saguenay service average well in excess of $1,000 per 20-foot container.

D. New Zealand Cargoes to Bermuda. Sailings from New Zealand are coordinated by the New Zealand Shipowners Committee, and their members are Blue Star Line, PRO, Shaw Savill, and New Zealand Shipping Line. These shipping lines offer three sailings per year from Timaru, Auckland, and Wellington to Bermuda. There is no fixed trading pattern for these vessels except that they come via the Panama Canal.

Potential for a Halifax-Bermuda Service

Potential exists for a shipping service between Halifax and Hamilton, Bermuda. The traffic would be (1) Canadian exports and (2) European and U.K. exports transshipped at Halifax from deep sea container lines. All the cargo would be containerized. The service would mirror that provided by Bermuda Express out of New York in combining local and distant cargoes.

Taking the deep sea container trade first, Atlantic Container Line and Dart Container Line service all of Northern Europe and the United Kingdom. Between the two lines, three sailings per week to Halifax are offered, providing a veritable blanket coverage of all major European ports (see attached service patterns, Exhibits 3a and 3b). Both lines are represented by substantial interests in these

Exhibit 3: Patterns of Ocean Container Ship Services

a. Atlantic Container Line

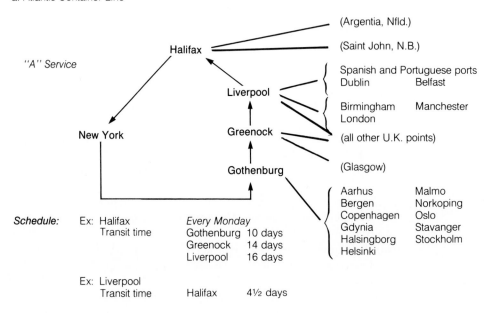

Schedule:	Ex: Halifax	*Every Monday*	
	Transit time	Gothenburg	10 days
		Greenock	14 days
		Liverpool	16 days
	Ex: Liverpool		
	Transit time	Halifax	4½ days

b. Dart Container Line

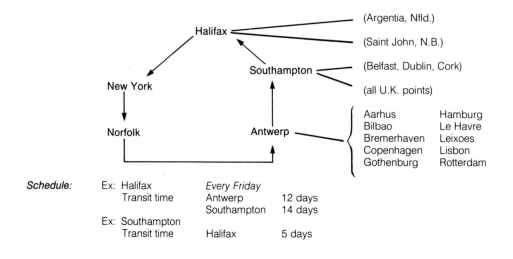

Schedule:	Ex: Halifax	*Every Friday*	
	Transit time	Antwerp	12 days
		Southampton	14 days
	Ex: Southampton		
	Transit time	Halifax	5 days

Exhibit 3 *(concluded)*

c. Zim Container Service

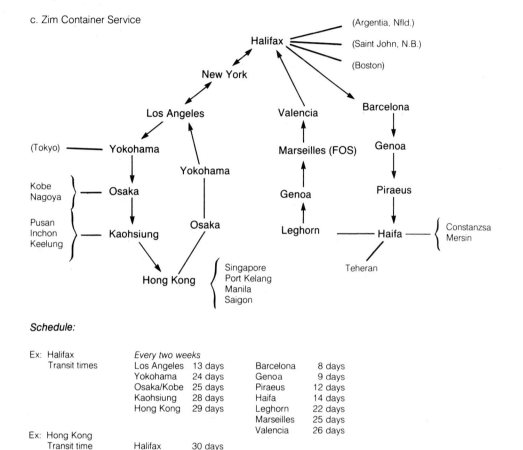

Schedule:

Ex: Halifax
    Transit times

Every two weeks

Los Angeles	13 days	Barcelona	8 days
Yokohama	24 days	Genoa	9 days
Osaka/Kobe	25 days	Piraeus	12 days
Kaohsiung	28 days	Haifa	14 days
Hong Kong	29 days	Leghorn	22 days
		Marseilles	25 days
		Valencia	26 days

Ex: Hong Kong
    Transit time   Halifax   30 days

Ex: Valencia
    Transit time   Halifax   7 days

Source: Atlantic Provinces Transporation Commission, *Directory of Ocean Containership Services.*

areas and have extensive sales forces and networks of consolidation depots already in place, allowing them to move quickly and effectively to generate cargo for a new system if they can be so motivated. In Southern Europe, the same can be said of Zim Container Service (see attached service pattern, Exhibit 3c). This strength in Europe and the United Kingdom is absolutely critical to the success of the Halifax-Bermuda service inasmuch as Europe and the United Kingdom will be the most significant contributors to the service in terms of volume and revenue. Strategically, then, the transshipment cargo (especially from Europe/U.K.) must be regarded as the base of the service and the Canadian cargo as an "add on."

The transshipment operation at Halifax has the advantage of serving all vessels from one dock, a situation which cannot be duplicated by Halifax's most formidable competitor—New York. At New York, containers must be loaded to or from mother ships at various points in New Jersey and then trucked to or from Pier 8 in Brooklyn (some 25 miles distant) to connect with the Bermuda-bound ship. This situation adds to the problem of control, and contributes at least $150 in the form of gate charges and trucking charges per 20-foot container. As the first port of call for westbound services of ACL, Dart Container Line, and Zim Container Service, Halifax also has an advantage over New York in terms of delivery time for containers originating in Europe.

On the matter of local Canadian cargo, substantial amounts now move via New York. This can be recovered if a quality transportation service is available. Quality in this context implies container availability (including temperature-controlled containers for reefer and chilled requirements), frequency (weekly appears to be the minimum acceptable frequency), and reliability. An outstanding example of a Canadian company shipping considerable volumes of food products via New York to Bermuda is McCain Foods of Florenceville, New Brunswick. If the level of service at Halifax was satisfactory, not only could the existing flow of traffic be captured, but it is likely that McCain would increase their penetration of the Bermudian market at the expense of U.S. suppliers.

Revenues and Costs

Bermuda General Cargo Imports by volume are shown in Exhibit 4. The traffic base for a potential Halifax-Bermuda service has the following sources:

Source of Imports	Tons
1. Europe/U.K.	24,830
2. Canada	11,838
3. New Zealand	2,446
4. U.S. West Coast	2,000 (est.)
5. Cargo originating in north New York State and U.S. Midwest	1,000 (est.)
6. Cargo that can be resourced from the U.S. East Coast	2,000 (est.)
Total annual tonnage for which Halifax system is competitive	44,114

We estimate that a Halifax-based service could capture 20,000 to 28,000 tons of this business. This is based on the following calculation:

Total annual tonnage potential: 44,114

Assume 100 percent of trade containerized and average tonnage/TEU is 8 tons. With 50 sailings per year, TEU available per sailing is 110, that is,

$$\frac{44,114}{8 \times 50}$$

Exhibit 4:   Bermuda General Cargo Imports (in tons of 2,240 pounds)

Year	New Zealand	Canada	Europe/United Kingdom	United States	Total
1968	—	—	—	—	97,036
1969	1,831	19,942	38,466	39,666 (1,237)	105,932
1970	2,085	20,774	39,142	48,529 (1,539)	113,404
1971	1,853	26,219	41,544	47,550 (775)	118,672
1972	2,456	20,807	34,166	43,860 (1,629)	104,148
1973	2,059	16,057	30,204	46,618	96,025
1974	2,446	11,838	24,830	49,603	89,707

1. Figures in parentheses in the U.S. column are tonnage moved via the U.S. West Coast (for example, Los Angeles). Direct sailings from the West Coast to Bermuda terminated in 1972. Most of this cargo still moves over the ports of San Francisco and Los Angeles via the Panama Canal on vessels of U.S. lines and is transshipped at New York.

2. In recent years, total tonnage to Bermuda has declined owing to a moratorium declared on major hotel construction effective 1973 through 1978. In addition, tourist activity was at a low level in 1974 due to the recessionary climate in the United States. However, an upturn was expected and importers in Bermuda felt that the 1974 import levels represented the bottoming out of a trend.

3. The U.S. tonnages include a significant amount of Canadian, Far East, and Europe/U.K. cargo moving in via New York, either by truck from Canada or transshipped from deep sea vessels in the case of Europe/U.K. and the Far East.

4. Cumulative totals of the annual tonnages for New Zealand, Canada, Europe, United Kingdom, and United States do not equal "total" figures on the above chart. This is due to the existence of small tonnages (usually less than 1,000 tons per annum) imported from countries other than those indicated.

5. A significant amount of air freight also enters Bermuda. In 1974 it amounted to 6,543 tons, 60 percent of which originated in the United States and 40 percent of which originated in the United Kingdom.

Source: Analytic Services Limited, Halifax, Nova Scotia.

Based on a strong competitive position in Europe and Canada, as well as a good position with respect to California and New Zealand, one could expect a penetration of 50–70 containers per sailing from a total of 110 available.

This forecast is based on a shipping rate of $800 round trip (Halifax to Hamilton and return) for a transshipped dry cargo 20-foot container. Reefer and chilled cargo would bear high rates (say $1,000) as would dry containers originating in Canada. The $800 rate is predicated on cargoes being able to pay $1,500 as a minimum rate from Europe/U.K. on a through rate to Bermuda, and deep sea lines requiring revenues of $700 per 20-foot container for the Europe/U.K. to Halifax portion.

Several comparisons suggest this to be a reasonable rate for a new service.

1. Bermuda Express quotes a round-trip rate for nonvolume movements of transshipped containers from New York to Bermuda of $1,017 per 20-foot container (exclusive of trucking charges and port costs).

2. On cargo from Europe/U.K., Bermuda importers have indicated that existing rates for a 20-foot container range from a low of $1,400 to a high of $2,600, according to origin and commodity. In fact, most of the freight is paying more than $1,800 per container.

3. Saguenay rates for a 20-foot container are, on average, well in excess of $1,000.

4. McCain Foods currently pays $1,300 per 20-foot container to ship its frozen foods to Bermuda through New York on the Bermuda Express Service. In addition, it incurs trucking costs of $500 per container that would be reduced if it shipped through Halifax.

A profit analysis based on 50–70 TEU per sailing is given in Exhibit 5.

Exhibit 5:   Profit Analysis Based on 50–70 TEU per Sailing

A.   Office costs:

Halifax Office	*Annual Expenses*
Manager	$20,000
Assistant manager	12,000
Clerk	9,000
Boarding officer	8,000
Secretary	7,000
Subtotal	56,000
Office	7,000
Total	$63,000

Office costs per sailing based on 50 sailings per year: $1,260.

This assumes that a separate office is established. If the service were integrated with an established agency, total cost would be less than half, that is, less than $630 per voyage.

B.   Ship operating costs:

These are based on a two-year time charter for a 100 TEU full container ship (cellularized), with an operating speed of 13 knots, consuming eight tons of fuel daily.

Halifax-Hamilton sailing time = 756 nautical miles ÷ 13 knots per hour
= 58 hours

Halifax-Hamilton return = 116 hours, leaving 52 hours per week for port time at both ports and an allowance for delays.

Per diem charter	=		$2,500–$2,800
Per diem fuel costs	=	8 × $110	$ 880–$ 880
		Range	$3,380–$3,680

365 days × ($3,380–$3,680)

Annual cost to operate vessel including fuel = $1,233,700–$1,343,200
Cost per sailing including fuel   = $ 24,674–$ 26,864

C.   Stevedoring costs:

Stevedoring at Hamilton ($60 average per TEU including overtime)
Based on 50 TEU per week = 3,000 × 2 = $6,000
Based on 70 TEU per week = 4,200 × 2 = $8,400

Stevedoring at Halifax ($65 average per TEU including overtime)
Based on 50 TEU per week = 3,250 × 2 = $6,500
Based on 70 TEU per week = 4,550 × 2 = $9,100

Exhibit 5 (*concluded*)

D. Port charges:

Halifax port charges:

Harbour dues	$ 55
Pilotage	150
Wharfage	100
	$305

Hamilton port charges:

Agency fees	$200
Pilotage	150
Other	150
	$500

E. Contingency:

Two hundred dollars per voyage is included to account for unforeseen expenses such as the use of tugs during adverse weather conditions and pilotage charges due to interharbour movages, as well as to pay for charterers' liability insurance.

Maximum total cost per voyage:

a.	Office costs	$ 1,260
b.	Ship costs	26,864
c.	Stevedoring—Halifax	9,100
	Hamilton	8,400
d.	Port charges	805
e.	Contingency	200
	Total	$46,629
	Revenue $800 × 70 TEU	$56,000
	Profit	$ 9,371

Minimum total costs per voyage:

a.	Office costs	$ 630
b.	Ship costs	24,674
c.	Stevedoring—Halifax	6,500
	Hamilton	6,000
d.	Port charges	805
e.	Contingency	200
	Total	$38,809
	Revenue $800 × 50 TEU	$40,000
	Profit	$ 1,191

The profit per voyage ranges between $1,191 and $9,371.

Source: Analytic Services Limited, Halifax, Nova Scotia.

Four Seasons' Yorkville Inn

In late 1976 Samuel Morrison a mortgage broker with Livingston, Teach & Co., of New York City, was reviewing a mortgage application for a five-star hotel in Toronto, Canada. The developer of the hotel was a 50–50 partnership of DWS Holdings, Inc., of New York, a private company, and Four Seasons Hotels, Ltd., of Canada, a public company. Four Seasons would operate the hotel which the application described as "a small luxury hotel offering service facilities equal to, or better than, those offered in the top hotels in Europe and the Far East."

Morrison, however, was concerned about the market viability of yet another, even if superior, "first-class" hotel in Toronto, an already "overbuilt" city. His reservations about the Toronto market had led him to question the entire project—whether a hotel was the best use for the land, whether the ownership agreement would cause any problems, and whether any lender might stand a good chance of getting burned by investing in the hotel.

Although the mortgage financing of a $30 million plus project would earn his company a healthy commission, Morrison knew that his career depended upon his being perceived as reliable and astute by his clients, the lenders who trusted him to bring them into good projects. And though long-term lenders were aware that hotels were among the riskiest of loans, Morrison wanted to make sure any recommendation he made to a potential lender directly addressed the project's risks and quantified them.

"There must be an easier way to make a living than crunching numbers," thought Morrison as he leaned back, cupped his hands over his head, and looked wistfully toward nothing in particular on the ceiling. Like many of his former colleagues at business school, Morrison felt more comfortable with what had been referred to, sometimes euphemistically, as the "qualitative issues," of which he now had many, including those addressed in the developer's market study (excerpts in the Appendix).

Morrison wondered whether the developers' position was as difficult as they had claimed. At his meeting with them they had pointed out that they had taken many of the critical risks already, for example, they had acquired the land, and spent money on terminating tenants, on predevelopment designs, and on obtaining the zoning change they needed. Now, they said, they were blocked and could do nothing until they got a favorable response from a long-term lender.

Morrison felt that if lenders believed the project could duplicate the success Four Seasons had had with its Inn on the Park in London, they might be attracted by the partners' plight and the opportunity to obtain an advantageous position in the project. Morrison thought, "I've got to decide for myself whether Yorkville will be a dog or a star and whether I should be a bear or a bull. Then it's a matter of *whom* to approach."

A History

The Project's Beginnings

Before making any contact at all with Four Seasons, DWS had been part of a joint venture which was constructing Hazelton Lanes, a mixed-use development of apartments and retail space in the emergent chic and elite Yorkville area of Toronto. Adjacent to the Hazelton Lanes project was a deficit-ridden shopping center which had been offered for sale in mid-1974. At that time DWS had just put Hazelton Lanes on the market, and already some retail space had been rented and a few apartments sold. Management felt that this initial evidence of market acceptance augured well for the success of the project, and they speculated that Hazelton's success might well rub off on adjacent properties. Therefore, in fall 1974 DWS acquired a 25-year lease on the shopping center, with an option to purchase within five years, reasoning that within five years the company could easily decide whether to improve the shopping center or to convert it to some other use which would better exploit its location.

The annual lease payments on the property were less than the finance costs of acquisition. Lease payments were $125,000, increasing to $250,000 within three years, as contrasted to a 10 percent to 12 percent cost of money on a purchasing price of $4.5 million. (DWS budgeted a $100,000 annual operating loss on the center during the holding period.)

In charge of the project was Jefferey Sussman, a Cornell graduate of 1965 and an experienced office broker who had been with DWS for some years—in fact, since the company had been founded as a joint venture by the well-known Louis Dreyfus Corporation and the Standard Life Assurance Company (see Exhibit 1). Through DWS's Hazelton Lane architect, Sussman met Isadore Sharp, president of Four Seasons Hotels, Ltd., a five-star hotel chain based in Canada. See Exhibit 2 for Four Seasons' financial statements and Exhibit 3 for a list of its hotels in operation and under development. Sharp said Yorkville was a prime site for a five-star hotel.

Sussman was immediately attracted to the five-star hotel concept because he and his colleagues stayed at such hotels themselves when they could. Furthermore, Sussman reasoned that because such hotels addressed a small, affluent

---

Exhibit 1: A Brief Description of DWS Holdings

DWS Holdings was formed in 1970 as a joint venture between the Louis Dreyfus Corporation and the Standard Life Assurance Company of Edinburgh, Scotland.

The Louis Dreyfus Corporation is a privately held international organization with interests in commodities, shipping, and banking. It owns a majority interest in DWS Holdings and is the active managing partner in the company.

Standard Life Assurance Company is one of the largest life insurance companies in Scotland.

DWS is involved in two aspects of the real estate business: purchase of existing buildings and purchase of land in growth markets for immediate and future development.

In pursuing these opportunities, DWS seeks investment return and asset appreciation commensurate with prudent risk management.

In both North America and Europe, DWS has selected properties and designed projects with consideration for a balancing of stable current income and of significant future increase of return and value.

From conception and design to completion of a project, DWS Holdings is prepared to carry through in all phases and types of real estate development—office, retail, commercial, and residential space.

Local partnerships for each of its projects or investments enable DWS to conduct an international real estate business while maintaining an understanding of the needs and requirements of the particular area involved.

Recognizing the stability and growth potential of Canada, DWS's initial ventures into this market are in the major cities of Montreal and Toronto. Completed projects and developments planned for these areas represent more than a quarter of a billion dollars in land and development costs.

---

market they were comparatively isolated from the effects of economic cycles. And though Toronto had some fine hotels, it had none catering solely to the very top of the market, as Sussman well knew. Despite the need to obtain a zoning change from the city, Sharp offered to share ownership and all development costs for the hotel on a 50–50 basis upon being assured of DWS's legal rights to the property. Sussman accepted the offer, and the general deal was confirmed by a handshake.

Unplanned Ownership

DWS, like most developers, was building Hazelton Lanes to the very limits of its allotted land and found that it could save $75,000 by using its adjacent leased land for storage of construction equipment and for forming Hazelton Lanes' foundations. DWS's attorneys felt that DWS had the right to sublet a portion of the shopping center land to the Hazelton project without getting the fee owner's permission. So counselled, the joint venture excavated a 25-foot-wide strip along the shared property line. Seeing this, the fee owner obtained a court order to stop work and tried to enjoin DWS from using the land by seeking another court order instructing DWS to restore the land to its original condition immediately. DWS countersued and was able to lift the stop-work injunction, but the second suit

Exhibit 2

FOUR SEASONS HOTELS, LTD.
Financial Statements
31st December, 1975

Operating results:

Revenue	$29,257,131
Gross profit	6,138,596
Net profit before taxes	3,241,850
Income taxes	1,737,276
Income before extraordinary items	1,504,574
Net income	1,504,574
Cash flow	3,446,654
Dividends on all classes of stock	600,355
Retained earnings at year-end	8,698,394

Assets

Current assets:	
Cash on hand and in bank	$ 829,714
Acounts receivable after allowance for doubtful accounts: 1975—$201,463; 1974—$239,914	2,728,034
Management fees receivable	120,130
Inventory of food, beverages, and supplies—at lower of cost or replacement value	1,083,004
Short-term loans receivable	1,638,929
Other amounts receivable and prepaid expenses	597,194
Loan receivable—South Side Development Limited	13,137,848
Total current assets	20,134,853
Deferred development and construction costs	3,148,546
Investments:	
South Side Development Limited	49,000
Real estate partnerships and joint ventures	2,094,799
Hotel joint ventures	110,715
Other	482,624
Total investments	2,737,138
Fixed assets:	
Land	2,995,590
Buildings	22,437,668
Furniture, furnishings, and equipment	13,298,993
Leasehold improvements (at cost)	1,721,740
Vehicles (at cost)	30,307
	40,484,298
Less: Accumulated depreciation	6,179,440
	34,304,858
Linen, tableware, and uniforms (inventoried at the lower of cost or replacement value)	2,237,499
Total fixed assets	36,542,357
Other assets:	
Unamortized financing costs	174,826
Unamortized preopening and opening expenses	4,385,288
Total other assets	4,560,114
Total assets	$67,123,008

Exhibit 2 (*concluded*)

Liabilities

Current liabilities:

Bank indebtedness	$11,500,368
Accounts payable and accrued charges	4,284,217
Long-term debt due within one year	546,016
Income taxes payable	1,412,081
Total current liabilities	17,742,682
Long-term debt	24,793,517
Deferred income taxes	4,785,943
Total liabilities	47,322,142

Shareholders' Equity

Capital stock:

Authorized:

2,000,000 first preference shares, with a par value of $10 each, issuable in series 6,000,000 common shares without par value

Issued and fully paid:

400,000 Series A first preference shares 6 percent cumulative, redeemable, convertible, with a par value of $10 each	4,000,000
3,002,960 common shares, without par value (1974—3,002,960 shares)	4,096,449
Retained earnings	8,698,394
Surplus arising from appraisal of fixed assets	3,006,023
Total shareholders' equity	19,800,866
Total liabilities and shareholders' equity	$67,123,008

looked as if it would drag on. A quick restoration, particularly at such an inopportune time—the foundations for Hazelton had not been completed — would have cost approximately $750,000. Because of its needs for zoning changes, construction delays, and an increased cost of money, DWS had already seen the cost of the Hazelton project increase 40 percent—from $10 million to about $14 million in three years. Fortunately, DWS had been able to pass along the increase to apartment buyers and retail outlet lessees, but another unforeseen increase was unwelcome, especially because of its up-front timing. To resolve matters and to escape the "shadow" of the court, DWS decided to exercise its option on the land. As Sussman put it, "The fee owner won the battle of wits and DWS acquired the land."

DWS then decided to get the current lessees out of the shopping center to avoid having to do so after the news of the sale became public, perhaps prompting some lessees to hold out for more money. Most left readily because the center was losing money. DWS told the few holdouts that no matter what future use the property was given, DWS would demolish the center and build around them. DWS had to pay only two lessees a "holdout" amount to leave.

Exhibit 3: Four Seasons' Operations and Developments

Existing operations:		
Toronto, Canada	Inn on the Park	609 rooms
	Four Seasons, Jarvis	164 rooms
Belleville, Canada	Four Seasons	125 rooms
Calgary, Canada	Four Seasons	387 rooms
London, England	Inn on the Park	230 rooms
San Francisco, California	The Clift Hotel	406 rooms
Israel	Four Seasons	130 investment coops
Montreal, Canada	Le Quatre Saisons	320 rooms
Vancouver, Canada	Four Seasons	410 rooms
Under development:		
Edmonton, Canada	Four Seasons	350 rooms
Paris, France	Four Seasons	400 rooms
Denver, Colorado	Four Seasons	650 rooms
Seattle, Washington	Four Seasons	350 rooms
Rome, Italy	Inn on the Park	387 rooms

The Hotel: Predevelopment

The partners for the hotel formalized their preliminary agreement which Sussman felt was unique in the hotel business. Each agreed to be responsible for 50 percent of the equity and debt to be put into the project. Four Seasons contracted with the partnership to operate the hotel for a fee of 3 percent of gross income and 17 percent of net income—after payment of expenses, debt service, taxes, and repayment of equity. The balance would be split evenly. Each partner appointed two members to an executive committee, and DWS appointed an additional person as project manager who would be responsible to the partnership, not just to DWS. Four Seasons entered the formal agreement despite the land's not yet being zoned for a hotel because Sharp felt any downside risk was covered by the property's location next to Hazelton. In describing why DWS wanted a partner, Sussman said:

> We wanted someone to take the same kind of risks we were. In Canada the stock market looks upon real estate in a more favorable light than in the United States and understands cash flow. Our partner is a public company but understands the real estate aspects of the project. They want the residual ownership of the property. Four Seasons realizes the difficulty of financing a hotel in which the operator has no risk. They know financiers are attracted by a quality operator's long-term commitment to a hotel.

The partners were able to obtain a two-year loan on the land to finance predevelopment work.[1] They then found themselves with an idea for a hotel on land not zoned for hotels in a city conscious of the need for balanced growth. In fact, Toronto had recently instituted a Holding By-Law which dictated that any project higher than 40 feet with more than 40,000 square feet in total usable space had to obtain site-plan approval from the city council. Describing the process, Sussman said:

> Toronto cares more about planning than any other city in the world except, perhaps, Paris. They are extremely cognizant of the planning process. They put the Holding By-Law in because the current zoning had received statutory approval in 1956. Since then the city has grown from a million-three to 3 million people. They felt they had to rethink the zoning for both the downtown core and surrounding areas.
>
> I believe, as a developer, that it is a great thing. It ensures the long-term viability of the city and, therefore, our project.
>
> The city was happy to deal with us, however, because we did Hazelton. Cities, politicians, and local residents are skeptical; unless you have a real history with people, it's "What have you done for me lately?" and I think their attitude is right. Once you build a building, if it isn't what they want, you ain't gonna take it down!

The Market

While developing their concept for the hotel, the partners had to consider the implications of the hotel building boom Toronto had just experienced (see the Appendix). Despite what many viewed as overbuilding in the Toronto market, Sussman agreed with the conclusion of the market study the partnership had authorized from one of the world's most authoritative hotel investment consultants:

> Nonetheless, there does appear to be a market for a five-star deluxe operation. Most cities in North America and Europe have one or two hotels, such as the Ritz Carlton, Chateau Champlain, and Bonaventure in Montreal; the Stanford Court in San Francisco; the Ritz Carlton in Chicago; the Latham in Philadelphia; the Houston Oaks in Houston; the Ritz Carlton in Boston; and the Four Seasons in London, which command considerably higher room rates than their competitors and often achieve occupancy levels up to 20 points above the city average. To achieve such results a hotel must not only provide excellent service and facilities but must also be recognized by the travelling public as a superior facility. Four Seasons has achieved such recognition with its London, England, venture.

In London, Four Seasons had built the now well-known Inn on the Park Hotel in Park Lane and entered into direct competition with world-famous hotels addressing the top end of the market—it was down the street from the Dorchester,

---

[1] The partners had the choice of borrowing Canadian dollars outright at a floating rate over Canadian prime or borrowing American dollars via London interbank financing; they did the latter and bought a long commitment ahead, thus locking their financing costs even though they had floating-rate financing. Because of the luck of the draw at the time, they locked themselves for the first year into paying 8.5 percent which compared favorably to the 13 percent they would have paid based on the Canadian prime.

across the street from the Ritz, and within walking distance of the new Barclay and the Connaught. In that area and during the worst period London hoteliers could recall, the Four Seasons Hotel had constantly run from 90 percent to 97 percent occupancy while having the highest average room rate in London. The partners felt a similar small, super-luxury hotel, offering personal services to the busy travelling executive would succeed in Toronto, despite its apparently overbuilt hotel market: "The London Inn on the Park is the standard to be achieved."

Developing the Concept

Feeling that no hotel in Toronto met the standard they sought, the partners used as models the top hotels in many North American and European cities and agreed to use the same architect who had designed Hazelton Lanes because of his knowledge of Toronto and its building-control procedures. He had also worked for Four Seasons on other projects and was familiar with its standard approaches to common elements, such as public space and "back of house" detail (for example, kitchen design). The partners gave him a program which listed the number and size of rooms, bathrooms and public rooms, types of fixtures, restaurant mix, and other details. The architect was instructed to do what he wanted within these constraints. Costing about $100,000, the plans took 15 months to draft and refine, largely because of the architect's need to work closely with the city on zoning matters. Exhibit 4 is a photograph of the architect's model of the proposed hotel. Exhibits 5 and 6 show how the new hotel fits into the Yorkville Area.

Upon receipt of the preliminary drawings and a preliminary zoning approval, the partners worked over the drawings seeking efficiency and cost cutting while trying to maintain the integrity of the five-star hotel concept.

> This was where some real give and take occurred. What had been single loaded corridors became double loaded. The arrangements of some larger suites were changed to create more rooms at a lower per-square-foot cost. Furniture, fixtures, and equipment were originally quoted at $12,000 per room; $2,000 to $3,000 was actually for the bedrooms themselves; the balance was for public spaces. It can be crazy—if you decide the television sets should have 19-inch screens rather than 17-inch, it can cost you an extra $100 times 300 rooms or $30,000. And there are dozens of choices like this ranging from the type of bathtub you use to the quality cloth you use on the furniture.

A summary of the requirements for the guest rooms appears in Exhibit 7.

Estimates and Financing

Agreeing on a concept and its details, the partners gave out a set of architectural, mechanical, and electrical "scope and intent drawings" to six contractors for

Exhibit 4

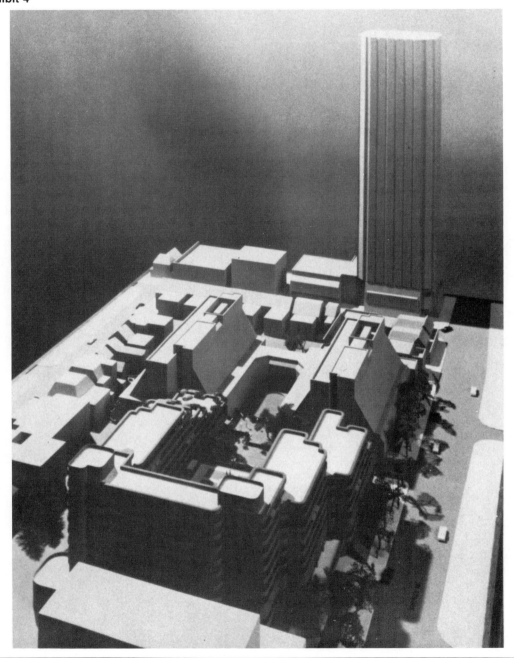

Exhibit 5

Summary of Pertinent Information

Location: Toronto, Ontario, Canada: Yorkville area. Subject property is situated in the block bounded by Avenue Road (west) and Hazelton Avenue (east) north of Bloor Street. With many renovated townhouses, combining both residential and retail space, Yorkville Village has become a thriving center of fashionable clothing stores, art galleries, fine restaurants and luxurious in-town residences.

Site: Dimensions of the site are roughly 317 feet by 267 feet, comprising a total of 84,639 square feet.

Zoning: CISL323, Commercial. Maximum above grade density permitted under this zoning is 253,000 square feet, of which not more than 25,000 square feet can be retail stores. Density of proposed hotel complex above grade is 252,889 square feet.

The Facility: This 294-suite luxury hotel will have a variety of restaurants and accommodations, a 3-level skylit meeting place, and shops with underground parking. The improvements will be contained in a U-shaped structure with 252,889 square feet of gross floor area above grade and 182,538 square feet of gross floor area below grade. 255 cars will be self-parked on three below grade levels.

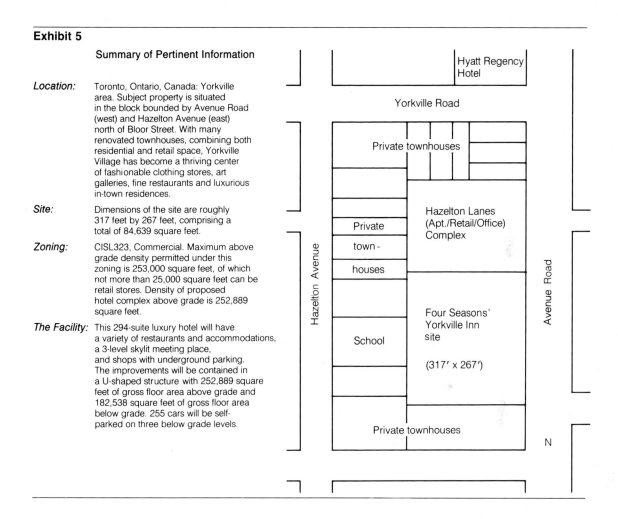

bidding on basic construction and mechanical and electrical work. The winning bidder was the contractor who was building the Hazelton Lanes project. A factor in his winning bid appeared to be his being able to come right off the Hazelton Lanes property to the new project without going through the time and expense of moving heavy construction equipment and relocating men. Even the lowest bid, however, was for a substantially higher amount than the partners had initially budgeted. They, therefore, agreed with the low-bid contractor that he would work toward the partners' originally budgeted figure—this evolved into a continuous "exercise" of design changes, refinements, and innovation. Sussman said:

> Now we had a $30–$35 million project and all we needed was financing. That size project meant that we would have to go outside the Canadian market to get financing—Canadian lenders can rarely lend more than $5–$10 million each because

Exhibit 6

of their size. And although hotels are difficult to finance anywhere, in Toronto because of the overbuilt situation we felt it would be especially hard. In addition, getting money anywhere was difficult because of the recession.

We felt we needed professional help so we got a mortgage broker. This eliminates shopping which can hurt a project in the long run. Shopping is just a bad thing—a turndown for any reason hurts you.

Brokers help in two or three ways—they're in touch with lenders and can take a deal to them. Because of their past integrity and reputation, they can give the important details of the project without being questioned and without disclosing the name of the developer, development, or location. Secondly, they can go to different people in the same firm without annoying them—something we couldn't do. Thirdly, insurance companies, and so forth, approach good mortgage brokers and tell them the amounts they wish to invest for x amount of time.

Mr. Morrison, the mortgage broker, claimed that because of Yorkville's high cost per room, $75,000 to $80,000 (see Exhibit 8) rather than the conventional average of $40,000 to $45,000, lenders would have to be convinced of the validity of the developers' projections which showed the hotel providing a substantial

Exhibit 7: Summary of Specific Requirement for Guest Rooms

Definite requirements:
Bedrooms:
1. Built-in TV with bedside controls and remote on/off.
2. Bedside digital clock radio.
3. Six duplex outlets.
4. Mini-refrigerator located in either bedroom or bathroom—whichever is most compatible with the room design.
5. Telephones to be located on the desk in all rooms including living rooms. Telephones to have long leads to permit use at both desk and night tables.

Bathrooms:
1. Telephone.
2. Oversize bathtubs and separate shower stalls in split-level suites.
3. Bidets in the bathrooms of the bedrooms of the split-level suites and 1½ module living room suites.
4. Lighting to be incandescent with full-width and full-height mirror to vanity.
5. In addition to the above, washroom accessories will be provided as Four Seasons standards.

Requirements subject to cost (separate price to be obtained):
Bedrooms:
1. Built-in pick-up boxes for guest shoe-shine service.
2. Heated dumb valet—to be reviewed.
3. Remote TV channel change.

Bathrooms:
1. 2'8" × 5'0" cast-iron tub in lieu of 2'6" × 5'0" pressed-steel tub.

Exhibit 8: Projected Cost—300 Rooms (in thousands)

Building costs:	
Demolition/site preparation	$ 100,000
Construction—building	13,000,000
Architect and engineer fees	825,000
Development fee	120,000
Interest during construction and financing fees	3,000,000
Taxes during construction	100,000
Insurance during construction	100,000
Contingency	500,000
Total building costs	17,745,000
Furniture, fixtures, and equipment	3,500,000
Design and procurement fee	105,000
Preopening management fee	120,000
Preopening (other)	800,000
Working capital/investment/banks	300,000
Land costs	9,025,000
Total projected cost	$31,595,000
Deficit operation	$ 1,000,000

operating income (see Exhibit 9). To convince the lenders of the partners' own faith in the projections, Mr. Morrison told them they would probably do best by initially seeking a floor loan with a commitment from the lender that over the next five-year period, based on the hotel's earnings and occupancy, it would provide the partners with more mortgage money. Such a commitment would probably involve the lender's charging an up-front fee of about 1 percent of the commit-

Exhibit 9: Pro Forma Operating Statement—300 Rooms (dollars in thousands)

	Year 1		Year 2		Year 3		Year 4	
	Amount	*Percent*	*Amount*	*Percent*	*Amount*	*Percent*	*Amount*	*Percent*
Occupancy		73%		76%		80%		83%
Average rate	$ 50.00		$ 55.00		$ 60.50		$ 65.34	
Gross operating revenue:								
Rooms	3,997	51	4,577	51	5,300	52	5,938	53
Food	2,289	29	2,564	29	2,872	28	3,130	28
Beverage	1,346	17	1,508	17	1,688	17	1,840	16
Telephone	200	3	223	3	251	3	278	3
Other departments	40	1	45	1	50	1	56	1
Total gross revenue	7,872	100	8,916	100	10,161	100	11,243	100
Department gross profits:								
Rooms	2,958	74	3,524	77	4,187	79	4,691	79
Food and beverage	727	20	896	22	1,003	22	1,094	22
Telephone	−30	−15	−27	−12	−23	−9	−25	−9
Other departments	−2	−5	−1	−3	−1	−1	−1	−1
Department gross profit	3,653	46	4,392	49	5,167	51	5,759	51
Other income	15	0	20	0	21	0	23	0
Gross operating income	3,668	47	4,412	50	5,188	51	5,782	51
Deductions from income:								
Administrative and general	630	8	669	8	732	7	798	7
Management fee	236	3	267	3	305	3	337	3
Advertising and business promotion	394	5	401	5	396	4	394	4
Utilities	195	3	218	2	244	2	270	2
Repairs and maintenance	195	3	224	3	255	3	288	3
Total deductions	1,649	21	1,779	20	1,931	19	2,087	19
Gross operating profit	2,019	26	2,633	30	3,257	32	3,696	33
Taxes and insurance	394	5	434	5	477	5	515	5
Net operating profit excluding retail	1,625	21	2,199	25	2,780	27	3,181	28
Retail profits	$ 539		$ 809		$ 1,178		$ 1,260	

ment. Morrison said he would need the partners' commitment to provide the balance of the capital which would be needed until the increased loan took effect. He advised the partners to expect an initial loan of between $16 million and $18 million. He said he hoped they could work it up to $24 million to $26 million once the project was fully occupied. In the meantime, they would have to make an

Year 5		Year 6		Year 7		Year 8		Year 9		Year 10	
Amount	*Percent*	*Amount*	*Percent*	*Amount*	*Percent*	*Amount*	*Percent*	*Amount*	*Percent*	*Amount*	*Percent*
	85%		85%		85%		85%		85%		85%
$ 69.26		$ 73.42		$ 77.82		$ 82.49		$ 87.44		$ 92.69	
6,446	53	6,833	53	7,243	53	7,678	52	8,138	52	8,627	52
3,349	28	3,584	28	3,835	28	4,103	28	4,390	28	4,698	28
1,969	16	2,107	16	2,255	16	2,412	17	2,851	17	2,762	17
305	3	326	3	349	3	374	3	400	3	428	3
61	1	65	1	70	1	75	1	80	1	86	1
12,131	100	12,916	100	13,751	100	14,642	100	15,590	100	16,600	100
5,093	79	5,398	79	5,722	79	6,065	79	6,429	79	6,815	79
1,170	22	1,252	22	1,340	22	1,433	22	1,534	22	1,641	22
−27	−9	−29	−9	−31	−9	−34	−9	−36	−9	−39	−9
−1	−1	−1	−1	−1	−1	−1	−1	−1	−1	−1	−1
6,235	51	6,620	51	7,030	51	7,464	51	7,926	51	8,417	51
25	0	26	0	28	0	30	0	32	0	34	0
6,259	52	6,646	52	7,058	51	7,494	51	7,958	51	8,451	51
849	7	904	7	963	7	1,025	7	1,091	7	1,162	7
364	3	387	3	413	3	439	3	468	3	498	3
388	3	413	3	440	3	469	3	499	3	531	3
296	2	320	3	345	3	373	3	403	3	435	3
317	3	342	3	369	3	399	3	431	3	465	3
2,214	18	2,366	18	2,530	18	2,704	19	2,891	19	3,091	19
4,045	33	4,280	33	4,528	33	4,790	33	5,067	33	5,360	32
546	5	579	5	614	5	651	4	690	4	731	4
3,499	29	3,701	29	3,914	28	4,139	28	4,377	28	4,629	28
$ 1,349		$ 1,443		$ 1,544		$ 1,652		$ 1,768		$ 1,892	

equity commitment totalling between $14 million and $16 million. Since $18 million wouldn't be enough to complete construction, the partners hoped they could borrow an additional $8 million and, therefore, limit the equity amount they would have to provide to only $6 million.

Sussman felt there was a strong possibility of an American lender's participating at an interest rate of 10 percent–10½ percent plus some type of participation in the project to bring the lender's yield up to around 11½ percent. The lender could possibly participate in gross income after a certain base income had been established, or perhaps in net income—though lenders (for example, REITS) were prohibited from such active participation. Perhaps the participation could take the form of a sale and leaseback of the land. A lender might well make a long-term

---

Exhibit 10: Projected Returns

Assumptions*			Four Seasons	DWS	Bank
Two years to projected occupancy	IRR NPV @ 10%		25% $4.4M	18% $4.8M	—
Two years (bank takes 3% of net income)	IRR NPV @ 10%		23.7% $3.9M	16.3% $1.24M	11.42% $1.4M @ 10.25%
Two years (bank takes 8% of net income)	IRR NPV @ 10%		21.1% $2.9M	13.2% $ .33M	12.3% $2.4M @ 10.25%
13% below pro forma revenues—8% less operating income	IRR NPV @ 10%		24% $3.9M	17% $1.7M	—
13% below pro forma— bank takes 3%	IRR NPV @ 10%		20.25% $2.4M	2.25% −$1.6M	9.7% −$.7M @ 10.25%

* These calculations are based on the following assumptions:
 Land cost: $9,025,000.
 Up-front fee for borrowing: $340,000.
 Cost: $32.5 million.
 Equity: $7.5 million; pattern of investment based on two-year lead time:

  Year 0: $1.5 million.
  Year 1: $3.0 million.
  Year 2: $3.0 million.

 Loan: $25 million; pattern of drawing it based on two-year lead time:

  Year 0: $ 5 million.
  Year 1: $10 million.
  Year 2: Refinance for the entire $25 million, leading to annual mortgage payments of $2.69 million at 10.25 percent interest, 30-year term.

Income projections are based on Exhibit 9 and include retail profits. Depreciation is over 40 years and is calculated on the Canadian 5 percent declining balance method, that is, 5 percent of the remaining depreciable balance is available each year.

In addition, Morrison calculated the break-even occupancy to be 73.3 percent during the second year of operations and 70 percent for each of the three years thereafter. However, for Four Seasons, receiving 3 percent of the years' income, the break-even occupancy was 3 percent less.

Morrison calculated the break-even point for room rates to be approximately $51 during the second year of operations and $46 for each of the three years thereafter.

investment as well as a loan. In any event, the partners could expect tough negotiations on the form and extent of lender participation. Anticipating the negotiations, Sussman said:

> We might say, well, if you think it's so good, instead of taking an effective 3 percent of net income—no matter how it's structured—why don't you take 5 percent, and instead of giving us $18 million as a floor, why don't you give us $21 or $24 million as a ceiling? Why don't you give us $27 million?

Morrison's Immediate Problem

If he were going to broker the deal successfully, Morrison knew he had to determine who would be taking what risks for what returns and the likelihood and extent of the downside for each of the parties. He had calculated rates of return and break-evens based on the partners' figures (see Exhibit 10) and had assembled some comparable figures to compare to those projected by the partners (see Exhibit 11). The question he had to answer first was, "What do the numbers mean?" Then it was a matter of deciding what to do.

Exhibit 11: Hotel Operating Comparables—1975

	Four Seasons (Projections for Yorkville Inn)	Canada		United States	
Hotel sales and expenses:					
Total sales	100%	100.0%		100.0%	
Room sales	52	48.5		54.9	
Food sales	29	28.0		25.5	
Beverage sales	17	18.3		10.5	
Minor operated department sales	4	2.8		5.7	
Other income		2.4		3.4	
Average room occupancy and rates:					
Average annual room occupancy (over 5 years)	73%–85%	64.9%		63.1%	
Average daily room rate (U.S. dollars) (over 10 years)	$50–$92	$28.99		$32.26	
Average rate per guest (U.S. dollars)		$22.58		$27.59	
Average room sales and expenses:					
Sales—average per room		$6,757		$7,344	
Department expenses:					
Payroll		$1,277	18.9%	$1,483	20.2%
Other		599	8.9	628	8.5
Total	26%	$1,876	27.8%	$2,111	28.7%
Department income	74%	$4,881	72.2%	$5,233	71.3%

Appendix: Four Seasons' Yorkville Inn— Excerpts from Market Study

Overview

There is every indication that the demand for first-class accommodation in the downtown core will continue to grow, although not at the same rate as in the past decade. For the period under review, we have projected a real growth in demand of 3.5 percent per annum which, in our opinion, is a conservative and realistic estimate.

On the basis of the projected growth rate, the average occupancy of first-class hotels should be approximately as follows:

1976	59%
1977	61
1978	63
1979	63
1980	65
1981	67
1982	70
1983	72

In this projection we have assumed that the proposed 300-room Four Seasons Hotel will be open throughout 1979 and that no other competitive first-class properties will enter the market. . . .

The City

While enjoying one of the fastest rates of urbanization of any North American city, Toronto has been able to avoid many urban-related problems and maintain a low incidence of crime. This has been instrumental in the city's ability to attract investment and provide employment whilst continuing to grow. The more rapid growth rate projected for the metropolitan area than for Metro itself is not an indication of centre city stagnation prevalent in many large American cities but is the result of greater land availability and lower cost outside the core area. . . .

The classification of building permits issued during 1973, 1974, and 1975 is as follows (in thousands of dollars):

	1973	1974	1975
Residential	$1,062,166	$ 728,717	$ 917,264
Industrial	249,820	255,536	183,557
Commercial	448,195	494,793	543,846
Institutional and government	164,453	139,748	190,705
Total	$1,924,634	$1,618,794	$1,835,372

Source: Statistics Canada, Building Permits 64–001, 1975.

It is significant that although the total value of building permits issued during the past two years did not reach 1973's record high, the value of commercial permits increased each year. As commercial activity has the greatest effect upon accommodation demand, the impact of activity generated by the structures being built today will be felt in the accommodation sector in two or three years (rather than the year permits are issued). . . .

Effect of Zoning

As a result, the two-year "Holding By-Law" was introduced in 1973 to ensure that all new development could be evaluated and would meet the desired goal of diversifying the activities in the central area. New development and zoning restrictions have been introduced, greatly reducing commercial densities within the core area. In addition, to further restrict office growth, By-Law No. 34–76 has been introduced.

> It is Council's objective to maintain the rate of growth in the Central Core below a level which, in Council's opinion, would result in an aggregate total of commercial office space in the Central Core of 61 million square feet by 1981, 64.5 million square feet by 1986, and 68 million square feet by 1991.

While such controls should limit growth in the downtown core, the net result should be very favorable to luxury accommodation development for the following reasons:

1. Office space rental rates in downtown Toronto should increase substantially. Already it is reported that a downtown building started today would require rental rates of at least $15 per square foot and a major building would require $20 per square foot. Such rental rates should ensure that the most sophisticated and commercially significant companies locate in the core. Representatives of and people doing business with such companies would be most willing and able to patronize five-star accommodation.

2. Studies by the City of Toronto Planning Board have shown that the current ratio of approximately 250 square feet of gross floor space per office employee is expected to increase over the next 10 years. The increase in floor space per employee will result from the increasing proportion of senior management accommodated in the core area.

3. Development controls will ensure that the core area remains the functional centre for government, financial, commercial, cultural, and entertainment activities; an area attractive to both business and pleasure travellers. . . .

Travellers to Toronto

The development of a highly efficient network of transportation has been a primary factor contributing to the growth of metropolitan Toronto.

The Toronto International Airport, located approximately 20 miles northwest of downtown Toronto, is the busiest airport in Canada and is serviced by the major Canadian airlines, U.S. carriers, and an increasing number of international airlines. An air traffic forecast prepared in 1973 predicted a 90 percent increase in traffic in the Toronto general area during the period covered.

Year	Number of Passengers (in Millions)
1974	8.15
1975	8.83
1976	9.52
1977	10.25
1978	11.04
1979	11.90
1980	12.80
1981	13.52
1982	14.57
1983	15.54

Source: Statistics Canada, Ministry of Transportation and Communication.

Hyatt Regency

The 32–storeyed, 516-room Hyatt Regency Toronto catering to the senior level commercial traveller, became Toronto's leading hotel in less than a year. It is situated just south of the proposed Four Seasons site, in the city's most elite shopping district, where the boutiques, theatres, antique shops, and restaurants of Yorkville and Bloor Street are added attractions to the hotel's guests.

Guest room rates begin at $35 single and $45 double; however, 70 percent of the guest rooms are categorized "deluxe" and "superior" and sell in the $40 to $52 per night range. These tastefully decorated guest rooms include such features as bay windows, king-and queen-sized beds, electric blankets, and electric alarm clocks. Regular one-bedroom suites are sold at rates from $85 to $97 and two-bedroom suites at $131 to $151. The hotel also has six executive suites, which include a spacious parlour and bar, at $175–$200 for one-bedroom suites, and $250–$300 for two-bedroom suites.

The facilities of the hotel include 7 meeting rooms, 10 small conference suites, and the elegant Regency Ballroom, capable of accommodating a reception of up to 1,000 persons or a banquet seating 600. In addition, the hotel houses Truffel's, Toronto's most expensive dining room.

The hotel maintains one of the highest standards of service in Toronto and achieves one of the highest occupancy levels and average room rates in the downtown area. To maintain the hotel's quality image, the operators will be investing approximately $300,000 in new room furnishings during calendar 1976.

While the Hyatt should certainly be a source of keen competition for the

Toronto Accommodation Supply, 1964–January 1976

	Number of Rooms	Total Number of Rooms Available at End of Year
Existing accommodations—1964:		
Anndore Hotel	120	
Ascot Inn	100	
Avion Motor Hotel	100	
Benvenuto Place	96	
Cambridge Motor Hotel	188	
Canadiana Motor Hotel	91	
Carriage House	110	
Conroy Hotel	73	
Constellation Hotel	285	
Four Seasons—Motor Hotel	164	
Holiday Inn West	200	
King Edward Sheraton	775	
Lord Simcoe	750	
Muir Park	122	
Park Plaza	355	
Royal York	1,481	
Regency Towers	62	
Skyline Hotel	100	
Seaway Hotel	156	
Seaway Towers	144	
Seaway Beverley Hills	108	
Valhalla Inn	146	
Westbury	600	
Waldorf Astoria	128	
Windsor Arms	90	
West Way	50	
Westminister	93	
Total	6,687	6,687
Expansions and new accommodations:		
1966—Strathcona Hotel	110	
1967—Inn on the Park	258	
Skyline Hotel (addition)	300	
	668	7,355
1968—Guild Inn	110	
Holiday Inn—East	205	
Sutton Place Hotel	228	
	543	7,898
1969—Holiday Inn—Don Valley	291	8,189
1970—Sutton Place Hotel (addition)	105	
Sherway Inn	89	
Town Inn	200	
	394	8,583

Toronto Accommodation Supply, 1964–January 1976 (*concluded*)

	Number of Rooms	Total Number of Rooms Available at End of Year
1971—Airport Hilton	270	
Cara Inn	211	
Holiday Inn—Airport	353	
Howard Johnson's Airport	260	
Inn on the Park (addition)	200	
Skyline Hotel (addition)	200	
	1,494	10,077
1972—Constellation (addition)	300	
Four Seasons Sheraton	1,466	
Holiday Inn Downtown	750	
Holiday Inn Yorkdale	252	
Hyatt Regency	516	
Inn on the Park	142	
	3,426	13,503
1973—Bristol Place Hotel	217	
Howard Johnson's Motor Lodge	110	
Mount Soudan	54	
	381	13,884
1974—Prince Hotel	406	
Ramada Inn	312	
Roehampton Place	111	
Skyline (addition)	200	
Travelodge	248	
	1,277	15,161
1975—Bond Place	300	
Harbour Castle	983	
Hotel Triumph	196	
Hotel Toronto	600	
Chelsea Inn	894	
	2,973	18,134
1976—Plaza II	250	18,384

proposed Four Seasons Hotel, it has established the luxury image associated with the Yorkville area. In essence, the success of the Hyatt is a stepping stone toward the type of luxury hotel envisioned by Four Seasons. . . .

There has been a rapid increase in the supply of both first-class and economy-type accommodation in Toronto during the past five years. This together with a depressed economy in 1975 has resulted in both reduced overall occupancies and a decrease in the rate of room price increases. (See Exhibit 1–A.)

At present it would appear that the market for first-class accommodation is

Exhibit 1–A: Historical Demand for First-Class Accommodation

Year	Room-Night Demand	Room-Night Supply	Occupancy of First-Class Hotels	City Average Occupancy	Percentage Change in Demand	Percentage Change in Supply
1967	548,675	728,175	75%	75%	Base	N/C
1968	573,871	811,395	71	69	+4.6%	+11%
1969	586,013	811,395	72	73	+2.1	N/C
1970	625,974	849,720	74	72	+6.8	+4.7
1971	592,310	849,720	70	68	−5.4	N/C
1972	831,979	1,217,032	68	67	+40.4	+43.2
1973	1,243,417	1,846,900	67	68	+59.4	+51.2
1974	1,403,644	1,846,900	76	74	+13.0	N/C
1975	1,438,465	2,195,475*	66	66	+2.5	+18.9
January and February, 1975	178,415	298,540	60	56	N/A	N/A
January and February, 1976	182,281	407,218†	45	51	+2.3	+36.4

N/C = No change.
* Includes Harbour Castle Hotel for eight months and Hotel Toronto for six months.
† Includes all competitive first-class hotels, adjusted for extra day in 1976.

more than satisfied and given a normal growth rate in demand, a period of approximately four years will be required before all hotels, on average, will be operating at economic levels of occupancy.

In spite of the above we remain firmly of the opinion that a market exists for a truly deluxe facility which in effect would attract the more affluent guests from those hotels which by today's standard are considered to be first-class operations.

Site Analysis

The site of the proposed Four Seasons Hotel is ideally suited to the development of a five-star property. Discussions with members of our firm in various cities in the United States confirmed that deluxe hotels in their respective cities were primarily located in areas similar to that of Yorkville.

During the past decade, Yorkville has developed from a "hippy hangout" to Toronto's most prestigious shopping area and a prime residential community. Projects now under development should further upgrade the image of the area. The most recent proposed planning guidelines for Metro Toronto devote considerable space to proposals for Yorkville, and include the following:

- Retain the high-quality retail character.
- Maintain and improve pedestrian access.
- Restrict high-density commercial growth to Bloor Street and maintain the low-rise character of Yorkville.

The North-Midtown area, of which Yorkville is a part, provides high-quality residences for approximately 5,000 persons. In addition, the boutiques and top-grade business concerns in the area employ approximately 30,000 people. This resident and worker population should provide the base demand for the proposed hotel's food and beverage facilities. In addition, Yorkville has become established as a retail and entertainment centre, attracting patrons from throughout the city.

Yorkville also attracts many Canadian and international visitors. The following quote from Metro plan illustrates:

> Bloor Street, between Park Road and Avenue Road, and the Village of Yorkville are well-known high-order retail areas serving a metropolitan and international clientele. (Some speciality Yorkville shops estimate that 90 percent of Saturday sales are made to visitors from the United States.)

While Yorkville has become established as a high-quality retail area, it is sufficiently close to the commercial core to attract business travelers. The success of the Yorkville area in attracting these people is evidenced by the ability of the Hyatt Regency and Park Plaza hotels to achieve considerably higher occupancy levels than the city's other first-class properties. Another hotel in the area, not generally well known, is the Windsor Arms. Despite minimal advertising, it caters to many affluent visitors to Toronto who desire the hotel's unobtrusive, relaxed atmosphere. We have not included the Windsor Arms in our listing of competitive facilities because of its relatively small size and the fact that it concerns itself primarily with the food and beverage market. . . .

The success of Hazelton Lanes should reinforce the image and character of the Yorkville area. This in turn would contribute to establishing the appropriate setting for the proposed five-star hotel. Although we have no doubt that Four Seasons can build a five-star hotel, it is imperative that the public accept the hotel as a five-star property.

We have been informed that at least one restaurant will be developed in the Hazelton Lanes project and have taken this into account in preparing our financial projections for the proposed hotel. . . .

Projected Patronage of a Five-Star Deluxe Hotel on the Proposed Site

Details of the Proposed Facilities

It is proposed that the Four Seasons Hotel consist of 300 rooms, approximately 20 with private terraces. We believe 300 rooms to be an ideal size for a deluxe hotel based on our analysis of similar properties in other cities. Properties of over 300 rooms are too large to give the personalized service demanded by the most discriminating guests, and smaller properties cannot derive appropriate economies of scale.

The proposed rooms are considerably larger than those offered by competitive hotels, the majority being approximately 400 square feet. In addition, the almost-square shape of many of the rooms offers the possibility of unique room layouts. We suggest that consideration be given to providing a retractable partition in each room to separate the sleeping area from the living area. Such a move would, in essence, turn each room into a suite and, if well done, could further the hotel's deluxe image. Furnishings and room arrangements similar to those provided by Ottawa's Carleton Towers Hotel, which we believe to be some of the best in Canada, would add to the deluxe, business-oriented atmosphere.

Food and beverage facilities will comprise:

- 125-seat specialty dining room.
- 100-seat coffee shop.
- 30-seat lobby bar.
- 60-seat pub on the main floor.
- 30-seat pool bar.
- 135-seat cocktail lounge.
- 30-seat delicatessen.
- 520 meeting/banquet seats composed of a 275-seat ballroom and five meeting rooms seating from 25 to 80 persons.

We believe the quantity and variety of food and beverage facilities to be ideal for a five-star hotel on the proposed site. Consideration should be given to the future expansion of the cocktail lounge and possibly of the pub. In general, the size and variety of food and beverage facilities of the proposed Four Seasons Hotel are in proportion to those of the very successful Hyatt Regency Hotel; however, as befits a five-star hotel, less emphasis is placed on meeting and banquet space. . . .

The payroll allocation to the Rooms Department is based on a staffing schedule to which current wage rates were applied and then adjusted for anticipated inflationary increase. The staffing schedule was based on the staff required to service a 75 percent annual occupancy and was not reduced for the lower occupancy levels projected for the initial years. Further, we have assumed that the Four Seasons will hire superior staff and pay wages accordingly. Employee benefits have been estimated to be approximately 14 percent of payroll in accordance with increasing government and union requirements.

Departmental expenses are based on the dollar amounts per occupied room currently expended by the city's first-class hotels. These amounts were subsequently adjusted for inflation. Travel agents' commissions were estimated at 1.1 percent of room sales. . . .

Projected operating results are given in Exhibit 1–B.

Exhibit 1–B: Projected Annual Hotel Operating Results* (dollars in thousands except rates per room)

	1979	1980	1981	1982	1983
Occupancy	63%	68%	72%	75%	75%
Average rate per occupied room	$ 53.00	$ 56.20	$ 59.50	$ 63.10	$ 67.00
Revenue:					
Rooms	$ 3,711	$ 4,248	$ 4,761	$ 5,260	$ 5,584
Food	2,360	2,560	2,761	2,958	3,129
Beverage	1,900	2,051	2,203	2,353	2,482
Telephone	182	206	232	256	271
Other income	52	59	67	74	78
Total	8,205	9,124	10,024	10,901	11,544
Departmental expenses:					
Rooms	981	1,057	1,138	1,216	1,290
Food and beverage	3,463	3,704	3,955	4,204	4,442
Telephone	206	227	248	269	284
Total	4,650	4,988	5,341	5,689	6,016
Gross operating income	3,555	4,136	4,683	5,212	5,528
Undistributed operating expenses:					
Administrative and general	640	686	733	782	827
Management fee	246	274	301	327	346
Advertising and promotion	328	347	360	371	381
Heat, light, and power	217	230	244	259	274
Repairs and maintenance	200	225	252	283	316
Total	1,631	1,762	1,890	2,022	2,144
House profit	$ 1,924	$ 2,374	$ 2,793	$ 3,190	$ 3,384

* This pro forma was prepared by the consultant and is somewhat less optimistic than the partners' own projections (see Exhibit 9).

Case 20

IKEA (Canada) Ltd.

Introduction

Bjorn Bayley, the president and general manager of IKEA Canada, reflected on the January 1985 meeting just completed with Anders Berglund, sales manager, and Mike MacDonald, controller. It had been one of their regular, informal end-of-the-day discussions on issues confronting IKEA. Today's discussion, a long overdue one, centered on a growth strategy for IKEA Canada. While walking to the car, Bjorn played back in his mind some of the points raised in the meeting.

"We are so busy with the everyday issues that sometimes we forget to address the more important matters such as where do we want to go with the Canadian IKEA operation," noted Anders.

Bjorn had agreed. "The everyday problems demand immediate solutions and can eat up a lot of time. However, we have to sort out our priorities for IKEA Canada's growth."

Mike added, "My recent trip east suggested that there is untapped potential in Southwestern Ontario that we should consider. The proposed new store in Toronto will help in that immediate market, but there is more that could be done in terms of servicing the other areas."

Then there is the mail order option which we continue to play with but perhaps are reluctant to really tackle," suggested Anders. "I know we have mixed feelings about this option."

Bjorn added, "We can't let the enthusiasm surrounding the recent developments in the United States detract from the attention needed for our Canadian operations. We have been and are likely to continue to be busy overseeing the opening of the first two U.S. stores. However, once expansion really takes off there, a separate U.S. organization will be established, and our efforts will be fully devoted to Canada."

Bjorn realized that some important points had been raised in the meeting. At the same time he realized that the issue should not be allowed to rest. He had closed the meeting with the following suggestion:

I think we all need to do more homework before we can sort out growth options for our Canadian operations. Can we agree to each do some analysis focusing on Southwestern Ontario and have a more formal meeting to discuss our positions in a month's time?

This case was prepared by Paul W. Beamish, Hugh J. Munro, and Thomas F. Cawsey of the School of Business and Economics, Wilfrid Laurier University. Copyright © 1986 by Wilfrid Laurier University.

Anders and Mike immediately checked their travel schedules and having judged the timing appropriate, agreed to meet in a month's time.

Background of IKEA

IKEA was an acronym taken from the name of the founder, Ingvar Kamprad, and the farm (Elmtaryd) and village (Agunneryd) in which he had opened his mail order business in 1943. By 1985 IKEA had become a well-known name in furniture retailing around the world. Kamprad was widely credited with revolutionizing furniture retailing and, in doing so, had gained 20 percent of the total Swedish market. In a relatively few years IKEA's international operations grew far larger than those in Sweden, and in 1984 provided 70 percent of group sales. With sales in 1984 of about U.S. $1 billion, IKEA was the world's largest furniture retailer. IKEA had approximately 15,000 items in its product range and a leading share in many markets in home textiles, kitchenware, and other household items.

Begun as a mail order operation out of Kamprad's home, it had blossomed to become an international chain, employing 8,300 in 70 retail outlets located in Sweden, Norway, Denmark, Holland, West Germany, Switzerland, France, Austria, Belgium, and Canada.

Recently IKEA entered the U.S. market with the opening of a store in Philadelphia. Further store openings in other major metropolitan areas in the Northeast United States were planned for the very near future. The intent was to oversee the initial U.S. operations with the management of IKEA Canada and establish a separate organization in the United States when the expansion was well underway.

The key to the IKEA success was its revolutionary approach to all phases of the business: design, manufacturing, product assortment, distribution, sales, and perhaps most importantly, management philosophy, which stressed flexibility and market orientation rather than long-range strategy.

In a general sense, the IKEA philosophy was best reflected by the following directive of Ingvar Kamprad:

> To create a better everyday life for the majority of people.

Consistent with the philosophy, the management of IKEA was to strive to offer a wide range of home furnishing items of good design and function, at prices so reasonable that the majority of people could afford to buy them.

The Canadian IKEA experience began in 1976 when stores were opened in Halifax and Vancouver as franchise operations. IKEA Canada expanded to six franchised stores by 1979 with the addition of outlets in Edmonton, Calgary, Toronto, and Ottawa. The original franchises were bought back by IKEA in 1979. In 1982 new stores were opened in Quebec City and Montreal to bring the total to eight stores. The sales performance of each of IKEA's Canadian outlets is presented in Exhibit 1.

Exhibit 1: IKEA Canada Sales (in thousands of Canadian dollars)

	Actual						Forecast	
	1979	1980	1981	1982	1983	1984	1985	1986
Vancouver	$ 4,428	$ 8,196	$12,122	$11,824	$12,885	$19,636	$21,800	$24,000
Calgary	1,451	4,782	7,379	8,550	7,420	7,848	8,700	9,500
Ottawa	528	3,265	5,730	6,914	8,352	9,015	9,700	10,500
Montreal					8,617	12,623	13,700	21,500*
Halifax	1,383	2,271	3,634	4,257	4,474	6,504	7,400	8,000
Toronto	3,562	6,246	11,231	13,191	16,249	18,318	20,500	23,000
Edmonton	3,067	4,540	6,506	7,474	8,075	8,743	9,700	16,000
Quebec City				5,057	8,284	9,027	10,000	10,500
Total	$14,419	$29,300	$46,611	$57,267	$74,176	$91,714	$101,500	$123,000

* Projected growth due to store size expansion.

Marketing

IKEA had its own unique product range which it distributed worldwide. An imperative requirement was that all articles should be suitable for the Scandinavian market. Once this range of products had been established, operations in individual countries could then select the products that they would like to carry from this set. Bjorn Bayley commented on how this procedure affected his operations.

> We have been quite fortunate here in IKEA Canada. We tend to lag Sweden by a year in terms of changes to our product offerings. What this means is that by the time we consider new offerings out of Sweden, we have a year's market performance data available to assist us. In essence, we have a surrogate "test market" in Sweden before having to make our selections. This has helped us considerably in formulating our product line changes.

In addition to IKEA's basic product range, individual operations such as Canada could develop and market a limited range of offerings that could be combined with the basic IKEA style. This range was usually very limited and specifically tailored to individual domestic markets.

IKEA's product range was directed at covering the total home area, indoors as well as outdoors, with loose as well as fixed home furnishings. The range also comprised tools and ornamental articles for the home and components for the different degrees of "do-it-yourself" in the home furnishing area. Furthermore, the range contained a smaller number of articles for public buildings (for example, desks, cabinets). However, this range was limited so as not to jeopardize the overall price picture. Marketing emphasis was placed on the essential products within each product group.

A critical component to the IKEA concept was their pricing policy. They strived to be the lowest-priced competitor within a particular quality range. This did not mean that the customer "pays less but gets less." IKEA attempted to focus its quality on those dimensions which were critical to the consumer. For example, the quality of a work top would be superior to the quality of the back of a bookcase that would never be seen. "Low price with a meaning" was their theme.

IKEA's ability to offer lower prices than competitors stemmed from the following cost advantages:

1. Designs and construction techniques that yielded cost efficiencies in production.
2. Purchasing economies associated with volume.
3. A worldwide network of specialized manufacturers who could produce components at the lowest cost (for example, often components for the same product were made by various manufacturers in different countries).
4. Lower transport and warehousing costs because the products were sold unassembled.
5. Store locations where rents were low.
6. Delegation of some responsibilities (for example, selection, delivery, and assembling) to customers.

IKEA's promotional activities were directed at achieving two objectives:

1. Educate the consuming public on the IKEA concept and its associated benefits.
2. Build traffic by attracting new customers to their stores and encouraging customers to make more frequent visits.

The prime promotional vehicle was the annual IKEA catalogue which was selectively mailed out to customers as well as being available in the stores. The mailings were prioritized by matching the demographic profile of an area within a store's metropolitan market with that of the store's target market. For example, the key demographic characteristics in the Toronto customer profile included the following:

Income: $35,000+.
Owned condominium or townhouse.
University degree.
White collar.
Primary age group: 35–44.
Secondary age group: 25–34.
Husband/wife both work.
Two children.
Movers.

With the exception of minor deviations (such as owning of single detached homes versus condominium), this "upscale" profile was fairly consistent among the other metropolitan markets.

Newspaper, radio, and television advertisements complemented the catalogue campaign. These advertisements were placed seven to nine times throughout the year and were designed to build traffic for the stores.

Finally, special project measures to educate the consuming public constituted the third thrust of IKEA's promotional efforts. These included more informative advertisements placed in magazines such as *Macleans* and *TV Times*. An example of IKEA's magazine and newspaper advertising is provided in Exhibit 2.

IKEA's 1984 promotional expenditures for the Canadian market totalled $6 million and were broken down as follows:

Catalogues (production, printing, mailing)	$2.5 million
Magazine advertisements	2.0 million
Newspaper advertisements	1.0 million
Radio	.3 million
Television	.2 million
Total	$6.0 million

The promotional support allocated to each store was determined by its share of IKEA's total sales in Canada.

Prices

Prices for household furniture in Canada had not increased at the same rate as other consumer items. With 1981 as the base rate (that is, 100) the all item consumer price index increased by 17.2 percent by the end of 1983. Over the same period the consumer price index for household furnishings advanced by 13.4 percent. The average cost of goods sold in 1982 for household furniture stores was 63.7 percent, leaving an average gross margin of 36.3 percent. Additional information on Canada's furniture market is contained in Appendix 1.

Competition

Many types of stores competed for consumers expenditures on home furniture and furnishings. The most well known were the department stores (such as Eaton's, Simpsons, Sears, and The Bay) which carried a range of traditional furniture offerings that were predominantly in the middle price quality range.

The upper end of the market was serviced by a wide range of specialty furniture stores that attempted to differentiate themselves by offering unique designs, custom services, selection within a specialized product category, and/or a combination of the above. Examples of these types of stores in the Toronto area included Atwoods-Ethan Allen Gallery, Art Shoppe, De Boer's, Morette's, and Sheila's.

Exhibit 2: Example of IKEA Advertising

Only you can screw up an IKEA kitchen.

It's simply a matter of nuts and bolts. And screws.

By following the fully illustrated instructions in every carton, you can completely assemble a new IKEA kitchen on your own.

After all, why should you have to pay for installation when you can do it yourself?

This is why we've designed our kitchens for simple and easy assembly. And why they come in easy-to-handle packages you take home yourself. Everything you do contributes significantly to the much lower price.

Compare the cost of an IKEA kitchen and you'll quickly realize it's the smart one to buy.

Affordability, of course, isn't everything. We understand your concerns about quality, too. Which is why every component of an IKEA kitchen is independently tested by the Swedish Furniture Research Institute. Their tests are tough. So you don't have to take our word for it,

Our flat, easy-to-handle cartons let you bring everything home yourself.

you can take theirs. Our choice of cabinets lets you build almost any kitchen your imagination can cook up. The wide variety of doors and drawerfronts opens up even more possibilities.

And from our remarkable choice of interior fittings you select the shelves, baskets and other space-saving accessories to complete your kitchen. Each item is sold separately, so you buy only what you need, not what someone else thinks you need.

Come to IKEA and get the complete story. And you can

talk to one of our trained kitchen experts. Better yet, why not call and make an appointment?

You'll find you really can put an IKEA kitchen together yourself.

All things considered, the only mistake you could make is buying your kitchen somewhere else.

Doors and drawerfronts come in a variety of styles and finishes. All tested for durability.

$1,015

Includes all System 210 components shown here, even the kitchen sink.

Full 160° hinges give doors a flush fit, with no visible hardware.

Ask for these free and informative brochures when you visit IKEA. And look for more kitchen ideas in our Catalogue.

SYSTEM 210

IKEA KITCHEN

IKEA 1985

VICTORIA · VANCOUVER · CALGARY
EDMONTON · TORONTO · OTTAWA
MONTREAL · QUEBEC CITY · DARTMOUTH

IKEA

Furniture warehouse operations that frequently advertised discount prices filled the bottom end of the furniture offerings. The trade-off here was not necessarily entirely with the quality of the offerings; it often entailed less service and less emphasis on image factors.

More recently KD, or knockdown, furniture had become very popular with consumers. KD furniture had come to signify durable, stylish, and affordable products that were assembled at home. In fact, IKEA called it QA furniture, for quick assembly.

The comments which follow from people in the industry provide some insights as to the reasons for the success of KD furniture.[1]

> You can now achieve any look at all with KD furniture. The collections are constantly updated, and the range of finishes is expanding as well. Though this type of furniture was originally produced in teak and pine, enamelled, lacquered, and laminated finishes and a large selection of wood stains are now available. It allows our customers to coordinate the new pieces with existing furniture items.
>
> Bill Mira, IDOMO

> These manufacturers and distributors were serving the needs of the new consumer group (young families, singles, nomads) before some of the larger North American companies could even determine what their new target market was about. What the young consumers are looking for now are very well designed items that are economically priced and that create an instant impact. They want to go out, shop around, and create a total environment in as little time and with as little money as possible.
>
> Mr. Stokan, retail consultant

> It's very nice looking and the price is right, but it won't stand up the way the high-end product will. I usually recommend that clients purchase the best products they can possibly afford. But when funds are very limited, KD furniture is a good alternative.
>
> Woody Milholland, designer

IKEA Canada and more recently IDOMO, a Toronto furniture dealer, had been successful with the KD product lines. IDOMO appeared to have capitalized on the excess demand in the Toronto market that IKEA developed but was not able to service.

IDOMO operated stores in Hamilton, Mississauga (across from IKEA), and the Downsview area of Toronto. In their catalogue—which was distributed free to many homes in southern Ontario—they noted that KD furniture means "savings in shipping charges from our suppliers with whom we do volume buying and savings to you in that we make it easy to carry home." With a motto of "All you need is a screwdriver," like IKEA, they emphasized uniquely designed self-assembly furniture. Like IKEA, there was a wide selection of furniture available in pine or painted hardwoods. Unlike IKEA, IDOMO had greater emphasis on the

---

[1] *The Globe and Mail*, Homes Section, January 12, 1985.

use of teak. Exhibit 3 notes the products offered in both the 96-page IDOMO and 144-page IKEA catalogues. Prices were roughly comparable.

Prices listed in the IDOMO catalogue were in effect for a full year. While they made every effort to ensure their supply and prices until the end of the period, because of currency fluctuations, alternate suppliers, or increases in materials, they reserved the right to make adjustments to prices and specifications. A mail order number in Toronto was provided in the IDOMO catalogue. Of late IDOMO had begun to employ an increased amount of television advertising.

IDOMO purchased goods from around the world and operated a number of their own Canadian factories. Their primary source of goods was Denmark. (As

Exhibit 3: Catalogue Tables of Contents

IKEA		IDOMO
Accenten	IKEA at your service	Bathrooms
Armchairs	Kitchen accessories	Bar stools
Audio furniture	Kitchen cabinets	Bedrooms
Baskets	Lighting	Clocks
Bath mats	Mail order forms	Coffee tables
Bathroom cabinets	Marketplace	Daybeds
Bed linens	Mattresses	Desks
Beds	Mirrors	Dining
Bedside tables	Mobelfakta (quality control)	Juvenile bedrooms
Bedspreads	Occasional tables	Kitchen accessories
Benches	Picture frames	Kitchens
Bookcases	Pillows	Mirrors
Buffets	Pillowcases	Occasional chairs
Care and cleaning instructions	Planters	Office furniture
Carpets	Plant stands	Room dividers
Chairs	Pots and pans	Sofas
Chair pads	Quilts	Sofabeds
Chests of drawers	Quilt bags	Stereo/video
Children's furniture	Rugs	Systems & bookcases
China	Savings coupons	Wardrobes
Clothes closets	Serving tables	
Coffee tables	Sheets	
Cookware	Shelves	
Cutlery	Shower curtains	
Desks	Sofas	
Desk chairs	Sofa beds	
Dining chairs	Stools	
Dining tables	Storage systems	
Fabrics	Store hours	
Floor tiles	Table bar	
Glassware	Toys	
Hall furniture	Wallpaper	
Hat stands	Wall units	
IKEA's glossary of terms	Window blinds	

their catalogue noted, "IDOMO loves Danes, especially these following quality factories that support us: A/S Domino Mobler, Tvilum Moebelfabrik, Marca Export Group, Ove Jensens Moebelfabrik, Viking Moebler, E. J. Moebler K/S, Soenderbro Moebelfabrik, Gangsoe, Invita A/S.")

The success of this furniture had prompted some full-line department stores such as Robinsons to augment their traditional offerings with a KD line. Although Sears had not taken direct aim at the IKEA business, they potentially represented the most-formidable competitor among the full-line department stores. In Canada, Sears had 75 stores plus 1,500 sales offices. Their total inventories (at cost) were over $600 million. Sears was the only national catalogue distributor among general merchandise retailers. Their low-cost catalogue operation put out 12 different catalogues a year. When Eaton's discontinued its catalogue operation, Sears picked up an additional $250 million in sales. With such a large number of stores and sales offices, not surprisingly Sears had a large in-house transportation network—in fact, owning 1,800 trucks.

IKEA Management

IKEA Canada was organized on an informal basis. IKEA's senior management consisted of Bjorn Bayley, Anders Berglund, and Mike MacDonald.

Bjorn Bayley joined the company in 1969. His mother worked closely with Ingvar Kamprad for many years providing a family tie to the worldwide organization. She named all IKEA products and was reported to have named a table after Bjorn. Bjorn took over what had been six franchise operations run out of Vancouver, Halifax, Toronto, Edmonton, Calgary, and Ottawa. He spent his earlier years familiarizing himself with the Canadian operation and evaluating the management. The previous franchise owners from Halifax had stayed with the operation after the purchase.

Anders Berglund had joined IKEA Canada in 1979 and had acted as controller in both Denmark and Austrian-Dutch divisions. Anders began as controller but had recently moved to head up sales. Mike MacDonald, the controller and only non-Swedish-born member of the senior group, had joined the Canadian company in January 1984.

Bjorn talked about his relationships with the worldwide organization.

> The first five years in Canada we didn't see anyone here. There were some social visits as executives travelled to see Canada, but we didn't have much visibility. We had a hard sell to do on the people in Almhult (the site of corporate head office in Sweden). Even though Ingvar now lives in Switzerland, the heart of the company still seems to be in the original town. When we visited there we took over Canadian flags, scotch—anything to create an impression. One year we even wore Stetsons and denims and went as cowboys.
>
> Now it is quite different. Once a year I meet with the executive group of 13 for about a week. I attend these meetings with Anders and Mike. Last year we skipped the meeting as there was no time. I do spend two or three five-day weekends a year

talking with Ingvar. We talk about a lot of things as he asks me for advice on a wide variety of matters and vice versa. Frankly, I could never leave IKEA.

Bjorn described the relationship with IKEA worldwide as follows:

It is very hard to measure what we are doing in Canada. IKEA worldwide executive group is looking at the long-term picture, not just short-term profits. They use a number of ratios to compare us with other countries and focus on profits and costs. Sales are not as important. We intend to be here for a long time so we don't want to go for short-run profits.

In Canada, the three of us run things out of the Vancouver head office. I don't like anyone between me and the store managers. Sometimes I have to see them as a group, but if I can, I travel to the stores a lot.

When asked for an organization chart, Anders had to have one drawn by hand as none existed. It was drawn in a circular fashion to reflect the nonhierarchical nature of how Anders believed the company operated. There appeared to be three central features of the organization. Central to everything were the stores, the retail operation. These reported directly to Bjorn although it was evident that there was a lot of interaction between all top management and the retail outlets.

The second feature of the structure was the direct reporting relationships that existed between IKEA Canada and IKEA Worldwide. Many of the policies and procedures were initiated and developed for the global network. Even with the distance and time delays in shipping things to Canada, this centralization was evident. Product line and production policies generally were made on a worldwide basis. Canada's role was to decide which part of the worldwide product offerings to retail in Canada.

This third feature of the organization's functioning was the local support staff for the Canadian operation. Canada was able to "local source" some of its product, that is, have it made in Canada. As well, the support staff in Vancouver was responsible for personnel policies and the overall operations of the Canadian stores.

Store managers were measured by a variety of criteria. Store performance played a key role. As well, however, store appearance, staff turnover, sales per square foot, and staff per sales dollar were also measured. One Canadian store had the lowest staff per sales dollar in the IKEA system worldwide. This was thought to be a bad thing since it meant that customers were unlikely to be served properly.

Performance was expected from store managers. One manager had been fired after top management decided he was incompetent. It was reported that he spent five days a week entertaining people for lunch and lived high on the company expense account, including gas expenses twice what was expected.

It was IKEA's philosophy to be continually innovative in store designs. With each new store opening, an attempt was made to incorporate in the layout the things that worked well with the existing IKEA stores as well as any new concepts that had been developed in the retail industry. Currently the Vancouver store (also the site of IKEA head office) was known throughout IKEA as the model store in Canada. It was the largest, most modern of the chain and was laid out in the fashion of the major European stores. The original store in Vancouver had been in a particularly bad location. The parking was inadequate, and the entire store had a "tacky" image. Because of this the decision was made to build an up-to-date facility when the lease arrangements permitted.

The appearance of the store confirmed that the plans for this new store had come to fruition. The store was laid out with considerable attention to colour coordination in order to give a total effect that promoted sales. Traffic flow through the store was well designed and allowed large numbers of customers to move about in relative ease. The layout and design of the Vancouver store contrasted strongly with the Toronto store which was crowded and suffered major inventory problems because of insufficient unloading space.

Despite the functional design and pleasing appearance of the Vancouver store, it had not performed to top management's expectations. They believed that the store was capable of 50 percent more sales through add-on sales and good promotion. There was also speculation that the Canadian consumers simply had a different spending pattern than the more-sophisticated European customers. In general, Canadian and American tastes lagged European ones by one or two years.

Of the 550–600 people employed by IKEA, approximately 120–125 worked in the Vancouver store. Twenty-nine of these were full-time nonmanagement, 20 were management, and approximately 75 were part-time.

Each store had five or six department heads appointed by Bjorn Bayley. (The sixth head was the restaurant manager if a restaurant existed.) Generally, department heads could expect to earn $25,000–$26,000, with the operations manager earning $28,000–$30,000 and the store managers earning $40,000 and up.

Each department head had his/her area of responsibility as described below:

— Operations department head was in charge of all nonsales-related departments (stock control, customer services, cash, mail order, and bulky items).
— Deco manager planned all displays and worked with the furniture and marketplace managers to plan promotions and sales.
— Furniture manager handled all furniture displays and sales.
— Marketplace manager handled all nonfurniture displays and sales.
— Stock controller was in charge of all in-store stock, damaged goods containers, and all communications with head office stock control.
— Restaurant manager was relatively autonomous and handled all restaurant activities.
— Personnel (not a manager) handled payroll and orientation but not hiring which was handled by the store manager.

The company hoped to maintain a reasonable gap in salary between the various levels in the organization. Assistant department heads generally received at least 10 percent more than employees. Department heads received a minimum of 10 percent more than assistant heads. Salaries for store managers varied widely depending on their performance and years with the company.

Bayley noted:

> Our philosophy is translated into "freedom with responsibility." We try to have everyone that works for us believe these things and act on these guidelines. In Canada, the store manager sets the store budgets and sales budgets. Generally they overestimate what they can do, and we have to push their estimates down. After these discussions he runs the store on his own within those guidelines. It's almost impossible to push the philosophy down to the cashier level, but we try.
>
> You must understand that this organization reflects the personality and wishes of its founder, Ingvar Kamprad. It is still privately owned. Ingvar has diversified into banks, an insurance company, oil, and other things, but this firm reflects the philosophy reflected in the poster, IKEA's soul. [See Exhibit 4.]
>
> We claim to be the "impossible price" store, the best price in Canada. If we can't match or beat our competition with a quality product and make 30–40 percent gross profit, then we drop the product or the line. Normally, our prices are 10–15 percent better than our competition. Our philosophy has always been one of good quality and low price. We check our competition and match or undercut their prices.
>
> One other aspect of our philosophy relates to the amount of cash that we have available at any time. IKEA Worldwide says that we have to have 12 percent of sales in short-term securities. The idea is that one region in the world could have a bad few years and the cash might be needed. When the Frankfurt store burned down, the money was used to rebuild. In Canada the money can be used for expansion purposes.

The controller, Mike MacDonald, had joined the company about a year earlier. He stated, "The management style was hard to understand at first. I received little direction and was just trying to do my job. I was responsible for my area, and there was no particular hierarchy to follow. The job certainly isn't 8 to 5! There are no particular deadlines for results, and you are the one pushing yourself, no one else. You just know what you are responsible for and have to do it."

IKEA management saw themselves as a dynamic management team determined to make a success of their company. They were committed to the philosophy espoused by Kamprad and worked hard to ensure that corporate performance met his high standards. Because of the location of their head office in Vancouver, managing IKEA Canada involved a lot of travel. Management's dedication was shown by their hectic schedules. In December 1984 and January 1985, for example, Bayley and MacDonald had each spent over two thirds of their time in either Europe, the United States, or other parts of Canada. These schedules involved considerable sacrifice on the part of management in that they spent a great deal of time both in travelling and then in catching up once they returned to Vancouver.

Exhibit 4

IKEA's soul.

It isn't hard to produce fine, expensive furniture. When money is no object, the job is easy. It's like farming. When the soil is rich, the farmer's job is a pleasure. But, to produce fine furniture that isn't expensive ... that's another field — IKEA's field.

IKEA's home is in Sweden's province of Småland. The soil of Småland is poor and rocky, and for hundreds of years Småland's farmers have broken their backs to clear their fields and cultivate their soil. They had a goal. They were stubborn. They struggled. And they succeeded.

IKEA's nature is rooted in Småland. We began here 25 years ago, and our head offices are still here in the small town of Älmhult. Our goal has been to produce and sell beautiful and functional Scandinavian furniture at prices that ordinary people can afford. It hasn't been easy. But we've been stubborn. We've struggled. And we've succeeded.

We've found new ways.

One cannot farm a rocky piece of land in the same way as a fertile field. It takes toil and sweat to clear the obstacles and solve the problems. New ways have to be found.

Assembled furniture is bulky. Expensive to transport, expensive to store, difficult to handle. IKEA has found ingenious ways to "flat-pack" nearly all of our furniture. It saves us time and money at every stage ... savings which are reflected in our low prices. Our customers assemble the furniture themselves, but are well-compensated for their work!

Salesmen are expensive, and can also be irritating. IKEA leaves you to shop in peace. We trust you to make wise decisions based on the objective information attached to every item in our showroom. Materials, measurements, and consumer testing results are all clearly stated. And if you have any questions, you'll always find help at our information desks.

You pick out furniture yourself, take it to the check-out counter, and take it home in, or on, your car.

We save money. You save money.

We manufacture differently

Before IKEA's time, all furniture was manufactured in furniture factories. From start to finish.

IKEA changed that. We create furniture with simplified elements that can be efficiently produced by specialized factories. Unfinished pine shelves are made right at the saw mills. Cabinet doors are produced by door factories. Metal frames are made in machine workshops. Cushions come directly from textile mills.

Rational mass production. Supply and demand. Our 50 million customers (per year!) demand a lot, and we've found ways to supply them with high quality at bargain prices.

Nothing is impossible

We love problems and challenges because they give us a chance to show off our ingenuity. For example, we've designed the "Fastest pin-back chair" in the west, or

east. You can assemble it yourself in 5 minutes, thanks to a clever little screw attachment we invented. This special screw allows us to "flat-pack" the chair, and sell it cheaper than any other pin-back chair on the market.

We've also invented an ingenious little snap lock for some of our table legs, which actually makes a table stronger and cheaper at the same time!

We have also created a sensational new cabinet system for kitchens, bathrooms, wardrobes, etc. which is sturdy, attractive, and functional — at a fraction of the price you would normally pay for comparable European quality.

Nothing is impossible.

IKEA's soul

IKEA's soul is in the right place. Like Småland's farmers, our values are down-to-earth. We have toiled hard in a difficult field to produce a sweet harvest...

We've succeeded. Scandinavian design and quality that you can afford.

That's IKEA.

Purchasing/Inventory Control

The IKEA product line in Canada included 6,000 separate article numbers with the top 200 lines accounting for 60 percent of the sales (within any line there are a number of article numbers; for example, BOJ represents one line). Management felt that one of IKEA's strengths was in managing the logistics associated with securing and moving volumes of such a variety of items from suppliers to customers worldwide. The basic flow of IKEA's products from suppliers to Canadian customers is depicted in Exhibit 5.

For the Canadian operation there were three basic management groups involved in purchasing and stock control. The first group was the stock supply department (three full-time people) located in the central service office in Vancouver. Their mandate was to forecast sales for all of Canada and then secure or "earmark" enough long-term stock from the central warehouses in Sweden to service the anticipated sales volume level. Sales for Canada were forecasted for up to three years in the future with more specific requests being placed twice a year—once for the September to January period, another for the February to August period. Actual volumes were allowed to vary 10 percent above or below the forecasted levels.

Stockout problems typically occurred when actual sales deviated significantly from forecasts and/or when suppliers could not deliver the promised products on time. While there were some problems initially in getting Canadian orders filled by suppliers in Sweden, management reported that the recent service had been very good. The majority of problems tended to rest with the high degree of uncertainty surrounding forecasts. As Bjorn noted, "You need a gambler in the stock supply job."

Purchasing a slightly higher stock did not necessarily mean lower stockouts because most stockouts occurred when IKEA could potentially have used twice as much stock as predicted. The trend had been to prefer stockouts rather than loading up the individual stores with excess stock. More stores could be serviced when the majority of inventory was stored in central warehouses. An example of the service levels achieved for the Canadian stores is provided in Exhibit 6.

Exhibit 5:   Flow of IKEA's Products

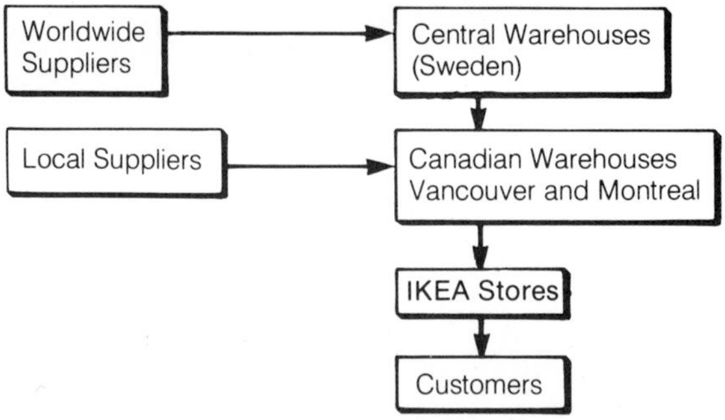

Exhibit 6:   Service Levels for Individual Stores in Canada (month of December 1984)

Store	V-Items*			K-Items†		
	Average	Low	High	Average	Low	High
Vancouver	89	67	100	92	83	100
Calgary	69	33	100	85	38	100
Ottawa	92	79	100	87	72	100
Montreal	88	50	100	87	67	100
Halifax	92	67	100	90	88	97
Toronto	71	25	100	80	61	100
Edmonton	90	63	100	90	72	97
Quebec City	80	63	100	90	72	100
Canada	84	74	96	86	71	97

* V = Critical items within a product line. Desired service level is 99 percent (that is, 99 percent of items within a product group are in stock at time required).
† K = Catalogue items within a product group. Desired service level is 90 percent.

The second level of involvement in stock control occurred at the individual store level. With the central service group having earmarked the stock required for all of the Canadian operations, it was the responsibility of the individual stores' stock control groups to draw on these stock reserves as needed (that is, short-term stock supply). Individual stores were given the directive of maintaining 13½ weeks of inventory on hand (10½ weeks in the store, 3 weeks in transit). The stores used an automatic reorder system which required that individual stores set their own order points and monitor their inventory on hand.

Typically, orders for a particular store were sent via computer to Sweden twice a week. The time between placing the order and delivery of the items ranged from six to eight weeks. The orders were filled from stock sent from the central warehouses in Sweden to the warehouses in Canada or, on occasion, directly from the suppliers.

The third level of involvement in IKEA Canada's stock control was local sourcing. In order to achieve its objective of offering an "impossible price," IKEA sought out low-cost manufacturers around the world. For most items this meant that purchases would not be made in Canada unless they were absolutely cheaper. However, to reduce the risk of stockouts for the very best selling items, IKEA tried to develop a Canadian supplier even if a slight premium had to be paid. Palle Jensen from the central service operation in Vancouver was in charge of securing local suppliers. Jensen reported directly to Inter-IKEA in Denmark, with only a dotted-line relationship to the Canadian general manager.

In 1984 the stock control group purchased $57 million worth of goods on IKEA Canada's behalf. Jensen's local suppliers contributed $12 million of this (up from $7 million the previous year) with the remaining $45 million being imports. With an average 18 percent tariff on imports plus associated transportation costs, this meant that some otherwise noncompetitive Canadian manufacturers were capable of becoming IKEA suppliers. Although substantial progress had been made in increasing the volume of stock obtained from local manufacturers, there were a number of significant impediments to further growth. These impediments were related to exchange rates, IKEA staff size, consumer attitudes, production efficiency, and raw material availability.

IKEA worked to a limited degree with the manufacturers to help them produce at a lower cost. To this end they provided detailed product specifications as well as other technical assistance, equipment leasing, and sometimes loans for cash flow.

Although IKEA was willing to work closely with its suppliers, it did not view itself as a manufacturer. In fact, it was against company policy to enter into any businesses that deviated from its strengths in furniture retailing.

In December 1984 IKEA Canada did provide some assistance to one of their local suppliers, Parrsboro Woodworkers Ltd. of Truro, Nova Scotia, which was forced into receivership. The supplier had been aided in its bid for financing by both orders and $1.2 million investment in machinery from IKEA. Modern equipment had been purchased to process the plentiful local supply of low-cost quality hardwood in the surrounding area. The management of IKEA Canada was also assisting in the search for a buyer for the Parrsboro operation.

IKEA Canada's Financial Position

IKEA's policy was to finance growth primarily through internally generated funds, that is, the funds available for IKEA Canada's growth were a function of the cash generated from its operations. The exceptions to this were expenditures for land and building which were usually carried via loans from banks. IKEA had a policy of owning their own land and buildings with the mortgaged portion a maximum 70 percent of the purchase amount and being repaid over 5 to 15 years.

IKEA Canada's successful track record yielded considerable flexibility with respect to financing growth. The sales history of IKEA Canada has already been summarized in Exhibit 1. Store sales were usually 70 percent furniture and 30 percent other (textile/carpet, lighting, accent/boutique/season). Markups were higher on nonfurniture items due to increased handling costs. Overall, gross profits were often around 25–35 percent. It was felt that this profit target was required in order to support their growth objective of 20 percent per year.

In terms of demands on IKEA Canada's financial position, management recognized that there would be continued pressure to upgrade or expand existing facilities when either the demand warranted it or the timing was appropriate (for example, lease expiring). Management was currently reviewing plans for store location moves in Montreal, Toronto, and Calgary. At the same time, management felt there were options that involved bringing the IKEA concept to untapped markets within Canada that warranted attention. It was believed that if managed carefully, the latter growth avenue could be supported with funds currently available and/or generated internally.

IKEA's Alternative Strategies for Growth

IKEA Canada has been steadily growing since opening its first Canadian store in 1976. Future growth was expected to occur along the following two fronts:

1. Increased penetration of existing markets within Canada.
2. Expansion into new market areas within Canada.

Management's philosophy toward growth reflected a preference for "deliberate, cautious moves" that could be primarily supported through internal financing as opposed to big-scale "major aggressive growth projects" requiring significant external support ("small sure steps" as opposed to "running with the risk of falling").

The specific growth avenue of immediate concern was increasing the penetration in the Southwestern Ontario market. IKEA currently had only the Toronto store in the Southwestern Ontario market, and this facility had been very successful to date, operating at or over capacity.

Management felt that there was significant potential remaining in both the Toronto area and the other relatively untapped metropolitan areas within Southwestern Ontario. Management had already made the decision to open a new and larger store in a new location in Toronto. From their perspective, there were the following basic options for pursuing growth opportunities:

1. Allow a second, larger store in Toronto to either complement or replace the existing store.
2. Establish a mail order business to service the untapped areas within the Southwestern Ontario market.
3. Open up another store within a different metropolitan area in Southwestern Ontario.
4. Combine some or all of the above approaches.

At a minimum, management felt there was considerable unrealized potential within the Toronto market that should be addressed. A recent study commissioned by management provided some insights into the existing store's current penetration of the Toronto market. This analysis suggested that there was considerable potential for further penetration of the Toronto area. The big issue remaining was determining how to realize this potential.

Current operational difficulties with the existing Toronto store were limiting its ability to capitalize on growth opportunities. It had one of the poorest service level records of all stores. Stockouts had become so prevalent that the store manager instituted a telephone campaign to fill back orders when the inventory became available. What was most surprising was that management estimated that almost 90 percent of customers were willing to wait for IKEA products. However, the entrance of copycat competitors like IDOMO suggested that improvements were necessary in order to prevent others from capitalizing on the potential that existed.

Because of the above problem and the unrealized potential, management had decided to open a second, larger store. This store was to be located in North Toronto, three kilometres west of Toronto's main thoroughfare (Yonge Street) and just north of the Trans-Canada Highway (Highway 401), which crossed through Toronto in an east-west direction. The issue remaining was whether to keep the existing store or to close it down. There would have to be enough demand either in the Toronto area or from surrounding areas to warrant keeping two stores in operation.

Another growth alternative involved increasing the number of stores to service more of the Southwestern Ontario market. This option warranted considerable analysis given the costs involved. For example, the proposed new store in Toronto was estimated to incur the following capital expenditures (in millions of dollars):

Land	$ 2.64 (12 acres @ $220,000/acre)
Building	6.50
Equipment/improvements	1.50
Total	$10.64

IKEA had a policy of using teams of existing employees who demonstrated expertise in particular areas (for example, deco, purchasing) to train and assist personnel for a new store. The costs associated with such a program were called buildup costs. Standard buildup costs for a new store independent of those listed above would also be incurred. These were estimated as follows:

Staff buildup	$ 750,000
Operational buildup	450,000
Services buildup	500,000
Advertising	800,000
	$2,500,000

In addition to these costs, it was estimated that approximately 11 weeks of inventory would be required for working capital purposes.

Management was unsure as to where a new store or stores should be opened. The population base would have to be large enough and contain a sufficient number of households who matched the profile of customers currently attracted to the IKEA concept. Any new store would have to comply with the performance requirements imposed on the existing stores. As a preliminary step in exploring

Exhibit 7:   Mail Order Sales for Canadian Stores, December 1983—December 1984

Store	Mail Order Sales (000)	Total Sales	Mail Order Percent of Total Sales	Mail Order Percent October 1982– November 1983
Vancouver	$1,453.5	$ 21,502.3	6.8%	5.6%
Calgary	773.8	8,988.9	8.6	3.0
Ottawa	177.2	10,061.7	1.8	1.3
Montreal	309.4	14,144.7	2.2	0.6
Halifax	1,653.3	7,220.4	22.9	14.7
Toronto	398.9	21,280.9	1.8	1.0
Edmonton	1,494.5	9,694.6	15.4	6.9
Quebec City	589.6	9,710.2	6.1	2.4
Total	$6,850.2	$102,603.7	6.7%	3.6%

this option, demographic characteristics of the major metropolitan areas within Southwestern Ontario were compiled (see Appendix 2).

An alternate approach for tapping the potential in Southwestern Ontario was to establish a more extensive mail order business. Management had been contemplating this growth option for some time. While the original thinking was to consider mail order as a means for augmenting business nationwide, management believed that focusing on the Southwestern Ontario market which offered considerable potential could serve as a good test of the viability of increasing the mail order thrust.

IKEA Canada currently did about $7 million a year mail order through their catalogue business. Forecasts for 1985 suggested that mail order business would likely reach $8.3 million. See Exhibit 7 for the breakdown of mail order sales by store. Approximately 3.6 million catalogues were distributed annually at a cost of $2.5 million. While these catalogues lent themselves nicely to mail order, they were a critical promotional component for IKEA's mainstream store operations and would exist without mail order sales. New catalogues were distributed at the beginning of the company's fiscal year, September 1. Prices quoted in the catalogue remained valid for the year.

Management's feelings about mail order were, at best, mixed. Len Laycock, the marketing manager, was considered the "champion" of the mail order option. From Len's perspective, if IKEA could generate the current level of mail order business without even trying, the potential had to be much greater.

Len had a vision of how this potential could be pursued. As an interim step, a separate mail order business could be established whereby an office could be set up for soliciting and processing customer orders. All catalogue sales would be channeled through this operation. The actual products would be shipped from inventory carried by the closest existing store. As it stands now, the options for the Ontario market would be either the Toronto or the Ottawa store. The mail order office would be responsible for marketing, order processing, inventory sourcing, shipping, and sales returns. The operation would likely require a manager, two or three support staff, promotional support, an extensive mailing list, telephones, and a computer. Len felt that it wouldn't be unrealistic to expect the first-year cost to run in the neighbourhood of $750,000. Once mail order sales began to flourish, Len felt that the individual stores could be relieved of the task of handling mail order related inventory and that this responsibility could be brought under the one umbrella established in the interim. A new central warehouse would be necessary with the associated costs (land and building) estimated to be around $5 million.

An alternative approach to that envisioned by Len involved integrating the mail order business with an existing store operation. A more concerted catalogue mailout would be required and likely targeted to those regions offering the greatest potential. Additional staff would be required (likely three or four), but the operation would basically be an extension of the existing business. With the increase in thrust on mail order, additional pressures would be put on inventory management and control in order to prevent further stockout problems from occurring.

Regardless of which mail order operation was adopted, Len knew that considerable analysis was required in order to effectively and efficiently target the incremental catalogue mailouts. The data that management compiled to assess the additional store(s) alternative would be of assistance in these determinations. One other aspect of the business that would change with an increased emphasis on mail order was transportation. Len felt that initially this could be handled by contracting out the transportation services as they did now. Once volume increased significantly, serious thought could be given to the idea of IKEA having its own fleet of transports to accommodate the needs of mail order customers.

The other senior managers at IKEA Canada expressed some serious reservations about going the mail order route:

"To date we have engaged in defensive mail order—only when the customer really wants it and the order is large enough. The separate handling, breaking down of orders, and repackaging required for mail orders would be too expensive and go against the economics-through-volume approach of IKEA," exclaimed Mike.

"Profit margins of mail order business tend to be half that of a store operation. There are more sales returns, particularly because of damages incurred in shipping. (The damaged returns with mail orders will likely double the normal rate of 2 percent). In fact, many of the items in our product line are not conducive to mail order shipping," added Bjorn.

Anders offered an additional concern. "It is difficult to know where to draw the market boundaries for a mail order business. We don't want to be substituting mail order customers for store visitors."

Len knew that he had some selling to do in order to get the others to share in his excitement for mail order. He was encouraged by his discussions with experts involved in direct marketing in the retail industry who suggested that catalogues and mail order are and will continue to play bigger roles in retail sales. The flavour of some of these sentiments is captured in *The Globe and Mail* newspaper article provided in Exhibit 8.

Management was unsure as to which growth option or combination of options would be most feasible or effective. They felt that there was considerable potential available in the Southwestern Ontario market. The concern was how best to apply the successful IKEA concept to capitalize on this potential. They realized that the decision was an important one requiring considerable thought and immediate attention. Whatever approach was adopted, all felt the choice would likely serve as a model for subsequent growth efforts in other markets in Canada and the United States.

Exhibit 8

Catalogues are Playing Bigger Role in Retail Sales
by Cathryn Motherwell

Catalogues are gaining greater importance in retail sales.

Although the Toronto-based Sears department store chain does not disclose sales figures for its 1,350 catalogue outlets (its consolidated 1984 sales totalled $3.4 billion), vice president of public affairs Bob Knox did acknowledge that catalogue sales are "a very substantial part of our business."

The Canadian Direct Marketing Association estimates that Canadians spend $1 billion a year on goods purchased from catalogues, but that figure is approximate because Sears does not report its catalogue revenue.

CDMA president Frank Ferguson said Sears' catalogue sales have been estimated at $250 million, but that figure may be a combination of catalogue sales and in-store sales generated by the catalogue.

"Everybody has to follow the Sears lead," he said. "They are the masters of the catalogue. No one knows what they know, and they keep it to themselves."

After Sears, the CDMA member with the largest annual catalogue sales is Regal Greetings and Gifts of Toronto, with $75 million, Mr. Ferguson said. The next major level of sales, $20 million, is shared by several companies.

Most of the new catalogues on the market are produced by existing retailers seeking to expand their markets beyond their own local areas. People keep catalogues for long periods of time to consult them, narrow down their choices, comparison shop, and then either order from home or visit a store to make their purchase.

The companies using catalogues agree that people have less time to go shopping, and as more women enter the work force, catalogue sales are expected to increase.

Exhibit 8 (*concluded*)

One catalogue proponent noted, "I see a bright future for catalogue sales, if done properly." The primary problem is the lack of people with catalogue business experience in Canada. As the industry develops, some of the expertise will come from people working in the packaged goods industries, he predicted.

But while it is anticipated that the Canadian consumer will become a more frequent user of catalogues, catalogue and mail order sales are not expected to approach the current level of activity in the United States.

Homeowners in selected areas south of the border can receive upwards of 20 unsolicited catalogues on their doorsteps each week, as businesses jostle for a portion of a market that is said to be approaching $100 billion (U.S.) in annual sales.

Catalogues are expensive undertakings, however. Presentation is important, and rising production and printing costs limit what some companies can produce.

Sears prints about 4 million copies of its catalogue, Mr. Knox said, but demand has been greater than supply. This year the company decided to charge $4 for its catalogue and offer a $4 discount when a purchase is made (regular customers receive a free catalogue).

Sears has also introduced computer ordering at its catalogue operations in the Toronto area.

To use the system, which is called Comp-U-Shop, a customer must have a Touch-Tone telephone and a Sears account. The person calls the company and is connected with a computer that verifies his or her identity, then takes the catalogue order and says whether the item is in stock and when it will be delivered.

Sears is also trying to improve its catalogue service to customers elsewhere in the country by giving catalogue order takers computer access so that customers will know if an item is in stock.

One of the common complaints about catalogue operations is that merchandise is ordered but never received, and businesses find that they are trying to counter consumers' bad experiences.

The CDMA does not condone its members taking payment for goods before they are shipped. It recommends that customers pay by credit card because if they are billed but do not receive the merchandise, the onus is on the business to prove that the goods were shipped.

Source: *The Globe and Mail*, Monday, May 6, 1985, p. B10.

Appendix 1: Canada's Furniture Market

Domestic Manufacturing

The Canadian furniture industry, excluding reupholstering, was composed of four subgroups, as follows:

— Household furniture, which includes wooden, metal, and upholstered furniture for the home.
— Office furniture, exemplified by products such as desks, chairs, tables, screens, and filing cabinets.
— Miscellaneous furniture and fixtures, which involves special items for schools, hospitals, hotels, stores, and so forth.
— The electric lamp and shade subgroup, entailing portable floor and table lamps and shades.

The industry, which was mostly located in Ontario and Quebec, consisted of some 1,400 establishments. Dominated by small-sized plants, 827 of the establishments employed less than 50 workers. About 60 percent had fewer than 20 employees and were, in a sense, handicraft operations. They developed on the basis of successfully serving regional markets and, to reduce transportation costs, had centralized about nine-tenths of production close to the large metropolitan markets of Ontario and Quebec.

The Statistics Canada report "Inventories, Shipments and Orders in Manufacturing Industries" revealed the following data on furniture shipments by Canadian manufacturers:

	1983	1984	Percent Change 1983–1984
Canadian shipments by manufacturers (in millions):			
Household furniture	$1,506	$1,552	3%
Office furniture	409	524	22
Total	$1,915	$2,076	8%

Data in this section was compiled from the 1984 Statistics Canada Market Research Handbook and a report, "The Canadian Furniture Market," prepared by Maclean Hunter.

The industry appears to have survived the economic difficulties of 1982 and there is some evidence of economic prosperity.

Domestic Consumption Including Imports

Domestic consumption of furniture (production + imports − exports) totalled about $1,866 million in 1984. Imports, which totalled $332 million, up 23 percent from 1983, accounted for approximately 18 percent of this domestic furniture consumption. Fifty percent of the imports in 1984 originated in the United States. The duties on American furniture imported by Canada were currently around 16.3 percent. The second leading source of Canadian imports was Taiwan (11 percent) followed closely by Italy (10 percent). Denmark was a distant fourth with 5 percent of the 1984 furniture imports.

Actual dollar imports of furniture for the years 1980–84 were broken down as follows (in thousands):

	Household Furniture	Office Furniture	Special Purpose	Total (Includes Mattresses and Lamps)
1980	$191,495	$23,807	$19,993	$243,542
1981	240,344	30,313	27,253	306,140
1982	156,982	24,429	25,644	213,843
1983	197,634	25,446	34,505	271,226
1984	234,301	33,699	45,980	332,373

Furniture exports in 1984 totalled $542 million, which was 26.1 percent of total furniture shipments. This represented an increase of 40 percent over 1983 and 75 percent over 1982.

Over 90 percent of Canadian furniture exports went to the United States. The depreciated Canadian dollar had significantly aided furniture export sales. Duties were as low as 3.1 percent on Canadian-made furniture entering the United States. With transportation constituting a significant portion of unit cost and many major U.S. markets being within one shipping day from Toronto or Montreal, the United States was expected to continue to provide good potential for Canadian-made furniture.

In 1984 total retail sales for household furniture stores in Canada were estimated to be $1,661 million. This represented a 7 percent increase over the 1983 total and 37 percent over the 1982 figure. The Statistics Canada report "Family Expenditures in Canada" showed that the average household expenditure on furniture totalled $487.40 in 1982.

Approximately 71 percent of 1984 sales were accounted for by independent retail stores with the remainder going to chain stores. Ontario's 1984 retail sales from household furniture stores were approximately $546 million with 59 percent stemming from independents and 41 percent from the chain stores.

The average sales per square metre (1982 data) for household furniture stores with appliances and furnishings was $1,555. For household furniture stores without appliances and furnishings, the sales were $907 per square metre during the same time period.

Furniture sales were fairly evenly distributed throughout the year. Deviations occasionally occurred in this pattern when the retail trade pursued aggressive promotions (for example, spring, early summer, and January).

The geographic distribution of retail furniture sales generally paralleled population distribution:

	1984 Population Distribution	1984 Sales Distribution
Newfoundland	2.4%	1.5%
Prince Edward Island	0.5	0.1
Nova Scotia	3.5	2.0
New Brunswick	2.9	2.2
Quebec	26.2	36.6
Ontario	35.6	36.0
Manitoba	4.3	3.5
Saskatchewan	4.1	3.6
Alberta	9.0	7.4
British Columbia	11.5	7.1
	100.0%	100.0%

Much of the retail sales were concentrated in the large metropolitan areas within a province. Metro Montreal accounted for 36 percent of Quebec's household furniture sales; Toronto, 34 percent of Ontario's; Winnipeg, 72 percent of Manitoba's; and Vancouver, 72 percent of British Columbia's. Together these four metropolitan centres accounted for 33 percent of Canadian household furniture store sales.

Appendix 2

Ecumene

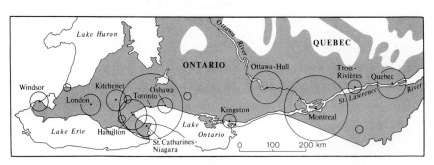

Urban population 1981

2800000
2000000
1500000
1000000
500000
250000
100001

○ 50000 - 100000

Census metropolitan areas with
a population of more than 100000
are shown by proportional circles

Case 21

Joseph E. Seagram & Sons, Limited

Introduction

Charles Bronfman, as part of his duties as chairman of Joseph E. Seagram & Sons, Limited, was reviewing the company's products and brands for the 1980 planning cycle. Seagram's Crown Royal continued its domination of the market for higher-price Canadian whisky, but there had been, from 1977 to 1980, a significant increase in both the volume and share of lower-priced Canadian whiskies, an area in which Seagram was not particularly active. Further, Seagram's dominance of the U.S. market through Canadian exportation of Seagram's Seven Crown, a dominance that began in 1934, had come to an end in 1978. The success of lighter spirits in general and Smirnoff vodka in particular had not been anticipated by Seagram.

In addition, historical expansion through acquisition and the introduction of new brands either to meet competitive threats or to capitalize on regional tastes had resulted in a proliferation of Seagram products in certain market categories. Seagram managers were beginning to question the absolute and relative profitability of some of these brands.

Finally, any product and brand management decisions would have to include the variables of the roles of company tradition and of the government. Joseph E. Seagram & Sons, Limited, and the parent Seagram Company in New York were managed by Charles Bronfman and Edgar Bronfman, whose father had been the dominant influence not only in the creation of the modern Seagram company and in the establishment of its values but also in the creation of the world whisky business. On the governmental side, the Canadian government and its provincial counterparts were not only regulators of the company's production, advertising, and distribution but were, simultaneously, competitors and customers of Joseph E. Seagram & Sons, Limited.

The following pages describe the company and the legacy of Mr. Samuel Bronfman, the distilling industry in Canada, and the status of Seagram's products and marketing strategy in 1980.

This case has been prepared by John Barnett, University of New Hampshire. Copyright © 1985 by John H. Barnett. Edited by Paul W. Beamish, 1986.

Background and Organization

In 1980 the Seagram Company was the largest distiller in the world. Within the Seagram Company, Charles Bronfman was charged with both worldwide and Canadian responsibilities. Worldwide responsibilities were part of Bronfman's duties as chairman of the executive committee of the parent Seagram Company. Canadian responsibilities stemmed from Bronfman's role as chairman of Joseph E. Seagram & Sons, Limited, the Canadian whisky[1] distilling and distribution subsidiary of the Seagram Company.

The organization of the Seagram Company and Joseph E. Seagram & Sons, Limited, is summarized below:

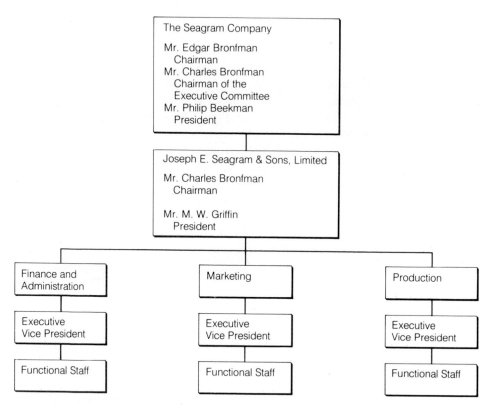

The parent company, the Seagram Company, had Mr. Edgar M. Bronfman, Charles's older brother, as chairman, Mr. Charles Bronfman as chairman of the executive committee, and Mr. Philip Beekman, formerly president of Colgate-Palmolive International, as president. While financial and accounting policies

---

[1] *Whisky*, when Canadian or Scotch, is spelled without an *e*, and the plural is *whiskies*. *Whiskey*, when American or Irish, is spelled with the *e*, and the plural is *whiskeys*.

including transfer prices were decided by the parent company, the Joseph E. Seagram & Sons, Limited executives were responsible for: marketing of all Seagram's products in Canada; all production and distilling within Canada (based upon sales forecasts for U.S. markets developed by the parent company); Jamaica and Israel international operations; and the implementation of any parent company policies that pertained to the Canadian subsidiary, Joseph E. Seagram & Sons, Limited. Eighty percent of the parent company's stockholders were Canadian, and annual meetings were held in Montreal. The company's stock was traded on the major American and Canadian Stock exchanges.

About 30 percent of Seagram stock was controlled by the Bronfman family.

Outside directors of the Seagram Company shown in the 1979 annual report included the chairmen of Power Corporation of Canada, Bell Canada, Bank of Montreal, Wood Gundy, and Canadian Pacific Limited, the senior partner of Goldman Sachs, and the president of Cemp Investments Ltd.

Reporting to Mr. Griffin as president of Joseph E. Seagram & Sons, Limited, were executive vice presidents for finance and administration (Mr. Babich), marketing (Mr. Roche), and production (Mr. Jellinek). The atmosphere at the Peel Street Seagram building was informal and collegial. The top executives often dropped into each others' offices to discuss problems in an operating manner that did not suggest rigid, formal chains of command.

In describing his personal views of career planning and employee selection, Mr. Bronfman discussed the importance of compatibility of personal goals, corporate objectives, and the goals of other managers. He commented, "Make sure that your fellow managers walk down the same side of the street with you. If you are interested in quality, don't associate yourself with the high-volume, mass merchandiser."

Charles Bronfman impressed people as a sensitive and thoughtful person, gracious if somewhat shy. The reserved manner was obviously only an occasional behavior pattern, as evidenced by the personal stories of his emotional opposition to the Quebec separatist movement and especially his quick and positive response to the opportunity to own the Montreal Expos. The Expos, a personal investment by Charles, was a source of satisfaction and interest to company personnel as well as to Charles, and indeed the whole nation rallied behind the Expos during their National League baseball play-off efforts.

The Beginning

Samuel Bronfman, Charles's father, operated a liquor mail-order business with his brother prior to World War I. Operating initially in the Prairie Provinces, the firm soon had warehouses and mail-order outlets throughout Canada. During the 1920s, however, the governments of each province took over the control and sale of liquor.

Samuel Bronfman then founded Distillers-Corporation Ltd. and built a distillery in the LaSalle suburb of Montreal to supply the new provincial liquor boards and commissions. In 1926 Distillers acquired the shares of Joseph E. Seagram & Sons, Limited, of Waterloo, a distillery founded in 1857. Also in 1926 the company entered into an agreement with The Distillers Company Limited of Great Britain, then the world's largest distilling firm. The initial arrangement, the company's first international venture, gave Seagram rights to well-known brands of Scotch whisky. Sales of Scotch exceeded Canadian whisky in the early 1920s, since Canadian distilleries had been shut down by government edict during World War I.

One of the most significant events in Seagram's history was Prohibition in the United States. Samuel Bronfman became convinced in the late 1920s that Prohibition was a failure and would be repealed. Seagram expanded production at LaSalle and Waterloo and began to mature whiskies in expanded warehouse facilities. Having acquired some American distilleries in the United States upon the repeal of Prohibition, Seagram postponed the immediate profits American distillers were making. Instead, Seagram shipped its four-, five-, and six-year-old whiskies from Canada, blended them with neutral distilled spirits, and produced aged spirits. The company introduced Seagram's Five Crown and Seagram's Seven Crown in August of 1934. In 60 days their whiskies were outselling all others throughout the United States. Seagram's Seven Crown held the number one brand position exclusively in the United States until 1978, when Bacardi's White Rum sales equalled Seven Crown.

International Operations

The company expanded further internationally after World War II. Early post-war expansion was directed at Mexico, Central America, and South America. Expansions were typically made in areas where company executives had some personal relationships. By mid-1972 an overseas subsidiary was active in Mexico, Costa Rica, Venezuela, Brazil, Argentina, France, Italy, and Germany. By 1980, operating plants of Seagram were found in 24 countries, and Seagram's products were sold in over 100 countries through 475 distributors.

The basis of the company's international sales was the "two-way street" concept. For example, Canadian, American, and Scotch whiskies were shipped to France and Italy, and French and Italian products were shipped to Canada, the United States, and Great Britain. This two-way street premise extended to all countries where Seagram facilities were located. Samual Bronfman referred to this policy as ". . . the spine of our business. It brings and holds together our worldwide operation."

In 1965 the Seagram Overseas Sales Company was formed. In each country where production facilities were located, the company maintained a marketing organization to sell locally produced products as well as imported products from other Seagram companies.

The Company in the 1970s

The Seagram Company enjoyed constant growth throughout its history with sales and assets passing $1 billion (U.S.) in 1968 and $2 billion (U.S.) in 1978. Exhibit 1 presents selected financial highlights of the parent company from the company's 1978 and 1979 annual reports.

The common stock of Seagram traded between $19 and $59 in the 1975–80 period, as shown in Exhibit 2.

Seagram's brands included Seagram's Seven Crown, the largest selling brand in the United States for over 30 years, V.O., Crown Royal, Chivas Regal,

Exhibit 1

THE SEAGRAM COMPANY, LIMITED, AND SUBSIDIARY COMPANIES
Financial Summary
(U.S. dollars in thousands, except per share amounts)

	1979	1978
For the fiscal year:		
Sales and other income	$2,554,096	$2,272,584
Operating income	277,971	235,383
Income before foreign exchange fluctuations and extraordinary items	199,622	93,029
Foreign exchange gains (losses)*	(19,322)	(2,465)
Net income	168,159	90,564
Per share—net income	$4.79	$2.58
Dividends	31,883	28,566
Dividends per share (Canadian currency)	1.07	.906
Working capital provided from operations	220,127	214,184
Capital expenditures		
Spirits and wine	44,167	43,551†
Oil and gas	138,795	111,973
Total income	$ 182,962	$ 155,524
At fiscal year-end:		
Total assets	$2,437,076	$2,297,666
Shareholders' equity	1,221,636	1,085,560
Shareholders' equity per share	$34.83	$30.95
Inventories	1,047,186	962,628
Property, plant, and equipment—		
Spirits and wine (net)	376,225	390,565
Oil and gas properties (net)	463,574	376,446
Short-term investments	6,683	30,438
Short-term debt	285,543	190,149
Long-term indebtedness	421,098	512,064
Stock price (Canadian currency)	34.25	28.63

The number of shares outstanding during the period was 35,077,400.
* Includes related tax effects.
† Excludes capital assets of $19,431,000 arising from the acquisition of The Glenlivet Distillers Ltd.

Exhibit 2: Selected Financial Statistics (figures in U.S. currency except dividends)

Year	Earnings per Share*	Dividends per Share*	Dividend Payout	Price Range
1975	$2.11	$ .80	38%	$37–$25
1976	2.30	.82	36	31⅝–19⅜
1977	2.48	.88	35	24–19¼
1978	2.58	.97	38	29–20⅜
1979	4.79†	1.12	23	42¼–27¼
1980				59–33

* 35,077,400 shares.
† Includes $2.15/share gain on change in British tax laws.
Source: *Moody's Handbook of Common Stocks*, Summer 1980.

Glenlivet, Barton and Guestier Wines (B & G), G. H. Mumm Champagne, Myers's Rum, Leroux liqueurs, and many others. The U.S. market had historically represented between 75 percent and 85 percent of total Seagram sales.

The Legacy of "Mr. Sam"

Joseph E. Seagram & Sons, Limited's first president was Charles's father, Samuel Bronfman, who built Seagram into the largest liquor company in the world through the growth and development of his North American operations. As well as initiating the first international operations and developing the "two-way street" philosophy of the firm in the international environment, Samuel Bronfman also introduced the campaign to drink moderately. The first moderate drinking campaign started in 1934. The first advertisement opened with the line, "We who make whisky say: 'Drink Moderately.'" Seagram received 150,000 complimentary letters including praise from clergymen. Samuel Bronfman died in 1971. Brian Murphy called Bronfman "the man who had done more than anyone else to shape the world whisky business in modern times."[2]

In a supplement to the 1970 annual report, "Mr. Sam" commented upon his 60 years of association with the Company:[3]

> It has been written of me that I have an instinct for dynasty. Be that as it may. I have been privileged to play a forceful part in the development of a great industry, and I have done so with the constant support of family, friends, and often the sons of friends. To me these generations of fond memories and loyal companionship are not the least part of the achievement.[4]

Bronfman described the early involvement of his sons in the firm:

> When my sons Edgar and Charles were in their teens, they began to spend their weekends and college summers in our LaSalle plant. Under the capable guidance of

---

[2] B. Murphy, *The World Book of Whiskey* (Glasgow–London: Collins, 1978).

[3] Samuel Bronfman, *From Little Acorns* (issued October 1970, Montreal).

[4] Ibid., p. 15.

our production experts, they acquired a great store of knowledge about our industry in general and our business in particular.

Following production experience, they gained a thorough foundation in administration and later in sales. Edgar, who is the older, at one time moved a desk into my office and was at my side daily observing, listening, asking questions, and gaining invaluable experience.[5]

Samuel Bronfman also described the development of Seagram's overseas business:

Scotland

Following Repeal in the United States, it was clear to me that if we were to become a truly great international distilling company, we must enter the Scotch whisky business.

With this thought in mind, I travelled to Scotland in 1935, called on my friend James Barclay, and through him acquired the Robert Brown Company which had been established in 1861. With this company as our base, we began immediately to lay down stocks of select Scotch whiskies for maturing.[6]

France

Our first business connection with France was made by the great Canadian ambassador—Seagram's V.O. Our next connection was made from the United States. There I brought in Oscar Wile to head our Browne Vintner Company. . . . Oscar had been in the importing business in America long before Prohibition and had many friends in the wine industry in Europe.

On one of his many visits to France, he became friendly with Rene Lalou, president of G. H. Mumm & Co. My son-in-law, Baron Alain de Gunzburg, who resides in Paris, was also a friend of Mr. Lalou. This tripartite friendship eventually led to our company taking a major position in Mumm, which was and is a public company[7]

Israel

In 1962 Charles was in Israel and became intrigued with the possibilities of developing a new liqueur which would be exclusive to Israel. . . . Using Jaffa oranges as the base, with time-consuming patience so necessary in creating a new liqueur, Charles and our experts evenutally solved the problems. . . . Appropriately, Charles named the new liqueur Sabra, a word to designate native-born Israelis. He went on to work closely with our packaging design people, and together they created a most distinctive package which reflects both the ancient and the modern.[8]

---

[5] Ibid., p. 26.

[6] Ibid., p. 34.

[7] Ibid., p. 38.

[8] Ibid., p. 45.

Mexico

> Several years ago my wife and I spend a holiday in Mexico. We weren't there very long before I was looking into possibilities for our business. I was greatly impressed with the progress Mexico was making toward becoming an industrialized nation and decided that we should build a plant there. . . . We have a very happy relationship with the Saenz family, who have the largest sugar business in the country and an interest in our company. Aaron Saenz is chairman and Aaron, Jr., affectionately known as "Chato," is president and takes a very active interest in our welfare.[9]

Venezuela

> For many years in Venezuela the Curiel Company were our agents and Benjamin Chumaceiro was associated with that firm. One day Benny came to me and explained that he had two sons and would like to go into business for himself to build an organization which later his sons would carry on.
>
> I was very much impressed with Benny Chumaceiro and agreed on the spot to join with him.[10]

Bronfman had strong ideas about the role of business in society. In his introductory comments to a 1942 book on Canada and its future, he wrote:

> The horizon of industry, surely, does not terminate at the boundary line of its plants; it has a broader horizon, a farther view, and that view embraces the entire nation.

Charles Bronfman discontinued his university studies to work full-time in the company. After the death of his father, Charles Bronfman became president of the company. One of many concepts of his father that Charles Bronfman continued was the emphasis on moderation in Seagram's advertising.

Production

The principal difference between Seagram and its main competition, Hiram Walker, Inc., was that Seagram aged the whiskies in casks (always of oak) instead of blending the whiskies first and then aging the blend. Seagram felt that this procedure gave them much greater control of the variables of the distilling business and thus greater flexibility, both of which led, it was felt, to a finer product. (The exterior of the Montreal headquarters building was emblazoned with the Seagram's motto of "Integrity, Craftmanship, Tradition.")

The distilling process resulted in large inventory investments and a long inventory planning cycle. Firms doing any significant maturing of whiskies had a high percentage of assets invested in inventories. Since alcohol evaporated, Seagram allowed for a 3 percent annual loss. The loss was automatically programmed into its production planning/inventory control procedures.

---

[9] Ibid., p. 47.

[10] Ibid., p. 49.

The planning cycle encompassed the ages of fine whiskies. For example, Crown Royal was a 10-year-old whisky. Joseph E. Seagram & Sons, Limited, had a Crown Royal production control system that in 1979 included the period 1969 to 1989, as 1969 whiskies were being bottled and 1979 whiskies were being laid down for blending and bottling in 1989.

The production cost control system at Seagram was one of standard direct cost. The administrative control of Canadian production was based on measures of efficiency and on a standard direct cost system. Operations were judged based on manhours of labour and various measures of costs, quality, and yields.

As Mr. Babich, the executive vice president for finance and administration, put it: "Under the old 1958 system, absorption costing did not permit the accurate evaluation of the individual production elements. To correct this situation, outside consultants and plant operating managers developed a system of standard direct costing." Mr. Babich further commented:

> The system required a six month's conversion period, and no one understood it. Some standards were wrong, but the system was implemented. After periods of monthly visits to question variances and to review standards, we finally developed a management tool that works.

This conversion process allowed for participation at all production levels in the development of the new cost system.

Initially, the Montreal executives set general objectives of yields and costs. Next the plant production manager and his staff set detailed standards for the next year, which had to be approved by Montreal, during the January to April planning cycle (the fiscal year ends 31 July). The plant manager's performance was evaluated based on his measures of cost, quality, and yield.

The Canadian production process was almost entirely self-sufficient, as the firm imported only minimal quantities (5 percent of its glass and 8 percent of its corn) from the United States. There were six production centres in Canada as follows:

Location	Number of Employees	Production
LaSalle (Quebec)	400	Production, bottling (rum, grain)
Amherstburg (Ontario)	300	Production, bottling (grain)
Waterloo (Ontario)	250	Production, bottling (grain)
Gimli (Manitoba)	160	Production, bottling (grain)
Beaupre (Quebec)	60	Production (grain)
Richibucto (New Brunswick)	60	Production, bottling (rum)

While LaSalle, Beaupre, Waterloo, Gimli, and Richibucto served primarily Canadian markets, the Amherstburg centre served U.S. markets.

The general distribution of cost and production was approximately as follows:

materials, 55 percent (grain, 38 percent, bottling, 17 percent); labour, 20–25 percent; overhead and profit, 20–25 percent.

The selling price of whisky is illustrated below:

Joseph E. Seagram & Co. Limited Sample Retail Price, 1980 (B Category—Ontario)

	Case of 12 Bottles	Per Bottle
Factory selling price F.O.B. plant	$ 23.00	$1.92
Add: Federal excise duty based on proof gallons	22.45	1.88
Subtotal	45.45	3.80
Add: 12% federal sales tax	5.45	.45
Subtotal	50.90	4.25
Add: Provincial liquor board markup	50.90	4.25
Subtotal	101.80	8.50
Add: Provincial tax @ 10%	10.20	.85
Retail price	$112.00	$9.35

Finance and Administration

Since New York headquarters established the transfer prices of Canadian production exports to the United States, Canadian administrative attention was focused as follows: (1) meeting New York estimated production requirements, (2) cost control and efficiency of production, and (3) Canadian marketing.

Production efficiency and control, as discussed above, were based on standards of yields and efficiencies. Marketing control and evaluation were based on share of the market reports and product contribution reports, including actual versus planned results. Appendix 1 presents excerpts from the monthly "Analysis of Canadian Performance" submitted to the top executives in Montreal. The financial and accounting reporting system produced share of market data 1 day, cost control and product contribution data 5 days, and plant operations data 11 business days after the end of the month.

Incentive Compensation

Top managers and executives in 1979 were undergoing a change in their evaluation and incentive programs. Where previously bonuses had been based on variance control for production executives and market shares for sales executives, incentives and evaluation began to include specific objectives and special projects. Appendix 2 describes this new plan.

Marketing

Seagram's marketing organization and strategy are discussed, along with a description of Seagram's products, beginning after the following section on the distilling industry in Canada. In general, marketing decisions of a strategic nature were made in Montreal and were communicated to regional operating marketing companies.

The Distilling Industry in Canada

Distilled spirits were made in Canada by 14 distillers operating 37 distilleries. These 14 private companies sold their product within Canada to the 10 provincial and 2 territorial governments, their sole Canadian customers.

Governmental regulation and control of the distilling industry included regulations of distilling, aging, labelling, warehousing, and shipping. This regulation was based on the Food and Drug Act and the Excise Act. Further, the provincial and territorial liquor boards retained all right to retail spirits to the public. The provincial and territorial liquor boards chose the brands they would list, display, and sell. With limited shelf space, distillers' salesmen were often asked, "What brand will you de-list if we agree to add your new brands?" These boards also granted licences to bars, restaurants, and pubs. Finally, each liquor board regulated advertising and sales activities, ranging from no advertising (New Brunswick, Prince Edward Island, and Saskatchewan) to various allowances for newspapers, magazines, and displays.

The provincial liquor control boards reported to various departments as follows: Alberta, Solicitor General; British Columbia, Consumer and Corporate Affairs; Manitoba, Tourism; New Brunswick and Newfoundland, Finance; Northwest Territories, Commissioner's Office; Nova Scotia, Highways; Ontario, Consumer and Commercial Relations; Prince Edward Island, Premier's Office; Quebec, Trade and Commerce; Saskatchewan, Environment; and Yukon, Commissioner's Office.

Monies from the provincial markup on liquor sales for provincial financing and from federal taxes on spirits for federal financing were very significant. For example, federal excise taxes and duties on spirits and beer exceeded $500 million annually in the late 1970s.

As shown in the sample retail price figures on the previous page, to the distillers' price of every case of spirits was added the federal excise duty and federal sales tax. The provincial liquor boards then added the freight charges, exchange rate, and differentials in the case of imported products to arrive at their cost. Thus, liquor boards, in effect, doubled their landed cost by adding provincial markup and on top of this added the provincial sales tax to arrive at the final retail price for each bottle. One government official commented: "What would you rather have us do, tax bread or booze?"

Across Canada in general about 50 percent of the population did not drink; of the 50 percent that were drinkers, approximately 30 percent would be classified as light drinkers and 20 percent as heavy drinkers. One interesting result of the range of drinking habits was the difficulty of market research, since respondents' replies on their drinking habits were suspect at best.

One industry spokesman noted that it was unlikely that any of the provincial liquor boards would allow dual distribution, for example, additional private distribution of alcoholic beverages, because of the tax revenue consequences. All provincial liquor boards across Canada had taken a serious look at the Quebec experience of distributing wine in grocery stores. Although beer had been distributed in the ''mom-and-pop'' stores for a number of years in Quebec, this policy was liberalized to extend to 20 brands of the inexpensive wines, 10 of which were the QLB-owned brands and the remaining 10 were all bottled in Quebec. These brands were among the least expensive on the QLB's wine list and carried a 20–25 cent premium in the grocery stores compared to the QLB price. The Quebec Liquor Board forecast about $6 million in sales of these inexpensive wines in private outlets. Nonetheless, the private distribution produced $50 million in sales and seriously affected the position of the liquor board's distribution outlet. The Quebec Liquor Board attempted to draw customers back into their outlets by introducing an advertising campaign. The revenue effects were especially detrimental to the Quebec Liquor Board because consumers had traded down to buy the less-expensive wines and avoid going to the QLB outlets. Thus, other wines that were distributed only through QLB outlets had suffered. The Quebec Liquor Board's absolute margins on these inexpensive wines were, of course, much less because they were lower-priced wines, notwithstanding the 100 percent markup. It was not clear what effect if any the QLB advertising strategy would have on reversing this distribution trend.

AM, FM, and TV regulations prohibited the advertising of spiritous liquors, but permitted the advertising of beer and wine. Although advertising on broadcasting stations came under federal jurisdiction, the provinces also exercised authority over the distribution and sale of alcoholic beverages, including their advertising and promotion. As a result, in certain provinces it was necessary to obtain clearance through the relevant liquor control boards or commissions as well as from the Canadian Radio-Television and Telecommunications Commission (CRTC) for beer and wine advertisements. As of 1980, Ontario, Quebec, Nova Scotia, Manitoba, and Alberta had this requirement. In Newfoundland, only CRTC clearance was required.

The main criterion in the approval of scripts was adherence to standards of good taste. In a time of quickly changing standards, perception of what was in good taste became highly individualistic.

Other standards applied by the committee were that advertising should not attempt to influence nondrinkers to drink, or be associated with youth or youth symbols. It should not attempt to establish a certain product as a status symbol, a necessity for the enjoyment of life, or an escape from life's problems. Finally, it should not show persons engaged in activity in which the consumption of alcohol was prohibited.

Commenting upon the regulation of advertising by federal and provincial bodies, Mr. Ed Nodwell, executive vice president and manager of the Montreal office of McConnell advertising, said:

Regulations governing the sale and promotion of alcoholic beverages have been with us for a long time, and I suppose those of us who work or have worked in that industry have simply adjusted to them to the point where we don't challenge their rationality.

In Quebec, a liquor ad running in a newspaper can have a maximum size of 1,200 agate lines, and two ads of that size may appear in any newspaper.

In Manitoba, the ad size can be 1,250 lines but only one advertisement per company per issue. I wonder what momentous events swing on that 50-line difference between Manitoba and Quebec?

That is only one of the old and small irritants we have come to accept. A few years ago British Columbia unilaterally decided that there would be no advertising in B.C. for any tobacco or alcoholic beverage product, creating confusion, cost, and inconvenience among advertisers, agencies, publishers, and everyone else involved in the challenged industries.

The Association of Canadian Distillers compiled the figures in Table 1 from data supplied by the provincial liquor boards. This data provides an extensive data bank for industry research.

Tastes varied substantially by province, as Table 2 shows.

Table 1: Total Sales of Spirits (cases of twelve 25-ounce bottles, in thousands)

	1974	1975	1976	1977	1978
Total spirits	20,326	20,799	21,710	22,270	22,845
Index 1974 = 100	100	102	107	110	112
Canadian whisky	8,485	8,459	8,799	8,912	9,100
Index 1974 = 100	100	100	104	105	107
Percent of total	41.7%	40.7%	40.5%	40.0%	39.8%
Domestic rum	2,805	2,842	3,014	3,091	3,267
Index 1974 = 100	100	101	107	110	116
Percent of total	13.8%	13.7%	13.9%	13.9%	14.3%
Domestic vodka	1,847	2,040	2,189	2,358	2,518
Index 1974 = 100	100	110	119	128	136
Percent of total	9.1%	9.8%	10.1%	10.6%	11.0%
Scotch whisky	1,424	1,466	1,535	1,575	1,554
Index 1974 = 100	100	103	108	111	109
Percent of total	7.0%	7.0%	7.1%	7.1%	6.8%
Gin (domestic and imported)	1,951	1,914	1,889	1,848	1,828
Index 1974 = 100	100	98	97	95	94
Percent of total	9.6%	9.2%	8.7%	8.3%	8.0%

Source: Compiled from data provided by provincial liquor boards.

Table 2: 1978 Usage by Spirit Class

Spirit	National Percentage by Volume		Provincial Percentage of Total		
			Low		High
Canadian whisky	39.8%	9.2%	Quebec	61.9%	Saskatchewan
Domestic rum	14.3	12.2	Quebec	47.1	Nova Scotia
Domestic vodka	11.0	4.8	Newfoundland	17.5	Yukon
Scotch	6.8	3.7	Prince Edward Island	9.3	British Columbia
Gin	8.0	3.6	Saskatchewan	32.6	Quebec

Seagram's Products and Marketing Strategy

Seagram's marketing strategy could be best summed by the three words that appeared on the House of Seagram crest, *Integrity, Craftsmanship* and *Tradition*. The legacy of the late Samuel Bronfman was quality blended whiskies. This tradition accounted for the bulk of Seagram's sales due to Five Star, V.O., and Chivas Regal. Mr. Sam's only one admitted mistake was late entry into the vodka market which grew rapidly without any significant Seagram entry in the field. Although Seagram had some late entries in the vodka market, one marketing manager of a competitor in vodka explained, "They [Seagram] were convinced that light drinks would never become a major factor in the liquor business even when it was changing right before their eyes. They were just complacent and arrogant." Seagram's senior management, however, commented that their interest was in quality and craftsmanship, attributes of blended whisky more than vodka.

Organization

After World War II, Seagram was organized on a regional sales basis. Each regional sales company dealt with a few brands in each province; very little advertising was done, and although all brands were available to each regional sales company, in general the larger brands grew. The sales company carried the little brands because they had no choice. Each regional sales company only dealt with a few or perhaps one province. In 1966, the company was reorganized into a national marketing organization. In this context, there were four national marketing companies within the House of Seagram: Joseph E. Seagram & Sons, Limited; Thomas Adams Distillers Ltd.; Canadian Distillers Ltd.; and International Wines and Spirits. Each managed its own brands, although Seagram added a centralized staff organization that provided research and planning.

These national companies had regional marketing branches. For example, in 1972–73, Seagram formed a series of regional marketing companies selling regional brands such as B. C. Special (British Columbia), Lord Selkirk rum and Pickwick gin (Manitoba), Montmorency (Quebec), and Flagship rum, Whitehall gin, and Atlantic whiskies (Nova Scotia).

These regional marketing companies served several important functions, including executive development. Several M.B.A.s were given assignments as directors of these regional companies. In directing the regional companies, their managers gained experience early in their careers in price competition and liquor board relations. The period was almost a "constant price war," as an industry observer noted.

Seagram's Advertising

Advertising was primarily newspaper and magazine advertisements showing the product, along with the moderation advertising as discussed earlier. That Seagram's promotional strategy revolved almost exclusively around the use of print as paid media was due in part to the provincial and federal restrictions on liquor advertising in broadcast media. The Broadcasting Act and various provincial trade legislations impinged upon the appearance of liquor advertising in broadcast media. British Columbia's former NDP government enacted an outright prohibition of all liquor and tobacco advertising. One prairie province also restricted liquor lifestyle ads, defining lifestyle advertising as any ad with people in it. To contend with this patchwork of overlapping piecemeal regulation across Canada, Seagram restricted itself principally to print media and largely restricted its creative strategies to "bottle and glass." In this manner, separate advertisements did not have to be prepared to correspond to each individual provincial regulation: instead, the ad conformed to the strictest of any province's regulations.

Pricing

Following its "craftsmanship" strategy, Seagram concentrated on the higher-price market segments. In absolute dollars, Crown Royal and V.O. were the most profitable brands. During the early 1970s, however, price competition became stronger within the industry. Canadian whisky, which was classified by price categories, A being the highest, saw a shift to the lower-price categories.

The Canadian market had an average growth rate of approximately 10 percent per year during the 1970–73 period. As one industry observer noted:

> This was perceived by the smaller distillers as offering an opportunity for growth. The small distillers introduced new products below existing floor pricing, most notably in the F category.

Seagram believed the profit margin in the F category was insufficient, and they did not enter this category until 1975. Some of the entries were repositioned from the E category and some were new entries. Two "fading" brands, Four Roses and, more recently, Lord Calvert, were repositioned in the F category. Neither brand bore the Seagram name because of a cannibalization risk against Seagram's best-selling brand, Five Star, in the E category.

Seagram aggressively marketed V.O. and Crown Royal, and these brands contributed the most significant amount of gross margin dollars. Captain Morgan was a successful brand in all three of the rum categories—white, light, and dark, although Bacardi's lead in the former two categories was substantial.

Certainly Bronfman's marketing decision had to encompass pricing, including tactics appropriate for the leader in an increasingly price competitive industry.

Brand Proliferation

In a 1980 two-page memo, the Seagram management listed all of their brands ranked from top to bottom in terms of gross contribution. Upon reviewing the brands on the second page of this memo, management inquired whether or not these "page-two brands" were in fact providing any net contribution. At that time, Seagram marketed over 82 different brands of distilled products across Canada. The answer given was that not all of these brands provided a profitable net margin to Seagram. Some of these unprofitable brands were carryovers from previous organizational structures. Some brands were marketed exclusively in one province. Other brands were marketed in only a few provinces.

In addition to pricing decisions, then, Mr. Bronfman had brand management decisions to make. Fortunately, the industry had a wealth of market data.

Market Data

Exhibit 3 presents Canadian whisky market-share data by manufacturer. Category rank indicated which price category (A = highest, F = lowest price) the brand was in and what rank it was within that category. Thus, Hiram Walker's Canadian Club was the largest seller overall and was first in the B category. Similarly, Seagram's V.O. was fourth overall in Canada whisky and second within the B price category. At one time Seagram boasted Canada's largest-selling Canadian whisky, Five Star; however, as this product category (E) declined, Five Star declined with it. Up to 1980, Five Star's sales levelled off, and share increased in the face of a declining category. This decline was due to an increase in both volume and share of the F (lower than Five Star) price category. The top four Canadian whiskies consisted of two Hiram Walker brands, Canadian Club and Walker's Special Old, and two Seagram's brands, Five Star and V.O. These were the one and two brands in the two largest categories. The more rapidly growing category was F, the low-priced whiskies which were introduced in 1971 in the western provinces. Ontario, Canada's largest Canadian whisky-drinking province, had a price floor, and the F category whiskies fell below this. The success of the F whiskies came largely in the west where "age claims" predominated the promotional strategies. For example, Carrington advertised a five-year-old whisky at a three-year-old price. Because of their lower price, the margin contribution in the F category was significantly lower. The C category whiskies were an odd in-between. In category D, the five- to six-year-old aged whiskies,

Exhibit 3

Canadian Whisky (25-oz. cases)

Brand (Distiller)	1977 Sales Volume	1977 Market Share	1978 Sales Volume	1978 Market Share	1979 Sales Volume	1979 Market Share	1980 Sales Volume	1980 Market Share
"A"								
1 Crown Royal (Seagram)	92,215	58 4%	102,717	61 9%	106,153	62 4%	106,892	64 7%
2 Alberta Springs (Alberta)	12,420	7 8	15,145	9 1	16,488	9 7	16,352	9 9
3 Captains Table (McGuinness)	11,648	7 4	11,631	7 0	12,034	7 1	11,262	6 8
4 Very Special Package (Corby)	9,179	5 8	8,075	4 9	8,709	5 1	9,232	5 59
5 Carleton Tower (Walker)	11,628	7 4	11,055	6 7	9,767	5 7	7,234	4 4
Total "A"	157,865	1 77	165,840	1 82	170,048	1 9	165,289	1 8
Total index, 1977 = 100	100		105		108		105	
"B"								
2 Seagram V.O. (Seagram)	457,638	23 3	503,529	25 5	489,634	24 1	491,933	22 3
7 Adams Antique (Seagram)	42,572	2 2	46,316	2 4	48,874	2 4	51,457	2 3
1 Canadian Club (Walker)	1,084,403	55 3	1,053,451	53 4	1,095,569	53 9	1,097,686	49 9
3 Wiser's DeLuxe (Corby)	138,780	7 1	152,015	7 7	174,463	8 6	205,202	9 3
4 Black Velvet (Gilbey, seed)					15,309	9	149,400	6 8
Total "B"	1,960,431	22 0	1,971,920	21 67	2,032,466	22 4	2,202,079	24 0
Total index, 1977 = 100	100		101		104		112	
"C"								
1 Schenley O.F.C. (Schenley)	42,497	16 6	130,200	42 6	136,591	51 0	149,918	60 3
2 Walker Imperial (Walker) seed	92,737	36 3	84,152	27 6	43,328	16 1	2	0 0
Total "C"	255,327	2 87	305,491	3 36	269,549	3 0	248,512	2 7
Total index, 1977 = 100	100		120		106		97	
"D"								
1 Seagram 83 (Seagram)	291,237	23 0	318,019	24 6	337,312	26 0	374,313	33 8
2 Adams Private Stock (Seagram)	160,504	12 7	164,158	12 7	173,852	13 4	176,947	16 0
14 H. Bay Fine Old (Seagram)	18,213	1 4	18,445	1 4	17,584	1 3	15,246	1 4
15 Canada House (Seagram)	17,403	1 4	15,642	1 2	14,697	1 1	11,892	1 1
1 Black Velvet (Gilbey)	332,449	26 2	325,884	25 1				
3 Walker Imperial (Walker)					43,824	3 3	128,164	11 6
4 McGuinness Gold Tassel (McGuinness)	88,852	7 0	94,155	7 3	93,988	7 3	94,541	8 5
6 Walker Gold Crest (Walker)	50,979	4 0	42,556	3 3	285,383	22 0	42,151	3 8
Total "D"	1,267,916	14 23	1,294,270	14 22	1,295,792	14 3	1,109,134	12 1
Total index, 1977 = 100	100		102		102		87	
"E"								
1 Five Star (Seagram)	849,106	21 1%	846,912	22 3%	830,286	22 8%	817,692	22 1%
11 Double Distilled (Seagram)	128,538	3 2	113,175	3 0	108,480	3 0	98,130	2 7
14 Gold Stripe (Seagram)	125,679	3 1	91,991	2 4	56,422	1 6	40,904	1 1
18 H. Bay F.O.B. (Seagram)	51,284	1 3	43,630	1 2	32,760	9	25,359	7
2 Walker Spec. Old (Walker)	653,463	16 3	571,444	15 1	556,535	15 3	563,034	15 3
3 McGuinness Silk Tassel (McGuinness)	341,976	8 5	356,441	9 4	358,814	9 9	385,122	10 4
4 Corby Royal Reserve (Corby)	266,448	6 6	264,096	7 0	269,929	7 4	294,936	8 0
12 G & W Bonded Stock (Walker)	154,263	3 8	113,770	3 0	88,740	2 4	75,186	2 0
Total "E"	4,018,264	45 09	3,794,313	41 69	3,639,196	40 1	3,693,506	40 2
Total index	100		94		91		92	
"F"								
6 H. Bay Special (Seagram)	44,384	3 5	68,636	4 4	78,724	4 7	89,638	5 1
7 Four Roses (Seagram)	30,296	2 4	62,793	4 0	73,605	4 4	84,304	4 8
20 Three Star (Seagram)	26,384	2 1	26,313	1 7	20,535	1 2	26,253	1 5
17 Lord Calvert (Seagram)	3,669	3	21,110	1 3	28,132	1 7	35,583	2 0
36 Atlantic Special (Seagram)	6,279	5	6,804	4			0	0
42 Homestead (Seagram)	4,912	4	1,825	1			0	0
1 Alberta Windsor DeLuxe (Alberta)	127,660	10 2	164,356	10 5	185,801	11 1	213,404	12 1
2 Carrington Can. Spirit (Alberta)	140,851	11 3	156,486	10 0	160,080	9 6	169,059	9 6
3 G & W Bonded Stock (Walker)	27,780	2 2	73,401	4 7	109,455	6 5	160,268	9 1
4 Silver Tassel (McGuinness)	42,065	3 4	87,756	5 6	117,935	7 0	137,078	7 4
15 Walker's 58 (Walker)	35,228	2 8	31,362	2 0	46,564	2 8	49,885	2 8
Total "F"	1,252,113	14 05	1,568,695	17 24	1,676,893	18 5	1,768,882	19 3
Total Canadian whisky	8,911,915		9,100,528		9,083,934		9,187,402	
Total index	100		125		134		141	
Total whisky index	100		102		102		103	

Seagram's 83 and Gilbey's Black Velvet, predominated. Crown Royal stood alone on top of the A category, 10-year-old aged whiskies.

Exhibit 4 presents data on Scotch, vodka, gin, and rum sales in cases. Again, all of Seagram's and also the most-popular brands regardless of manufacturer are shown, with category ranking indicated to the left of the brand name. Distillers' Johnnie Walker Red was Canada's leading selling Scotch, followed by Gooderham's Ballantines. Overall, the Distillers brands, Johnnie Walker, Dewar's Black and White, and Dawsons, comprised better than a third of the Canadian Scotch market. Hobb's Cutty Sark ranked third, followed by Gilbey's J & B. Seagram's Chivas Regal had a 3.8 market share on a case basis but due to its price accounted for a larger market share on a dollar basis. Smirnoff brand vodka accounted for almost half the vodka sales in Canada. Gordon's, distributed by Seagram, was Canada's largest selling domestic gin, followed by Gilbey's, while Meaghers' imported Beefeater was the single best selling Canadian brand. The sale of each of these brands varied considerably on a province-by-province basis.

Based upon product portfolio management concepts, which are described in Appendix 3, the casewriter had the following observations:

Category A: Seagram's star, Crown Royal, enjoyed 65 percent of the market and had a 16 percent growth in a plus 5 percent growth category.

Category D: Walker Imperial, with 11 percent market share in Category D, was repositioned down from Category C. Some of its share may have been at the expense of Walker Gold Crest, which dropped from almost 300,000 cases to 40,000 cases following Imperial's introduction. At the same time, Gilbey took Black Velvet (300,000 cases in 1977) up to Category B (150,000 cases in 1980).

Category F: Seagram's F category products ranged from a 1977 to 1980 growth of 870 percent (Lord Calvert) to 0 percent growth (Three Star), while Walker went from 480 percent (G & W) to 42 percent (58).

Scotch: Walker's Ballantine grew at 3 percent to an 11 percent market share versus Chivas Regal's minus 14 percent growth with 3 percent market share.

Vodka: Seagram discontinued several brands, but no brand challenged Smirnoff.

Rum: Seagram's several brands had insignificant market share, except Morgan's 12 percent (versus 42 percent for Bacardi). Morgan's growth was 16 percent versus Bacardi's 6 percent.

The American Market and Long-Term Trends

As Mr. Bronfman turned to the Canadian marketing plan, he kept in mind certain trends in the United States.

1. While Canadian whisky had increased from 9 percent to 12 percent of total spirits consumed in the last decade in the United States, vodka had grown from 11 percent to 19 percent. Bourbon fell from 24 percent to 15 percent and blends from 21

Exhibit 4

Brand (Distiller)	1977 Sales Volume	1977 Market Share	1978 Sales Volume	1978 Market Share	1979 Sales Volume	1979 Market Share	1980 Sales Volume	1980 Market Share
Top Brands—Total All Categories								
Dry Gin (25-oz. cases)								
1 Gordon's (Seagram)	250.044	20 4%	251.313	20 5%	247.276	20 9%	243.510	20 5%
4 White Satin (Seagram)	69.970	5 7	71.414	5 8	84.143	7 1	94.272	7 9
10 Seagram Ex Dry (Seagram)	20.339	1 7	27.572	2 2	30.989	2 6	31.840	2 7
12 King Arthur (Seagram)	41.601	3 4	38.921	3 2	29.588	2 5	27.920	2 4
15 Silver Fizz (Seagram)	29.315	2 4	24.470	2 0	24.141	2 0	21.561	1 8
16 Vickers (Seagram)	17.593	1 4	21.407	1 7	16.595	1 4	18.392	1 6
23 Hudson's Bay London Dry (Seagram)	12.961	1 1	11.910	1 0			0	0
2 Gilbey's (Gilbey)	234.213	19 1	221.034	18 0	204.869	17 3	182.066	15 3
3 Schenley London Dry (Schenley)	62.295	5 1	77.397	6 3	83.450	7 0	98.713	8 3
7 Walker's Crystal (Walker)	33.337	2 7	29.210	2 4	36.918	3 1	42.910	3 6
Total domestic dry gin	1.223.907	62 9%	1.228.093	63 8%	1.184.751	65 7%	1.189.301	68 0%
Total index	100		100		97		97	
Rum (25-oz. cases) White								
2 Captain Morgan (Seagram)	218.846	11 4%	230.456	11 4%	243.529	12 1%	255.012	11 9%
7 Myers's White (Seagram)	22.063	1 2	23.769	1 2	46.329	2 3	52.735	2 5
9 Wood's White Sail (Seagram)	56.065	2 9	54.304	2 7	49.861	2 5	49.726	2 3
21 Tropicana (Seagram)	13.452	7	12.610	6			0	0
15 Hudson's Bay (Seagram)	8.103	4	10.697	5	16.622	8	18.364	9
26 Atlantic Flagship (Seagram)	6.621	3	8.422	4			0	0
34 Whistler (Seagram)	848	0	2.715	1			0	0
40 Trelawny (Seagram)	678	0	1.748	1			0	0
1 Bacardi Carta Blanca (FBM)	851.823	44 3	889.322	44 1	872.689	43 2	902.732	42 5
3 Ron Carioca (Schenley)	143.128	7 4	147.125	7 3	141.015	7 0	165.738	7 8
11 Maraca Deluxe (Walker)	49.409	2 6	46.784	2 3	43.077	2 1	40.803	1 9
12 Gov'ment House (Walker)	10.926	6	20.214	1 0	30.244	1 5	38.336	1 8
Total white, domestic	1.924.082	62 26%	2.016.616	61 72%	2.018.272	61 4%	2.135.608	62 2%
Total index	100		105		105		111	
Rum (25-oz. cases) Light								
4 Captain Morgan Gold (Seagram)	52.244	8 4%	51.796	7 9%	50.744	7 6%	51.694	7 6%
1 Bacardi Carta de Oro (FBM)	180.164	29 0	185.437	28 3	185.740	27 9	193.048	28 5
2 Lambs Palm Breeze (Corby)	119.669	19 3	118.326	18 1	116.648	17 5	113.178	16 7
3 Gov Gen. Light (Gilbey)	101.030	16 3	96.073	14 7	88.825	13 3	78.235	11 6
Total light, domestic	620.517	20 08	654.269	20 02	666.251	20 27	676.388	19 7
Total index	100							
Dark								
2 Captain Morgan Black (Seagram)	139.666	25 5	139.151	23 3	136.031	22 6	137.331	22 1
4 Wood's Old Navy (Seagram)	28.774	5 3	34.089	5 7	34.311	5 7	37.295	6 0
1 Lamb's Old Navy (Corby)	160.562	29 4	142.545	23 9	147.276	24 5	149.924	24 2
3 Screech (NLC)	10.318	1 9	51.840	8 7	50.084	8 3	51.739	8 3
Total dark, domestic	545.989	17 67	596.475	18 26	601.638	18 3	620.455	18 1
Total domestic rum	3.090.588	87 47	3.267.361	89 91	3.286.161	91 0	3.432.451	91 1
Total index	100		106		106		111	
Scotch Whisky (25-oz. cases)								
10 Chivas Regal (Seagram)	55.603	3 5%	58.427	3 8%	54.969	3 6%	47.923	3 2%
12 St. Leger (Seagram)					0	0	39.409	2 6
15 Queen Anne (Seagram)					0	0	30.128	2 0
100 Pipers (Seagram)	16.859	1 1	11.872	8	0	0	0	0
Black Watch (Seagram)	4.262	3	5.857	4	0	0	0	0
20 Hudson's Bay Best Procurable (Seagram)	5.526	4	5.572	4	11.865	8	18.684	1 2
Passport (Seagram)	4.313	3	3.641	2	0	0	0	0
1 J. Walker Red (Distillers)	215.612	13 7	222.456	14 3	202.484	13 4	210.229	13 8
2 Ballantines (Walker)	155.264	9 9	158.707	10 2	157.968	10 5	159.746	10 5
3 J & B (Gilbey)	99.121	6 3	99.476	6 4	101.649	6 7	105.295	6 9
4 Cutty Sark (Hobbs)	112.810	7 2	106.400	6 8	93.254	6 2	84.167	5 5
Total	1.575.487	100 0%	1.554.432	100 0%	1.511.350	96 4%	1.519.197	95 9%
Total index, 1977 = 100	100		99		96		96	
Vodka (25-oz. cases)								
13 Bolshoi (Seagram)	60.085	2 6%	54.529	2 2%	49.564	1 9%	41.803	1 6%
16 Prince Igor (Seagram)	47.504	2 0	40.260	1 6	37.586	1 5	38.778	1 4
18 Hudson's Bay (Seagram)	10.655	5	23.246	9	22.374	9	28.517	1 1
Gordons (Seagram)	19.846	8	20.322	8			0	0
Nikolai (Seagram)	20.665	9	17.462	8			0	0
Natasha (Seagram)	6.636	3	6.969	3			0	0
Moichev (Seagram)	6.149	3	6.527	3			0	0
Kolomyka (Seagram)	1.205	1	4.073	2			0	0
1 Smirnoff (Gilbey)	1.125.235	47 7	1.131.132	44 9	1.008.055	39 5	993.277	36 7
2 Alberta (Alberta)	158.782	6 7	170.986	6 8	185.501	7 3	198.259	7 3
3 McGuinness Red Tassel (McGuinness)	138.443	5 9	171.968	6 8	150.836	5 9	165.485	6 1
10 Crystal (Walker)	26.758	1 1	27.742	1 1	42.427	1 7	50.397	1 9
11 G & W Skol (Walker)	33.593	1 4	30.717	1 2	41.911	1 7	50.152	1 9
Total vodka domestic	2.358.331		2.517.584		2.552.013		2.705.281	
Total index, 1977 = 100	100		107		108		115	

* Summing the volume for brands identified and their respective market shares will not equal industry volume. To illustrate, the total Scotch whisky figure, $1,575,487, is for the total sales in the industry by all brands of Scotch whisky, not just the nine brands identified. Also, the market share percentages are for the identified brands only, which represent only their respective part of the total market.

Source: Association of Canadian Distillers, *Consolidated Brand Report* (Ottawa: 1978, 1980).

percent to 9 percent. Seagram's Seven Crown, which had been the best-selling brand in the United States since the end of Prohibition, was now third with 6 million cases in 1979 versus 6 million cases of Smirnoff and 7 million cases of Bacardi rum.

2. Americans could no longer be categorized as single-product (bourbon, gin, or Scotch) drinkers, as the last decade saw the spread of exotic drinks, cordials, and wines.

3. While the adult population was increasing and drinking ages being lowered, consumption increased at an annual rate of less than 2 percent in the American market.

Mr. Bronfman knew it was important to consider the possibility of similar trends in Canadian consumption, as he reached decisions on product pricing, promotion, and brand management.

Appendix 1:   Analysis of Operations
(Excerpted and Amounts Omitted)

Interest—Long-Term

The latest outlook of XXX is XXX worse than the original plan because the devaluation of the Canadian dollar has added to the Eurobond interest cost which is payable in U.S. currency.

Foreign Exchange Gain

The latest outlook of XXX is XXX better than originally forecasted due to the devaluation of the Canadian dollar. The original plan was based on an exchange rate of XXX, while the rate used for the outlook is XXX.

Domestic Marketing Contribution

Net contribution is now expected to reach XXX or XXX below original plan.

A shortfall in volume and higher planned advertising and research expenditures are expected to be largely offset by some XXX million extra due to the April 1st price increases:

Due to volume (down XXX c/s)	XXX
Due to price increase	XXX
Change in imputed cost of wines	XXX
Increase in brand advertising	XXX
Increase in other expenses	XXX
	XXX

U.S.A. Marketing Contribution

Changes in volume account for improved contribution for both the seven months actual and the latest outlook for the year.

Export Marketing Contribution

Contribution is better than plan after seven months due to a prior year adjustment of marketing expenses. This adjustment also accounts for the variance between the original plan and latest.

Shipment Volume Analysis

A. *Seagram*—Total shipments are expected to be XXX cases below original plan for the year.

To the end of February, shipments are XXX cases below plan which would indicate volumes would firm up during the last five months.

V.O. shipments are projected to be XXX cases below plan at XXX cases, compared to XXX cases last year. After the first seven months, shipments are XXX cases under plan, with shortfalls of XXX cases in Ontario, XXX in Quebec, XXX in British Columbia, and XXX in Alberta.

Five Star is expected to be XXX cases below plan at XXX cases, compared to XXX last year. For the seven-month period, actual shipments are XXX below plan with shortfalls of XXX cases in Ontario, XXX in British Columbia, XXX in Saskatchewan, and XXX in Manitoba.

B. *U.S.A. Market*—Total shipments to date are XXX cases above plan and are expected to be XXX cases above plan for the year. This expected improvement is primarily due to higher inventories in Detroit and Champlain. The latest outlook for year-end inventory levels at these warehouses is XXX cases higher than originally forecasted, of which XXX cases are V.O. and XXX are Crown Royal.

To the end of February, actual shipments of V.O. are XXX cases above plan, and in the latest outlook V.O. is XXX cases above. Crown Royal shipments are XXX cases higher than plan to date and are expected to be XXX cases higher by year-end.

Administration

Total year expenditures are now projected at XXX, XXX higher than original forecast. After the first seven months, administration is XXX over forecast.

Production Overhead

The latest projection for the year is XXX, 2 percent lower than original forecast. While labour and expense variances are XXX better than the original plan to date, they are expected to be only XXX better by year-end, principally due to the effect of the new contracts.

Unfavourable grain purchase price variances originally forecast as nil are XXX to date, and the latest outlook for the year projects this to grow to XXX. Other purchase price variances originally forecasted at nil are now expected to be XXX for bottling materials, XXX for molasses, and XXX for fuel and electricity.

Appendix 2: Corporate Incentive Bonus Plan B

This plan is based on the attainment of approved goals and objectives. It is applicable to designated executives and managers in administration, marketing, and production division.

In each fiscal year, the president will allocate an amount of money that can be used in each division for distribution to eligible participants.

Procedure

A. Establishing goals
   1. It is the responsibility of each participant to set goals for each fiscal year and to have these accepted by his manager.
   2. One or two goals related to each major job responsibility should be formulated and reviewed with the manager.

   A list of the agreed goals will be established in writing.

B. Defining goals
   1. Goals are the end results to be achieved within a stated period of time, usually one year.
   2. Goals should be stated in terms of the results to be accomplished—not as activities or tasks of the individual.
   3. Goals must be expressed precisely in measurable terms, not as generalized statements about improvements.

C. Types of goals
   Each goal shall be categorized in one of the following types:

   Type 1 — *Normal activity goals*—These pertain to the regular requirements and responsibilities of the individual's job. They should involve improvement of existing performance levels and/or maintenance of established standards.

   Type 2 — *Extraordinary activity goals*—These are goals of an innovative nature over and beyond the usual responsibilities. They involve some original, new, or different way to produce desirable results.

   Type 3 — *Long-term project goals*—These involve projects which have potential for improving corporate profitability or position but which may not be completed within the current year.

In order to have a balanced set of objectives, each participant's goals should include some of each type.

D. Reviewing progress

1. At four-month intervals, the subordinate and his manager will discuss progress toward achievement of each goal and revise goals which are found to be unrealistic.

2. At the end of the year, the subordinate will prepare a written statement of his goals and achievement.

3. He and his manager will discuss this statement, their objectives being (1) to agree, as completely as possible, on what has and has not been accomplished; (2) to determine causes for any lack of achievement; and (3) to make plans, as needed, for improved future performance.

4. The subordinate will prepare a written summary of the agreement and conclusions reached in 3.

E. Evaluation of accomplishment

The extent of achievement will be determined as follows:

1. Determine general performance level: For each goal, select which of the five column headings best described the employee's accomplishment, that is, "Major Goal Overachievement," "Definitely Exceeded Goal," "Substantially Achieved Goal," and so on.

Performance Level

Major Goal Overachievement	*Definitely Exceeded Goal*	*Substantially Achieved Goal*	*Definite Goal Shortfall*	*Major Goal Shortfall*
80–100 points	60–80 points	40–60 points	20–40 points	0–20 points

Appendix 3:   Note on Product Portfolio Management

Product portfolio as developed by the Boston Consulting Group emphasizes the assumed relationship between market share and per-unit profitability. As market share increases and as the total industry growth increases, the experience curve effect on production costs makes market share in a growth industry attractive through its relative profits. Product portfolio managers, then, should analyze products by means of a growth and market share matrix, using a circle of proportional size for each single product's sales. As growth slows or market share declines, proceeds from declining products should be invested in ones with increasing market shares or relative growth, unless reinvestment in slow growth and declining share is the only alternative. Underlying the movement of products over the matrix are the industry and company's decisions and the product life cycle itself.

The growth and market share matrix may be summarized as follows:

		Market Share *(Directly Correlated with Funds Source)*	
		High	*Low*
	High	Star products	Question marks
Industry/Product *Growth Rate* *(Directly Correlated with Funds Use)*	*Low*	Cash cows	Dog products

The best portfolio strategy is utilizing funds from cash cows to make star products from question marks.

After a product portfolio analysis is completed for the firm and its competitor, the strategist then assesses one's own position versus the industry in general and competitors in particular, funds balance and the distribution of products, and the movement or trend of products over a period of several years.

Case 22

Kolapore, Inc.

In January 1986 Mr. Adriaan Demmers, president and sole employee of Kolapore, Inc., a firm based in Guelph, Ontario, specializing in the importation, processing, and sale of high-quality souvenir spoons, was becoming increasingly frustrated with the pace at which his business was developing. Over a two-year period, Demmers had taken his idea of importing souvenir spoons from Holland to Canada to annual sales of nearly $30,000. He believed the potential existed for well over $100,000 in Canadian sales plus exports to the United States. This success to date had been a strain, however, on Demmers's limited financial resources and had not provided any compensation for the long hours invested. Demmers was beginning to question if he was ever going to have the major breakthrough which he had always believed was "just around the corner."

Recently, Demmers had accepted a full-time position with another firm in an unrelated business. While Demmers realized that he could continue to operate Kolapore, Inc., on a part-time basis, he wondered if he should "face reality" and simply fold up the business or try to sell it. Alternately, Demmers could not occasionally help wondering if he should be devoting himself full-time to Kolapore.

Background

In February/March 1984 Demmers conducted a feasibility study of starting a business to market souvenir spoons. His idea was to offer a high-quality product depicting landmarks, historic buildings, and other unique symbols of the area in which the spoons were to be sold.

There were numerous spoons on the market, but most tended to be for Canada or Ontario rather than local sites of interest and were generally poorly made and not visually appealing. There were few quality spoons, and the ones that did exist were priced in the $15–$40 range.

Sources of spoons were examined and quotations were received from firms in Canada, the United States, and the Netherlands (Holland). The search process for a country from which to source the spoons was a limited one and was settled quickly, thanks to Demmers's Dutch heritage, the existence of a well-recognized

This case was prepared by Professor Paul W. Beamish, School of Business and Economics, Wilfrid Laurier University. Copyright © 1986 by Paul W. Beamish.

group of silversmiths in Schoonhoven, plus a particular company which already had over 40 Canadian specific dies and lower prices.

Demmers felt the key factors for success were good quality product, using designs of local landmarks, and an eye-catching display. He felt displays should be located in a prominent position in retail stores because souvenir spoons are often bought on impulse.

As part of his feasibility study, Demmers conducted a market analysis (including customer and retailer surveys), a competitive analysis (both manufacturers and distributors), and developed an import plan, marketing plan, and financial projections (including projected breakeven and cash flows). Excerpts from this study follow.

1.   Market Analysis

The market for souvenir spoons consists of several overlapping groups—primarily tourists and the gift market. There are also groups interested in spoons for more specialized purposes such as church groups, service clubs, associations, and others. These are very specialized and for special occasions.

A random telephone survey conducted in March 1984 of 50 people in Guelph revealed that 78 percent owned souvenir spoons. Forty-six percent of those people had purchased the spoons themselves, while 54 percent had received them as gifts. In total, almost 25 percent of the people in the sample collected souvenir spoons or had a rack on which to hang them. Retailers indicated that sales occurred primarily during the summer months and at Christmas time. Twelve retail outlets were visited to obtain information regarding quality, sales, and prices. Background on a selection of these retailers is summarized in Appendix 1.

There was a high awareness of souvenir spoons in the market, but the product quality was generally at the low end of the market. For example, rough edges on the bowls were common, and the crests on the spoons were often crooked. In fact, one manufacturer's spoon had a picture of Kitchener City Hall which was out of focus and off-center. (Terms concerning souvenir spoons are explained in Appendix 2.)

A limited variety of spoons was often available, and few of the spoons were of local points of interest even though these were the spoons that were most in demand. One retailer noted that of a total of 140 spoons sold in 1983, 106 were one variety, a spoon with a relief design in plastic of a Conestoga wagon. This was the only unique spoon Demmers found in the area "other than the cheap picture spoons."

There was no advertising for souvenir spoons due to the nature of the product and the lack of identification with a particular brand.

Souvenir spoons appeared to be a low priority in many producing companies, with little marketing effort made to push the products. Even the packaging was of poor quality; often, boxes were not supplied for gift wrapping.

The sale of spoons was viewed as seasonal by some retailers. Point-of-purchase displays were removed once the summer rush was over in many instances.

Spoons were not prominently displayed in most stores, yet they are largely an impulse item. In several stores they were kept in drawers and only taken out when requested.

2. Competitive Analysis

Souvenir spoons essentially serve two customer functions: as gifts or commemoratives. They can be used as gifts for family, friends, or special occasions such as Christmas. They can also serve as a commemorative token of having visited somewhere or for a special anniversary (for example, The Province of Ontario's 200th anniversary). They can be either functional (used for coffee or teaspoons) or may be used for decorative purposes (hung in a spoon rack or put in a cabinet).

Competition comes from all other gift items and all other souvenir items in approximately the same price range.

Demmers identified 11 companies that distributed souvenir spoons in the Southwestern Ontario area and gathered what data he could—much of it anecdotal—on each. This process had provided encouragement for Demmers to proceed. Background on these suppliers is summarized in Appendix 3.

Southwestern Ontario contained a number of large urban areas including Toronto (over 2 million people), Hamilton/Burlington, Kitchener/Waterloo, and London with over 300,000 people in each, plus many smaller cities such as Guelph. Guelph was located roughly in the centre of the triangle formed by Toronto, Waterloo, and Burlington and was within an hour's drive of each.

3. Importing

To import goods into Canada on a regular basis in amounts over $800, an importer number was required. This was available from Revenue Canada, Customs and Excise. Requirements for customs were an advise notice from the shipper and a customs invoice. These were available in office supply stores. A customs tariff number and commodity code were also required to complete the customs B3 form.

Souvenir spoons of either sterling silver or silver plate were listed in the customs tariff under number 42902-1. The Netherlands has Most Favoured Nation status, so the duty was 20.3 percent. On top of the cost of the merchandise (excluding transportation and insurance but including duty), there was a further 10 percent excise tax and 10 percent federal sales tax.

A customs broker could be hired to look after the clearing of goods through customs. Rates were approximately $41 plus $3.60 for every thousand dollars of value, duty included.

Insurance on a shipment of less than $10,000 costs a fixed fee of about $150 with insurance brokers. This can be reduced if insurance is taken on a yearly basis, based on the expected value of imports over the year. Freight forwarders charge approximately $2.00 per kilo regardless of the total weight of the shipment.

The importing can be easily handled without help on small shipments such as spoons. The product can be sent by airmail and insured with the post office. It can also be sent to a small city like Guelph rather than Toronto, and this avoids the busy Toronto customs office and possible delays of several days. The customs office in Guelph can easily clear the goods the same day they arrive.

Product

The proposed souvenir spoons would be a high-quality product with detailed dies made to give them a relief design far superior to any competitive spoons (except for those retailing in the $30 range). These spoons are available in silver plate and alpacca which makes them similar to jewellery.

Designs would be of specific points of interest. In the Kitchener-Waterloo area, for example, possible subjects would include Seagram Museum, Schneider House, Doon Pioneer Village, university crests, and city crests. Kitchener-Waterloo would be printed under the picture, also in relief in the metal, along with the title of the particular picture.

4. Marketing Plan

See Figure 1 on opposite page.

Price Points

$2.25	—	Metropolitan Supplies—nickel-plated.
$4.50–$6.00	—	Breadner Manufacturing—rhodium-plated and silver-plated. Candis Enterprises. Gazelle Importers.
$7.00–$8.00	—	Oneida or Commemorative—simple designs with engraved insignia. Appear to be made of a silver alloy.
$10.00–$14.00	—	Proposed price range for retail. — Quality comparable to $30.00 spoons, but silver content is lower. — Detailed designs of local landmarks. — Variety of 6–10 spoons in each market.
$30.00 and up	—	Breadner — Sterling silver. — Fine workmanship. — Very limited variety of designs.

Figure 1

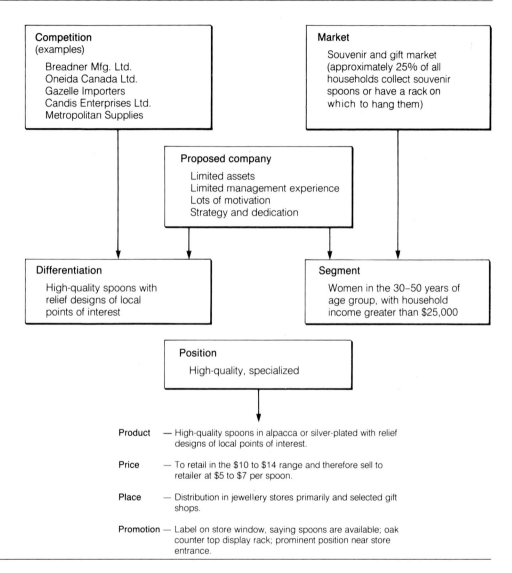

Place

Because souvenir spoons are purchased on impulse, locations with high traffic are essential. Jewellery stores and gift stores in malls and tourist areas are probably most suitable in this respect.

Due to the price range proposed and the quality of the merchandise, the quality and image of the store has to be appropriate. This would eliminate discount jewellery stores and cheap souvenir shops for the aforementioned reasons. Secondly, it would not please higher-end retailers if the same spoons were sold for less in the same area and would likely restrict distribution in the appropriate channels.

Jewellery stores are perceived by many people as selling expensive, luxury items that are not part of one's everyday needs. For this reason it would be helpful for these stores to have a window display.

Promotion

Each retail location will carry a minimum product line of six varieties of spoons: one with a Canadian theme, one with a provincial theme, and at least four spoons with designs of local landmarks or points of interest.

The packaging will be suitable for gift wrapping, so will likely consist of a small box with a clear plastic cover.

Each retail location will have an oak countertop display rack. There will be a relatively high cost to the displays initially, but they will attract attention and convey the quality of the spoons. Different sizes can be made depending on the number of spoons for a particular market.

Because souvenir spoons are primarily an impulse purchase, location in the store is important and should be near the entrance or have a window display. This is something which can be controlled only by persuading the retailer that this would increase the turnover and consequently his profits.

5. Finance

Contribution margin per spoon has been calculated using the most conservative numbers and at a wholesale price of $3.50. Typically, retailers would mark prices

Table 1: Forecast Variable Costs and Margins of Spoons

	Alpacca	*Silver Plate*
Quote by Dutch manufacturer (Zilverfabriek) (in guilders) 1 guilder = $.43 Cdn.	2.20 guilders	3.10 guilders
Factory cost in $Cdn.	$0.95	$1.33
Duty @ 20.3 percent	.19	.27
Cost, duty included	$1.14	$1.60
Federal sales tax @ 9 percent	.10	.14
Federal excise tax @ 10 percent	.11	.16
Freight and insurance	.10	.10
Cost	$1.45	$2.00
Contribution margin	$2.05 to $3.55	$1.50 to $3.00
Cost to retailer	3.50 to 5.00	3.50 to 5.00
Retailer markup	3.50 to 5.00	3.50 to 5.00
Retail price	7.00 to 10.00*	7.00 to 10.00

* These prices are lower than originally forecast due to Demmers's recognition that a $10 to $14 retail price was too high.

Table 2: Forecast Breakeven

Distribution costs (transportation)	$ 4,000
Rent expense (work from home)	—
Salary	15,000
Office supply costs (including telephone)	1,000
Inventory costs	1,000
Merchandising expenses (displays and boxes)	3,000
Investment in dies (10 @ $125 each)	1,250
Total fixed costs	$25,250

$25,250/$1.50 = 16,833 spoons
$25,250/$2.05 = 12,317 spoons
$25,250/$3.00 = 8,416 spoons

---

up by 100 percent (see Table 1). The contribution margins worked out to $2.05 on alpacca spoons and $1.50 on silver-plated spoons.

The breakeven, assuming costs of $25,250 per year and a contribution margin of $2.05, would be sales volume of 12,317 spoons with sales value of $43,110 (see Table 2). Assuming the spoons would be introduced in the Toronto market and distribution obtained in 100 retail locations, this means sales of 124 spoons per store.

Upon graduating from a university business school in April 1984, Demmers planned to devote his efforts to Kolapore. He felt that while there could be a short-term financial drain, his cash balance would be positive at the end of the second month of operation (see Table 3).

Subsequent Events

Soon after graduating in April, it became clear to Demmers that Kolapore was not going to realize forecast sales of $28,000 by September 1984. Due to delays in

---

Table 3: Forecast Cash Flow, May–August 1984

	May	June	July	August
Cash	$ 3,000	$ (750)	$ 1,000	$ 7,500
Disbursements:				
Moulds	1,250	—	—	—
Purchases	—	7,250	—	7,250
Promotion expenses	2,000	1,000	—	—
Car expenses	500	500	500	500
Total disbursements	3,750	8,750	500	7,750
Net cash	(750)	(9,500)	500	(250)
Receipts:				
Accounts receivable	—	10,500	7,000	10,500
Cash balance (to be borrowed)	$ (750)	$ 1,000	$ 7,500	$ 10,250
Terms n/30.				

getting shipments from Holland and difficulty in obtaining distribution in Canada, sales were only $1,830 over the summer. A number of assumptions in the original feasibility study (as described in the first section) had proven incorrect:

1. The number of dies ultimately required (each of which costs $125) was not going to be 10 but closer to 50.
2. The federal sales tax rate had increased to 10 percent from 9 percent.
3. Duty was payable on the dies themselves as well as on the spoons at the rate of 20.3 percent excise tax plus federal sales tax.
4. Delivery time for new dies was closer to six months than the forecast 10–12 weeks (the artist had been ill for several months). Several orders were cancelled during this period as a result.
5. Packaging costs per spoon were closer to 32 cents per unit than the estimated 10 cents.
6. Distribution had been difficult because the large chain stores which dominated the market all had established suppliers.
7. The target market was not nearly as upscale as originally envisioned. Although Kolapore's spoons were readily identifiable as being of superior quality, most customers would only pay a maximum of $7–$8 retail for any spoon. Demmers had estimated the total Canadian souvenir spoon market at about $1.5 million annually. Within that, a very small portion was for sterling silver (where Demmers could not compete), about $450,000 was at the $7 retail price point where Demmers was selling (some of his competitors were promoting similar or poorer-quality spoons at the same price), with the balance of the market reserved for lower-priced/lower-quality spoons.

The goal of 100 stores by September 1984 was still a long way off.

Demmers had also discovered that the chain stores plan all their buying from 6 to 12 months in advance. Because many of the spoons he had designed did not arrive until September 1984, this meant that he had missed much of the tourist season (and nearly all of the Christmas market).

On the positive side, the Dutch guilder had depreciated relative to the Canadian dollar. In September 1984 it cost Canadian $0.39 for 1 guilder rather than $0.43 as forecast. In addition, delivery times for spoons from existing dies required three to four weeks rather than the expected four to six weeks, and the cost of display cases was only about $16.00 each. These were made of plastic rather than the originally envisioned oak.

Although Kolapore was showing a negative cash balance at the end of August 1984 (see Table 4), sales began to improve in September (see Table 5), growing to nearly $16,000 by the end of the first full year of operation (see Tables 6 and 7 for financial statements). A financial loss of $1,800 was incurred for the first year of operation, and this took no account of the countless hours Demmers had invested.

Table 4: Actual Cash Flow, 1984

	May	June	July	August
Cash	$2,600	$1,000	$ 950	$ 530
Disbursements:				
Purchases	1,000	550	870	1,460
Expenses	1,000	80	300	300
Total disbursements	2,000	630	1,170	1,760
Net cash	600	370	(220)	(1,230)
Receipts:				
Accounts receivable	400	580	750	1,100
Cash balance	$1,000	$ 950	$ 530	$ (130)

Since the business was not yet self-supporting, in September 1984 Demmers had begun to look for other sources of income.

Between September 1984 and January 1986 Demmers worked for five months in a fibreglass factory, acquired a house in Guelph in which he was able to live and to rent out rooms, sold Bruce Trail calendars on a commission basis, worked at organizing and selling several ski tours (which did not take place), and opened an ice-cream store in a regional resort area (Wasaga Beach). Due to a low volume of traffic, this latter venture in the summer of 1985 resulted in an $8,000 loss. In the fall of 1985 Demmers accepted a position as production manager for a weekly newspaper in Guelph.

By this time, Demmers was selling direct to retailers in 20 towns and cities in Ontario and through five chains: Simpsons and United Cigar Stores and, to a much smaller extent, Eaton's, Birks, and Best Wishes. Other chains such as The Bay, Sears, and Woolco had been approached but so far without success. Demmers was hoping to find the time so that he could approach the buyers at K mart, Zeller's, Consumer's Distributing, Robinson's, Woodwards, and others.

Kolapore spoons were sold in Simpsons stores from Windsor, Ontario, to Halifax, Nova Scotia, and in 18 United Cigar Store locations in southern Ontario.

Table 5: Actual Sales, 1984–1985

May	$ 400
June	580
July	750
August	1,100
September	2,600
October	2,540
November	1,500
December	1,400
January–March	4,923

Table 6

KOLAPORE INC.
Balance Sheet
As at March 31, 1985
(Unaudited—See Notice to Reader)

Assets

Current assets:
Cash	$1,708
Accounts receivable	1,763
Inventory	2,873
Total current assets	6,344
Incorporation expense	466
Total assets	$6,810

Liabilities

Current liabilities:
Accounts payable and accruals	$ 268
Due to shareholder (note 2)	8,342
Total liabilities	8,610

Shareholders' Equity

Retained earnings (deficit)	(1,800)
Total liabilities and shareholder's equity	$6,810

Notice to reader: These financial statements have been compiled solely for tax purposes. I have not audited, reviewed, or otherwise attempted to verify their accuracy or completeness.

Guelph, Ontario   Chartered Accountant
May 2, 1985

Four months after Demmers's first delivery to the chain outlets in the summer of 1985, about half the stores were sold out of Kolapore spoons. Neither chain would reorder stock part way through the year.

To sell direct in some of the smaller cities, Demmers's practice had been to drive or walk through the main shopping areas, stopping at jewellery stores or other likely retail outlets. If he was unable to meet with the store owner, he would usually leave a sample and a letter with some information (see Exhibit 1 for a copy of the letter). Demmers's experience had been that unless he personally met with the right person—which sometimes took three or more visits—no sales would occur. When he was able to meet with the owner, his success rate was over 70 percent. To sell direct in larger centres such as Toronto (where he had 40 customers), Demmers had focused his efforts on hotel gift shops. Having established these customers, he could now visit all 40 customers in Toronto personally in two to three days.

By year-end, Demmers had access to a pool of 89 Canadian-specific dies. Demmers's supplier in Holland had 46 dies in stock which another Canadian from

Table 7

KOLAPORE INC.
Statement of Income
Year Ended March 31, 1985
(Unaudited—See Notice to Reader)

Sales	$15,793
Cost of sales:	
Inventory at beginning of year	—
Purchases	8,453
Duty and freight	2,288
Dies	3,034
	13,775
Less: Inventory at end of year	2,873
Cost of sales	10,902
Gross profit	4,891
Expenses:	
Office	657
Samples	582
Auto expenses	1,137
Car allowance	3,900
Bank interest and charges	139
Advertising	26
Accounting	250
Total expenses	6,691
Net profit (loss) for the year	$(1,800)

Notes: 1. Significant accounting policies:
KOLAPORE INC. is a company incorporated under the laws of Ontario on April 6, 1984, and is primarily engaged in the importing and selling of souvenir spoons.
The accounting policies are in accordance with generally accepted accounting principles.
Inventory is valued at lower of cost or net realizable value.
Incorporation expense is not amortized.
2. Due to shareholder is noninterest bearing and payable on demand.

Western Canada had had designed. Spoons based on these dies were no longer being sold anywhere as far as Demmers could tell.

For the most part Demmers was selling spoons based on his own designs. (For those spoons which Demmers had had designed, he had exclusive rights in Canada). In less than two years he had 43 more dies made up (see Exhibit 2 for a complete list). In some cases Demmers had asked a particular company/group to pay the cost of the dies; in others, such as for universities, he had built the die cost into his price for the first shipment; while in others he had simply gone ahead on his own with the hope that he could achieve sufficient sales to justify the investment.

There was a wide variability in the sales level associated with each spoon. Sales from his best-seller—the Toronto skyline (which depicted major buildings and the CN Tower)—were about 1,000 spoons a year. Demmers's second best selling spoon in

---

Exhibit 1: Kolapore, Inc., Letter of Introduction

Kolapore, Inc.
P.O. Box 361
Guelph, Ontario
N1H 6K5

Dear

   Kolapore, Inc., would like to offer you the opportunity to have your own design on a spoon made up in metal relief, for example, a logo, code of arms, crest, building, or whatever you would like.

   There is always a large market for souvenir spoons of unique design and high quality. Kolapore Collection Spoons fit this category extremely well and are priced very competitively.

   The spoons are available in silver plate at $3.50 per spoon. This price includes a gift box, federal sales tax, and shipping.

   The minimum order is 100 spoons to get a new design made up, and there is also a one-time die charge of $125.00 to help offset the cost of making the new die. Delivery time is approximately three months if a die has to be made up; subsequent orders will take four to six weeks.

   The dies for Kolapore Collection Spoons are made by master craftsmen in Schoonhoven, Holland, the silversmith capital of the world. The spoons themselves are made in Canada. As a result, the quality of the spoons is exceptional and recognized by the consumer at a glance.

   I trust that this is sufficient information. I look forward to hearing from you. If you have any questions or concerns, please don't hesitate to contact me. Thank you for your time and consideration.

                              Sincerely,

                              Adriaan Demmers
                              President

Toronto was 300 units of Casa Loma. (For a list of some of the major tourist sites in Toronto, see Exhibit 3). This spoon had quickly sold out on site in 10 days. (However the buyer had been unwilling to order more part way through the year). Spoons with other Toronto designs were selling less than 50 units a year.

By December 1985 inventories had increased and Kolapore, Inc., was still showing a small loss (see Table 8). Any gains from changes in the rate of import duty on spoons (20.3 percent in 1984 to 18.4 percent in 1986) had been negated by changes in federal sales tax (9 percent in 1984 to 11 percent in 1986) and exchange rates. The fluctuating Dutch guilder was at a two-year high relative to the Canadian dollar. From a March 1984 value of Cdn. $0.43, the guilder had declined

Exhibit 2: Kolapore Collection Spoons—Designs Available

Canada:
  Deer
  Elk
  Caribou
  Cougar
  Mountain goat
  Moose
  Bighorn sheep
  Grizzly bear
  Salmon
  Coast Indian
  Indian
  Coat of arms
  Mountie
  Maple leaf

Province of Ontario:
  ✔ Trillium
  ✔ Windsor, Ambassador Bridge
  ✔ Sarnia, Bluewater Bridge
  ✔ Chatham, St. Joseph's Church
  ✔ London, Storybook Gardens
  ✔ Woodstock, Old Town Hall
  ✔ Stratford, swan
  ✔ Kitchener, Schneider Haus
  ✔ Waterloo, The Seagram Museum
  ✔ Waterloo County, Mennonite horse and
      buggy
  ✔ Elora, Mill Street
  ✔ Guelph, Church of our Lady
  ✔ Guelph, Credit Union
  ✔ Guelph, St. Joseph's Hospital
  ✔ Kitchener-Waterloo, Oktoberfest
  ✔ Hamilton, Dundurn Castle
  ✔ St. Catharines, Old Court House
  ✔ Niagara Falls, Falls, Brock Monument, and
      Maid of the Mist
  ✔ Acton, Leathertown (hide with buildings)
  ✔ Toronto, skyline
  ✔ Toronto, City Hall
  ✔ Toronto, St. Lawrence Hall
  ✔ Toronto, Casa Loma
  ✔ Kingston, City Hall
  ✔ Ottawa, Parliament buildings
  ✔ Collingwood, Town Hall
  ✔ Owen Sound, City crest
University and community college crests/coats of
    arms:
  ✔ Wilfrid Laurier
  ✔ Waterloo

  ✔ Carleton
  ✔ Guelph
  ✔ York
  ✔ Western
  ✔ Windsor
  ✔ McMaster
  ✔ Brock
  ✔ Fanshawe
  ✔ Humber
Province of Quebec:
  Montreal, skyline
  Montreal, Olympic Stadium

Province of Nova Scotia:
  Bluenose (schooner)

Yukon Territory:
  Coat of arms
  Gold panner

Province of British Columbia:
  Coat of arms
  Prince George
  Victoria, Parliament buildings
  Victoria, lamp post
  Victoria, Empress Hotel
  Nanaimo, Bastion
  Dogwood (flower)
  Totem pole
  Kermode Terrace
  Smithers
  Northlander Rogers Pass, bear
  Northlander Rogers Pass, house
  Kelowna, The Ogopogo
  Okanagan. The Ogopogo
  Vancouver, Grouse Mountain/skyride/chalet
  Vancouver, Grouse Mountain skyride
  Vancouver, Grouse Mountain skyride/cabin
  Vancouver, Cleveland Dam
  Vancouver, The Lions
  Vancouver, The Lions Gate Bridge

Province of Alberta:
  Banff, Mount Norquay
  Banff, Mount Rundle
  Banff, Banff Springs Hotel
  Calgary, bronco rider
  Edmonton, Klondike Mike
  Wild Rose (flower)
  Oil derrick
  Jasper
  Jasper sky tram

Note: Check mark denotes those made up on Demmers's initiative.

Exhibit 3: Some Major Tourist Sites in Toronto

1. Metro Zoo
2. CN Tower
3. Casa Loma
4. Royal Ontario Museum (ROM)
5. Black Creek Pioneer Village
6. Art Gallery of Ontario (AGO)
7. Canada's Wonderland
8. Ontario Place
9. The Ontario Science Centre

Table 8

KOLAPORE INC.
Statement of Income
Eight Months* Ending November 30, 1985
(Unaudited)

Sales	$21,000
Cost of sales:	
Inventory at beginning of year	2,873
Purchases	12,000
Duty and freight	3,500
Dies	1,950
	20,323
Less: Inventory at end of year	5,000
Cost of sales	15,323
Gross profit	5,677
Expenses	6,500
Net profit (loss) for the year to date	$ (823)

* Annual sales expected to be $30,000.

---

to $0.36 in February 1985 and climbed to $0.50 by December 1985. Partially due to these exchange fluctuations, during the past eight months, Demmers had also arranged for the spoons to be silver plated at a cost of 40 cents each in Ontario. This had resulted in a saving of 15 cents a spoon (which varied with the exchange rate). More significantly, because many spoons were purchased as souvenirs of Canada, by adding sufficient value by silver plating in Canada, the imported product no longer had to be legally stamped, "Made in Holland." In fact, the packaging could now be marked "Made in Canada." Demmers was quite optimistic regarding the implications of this change because a number of potential store buyers had rejected his line because it did not say "Made in Canada." Demmers's supplier was upset, however, with the change.

Meanwhile, the feedback he was receiving from many of his customers was positive—in most cases they were selling more of his spoons than any other brand. Some customers, in fact, had enquired about other products. Since he had so far not experienced any competitive reactions to his spoons, Demmers was thinking of investigating the possibility of adding ashtrays, letter openers, key chains, lapel pins, and bottle openers to the product line in 1986—if he stayed in business. Each one of these products could have a crest attached to it. These crests would be the same as those used on the spoons and would thus utilize the dies to a greater extent. The landed costs per metal crest from the same supplier would be 85 cents. Demmers contemplated attaching these crests himself onto products supplied by Canadian manufacturers. However, initial investigations had revealed no obvious economical second product line.

Demmers also planned to phase out alpacca imports—all products would now be silver plated. In fact, Demmers was also wondering if he should acquire the equipment and materials in order to do this silver plating and polishing himself.

With no lack of ideas, many of the original frustrations nonetheless remained. The buyers at major chains such as Eaton's and Simpsons had changed once again, and because they did not use an automatic reorder system, new appointments had to be arranged. This was as difficult as ever. Also, Demmers still had not been able to draw anything from the firm for his efforts. These factors, coupled with his lack of cash and the demands of his new full-time position, had left Demmers uncertain as to what he should do next. With the spring buying season approaching—when Demmers would normally visit potential buyers—he realized that his decision regarding the future of Kolapore could not be postponed much longer.

Appendix 1: Survey of Spoons Carried by Local Retailers in Guelph and Kitchener-Waterloo Region

- A Taste of Europe—Delicatessen & Gift Store
  Guelph Eaton Centre
  — A selection of spoons from Holland with Dutch designs.
  — One with the Canadian coat of arms which looked good.
  — Rhodium-plated spoons—$5.98 per spoon.
  — Well displayed at front of store.

- Eaton's—Guelph Eaton Centre
  — Breadner spoons with maple leaf or Canadian flag and "Guelph" stamped in the bowl.

- — Rhodium-plated—$4.98.
- — No display and hard to find.
- Pequenot Jewellers—Wyndham Street, Guelph
  - — Carry Candis spoons, which look cheap and do not sell very well.
  - — $4.98.
  - — Poorly displayed.
- Smith & Son, Jewellers—Wyndham Street, Guelph
  - — Do not carry souvenir spoons because they are not in line with the store's image. They often get requests for them.
- Franks Jewellers—King Street, Waterloo
  - — Carry Breadner spoons with the Waterloo coat of arms.
  - — Rhodium-plated spoons—$4.50 per spoon.
  - — Not on display but kept in drawer.
  - — Sell less than 12 per year.
- Copper Creek—Waterloo Square Mall, Waterloo
  - — Candis spoons—$5.00 each.
- Birks—King Centre, Kitchener
  - — Carry Oneida and Breadner spoons.
  - — Rhodium-plated spoons for $5.98.
  - — Oneida spoons were $8.95 and looked like a silver alloy.
  - — Sterling silver Breadner spoons for $31.95.
  - — Displayed in a spoon rack, looked good.
  - — Birks regency spoons with crest of each province, $12.50.
- Eaton's—Market Square, Kitchener
  - — Breadner spoons, two types for Canada only.
  - — Rhodium-plated—$4.98 each.
- Young's Jewellers—King Street, Kitchener
  - — Rhodium-plated Breadner spoons, $4.50 each.
- Walters Jewellers
  - — Against chain policy to carry souvenir spoons because of poor quality and low turnover.
- Peoples Jewellers
  - — Do not carry souvenir spoons.
- Engels Gift Shop—King Street, Kitchener
  - — Carry Breadner, Oneida, Gazelle, and Metropolitan.
  - — Altogether about 20 varieties.
  - — Well displayed near entrance of store; prices range from $2.25 for Metropolitan spoons to $7.98 for Oneida spoons.
  - — Saleslady said they sell hundreds every year, mostly in the summer.

Appendix 2:   Terms Concerning Souvenir Spoons

Crest	—	Emblem, either metal, plastic, or enamel, that is affixed to a standard spoon.
Picture spoon	—	Spoon with a picture under plastic which is heat moulded to the spoon.
Relief design	—	Spoon with an engraving or picture which is moulded into the metal of the spoon.
Enamel	—	Opaque substance similar to glass in composition.
Plated	—	Thin layer of metal put on by electrolysis.
Rhodium-plated	—	Shiny "jeweller's metal" which does not tarnish (no silver content).
Silver-plated	—	Silver covering on another metal (such as steel).
Sterling silver	—	Alloy of 92.5 percent silver and 8.5 percent copper, nickel, and zinc.
Alpacca	—	Alloy of 82 percent copper and 18 percent nickel.

Appendix 3:   Souvenir Spoon Suppliers

Breadner Manufacturing Ltd.

Breadner appears to have national market distribution and includes two major retailers, Birks and Eaton's. According to some of the store managers interviewed, their sales of souvenir spoons in each location was low. Several retailers also expressed dissatisfaction with the Breadner line because of the slow turnover. Typically, there was a basic design for the spoon which did not change except for a different crest glued on for the different locale.

Breadner has been in the jewellery business since 1900 and has a plant in Hull, Quebec. They manufacture to order various types of pins, medals, and advertising specialties but advised Demmers that in general they use their entire output of souvenir spoons for their own sales.

They have many varieties of spoons in their catalogue and an established distribution system across the country. Demmers recognized the possibility that they could upgrade their selection in a short time span to compete directly with his intended selection of spoons.

Typical retail prices for Breadner spoons were $4.50 and up, the cost to the retailer being $2.25 and up. Breadner's high-end sterling silver spoons were available at Birks for $31.95, with the cost to Birks estimated at about $15.00 per spoon. Both rhodium-plated and silver-plated spoons were available, but rhodium-plated was more common. Silver-plated spoons were not carried.

Candis Enterprises Ltd.

Candis is located in Willowdale, Ontario. This company has good distribution in gift shops (for example, the 650-outlet United Cigar Store Chain) and in some jewellery stores. They have a line of rhodium-plated spoons marketed under the MaR-VEL name and silver-plated spoons under the Candis name.

Their strategy appears to be one of putting out a large variety of spoons for each place in which they sell. However, the quality seems to be toward the low end: many of the spoons have rough edges on the bowls and there is no detail in the dies.

Wholesale cost ranges from $2.00 per spoon for a rhodium-plated picture spoon to $3.25 for a silver-plated spoon with a five-colour ceramic crest.

Metropolitan Supplies Ltd.

Metropolitan Supplies is located in Toronto and distributes its goods across Canada primarily to gift shops and souvenir shops in tourist areas. This company deals with all sorts of souvenirs and novelty items. They have a large selection of spoons, each of which can be crested to suit the buyer. The quality of the spoons is at the low end. Prices range from $0.55 per spoon (wholesale) for iron and nickel-plated spoons to $2.00 per spoon for silver-plated spoons.

Gazelle Importers and Distributors

Gazelle Importers and Distributors is located in Grimsby, Ontario. They previously imported spoons from Holland but later manufactured in Ontario. Their spoons are sold under the Gazelle name. They retail for $5.95 and, therefore, presumably cost the retailer about $3.00. Spoons have designs for Ontario and Canada but nothing local. Quality seems about the same as Breadner's less-expensive line.

Oneida Canada Ltd.

Oneida is located in Niagara Falls, Ontario, and is a division of Oneida Ltd. in the United States. The Niagara Falls plant manufactures stainless steel and silver-plate flatware. Their product is distributed in several jewellery stores including Birks and gift shops. The quality is better than any other spoons except for Breadner's sterling spoons. Prices are also somewhat higher with a retail price of $7.98, giving a probable cost to the retailer of about $4.00 per spoon. There is little variety. All spoons come in one design with a different engraving in the top of the spoon.

Commemorative Spoons

This firm is located in Ottawa and sells spoons in the $6.95–$8.95 range. They have three basic designs (supplied by Oneida). They have large accounts with Simpsons and Cara and frequently deal with clubs for whom they make up special spoons for fund-raising.

Hunnisett and Edmunds

This is a distribution company which specializes in selling to card shops and variety stores. They use a somewhat unique packaging system—selling via fly-top displays of 12 spoons.

Parsons-Steiner

This firm is located in Toronto. The quality of the product is low. Retail prices range from $1.99 to $5.98. Spoons tend to be picture spoons, and the least-expensive ones appear to be made of cast iron with a decal attached.

Boma

This company is located in Vancouver, British Columbia. The quality is very good. Spoons are made out of pewter with designs of such things as totem poles. Retail prices range from $10 to $20.

Aalco Souvenirs

Located in Vancouver, this company carries over 300 "three-dimensional" models of spoons. They are made in Canada and are nickel plated with a white gold flash. Aalco's products are distributed across Canada. They also carry other souvenir items such as bells, bottle openers, key chains, lapel pins, and charms. Prices for spoons range from $2.50 to $3.00 each.

Souvenir Canada

Located in Downsview, Ontario, and operating throughout Canada and the United States, this company carries spoons with plastic decals, key chains, bottle openers, bells, lapel pins, mugs, plates, glasses, clothing, and special promotional items. They have been in business for about 10 years and use standardized spoons with crests attached. Retail price per spoon is $3.00.

Case 23

Larson Incorporated (Revised)

David Larson, vice president of international operations for Larson Inc., was mulling over the decisions he was required to make regarding the company's Nigerian operation. He was disturbed by the negative tone of the report sent to him on January 4, 1979, by the chief executive officer of the Nigerian affiliate, George Ridley (see Exhibit 1). Larson believed the future prospects for Nigeria were excellent and was concerned about the action he should take.

Company Background

Larson Inc. was a Montreal-based multinational corporation in the wire and cable business. Wholly owned subsidiaries were located in the United States and United Kingdom, while Mexico, Venezuela, Australia, and Nigeria were the sites of joint ventures. Other countries around the world were serviced through exports from the parent or one of its subsidiaries.

The parent company was established in 1925 by David Larson's grandfather. Ownership and management of the company remained in the hands of the Larson family and was highly centralized. The annual sales volume for the corporation worldwide approximated $575 million in 1978. Revenue was primarily generated from the sale of power, communication, construction, and control cables.

Technical service was an important part of Larson Inc.'s product package, so the company maintained a large force of engineers to consult with customers and occasionally supervise installation. As a consequence, licensing was really not a viable method of serving foreign markets.

Background on Nigeria

Covering a geographic area slightly larger than either Ontario or British Columbia, Nigeria is located in the west-central part of the African continent. With 85 million people, in 1979 it was the most populous country in Africa, in fact the ninth most populous nation in the world. From 1970 to 1979 it had an annual population growth rate of 2.5 percent. Its population by the year 2000 was estimated to be 149 million. About 47 percent of the population was under 15 years of age.

Seventy-five percent of the labour force was in agriculture, and about 20 percent of the population lived in urban centres.

This case was prepared by I. A. Litvak, York University. Copyright © 1984 by I. A. Litvak. Revised by Paul W. Beamish, 1986.

The gross national product (at market prices) in 1979 was about U.S. $85 billion. This was about one third that of Canada. Nigeria's GNP was the 23rd highest in the world, with a growth rate from 1970 to 1979 of 5.3 percent. This was one of the highest growth rates in the world—fuelled in part by export sales from Nigeria's large oil reserves.

The Nigerian Operation

Larson Inc. established a joint venture in Nigeria in 1974 with a local partner who held 25 percent of the joint venture's equity. In 1978, Larson Inc. promised Nigerian authorities that the share of local ownership would be increased to 51 percent within five to seven years. Such indigenization requests from developing country governments were quite common.

Sales revenue for the Nigerian firm totalled $28 million in Canadian funds in 1978. Of this revenue, $24.5 million was realized in Nigeria, while $3.5 million was from exports. About 40 percent of the firm's Nigerian sales ($10 million) were made to various enterprises and departments of the government of Nigeria. The company was making a reasonable profit of 10 percent of revenue, but with a little bit of luck and increased efficiency, it was believed it could make a profit of 20 percent.

The Nigerian operation had become less attractive for Larson Inc. in recent months. Although it was believed that Nigeria should become one of the key economic players in Africa in the 1980s and that the demand for Larson's products would remain very strong there, doing business in Nigeria was growing more costly. Furthermore, Larson Inc. was becoming increasingly unhappy with its local partner in Nigeria, a lawyer who was solely concerned with quick "paybacks" at the expense of reinvestment and long-term growth prospects.

David Larson recognized that having the right partner in a joint venture was of paramount importance. The company expected the partner or partners to be actively engaged in the business, "not businessmen interested in investing money alone." The partner was expected to hold a substantial equity in the venture. In the early years of joint venture, additional funding was often required, and thus it was necessary for the foreign partner to be in a strong financial position.

The disillusionment of George Ridley, the Nigerian firm's CEO, had been increasing since his early days in that position. He was an expatriate from the United Kingdom who, due to his background as a military officer, placed a high value upon order and control. The chaotic situation in Nigeria proved very trying for him. His problems were further complicated by his inability to attract good local employees in Nigeria, while his best expatriate staff requested transfers to Montreal or Larson Inc.'s other foreign operations soon after their arrival in Nigeria. On a number of occasions, Ridley was prompted to suggest to head office that it reconsider its Nigerian commitment.

David Larson reflected on the situation. He remained convinced that Larson Inc. should maintain its operations in Nigeria; however, he had to design a plan to increase local Nigerian equity in the venture to 51 percent. Larson wondered what should be done about Ridley. On the one hand, Ridley had been with the company for many years and knew the business intimately; on the other hand, Larson felt that Ridley's attitude was contributing to the poor morale in the Nigerian firm and wondered if Ridley had lost his sense of adaptability. Larson knew Ridley had to be replaced, but he was unsure about the timing and the method to use, since Ridley was only two years away from retirement.

Larson had to come to some conclusions fairly quickly. He had been requested to prepare a plan of action for the Nigerian operation for consideration by the board of directors of Larson Inc. in one month's time. He thought he should start by identifying the key questions, whom he should contact, and how he should handle Ridley in the meantime.

Exhibit 1: The Ridley Report

In response to the request from head office for a detailed overview of the Nigerian situation and its implications for Larson Inc., the following report was prepared. This report will attempt to itemize the factors in the Nigerian environment that have contributed to the problems experienced by Larson Inc.'s joint venture in Nigeria.

The Nigerian Enterprises Promotion Decrees

1. There can be no doubt that the Nigerian Enterprises Promotion Decree of 1977 represents very severe and far-reaching indigenization legislation. The cumulative damaging effects of the decree have been exacerbated by some aspects of its implementation. In particular the valuation of companies by the Nigerian Securities and Exchange Committee has in many cases been unrealistically low. This has represented substantial real-capital asset losses to the overseas companies concerned, which had no opportunity of appeal to an independent authority. This unsatisfactory aspect has been made worse by the difficulties and delays experienced by many companies in obtaining foreign currency for the remittance of proceeds from the sale of shares. A disquieting feature has been the enforced imposition, in certain cases, of a requirement to issue new equity in Nigeria instead of selling existing shares with the consequent ineligibility to remit even part of the proceeds from Nigeria and a dilution of value to both Nigerian and foreign shareholders. Another aspect causing great concern is related to the time constraint for compliance, particularly as the Nigerian authorities concerned appear to be literally snowed under with applications. There is also doubt as to the continuing ability of the market to absorb the very large amount of equity that must inevitably be offered for sale within a period of a few months.

Remittances

2. In addition to the problems of remittances of the proceeds from the sale of shares under the 1977 decree, there has been a steadily increasing delay in the granting of

---

Exhibit 1 (*continued*)

foreign exchange for remittances from Nigeria, such as payment for supplies and services from overseas. Whereas early this year delays of about three months were being reported, delays of up to eight months or even more are now not unusual. Larson Nigeria cannot continue to operate effectively if it is unable to remit proceeds and pay bills in a reasonable time frame. It is in the position of importing $5.5 million (Cdn.) in products and services annually. These delays in remittances, coupled with delays in payments (see paragraph 4(*a*) below), also raise problems related to export guarantees, which normally are of limited duration only.

3. A problem regarding remittances has arisen as a result of the Nigerian Insurance Decree No. 59, under which cargoes due for import to Nigeria have to be insured with a Nigerian-registered insurance company. Though claims related to cargo loss and damage are paid in Nigeria, foreign exchange for remittance to pay the overseas supplier is not being granted on the grounds that the goods have not arrived.

Problems Affecting Liquidity and Cash Flow

4. A number of problems have arisen during the last two years or so that are having a serious effect upon liquidity and cash flow, with the result that local expenses can be met only by increasing bank borrowing, which is not only additional cost but also becoming more difficult to obtain. These problems include:

(a) Serious delays in obtaining payment from federal and state government departments for supplies and services provided, even in instances where payment terms are clearly written into the contract concerned. This is particularly true for state governments where payment of many accounts is 12 months or more in arrears. Even when paid, further delays are experienced in obtaining foreign currency for the part that is remittable abroad. This deterioration in cash flow from government clients has in turn permeated through to the private clients.

(b) The 1978 federal budget measures, whereby companies are required to pay tax in advance of audited accounts, with the result that over a period of about 12 months Larson Nigeria is faced with paying virtually two years' tax.

(c) The requirement for 100 percent deposit on application for some letters of credit.

(d) The fairly recent requirement by the Nigerian Port Authorities for the payment of 50 percent of customs duty before a ship is even permitted to berth.

Incomes and Prices Policy Guidelines

5. Many of the guidelines issued by the Productivity, Prices and Incomes Board are a direct discouragement, as they make operations in Nigeria increasingly less attractive in comparison with other areas in the world. Among these guidelines are:

(a) Continued restrictions on wage and salary increases, fees for professional services, audit fees, and so forth.

Exhibit 1 (*continued*)

(**b**)   Unrealistic restrictions on price markup for many imported goods. The permitted markup of 25 percent is totally inadequate to meet the very high operating costs in Nigeria and to provide good sales and aftersales service.

Dividends

6.   While Larson Inc. welcomed the raising of the level of dividend restriction from 30 percent gross (16½ percent net) to 40 percent gross (20 percent net) of issued capital, the exclusion of script/bonus issues past October 1, 1976, is still a matter of concern where profits that would otherwise have been available for remittance have been reinvested. It seems inequitable that investors, both indigenous and foreign, should not receive a return on this reinvestment. Furthermore, it results in an artificial dilution of share value for both indigenous and overseas shareholders.

7.   The regulations regarding interim dividends are also a matter of concern. The requirement to pay advance income tax on such dividends prior to the due date for payment of tax on the full year's income is unreasonable, and the rule under which remittance to overseas shareholders have to await final account is discriminatory.

Offshore Technical and Management Services

8.   Restrictions on the reimbursement of expenses to the parent company for offshore management and technical services are a cause of great concern, since such services are costly to provide.

Professional Fees

9.   The whole position regarding fees for professional services provided from overseas is most unsatisfactory. Not only are the federal government scales substantially lower than in most other countries, but the basis of the project cost applied in Nigeria is out of keeping with normally accepted international practice. The arbitrary restriction on the percentage of fees that may be remitted is a further disincentive to attracting professional services. Moreover, payment of professional fees in themselves produce cash flow problems exacerbated by long delays in payments and remittance approvals (referred to above).

Royalties and Trade Marks

10.   The Nigerian government's apparent unpreparedness to permit payment of royalties for the use of trade marks for a period of more than 10 years is out of keeping with the generally accepted international practice.

Expatriate Quotas, Work Permits, and Entry Visas

11.   It must be recognized that expatriate expertise is a very important element for this business, but expatriate staff is very costly. Unfortunately, at the present time there are a number of difficulties and frustrations, such as the arbitrary cuts in expatriate quotas at

Exhibit 1 *(concluded)*

very short notice and the delays in obtaining, and in some cases the refusal of, entry visas and work permits for individuals required for work in Nigeria.

Expatriate Staff

12. In general the conditions of employment and life in Nigeria are regarded as unattractive as compared with many other countries competing for the same expertise. This is due partly to the general deterioration in law and order, to the restrictions on salary increases, to the restrictions placed on home remittances, to the unsatisfactory state of public utilities such as electricity, water, and telecommunications, and to general frustrations related to visas and work permits, mentioned above. The situation has now reached a stage where not only is recruitment of suitably qualified skilled experts becoming increasingly difficult, but we are also faced with resignations and refusals to renew contracts even by individuals who have worked and lived here for some years. Furthermore, the uncertainty over the length of time for which employment in Nigeria will be available due to doubts whether the necessary expatriate quotas will continue to be available to the employer is most unsettling to existing staff. This and the restriction of contracts to as little time as two years are important factors in deterring the more highly qualified applicants from considering posts in Nigeria. This is resulting in a decline in the quality of expatriate staff it is possible to recruit.

Public Utilities

13. The constant interruption in public utility services not only affects the morale of all employees but has a very serious impact upon the operation of the business itself. Unless reasonable and continuing supplies of electricity, water, and telecommunications can be assured, the costs related to setting up and operating escalate.

Continuity of Operating Conditions

14. The general and growing feeling of uncertainty about the continuity of operating conditions is a matter of considerable concern. It would seem that this uncertainty is engendered by a whole range of matters related to short notice changes (sometimes even retrospective) in legislation and regulations; imprecise definition of legislation and regulations, which lead to long periods of negotiation and uncertainty; delays between public announcement of measures and promulgation of how they are to be implemented; and, sometimes, inconsistent interpretation of legislation and regulations by Nigerian officials.

Bribery

15. Surrounding many of the problems previously listed is the pervasive practice of bribery, known locally as the "dash." Without such a payment, it is very difficult to complete business or government transactions with native Nigerians.

Case 24

Laval Structures Ltd.

On April 3, 1977, the bankers to Laval Structures Ltd., a Quebec-based home builder, called a meeting with the partners in Laval Structures—Jean and Pierre Montreaux. At this meeting, executives from Roy-Nat, the primary lending company, expressed their dissatisfaction with the company's performance. They wanted to know why the numerous problems had occurred and what was going to be done about the current crisis. More to the point, they announced that Roy-Nat intended to call its loans in two weeks' time unless the explanation and recovery plan were satisfactory. With this news, the Montreauxs hurriedly left the meeting.

Background

Laval Structures Ltd. commenced operations under Jean and Pierre Montreaux, owners and managers of two small companies in Laval, Quebec. The two businesses which they operated were Montreaux and Frere Construction Co., which built small houses under contract and on speculation, and Montreaux Engineering Lumber, which sold building materials and prefabricated chalets and houses. In 1959 they expanded through the purchase of a sand and gravel pit on 130 acres of land located in the area. A new company, Montreaux Gravel Pit Ltd., was formed to develop the gravel and sand business.

In 1962 they decided to expand the gravel pit operations through the purchase of new equipment for sifting and loading sand and gravel. As part of this expansion they sought and secured a loan for $150,000 from Roy-Nat. The lending company was impressed with the purity of the reserves (estimated at 1 million yards) and the integrity and good credit rating of the owners. The balance sheet of Montreaux Gravel Pit upon which they secured the loan is shown in Table 1.

The sales of Montreaux Gravel Pit Ltd. are found in Table 2. The first year of profitability for the company was in 1966 when it earned $5,000. By using the profits from their other companies, they established a reputation for prompt loan payments and good financial management.

The two other businesses of the partners were conducted through limited partnerships. The Montreaux Engineering Lumber was the more profitable and

Table 1

MONTREAUX GRAVEL PIT LTD.
Balance Sheet
November 30, 1962
(in thousands)

Assets		Liabilities	
Current assets:		Current liabilities:	
Cash	$ 4	Current	$ 24
Receivables	28	Bank loan	30
Inventory	20	Notes and liens	55
Prepaid expense	2	Total current liabilities	109
Total current assets	54		
Fixed assets:		Other liabilities:	
Land	18	First mortgage	135
Sand pit	133	Liens	78
Machinery	150	Notes (long term)	14
Rolling Stock	29	Total other liabilities	227
Total fixed assets	330	Net worth	48
Total assets	$384	Total liabilities and net worth	$384

expanding component of the business. The sales and profits of this business are shown in Table 3.

On a combined basis for all the various companies and businesses, Jean and Pierre Montreaux reported sales and profits as shown in Table 4.

The businesses were short of working capital as a result of the necessity of expanding their facilities and equipment. The cousins were, however, anxious to grow and expand. This desire for growth led them into three directions:

1. In 1967 through the Montreaux Gravel Pit Ltd., they again sought additional loans from Roy-Nat. Funds were provided which brought their outstanding loans to the original figure of $150,000. Up to 1967, loan payments had been made on schedule.

2. The Montreaux Engineering Lumber Co. began to add other prefabricated

Table 2: Sales of Montreaux Gravel Pit Ltd. (dollars in thousands)

Year	Sales
1960	$ 70
1961	192
1962	209
1963	205
1964	233
1965	259
1966	305

Table 3: Sales of Montreaux Engineering Lumber (dollars in thousands)

Year	Sales	Profits
1963	$ 715	$ 3
1964	808	5
1965	1,096	20
1966	1,741	40

components to their line of houses and chalets—premanufactured trusses and walls. The company had built facilities in the early years for the manufacture of houses and chalets. The workshop, with the new products, varied in employment from 75 to 150 people. In 1966 the company sold 100 prefabricated houses. The houses represented only one third of sales, while the trusses and prefabricated wall units represented two thirds of sales.

The original chalet model line was expanded by the addition of two standardized houses. One size was 24 feet by 36 feet, and the other was 24 feet by 50 feet. Prices varied between $8,000 and $11,000. The houses were erected by local contractors, who built foundations and installed wiring, plumbing, and heating.

3. The Montreaux Gravel Pit Ltd. planned to become the financing agent for an International Village to be erected to accommodate visitors to Montreal's Expo '67. Although this project was not funded, the company sold its components to build the Place d'Afrique at Expo '67 and a 350-room motel.

Table 4: Sales and Profits of Montreaux Businesses (dollars in thousands)

Year	Sales	Profits
1963	$1,866	$22
1964	2,651	(31)
1965	3,142	(8)
1966	Not available	47

Laval Structures Ltd.

The companies of the cousins were operated in various legal forms. Montreaux Gravel Pit was a limited company, while the other companies were partnerships. Several of the minority partners held various parts of the company through liens and mortgages. When one of the silent partners died, his estate demanded payment of the value of its interests. In order to solve these and other financing problems, in 1968 the various companies were reorganized under the name Laval Structures Ltd. In this new company Jean Montreaux held 54 percent of the shares and Pierre held 44 percent. The remaining fraction was used to settle the claims and interests of the various minority partners. Roy-Nat was approached to

Table 5: Combined Sales and Profits of Laval Structures Ltd. (dollars in thousands)

Year	Sales	Profits
1967	$3,758	$95
1968	3,976	25
1969	4,803	3
1970	4,806	35

assist in financing the new company and increased its loan commitment to $235,000. The combined sales and profits of Laval Structures Ltd. is found in Table 5.

By 1968 the company had established itself as a leading producer of prefabricated housing and components. It was estimated that it held 80 percent of the Quebec market. Its only competitor was Alcan. The housing section of the business, which had an excellent reputation as a producer of quality components, represented 70 percent of the total sales of the corporation.

Expansion and Growth

The major growth of the company began in 1970. In 1971 it formed a joint venture to build 600 homes in a community south of Montreal. This joint venture was planned to last for four years (until 1975). The venture proved very profitable and assured a steady market of about 150 homes annually. Another 200 houses were sold to a mining company. In order to meet the demand, the company began a move to shift work. The demand for houses was seasonal, and often houses could be transported and erected only during the summer months in northern areas. Nonetheless, the market for prefabricated units appeared very promising. The company, however, was unable to make substantial inroads in Montreal, where almost 62 percent of the people lived in rental quarters, but its products were sold in the suburbs.

Laval Structures foresaw a rising demand for their products. The period 1970–71 was one of increases in the number of housing starts, as shown in Table 6.

In anticipation of increased sales and markets, the plant at Laval was expanded. In 1971 the company was capable of producing 25 houses per week. In 1972 the facilities were expanded further to increase the capability to 40 units per week. A construction company was formed to work in northern Quebec, erecting the prefabricated units. This latter company purchased lots, developed subdivisions, and performed the total installation for the customer.

By 1972 Laval Structures Ltd. offered 22 different models of chalets and houses which ranged in price from $7,500 to $9,000 (F.O.B. Laval). The balance sheet of the company for December 31, 1971, is contained in Table 7.

Table 6:   New Dwelling Starts by Province (population centres of 10,000 or over)

Year	Atlantic Provinces	Quebec	Ontario	Prairies
1970	5,326	40,041	66,497	21,893
1971	7,359	42,116	78,476	32,249
1972	9,483	47,109	91,114	31,416
1973	11,963	49,169	92,211	29,510
1974	9,970	39,374	71,519	24,959
1975	11,748	43,141	67,644	32,744
1976	10,882	53,491	71,301	44,513

Source: Canadian Housing Statistics, 1979, Statistical Services Division, Canada Mortgage and Housing Corporation, Ottawa, March 1980, p. 5.

Table 7

LAVAL STRUCTURES LTD.
Balance Sheet
As of December 31, 1971
(in thousands)

Assets		Liabilities	
Current assets:		**Current liabilities:**	
Cash	$ 57	Bank loans	$ 865
Accounts receivable	1,731	Accounts payable	1,066
Inventory	763	Tax payable	87
Prepaid expenses	12	Other	109
Total current assets	2,563	Total current liabilities	2,127
Fixed assets:			
Land and buildings	578	**Long-term liabilities:**	
Reserve	(175)	Long-term debt to	
Machinery and equipment	424	shareholders	402
Reserves	(270)	Other	222
Vehicles	367	Total long-term liabilities	624
Reserves	(153)	Deferred taxes	29
Furniture and quarry	39		
Reserves	(24)		
Total	1,408	**Net worth:**	
Less: Reserves	(622)	Shareholders' equity	610
Total fixed assets	786	Total liabilities and	
		shareholders' equity	$3,390
Other assets:			
Mortgage receivable	6		
C/V life insurance	10		
Finance charges	25		
Total other assets	41		
Total assets	$3,390		

The Management at Laval Structures

The two cousins who had started Laval Structures Ltd. occupied senior-level positions in the company and continued the same management style they had used in the earlier years. Management responsibilities were shared, while the day-to-day operations were carried on by a minority shareholder in the company. A plant manager oversaw the operations of the assembly area. The success which they enjoyed permitted the owners extended southern vacations and substantially improved their lifestyles. Financial statements were prepared on an annual basis, orders were filled as they were received, and the downturn in orders was accompanied by variations in plant employment.

In 1974 Roy-Nat encouraged the owners to restructure the company. A sales manager was hired along with a controller and a production manager. However, the first appointee to the position of production manager was fired after only a few months. The lending group encouraged the company to prepare pro forma budgets and monthly financial reports, instead of the previous annual ones. The minority shareholder, who had been the effective manager of the operations, purchased the northern Quebec construction company and left Laval.

Following this brief attempt to restructure the company, the cousins resumed their past habits. There was to be no director of production or finance and no formal organization structure. They based their operational decisions and their sales efforts on their desire to grow and expand, and their familiarity with the market—even though they had no cash controls, cost records, nor market analyses.

Laval Structures Ltd. expanded its sales efforts from Quebec into the Maritimes and the United States. The company noted with pride that its buildings were approved in all 50 states. Structural units for motels, apartments, and schools were added to the product line. Sales of housing units (single-family houses) for the years 1972–1975 were as follows: 1972—1,100 units; 1973—1,435 units; 1974—1,203 units; 1975—1,076 units.

The breakdowns of dwelling starts by province and metropolitan area are found in Tables 8 and 9. Table 10 illustrates the dwelling unit type and tenure by 1976 census metropolitan areas.

The desire for further expansion led the company into the Ontario market in 1974 through the purchase of a bankrupt construction company in Kingston. The company, along with its assets and liabilities, was purchased for $1. The cousins considered this a bargain, since no initial capital investment was required. A manufacturing operation was established under a general manager. During the first year of operations the company sold 50 houses and secured a contract for an additional 200 houses. Although the company had expected to sell 500 houses and had built the plant for this level of sales, the Ontario market did not meet their expectations. In 1975 the construction company, along with the facilities for the manufacturing of homes, was sold for a loss of $1,005,000. The company felt that the general manager had not performed adequately, and he was fired. See Appendices 1 and 2 for 1973–75 financial statements.

Table 8:   New Dwelling Starts by Province by Type (population centres of 10,000 and over)

Year	Atlantic Provinces	Quebec	Ontario	Prairies
		Single Detached		
1970	2,110	11,096	13,978	7,720
1971	2,953	13,173	21,996	11,562
1972	4,926	19,414	27,818	15,173
1973	5,964	19,172	27,921	16,905
1974	5,376	20,664	22,577	16,947
1975	6,103	22,012	23,854	19,100
1976	5,463	23,219	22,617	19,641
		Apartment and Other		
1970	2,449	23,765	40,428	9,438
1971	3,129	25,972	42,544	15,439
1972	3,104	24,150	46,855	12,274
1973	4,523	27,164	45,436	10,086
1974	3,243	16,698	33,988	4,994
1975	3,704	18,729	23,664	7,999
1976	4,179	27,549	23,387	14,063
		Semidetached, Duplex, and Row		
1970	767	5,180	12,091	4,735
1971	1,277	2,971	13,936	5,248
1972	1,453	3,545	16,441	3,969
1973	1,476	2,833	18,854	2,519
1974	1,351	2,012	14,950	3,018
1975	1,941	2,400	20,126	5,645
1976	1,240	2,781	25,297	10,809

Source: Canadian Housing Statistics, 1979, p. 11.

By 1975 the construction process had become formalized and highly structured. Houses were built in halves and joined together in the field. Although the houses looked like two trailers, when joined they made an attractive small house. The company had devoted a great deal of their capital to improvements in the facilities and buildings. In 1973 the company spent $247,000; in 1974, $72,000; and in 1975, $478,000. By early 1975 the plant represented a moderate-sized factory with five separate buildings. The plant operated 16 hours per day, 5 days per week in the summer. In winter, production and employment dropped about 50 percent. At capacity, the plant employed 700 people. The major assembly work was conducted in a 65,720-square-foot building. A preassembly building of 21,415 square feet prepared components for the production line. The other buildings were used for a welding shop, storage, and offices.

The company relied upon agents in the field to sell the houses, secure lots, erect the buildings, and install the needed wiring, plumbing, and heating. Ninety

Table 9:   Dwelling Starts by Metropolitan Area

Area	1970	1971	1972	1973	1974	1975	1976
Calgary	6,740	8,801	7,047	6,981	6,487	7,872	11,360
Chicoutimi-Jonquiere	860	791	1,425	1,581	1,463	1,261	964
Edmonton	6,330	11,286	9,500	7,384	5,362	8,647	12,370
Halifax	2,343	2,551	2,540	4,181	3,095	2,708	3,499
Hamilton	4,545	5,408	8,321	8,708	5,968	6,720	5,490
Kitchener	3,075	3,905	5,349	5,054	4,085	3,380	3,926
London	2,738	5,192	5,444	3,872	3,311	3,783	3,318
Montreal	23,017	22,285	24,731	30,700	24,758	26,702	37,531
Oshawa	1,302	1,571	1,832	1,821	1,589	2,376	3,500
Ottawa-Hull	11,345	11,141	14,887	15,511	9,709	7,156	7,059
Ottawa	8,204	8,603	10,808	11,951	7,327	4,122	5,117
Hull	3,141	2,538	4,079	3,560	2,382	3,034	1,942
Quebec	6,421	8,274	8,420	4,648	3,209	4,884	5,427
Regina	418	1,307	1,304	1,366	2,271	2,982	3,070
St. Catharines-Niagara	1,810	2,814	4,219	3,937	3,233	3,195	4,167
Saint John	498	1,048	1,608	1,085	1,139	2,283	1,732
St. John's	679	1,222	1,307	1,705	1,876	2,151	1,386
Saskatoon	259	498	877	1,342	1,232	2,486	2,965
Sudbury	1,961	3,761	1,685	933	449	922	1,058
Thunder Bay	722	515	1,139	1,355	874	919	1,491
Toronto	32,423	35,209	38,695	37,697	29,580	26,457	26,555
Vancouver	13,437	15,553	16,210	17,334	14,452	13,315	16,702
Victoria	2,559	3,102	4,192	4,013	2,630	3,980	4,439
Windsor	1,956	2,214	2,983	2,033	2,602	1,643	2,002
Winnipeg	6,661	7,726	9,134	7,698	5,628	5,294	6,718
Total	132,099	156,174	172,849	170,939	135,002	141,116	166,729

Source: Canadian Housing Statistics, 1979, p. 6.

agents, who were often local contractors or building supply companies and were price-sensitive to the market demands, operated in Quebec.

The 1976–1977 Crisis

The company's sales were concentrated almost 80 percent in Quebec and 10 percent each in Ontario and the Maritime provinces. There were 25 models of homes which sold for an average price of $15,000. Since the company began operations in 1968, several other competitors had entered the field. One company was located in Quebec City, and a competitor near Montreal produced similar products. Each of these competitors was small and had not enjoyed the growth of Laval Structures. The competitors were also considered inferior in the size of their plants and facilities as well as in their variety of offerings. These companies concentrated in the house-building area and did not produce components for schools, motels, and apartment buildings. The major competitor was Atco.

In 1975 the company secured a contract for 155 furnished houses as part of the

Table 10

Metropolitan Area	All Dwellings	Dwelling Type (Percent)				Tenure (Percent)	
		Single Detached	Semidetached and Duplex	Row Housing	Apartment and Other	Owner Occupied	Rental
Calgary	155,155	58.5%	11.3%	4.9%	25.3%	58.4%	41.6%
Chicoutimi-Jonquiere	33,850	47.8	25.2	1.7	25.4	60.9	39.1
Edmonton	179,635	55.9	6.9	6.2	31.1	55.6	44.4
Halifax	81,845	48.1	12.7	3.6	35.6	55.7	44.3
Hamilton	172,515	58.8	7.1	4.9	29.1	63.8	36.2
Kitchener	87,880	53.8	10.8	5.4	30.0	60.4	39.6
London	91,770	56.1	8.1	5.8	29.9	57.8	42.2
Montreal	924,635	24.2	7.7	2.2	66.0	38.2	61.8
Oshawa	41,445	60.2	12.2	3.9	23.7	67.7	32.3
Ottawa-Hull	225,105	41.8	12.3	9.0	36.9	51.5	48.5
Quebec	164,600	36.5	12.4	2.0	49.1	46.2	53.8
Regina	49,790	66.9	5.2	2.7	25.2	65.3	34.7
St. Catharines-Niagara	97,395	69.7	9.5	2.3	18.5	72.2	27.8
Saint John	34,065	43.4	15.7	3.0	37.9	55.3	44.7
St. John's	36,800	50.2	23.2	11.5	15.1	68.5	31.5
Saskatoon	44,800	63.2	10.7	2.6	23.5	63.3	36.4
Sudbury	45,710	57.1	13.3	3.5	26.1	61.6	38.4
Thunder Bay	37,270	70.4	10.0	1.9	17.7	72.0	28.0
Toronto	909,530	39.8	13.3	4.9	42.0	55.8	44.2
Vancouver	407,560	56.9	5.8	2.5	34.8	59.4	40.6
Victoria	81,005	58.0	5.7	2.5	33.8	60.9	39.1
Windsor	80,190	67.0	8.6	3.7	20.6	69.6	30.4
Winnipeg	197,305	58.5	7.1	2.6	31.8	59.0	41.0
Canada	7,166,095	55.7%	9.4%	3.0%	31.8%	61.8%	38.2%

Source: Canadian Housing Statistics, 1979, p. 98.

James Bay Hydro Project. The joint venture in the town south of Montreal was also coming to a close.

Since 1974 the company had tried to sell its products abroad to take advantage of the rising demand for housing in Saudi Arabia and countries in South America. The cousins had made several trips abroad in search of these sales, and in late 1975 the company sold 50 houses for a new housing project in Libya and 100 houses to a South American government. The Libyan contract was expanded in early 1976 by an additional 70 houses.

In late 1975 the company was short of working capital. It requested and received a loan of $600,000 from Roy-Nat, of which $300,000 was for the plant which was built in 1975 and the remainder for the financing of contracts it had received from abroad. On the basis of its foreign contracts and expected sales in Quebec, the company prepared pro forma financial statements for 1976 which are found in Appendices 3 and 4. The order of $2.8 million from Libya and the $1.2 million order for South America are included in these figures.

Before the formal year-end financial statements were available for 1976, the company again approached its lending sources. Roy-Nat increased its commitment to $1 million. A chartered bank was approached and made a working capital loan to finance the order. This loan from the chartered bank would ultimately reach $4 million. (See Appendix 5.)

In the early months of 1977 the formal statements for Laval Structures became available. Sales of houses had totalled 694, rather than the 1,650 projected. In the first five months of 1977 the company shipped 183 houses and had total orders for 195 (including the foreign contracts).

Laval Structures manufactured 100 houses for the Libyan order, crated them for shipment, and transported the houses to the Port of Montreal for shipment in the spring of 1977. The Libyan buyers refused to honour the order and refused acceptance. The South American order was not completed.

In early 1977 the company's working capital was in serious condition. In the first three months the company lost $770,000. Roy-Nat investigated the financial affairs of the company and discovered that it had more than $1 million in accounts payable that were over 45 days old and had total bank loans and accounts payable of $7,181,623. With this knowledge, Roy-Nat called the meeting for April 3.

APPENDIX 1

LAVAL STRUCTURES LTD.
Income Statements
For the Years Ending December 31, 1973–1975
(in thousands)

	1973	1974	1975
Sales	$19,300	$19,300	$21,800
Cost of goods sold	17,700	17,400	19,800
Gross profit	1,600	1,900	2,000
Cost of transport and erection	204	275	390
Operating income	1,396	1,625	1,610
Income from joint venture	195	71	954
Total income	1,591	1,696	2,564
Expenses:			
Sales	306	462	330
Administration	738	887	1,142
Finance	170	181	374
Loss or gain on sale of assets	15	2	(2)
Total expenses	1,229	1,532	1,844
Gross profit	362	164	720
Taxes current	96	115	384
Tax credit	(2)	46	(62)
Net income	$ 264	$ 95	$ 274

APPENDIX 2

LAVAL STRUCTURES LTD.
Balance Sheets
As of December 31, 1973–1975
(in thousands)

	1973	1974	1975
Assets			
Current assets:			
Cash	$ 22	$ 21	$ 385
Accounts receivable	2,200	1,200	2,250
Notes receivable	25	10	50
Joint venture equity	101	103	284
Inventories	2,500	1,850	3,300
Advances to affiliated companies	323	935	—
Prepaid expenses	142	92	9
Prepaid taxes	92	—	—
Total current assets	5,405	4,211	6,278
Investments	16	16	6
Fixed assets:			
Land and buildings	1,775	1,825	1,400
Reserve (depreciation)	(650)	(800)	—
Total fixed assets	1,125	1,025	1,400
Other assets	30	17	284
Total assets	$6,576	$5,269	$7,968
Liabilities			
Liabilities:			
Loans	$1,700	$1,700	$ 830
Cheques outstanding	—	177	1,038
Accounts payable	2,900	1,000	3,300
Deposits	—	80	77
Tax payable	197	106	103
Deferred income tax	58	126	476
Current due on notes	151	205	235
Total liabilities	5,006	3,394	6,059
Due directors	88	74	64
Long-term debt	677	1,064	927
Shareholders' equity	805	737	918
Total liabilities and shareholders' equity	$6,576	$5,269	$7,968

APPENDIX 3

LAVAL STRUCTURES LTD.
Pro Forma Balance Sheet
For the Year Ending December 31, 1976

Assets

Current assets:

Cash	$ 463,728
Accounts receivable	2,085,000
Notes receivable	—
Joint venture equity	307,000
Inventories	2,236,250
Prepaid expenses	—
Total current assets	5,091,978

Other assets:

Investments	400,000
Other	70,441
Fixed assets	1,700,000
Total assets	$7,262,419

Liabilities

Liabilities:

Loans	—
Outstanding cheques	$ 200,000
Accounts payable	1,430,000
Deposits	75,000
Income tax payable	1,046,478
Deferred income taxes	425,000
Current due on notes	237,704
Total liabilities	3,414,182
Due directors	63,921
Long-term debt	1,120,422
Shareholders' equity and retained earnings	2,663,894
Total liabilities and shareholders' equity	$7,262,419

APPENDIX 4

LAVAL STRUCTURES LTD.
Pro Forma Income Statement
For 12 Months Ending December 31, 1976

Sales	$25,550,000
Cost of sales	22,310,000
Gross profit	3,240,000
Net cost of transportation and erection	24,000
Operating income	3,216,000
Income from joint venture	900,000
Total income	4,116,000
Expenses:	
Selling	305,044
Administration	1,036,799
Financial	362,802
Profit (loss) on sale of fixed assets	295,355
Total expenses	2,000,000
Income before taxes	2,116,000
Income taxes	996,000
Net income	$ 1,120,000

APPENDIX 5

LAVAL STRUCTURES LTD.
Balance Sheet
For 11 Months Ending November 30, 1976
(in thousands)

Assets

Current assets:

Cash	$ 27
Accounts receivable	4,468
Deposits	835
Advances to affiliated companies	463
Joint venture	65
Inventory	2,645
Other	231
Prepaid expense	53
Taxes receivable	21
Total current assets	8,808

Other assets:

Equity in affiliates	766
Cash value—life insurance	2
Total other assets	768
Total current assets and other assets	9,576
Fixed assets	2,801
Reserve	(1,011)
	1,790
Total assets	$11,366

Liabilities

Current liabilities:

Bank loans and cheques outstanding	$ 4,038
Deposits for loans	835
Accounts payable	2,471
Deposits—houses	60
Current debts—long term	234
Taxes payable	614
Total current liabilities	8,252

Other liabilities:

Long term debt	1,370
Other	93
Shareholders' loans	52
Taxes	54
Total other liabilities	1,569

Capital account:

Shareholders' equity	1,545
Total liabilities and shareholders' equity	$11,366

LAVAL STRUCTURES LTD.
Income Statement
For 11 Months Ending November 30, 1976
(in thousands)

Sales	$16,730
Cost of goods sold	12,020
Fabrication and erection	2,710
Gross profit	2,000

Cost of sales:

Sales	220
Administration	1,252
Finance	508
Total cost of sales	1,980
Gross profit on operations	20
Gain on sale of assets	15
Profit before taxes	$ 35

Living Lettuce Ltd.

In May 1985 Mr. Odin Melvaer, manager of Living Lettuce Cambridge, a small producer of hydroponically grown lettuce, was seeking financing for a new facility. Melvaer, age 64, hoped to establish an operation with a production capacity of 2 million heads of lettuce annually. This would be 10 times the size of the current facility and would make Living Lettuce easily the largest hydroponic lettuce grower in Canada.

Earlier Melvaer had visited John Dingemans, owner of Spring Time Nursery in England. Dingemans produced 4.5 million head of hydroponically grown lettuce annually with the help of a computer installation that monitored 19 separate growing parameters. This automated system, designed by Dingemans, was capable of creating ideal growing conditions for lettuce year-round and was believed adaptable to the Canadian climate.

As a result of his visit to England, Melvaer was able to verbally obtain the North American rights to Dingemans' system. Several stipulations attached to this agreement included Dingemans' right to oversee the start-up of the first operation which was required to be located at the current site in Cambridge, Ontario.

Plans were drawn up for the new greenhouse facility. However, a lack of financing was holding back construction. While the Canadian Imperial Bank of Commerce had agreed to lend Living Lettuce Cambridge $900,000, additional capital was still required, and it was decided to seek outside equity investors to finance the balance. With this in mind, Melvaer had developed a 24-page business plan and a 12-page set of detailed financial projections for presentation to potential investors. These summaries were available in two separate coil-bound reports.

Although Melvaer's initial efforts to raise private financing over the past year had been unsuccessful, he remained confident that investors would ultimately share his enthusiasm for the viability of the project. From his perspective, the two primary issues requiring resolution were whom to approach and what terms to offer them.

The section which follows is a verbatim copy of Living Lettuce Cambridge's business plan and includes excerpts from projected financial statements and the bank agreement. Section three provides additional background on the Canadian hydroponic market and other information gathered by the case writer.

This case was written by Professor Paul W. Beamish with the assistance of Mr. Richard A. Rigby. Copyright © 1986 by Wilfrid Laurier University.

TABLE OF CONTENTS

PLAN SUMMARY

To raise required capital to erect a 2⅓ acre hydroponic greenhouse.

This unit will produce over 2 million heads of lettuce at the lowest cost per head. Lettuce requires, five weeks in the summer and eight weeks in the winter, growing time from sowing to harvest.

This unit is a duplication of an existing unit (Spring Time Nursery) in England. The owner, Mr. John Dingemans, will be the consultant for the project for five years. He has already adapted this greenhouse to our Canadian climate (heavier structure due to our snow-load, heavier glass to withstand hail, etc.). The greenhouse will be insured for hail and snow damage.

His operation and financial statements (for last four years) are available for your inspection. What we are going to do here has been a successful operation in England for four years.

* page numbers refer to those in original business plan.

Business Plan
Page 1

489

Not only will we be producing the best lettuce in Canada, but tomatoes, cucumbers, spinach and peppers, as well.

Also we will we be expanding into the fresh herb market which should increase our sales by 30% but only increasing costs by about 8% (250 restaurants at $30.00 per week). No one in presently supplying fresh herbs in Ontario on a year-round basis. Distribution will be done by existing dry herb company.

Our team has at least four years of successful production and sales of these products that no one else has in Ontario and in the United Kingdom.

WHAT IS LIVING LETTUCE?

In 1977 the Canadian Company LIVING LETTUCE LTD., Grand Valley, Ontario, started to develop a completely independent method for growing lettuce, vegetables and herbs on a hydroponic basis.

By 1979 the development of this special hydroponic process had advanced to the point that the Company LIVING LETTUCE CAMBRIDGE was able to start growing and selling lettuce on a commercial basis, approximately 200,000 heads of lettuce per year are produced. (greenhouse size - 300 ft. by 25 ft).

At the beginning of this year LIVING LETTUCE LTD. finalized a cooperation agreement with one of the most experienced European Producers of hydroponic lettuce (Spring Time Nursery), with the goal to utilize the research work of both companies and to build large scale greenhouse facilities on the North American Continent.

Founder and President of LIVING LETTUCE LTD. and initiator of the special "Living Lettuce Hydroponic Growing System" is Mr. Paul Hilger, Toronto, Canada. Mr. Paul Hilger has agreed to contribute to the Investment Company his complete Know How, the established Registered Tradename of "Living Lettuce" as well as the Lettuce Production Plant in Cambridge, known as LIVING LETTUCE CAMBRIDGE.

BUSINESS PLAN FOR LIVING LETTUCE CAMBRIDGE

BUSINESS DESCRIPTION

Hydroponic Greenhouse—300′ × 400′ (Production Area). To produce 2 million head of lettuce annually. Customers to include A&P, Dominion and Safeway also better class restaurants in Toronto, Kitchener and area. Living Lettuce Limited using three experimental greenhouses have developed a system of hydroponically growing lettuce using Dr. Cooper's nutrient film technique. After 4 years of research and development in Grand Valley a new model house was built at Cambridge (April 1982). This house produces more lettuce (250,000 hd/yr) than the combines production of the other three (these have since been torn down). Living Lettuce Cambridge

Business Plan
Page 2

has now been producing for two years. In 1984 Living Lettuce Cambridge increased production by 25%. This was possible by further refinement of our growing techniques and qualified staff.

In our staff we have an Agronomist, Kathy Harder, University of Guelph graduate in Horticulture. She has three years experience in greenhouse growing in England. She is very competent and conscientious.

Odin Melvaer has two years mechanical enginnering at Queen's. He joined the RCAF (in 1943), three years architechture at the University of Toronto, and was employed as technical representative for Fiberglass Canada Ltd. for 7 years and Flintkote for 5 years.

He managed and eventually owned a polystyrene manufacturing plan in Toronto (Perfoam). He developed foam insulation, distribution and sales to all lumber yards in Ontario. He owned a small beef farm north of Toronto (Charlois and Hereford cattle). He also owned a small country hotel in New Dundee from 1972 to 1974. After selling, he was sales engineer for Duriron Canada Ltd. until 1981. Since then he have been involved with Living Lettuce.

Along with the day to day management of the greenhouse we have developed a new and better system of feeding the lettuce. We have assisted in developing better carbon dioxide distribution and we are working on an air-to-air heat exchanger, to better control humidity in the greenhouse.

Financing of Living Lettuce Cambridge has been by Mr. Hilger and myself. Living Lettuce Cambridge is a limited partnership between Mr. Hilger 75% and myself 25%.

Mr. Paul Hilger is Chairman of the Board and sole owner of Kalander-walzenfabrik, Bauart ECK Hilger & Co., Dusseldorf. The company has been established since the late 1800's. The company's world wide sales are approximately $5,000,000 per year.

MARKET ANALYSIS

Ontario imports 207,000,000 lbs. of lettuce yearly from California and Mexico. It is of inferior quality does not keep well, has a bland taste, ⅓ is thrown away, must be washed (for pesticides and fungicides) and the retail price varies from $0.60 to $1.49 per head. A combination of two factors will make imported lettuce prohibitive during the next decade; the cost of transportation will double and the shortage of water will eliminate many of the present producers. Also two tons of ice are shipped in each rail car load of lettuce leaving California.

In contrast our lettuce is grown in a controlled environment. All liquids are treated with ultra violet to control bacteria and fungi. You do not even wash Living Lettuce.

The lettuce is packaged in a plastic bag complete with its roots and 1½ ozs. of nutrient which is why we call it *"Living Lettuce"*.* It will keep in a cooler or a refridgerator for 10 days. You just take the plastic bag and lettuce and put it in a mug or glass (to keep it upright) and store. When required just pull down the plastic bag, use what is required and return to the fridge. There is no waste, you just enjoy! (*Registered Trademark)

We are not affected by weather, hence, our production is consistent and forecastable. We produce our product all year. We can deliver biweekly. Due to our location (on Highway 401) the A&P, Dominion and Safeway trucks go right by the greenhouse coming back from deliveries to Western Ontario empty, this will cut out costs of delivery.

Over the last twelve months we have worked closely with Mr. Jim Diodadi—Produce Manager of the A&P Company. We developed a special metal rack to display our lettuce in 100 of their stores. Attached was a sign explaining the nature of the product. We found from our market analysis that people will pay for quality and products free from chemicals. Our product sold at prices from $1.29 to $1.49 while local lettuce was priced at $0.69 to $1.19. We were shipping 200 cases per week (all we could spare) at $0.80 per head. We subsequently imported similar lettuce from England and sold to the market at the same price for a profit.

With this new large (2½ acre) greenhouse we will be able to reduce cost per head by 50%. We will continue to sell our "carriage trade", the restaurants at $1.00 per head and our chains at $0.80 per head. This translates into a guaranteed top quality product, ample and consistent supply at a fixed price for twelve months. Lettuce now becomes a headache the *chef and produce buyer does not have*.

MARKET SIZE AND TRENDS

From Statistics Canada—imported vegetables are:

	1981	1982	1983
Lettuce	202,285	195,510	207,540
Tomatoes	108,284	100,820	139,575
Cucumbers	32,390	27.234	31,610

NOTE: Figures are/1,000 lbs.

From these figures our projected sales of 2,000,000 is about 1% of total lettuce imported. since this includes all types of lettuce, we are going to have to educate the public into buying our Boston Bibb Lettuce in preference to California Iceberg Lettuce.

By analysis we can show (see previous page*) our lettuce is much 2igher in mineral content. The flavour is much superior because it is always fresh. With our costs remaining fairly stable and with the increasing cost of transportation, the future looks very encouraging.

Business Plan
Page 4

A STATEMENT OF PRINCIPLE

Living Lettuce is grown totally WITHOUT pesticides and fungicides. Instead, we made our solar greenhouses insect-proof by installing mesh screens across all air intakes, and sealing all gaps and seams. Fungi are eliminated by illuminating the irrigation water with the ultraviolet part of the solar spectrum. We have followed this policy successfully since we started in 1977.

Our Living Lettuce is also totally free of dust, dirt, sand, grit, industrial pollution and atmospheric fallout, since we grow it in a closed environment. Because of this, and because washing leaches nutrients and flavour from the lettuce leaf, we recommend that our lettuce NOT be washed before serving.

Our lettuce is raised in a mixture of peat moss and limestone, fed with well water and pure mineral nutrients. These comprise Epsom salts, natural gypsum, potash, etc., plus chelated minerals (iron, zinc, boron, copper) of the type used as food supplements for human nutrition. As a result of these ideal growing conditions, Living Lettuce has a consistently higher content of dry matter, fiber and trace minerals than typical imported lettuce:

Mineral Analysis of Lettuce (average % of dry matter)	Imported Lettuce	Living Lettuce
Phosphorus	0.450%	1.000%
Potassium	3.250%	13.000%
Calcium	1.500%	2.000%
Magnesium	0.500%	0.700%
Zinc	0.005%	0.008%
Iron	0.006%	0.010%

Analysis by the Plant Analysis Laboratory, University of Guelph, Ont.

It is an indication of our reputation for clean and pure lettuce that we at Living Lettuce Limited have been asked by the Canadian Organic Certification Organisation (C.O.C.A.) to assist in writing the standards for greenhouse lettuce.

It is no surprise that food as pure and nutritious as our Living Lettuce also tastes better. Try it and see why our lettuce has been the exclusive choice of 60 of the finest restaurants in Toronto and area since early 1979.

LIVING LETTUCE

RR#33   Cambridge   Ontario

N3H 4R8   (519)-653-7951

Business Plan
Page 5

To compare the present (imported) field grown Boston Bibb used in Ontario is not realistic. The heads are very small, the quality is poor and the price is high, around the $1.00 range. From experience we know when "Living Lettuce" is available in an A&P store, even at $1.49, the imported Boston does *not* sell.

Using our past history with A&P, Dominion and Safeway stores and keeping in mind they sold this lettuce anywhere from $1.29 to $1.49, both Dominion and A&P sold 200 cases per week. Since our supply was limited only certain stores actually received the product; the average for 40 stores was five cases per week. With unlimited supply and some advertising by the chains we should be able to bring this average up to seven cases per week (they now average 156 cases Iceberg per week). Using 125 stores at seven cases per week × 52 weeks = 45,500 cases **OR**

455,000 hds.	A & P
200,000 hds.	Dominion
100,000 hds.	Safeway
600,000 hds.	Loblaws
150,000 hds.	Misc. Zehrs, Dutch Boy, Red & White, etc.
1,505,000	TOTAL

A New York marketing firm did a market survey of New York and Toronto and there are 6,000 top quality restaurants in New York City compared to 600 in Toronto, there must be another 600 in the surrounding area.

For four years we have been servicing restaurants such as Fentons, Harbour Castle and King Edward, who average about 15 cases per week. If we can cover 600 of them this amounts to 600 × 15 cases weeks × 10 hds/case = 468,000 heads per year.

Well within our delivery range are the cities of Buffalo and Detroit with tremendous potential.

COMPETITION

Living Greens:

In Orangeville—standard Westbrooke Greenhouses—about half our present capacity.

Mike Adamson and ?. He worked at Living Lettuce Ltd. in Grand Valley for two years, was in charge of maintenance and drove the truck on deliveries. He sells to restaurants in the Orangeville area and Toronto. He also sells at the Food Terminal. He has attempted to take some of our bigger accounts by price cutting but we have retrieved them (King Edward, Four Seasons, CN Tower).

ADVANTAGES OF LIVING LETTUCE

— tastes better
— no washing or preparation required
— more nutritious
— keeps longer
— yearly supply
— not affected by weather
— free of pesticides
— free of fungicides

PRODUCT DESCRIPTION

— a living product — lasts longer
— needs no washing
— no pesticides
— no fungicides
— no waste
— superior taste
— available yearly
— competitively priced

PROPRIETARY POSITION

—Our six years experience in Nutrient Film Technique (NFT) lettuce growing at Grand Valley.

—Our further experience gained at Living Lettuce Cambridge on lettuce, tomatoes, cucumbers and herbs over the past two years we have developed the system to give us a two year advantage.

—By hiring Mr. John Dingemans as our exclusive consultant we have access to his four years lettuce experience, not only for his knowledge of NFT, but also his greenhouse has been computer controlled for four years.

The records show his growing and harvesting system produces top quality lettuce (their standards are much stricter than ours) at the lowest per head cost.

OTHER BARRIERS TO COMPETITORS ENTRY

This system of growing using the Nutrient Film Technique was developed in England by Mr. Allan Cooper in 1972. It differs from other hydroponic systems in that the nutrient is continuously flowing over the root system of the cultivar. Previous systems had the nutrient pumped up to the root system at intervals to try to

Business Plan
Page 7

imitate the way the rain is exposed to the root system in the field. Dr. Cooper's system was ridiculed at its inception because people felt the roots would die due to a lack of oxygen.

His system has since proven itself to these growers who use his system and adapted it to their particular conditions, i.e. light intensity, well water and rain water analysis, temperature (maximum and minimum), crop desired and market demands.

Once you have solved those problems (it can take six months), then you must "fine tune" the nutrient system (it is adjusted twice a month, once you know what you are doing) to adequately feed the plants but not allow a salt build-up in the root system. Also humidity and temperature are vital; humidity to allow transpiration and temperatures are to be kept at ideal levels day and night.

To all of this, you add the growers inane sensibility to the atmosphere in the green house which tells him something is not right before the alarm system is aware there is a problem.

Through using the NFT system we have learned that plants react differently in a NFT greenhouse than in a field. They are healthier, more disease resistant, more forgiving of human mistakes and more tolerant of temperature extremes (we have produced *good* lettuce at 95 degrees fahrenheit in the greenhouse for five days).

RESEARCH AND DEVELOPMENT ACTIVITIES

We have produced tomatoes, cucumbers, three other types of lettuce, peppers, spinach and herbs on a test basis.

Leaf Lettuce of various types can be grown now—Romaine and other types of Head Lettuce are about one year off (this is the word we get from Holland where the seed development is being done). The lettuce we are now growing took seven years to develop. Tomatoes, peppers and cucumber seeds are available now. Spinach is also about one year away.

This brings us to herbs. We have been growing several different varieties (basil, chives, parsley, water cress, dill, etc.) and are almost ready to go into production of the most popular ones.

Since fresh herbs are not available during winter in Canada as yet, we have been working with a green house operator in New York City. He started growing lettuce but switched to herbs because of the demand. The business grew so quickly he is now building a 14 unit Dutch Greenhouse ($1.1 million) to meet demand and in the meantime he is importing from California and New Zealand.

REGULATORY REQUIREMENTS

As yet we have no lettuce board and lets keep it that way. Since all our crops are edible we are classified as an agricultural business with the inherent tax advantage thereof.

PRODUCT EXTENSION

Although our first greenhouse will be predominantly lettuce (herbs will be grown in pots suspended from pipes between columns), we can foresee our future units in other areas growing, three types of lettuce, cucumbers, tomatoes and herbs. This will increase revenue per square foot of greenhouse and shorten delivery distances.

MARKET STRATEGY

Restaurants

We will use our herb production as the "door-opener" for our lettuce. Not all restaurants use Boston Lettuce now (a lot more of them will be in the near future) but they *all* do use herbs and we will be able to supply them fresh *all* year.

Chain Stores

In order to familiarize the public with "controlled environment" products we propose to set up in all the produce departments one specific counter for top quality organically grown product, free from pesticides or fungicides. These units will be sectional so when you have four products available (lettuce, tomatoes, cucumbers, peppers), you use four units. The counter will be properly labelled (standard logo) so that the public become aware of the inherent quality, taste, etc. that is common to all hydroponic produce and hence will pay a higher price for them.

TARGET MARKETS

As previously mentioned under market analysis we have forecast our sales to our major chains as follows:

A & P	455,000 hds	6,000,000 hds
Dominion	200,000 hds	3,000,000 hds
Safeway	100,000 hds	1,500,000 hds
Loblaws	600,000 hds	9,000,000 hds
Misc.	150,000 hds	2,000,000 hds
	1,500,000 hds	21,000,000 hds (potential)

A & P alone sell about 6,000,000 heads of Iceberg Lettuce annually now; so with some co-operative promotion and advertising we should be able to get more than 1%.

PRICING

As previously stated we will sell to restaurants at $1.00 per head and the chain store at an average of $0.80 per head. During peak production (April-October) we will sell grocery stores at $0.70 per head and during the winter months (November-March) at $0.90 per head.

We now have the option of selling all of restaurant lettuce "Kouri Foods Inc." at $0.80 per head (See letter of intent). Mr. Paul Kawaja, owner of Kouri Foods will pick up the lettuce in Cambridge and delivery to all his existing customers in Ontario and Quebec. His other company "Vienna Meats" is now servicing about 500 restaurants in Ontario.

ADDENDA TO EXPORTS

From our location on the 401 highway at Cambridge, we can economically service Buffalo, Cleveland and Detroit. They purchase more than

$25,000,000 lettuce annually,
41,000,000 tomatoes annually,
15,000,000 cucumbers annually.

With the new greenhouse, we can supply these markets twelve (12) months a year and compete on price with California imports. California lettuce costs 15 cents to produce and 20 cents to ship to the U.S. Eastern Seaboard (35 cents U.S. = 45 cents Cdn.) Our cost F.O.B. Detroit is 15 cents per head Canadian.

CHICAGO

Since most transports are now privately owned, they book their loads through a broker. The pay-load is the outgoing trip and they are willing to take a return load for expenses. Since there are many loads coming in from Chicago, we can ship the lettuce back at the reduced rate. At this rate, it costs 0.002 cents per head to export a full load of lettuce to Chicago.

There is a successful five(5) acre hydroponic lettuce greenhouse in Decator, Illinois which sells its total production to two(2) food chains in Chicago.

SALES PLAN

We will not be through distributors except for the food terminal during peak production periods.

We will use our driver as our salesman for the restaurants. The contract sales will be handled by myself.

Business Plan
Page 10

PROMOTION

Restaurants:

Using the herb as the entry, we feel sure this will help to vastly increase the number of restaurants using our lettuce. Once we have adapted sections of the greenhouse for cucumbers and tomatoes, they also will assist in expanding our restaurant base.

Chain Stores:

Here we must allocate a budget work in conjunction with the chains to convince the public to try our lettuce.

STEP 1

Displaying lettuce with our existing wire racks and new signs—we must stress:

taste	available all year
quality	constant price
no waste	Canadian grown
no pesticides	no fungicides

STEP 2

Special TV spots using the same type as Loblaws are using now—having a Vice-President show the product and stress its Canadian origin.

Also explaining our present dependence on U.S. production for many of our daily vegetables. If we do not encourage Canadian production, these vegetables will become prohibitively expensive. If we can just get 5% of the market (10,000,000 heads) we will need four more greenhouses.

Continuous working with the District Managers of the chains to explain to their staff what "Controlled Environment" is all about. Checking displays, it is important to train them to display about ½ of the expected sales, to keep the product looking fresh and attractive.

SERVICE OPERATION

Location:

Right on Highway 401 and next to Doon-Blair exit. All our major customers' trucks go right by our greenhouse returning to Toronto empty.

Business Plan
Page 11

499

Within a 100 km radius we have the Toronto, Hamilton, Guelph, Kitchener, Stratford, London, etc., an enormous market.

Cambridge has been hit hard with company closures and hence unemployment is very high. There are a lot of good personnel available who would appreciate a permanent and interesting job.

Our major suppliers are Plant Products in Toronto, ASB in Kitchener and Millbrook Warehouse in Millbrook, easy access for our truck to pick up supplies, rather than pay freight. Since we are classified as an agricultural and a small business we are taxed accordingly.

Again our utility costs will be based on volume and on an agricultural rate.

Facilities and Equipment:

Since we are in essence duplicating Mr. John Dingemans' operation in Stotfold, England (ours will be a trifle smaller, 62 houses vs 40 houses), as you can see by the copies of quotations enclosed, all the equipment required for the efficient operation of the greenhouse have been included. Mr. Dingemans and I spent two days at the greenhouse manufacturers factory in Holland to go over every detail. Naturally all the latest developments in the industry will be included. Thicker glass, heavier structural members (for snow load in our climate), larger and more automatic opening windows (for better cooling), larger main gutters to drain off snow melt, reverse osmosis water system, etc.

Our computer will be identical to Mr. Dingemans' so we will be able to exchange directly any problems.

The enclosed list of equipment and building required demonstrate the thoroughness and the attention to detail we exercised in pricing this project.

Since the floor of the greenhouse will actually be the beds where the lettuce will grow we have retained J.T. Donald consulting Engineers. They will supervise bore holes on the site and write complete specifications for the concrete slab including the expansion joints. They will specify the epoxy topping and supervise its placement.

The greenhouse itself will be completely erected, including heating, cooling, ventilation and operating by V & V Noor-Dland's branch from New York. The manual labour will be hired locally and be subsidized by the government.

MANAGEMENT AND ORGANIZATION

Chairman of the Board: Mr. Paul Hilger

Consultant—Mr. John Dingeman who has owned and operated profitably the identical operation in England. He will also oversee the construction of the greenhouse and its operation for five years. This will be done by telestar transmitted computer data.

Manager—Mr. Odin Melvaer, who has managed Living Lettuce Cambridge for two years. My duties include greenhouse supervision, sales to both restaurants and chains, product development with the chains (display racks and signs), and research and development of other products (tomatoes, cucumbers and herbs, etc.).

Supervisor (*Agronomist*)—Kathy Harder. She has been responsible for the day to day operation of Living Lettuce Cambridge, including growing tomatoes and other types of lettuce and herbs.

Office Manager—Mrs. Lorraine Melvaer. She has been responsible for the company's books, inventory control, weekly delivery, production and personnel.

Staff—We presently have two full-time persons and two part-time people to form the nucleus of the staff we will require. Our present driver-salesman will continue to deliver to restaurants.

ODIN MELVAER—General Manager

I joined Living Lettuce Limited in 1981 and worked with Helmut Julinot for one (1) year on sales promotion.

For two (2) years, assisted in the design of certain phases of the new greenhouse. This included CO_2 enrichment, new grow lights, and trough design. Also supervised construction of the greenhouse.

Once the greenhouse was completed, I was responsible for crop production, sales at both levels (chain stores and restaurants).

After encountering numerous lettuce leaf problems (brown edges, poor colour, deformaties), I developed a new nutrient feeding system using reverse osmosis water. This has eliminated leaf problems and greatly simplified quality control. Our production this year is up 25%.

By using a heat recovery system developed in conjunction with the University of Waterloo, we can now effectively reduce the humidity in the greenhouse and reduce our heating costs by 20%.

Business Plan
Page 13

Dr. Alan Cooper (responsible for developing the NFT system) has agreed to assist Living Lettuce in setting up the first installation of his new hydroponic system for tomatoes and cucumber production in North America.

TIMING

First Month —prepare site and put in foundation for ancillary building
　　　　　　　—order greenhouse
Second Month—erect ancillary building
Third Month —unpack containers containing greenhouse components and store in ancillary building
　　　　　　　—erect greenhouse
Fourth Month —pour slab and seed
Fifth Month —plant greenhouse
Sixth Month —IN PRODUCTION

FINANCIAL INFORMATION

How Much Money Do We Need?

First Month

Existing Greenhouse and Tech.	$300,000	
Land Purchase	100,000	
site preparation	14,000	
consulting engineers	3,500	
well	2,500	
propane installation	2,500	
greenhouse & chiller	70,000	
misc. (office, phone, etc.)	7,500	
	$500,000	$ 500,000

Second Month

ancilliary building	$140,000	
wages, etc.	20,000	
	$160,000	$ 160,000

Third Month

consulting engineers	$ 3,500	
ancilliary building bal.	100,000	
misc. (salaries, etc.)	50,000	
greenhouse (trucks)	420,000	
	$573,500	$ 573,500

Fourth Month

concrete slab	$350,000	
N.F.T. Equipment	11,200	
	$361,200	$ 361,200

Fifth Month

piping	$ 10,000	
computer	60,000	
misc.	40,000	
greenhouse	420,000	
	$530,000	$ 530,000

CONSTRUCTION TOTAL:		$2,124,700

BREAKDOWN OF GROWING FACILITIES

V & V Noorland Greenhouses	$ 750,000
Computer and Installation	60,000
Soil Block Making Machine	5,500
Fork Lifts	11,000
Boilers	60,000
JT Donald Consulting Engineers	
—Floor Slab	7,000
Diesel and 20′ Insulation Van	34,000
	26,000
Compost Mixer	3,200
NFT Piping	10,000
NFT Equipment	3,000
Vacuum Chiller	80,000
Filters	5,000
TOTAL	$1,054,700
Contingency Fund	80,000
	$1,134,700 $1,134,700

ANCILIARY BUILDING

Existing Greenhouse and Technical Knowledge	$ 300,000	
Ancillary Building	240,000	
Foundation and Slab	350,000	
Property Purchase	100,000	
Total	990,000	$ 990,000
		$2,124,700

A & P REPORT

This document has two main objects:

1) To justify a completely separate space for the best quality produce available. Hydroponically grown fruit and vegetables not only qualify as to quality, but are predictible and reliable. In order to assist A&P this continuity of supply, we must

know what produce of this standard is available; where it is available and how much A&P would need.

Once these products have been located and scheduled, they must be readily recognizable. This can be done by a large, bright green plastic logo, having a symbol or phrase identifying it. The symbol "Q-1" comes to mind. Both shipper and receiver will be able to identify the produce and give it the attention it requires.

2) To establish the market for these products so we can intelligently plan future greenhouse sizes and locations so that Ontario can produce these products. Dr. Frank Schales, Associate Professor of Horticulture, University of Maryland, in his presentation pointed out, that the same care must go into the packaging, storage and shipping as goes into production. This will require training of A&P's receiving staff and the airlines handling crew.

While at the International Hydroponic Conference in Honolulu, we met with representatives of many of the world's largest fruit and vegetable growers (Dole, Pepperidge Farms, D.R.A. (5 acres under glass, growing various vegetables.) We also made contact with two companies in Japan, one produces strawberries hydroponically, the other, mushrooms and different types of sprouts (radish, watercress and endive.) Dr. Takakura assured me they are looking for business. From the Dutch representative we was given names of their best hydroponic growers. Their products include peppers, egg plant, leeks, radishes, strawberries, cucumbers and tomatoes. From England we can buy strawberries, tomatoes and cucumbers. Other countries we made contact with were; Israel (some of the most exotic plants I have ever seen; in their own hydroponic pots, complete with a light underneath making the plant a work of art), Italy and Australia.

From the above paragraph, you can see that continuity of supply, variety and quality are available. It only requires someone to co-ordinate the requirements of A&P, both as to quantity and timing. This would ensure a continuous supply of the best quality produce for the designated "Q-1" display counter all year. Since all of these products are grown in controlled environment greenhouses, their supply should be extremely reliable. Monthly promotions can be scheduled well in advance to take advantage of market conditions.

In order to establish the viability of a special area for our "Q-1" products, I conducted a small demonstration at "Mr. Grocer" in Waterloo March of 1985. We set up a suitable display of our lettuce, provided a mild salad dressing and asked customers to sample the lettuce. I also had a display of hydroponic herbs (Sweet Basil and Parsley), which was sampled by the customers. We wound up selling all the Parsley and Sweet Basil.

Approximately 150 people filled out the attached questionnaire. From these people we learned the following:

Business Plan
Page 17

505

71%	had not tried hydroponic products before.
97%	said they would like to try our lettuce.
100%	described the product as excellent in taste and appearance.
86%	said they would expect to pay more for quality hydroponic products.
100%	favoured a separate department in produce to feature "Q-1".
93%	would like to see a variety of hydroponic fruits and vegetables.
96%	wanted more information on hydroponics.

HONOLULU HYDROPONIC CONFERENCE

While attending the Worldwide International Conference on Hydroponics in Honolulu from February 18 to 22, 1985, I was priviliged to not only meet Dr. Allen Cooper, but also to spend about two hours with him, discussing his revolutionary new simplification of "N.F.T." Nutrient Film Technique is the system we are presently using at Living Lettuce. His presentation outlined the progress that Ariel Industries (the company he is now representing) has made during the last 5 years.

I will not go into great detail of his new system now, except to point out that this modified N.F.T. system has been symplified to such a degree, that it can now be successfully used in the Third World. With the boon of this application to their food production the potential is staggering. One of the crops that has been especially successful has been potatoes.

I asked Dr. Cooper if this new method would also apply to lettuce production. His immediate reply was an emphatic NO! This new system has been primarily designed for crops that have three stages in the growth cycle; vegetative, blossoming and fruiting. After explaining to him that we were in the final stages in our proposed greenhouse expansion, I asked him if he would take the time to look at our Business Plan. After taking a cursory glance at the plan, he had two comments to make. 1) our consultant, Mr. Dingemans, was an exceptionally qualified and financially successful grower and 2) our choice of greenhouse (V&V Noorland) was excellent.

Dr. Cooper devised the Nutrient Film Technique and the existence of N.F.T. cropping is to a great extent due to his persistence and determination in the face of initial scepticism. With the spread of N.F.T., his experience has become international, ranging from N.F.T. tomato and cucumber cropping under artificial light in Alaska to the production of N.F.T. hybrid Napier grass for feeding the milking herds in India.

He is, undoubtedly, the world's foremost authority on Nutrient Film Technique.

N.B. Plan Summary from p.1 was repeated on p.24 of Business Plan.

BANK AGREEMENT*

Introduction

Canadian Imperial Bank of Commerce takes pleasure in being afforded this opportunity to present the following banking services proposal to Living Lettuce Toronto. Our proposal is based on the recent information which you have kindly made available to us and we have assumed that this information fairly reflects your business and financial circumstances.

No doubt our approach to credit accommodation and account operation is of prime importance to the Firm. Accordingly, we have devoted particular attention to these matters and trust you will find the related commitments to your complete satisfaction. We have also taken this opportunity to familiarize you with some of the various other banking services which are available and which could be readily adapted to your requirements should you so desire.

Of prime concern to us is our ability to provide new and existing customers with the best possible service and assistance. In this regard, it is our view that the Commerce has the expertise and level of qualified personnel to effectively accomplish this and therefore we look forward with confidence to the prospect of being appointed the Firm's banker in the near future.

Credit Arrangements

The following credit facility has been approved at the pleasure of the Bank and is subject to normal annual review, next scheduled for September 30, 1986, or sooner should conditions so dictate:

Limits

1. $ 50,000.00   Demand Loan (Operating Loan)
2. $100,000.00   Farm Improvement Loan
3. $750,000.00   Fixed Rate Farm Loan
4. $ 10,000.00   Corporate Visa Account.

Interest Rates and Other Charges:

1. The Bank's Prime Lending Rate, plus ¾%, payable monthly, not in advance.
2. The Bank's Prime Lending Rate, plus 1%, payable monthly, not in advance.
3. The interest rate and other conditions specific to Fixed Rate Farm Loans are to be established immediately prior to drawing down the funds. The current rates are as follows:

* This was on Bank letterhead paper.

Business Plan
Page 19

1 year term	11.25%
2 year term	12.25%
3 year term	12.75%
4 year term	13.00%
5 year term	13.25%

4. $20.00 per card plus standard interest rate as set out in the cardholder agreement.

Summary

The Bank is sincere in its desire to be appointed Banker for Living Lettuce Toronto. We are prepared to do whatever is necessary to ensure you will benefit from a decision to conduct your banking business with the Commerce.

The personnel at Main & Water Streets, Cambridge branch have the experience to handle the Firm's account in an efficient and professional manner, and look forward to establishing a long and mutually beneficial association.

Your acceptance of the terms of this banking proposal should be in writing and reach us on or before December 31, 1985, after which date, if not accepted or extended by mutual agreement, this proposal shall automatically lapse without further notice.

Our thanks are extended to you again for the opportunity to present this proposal. Please contact the undernoted should you want to discuss anything further.

Mr. Hubert A. Will	Mr. Len Van Geest
Manager	Account Manager
Main & Water Streets	Main & Water Streets
Cambridge, Ontario	Cambridge, Ontario
(519) 621-5030	(519) 621-5030

Business Plan
Page 20

508

Ernst & Whinney   Chartered Accountants

706-101 Frederick Street
PO Box 2757
Kitchener, Ontario N2H 6N3

519/578-8540

COMMENTS ON FINANCIAL PROJECTIONS

Mr. P. Hilger and Mr. O. Melvaer
Living Lettuce

We have reviewed the accompanying financial projections of Living Lettuce
dated March 22, 1985, consisting of annual projected balance sheets as at
May 31, 1986 to 1990 and annual projected income statements, projected
statements of changes in financial position and projected statements of
cash flows* for the five years ended May 31, 1986 to 1990. Our review
consisted primarily of enquiry and comparison together with such test of
compilation as we considered necessary in the circumstances.

Based on our review, in our opinion, these financial projections are compiled
on the basis of the assumptions and accounting policies disclosed in the
accompanying notes.

We do not express an opinion as to whether the results for the projection
period will approximate those projected because the financial projections
are based on assumptions, made by management, regarding future events which
by their nature are not susceptible to independent substantiation.

In accordance with the terms of our engagement, we have no responsibility
to update our review for events occurring after the date of our comments.

March 22, 1985   *Ernst & Whinney*

* Not included in case

509

PROJECTED BALANCE SHEETS
LIVING LETTUCE

			May 31		
	1986	*1987*	*1988*	*1989*	*1990*
ASSETS					
CURRENT ASSETS					
Cash	$ 444,700	$1,248,900	$2,085,400	$2,950,850	$3,853,300
Accounts receivable	36,600	39,000	40,200	44,400	45,600
Inventory	46,500	52,800	54,700	57,500	59,500
	527,800	1,340,700	2,180,300	3,052,750	3,958,400
PLANT AND EQUIPMENT					
Existing facility	300,000	300,000	300,000	300,000	300,000
New facility	1,453,700	1,453,700	1,453,700	1,453,700	1,453,700
	1,753,700	1,753,700	1,753,700	1,753,700	1,753,700
Less accumulated depreciation	116,500	273,400	430,300	587,200	744,100
	1,637,200	1,480,300	1,323,400	1,166,500	1,009,600
DEFERRED CHARGES	24,000	18,000	12,000	6,000	—
	$2,189,000	$2,839,000	$3,515,700	$4,225,250	$4,968,000
LIABILITIES AND INVESTORS' EQUITY					
LONG-TERM DEBT	$ 777,600	$ 734,800	$ 685,400	$ 628,800	$ 563,700
INVESTORS' EQUITY					
Capital investment	1,200,000	1,200,000	1,200,000	1,200,000	1,200,000
Retained earnings	211,400	904,200	1,630,300	2,396,450	3,204,300
	1,411,400	2,104,200	2,830,300	3,596,450	4,404,300
	$2,189,000	$2,839,000	$3,515,700	$4,225,250	$4,968,000

APPROVED BY:

_____Mr. P. Hilger

_____Mr. O. Melvaer

See significant management assumptions

PROJECTED INCOME STATEMENTS
LIVING LETTUCE

	Year Ended May 31				
	1986	*1987*	*1988*	*1989*	*1990*
Sales	$946,000	$1,655,200	$1,708,800	$1,767,000	$1,826,000
Cost of sales					
Inventory, beginning of year	—	46,500	52,800	54,700	57,500
Material purchases	94,100	133,800	139,300	145,500	151,100
Direct labour	178,200	217,200	223,600	232,000	239,300
Overhead expenses	177,300	182,800	189,500	197,100	205,100
	449,600	580,300	605,200	629,300	653,000
Inventory, end of year	46,500	52,800	54,700	57,500	59,500
	403,100	527,500	550,500	571,800	593,500
Gross profit	542,900	1,127,700	1,158,300	1,195,200	1,232,500
Expenses					
Selling, general and administrative	103,440	118,720	121,240	123,820	126,420
Consulting fees	31,560	53,280	54,660	56,130	57,630
Depreciation	116,500	156,900	156,900	156,900	156,900
Interest on long-term debt	80,000	106,000	99,400	92,200	83,700
	331,500	434,900	432,200	429,050	424,650
NET INCOME	$211,400	$ 692,800	$ 726,100	$ 766,150	$ 807,850

See significant management assumptions

PROJECTED STATEMENTS OF CHANGES IN FINANCIAL POSITION
LIVING LETTUCE

	Year Ended May 31				
	1986	1987	1988	1989	1990
SOURCES OF FUNDS					
From operations					
Net income	$ 211,400	$ 692,800	$ 726,100	$ 766,150	$ 807,850
Charges to income not involving working capital					
Decrease in deferred charges	6,000	6,000	6,000	6,000	6,000
Depreciation	116,500	156,900	156,900	156,900	156,900
TOTAL FROM OPERATIONS	333,900	855,700	889,000	929,050	970,750
Increase in bank loan	800,000				
Equity investment	1,200,000				
TOTAL SOURCES OF FUNDS	2,333,900	855,700	889,000	929,050	970,750
APPLICATIONS OF FUNDS					
Repayment of bank loan	22,400	42,800	49,400	56,600	65,100
Additions to plant and equipment	1,753,700				
Deferred consulting fee	30,000				
TOTAL APPLICATIONS OF FUNDS	1,806,100	42,800	49,400	56,600	65,100
INCREASE IN WORKING CAPITAL	527,800	812,900	839,600	872,450	905,650
Working capital at beginning of year	—	527,800	1,340,700	2,180,300	3,052,750
WORKING CAPITAL AT END OF YEAR	$ 527,800	$ 1,340,700	$ 2,180,300	$ 3,052,750	$ 3,958,400
WORKING CAPITAL IS REPRESENTED BY					
Current assets	$ 527,800	$ 1,340,700	$ 2,180,300	$ 3,052,750	$ 3,958,400

See significant management assumptions

SIGNIFICANT MANAGEMENT ASSUMPTIONS
LIVING LETTUCE
June 1, 1985 to May 31, 1990

The following significant management assumptions form an integral part of the accompanying financial projections. These assumptions are not an all-inclusive list of all assumptions used in the preparation of the accompanying financial projections and all assumptions used were based on information with respect to circumstances and conditions existing as at March 22, 1985. Actual results will vary from the accompanying projections and the variations may be material.

A. Equity Assumptions

Living Lettuce will be organized as a limited partnership.
Equity investment of $1,200,000 will be obtained.
Debt financing of $800,000 at 14% on a five year term loan basis, amortized over 10 years will be obtained. Blended principle and interest payments will be $12,400 per month.
All income is retained in the partnership and no distribution is made to the partners during the projected period. No interest is earned on excess cash in the business.

B. Investment Assumptions

The existing greenhouse facility will be purchased by Living Lettuce for $300,000.
The new greenhouse facility will be constructed at a cost of $1,453,700.
Construction will commence June 1, 1985, with the first crop being harvested November 1, 1985.
Exchange rates are 3.20 Dutch Guilders equals $1.00 U.S. and $1.00 U.S. equals $1.30 Canadian.
No capital expenditures are required during the projected period.

C. Sales Assumptions

Existing facility
The existing facility will produce lettuce until October 1985 when it will be converted to herb production and research and development. Revenue from herb production is $6,000 per month in the first year and increases 10% per year thereafter.
New facility
Lettuce production is at the rate of 2,000,000 heads per year for the first two years. A ready market is assumed for this production. Revenue is defined as follows for the first two years:

SIGNIFICANT MANAGEMENT ASSUMPTIONS—Continued
LIVING LETTUCE

C. Sales Assumptions—Continued

| | | April–October | | November–March | |
Sales to	Percent of Volume	Percent of Production	Selling Price	Percent of Production	Selling Price
Restaurants	25%	65%	$0.80	35%	$0.80
Grocery stores	75%	65%	$0.70	35%	$0.90

All prices are F.O.B. facility.
Increases in production and prices will produce a 3% annual revenue increase in years three to five.
General
Receipts of sales revenue is 75% in month of sale, 20% in subsequent month and 5% in second subsequent month.

D. Costs of Production Assumptions (New Facility)

Materials
Material costs are at an annual rate of $120,000 in the first year and are incurred in relation to production.
Material costs increase 3% in year two and 4% annually thereafter.
All purchases are paid in the month incurred.
Labour
Labour costs are at an annual rate of $160,000 in the first year and are incurred in relation to sales revenue.
Labour costs increase 2% in year two and 3% annually thereafter.
Labour costs are paid in the month incurred.
Overhead expenses
Repairs and maintenance are $2,000 per month for three years and increase 2% annually thereafter.
Utilities are at an annual rate of $120,000 in the first year and increase 5% thereafter.
Land is leased on a five year lease with a five year renewal option at an annual rate of $14,400 for the first five years.
Overhead costs are paid in the month incurred.

D. Costs of Production Assumptions (New Facility)—Continued

Selling, general and administrative expenses
The manager's salary is $36,000 per year for five years, plus 2% of sales from the new facility.
Other expenses are at an annual rate of $50,000 in the first year and increase 3% annually thereafter.
Selling, general and administrative expenses are incurred evenly through the year and are paid in month incurred.
Other costs
The consultant is paid a $30,000 retainer plus 3% of sales from the new facility.

E. Accounting Policies

Living Lettuce will be organized as a limited partnership and accordingly is not liable for income taxes. Income taxes are the responsibility of each investor.
Depreciation is on a straight-line basis over the estimated useful lives of the facilities, which are estimated as follows:

Existing facility - 5 year life
New facility - 15 year life

The initial consulting fee of $30,000 is deferred and amortized over five years, the life of the consulting agreement.

All amounts are stated in Canadian dollars.

Section III: Additional Information

This section contains additional information regarding various aspects of the business plan which Melvaer could bring to the attention of potential investors.

1. The Ontario Lettuce Market

The total amount of lettuce imported through the Ontario Food Terminal in 1985 was 100,584,000 pounds. This converted to 48,280,320 head of lettuce (24 head = 50 pounds). During 1985 the price of lettuce ranged from a low of 54 cents per head to a high of 91 cents at the Ontario Food Terminal. The average price was 68 cents. Using the average price, $32,830,617 of lettuce was imported through this terminal in 1985.

Melvaer estimated that 85 percent of the lettuce imported was California iceberg. This strain of lettuce had been developed over 30 years. Iceberg lettuce was developed to withstand long transportation hauls with the lettuce packed in ice to keep it fresh. The market had grown accustomed to its crispness and would be hard pressed to substitute its use in certain applications. In salads, for example, iceberg lettuce was ideal because it kept longer than hydroponic lettuce. On the other hand, hydroponic lettuce was suitable for short-term applications such as sandwiches. Melvaer felt that iceberg lettuce could be hydroponically grown within two years.

2. The Food Store Market

According to Mr. Jim Diodadi, VP-Produce, A&P Food Stores, inconsistent delivery and insufficient supply of hydroponic lettuce were the major problems experienced by A&P. As a result of these problems, local store outlets often turned to their own, typically local, source of supply for hydroponic lettuce instead of counting on supplies from the central warehouse in Toronto. In 1985 A&P stores were dealing with four suppliers of hydroponic lettuce, and Diodadi felt that all four, including Living Lettuce Cambridge, were trying to develop processes that would provide them with a reliable product at a low cost. Diodadi aimed to secure a reliable supplier who could provide enough quality lettuce at a low cost for all of A&P's requirements. A&P's needs alone could exceed 500,000 heads annually with the support of an aggressive marketing effort.

Diodadi considered Living Lettuce Cambridge a prime candidate for becoming A&P's major supplier of hydroponic lettuce if it was capable of increasing capacity and reducing costs. This would be a natural extension of the existing joint effort by both Living Lettuce Cambridge and A&P in the design and installation of special display racks for hydroponic lettuce in over 200 A&P outlets. According to Diodadi, this concept could be developed further to other hydroponic vegetables, and a separate produce section could be set up with special display racks installed for hydroponic products.

Melvaer foresaw Living Lettuce using a promotional film clip in vans stationed at A&P outlets to educate the public about the benefits of hydroponically grown lettuce. In addition, the staff at A&P produce outlets would be taught the benefits of this product and how it should be displayed and cared for.

One A&P produce manager stated that in terms of hydroponic lettuce, leaf lettuce usually outsold Boston Bibb by 2 to 1. This manager calculated that on average, A&P could sell 20 cases of hydroponic leaf lettuce weekly when sufficient supplies were available.

3. The Restaurant Market

Living Lettuce Cambridge was supplying approximately 35 restaurants. Melvaer calculated that these restaurants would purchase close to 200,000 head of lettuce annually. Some hotels, such as The Prince in Toronto, had been importing lettuce by flying it in from Holland for up to $4 per head. Melvaer stated that Kouri Foods Inc. (acting as a distributor for Living Lettuce) would help Living Lettuce Cambridge increase its share of the restaurant market. Apparently Kouri Foods dealt with 600 restaurants in Ontario and 500 in Quebec. Therefore, by selling produce to Kouri, Living Lettuce would have a distributor who would be able to potentially increase its restaurant customers to 600 at 15 cases per week.

Melvaer saw the sale of fresh basil and other herbs to restaurants in the middle of February as a good lead-in to lettuce sales. After the new hydroponic facility was constructed, Melvaer planned to use the existing building for growing herbs.

4. The Competition

According to Melvaer, many hydroponic producers of lettuce had gone out of business. He cited a lack of process knowledge, financial problems, and poor marketing as reasons for a low success rate in Canadian hydroponics.

Melvaer saw very little competition and believed there were maybe three "mom-and-pop" operations in the area. Two producers of hydroponically grown lettuce—Hilltop Gardens in Aylmer and the Strathroy Lettuce Factory—serviced the London, Ontario, market, 50 miles west of Living Lettuce Cambridge.

5. Hydroponic Vegetables

Diodadi felt there was a bright future for hydroponically produced vegetables. He pointed to the fact that, for health reasons, customers were concerned about the high use of fungicides on field crops as a prime reason for a shift to hydroponic produce. The natural flavour of hydroponic vegetables was another quality consumers were increasingly demanding, said Diodadi.

Apparently A&P had approached the Federal Ministry of Agriculture to lend their support for hydroponic producers. Diodadi stated that funding, possibly in the form of grants, was needed to develop hydroponic growing in Canada. The major benefit for Canada would be the development of year-round vegetable production. This would alleviate the high dependence on imported produce during the winter months. According to Diodadi, the government was receptive although no programs had been announced.

When asked specifically about Living Lettuce Cambridge, Diodadi spoke positively about its efforts to lower costs through the acquisition of Dingemans' automated system. He recognized that Spring Time Nursery was a pioneer of hydroponics in Europe through the development of an automated growing system and felt that Canadian hydroponic producers had to cut costs to learn to grow efficiently before hydroponics would begin to experience the growth potential he foresaw. Living Lettuce Cambridge would be able to benefit in these areas with the implementation of Dingemans' system, according to Diodadi.

Tomatoes, cucumbers, spinach, and peppers had been produced hydroponically in Holland and imported to Canada. Melvaer felt that Living Lettuce Cambridge would be producing these other vegetables, in addition to lettuce, within three years. He stated, however, that this would not be attempted until the new lettuce operation was running efficiently and was competitive with California and Mexican imported lettuce.

6. Paul Hilger's Plans

Paul Hilger was trying to divest his equity position in Living Lettuce Ltd. and Living Lettuce Cambridge. He cited other commitments as the reason for this and felt that he could not devote time to the operation of this company. He would sell his equity in both companies for $100,000 when new investors were secured and an additional $100,000 within one year of that date. Melvaer was attempting to convince him to keep some of the $200,000 invested in stock of Living Lettuce Ltd.

7. Equity Financing

Malvaer felt that an $800,000 investment would likely secure 25 percent equity in Living Lettuce Ltd. and probably a majority share of Living Lettuce Cambridge. This, however, was completely negotiable. Melvaer would want to maintain operational control of the Cambridge operation. If Hilger continued his plans to completely pull out of Living Lettuce, the only equity holders would be the new investors and Melvaer.

8. Additional Living Lettuce Sites

Living Lettuce Ltd. would receive an up-front fee, a five-year management contract, and a percentage of equity in any additional sites. Melvaer felt that one year (depending on background) would be needed to train the operator of a new Living Lettuce operation.

Exhibit 1 provides several illustrations of the Living Lettuce Cambridge operation.

Exhibit 1

Mr. Odin Melvaer
with lettuce halfway
through the
growing cycle.

Packing
operation.

Living Lettuce
Cambridge.

Magna International Inc.

By mid-1986 annual sales of Magna International Inc. were projected to top $1 billion for the first time. As Canada's largest manufacturer of automotive parts, Magna's corporate objectives of having an average of $100 of its auto parts built into every North American car was also in sight.

Although company founder Frank Stronach and his management team continuously espoused a "small is beautiful" philosophy, their dreams for Magna were by no means small. Stronach stated in 1985 that he was intent on creating "one of the largest corporations in North America" and that he felt Magna could maintain 30 percent annual growth for many years. By 1986 it was also clear that Magna was committed to a strategy of increased internationalization of its operations. These goals clearly raised questions about the appropriateness of Magna's current operating philosophy and organization for the planned growth.

Frank Stronach and Magna International

In 1985 Magna's flamboyant chairman and chief executive officer, Frank Stronach, was the highest-paid executive in Canada with a salary of $1.85 million. Many felt this was justified given Magna's almost unprecedented 30 percent annual growth in sales and profits over the last 15 years. Exhibit 1 provides financial statements from Magna's 1985 annual report detailing the company's financial performance.

The company in its original form was founded in 1957 by its controlling shareholder, Chairman and CEO Frank Stronach. By 1986 it employed more than 7,500 people in approximately 65 Canadian and 5 American plants and in 1 additional plant in West Germany. In 1984 75 percent of sales were to U.S. customers. Magna's primary customers were the various operating divisions of Ford, General Motors, Chrysler, and AMC—the "Big Four" North American auto manufacturers. In fact, 95 percent of their products went into North American cars.

The history of Magna was really the entrepreneurial life story of Frank Stronach, who immigrated to Canada from Austria in 1954. Trained as a tool and die maker, Stronach invested what little savings he had and opened up his own

This case was written by Paul W. Beamish and William Webb, School of Business and Economics, Wilfrid Laurier University. Copyright © 1986 by Wilfrid Laurier University.

Exhibit 1

10-Year Financial Summary

Magna International Inc.
(Canadian dollars in thousands except per share figures)

	1985	1984	1983	1982	1981[1]	1980	1979	1978	1977	1976
Operations Data										
Sales	**$690,400**	$493,559	$302,451	$226,534	$232,114	$183,456	$165,738	$128,189	$80,953	$55,010
Income from operations	**69,430**	57,124	25,473	9,055	12,054	9,249	15,924	12,899	8,185	5,734
Net income[4]	**43,191**	31,480	14,647	5,265	6,911	5,640	8,455	6,595	4,093	2,786
Extraordinary items						(1,922)	272	795		
Basic earnings per Class A and Class B share[2,3]	**$2.00**	$1.93	$1.10	$0.49	$0.64	$0.34	$0.89	$0.80	$0.48	$0.36
Fully diluted earnings per Class A and Class B share	**$1.93**	$1.85	$1.07	$0.44	$0.57	$0.33	$0.78	$0.68	$0.47	$0.32
Depreciation	**24,322**	15,044	11,267	9,325	9,188	6,154	4,506	3,349	2,210	1,416
Cash flow from operations	**85,974**	55,945	32,522	14,604	14,672	12,052	15,275	13,160	7,542	5,171
Dividends declared per Class A and Class B share[2,3]	**$0.48**	$0.31	$0.13[5]	$0.13	$0.18	$0.18	$0.14	$0.10	$0.06	$0.03
Financial Position										
Working capital	**64,121**	79,804	48,291	31,792	30,792	28,223	19,174	15,351	7,412	4,925
Capital expenditures	**222,878**	110,239	29,806	17,434	21,052	23,630	23,085	16,231	8,584	3,456
Fixed assets (Less accumulated depreciation)	**357,371**	179,817	87,388	70,553	74,074	62,629	47,089	30,269	19,387	8,940
Long-term debt	**103,997**	96,497	42,159	55,554	56,308	45,830	30,441	19,588	10,238	4,627
Equity relating to Class A and Class B shares	**297,935**	143,566	81,590	41,071	39,631	33,792	32,086	23,270	15,226	9,646
Equity per Class A and Class B share[2,3]	**$12.44**	$8.43	$5.59	$4.13	$3.84	$3.35	$3.18	$2.41	$1.68	$1.25

[1] *1981 and prior figures include sales and income from Aerospace/Defence operations sold effective August 1, 1981.*
[2] *Adjusted for years prior to 1979 to give effect to the capital reorganization during 1979.*
[3] *1983 and prior figures adjusted to give effect to the stock dividend issued June 1983.*
[4] *Before extraordinary items.*
[5] *In addition, stockholders received a special stock dividend issued June 1983.*

tool and die shop in a rented Toronto garage while still in his mid-20s. Business was good in the first two years, and Stronach soon employed 30 people. When his foreman told him that he wanted to leave and start his own business, Stronach offered the man part ownership in the business in order to keep him. The foreman stayed and set up the company's second tool and die shop. This was the first glimmer of what was to be part of Magna's future strategy for corporate growth — decentralization with equity participation by its employees.

Stronach summed up his feelings and reasons behind the philosophy: "If I lose a good person, I'm losing somebody who could be a competitor. I want those people in my camp. That's what business is all about—people management."

By 1969 Stronach owned eight plants that were run autonomously. In order to implement a plan to facilitate employee share ownership, he merged with the publicly traded Magna Electronics Corporation, substituting *International* for the word *Electronics* to reflect the company's broad range of products and greater ambitions.

For the next 15 years Magna grew almost continually at an annual rate of 30 percent or more and by 1985 was opening one new factory every six to eight weeks to keep pace with demand. Its product lines had grown to over 4,000 different components and assemblies, encompassing parts for nearly every section of the automobile. Exhibit 2 provides a list of product families manufactured by each of Magna's operating groups in 1984. Some products were manufactured to customer specifications while others were designed by Magna's staff and sold as original equipment based on their innovative designs.

The Magna "Success Formula"

Magna consistently performed well in the cyclical auto-parts industry whose performance followed the auto industry's traditional four-year up-and-down cycle. One investment analyst commented that Magna had "the best growth record and highest returns on equity in the business." Exhibit 3 provides a brief analysis of the auto-parts industry and shows Magna's financial performance in comparison with three other major auto-parts manufacturers.

Many explanations were offered to explain Magna's unequalled success. In the end, however, it seemed to boil down to the company's ability to manufacture the highest quality product at the lowest possible cost.

Some observers, including Magna's management and, especially, Frank Stronach, attributed its success to Magna's unique "corporate culture" whose key elements were embodied in the company's "Corporate Constitution," published for the first time in Magna's 1984 annual report. The stated purpose of the constitution was to "define the rights of employees and investors to participate in the company's profits and growth and impose discipline on management." Stronach thought that Magna might be the only company in the Western world with a corporate constitution which guaranteed employee rights and imposed discipline on management. Exhibit 4 shows the Magna Corporate Constitution, and Exhibit 5 gives some excerpts from the 1985 annual report that demonstrate the constitution in practice at Magna.

Other critical components of the corporate culture included a commitment of keeping all Magna plants small with a maximum of 100 employees each, an emphasis on research and development, and rewards for both management and

Exhibit 2: Magna Product Directory

CMT Group:

Seat track mechanisms
Window winding regulators
Hand brake assemblies
Hood hinges
Door hinges

Door latches
Hood latches
Trunk latches
Clutch and brake pedal assemblies

Decorative Products Group:

Front bumper and grille fascia
Rear bumper fascia
Rocker panels
Wheel house opening mouldings
Window channels
Weather strip channels
Headlamp retainers
Centre hood mouldings

Windshield mouldings
Rear window mouldings
Drain trough mouldings
Exterior window mouldings
Tail light bezels
Rocker panel mouldings
Body side mouldings

MACI Group:

Cooling fan motors
Heating fan motors
Windshield wiper motors
Immersible fuel pumps
Thermostatic air controllers
Magnetic capsule switches

Relay switches
Instrument clusters
Fuel control devices
Electronic tone and voice
    synthesized alarms
Electronic fluid level devices

Magna Manufacturing Group:

Aluminum bumper reinforcements
Shock absorber towers
Rear cross members
Fuel tank straps
Sill plates
Scuff plates
Alternator fans
Motor mounts
Canister support brackets

Glove box doors
Seat belt anchors
Heat shields
Catalytic converters
Thermostat housings
Water pumps
Instrument panel supports
Headrests

Maple Group:

Poly V crankshaft pulleys
Power steering pulleys
Alternator pulleys
Automatic Poly V belt tensioners
Water pump pulleys

Compressor pump pulleys
Two speed accessory drive system
Oil strainers
Oil pick-up tubes
Dip-stick tubes

Exhibit 3: Market Overview

The auto-parts market can be divided into eight sections. Passenger car, light truck, medium and heavy truck, and off-highway vehicles give the four major sections, and each of these can be broken into original equipment (O.E.) and aftermarket. A further subdivision could be made in aftermarket between the original equipment aftermarket and the third-party aftermarket. That subdivision is not considered here.

Most auto-parts companies cover more than one segment, so companies can be competitors with some products and not with others. Competitors also depend upon whether a company is in the original equipment market or aftermarket. Canadian aftermarket firms concentrate on the Canadian market because of the duty collectible in crossing the Canada-U.S. border. Original equipment, on the other hand, is duty free under the autopact, and therefore firms in both Canada and the United States compete for this business.

The business cycles for original equipment and the aftermarket tend to be counter-cyclical. When new vehicle sales are down, the sales of replacement parts tend to be up, thereby giving some protection to firms that are in both market segments.

The companies below have the following characteristics:

Budd Canada	Passenger	O.E. and aftermarket
	Light truck	O.E.
Hayes-Dana	Passenger car	O.E. and aftermarket
	Light truck	O.E. and aftermarket
	Medium and heavy truck	O.E. and aftermarket
	Off-highway vehicles	O.E. and aftermarket
Magna International	Passenger car	O.E. and aftermarket
	Light truck	O.E. and aftermarket
Long Manufacturing	Passenger car	O.E. and aftermarket
	Light truck	O.E. and aftermarket
	Medium and heavy truck	O.E. and aftermarket
	Off-highway vehicles	O.E.

Industry Overview for 1984

Sales of cars and light trucks again increased by 19 percent. The market for other trucks and off-highway vehicles did not improve.

Statistical process control and just-in-time delivery were taken up by the whole auto-parts industry. The new threat to the auto-parts industry was the statement from the manufacturers that the supplier base was to be cut 50 percent within three years to reduce their overhead in dealing with suppliers and to increase control.

Budd Canada in 1984

Budd had a good year in 1984. Sales increased by 36 percent, and net profits were $11.2 million compared to 1983's loss of $2.2 million.

Exhibit 3 (*continued*)

This was due to several factors:

- General administration expenses were kept under control and resulted in expenses as a percentage of sales of only 8 percent compared with their historical average of about 10 percent.

- Cost of goods sold was reduced even lower than the 1980 level (81.2 percent compared with 84.9 percent in 1980). This was the result of the fully utilized Kitchener plant which in turn was because of the increased sales and productivity gains made with the recent plant additions.

Budd not only showed a good profit in 1984, they also outperformed the market in terms of the net profits/net sales ratio. Their return on investment ratios compared favourably with the industry averages.

The working capital management ratios show that Budd compares favourably with other companies. Aggressive management of accounts receivable shows a decrease in days receivable from 78 to 58 days.

Liquidity and solvency ratios show an excellent position.

Hayes-Dana in 1984

The year 1984 saw Hayes-Dana sales increase by 31 percent and profitability increase by 170 percent. The favourable picture comes from

- Improving the cost of goods sold percentage by 3.5 percent of sales, resulting in a favourable variance of $11.9 million.

- Depreciation expense was not at the 1983 levels, resulting in an additional favourable variance of $2.5 million. This plus the increase in investment income were offset by increased operating expenses of a full 1 percent of sales, resulting in an unfavourable variance of $3.9 million.

Days receivable again continued to increase, in a year where all other manufacturers studied managed to reduce their collection period. Inventory turnover improved but still lagged the industry. These working capital items accounted for $24 million of the funds available. As well, plant additions of $9 million and an increase of investment in affiliates used the funds raised from increasing current loans and other liabilities and from increasing long-term debt.

The end-of-year inventory at Hayes-Dana was higher than in other companies. Cost of goods sold was improving but was not at the level Budd had achieved.

The $9 million plant addition in 1984 should improve their operating expense ratio in upcoming years. It would be reasonable to assume that Hayes-Dana could achieve the 81 percent cost-of-goods-sold level that Budd and others have achieved.

Magna in 1984

Magna's sales increased 63 percent in 1984, and net profits more than doubled. Magna obtained more than its share of the improving market in 1984, when we see the other companies' sales increase somewhere from 30 to 40 percent. The very favourable net

Exhibit 3 (*concluded*)

profit results can be explained by the management of operating expenses. Operating expenses as a percent of sales dropped from 85.3 percent to 74.9 percent; this level of operating expense reduction was not achieved by any of the other three companies.

Accounts receivable management was excellent, reducing the days receivable from 68.8 days to 63.9 days, the lowest it had been since 1980. It still remained significantly higher, however, than the other companies studied.

Inventory management resulted in a slight drop of inventory turns; the result was, however, well within the results obtained by the other companies studied.

Plant expenditures for the year totalled $107 million; this obviously had a good effect on the operating expense reduction discussed above. The plant expansion was funded by an increase in long-term debt of $54 million and a stock offering which raised an additional $35 million.

At year-end 1984, Magna is in a favourable liquidity and solvency position relative to the other companies studied.

Long Manufacturing in 1984

Long's sales increased to $49.5 million, up 39 percent from 1983. Return on equity at 41 percent was the best of the companies studied.

Long was driving down debt. The success was shown in the long-term debt to total assets ratio, dropping to the low of the group of companies studied, and the common stock equity to total assets ratio, rising to a more usual level of 26 percent. This was achieved by paying off $6 million of the $7 million of long-term debt and an additional $1.1 million of current debt.

The current ratio remained at 1.1, and the quick ratio dropped slightly to 0.5. Accounts receivable were brought down to 35 days, and inventory turns rose again, up to 9.3, both better than the other three companies.

workers through an attractive profit-sharing plan and a range of social benefits from day care for employees' children to a recently opened company-owned conservation and recreation area.

Organization and Operating Structure

Exhibit 6 illustrates and describes Magna's unique operating structure which consisted of three levels of responsibility: the operating unit, group management (in charge of an operating group), and executive management.

At the operating unit or individual factory level, maximum employment was kept to no more than 100 workers because of Stronach's belief that management and employees should maintain close working relationships and that smaller units sparked individual initiative and a degree of entrepreneurship. Stronach felt that a "family relationship" should exist among co-workers and management with each person knowing the name of all his fellow employees.

Exhibit 4

Magna's Corporate Constitution

Board of Directors
Magna believes that outside directors provide independent counsel and discipline. A majority of Magna's Board of Directors will be outsiders.

Employee Equity and Profit Participation
Ten per cent of Magna's profit before tax will be allocated to employees. These funds will be used for the purchase of Magna shares in trust for employees and for cash distributions to employees, recognizing both performance and length of service.

Shareholder Profit Participation
Magna will distribute, on average, 20 per cent of its annual net profit to its shareholders.

Management Profit Participation
In order to obtain a long term contractual commitment from management, the Company provides a compensation arrangement which, in addition to a base salary comparable to industry standards, allows for the distribution to corporate management of up to 6 per cent of Magna's profit before tax.

Research and Technology Development
Magna will allocate 7 per cent of its profit before tax for research and technology development to ensure the long term viability of the Company.

Social Responsibility
The Company will contribute a maximum of 2 per cent of its profit before tax to charitable, cultural, educational and political institutions to support the basic fabric of society.

Minimum Profit Performance
Management has an obligation to produce a profit. If Magna does not generate a minimum after-tax return of 4 per cent on share capital for two consecutive years, Class A shareholders, voting as a Class, will have the right to elect additional directors.

Major Investments
In the event that more than 20 per cent of Magna's equity is to be committed to a new unrelated business, Class A and Class B shareholders will have the right to approve such an investment with each class voting separately.

Constitutional Amendments
Any change to Magna's Corporate Constitution will require the approval of the Class A and Class B shareholders with each class voting separately.

(Copies of the complete Constitution can be obtained from the Corporate Secretary's office.)

Exhibit 5:   Excerpts from 1985 Annual Report: Corporate Constitution in Practice

Magna's continued growth is based upon our unique corporate culture which allows the company to make a better product for a better price.

Our culture recognizes that it takes three ingredients to be successful in business, namely: management, employees, and capital. Furthermore, it requires that each of these ingredients has a right to share in the profits that it helps to generate. This foremost principle and other operating principles are enshrined in Magna's Corporate Constitution.

We in management continuously search for ways to stimulate employees to achieve greater productivity. In recent years this has been partially accomplished through the introduction of new technology. At Magna we continue to emphasize the human capital as we introduce technology in a manner that does not result in the displacement of employees. We are focusing on productivity improvements through new technology as a means of continuing to upgrade wages for production employees in the years ahead while maintaining our competitive position in the marketplace.

Management's primary responsibility is to demonstrate to employees that we care for their well-being particularly with regard to wages, environment, safety in the workplace, fairness and equal opportunity for advancement. We are committed to these principles and intend to strengthen further our Human Resources department to make sure that our standards are maintained. A structure like this can only function through total openness. It is an education process. In our view the employees must fully understand the competitive factors facing the company as well as the facts surrounding our financial structure. I like to see employees reading the financial section of the papers in the morning, realizing that they are shareholders of Magna. In fact, at this stage, our manufacturing and office employees own more than $30 million of Magna stock.

Members of management are also large shareholders in the company. The value of their shares amounts to approximately $30 million, and accordingly, they have an interest in protecting the value of their investments. It is important for a healthy, growing company to have a strong equity base in relation to debt, but we are sensitive to the effect of equity dilution on our ability to maintain investor confidence. Accordingly, we try to balance issues of new equity with growth in earnings per share.

Sales growth translates into the need for new production facilities. As a result, Magna's investment in land and buildings continues to increase. Management utilizes Magna's job creation capability to obtain favourable terms when purchasing land. We also seek joint venture partners to assist in the development of those lands. Our objective is to minimize Magna's capital outlay for land so as not to divert capital from our automotive components manufacturing activities.

Quality Assurance

Quality is stressed throughout Magna—our success has been built on it—our future depends on it. We continue to train employees at all levels in matters relating to quality including the use of sophisticated measuring devices and statistical process control techniques. As a result of efforts in the area of quality, our operating units received many quality awards from our customers. Magna is dedicated to supplying automotive components and systems which are "world class" in quality and value.

Exhibit 5 (*continued*)

Human Resources

Magna's greatest asset is its motivated work force. We continuously strive to provide a positive, safe, and fair environment for all employees.

With this in mind we continue to expand our Human Resources department at the group and corporate offices and sponsor seminars which stress the importance of good communications between management and employees. Wherever possible, productivity gains are recognized with improved wages and expenditures to improve the working environment.

During the year we introduced "Magna People," a bimonthly newsletter about Magna and its people. Simeon Park, which opened officially in June 1984, saw the introduction of many employee organized functions, both winter and summer. The allocation to our Employee Equity Participation and Profit Sharing Program amounted to $8.3 million in 1985 compared to $6.4 million last year.

Other Employee Programs

We provide a number of other programs for our employees including the following:

A. Simeon Park

Magna has developed a recreational park on 100 acres of natural countryside just north of Toronto. This park, available to all Magna employees and their families, features a 23-acre lake, sports and recreation facilities including children's playgrounds, tennis and volleyball courts, soccer fields, a baseball diamond, barbecue pits and picnic areas, nature trails, fishing docks, and a large swimming pool.

The park is readily accessible to the majority of Magna's employees. During 1985 it was used extensively for company picnics, competitive team sports, and casual family outings.

B. Industrial Campus Concept

To provide employees with an improved work environment, Magna is developing an industrial campus which will consist of a cluster of 10–20 small autonomous plants together with the related group office and product development centre supported by social and recreational facilities such as day care, a medical office, and educational and sporting facilities.

In 1985 three new plants went into production in our first campus being developed in Newmarket, Ontario. A new group administration office and product development centre associated with these plants also opened during the year. Two additional plants were under construction at year-end. Land for other campuses is being assembled in preparation for our future growth.

Exhibit 5 (*concluded*)

C. Technical Training Centre

Consistent with our commitment to high-quality in-house technical strength, Magna opened its first technical training centre in the fall of 1984. The school is equipped with modern classroom and shop facilities and the latest in machinery and equipment.

On completion of their training, apprentices will work in a Magna operating unit to complete the requirements for trade qualification.

The purpose of the centre is to help fulfill Magna's demand for skilled tool and die makers and other technical trades. These students will also receive training in management practices.

D. Continuing Education

Magna encourages all employees to improve continually their skills and education. For this reason, we offer in-house training and education in areas of communication, safety, quality control, microcomputer applications, and management skills.

Social Responsibility

Magna believes it has a responsibility to support the basic fabric of society. We fulfill this obligation by giving financial assistance and contributing our time to programs and projects in the areas of health and welfare, youth, the advancement of art and culture, education, and in support of the political process. Examples of the programs we support include:

A. University Teaching and Research Support

Magna currently provides financial support to four universities for teaching and research concerning entrepreneurship and fair enterprise.

B. Student Sponsorship

Each year Magna sponsors a number of outstanding students to attend the GMI Engineering and Management Institute in Michigan. GMI is a private university offering degrees in engineering and industrial administration.

Sponsorship guarantees students financial support and planned work assignments in Magna plants as well as the offer of a full-time position with Magna upon graduation.

"Communication is very important. If you have a few thousand people under one roof, you need a hundred thousand rules. You lose the human touch. You create a faceless kind of management," said Stronach, adding that Magna's environment simply created "a damned good atmosphere to work in!"

Every Magna factory was unique in its own right, with its own product mandate, R&D department, and production and profit objectives established by

Exhibit 6: Operating Structure

Operating Unit

Each operating unit is directed by a general manager and an assistant general manager who have complete authority and responsibility for the operation of their unit within broad guidelines established by executive group management. These decentralized units generally employ approximately 100 people thus giving the management teams close contact with staff and immediate control of all matters affecting personnel, product quality, efficiency, and profitability of the unit.

Group Management

The operating units are grouped—geographically and by markets—under the direction of a group management team which is accountable to executive management. A group vice president is responsible for all areas of activity in his group and is supported by marketing, financial, and human resources executives.

Each group has its own sales team which maintains the day-to-day contact with the customers, the group office, and the operating units.

The group financial staff monitors all financial activities including capital spending and operating results. Each group has its own quality control and human resources personnel which review the operating unit's performance and serve as a resource to the units.

Group management also oversees research and technology development conducted for their group.

Executive Management

Executive management is responsible for establishing policies consistent with the company's philosophy as developed by the board of directors.

Strategic planning is a priority of executive management. This involves the identification of specific products and technologies that Magna must develop in order to meet the challenges of an evolving marketplace. It also includes the establishment of management teams capable of implementing Magna's marketing, quality, human resources, and financial goals and objectives. As part of its responsibilities, executive management secures and allocates financial resources and, together with group management, monitors the performance of the operating units.

The corporate office serves as a resource to the groups and operating units in the acquisition of capital equipment, raw materials, and services.

This system allows the groups and operating units to benefit from Magna's corporate buying power when it is to their advantage. However, responsibility for product quality and delivery rests with each operating unit, and accordingly, the units make purchases from whatever source best meets their individual requirements.

Exhibit 6 (*concluded*)

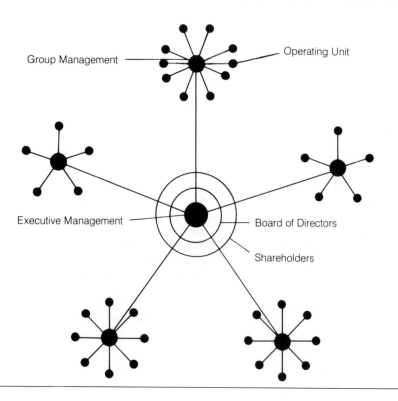

that unit's management team. Every employee had access to management, and since each earned shares in the company through a profit-sharing plan, they were likely to come forward with assembly-line suggestions to improve quality or cut costs—suggestions that could lead to promotion, more profits to share, and increased equity participation. The small scale of each unit's operations and Magna's emphasis on factory-floor technical skills (promoted by in-house technical education and upgrading programs) resulted in a high degree of flexibility and an ability to adapt quickly to changes in manufacturing operations.

Growth at the operating unit level, as for all levels of Magna, was somewhat "organic" in nature, rather than "planned" in the traditional sense. When a particular unit (factory) could no longer keep pace with demand and was running three shifts of 100 people on a 24-hour schedule, the unit's general manager would be allowed to build a second factory. If more factories had to be built for a common product line, these might eventually form the basis of a new management group with the former general manager as group vice president. As this suggests, Magna had a rather unusual and interesting method of delegating responsibility and controls between the executive management, group management, and the operating units. Magna's unit general managers were given 100 percent control, authority, and responsibility for their units, with the requirement that they clearly identify themselves as part of Magna International when communicating with suppliers or customers.

This high degree of decentralization did give rise to a number of trade-offs at the operating-unit level. Magna realized higher transportation costs in shipping from widely dispersed locations to the automotive assembly plants of the major manufacturers; however, significant quantities were still shipped such that discounts were not completely foregone.

Some diseconomies also arose from the lack of centralized purchasing of raw materials. Each unit dealt with its own suppliers, but frequently general managers in the same operating group would cooperate to secure volume discounts when available.

Administrative costs were duplicated in some cases since each operating unit had its own personnel, accounting, and other staff departments, but management felt that, in general, the benefits of decentralization outweighed its costs.

At Magna, financial control was maintained by accountants at each of the group offices and operating units. Each operating unit was required to submit a business plan for the year outlining the operating and capital budget to group management. These plans were assessed by the groups and submitted to corporate executive officers for final approval.

Once approved, the groups and operating units set out independently in pursuit of their defined business goals. Performance was monitored monthly using uniform financial reports comparing actual operating results to budget and measuring capital spending against plan.

Although organic, growth was not indiscriminate at the factory level and was monitored by group management which worked within the broad corporate policy set by executive management. Executive management consisted of Frank Stronach and a handful of senior executives. Corporate headquarters were housed in a two-storied office in a suburban Toronto business park and consisted of a 100-person staff.

Operating units were grouped geographically and by market under one of five group management teams which were destined to divide and form more groups as Magna expanded. Each group was responsible for specific technologies and product lines and had its own marketing, R&D, and planning responsibilities.

On average, each group management nucleus had 10 to 15 factories responsible to it. Magna's strategy was to keep these factories close together geographically, wherever possible, and as the company grew sufficiently, to develop its own industrial parks.

In 1985 Magna consisted of five management groups: the CMT Group (Creative Mechanical Technologies), the Decorative Products Group, the MACI Group, the Magna Manufacturing Group, and the Maple Group. The products manufactured by each group in 1984 are found in Exhibit 2.

Equity Participation

Frank Stronach maintained that employees had "a moral right to some of the profits they help generate. . . . If they get profit and they put it into the company equity, there's a sort of discipline which helps the employee. We've got some people on machines who've got $30,000 sitting there. That's a lot of money for an average person."

In keeping with Stronach's belief, Magna had a type of deferred profit-sharing program for its employees to reward productivity and loyalty. Employees were awarded a point for every $1,000 they earned and a point for each year they stayed with the company. The more points they had accumulated, the greater their share in the fund. Each year 7 percent of profits before tax were transferred to an employee equity trust fund. Employees received quarterly statements of how many shares they owned and their value. If an employee left within two years, his shares reverted to other employees. After his third year with Magna, he owned a percentage which increased until the 10th year when it became completely his, even if he left. In Magna's earlier years, profit sharing was available only to middle management but was expanded to cover all employees in 1978.

Magna's senior management team of about 20 executives enjoyed a separate profit participation program for which 6 percent of before-tax profits were set aside. The result was some very generous bonuses in addition to their competitive salaries, but Frank Stronach had no qualms about this, stating, "Good management doesn't come cheap—I don't come cheap." In addition to Stronach, the compensation received by four other Magna executives placed them among the 15 most highly paid managers in Canada in 1985.

Exclusive of the top executive, Magna's approximately 250 managers owned about 12½% of the company. The over 7,000 workers held about the same equity position.

Although Magna's workers enjoyed equity participation, their hourly salaries were low by industry standards—approximately $6 per hour in 1985. Some estimated that Magna, without a single union in any of its plants, therefore had an hourly wage burden about half the size of its unionized competitors—a substantial competitive advantage in an industry where cost control was a key success factor. Stronach maintained that increases in productivity were resulting in rising wages at Magna and that Magna would soon be catching up in terms of hourly wage rates. But low hourly wages and the lack of a union in any of its plants made Magna a favourite target of attacks by the United Auto Workers (UAW) union.

Magna and the UAW

Magna seemed to be an impregnable target for union organizers—a fact which some industry followers felt was vital to Magna's success. Stronach himself did not appear to harbour anti-union sentiments, stating, "Unions can be part of free enterprise because society needs checks and balances," and, "If you run a lousy ship, you deserve a union."

Regardless of the sincerity of these views, Stronach had the grudging respect of his UAW adversaries. Buzz Hargrove, administrative assistant to Canadian UAW leader Bob White, knew Frank Stronach personally and said, "I didn't agree with his ideology or his philosophy, but I thought he was a well-motivated, decent human being."

In one instance, in 1978, the UAW was granted automatic certification at one of Magna's Toronto plants because of management interference in the organizing drive. However, some union cards were burned, the UAW failed to negotiate a contract, and it was then voted out by the Magna employees. The negotiations stalled on the single issue of the now mandatory Rand formula (where all employees in the bargaining unit must pay union dues regardless of whether they choose to become union members), but in the UAW's opinion, this issue was irrelevant because Magna had really just chosen to dig in its heels.

Buzz Hargrove said, "Frank Stronach and I had lunch together one day, and he told me that their strategy was essentially to find an issue that they knew we would not agree to that would force us to strike the plant in order to try to get an agreement, and they would just let the thing sit. They wouldn't try to run the plant or hire scabs, but to all intents and purposes, the plant would remain closed as long as there was a picket line. Whether it took a year, or two, or three, or forever, it didn't matter. They were not going to have a union in their shop." Hargrove continued, "We have no alternative but to continue . . . and probably even step up . . . our efforts to organize Magna. We can't have a major segment of the automotive parts industry unorganized."

It was possible that the UAW would be aided in subsequent attempts to organize Magna by the company's ongoing strategy to cluster its five management groups and their related plants into industrial campuses. Frank Stronach, in a 1985 interview, admitted that he was concerned by the threat of renewed UAW action because, "It's always a concern if someone would interfere with your environment, with your philosophies, with your basic framework." In an interview a year earlier, he had claimed;

> I don't believe the UAW would really get out to organize us. They would if they heard complaints, or if the employees were unhappy. . . . We try to provide a better alternative. We say that if we had unions, we would lose individually because everything is then divided into group one, group two, group three. Such groups stop a person from voicing his opinion. This is the danger when one body or one group gets too strong; it's too structured and the individual gets lost. . . . Three or four years ago we had two people in labour relations. Now we have a department with 10 people. We employ a labour lawyer whose function is to make our managers understand that we insist on certain principles and standards. His job is not to squeeze employees but to educate managers.

Corporate Strategy

Magna had a clear set of corporate objectives and a strategy for achieving them. As Magna's success became well-known, its senior executives, especially Frank

Stronach, were increasingly sought out for interviews. Features appeared repeatedly in newspapers, popular magazines, on television, and even in books, which described Magna's objectives and plans for realizing them.

The company's primary objective was to become the most diversified supplier of parts, components, and assemblies to the North American automotive industry and to steadily increase its dollar share of total industry sales from its 1985 level of 1 percent. Magna intended to accomplish this by increasing its average "penetration level" or the average dollar value of Magna parts that went into every North American automobile.

Over the period 1979 to 1985 Magna's penetration level had risen from $8.95 to $49.00 with a goal of $100 per vehicle by 1988. The company exceeded the $100 goal in the middle of its 1986 fiscal year.

Management consistently referred to a three-pronged strategy that it felt would allow Magna to sustain its remarkable growth and achieve its objectives: (1) continued increases in market share for existing Magna products; (2) introduction of new products and technologies to the marketplace, driven by ongoing in-house research and development and through joint ventures with partners who were leaders in product design and manufacturing capabilities; and (3) manufacturing and marketing of modular assemblies using a variety of Magna parts and components. For example, instead of manufacturing cooling fans and radiators independently, Magna intended to market one complete unit that included a fan, radiator, and shrouds and could be bolted directly into a vehicle on an assembly line.

In addition to its diversification strategy of building ever-greater numbers of parts and components, Magna simultaneously pursued an ongoing strategy of vertical integration. This was mainly in the form of backward integration, described by many as a key reason for Magna's success as it allowed the company to reduce costs and respond quickly and flexibly to design changes by its customers. Magna integrated vertically by undertaking its own tool and die making—the company's original business—and by developing and applying its in-house expertise in robotics and computer-aided-design/computer-aided-manufacturing (CAD/CAM) to equip Magna for the so-called factory of the future. There was even speculation that a Magna company, which had designed and built its own robotics system, might market the systems as another product in the future.

Magna's medium-term strategy was to geographically cluster its operating units and their plants into "industrial campuses," each with an infrastructure of company-supported social and recreational services, such as day care, medical, educational, and fitness centres. Each campus would consist of a cluster of 10 to 20 small autonomous plants, with the related operating group's office and product development centre located on the campus as well. The goal of this concept was to enhance the working environment for Magna employees. Stronach estimated, "Fifty cents spent on something like day care in our campuses will return $1.50 in increased productivity." Magna's first campus was begun in Newmarket, Ontario, in 1985 with three new plants and associated offices. Land for other campuses was quickly being assembled in anticipation of future growth. An announcement had also been made that Magna would begin construction of another 10 to 20 factory industrial campuses on a 26-acre parcel of land in Waterloo, Ontario, in 1986.

One strategy for dealing with the company's rapid growth was raised by Jim McAlpine, Magna's executive vice president and chief financial officer, who suggested in a 1985 interview that Magna intended to spin off at least one of its operating units by selling or distributing shares to the public in 1986. Magna would retain at least 52 percent of the unit's shares, 20 percent would be given to the unit's employees, 5 percent would go to management, and the remainder would probably be distributed to the public through an equity issue or divided plan. Such a strategy would reinforce Magna's corporate philosophy of decentralization. McAlpine added, ''A spin-off allows our management teams to continue to grow as managers. We hope it reduces the buildup of bureaucracy.'' It seemed that Magna International's main role in the future might be that of a holding company or a birthplace for a number of new companies.

International Activities

An increasingly important component of Magna's corporate strategy was the recognition of the emphasis on international activity within the automobile industry. By 1985 Magna's international activities, on a number of fronts, had been relatively modest but had resulted in the development of relationships that management felt would position the company to take advantage of a variety of opportunities. The 1985 annual report stated, ''With patience and persistence, we will be able to build successfully upon these relationships and establish Magna as a participant in the key automotive markets of the world.''

Magna's international activities before 1986 had consisted primarily of joint ventures with foreign companies where Magna's goal was to acquire new technologies and knowledge of new products and processes. Magna sought joint ventures to build a technology base quickly. Frank Stronach said, ''It's too time-consuming to do it on our own. . . . We don't want to re-invent the wheel constantly.'' A list of some major joint ventures that Magna had been involved in up to 1986 is provided below. In 1985 Magna was in 13 active joint ventures.

Typical Joint Ventures Undertaken by Magna International Inc.

Joint Venture Partner	Partner's Nationality	Part Produced
1. Philips Group	Dutch	Electronic components
2. Veglia SA	French	Instrument clusters for Renault
3. Chausson	French	Aluminum radiators for Renault
4. Webasto GmbH	West German	Sun roofs
5. Willibald Grammer	West German	Foam technology for seats
6. Brown, Boveri et Cie AG	Swiss	Power trains for electric vehicles

Typical joint ventures entered into by Magna were those with two French auto-parts suppliers. With Veglia SA, a French producer of dashboard equipment, Magna set up Invotek Instruments of Toronto to manufacture instrument clusters for the Renault Alliance and Encore. In 1984 with Societe Anonyme des Usines Chausson, a Renault subsidiary, Magna established Thermag Industries Inc. of Mississauga. The purpose was to produce aluminum radiators for Renaults built in North America by AMC, instead of shipping radiators from France. An $8 million plant was to be built with production to begin in 1986. Magna took a 60 percent interest in the venture in order to gain access to technology and markets, while Chausson took the minority 40 percent interest and supplied its technology.

In July 1984 Magna signed a joint venture agreement with the Japanese parts manufacturer Niles Buhin Co., at a time when Japanese manufacturers were beginning to try to increase their penetration of the lucrative North American market. Simultaneously, Magna began negotiating with four or five other Japanese companies for similar ventures that Frank Stronach felt could bring Magna hundreds of millions of dollars in revenues over the next few years.

Niles Buhin was an electronics components maker and, unlike many Japanese parts suppliers, did not belong to a particular car-making group, although most of its business was with Nissan and Mitsubishi. At the time, Niles Buhin had sales of $150 million while Magna's sales were $302 million.

Magna was again seeking access to advanced technology, primarily in electronics and lightweight materials while Niles Buhin saw the venture as a good way to gain entry to a large and growing market far from their domestic bases. They were being encouraged to do so by the large Japanese carmakers who wanted the parts makers to follow them to North America; but because Japanese vehicle production would be insufficient to support them, the Japanese parts manufacturers required access to the big U.S. manufacturers as well. Some planned to try this on their own, but many saw joint ventures, like the one between Magna and Niles Buhin, as a better alternative.

Japanese manufacturers were extremely sensitive about labour problems, but Magna's main selling point to the Japanese was its record of good labour relations. Management was of the opinion that the Japanese felt "quite comfortable" with Magna.

According to its 1985 annual report, in seeking additional joint ventures with the Japanese, Magna's primary targets were the Japanese vehicle manufacturers who had, or were planning to locate, production facilities in North America as well as their suppliers who were exploring opportunities to do business in North America. Magna's strategy was to demonstrate to the manufacturers that it could provide "world class" products in terms of quality and value. With Japanese part suppliers, Magna sought to develop forms of cooperation in North America where both parties could contribute and prosper.

By 1985 Magna had licensed one of its products to Japanese parts suppliers for production and sale in Japan and had acquired licenses to manufacture and sell certain Japanese products in North America. The company was also in the midst of establishing a trading company with a Japanese parts supplier to coordinate the supply of certain products manufactured by Magna to one of the Japanese automakers located in North America.

In 1985 a tooling and production facility had been established in West Germany to supply European OEMs. Contracts had also been signed to supply some North American produced components to two German automakers.

An agreement was signed late in the year to establish a joint venture in the People's Republic of China to manufacture components for the Chinese auto market.

As fiscal 1986 approached, it was increasingly clear that Magna International was stepping up the pace of its international activities with ambitious hopes for the future of these operations.

Magna's Future Prospects

As fiscal 1986 came to a close, it was becoming evident that the company Frank Stronach had built up from a rented Toronto garage might be coming to a crossroads in its history. A number of questions and issues required resolution.

It appeared certain that the company's strong growth would continue unabated for at least the next few years. However, one could not help but wonder if Magna's traditional success formula would be adequate to accommodate further phenomenal growth. Would continued growth and the spinning-off of new companies make it easier for the UAW to finally unionize some of Magna's factories, and what repercussions would such an event have on Magna as a whole?

There had been a trend for the North American automakers to source 100 percent of their components in one place to ensure consistency. Certainly, no company in Canada was better positioned than Magna to make the most of the trend. Yet would this trend continue?

Magna's increasing international activities seemed to be the next logical step in the company's uninterrupted growth, but concern existed about how this would fit into Magna's current organizational structure which emphasized geographical clustering and a commonality of product lines among related operating units. Would modifications or exceptions to the Magna "formula" have to be made to accommodate these relatively new activities that were growing rapidly in relative importance?

Stronach's dynamic, entrepreneurial personality and vision undoubtedly accounted for a considerable measure of Magna's success. How would this role change as Magna continued to grow and Stronach became a smaller part of Magna's operations? One observer had noted that Stronach seemed to have all the pieces in place so that any of his chief executives could manage the company quite well. Yet others wondered what effect his retirement might have on the company.

Frank Stronach once called Magna International's Corporate Constitution "perhaps the most important chapter in western industrial society in many years

. . . that I believe will have an enormous bearing in the future structure of corporations [and] law making." As the new fiscal year approached, one could not help wondering whether that document was well suited to guide Magna International and other corporations into the 1990s.

References

Arnott, Sheila. "What Our Top Executives Are Earning." *The Financial Post*, May 1986.

Avery, Nick, and Alison Burkett. "Comparison of the Auto-Parts Market 1981–1984." Wilfrid Laurier University MBA Report, November 27, 1985.

Barnes, Kenneth, and Everett Banning. *Money-Makers! The Secrets of Canada's Most Successful Entrepreneurs*. Toronto: McClelland & Stewart, Ltd., 1985.

"Everybody's Business." Global television program. Various video excerpts re: Magna International, Inc.

Galt, Virginia. "Decentralizing, Worker Participation Plans, Help Put Magna on the Road to Recovery." *The Globe and Mail*, July 6, 1981, B1, B5.

Harrison, Douglas. "Franco-Canadian Economic Bonds Are Increasing." *Kitchener-Waterloo Record*, February 17, 1985, B9.

Hart, Matthew. "Frank as He'll Ever Be." *The Financial Post Moneywise Magazine*, May 1986, pp. 64–67.

Koch, Henry. "Magna Spinoffs to Spur Waterloo Growth: Carroll." *Kitchener-Waterloo Record*, January 23, 1985, B9.

Lilley, Wayne. "Small is Beautiful." *Canadian Business* 57, no. 6 (1984), pp. 170–71.

"Magna Executive Optimistic about Firm's 1985 Showing." *The Globe and Mail*, August 3, 1985, B5.

Magna International Inc. *Annual Report 1984*. 1984.

———. *Annual Report 1985*. 1985.

"Magna International Inc." *Toronto Stock Exchange Review*, November 1984, pp. 1–4.

"Milner, Brian. "Magna, Japanese Firm Form Joint Venture." *The Globe and Mail*, July 30, 1984, B1.

Partridge, John, "Small Is Beautiful to Magna Chief but He Still Aims to Be the Biggest." *The Globe and Mail*, January 5, 1985, B1, B3.

Waddell, Christopher. "Magna Chairman Sells Shares but Remains Firmly in the Saddle." *The Globe and Mail*, December 7, 1984, B1, B2.

———. "Magna Hopes to Be Supplier for GM's Saturn." *The Globe and Mail*, April 19, 1985, B3.

Walker, Dean. "The Capitalist's Gospel According to Frank Stronach." *Executive*, May 1984, pp. 46–49.

Wilson, Sharon E. "The Best of Both Worlds: How Large Corporations Can Benefit from Decentralized Manufacturing." Wilfrid Laurier University Report, August 1985.

Case 27

Michael Bregman

In July 1980 Michael Bregman was preparing a strategy to expand his fledgling Canadian restaurant business. During the last eight months he had started pilot locations for two different restaurant concepts. The first was "Mmmuffins" (as in, "Mmm, good!"). This was a take-out bakery operation offering a wide variety of fresh, hot muffins (baked on premises) together with accompanying beverages. The second was "Michel's Baguette," a more elaborate French bakery cafe. Baguette offered a take-out counter for a variety of French croissants and breads (also baked in the restaurant) as well as an on-premises cafe with soups, salads, sandwiches on fresh bread, an omelette bar, and fresh croissants.

Michael hoped to build a substantial restaurant chain with one or both of these concepts. Even though the two pilots were just underway, a flurry of construction of new shopping centers across Canada appeared to offer a unique opportunity for rapid growth. In fact, one major developer was negotiating with Michael for a package of locations right now. The package included some locations Michael felt would be good, but the developer also wanted commitment to some locations Michael felt would do poorly.

Such a deal would be a major undertaking for his young company. It would heavily influence the company's direction during the crucial formative years. Yet Michael was still considering the merits of franchising versus internal growth and evaluating the relative attractiveness of the two restaurant concepts. He wanted to make conscious strategic decisions in these areas before he committed to any course of action.

Background

Michael Bregman was a native of Canada. After earning a degree in finance from Wharton at the University of Pennsylvania, he entered directly into the MBA program at Harvard from which he graduated in 1977. Michael sought a job in the food business because of an interest he had developed due to his family's long association with that industry.

Michael's grandfather had built a successful bakery as had Michael's father,

Lou Bregman. In 1971 Lou Bregman had purchased Hunt's and Woman's Bakery (Hunt's) division from the Kellogg Company which Lou had been supplying. The division had been losing money on annual sales of about $20 million, but under Lou Bregman's guidance soon prospered. Hunt's sold bakery products to 130 company-owned retail stores and to 370 supermarkets. Michael had worked after school and in summer jobs in various restaurants and bakeries.

> I joined Loblaws, a Canadian chain that was perceived as being a very stodgy supermarket company. Everybody thought I was crazy because I had offers from some of the big consulting companies and investment banks, places that I should be going. But at Loblaws I would be working for a new president with no experience in supermarketing right in the midst of a turnaround. I would call him a marketing genius and really went to work for him rather than the company.

Michael worked on corporate development projects including the launch of no-name (unbranded) products in Canada which was very successful. But things were not going as smoothly at Hunt's. Lou Bregman was having disagreements with his majority partners (who were in the real estate business) as the result of some difficult financial times. The company was in a turmoil, and Lou asked Michael to join Hunt's to see if he could help out. Michael agreed in June of 1978 and was put in charge of the retail division. Lou concentrated on the central bakery operations, and the other partners attempted to provide overall direction. Michael quickly found himself at odds with the other managers and strongly disagreed with what he thought were stupid decisions. He stayed only at his father's urging until December 1978, then resigned.

> I must say that I felt pretty defeated at the time. I'd worked so hard and had accomplished so little. I'd fought a lot, and I've never been much of a fighter, but I also can't do anything unless I believe in it. It was a difficult time.
>
> I didn't know what I was going to do. I'd always planned all along to start my own business at some time. I didn't know what or when, but I did know I wanted to do it quickly because I think it gets harder and harder as life goes on and you have all sorts of commitments.
>
> I went out for lunch one day with my old boss from Loblaws who suggested I go back to them again. I really hadn't thought of that but had simply been keeping in touch. I told him I couldn't really make a long-term commitment because my heart was in starting my own business. He said that would be all right, that he could put me on a short-term assignment. It took about five minutes worth of convincing for me to agree.

Evolution of a Start-Up

As his first project, Michael was asked to recommend a strategy for Loblaws in-store bakeries: What should they be? Should they be bake-off stores of frozen products (baking prefrozen doughs) or scratch bakeries? Should Loblaws have them? He prepared a similar study of the deli department. Michael was then asked to implement his recommendations in the bakery area and became director of bakery operations, a new position. He worked closely with the manager of bakery operations who was oriented to the day-to-day management more than to strategy and planning for the department. Bakeries became important to Loblaws new super stores which were designed to provide greater variety and savings than traditional supermarkets. Bakery products were successful in drawing customers to the stores with store-baked crusty bread and rolls.

> Somewhere along the way, a small businessman visited me. He thought we should sell his muffins in our stores. We have taken muffins for granted: they'd been around forever and were sort of stable and unexciting—what do you do with a muffin? All of a sudden this fellow comes in with these giant muffins, much larger than any we'd ever seen. We sold our small muffins for 15 cents each; we'd have to retail his at 45 cents.
>
> Naturally everybody was against them just on price. But I decided to test them in two of the most affluent stores. They went like crazy; it was wild. We kept upping the orders, and we could never keep them in stock. We didn't promote them, just put them in the counter, but there was immediate appeal. That triggered something in me. Seeing that here you could take a very drab product and make it exciting. And I thought you could do more with it than I saw him do.

Despite Michael's interest in the food industry and fascination with the performance of the large muffins, he really didn't like the bakery business:

> It always seemed to be an old man's game, a tired industry that was declining and very production oriented, very unexciting. Over 75 percent of the retail bakeries in North America had closed between the early-60s and mid-70s. Before that, the retail baking industry was composed of hundreds of independent skilled bakers who had come over from Europe and opened up shops and carried on as they had in Europe. The little shops handled 200 or 300 items, mostly, if not all, made by hand. You needed skilled bakers to continue who became very expensive and in short supply.
>
> Mom and pop were willing to work crazy hours and take low salaries because they wanted their own bakery. But by the mid-70s those same skilled people could get jobs in any supermarket in the country, earn $25,000, work 37–38 hours, have terrific benefits and no headaches. That together with the shift of customers to the shopping centers really put an end to most of that business.
>
> The pressure really began with the bakery chains, like my father's, that were serviced from central plants. But then the supermarkets started doing in-store baking, selling a fresher product at a lower price. Gas had gone crazy, and it had become prohibitive to deliver fresh products from a central facility to many small shops daily or twice a day. And the supermarket had a different view of the baking business. They were very price conscious. They weren't in the baking business to make money but to draw customers to buy other things. The last thing they wanted to do was to draw a customer into the store and see a bakery that had prices that were too high. Their cost systems were often really rather silly and ignored investment and overhead and value of the space used by an individual area. Some supermarket departments, like the bakeries, were really much more expensive marketing tools than they thought. But the supermarkets tended to just look at the total bottom line as a contribution number. Looking at these things, it was easy to be negative about the industry.

Then I started to feel there was a massive opportunity out there! People still liked baked goods, and they hadn't been supplied with them in the right fashion. As I thought in general terms of what was going to happen to the retail baking industry, I felt that the stores were going to get smaller and the industry would have to specialize in one or two lines of products. Also you'd surely have to bake on premises to create the freshness that no one else could duplicate. That's really the key component of quality in our industry. I also reminded myself that the retail baking business is primarily based on impulse sales and location is extremely important.

I guess I had all of this in mind in May 1979 while my father and I were driving to a restaurant show in Chicago. For the first time it really occurred to me: Why don't we open a muffin shop? We sort of chuckled—what a stupid idea. Later I began to think, why not? There's not a lot of money to lose and a lot to gain if it worked. It was totally different than anything we'd seen in North America.

During the summer, I began investigating some space in the Eaton Centre. This was Toronto's principal downtown shopping complex with over 3.7 million square feet of space. The Eaton Centre was directly connected to three subway terminals and had 200,000 office workers within easy walking distance. It was anchored by two major department stores and two office towers. There were over 300 retail shops and restaurants in the complex. Their leasing agent was pretty skeptical but was willing to lease some space. In August I committed to lease 350 square feet at $15,000 a year or 8 percent of sales, beginning December 1. Now I needed to develop my shop.

In the meantime, Lou Bregman had sold his interest in Hunt's and had considered retirement. Yet when he had the chance to buy a downtown Bagel Nosh store that had gone bankrupt, he decided to develop a new full-service restaurant and bakery called Bregman's. Michael was helping his father get started with that, and Lou Bregman co-guaranteed the lease obligations with Michael for the muffin shop.

In addition to his duties at Loblaws, helping his father's new venture, and planning his muffin shop, Michael found himself drawn into yet another start-up:

My wife and I had honeymooned in France when we were married in May 1978. I really fell in love with their croissants. I couldn't believe how great they were. I'd never tasted a decent croissant in North America. They were all weak imitations, and I thought this would be a great product to bring over here. I had seen a few French bakery stores in Chicago and New York, but very few. I knew that this would be something to pursue in the future.

As we were settling our lease deal for the muffin shop in the Eaton Centre, I mentioned to the leasing agent that I had heard that a French bread chain, Au Bon Pain, was coming to the center. He was surprised I'd heard of it but said they had some problems with them. I said I was planning to get in the same business, and he got very excited. He called his boss and very quickly offered to negotiate with us. Space in the Eaton Centre was very difficult to obtain and seemed to me to be one of the best possible locations. So we leased the space and decided to do our French bakery, too. Again, we personally guaranteed the leases.

Despite the serendipitous opening at the Eaton Centre, Michael's commitment to the French bakery restaurant was not a spur-of-the-moment decision. He had been actively investigating the possibilities of both the muffin shop and the French bakery since the Chicago show in May. Because the French bakery would require much more capital, Michael had prepared a short business plan which he circulated to three or four people he thought might invest. One was Ralph Scurfield of Calgary, president of the NuWest Group, the largest homebuilder in North America. Michael had met him while Ralph was enrolled in an executive program at Harvard. Michael had done a field study for NuWest and had kept in touch with Ralph. Now Ralph said that he knew very little about the restaurant business but that he did know Michael Bregman and would be willing to bet some money on him. A long negotiation ensued as Michael sought locations for the muffin shop or for the French bakery. They reached agreement in the fall:

> We capitalized the company with $450,000. My father and I each put in $62,500 in common stock and Ralph put in $125,000 in common stock and an additional $200,000 in preferred shares. I had a net worth of about $8,000 and got a loan for my share. I had to get my wife, mother, and father to co-sign and my parents to put their house up. It scared the daylights out of me. If things went wrong, it wouldn't sink them, but I didn't know how I could live with it.
>
> I would take a salary cut to $25,000 a year, which together with my wife's income would just about let us live and cover the loan. The contract ended up 60 pages long with 5 pages of basics and the rest disaster clauses. I would have tie-breaking power unless things went wrong and would also have to get Ralph's approval for capital expenditures over $5,000. The initial spending requirements were approved as part of the agreement. There was also a complex redemption plan for the preferred which included penalties for not making the five-year schedule.

The fall of 1979 was frantic as Michael managed to get both of his projects underway. Although he and his father had been in the baking business, neither of them were familiar with the special processes needed for muffins of this type nor with French baking. At the same time Michael was working to design the stores, he had to find and test muffin recipes and learn to operate the specialized French baking equipment. Part of his strategy was to use the very best help he could find. For design, he employed Don Watt & Associates, one of Canada's premier designers. The equipment suppliers were also very helpful in the strenuous task of laying out all of the necessary customer service and baking equipment in 350 square feet for the muffin shop. Michael also found a French baker who lived in Washington who agreed to come up just before the bakery opened to teach several bakers how to bake French bakery products.

Somehow they got underway. Michael left Loblaws at the end of November 1979, and Mmmuffins opened December 15. Michel's Baguette began construction at that point and opened in April 1980. It was not a time Michael would like to repeat.

Evaluating the First Efforts

By July the two stores were beginning to stabilize, and Michael was preparing to expand. He reviewed the state of each operation to help him decide what directions he might take.

Exhibit 1:   Store Designs

He was pleased with both store designs and concepts. The extra expense and effort he had put in store planning had been well worth the investment. Both facilities were attractive and inviting (see Exhibit 1). As for product selections, they had developed recipes for over 15 varieties of muffins which could be made from four different base mixtures. About 10 would be offered at any point in time. At Baguette, the menu appeared workable and was proving to be a popular range of choices (see Exhibit 2).

Sales for both stores had been encouraging, and costs were beginning to become steady. He now had seven months of experience with Mmmuffins and three months with Baguette. Exhibit 3 is a record of sales and variable costs for the two stores. Exhibit 4 is a year-to-date financial statement showing the total performance and financial position.

After hectic start-up periods, the operations of each store were now also satisfactory. As expected, they were very different from each other. The Mmmuffins store had only 350 square feet of space. That small area had to contain

Exhibit 1 (*continued*)

room for supply storage, preparation of raw materials and mixes, baking, clean-up, and the retail service counters. Michael described how this worked:

> I think our design was one of the very most important reasons behind our early success. Don Watt was able to create the magnet to draw customers in the first time. If they liked our product, liked our service, they'd come back. They came in first because of the color, the lighting, the photography—it's just a different showcase.
>
> The design also worked well functionally. There's just enough space to do everything, but no extra space to become cluttered or dirty and not be corrected. The customer cannot see the preparation area, but the manager can easily keep track of all activities. The total staff complement for the store runs between 6 and 12 people including part-timers, depending on the part-time mix. You need one manager and one assistant to cover the shifts. There are sales people at the counter and bakers. You can trade off some during slack buying periods. Service at the counter is fairly simple, and you can train a baker in two days from start to finish. You could almost get this down to two hours for most of the functions.
>
> Although we didn't really know what we were doing when we opened, we soon

Exhibit 1 (*concluded*)

Exhibit 2: Michel's Baguette—Product Line Highlights

Bakery		*Cafe*	
Bread:	Baguette	Salads:	Julienne
	Boule		Nicoise
	Alpine		Spinach
	Mini-baguette		Side salad
	Whole wheat baguette		Salad du jour
Croissants:	Butter	Soups:	Yellow pea with ham
	Almond		Soup du jour
	Petit Pain Au Chocolat	Quiches:	Bacon
	Raisin-custard		Spinach
	Cream cheese		Mushroom
	Cheddar cheese	Omelette bar:	Cheddar cheese
	Ham and cheese		Ham
	Apple cinnamon		Swiss cheese
	Blueberry		Green pepper
	Cherry		Onion
		Sandwiches:	Ham and cheese
			Roast beef
			Tuna
			Chicken salad
			Egg salad
			Cream cheese
			Swiss cheese
			Le Hero
			Le Jardin
			Roast beef and herb cheese
		Beverages:	Coffee
			Tea
			Milk
			Soft drinks
			Juices
			Perrier
		Croissants:	(As in bakery)

learned better ways to do things. We got better at finding and selecting specialized preparation equipment that fit our particular needs. Since we bake right from scratch using no commercial mixes, every extra efficiency helped. We learned what items we could make ahead of time and better ways to store them. This is really important when you begin baking early in the morning before opening and continue throughout the day.

I knew that if we were going to grow, we'd have to systematize the operation, so during the first months I wrote an operating manual with everything from opening procedures to how to clean the store, to recipes, to baking procedures, to how to greet customers and work the counter—everything. I found it one of the most-grueling experiences I had ever been through in my life. I was working behind the

Exhibit 3: Initial Operating Results

Period Ending	Number of Weeks	Amount of Sales	Average Sales per Week	Percent Food, Supplies	Percent Labour	Percent Food, Supplies, and Labour
Mmmuffins:						
January 19, 1980	5	$ 9,010	$ 1,802	38.2%	38.8%	77.0%
February 16	4	10,866	2,716	36.3	29.8	66.1
March 15	4	14,901	3,725	24.5	23.9	48.4
April 12	4	17,250	4,312	28.0	22.5	50.0
May 10	4	16,696	4,174	34.6	25.6	60.2
June 7	4	17,346	4,337	38.5	25.4	63.9
July 5	4	20,602	5,150	31.1	21.0	52.1
Highest week's sales—June 21—$5,574						51.4%
Michel's Baguette:						
May 10	4	44,470	11,118	37.7	33.5	68.2
June 7	4	52,921	13,230	27.4	25.4	52.8
July 5	4	65,487	16,372	25.9	23.1	49.0
Highest week's sales—June 21—$17,289						48.7%

counter myself during those opening months and was learning how important those controls and procedures were.

I also learned how important the manager was. As Baguette opened and I left the Mmmuffins store under the supervision of a manager I had hired, little problems started to arise—fighting among the staff, quality being a little less consistent than it should have been. I'm sure there was fault on both sides, but I found that the manager constantly needed attention.

But all in all, I was very pleased.

As a much larger and more complete bakery and restaurant, Michel's Baguette was much more complex:

Baguette had 2,500 square feet of space which was really a bit too tight. This had a larger food preparation, baking, and storage area, a take-out bakery counter, the cafeteria-style serving line, and an on-premises eating area with seats for 35. Once again, our physical design was an important asset. Our store helped attract customers at the same time that it worked well functionally in a very tight space.

With a larger menu, there were many more tasks to perform. There was a total staff of 55 to 60 people, including part-timers. You really need a very qualified head manager to be the general manager of the overall business as well as two assistant managers who have the capability to be the acting general manager when the general manager isn't there. You need a head baker who is a skilled baker and can guide the whole production area of the store. There are kitchen prep people, two kinds of service people, cafeteria counter people who actually prepare your portions, the salads, and sandwiches. Most of these jobs are more complex than those at Mmmuffins, and the baking is particularly difficult. It takes 20 steps to make croissants, and the breads also have more steps and are more demanding than making

Exhibit 4:   Financial Statements

MICHAEL BREGMAN
Balance Sheet
June 30, 1980
(unaudited)

Assets

Current assets:	
Term deposit	$120,000
Receivables	1,525
Inventory	6,669
Prepaid expenses	15,345
Deferred charges	1,062
Deferred income taxes	7,250
Total current assets	151,851
Equipment and leasehold improvements	400,741
Incorporation expense—at cost	7,151
	$559,743

Liabilities

Current liabilities:	
Bankers' advances	$ 1,436
Payables and accruals	124,736
Dividend payable	4,500
Total current liabilities	130,672

Shareholders' Equity

Share capital	450,000
Deficit	(20,929)
Total liabilities and shareholders' equity	$559,743

Statement of Loss and Deficit
Period from Inception, December 4, 1979 to June 30, 1980
(unaudited)

Sales	$269,428
Cost of sales	169,919
Gross operating profit	99,509
Store expenses	78,473
Income from store operations	21,036
Other income—interest	14,972
	36,008
Administration expenses	55,187
Net loss before income taxes	(19,179)
Deferred income taxes	7,250
Net loss	(11,929)
Dividends	(9,000)
Deficit, end of period	$(20,929)

Exhibit 4   *(concluded)*

Internal Statements of Operations
Inception to July 5, 1980*

	Mmmuffins	Michel's Baguette
Sales	$106,404	$162,745
Food costs	35,090	44,861
Gross profit	71,314	117,884
Operating expense:		
Supplies	6,083	7,259
Labour	29,249	52,333
Total operating expense	35,332	59,592
Gross operating profit	35,982	58,292
General expenses	2,228	1,992
Occupancy costs	19,411	35,609
Administrative costs	5,442	8,137
Total expenses	27,081	45,738
Net profit from operations	8,901	12,554
Add: Depreciation and amortization	5,367	9,005
Cash flow from operation	$ 14,268	$ 21,559

* Note: Slightly different period than prior statements.

muffins. There are many delicate areas where you can ruin the product, but I must say that we brought in the right equipment from France and, with care, can consistently make excellent products. All of the baked goods and other items are made from scratch and are continuously baked throughout the day.

I began to spend most of my time at Baguette once it opened and again had to learn as we went. This would take more effort to systemize, and I hadn't written a manual here yet. I was lucky in hiring some good bakers and restaurant managers to help me out. I went after managers that I had heard did a good job for other restaurants in the city and was able to get two to join me. They both worked out very well.

The primary appeal of each concept was absolute freshness and quality of baked goods. As Michael looked at the two operations, he was satisfied that they each properly reflected the key conceptual definitions he felt were critical to their success: hard-to-replicate standards of quality with costs kept to acceptable levels by careful specialization, organization, and store design. Michael described how these worked together:

For superior quality our recipes are based on using fresh eggs, buttermilk, and other very perishable items—very expensive, very hard-to-handle items. Bakeries don't use fresh eggs; they use powdered or frozen. But we decided we would use fresh. We didn't care about any of the rules; we would be better than anybody. But this created very difficult production problems. You can't make too much at once, and you can't make too little because it's a waste of time. The mixes and products aren't very storable, you can't freeze them, and you can't keep them for more than a day.

Besides ingredients, we control our quality by specializing. This means making limited types of baked goods in the best possible way and then providing only those menu items needed to support the specialized baking operation. With Mmmuffins this is practically absolute: There are only muffins and beverages. The bakery for Baguette is simply too capital-intensive for the menu to remain that simple. So we combine the bakery with a restaurant. Having the fresh croissants and fresh bread to make sandwiches helps the restaurant, and the sampling that goes on in the restaurant spills over and helps the bakery. The restaurant and bakery counter also have different peak times, so you have better distribution for the bakery equipment, and your service people can sway back and forth. But other than the baking, we do no cooking! It's just an assembly operation. We assemble salads, cut meat, cut cheese. But except for omelettes, we don't fry anything, we don't boil anything, we don't cook. Other than the baking, in terms of the back of the house, it's a very simple restaurant.

The stores' layouts and service delivery systems are designed to support efficiently each menu concept. Both provide efficient preparation areas. Both have ovens prominently situated in view of shoppers and passersby—the sight and aroma of fresh baking are major merchandising tools. At Mmmuffins, we have very efficient customer handling along with some innovative packaging for quantity purchases. At Baguette, we selected a cafeteria line for the restaurant to go along with the counter service for the take-out bakery. This is one step up from the fast-food joint where you have to fight for a seat and eat from a tray with disposables. We use better dinnerware, metal utensils, and glasses. This is a step down from the full-service restaurant where you are served by waitresses. We selected this because I felt strongly that in the mall environment, people want to eat quickly but in some comfort.

Considering Franchising

With both Mmmuffins and Baguette well started, Michael began to consider expansion. He felt there should be many opportunities for good restaurants and specialty food stores despite competition ranging from retail bakeries and super-markets to fast-food operations, to full-service restaurants. Almost all of these types of competitors would be present—clustered in large shopping areas and malls. This was true for the first Mmmuffins and Baguette locations. Yet both had held their own in the very competitive and highly visible Eaton Centre. The question was how to expand. Michael had two concepts, limited experience, and limited resources. How could he best capitalize on his work to date to build a significant restaurant business?

One avenue of growth he could pursue was franchising. Certainly enough others had chosen this method to make franchising a very important factor in the Canadian and U.S. economies. A *Foodservice & Hospitality Magazine* survey estimated that franchising represented 16.5 percent of the total Canadian food service and lodging industry in 1979. This market share was increasing. Survey respondents reported a 29 percent increase in total food service franchise sales resulting from a 10.5 percent increase in total units operating and a 17 percent increase in average sales per unit (to $381,443).

For U.S. firms, franchised units accounted for approximately one quarter of all food service sales. Exhibit 5 lists several characteristics of U.S.-owned

---

Exhibit 5:   Characteristics of U.S.-Owned Restaurant Franchisors (1978–80)

Table A: Restaurants (all types)* (dollars in thousands)

				Percent Changes	
Item	1978	1979†	1980†	1978–1979	1979–1980
Total number of establishments	55,312	59,928	66,672	8.3	11.3
Company owned	15,510	16,781	18,549	8.2	10.5
Franchisee owned	39,802	43,147	48,123	8.4	11.5
Total sales of products and services:	$21,100,788	$24,591,880	$28,990,499	16.5	17.9
Company owned	6,733,545	7,816,198	9,111,129	16.1	16.6
Franchisee owned	14,367,243	16,775,682	19,879,370	16.8	18.5
Total sales of products and services by franchisors to franchisees:					
Merchandise (nonfood) for resale	33,013	37,534	48,656	13.7	29.6
Supplies (such as paper goods and so forth)	170,889	231,017	287,379	35.2	24.4
Food ingredients	298,063	383,774	481,004	28.8	25.3
Other	46,817	53,728	40,771	14.8	−24.1
Total	548,782	706,053	857,810	28.7	21.5

* See Tables C and D on the next page.
† Data estimated by respondents.

Table B: Restaurants (all types)*: Distribution by Number of Establishments—1978 (dollars in thousands)

	Franchising Companies	Establishments		Sales	
Size Groups	Number	Number	Percent	(Amount)	Percent
Total	388	55,312	100.0%	$21,100,788	100.0%
1,001 and greater	12	27,750	50.2	11,400,272	54.0
501–1000	11	8,925	16.1	3,513,637	16.7
151–500	34	8,833	16.0	2,928,603	13.9
51–150	59	5,580	10.1	1,712,930	8.1
11–50	153	3,642	6.6	1,360,850	6.4
0–10	120	582	1.0	184,496	0.9

* See Tables C and D on the next page.
Source: U.S. Department of Commerce, "Franchising in the Economy 1978–1980," January 1980.

Exhibit 5 *(concluded)*

Table C: Restaurants, 1978–1980*: Distribution by Major Activity

Establishments

Major Activity	Firms	1978			1979			1980		
		Total	Company Owned	Franchisee Owned	Total	Company Owned	Franchisee Owned	Total	Company Owned	Franchisee Owned
Total	388	55,312	15,510	39,802	59,928	16,781	43,147	66,672	18,549	48,123
Chicken	31	6,708	1,870	4,838	7,193	2,011	5,182	7,826	2,197	5,629
Hamburgers, franks, roast beef, and so forth	117	26,038	4,648	21,390	27,833	5,077	22,756	30,651	5,695	24,956
Pizza	66	7,542	3,042	4,500	8,355	3,288	5,067	9,434	3,577	5,857
Mexican (taco and so forth)	29	2,329	993	1,336	2,527	1,044	1,483	2,913	1,183	1,730
Seafood	11	2,297	899	1,398	2,444	901	1,543	2,704	966	1,738
Pancakes, waffles	15	1,441	363	1,078	1,577	418	1,159	1,770	491	1,279
Steak, full menu	86	7,924	3,479	4,445	8,756	3,813	4,943	9,771	4,180	5,591
Sandwich and other	33	1,033	216	817	1,243	229	1,014	1,603	260	1,343

* Estimated by respondents for 1979 and 1980.

Table D: Restaurants, 1978–1980*: Distribution by Major Activity (sales—dollars in thousands)

Major Activity	Firms	1978			1979			1980		
		Total	Company Owned	Franchisee Owned	Total	Company Owned	Franchisee Owned	Total	Company Owned	Franchisee Owned
Total	388	$21,100,788	$6,733,545	$14,367,243	$24,591,880	$7,816,198	$16,775,682	$28,990,499	$9,111,129	$19,879,370
Chicken	31	2,034,012	653,977	1,380,035	2,247,838	765,738	1,482,100	2,563,755	899,485	1,664,270
Hamburgers, franks, roast beef, and so forth	117	10,862,837	2,589,465	8,273,372	12,961,887	3,038,923	9,922,964	15,521,446	3,595,801	11,925,645
Pizza	66	1,735,279	696,364	1,038,915	2,007,066	776,902	1,230,164	2,364,317	903,182	1,461,135
Mexican (taco and so forth)	29	602,376	304,697	297,679	648,100	315,922	332,178	766,692	377,652	389,040
Seafood	11	563,827	216,486	347,341	667,098	260,633	406,465	772,794	299,624	473,170
Pancakes, waffles	15	601,029	139,899	461,130	681,728	164,023	517,705	834,135	216,290	617,845
Steak, full menu	86	4,531,709	2,104,623	2,427,086	5,170,218	2,461,797	2,708,421	5,883,140	2,779,340	3,103,800
Sandwich and other	33	169,719	28,034	141,685	207,945	32,260	175,885	284,220	39,755	244,465

* Estimated by respondents for 1979 and 1980.

Exhibit 6: Top 25 U.S. Franchise Restaurant Systems

Franchise System	1974	1978	1979	Percent Change 1974–1979	Percent Change 1978–1979
Growth in systemwide sales, 1974–1979 (dollars in millions)					
McDonald's	$1,943.0	$4,575.0	$5,385.0	177%	17.7%
Kentucky Fried Chicken[t]	925.5	1,393.4	1,669.0	80	19.8
Burger King[t]	467.0	1,168.0	1,463.0	213	25.3
Wendy's	24.2	783.0	1,000.0*	4,032	27.8
International Dairy Queen[t]	590.0	823.2	926.0	57	12.5
Pizza Hut	232.0	702.0	829.0	257	18.1
Big Boy	484.0*	660.0*	750.0*	55	13.6
Hardee's[t]	280.0	564.6	750.0	168	32.8
Arby's	120.0	353.0	430.0	258	21.8
Ho Jo's	300.0*	425.0*	425.0*	42	0.0
Ponderosa[t]	183.0	328.5	406.9	122	23.9
Church's	126.9	345.0	405.7*	220	17.6
Bonanza	190.0	346.0	378.0	99	9.2
Tastee Freez[t]	267.9*	353.8*	350.0*	31	(1.1)
Long John Silver's[t]	45.5	283.4	342.0	652	20.7
Sonic Drive-ins[t]	52.1	291.7	336.0	545	15.2
Burger Chef[t]	250.0	301.0	335.0	34	11.3
Taco Bell[t]	71.1*	212.0*	320.0*	350	50.9
Western Sizzlin[t]	100.0	217.3	278.1	178	28.0
Dunkin' Donuts	163.3	249.4	283.8	74	14.0
A & W	174.4	247.5	255.0	46	3.0
Arthur Treacher's	48.3	191.5	226.3	369	18.2
Sizzler[t]	85.5	181.8	225.9	164	24.3
Perkins Cake n Steak	75.0*	200.0*	223.0*	197	11.5
Pizza Inn	58.6	165.8	189.0*	223	14.0
Growth in number of units 1974–1979					
McDonald's	3,232	5,185	5,747	78%	10.8%
Kentucky Fried Chicken[t]	4,627	5,355	5,444	18	1.7
Burger King[t]	1,199	2,153	2,439	103	13.3
Wendy's	93	1,407	1,818	1,855	29.2
International Dairy Queen[t]	4,504	4,820	4,860	8	0.8
Pizza Hut	1,668	3,541	3,846	131	8.6
Big Boy	881	1,041	1,100	25	5.7
Hardee's[t]	924	1,125	1,231	33	9.4
Arby's	439	818	928	111	13.4
Ho Jo's	922	882	867	(6)	(1.7)
Ponderosa[t]	389	588	636	63	8.2
Church's	565	970	1,125	99	16.0
Bonanza	550	700	675	23	(3.6)
Tastee Freez[t]	2,215	2,022	2,000*	(10)	(1.1)
Long John Silver's[t]	208	1,001	1,007	384	0.6
Sonic Drive-ins[t]	220	1,061	1,182	437	11.4
Burger Chef[t]	950	853	831	(13)	(2.6)
Taco Bell[t]	562	877	1,100	96	25.4
Western Sizzlin[t]	140	319	400	186	25.4

Exhibit 6 *(concluded)*

Franchise System	1974	1978	1979	Percent Change 1974–1979	Percent Change 1978–1979
Dunkin' Donuts	780	956	1,007	29	5.3
A & W	1,899	1,500	1,306	(31)	(12.9)
Arthur Treacher's	250	730	777	211	6.4
Sizzler[†]	256	352	402	57	14.2
Perkins Cake n Steak	183	342	400*	119	17.0
Pizza Inn	336	743	760	126	2.3

Includes U.S. and foreign sales and units.
* Estimated.
[†] Fiscal year-end figures (remainder are calendar year-end figures).
Source: *Restaurant Business*, March 1, 1980.

restaurant franchisors for 1978 with projections for 1979 and 1980. About 40 percent of all U.S. franchised restaurants were located in California, Texas, Ohio, Illinois, Michigan, or Florida. A January 1980 study by the U.S. Department of Commerce noted:

> The entry into the restaurant franchising system mostly by small companies continued in 1978 with a net gain of 38 franchisors, bringing the total to 388. During 1979, 17 franchisors with a total of 227 restaurants, 198 franchisee-owned, went out of business while 13 franchisors with a total of 168 restaurants, 84 franchisee-owned, decided to abandon franchising as a method of marketing.

> Big franchisors with over 1,000 units each increased to 11 to 1978 from 8 a year earlier. These 11 franchisors had 27,750 restaurants, 50.2 percent of all franchised restaurants, and accounted for $11.4 billion in sales, 54 percent of the total. Compared with 1977, the 8 franchisors with over 1,000 units each had 45 percent of the total units and 47 percent of the sales.

> Menu expansion and diversification continues on the increase to meet the mounting competition from other chains and to enlarge customer counts that have been adversely affected by higher food costs and periodic gasoline shortages. The higher costs of cosmetic and structural construction changes are forcing fast-food franchisors to reevaluate their investment in design and cast their decor changes more and more in marketing terms.

Growth statistics of the 25 largest U.S. franchise restaurant systems are shown in Exhibit 6.

While franchising was one means to achieve growth for either Mmmuffins or Baguette, it would impose additional complexities in doing business. A franchisee is an independent businessperson with personal capital at risk and a fair amount of management flexibility. In addition to the demands inherent in such relationships, there was increasing government regulation of franchise offerings and operations. In October 21, 1979, a new U.S. Federal Trade Commission rule requiring comprehensive disclosure statements for prospective franchisees became effective. Sixteen separate states also required various types of disclosures (although some states accepted a uniform format). Canada had no such comprehensive disclosure requirement, but many felt there was a need for one and expected such a rule in Canada in the future. Some pressure for such regulation came from established franchisors who were worried about the effect that a few incapable, overconfident, or unscrupulous franchisors might have on the industry.

The areas of disclosure required by the new U.S. law illustrate the many aspects of the business and the relationship that must be considered in franchising. These include:

— Specific background information about the identity, financial position, and business experience of the franchisor company and its key directors and executives.
— Details of the financial relationship including initial and continuing fees and expenses payable to the franchisor.
— Requirements for doing business with the franchisor or affiliates (such as purchase of supplies from a franchisor source) and any realty fees, financing arrangements, or other financial requirements.
— Restrictions and requirements for methods of operation placed on the franchisee.
— Termination, cancellation, and renewal terms.
— Control over future sites.
— Statistical information about the number of franchises and their rate of terminations.
— Franchisor-provided training programs and other support.

Even without disclosure requirements, it was considered a good idea to develop policies and practices for dealing with franchisees for the long term before opening the first operation. One reason for this was a general desire for consistent treatment of franchisees. Some examples of current practices of Canadian franchisors are summarized in Exhibit 7.

Increased regulation was not the only area of change going on in franchising. There was ever-increasing competition in Canada as more U.S. franchisors sought new markets in other countries. The need for better communication with franchises had started a trend of development of franchisee advisory councils by franchisors. The ultimate roles of these councils was still evolving. There was also a fairly constant trade back and forth between franchisors repurchasing units for company ownership and company-owned units being franchised.

A Question of Strategy

The question of using franchising as a means of expansion was only one aspect Michael needed to consider in planning for growth for his restaurant business. A fundamental question was how suitable were his concepts for wide use? He had started and managed both current units personally. How well would they "travel"? Both concepts depended on fresh baking which made them more

Exhibit 7: Sample Canadian Franchise Terms, February 1980

Franchisor (Franchise)	History, Current Status, and Expansion Plans	Franchise Requirements and Costs	Services Offered to Franchisee
Mister Donut of Canada Ltd. (Mister Donut)	—Established 1955 —55 franchised units in Canada —715 franchised units in United States, Japan —Locations: Ontario, 43; Quebec, 9; British Columbia, 2; Alberta, 1 —Canadian sales $10 million —10 operations to open in 1980	—Initial fee, $10,000 —Royalty fee, 4.9 percent of gross sales —Advertising fee, .5 percent —Current equipment package, $50,000	—Opening supervision —Field supervision —Classroom training —Newsletter —Site selection —Lease negotiation
McDonald's Restaurants of Canada Ltd. (McDonald's Restaurants)	—Established 1967 in Canada —156 franchised, 168 company owned —Total Canadian sales, $500 million —45 new units planned across Canada	—Franchise fee, $10,000; initial investment, $190,000; total cost is around $400,000 —Percentage rent plus royalty fee —Total commitment by sole operator to run operation —4 percent advertising fee	—Continual consultation of operation —Marketing —Training —Personnel —Real estate
The Harvest Inn, Inc. (The Pantry Family Restaurant)	—Established 1975 —5 units company owned, 2 franchised, all in British Columbia —Full-service restaurant for breakfast, lunch, and dinner —4 additional units are planned for British Columbia	—$20,000 initial fee —Royalty fee, 4 percent gross —Advertising fee, 2 percent	—Full turnkey service including site selection, interior design —Accounting, training, and personnel selection

Exhibit 7 *(concluded)*

Franchisor (Franchise)	History, Current Status, and Expansion Plans	Franchise Requirements and Costs	Services Offered to Franchisee
Burger King Canada Ltd. (Burger King)	—Established 1976. 27 franchised units and 10 company owned; 2,650 worldwide; British Columbia, 2; Alberta, 2; Ontario, 30; Prince Edward Island, 1; New Brunswick, 1; Nova Scotia, 4 —26 franchised units planned for Ontario, New Brunswick, British Columbia, Nova Scotia, Alberta —Menu includes hamburgers and specialty sandwiches	—Initial fee, $40,000 —4 percent royalty fee —4 percent advertising fee	—Complete service package
Smitty's Pancake Houses Ltd.	—Established 1959; now has 86 franchised and 6 company owned; 3 in Hawaii. —Total sales, $59 million —16 units planned for 1980	—Initial fee, $25,000 over 70 seats, $25,000 under 70 seats	
Country Style Donuts Ltd.	—Established 1962 —66 franchised, 4 company owned, 4 in United States; Alberta, 5; Saskatchewan, 1; Manitoba, 3; Ontario, 55; Quebec, 5; Nova Scotia, 1 —Total sales, $15 million —14 new units planned for Alberta, Ontario, and Saskatchewan —Menu includes coffee and donuts	—Initial fee, $85,000 ($2,500 deposit; $27,500 for construction; $50,000, equipment contract; $5,000, inventory) —Royalty fee, 4.5 percent of gross —2 percent advertising fee	—Turnkey operation —4-week training course —Supervisory assistance on opening —20-year franchise term

Exhibit 8: Estimated Capital Requirements of Additional Stores

Mmmuffins:

Equipment package	$15,000
General construction (including fixtures and leasehold improvements)	40,000–60,000
Opening supplies and inventories	5,000
Miscellaneous (design, insurance, permits, preopening salaries, opening promotion, landlord chargebacks, working capital)	10,000
Total	$70,000–$90,000*

Michel's Baguette:

Equipment package	$145,000
General construction (including fixtures and leasehold improvements)	170,000–235,000
Furniture and supplies	35,000–45,000
Miscellaneous (working capital, design, permits, opening promotion, preopening salaries, advance rent)	20,000–40,000
Total	$370,000–$465,000*

* These are stand-alone estimates. If franchised, any franchise fee would be an additional requirement.

demanding than many franchises. Other stores offering similar baked goods (donuts, cookies, or other items) used premixed ingredients, premade frozen products to be baked in the units, or simply distributed centrally baked products.

Michael also had to include the capital requirements and likely performance of additional units of either type in his planning. His estimates of capital requirements for new locations are shown in Exhibit 8. His estimates of stand-alone operating results if operated by a franchisee are shown in Exhibit 9.

Finally, no matter what methods of growth he might choose, his location strategy would be critical. Where would his concepts best fit? One aspect was the type of location and surrounding demographics. Another would be geographic— how far away and Canada versus the United States. Even within Canada, there were very different demands between the more stable eastern portion and the rapidly growing western area. Should he concentrate on finding more established and stable locations in the east or should he take advantage of the many openings in new centers a construction boom in the west was creating? What differences were there between good locations for Mmmuffins and good locations for Baguette?

An Offer of Locations

To help learn about possible locations that might be available, Michael began talking with major Canadian development companies. One important firm was Real Estate Canada (REC) which developed and controlled a large number of shopping malls across Canada. After preliminary discussions, REC offered Michael locations for Mmmuffins stores in one new mall and one mall expansion, both in Toronto suburbs. This was an important developer, and Michael felt the locations would be good for Mmmuffins, so he agreed, and they shook hands on the deal.

Exhibit 9:   Estimated Earnings Potentials

MMMUFFINS
Potential Annual Cash Flow*
(350-square-foot mall location)

	Weekly Sales					
	$3,000		**$4,000**		**$5,000**	
	Amount	*Percent*	*Amount*	*Percent*	*Amount*	*Percent*
Annual sales	$156,000		$208,000		$260,000	
Food cost (1)	48,360	31.0%	62,400	30.0%	78,000	30.0%
Selling supplies	7,020	4.5	9,360	4.5	11,700	4.5
Labour (including benefits) (2)	31,200	20.0	37,440	18.0	41,600	16.0
Gross operating profit	69,420	44.5	98,800	47.5	128,700	49.5
Operating expenses:						
Royalties	9,360	6.0	12,480	6.0	15,600	6.0
Telephone	500	.3	500	.2	500	.2
Utilities	3,500	2.2	3,800	1.8	4,000	1.5
Uniforms and laundry	600	.4	600	.3	650	.3
Advertising	3,120	2.0	4,160	2.0	5,200	2.0
Repairs and maintenance	800	.5	800	.4	800	.3
Insurance	900	.6	900	.4	900	.3
Total occupancy (rent) (3)	16,800	10.8	17,500	8.4	21,000	8.1
Depreciation and amortization (4)	7,000	4.5	7,000	3.4	7,000	2.7
Miscellaneous (5)	1,560	1.0	2,080	1.0	2,600	1.0
Total operating expenses	44,140	28.3	49,820	24.0	58,250	22.4
Earnings before interest and tax (6)	25,280	16.2	48,980	23.5	70,450	27.1
Add: Depreciation and amortization (7)	7,000	4.5	7,000	3.4	7,000	2.7
Cash flow before interest, tax, and franchisee compensation	$ 32,280	20.7%	$ 55,980	26.9%	$ 77,450	29.8%

* Post start-up; no operator/franchisee compensation is included.
See notes below.

Notes to Mmmuffins cash flow projections:
(1)   Based on prices of 60–65¢ per muffin, $3.45 for six, and 40¢ per cup of coffee.
(2)   Based on 70-hour weekly selling period with hourly wages of $3.75–$4.75 for baking staff, $3.50–$4.00 for full-time selling staff, and $3.00–$3.50 for part-time staff. Owner-operator's compensation is not included.
(3)   Total occupancy includes all services for which landlord invoices including rent, merchants' association fees, common area charges, HVAC, realty taxes, and so forth. Total occupancy may vary depending on location. We have assumed base rent of $40 per square foot for a 350-square-foot store or 7 percent of sales (whichever is greater) plus $8 per square foot in "extras."
(4)   Depreciation and amortization is calculated by applying the straight-line method on $70,000 over 10 years.

Exhibit 9 (*continued*)

    (5) Miscellaneous expense may include cash shortages, licenses and permits, office supplies, professional fees, and so forth.

    (6) Earnings before interest, tax, and franchisee's compensation is expressed as such due to wide variances in compensations paid, amount of debt to service, individual's accounting treatment of expenses, and so forth.

    (7) Depreciation, being a non-cash expense, is added back to illustrate total cash generated before interest, tax, and franchise compensation.

BAGUETTE
Potential Annual Cash Flow*
(3,000-square-foot mall location)

	Weekly Sales					
	$14,000		**$18,000**		**$22,000**	
	Amount	*Percent*	*Amount*	*Percent*	*Amount*	*Percent*
Annual sales	$728,000		$936,000		$1,144,000	
Food cost	232,960	32.0%	299,520	32.0%	354,640	31.0%
Selling supplies	21,840	3.0	28,080	3.0	34,320	3.0
Labour (including benefits) (1)	203,840	28.0	243,360	26.0	286,000	25.0
Gross operating profit	269,360	37.0	365,040	39.0	469,040	41.0
Operating expenses:						
Royalties	43,680	6.0	56,160	6.0	68,640	6.0
Utilities (2)	14,000	1.9	15,000	1.6	17,000	1.5
Telephone	700	.1	700	.1	700	.1
Uniforms and laundry	2,200	.3	2,600	.3	3,000	.3
Advertising (3)	7,280	1.0	9,360	1.0	11,500	1.0
Repairs and maintenance (4)	5,000	.7	6,000	.6	7,000	.6
Replacements (5)	3,500	.5	4,500	.5	5,500	.5
Insurance	3,000	.4	3,000	.3	3,000	.3
Total occupancy (rent) (6)	75,000	10.3	77,000	8.2	89,500	7.8
Depreciation (7)	30,000	4.1	30,000	3.2	30,000	2.6
Miscellaneous (8)	7,280	1.0	9,360	1.0	11,500	1.0
Total operating expenses	191,640	26.3	213,680	22.8	247,340	21.6
Earnings before interest and						
tax	77,720	10.7	151,360	16.2	221,700	19.4
Add: Depreciation (9)	30,000	4.1	30,000	3.2	30,000	2.6
Cash flow before interest, tax,						
and franchisee compensation	$107,720	14.8%	$181,360	19.4%	$251,700	22.0%

* After six-month start-up period; no operator/franchisee compensation is included.
See notes on the next page.

Exhibit 9 (*concluded*)

Notes to Baguette cash flow projections:
(1) Based on 70-hour weekly selling period with hourly wages of $4.00–$5.00 for baking staff, $3.50–$4.50 for full-time service, food preparation and bussing staff, and $3.25–$3.75 for part-time staff. Management salaries included: assistant store manager at $14,500 per year, head baker at $15,600 per year. Owner-operator's salary is not included.
(2) Based on actual experience in Toronto store. Utility expenses may vary widely depending on location, use of gas versus electric oven, hours of operation, and so forth.
(3) One percent allocation is for local advertising and promotion. At this time the franchisor does not maintain a national advertising fund.
(4) As most equipment is under warranty, first-year repair expenses should be lower than projections. Actual cost in future years will vary considerably due to periodic breakdowns, preventive maintenance program, use of equipment, and so forth.
(5) Replacements include costs of replenishing supplies of utensils, dishware, cutlery, trays, and so forth.
(6) Total occupancy includes all services for which landlord invoices: rent, merchants' association fees, common area charges, heating, ventilation, and air conditioning, realty taxes, and so forth. We have assumed a base rent of $18 per square foot for a 3,000-square-foot store or 6 percent of sales (whichever is greater) plus $7 per square foot in nonrent "extras." Actual total occupancy costs will vary for each location and should be evaluated individually.
(7) Depreciation is calculated by applying the straight-line method on $360,000 over 12 years.
(8) Miscellaneous expenses may include professional fees, licenses and permits, cash shortages, office supplies, and so forth.
(9) Depreciation, being a noncash expense, is added back to illustrate total cash generated before interest, tax, and franchisee's compensation.

Later, while lawyers were completing the legal paperwork, things changed. REC came back and said they wanted to include another location in Manitoba in central Canada in the agreement:

They said they were creating a package for me: the two Toronto locations and Manitoba in the west or nothing. And being the naive kid that I was, I got extremely upset. But we had a deal! I'd already told my partner about my plans for Toronto and that was OK, but the town in Manitoba had only about 50,000 people and was a thousand miles away. It was a rural environment and difficult to reach.

So I told them that we were just a young chain, and we just wanted to do a few stores at a time. They said, "No, that's the way it has to be." They had a brand new mall and needed to fill the space.

In the excitement of the offer of the initial two locations, Michael had been somewhat swept away with events. Now he was confronted with a more difficult situation than he had anticipated and felt he should pause to rethink his overall company strategy before reacting to this new offer. How should he make his company grow? How fast? How should he divide his efforts between the two concepts? Now he realized he should answer these questions before he went ahead with any expansion deal.

Case 28

Mike's Submarine Sandwiches Limited

As we see it, we may now be approaching saturation in the Quebec market. We may have to start to look at another metropolitan area as a base from which to spread out and repeat what we have done in the province of Quebec, rather than spread out helter-skelter with single stores.

These were the words of Mr. Lars Muller, president of Mike's Submarine Sandwiches, a rapidly growing fast-food chain which specialized in submarine sandwiches and pizzas. Mike's Submarine had grown primarily in the Montreal vicinity in the province of Quebec, and in early 1978 the management of Mike's were investigating three alternative metropolitan areas for future growth. They had tentatively concluded that the most favourable location for expansion was Boston, Massachusetts, and were about to consider the various details involved in such a move.

The Origins of Mike's Submarine

Mike's Submarine Sandwiches Limited was established in Montreal in March 1967 by the Marano brothers, who had seen a similar concept operating in the United States. Later that year the company was incorporated under federal charter as Mike's Submarine Sandwiches Limited.

The company's products—submarine sandwiches and pizzas—won immediate favour, and the brothers proceeded to open additional outlets. The four brothers, Antonio, Michael, Dominico, and Aldo, divided the responsibilities amongst themselves, including those for store operations, new sites and construction, and the franchising of outlets which began in 1969.

In the latter part of 1969 Mike's was brought to the attention of Mr. Austin C. Beutel and his associates as an investment possibility. Beutel explained: "My group was interested in investments in smaller companies as developing enterprises, turnarounds, and emerging companies, and Mike's fitted the criteria for investment, so we proceeded."

Commenting on the earlier days of the restaurant operation, Muller stated that the investment people were impressed with the Maranos' ability to "punch things through" and their willingness to work 24 hours a day if necessary.

This case is based on two cases prepared by Professor W. H. Ellis of McGill University. Copyright © 1978 by W. H. Ellis. Edited by Mark C. Baetz, 1986.

Muller commented further:

> The Maranos went and opened up stores but really were better small business managers than corporate managers. For all of the good things that they did, they really never understood the basic principles of finance. They looked at the till and the bank balance, and everything looked rosy. When the creditors or the tax man came in, they were in trouble. Two weeks afterwards, if sales were good, they were flush again. You can't finance that way, and you can't build a company that way.

Antonio (Tony) resigned from the company's management in 1972 and acquired C. Segatore Bakery Company Limited. He subsequently supplied bread and other food products to Mike's and many of its franchises. During fiscal year 1976 purchases by Mike's from Segatore Bakery amounted to nearly $125,000.

Two years after Tony's resignation, Michael Marano, who had become the chief operating officer of the company, and his brother Dominico, an employee, both resigned.

Following these resignations, Mr. Michael Hockenstein was appointed president of Mike's on October 1, 1973, with the responsibility of overseeing all the company's operations. Hockenstein was a chartered accountant by training who had previously operated a small computer service company and had worked for eight months as an analyst for Mr. Beutel.

The last of the Marano brothers, Aldo, served as second in charge to Mr. Hockenstein until February 1975 when he resigned to acquire a franchise. Three months later, Hockenstein himself resigned and was replaced in May 1975 by Mr. Lars Muller as president of Mike's Submarine Sandwiches Limited.

Management and Organization Structure

Mr. Muller became president of Mike's at the age of 35. He had embarked upon a university career but "just got fed up with it" and joined an investment house because "it seemed like a nice place to work and I had read somewhere that the closer you are to the money, the easier it is to make it." Muller's activities in the securities business and involvement in corporate finance led to his association with Beutel. On becoming president of Mike's, Muller was also appointed secretary-treasurer of its parent company, Restaurant Holdings of Canada Limited (see Exhibit 1 for organization structure).

Mike's supervisory staff consisted of Mr. Peter Deros, vice president, and Mr. Steve Deklaras, operations manager, who worked directly with the franchisees to maintain the company's quality standards and overall image.

Deros joined Mike's in February 1975 at the age of 27. He had had 10 years' experience in the fast-food industry, and his functions were described as being concerned with the selection of the franchisees, problems related to the start-ups of the stores, and "working deals." His responsibilities also included quality control and supplies. "I want him out there helping to get the stores opened," stated Muller.

Exhibit 1: Mike's Submarine Sandwiches Limited (Organization Chart, June 1977)

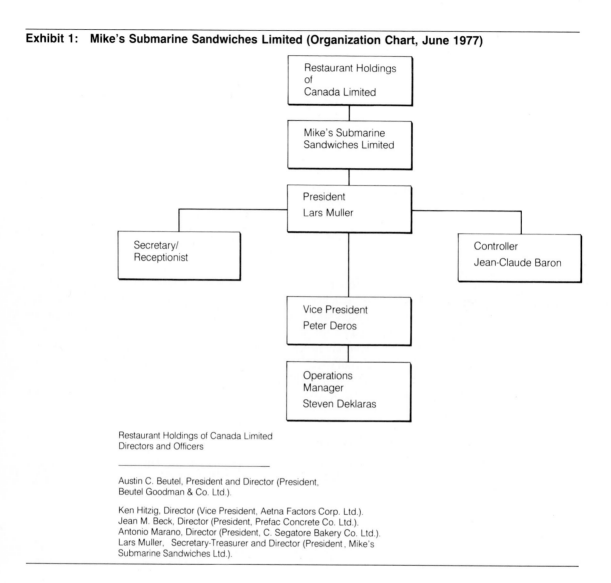

Restaurant Holdings of Canada Limited
Directors and Officers

Austin C. Beutel, President and Director (President, Beutel Goodman & Co. Ltd.).

Ken Hitzig, Director (Vice President, Aetna Factors Corp. Ltd.).
Jean M. Beck, Director (President, Prefac Concrete Co. Ltd.).
Antonio Marano, Director (President, C. Segatore Bakery Co. Ltd.).
Lars Muller, Secretary-Treasurer and Director (President, Mike's Submarine Sandwiches Ltd.).

Deklaras, 26, who joined Mike's a short time after Deros, was the "franchisee's services man," working closely with Deros at the operational level. His duties were described as the day-to-day contact with the franchisees, "everything from money problems to moral support, spending 95 percent of his day on the road." The service aspect was considered by management to be a critical facet of franchising relationships, "requiring a salesman-type background," which Deklaras had had. "He gets the things done and he does them nicely," was the view expressed by Muller.

The remaining head office staff consisted of a controller-accountant and a bookkeeper-typist who worked directly with Muller. Muller himself estimated that he spent about 50 percent of his time on the control aspect of Mike's, with the remainder being spent "in the field or on site selection."

The members of the board of directors of Mike's Submarine Sandwiches Limited were all representatives of the parent company, Restaurant Holdings of Canada Limited, which in turn held all of Mike's stock.

Beutel, as president of the parent company, described his role relative to Mike's as "one largely of liaison with Lars Muller, representing the financial interest. The other directors and I are consulted on advertising strategy, growth strategy, and general business policies. In this latter area, I do spend a lot of time, but the day-to-day operations, control, and details are left to Mr. Muller."

As an overall comment on Mike's organization, Muller commented: "As a policy, I want to be about one man short at all times. That means everybody is going to have to stretch a little."

Company Strategy and Objectives

Mike's Submarine Sandwiches Limited was conceived by Beutel and his associates as being in the business of establishing, franchising, financing, and to a lesser degree, operating fast-food establishments specializing in submarine sandwiches and pizzas. While the company was founded initially as a restaurant operation, it quickly began to franchise stores, and over the years the ratio of franchised to company-owned and operated stores had increased substantially (see Table 1).

The majority of stores (21 out of 28 in mid-1977) were located in the greater Montreal area, with four being in the Quebec City area and two in Eastern Ontario. All locations were leased for varying periods of time, except for a location owned by the parent company. Also, with two exceptions, the leases were in the name of Mike's, while in one other instance, the franchisee was the property owner. Elaborating further on the basic concepts of Mike's, Beutel made the following comments dealing with various facets of the operation:

Table 1: Stores in Operation

	Company Owned	Franchised	Total
October 1971	4	7	11
December 1972	6	3	9
December 1973	8	3	11
December 1974	3	10	13
December 1975	2	16	18
December 1976	4	21	25
June 1977	2	26	28
December 1977 (estimated)	2	31	33

We decided that the proper concept, given our limited resources of manpower and finances, was the franchise route, and so we proceeded not only to franchise out the restaurants we had but kept in mind that every future restaurant would be built for the purpose of franchising out.

Really, you might say that we are in the financing business more than we are in the submarine business or food business.

Our basic strategy is to maximize the return to the investor group. This means that we are trying to build a chain of restaurants by acquiring a strong consumer franchise within a geographic area which is continually expanding. Someone will come along and be prepared to buy the whole damn thing from us at a price that will reflect considerable goodwill for the market niche that we have built for ourselves.

We have tried to build the chain as rapidly as possible and focus all our resources, people, and money on the name and concept of Mike's as we know it, to become the dominant factor in our narrowly defined product line in a given market area because that is when you are in a position to be a leader.

It is basically a marketing game from the point of view of the public, and you are best off in a marketing game as we see it to have as much saturation and exposure as possible within a given market area. You then have the best economies of scale in advertising and promotion costs.

We made a pretty clear decision when Mr. Muller came in (after fumbling for a number of months) to focus on the Mike's concept and build the Mike's operation with the limited resources of people and money we had. We were not going to try to acquire a number of diverse operations under the same parent company—not even acquire a number of different restaurant operations—but just focus on the very narrow concept of submarines and pizzas under Mike's name.

The role of management today is to select sites, build and equip the restaurant, find a franchisee, make the deal with the franchisee, and supervise him to make sure that the standards of quality are maintained and that he is reporting properly—that is, presenting the right thing to the customer, doing that repeatedly, and paying us the agreed share.

We train the people, we supervise them, and we inspect, but really the money that the company is going to make is based on its sources of revenues, that is, franchise payments for the stores and royalties on sales.

The success of the operation will be a function of the success of the individual franchisees. But really we make our money as a finance and royalty company.

Financing and Corporate Performance

New Venture Equities Ltd., a venture capital affiliate of Beutel Goodman and Company Limited and others had initially advanced Mike's $150,000 in 1969, on a term basis, repayable in three to five years, for which they received, in partial consideration, 50 percent of the equity of Mike's. Representatives of New Venture Equities were elected to the board of the company.

On May 14, 1972, Rawhide Resources Limited, the name by which Restaurant Holdings of Canada Limited was then known, acquired all of the issued and outstanding shares of Mike's Submarine Sandwiches Limited for 1 million shares of its common stock then valued at $45,000.

At the time of the transaction, Mike's had a deficiency of net assets amounting to $95,000 so that the purchase consideration exceeded the net assets acquired by $140,000. In the 33 weeks remaining in 1972 Mike's had sales of $669,000 and net earnings of $20,900. During the year 1973 sales virtually doubled to $1,371,000, with net earnings of nearly $38,000 derived from the operations of 10 stores.

While the year 1973 saw rapid price increases in ingredients and escalating wage costs, the management of Mike's believed the return on investment and the commitment of funds in the establishment of new locations under Mike's banner were extremely attractive. Accordingly, the company pursued a program of expansion focused on the greater Montreal area and adjacent territory.

By the end of 1975 there were 18 stores in operation of which all but two were franchised. This year saw the conversion to and emphasis on franchised rather than company-operated locations. The immediate effect of this policy change was that corporate sales volume declined but was replaced by increased franchise sales and fees.

The direction of Mike's management activities became centered on securing new locations, providing leasehold improvements and equipment, enlisting franchisees, and supervising the franchise operations. Management was now of the opinion that the most serious limitation to growth was the availability of capital funds to invest in equipment and leasehold improvements and to finance the franchisee receivables.

The average cost per outlet in 1976 was estimated at about $50,000, depending on such factors as location, size, and existing facilities. At this time, it was believed that $250,000 would provide the company with sufficient funds for five or six outlets. These funds, together with down payments received and excess cash flow over repayments to the bank, would provide the company with sufficient funds to open up 8 to 10 stores per annum on an ongoing basis. To this end, an arrangement was made for revolving bank credit, first for $250,000 and later increased to $400,000 in April 1977.

The bank credit line was limited to 75 percent of the next 36 months of franchise payments receivable and was secured by such receivables, by the real estate owned by the company, and by a floating charge on all the company's assets. The franchise payments receivable consisted of the payments owed to the company by franchisees and were created contractually at the time a franchise was sold. Typically, the franchisee made an agreed-upon down payment, and the balance was payable monthly over five years in 60 even installments, principal and interest blended. Restaurant Holdings, as owner of 100 percent of Mike's shares, guaranteed the bank debt. The financial performance of Mike's from 1972 to 1977 is presented in Exhibits 2 and 3.

Competition

"Everybody in the whole fast-food industry is our competitor," explained Muller. There were approximately 89 fast-food franchise operators reported to be in

Exhibit 2

RESTAURANT HOLDINGS OF CANADA LIMITED
Consolidated Statement of Earnings and Retained Earnings
For the Years Ended December 31

	1977	1976	1975	1974	1973
Total restaurant sales (memorandum only—unaudited)	$6,655,000	$4,574,000	$2,598,131	$1,934,990	$1,370,790
Revenues:					
Company restaurant sales	504,555	530,396	687,663	1,054,520	844,819
Franchise sales and fees	716,801	399,094	230,083	118,347	167,149
Other	50,964	55,528	24,636	4,590	3,754
Total revenues	1,272,320	985,018	942,382	1,177,457	1,015,722
Costs and expenses:					
Company restaurants	440,684	460,253	636,716	1,114,398	932,268
Administrative and other	460,171	273,076	192,347		
Interest on long-term debt	15,865	15,000	13,406	6,249	14,125
Depreciation and amortization	143,837	97,687	46,975	47,244	31,454
Total costs and expenses	1,060,557	846,016	889,444	1,167,891	977,847
Earnings before income taxes and extraordinary item	211,763	139,002	52,938	9,566	37,875
Provision for income taxes—current	35,323	16,425	17,504	5,252	20,784
—deferred	62,109	48,439	10,764	—	—
Total provision for income taxes	97,432	64,864	28,268	5,252	20,784
Earnings before extraordinary item	114,331	74,138	24,670	4,314	17,091
Extraordinary item	—	7,219	10,623	5,252	20,784
Net earnings	$ 114,331	$ 81,357	$ 35,293	$ 9,566	$ 37,875
Earnings per share:					
Before extraordinary item	$ 0.315	$ 0.214	$ 0.088	$ 0.017	$ 0.0879
Extraordinary item	—	0.021	0.037	0.021	0.1010
Net earnings per share	$ 0.315	$ 0.235	$ 0.125	$ 0.038	$ 0.1889
Source of funds:					
Provided from operations:					
Earnings before extraordinary item	$ 114,331	$ 74,138	$ 24,670	$ 4,314	$ 37,875
Charges not requiring cash outlay	—	—	—	—	—
Depreciation and amortization	143,837	97,687	46,975	47,244	31,454
Deferred income taxes	52,217	48,439	10,764	—	—
Total from operations	310,385	220,264	82,409	51,558	69,329
From other sources:					
Recovery of income taxes on application of losses of prior years	—	7,219	17,504	5,252	—
Increase in long-term debt	50,000	—	—	—	—
Exercise of employee stock options	18,250	11,000	—	—	—
Issue of shares in exchange for convertible debt of the subsidiary company-contra	—	—	100,000	—	—
Issue of long-term debt	—	—	150,000	—	—
Other	—	—	—	750	2,440
Total sources of funds	378,635	238,483	349,913	57,560	71,769

Exhibit 2 *(concluded)*

	1977	1976	1975	1974	1973
Use of funds:					
Addition to fixed assets	$ 680,277	$ 349,100	$ 333,931	$ 142,571	$ 28,977
Conversion of long-term debt of subsidiary-contra	—	—	100,000	—	—
Increase in deposits	3,458	10,595	4,922	2,773	45
Total use of funds	683,735	359,695	438,853	145,344	29,022
Increase in working capital deficiency	305,100	121,212	88,940	87,784	(42,747)
Working capital deficiency at beginning of year	366,181	244,969	156,029	68,245	110,992
Working capital deficiency at end of year	671,281	366,181	244,969	156,029	68,245
Retained earnings (deficit) at beginning of year	21,199	(60,158)	(95,451)	(105,017)	(142,892)
Net earnings for the year	114,331	81,357	35,293	9,566	37,875
Retained earnings (deficit) at end of year	$ 135,530	$ 21,199	$ (60,158)	$ (95,451)	$ (105,017)

Canada in February 1977. Trade sources believed that McDonald's Restaurants of Canada Limited would continue to set the pace in hamburger houses and fast foods. Scott's Restaurants Company Limited, the largest operator of Kentucky Fried Chicken outlets, reportedly dominated the take-out chicken business. Foodex Systems Limited (Ponderosa) was expected to hold its lead in budget steak houses for the family restaurant sector.

In 1977 in the metropolitan Montreal area alone, McDonald's had 23 outlets; Kentucky Fried Chicken, 51; Harvey's 22; and Mr. Submarine, probably more closely competitive with Mike's, 4. There was no indication that any of these particular companies was content to remain with those numbers. For example, in 1977 the executive vice president for marketing at McDonald's stated: "A very important part of our growth now is going to be taking business away from competitors." Nevertheless, other fast-food companies were entering the market (Big Daddy's, Pizza Hut).

Competition for good surburban sites was also more intense, with prices rising appreciably. One company chain reported that its first stores in 1953 cost only $15,800 for land and building. By 1977 prices were rising that much in a single year.

There was quite a variation in the installation costs facing the various firms in the fast-food industry. Store-front chain family restaurants cost $90,000 to $120,000 to build and equip. Drive-ins with eating facilities were said to cost $240,000 to $260,000 and upwards. The big chains such as McDonald's faced installation costs of $500,000 to $1 million, with companies like Harvey's coming in at about $150,000 to $180,000. Mike's needed to spend up to $150,000, whereas Pizza Hut's installation costs were over $200,000.

Exhibit 3

RESTAURANT HOLDINGS OF CANADA LIMITED
Consolidated Balance Sheet
For the Years Ended December 31

Assets

	1977	1976	1975	1974	1973
Current assets:					
Cash	$ 5,842	$ 485	$ 132	$ 37,752	$ 80,933
Accounts receivable	40,920	13,928	19,898	19,919	13,201
Inventories at the lower of cost or net realizable value	3,286	5,829	4,521	26,247	21,175
Prepaid expenses	34,011	18,915	12,239	8,449	11,416
Total current assets	84,059	39,157	36,790	92,367	126,725
Fixed assets	1,325,388	788,948	537,535	250,579	155,252
Balances receivable on sale of franchises-contra	1,231,580	585,727	414,946	115,934	4,462
Intangible asset arising from acquisition of subsidiary	171,952	171,952	171,952	171,952	171,952
Other assets	24,340	20,188	9,593	11,552	11,885
Total assets	$2,837,319	$1,605,972	$1,170,816	$ 642,384	$ 470,276

Liabilities

	1977	1976	1975	1974	1973
Current liabilities:					
Bank advances	$ 479,183	$ 163,253	$ 46,477	$ 34,785	$ 34,014
Accounts payable and accrued liabilities	246,278	240,517	235,282	213,611	160,956
Income taxes payable	20,689	1,568	—	—	—
Deferred income taxes	9,190	—	—	—	—
Total current liabilities	755,340	405,338	281,759	248,396	194,970
Long-term debt	200,000	150,000	150,000	100,000	102,356
Unearned income on sale of franchises-contra	1,231,580	585,727	414,946	115,934	4,462
Deferred income taxes	112,122	59,203	10,764	—	—
Total liabilities	2,299,042	1,200,268	857,451	464,330	301,788

Shareholders' Equity

	1977	1976	1975	1974	1973
Capital stock:					
Authorized—991,540 shares without par value					
Issued—353,540 shares (1975—342,540)	402,747	348,505	373,505	273,505	273,505
Retained earnings (deficit)	135,530	21,199	(60,158)	(95,451)	(105,017)
Total liabilities and shareholders' equity	$2,837,319	$1,605,972	$1,170,816	$ 642,384	$ 470,276

The annual store volumes of firms such as Pizza Hut were under their construction costs, but Mike's store volumes were close to double the construction costs. According to Muller: "These numbers give us the leeway to gain new contracts."

Physical Plant

There was no standard design for Mike's stores although the logo on the exterior and the interior decor of all stores was intended to provide a similarity for the company's outlets.

In 1977 six of the locations had drive-in and parking facilities, whereas the majority, particularly in the downtown or urban areas, were located in leased buildings that provided ready access for walk-in traffic.

The stores ranged in seating capacity from the smallest at 24 persons to the largest which was able to seat 130 persons. They all featured Mike's red-orange colour combinations on walls, counters, and printed matter, including menus, and all served the same standard product at the same prices. All of the stores had sit-down facilities and, with the exception of two, offered delivery of the company's product at approximately a 10 percent differential.

The lack of parking facilities was thought by a franchisee to be a serious inhibitor to his particular sales growth:

> I know that customers will circle around once looking for a place to park, and if they can't find one, I have lost a sale. Hopefully they will come back another time, but I can't be sure.

Site Selection

In general, downtown locations with high traffic flow were favoured by some operators. However, the advantages of high exposure had to be weighed against five-day business activity and high site costs downtown, as opposed to seven days in the suburbs and something in between for intermediate locations in semi-industrial and semi-residential areas.

In discussing site selection, Muller noted: "The only thing that I want to see is concentration—as many people within a mile or a mile and a half as we can get. In Montreal that is about 100,000. One of my favourite ways to determine the feasibility of a site is just to sit on the curb and count the people going by—it is really that simple."

A mixture of commercial and residential populace was another criterion considered in the selection of new Mike's sites. With such a location the store would be able to obtain two meals per day instead of one. In the downtown area, they get lunch and the evening meal. The heavy industrial areas were a source of "massive" lunches and no evening meals, whereas in the residential area few lunches tended to be served, but the evening meals were large.

A further comment was made by Beutel on the company's site selection policy:

> Because we started in Montreal and are now a dominant factor there, maybe it will support more stores per given population than other areas where others may be established and aren't waiting for us. It is a matter of clawing your way in where there is service already and then, as the years go on and the product has become more accepted, we may find, as McDonald's and others have found, that an area that may have started on a 1:100,000 basis, can now support 1:50,000.

The company had extended its store operations to Cornwall and Kingston, 80 and 190 miles to the west, and to the Quebec City area, 160 miles to the east, with other stores opened or opening in the more northerly region of Quebec. Speaking of Quebec City, Beutel remarked, "Quebec City is just so large, and our fourth store will be opening there next month and that will be it. We may look for a fifth and possibly a sixth but no more."

Mike's management was reluctant to spread their sites too far afield:

> If you are going to take an isolated trading area where there is no spillover from a big city and the maximum it can support is one store, you will find that the economies of scale in terms of procurement and advertising promotion are against you. You will have another store, but it will be marginal, tough to service, and expensive to supervise.

Franchise Operations

Under Muller's direction, franchise sales and store openings had moved ahead aggressively so that by the end of 1977 there were two company-owned and 31 franchised stores for a total of 33.

Franchisees who had been in operation prior to 1975 felt that there had been a definite lack of guidance and direction from head office but that it had been remedied by the appointment of Muller. Muller, in turn, believed that the organization had to be just as concerned about the profitable performance of the franchisee's operations as it was for those owned by the company.

Franchises were awarded on the basis of the availability of a suitable franchisee, both in terms of financial resources and managerial competence. The franchise agreement provided for a level of performance for which failure to comply could result in the loss of the franchise privilege.

Mike's main attention was now focused on seeking out suitable locations, arranging for leasehold improvements and equipment for the outlets, and seeking franchisees to take over the operations. In addition, the company supervised quality and housekeeping standards, assisted franchisees with their operational problems, provided menus, and wherever possible, arranged for supplies through a designated commissary arrangement which afforded the company a nominal advertising allowance.

The company did not sell or lease real estate, fixtures, or equipment to its franchisees. The franchise agreement conveyed the right to use these fixed assets and to exploit the company's name and goodwill.

Franchisees purchased their own food and supplies. However, to enable Mike's and its franchisees to obtain the most advantageous prices and, at the same time, assist in the preservation of uniformity and quality, Mike's arranged contracts with a number of major suppliers and encouraged its franchisees to participate.

Despite this assistance (and similar to the experiences of many other companies in the fast-food industry), not all of Mike's units had been as successful as had been anticipated when they were opened. By mid-1977 a total of four stores had been closed, basically due to poor site locations and/or lack of attention on the part of the franchisee. Management now believed there would be considerably less opportunity for a repetition of similar situations where either the company had to take a store back or the franchisee would have to cease operations.

In discussing the control of the operation, Beutel remarked:

> Each Friday I have the sales figures for each store for the week ending the previous Sunday. Our year is divided into 13 four-week periods, and we budget on that basis. By looking through, I know how each store has done relative to the same week last year, how it is doing relative to budget. What I frequently do is look at the stores that are out of kilter. Most of our stores have been doing better than forecasted, but where there is a negative variance, I ask questions. It could be because there is a particular depressing factor in the area or any number of reasons. One of the suspicions is that you have a lousy manager there and he is scaring customers away.

Although franchisees had been interested in acquiring more than one outlet and had made this view known to management, Beutel said that from his experience, "in the few times we have tried it, it just hasn't worked. We have found that our successful franchisees, and most of them are successful, are those who own and operate a single store. The guy's own money is on the line, and the best operation follows when he is working in the store full-time."

Franchisee Selection

"Management, and this includes our franchisees, is the single greatest recurring problem we have," reported Beutel in discussing this aspect of the company's operations. This problem was by no means unique to Mike's and was a theme repeated time and again by many operators in the fast-food industry. Many of the large chains had extensive training programs, ranging from the nearly $10 million spent by McDonald's through its Hamburger University, Elk Grove, Illinois, down to the small operator who relied on the selection of friends and relatives who had little or no experience in the business. However, one report stated, "Entrepreneurial spirit is starting to give way to professional management techniques."

In Mike's experience, the franchisee most likely to succeed "tended to be an eager fellow who was anxious to make money, generally had a fairly limited education, in most cases was an immigrant, and was not afraid to work very hard for long hours and to get his hands dirty.''

Most of the franchisees were people who had worked in Mike's stores as chefs and cooks or were relatives or good friends of the existing franchisees.

Expanding on Mike's franchisee selection policy Beutel commented:

> We went the franchise route because the incentive is built into the franchisee. He has put up his own bucks and because of the leverage of the business, he can make a much bigger buck on his own. He tends to make his own decisions right on the spot rather than waiting for head office to make them. You have delegated out the responsibility automatically by virtually making him his own boss. The big decision occurs when one guy comes up and he has the $15,000 and another guy has a lot of valuable experience but doesn't have the $15,000. Sometimes you make a mistake and sometimes you are pleasantly surprised. But in our experience we know within a fairly short time period whether we have selected correctly or not.

Franchise Financing

The company was prepared to franchise a store at the time of its opening for a down payment usually between $5,000 to $15,000 and a total price which exceeded the cost to the company of the equipment and leasehold improvements by approximately $5,000 to $10,000. Part of this excess over cost was spent in preopening expenses, promotional efforts at the time of opening, and occasional head office assistance. The balance of the franchise sale carried varying interest rates ranging from 8 percent to 12 percent per annum and payable in equal monthly installments varying from 48 months to 60 months and occasionally longer.

The major function of the company was the creation of restaurant locations and equipping and improving them so as to increase the number of franchised outlets which in turn would enlarge the base on which the company collected its 7 percent royalty payments.

All leasehold improvements and equipment were purchased either for cash or on a short-term unsecured credit basis from suppliers.

The growth and profitability of Mike's was the direct function of sales at the consumer level, and since these were a function of the number of outlets, the company's objective was to continue opening stores and franchising them. This activity required outside financing as the total cost of equipping a store substantially exceeded the down payment received.

Commenting on the franchisee financing aspects of the operation, Beutel stated:

> Because of the acceptance of our products and because our stores have been gaining momentum rapidly, we have changed our numbers. Our fee structure is quite frankly geared to what the market will bear. It has changed a fair amount in the past two years. Part of that reflects inflation and part reflects our ability to command a premium.

We normally look for anywhere between $10,000 and $20,000 down. On the other hand, if it is a man that we know and have a lot of confidence in, we might be prepared to take $5,000 down, $5,000 in three months, and $5,000 in six months in addition to the regular schedule of payments. The most we have ever received as a down payment was $20,000.

Marketing

"We are serving a product that is almost tailor-made for our market," reported Muller in discussing Mike's market and promotional approach. Basically, this market was believed to be composed essentially of industrial and office workers, ethnic groups, and on the whole, the 18- to 40-year age group.

"We are creating a product that we are selling, but the product we are creating is stores. We own the proprietary rights to the concept that we have and to the name. What we really sell to the franchisee is the right to exploit our name, our menu, and to benefit from the services that head office provides by way of advertising, identification, supervision, quality format, and so on," reported Beutel.

Mike's marketing strategy was to open up stores and establish a primary position in its market. Muller, in commenting on the company's progress to date, said, "I don't know if 50 percent sales growth is an achievable objective, but it is looking good so far."

Beginning in 1977 there were two issues uppermost in the minds of Mike's management with regard to its market development: (1) the saturation of Quebec and (2) what to do, if anything, toward expanding into another major market area.

So far as the existing market in Quebec was concerned, an examination of the sales of each outlet, week by week, year by year, indicated that store sales had built rapidly to a given plateau and thereafter had grown slowly in line with certain population factors, growing acceptability of the products, and inflation. In terms of number of stores, Muller believed that Quebec would be saturated at about 45 stores. Nevertheless, the increase in the number of stores in recent years had not cut into the sales of the existing outlets. As far as the company could determine, the fluctuations in an individual outlet, apart from seasonal factors, were the result of the particular manager's or franchisee's skills. In other words, certain stores had displayed declining trends at various periods of time, and when the manager or franchisee had been replaced, the trend had been reversed.

The impact of more outlets seemed to afford the company the opportunity for increasing exposure. This, in turn, led to increased popularity and acceptability and a larger base for advertising and promotional efforts. With this in mind, management set aside a budget of approximately 1.5 percent of sales for advertising and promotion but, since 1975, had been spending nearly 2 percent annually. By comparison, McDonald's was reported to set aside 4.5 percent of all store revenues for advertising, promotion, and charitable projects. In 1976 the company spent $50,000 on radio spots, in the print media, and for the production of the company's menus.

Television was used for the first time in 1977, when the budget was increased to $125,000. In addition to the other promotional media used previously, a theme song was developed—"We are trying to create an image."

Other merchandising material such as T-shirts and stickers were made available for franchisee use as well as part of the company's overall campaign.

The Future

In 1977 comments on the future of the fast-food industry were sprinkled with conclusions such as "Either for convenience or sheer pleasure, the forecast is that many Canadians will soon be eating two meals out of three away from home." Similar trends had also been forecast for the United States with three out of four being suggested as indicative of the future in that country.

While the eating-out market was expected to continue a growth pattern, the sailing was not expected to be quite as smooth as it had been in the past. (See the Appendix.) Amongst the reasons frequently cited were the escalation of costs and overexpansion, particularly in certain segments of the industry and in certain areas of both Canada and the United States. Furthermore, as competition became more intense, the marketing role was expected to become a more important function as firms struggled to capture not only increasing primary demand but more and more market share from each other.

Fully cognizant of the many problems facing the future not only of the industry in general but of Mike's Submarine Sandwiches in particular, Beutel summarized his thinking about the company's future moves:

> We have a small but dynamic head office group whose focus has been on selecting locations and opening stores, finding the franchisees for them, and so on. We have pretty well saturated the Quebec market area where we started.
> We could say we have done a job here, sit back, and with a minimum of supervision and effort clip the coupons by collecting the fees and returning the money to the shareholders. Or we could say we want to go to another major metropolitan area or major marketing area. For the first store in that new area, there would be no exposure and there would be all the front-end expenses of starting, and the second time around is always more expensive than the first time.

Alternative Markets for Future Growth

The rule of thumb which guided Mike's Submarine market and site selection was the ratio of approximately one site per 100,000 population, preferably in relatively concentrated clusters. A new market would have to be a major centre, with local sources of supply for ingredients as well as advertising media, which could support a sufficient number of stores to justify administrative personnel and serve as a base for further outward expansion.

For instance, Quebec City could support four or five stores but not a permanent regional office nor become a base for further outlets. Therefore, using Montreal as the centre, a series of concentric circles were drawn with a maximum radius of 300 miles, representing about one hour's flying time from the focal point. Three major markets fitting the rule-of-thumb criteria became readily apparent: (1) Toronto, Ontario, (2) the Albany-Schenectady area, and (3) Boston, Massachusetts. Each location was then evaluated as follows:

(1) Toronto, Ontario

The Greater Toronto area had a population of just over 2.2 million, making it the largest metropolitan centre in Canada. The city had been experiencing rapid growth for several years and had a diversified and growing ethnic population. It would be relatively easy to arrange for supplies and promotional activity, and banking arrangements would be an extension of existing credits. However, the number of fast-food outlets appeared to be approaching saturation, and store rentals had escalated in recent years. It would also be difficult to obtain desirable locations. Furthermore, in the sale of submarine sandwiches there was one dominant supplier, Mr. Submarine, whose base was Toronto, with over 150 outlets throughout the city and a substantial advertising budget.

(2) Albany-Schenectady, New York

The major attraction to this area is that it fell well within the prescribed radius limit from Montreal, although airline connections were not as frequent and travelling time would actually be increased over the other two prospective locations. Furthermore, while the area could serve as a base for expansion eastward into populated New England, westward to upstate New York cities, and southward toward New York and New Jersey, the metropolitan region itself did not seem to possess the necessary vitality and appeal. Finally, there were a number of Mike's Submarine shops, independently owned and now completely unrelated, that would have created an identity problem. Thus, the "uncomfortable" feel and competitive situation in this area persuaded the company to consider the one other market possibility.

(3) Boston, Massachusetts

Studies of this area showed that the northeast part of the United States, particularly Massachusetts, had a lower concentration of fast-food shops relative to population than most of the other market areas under consideration. Boston was the home of the "Hero Sandwich," and there were a lot of such shops, hence a basic familiarity with the submarine concept. There was no dominant supplier in contrast with the situation in Toronto. Another feature that seemed to be attractive about Boston was the relatively dense population not only in the metropolitan area itself but along the corridor toward New York City. Even if New York City itself was by-passed, Mike's believed that there would be considerable potential in moving gradually into adjacent areas that would easily support the 1:100,000 ratio mentioned previously.

The Boston market was not without its drawbacks. Boston had quite different population concentrations compared with Montreal and was considerably more spread out. Some sections of downtown Boston tended to become virtually vacant in the evenings, and that was hardly conducive to maximum utilization of a fast-food outlet, even with a concentrated populace. The traffic patterns were vastly different to those in Montreal so that additional studies would be required in order to define desirable locations. There appeared to be a higher proportion of the greater Boston population living in single-family dwellings than was the situation in Montreal resulting in a much more scattered pattern.

While Boston was an appealing place to live, Mike's would have to establish completely new banking connections as its Canadian arrangements could not include the security of foreign-based assets. Further, the decline of the Canadian dollar made for difficulty in currency transactions and foreign exchange complications. Finally, Mike's would have to arrange for new suppliers of everything from equipment to ingredients to services and deal with a completely different set of rules, not only locally but nationally.

The Next Move

After reviewing the advantages and disadvantages of each location, Beutel and Muller concluded that Boston was the preferable location. Beutel described the next move:

> We went down to Boston and were introduced to people in the real estate business by friends whose opinions we respected. We toured the areas and, granted that we had a bias that we were ready to be impressed, we came away with a favourable feeling that we should proceed.

Appendix: The Fast-Food Industry

The fast-food franchise operator in Canada, based on recent trade information, had shown a "sizzling" growth rate in recent years, even more dynamic than that of the United States.

Fast-Food Franchise Operations

	Canada		Percent Increase in Canada	Percent Increase in the United States
	1974	*1976*		
Number of units	1,952	2,606	33.5%	20%
Total sales	$449 million	$764 million	69.8	32
Average sales/unit	$230,000	$293,000	27.4	10

Source: *Food Service and Hospitality*, February 1977.

The average sales per unit in Canada in 1976 was higher than the $275,000 U.S. average. Comparative data in share of market by menu type showed significant variations from the U.S. pattern.

Fast-Food Menu Operation, 1976

Major Menu Item	Percent in Canada	Percent in United States
Hamburgers, franks, and roast beef	43%	54%
Steak	5	15
Chicken	40	13
Pizza	7	8
Seafoods	1.5	3
Other (pancakes, sandwiches, ice cream)	16	10

Source: *Food Service and Hospitality*, February 1977.

The main reasons cited for the growth of the franchised operators in foodservice and lodging sectors were:

1. Franchise operations were usually controlled by professionals skilled in all operating areas. These skills were made available to every franchisee and substantially improved their operating efficiency and effectiveness.
2. Efficiency in marketing and "brand" recognition attracted new and repeat customers while reducing unit promotion and advertising costs as a percentage of sales.
3. Development costs of establishing and operating units were spread over a larger base, both in number of locations and number of customer transactions. Improved profits and lower consumer prices were, therefore, possible.
4. Ability of multiunit operators to buy in larger quantities meant lower unit prices, better uniformity in products or services provided, and greater efficiency in staffing and operations.
5. The franchise operator was less vulnerable if a local market condition reduced sales or profitability in one or several units. Single unit operators could be very vulnerable to local conditions.
6. Franchisors have taken increasing advantage of technology, particularly the availability of new, improved equipment and more efficient methods of operation.
7. Better financing and banking was available under the umbrella of a franchise group, whether or not franchisors were directly involved in the financing through funding or guarantees. Improved confidence on the part of the funds supplier meant more funds were available, often at a lower rate.

Case 29

Note on Licensing

What Is Licensing?

Licensing, in its basic form, is a contractual arrangement whereby the licensor (firm) allows its technology, patents, trademarks, or other proprietary advantages to be used by the licensee (another firm) for a fee. Licensing is a strategy for technology transfer and, internationally, a stage in the firm's "internationalization process" that requires little time or depth of involvement in foreign markets, in comparison to export strategies, joint ventures, and foreign direct investment (FDI).

When Is Licensing Employed?

The advantages to be gained by licensing depend on the technology, firm size, product maturity, and extent of the firm's experience. There are a number of internal and external circumstances that may lead a firm to employ a licensing strategy:

1. The licensee has existing products or facilities but requires technology, which may be acquired more cheaply or quickly from third parties (licensors) than by internal R&D; the need may be of limited extent or duration.

2. The licensor wishes to exploit its technology in secondary markets that may be too small to justify larger investments; the required economies of scale may not be attainable.

3. The licensee wishes to maximize its own business by adding new technologies.

4. Host-country governments restrict imports and/or FDI; or the risk of nationalization or foreign control is too great.

5. Prospects of "technology feedback" are high (that is, the licensor has contractually ensured himself of access to new developments generated by the licensee and based on licensed knowledge).

6. Licensing is a way of testing and developing a market that can later be exploited by direct investment.

This note was prepared by Paul W. Beamish and William Webb. Copyright © 1986 by Paul W. Beamish.

7. The licensee is unlikely to become a future competitor.

8. The pace of technological change is sufficiently rapid that the licensor can remain technologically superior and ahead of the licensee, who is a potential competitor.

9. Opportunities exist for licensing auxiliary processes without having to license basic product or process technologies.

10. A firm lacks the capital and managerial resources required for exporting or FDI but wants to earn additional profits with minimal commitment.

Risks Associated with Licensing

1. Most importantly, the licensor risks the dissipation of its proprietary advantage, since the licensee acquires at least a portion of the advantage via licensing. Thus, the licensor should try to ensure that its licensee will not be a future competitor.

   Licensed trademarks remain the licensor's property in perpetuity whereas licenses normally have a finite lifetime. A licensor may retain considerable bargaining power in proportion to the perishability of the licensed technology and the licensor's ability to provide a continuing supply of new technology in the future.

2. The licensor risks its worldwide reputation if the licensee cannot maintain the desired product standards and quality or if it engages in questionable practices.

3. Profits to the licensor may not be maximized since their involvement in the licensed markets is indirect.

Why Is Canada an Attractive Market for Licensing?

1. Canada has no regulatory scheme governing licensing unlike some countries where licenses are not valid until government approval or registration is completed.

2. Investment Canada (the successor organization of the federal Foreign Investment Review Agency) regulations do not apply to licensing unless it relates in some way to the control of a Canadian business enterprise.

3. Licenses granting exclusive rights to certain products or territories are allowed in Canada, except in rare cases when the government prohibits it because competition will be substantially lessened.

4. Canada does not have any foreign exchange controls or other restrictions on royalty payments (license fees). A ''withholding tax'' of 25 percent on royalty payments to nonresident licensors is applied but is reduced to 15 percent or less if the payments are to a licensor in one of 32 countries with which Canada has favoured-status tax treaties.

5. Canadian license agreements enjoy the benefit of freedom of contract. The

parties may, for the most part, create their own legal framework by the manner in which the contract is written.

Major Elements of the License Agreement

The license agreement is the essential commercial contract which specifies the rights to be granted, the consideration payable, and the duration of the agreement. The licensed rights usually take the form of patents, registered trademarks, registered industrial designs, unpatented technology, trade secrets, "know-how," or copyrights. The particular rights in a definable product and, therefore, the license agreement should make explicit reference to the product as well as to the underlying "intangible" or "intellectual" property rights.

Although no definitive standard form exists for these agreements, there are certain points which are typically covered in such a contract. In many cases, licensors will have developed "standard" forms for these contracts, based on their past experiences in licensing.

Typically, a license agreement will include the following:

1. A clear and correct description of the parties to the agreement, identifying the corporate names of each party, its incorporating jurisdiction, and its principal place of business.

2. A preamble or recitals describing the parties, their reasons for entering into the arrangement, and their respective roles.

3. A list of defined terms for the purposes of the particular contract in order to simplify this complex document and to eliminate ambiguity or vagueness (for example, definitions of the terms *licensed product*, *net profit*, *territory*, and so forth).

4. A set of schedules, in an exhibit or appendix, where necessary, to segregate lengthy detailed descriptions of any kind.

5. The grant which is fundamental to the agreement and explicitly describes the nature of the rights being granted to the licensee.

6. A description of any geographical limitations to be imposed on the licensee's manufacturing, selling, or sublicensing activities.

7. A description of any exclusive rights to manufacture and sell which may be granted.

8. A discussion of any rights to sublicense.

9. The terms relating to the duration of the agreement, including the initial term and any necessary provisions for the automatic extension or review of the agreement.

10. Provisions for the granting of rights to downstream refinements or improvements made by the licensor in the future.

11. Provisions for "technological flowback" agreements where some benefit of improvements made by the licensee revert to the licensor. The rights to

the future improvements by either the licensor or licensee are often used as bargaining chips in negotiations.

12. Details regarding the royalties or periodic payments based on the use of licensed rights. The percentage rate of the royalty may be fixed or variable (based on time, production level, sales level, and so forth), but the "royalty base" for this rate must be explicitly defined. Some methods of calculating royalties include percentage of sales, royalties based on production, percentage of net profit, lump-sum payments, or payment-free licenses in cross-licensing arrangements.

   There are no hard and fast rules for establishing royalty rates. One arbitrary rule (see Contractor) is the "25 percent rule of thumb" which suggests that the licensor aim for a 25 percent share of the licensee's related profits and then convert this profit level to a certain royalty rate. Others suggest that licensors will often specify a minimum or target absolute compensation. This can be derived from technology transfer cost considerations or a judgment of how much it may cost the prospective licensee to acquire the technology by other means or from an "industry norm." Royalty escalation clauses and the currency of payment should also be specified.

13. Specification of minimum performance requirements (for example, minimum royalty payments, unit sales volumes, employment of named personnel, minimum promotion expenditures, and so forth) to ensure the "best efforts" of the licensee in order that the license potential is fully exploited.

14. Other clauses common to most license agreements, including those to protect the licensed rights against licensees and third parties and those regarding title retention by the licensor, confidentiality of "know-how," quality control, most-favoured-licensee status, the applicable language of the contract, and any provisions with respect to the assignability of rights by the licensee.

The above list of elements common to most license agreements is, by no means, exhaustive. For a more detailed checklist for license agreements, see the Appendix which follows. It must be noted that every contract to a license agreement is unique in some way, and therefore, great care should be taken in its negotiation and formal documentation.

References

Contractor, Farok, J. "A Generalized Theorem for Joint-Venture and Licensing Negotiations." *Journal of International Business Studies*, Summer 1985, pp. 25–47.

Robock, Stefan H., and Kenneth Simmonds. *International Business and Multinational Enterprises.* 3rd ed. Homewood, Ill.: Richard D. Irwin, 1983.

Rugman, Alan M., Donald J. Lecraw, and Laurence D. Booth. *International Business: Firm and Environment.* New York: McGraw-Hill, 1985.

Stitt, Hubert J., and Samuel R. Baker. *The Licensing and Joint Venture Guide.* 3rd ed. Toronto: Ontario Ministry of Industry, Trade, and Technology, 1985.

Appendix: Note on Licensing

Checklist for License Agreements

Parties
Name of licensor_____
Address_____
Principal office_____
Incorporated in_____
Short title_____
Name of licensee_____
Address_____
Principal office_____
Incorporated in_____
Short title_____

Recitals
Licensor owns inventions ____ patents ____
patent ____ applications ____
industrial designs ____ trade marks ____
know-how ____
Licensor represents that it has the right to grant
a license relating to_____
Licensee represents_____
Licensee desires license relating to_____

Definitions
Define "the products" covered by a limited
license. If certain types of inventions only are
covered, define "the inventions". Define
"patents", "trade-marks", "registered designs",
"copyrights", "know-how", "net sales",
"territory". Adopt other defined terms as needed.

Date of Agreement
From date hereof_____
From some specific date_____
Effective date_____
When approved by_____

Grant
Patents_____
Trademarks_____
Registered designs_____
Copyright_____
Know how_____
Existing future
improvements by licensor_____
  In licensed inventions
  or know how_____
  In same field or for
  similar applications_____
All rights to use know-how and practise
inventions ____ and to make, use and sell
products ____
Exclusive_____
Exclusive except as to licensor_____
Exclusive for ____ years and non-exclusive
thereafter
Non-exclusive_____
Irrevocable_____

With right to grant sub-licences_____
  To make (manufacture)_____
  To have made for own use_____
  Unlimited_____
To use_____
To sell_____
To lease ____ rent ____

Nature of know-how
  Invention records
  Laboratory records
  Research reports
  Development reports
  Engineering reports
  Pilot plant design
  Production plant design
  Production specifications
  Raw material specifications
  Quality controls
  Economic surveys
  Market surveys
  Promotion methods
  Trade secrets
  List of customers
  Drawings and photographs
  Models, tools and parts
  Other (specify)
  Know-how not confidential
  Know-how confidential
    Employees to be bound
    Subcontractors and sublicensees to be bound
  If patents held invalid:
    Know-how payment stops
    Know-how payment continues

Territory
All countries ____ all countries except ____
(specify)

Restrictions
Limited to specified field_____
Limited to specified territory_____
Subject to prior license_____
Subject to licensor's right to make ____
have made ____ use ____ sell ____

Sub-Licenses
To any other party_____
To nominees of licensor_____
At specified consideration_____
Limitations_____
Consideration to be shared
with licensor_____
Copies to be furnished to licensor_____

Term
For ____ years.
Until (specify date)_____
Until some future event (specify)_____
For the life of any patent_____
Until specified notice of
termination_____
Extension of term_____

Automatic unless notice of
termination_____
Automatic if minimum
performance achieved_____
Automatic except for terms (e.g. royalty rate)
to be negotiated or arbitrated_____
Good faith negotiations to
extend_____

Consideration
Lump sum payment_____
Single payment_____
Instalments_____
Royalty, per cent of profits _____ gross sales_____
net sales, specific amount (specify) _____
per unit (specify) _____ other _____
Payment in Canadian dollars:
    At then current rate of exchange
    At rate of _____ dollars for _____ (foreign
    currency)
    If exchange rate decreases or increases by 5%
    the payments shall decrease or increase by like
    amount
    Exchange rate shall be that
    published in_____
Payment in currency other
than Canadian_____
Stock of licensee (specify)
    Stock of existing company _____ new
    company _____
    Value of the shares of stock shall be market
    value at date of agreement _____ book
    value _____
    Stock shall have full voting rights _____
    non-voting _____
    Stock shall have value not less than $_____
    Stock shall represent not less than _____ per
    cent of the issued shares
    Licensor shall have the option to acquire
    additional shares at market value _____ book
    value _____
Licensor shall have option to appoint directors:
    with full voting rights _____ non-voting _____

Minimum Royalty
Amount per calendar year _____ per 12-month
period _____
Payable in advance
Payable at end of calendar year _____ of 12-month
period _____
Credited against earned royalties:
Yes _____   No _____

Inspection of Licensee's Accounts
Not permitted
Permitted:
    at any time during business hours
    at specified times
    by licensor's authorized representatives
    by accountants

Acknowledgement of Licensor's Title
Not admitted

Admitted by licensee
If patents held invalid, then:
    Licensee may terminate:
    as to invalid claims _____
    entire agreement _____

Statements of Earned Royalty
Quarterly, within _____ days of end of quarter
Annually, within _____ days of end of year
Other periods (specify) _____
In writing and certified before notary public
With names and addresses of sub-licensees
With copies of sub-licenses
Together with payment of royalty accrued

Inspection of Licensee's Accounts
Not permitted
Permitted:
    at any time during business hours
    at specified times
    by licensor's authorized representatives
    by accountants

Acknowledgement of Licensor's Title
Not admitted
Admitted by licensee
If patents held invalid, then:
    Licensee may terminate:
        as to invalid claims _____
        entire agreement _____

Improvements by Licensee
Not included
Included for products (specify)
    Automatically owned by licensor
    Licensed to licensor automatic
    Licensor's option-free royalty
    For term of agreement _____ for specified
    term _____
    For territory of license _____ for specified
    territory _____

Diligence by Licensee
No obligation
Licensee will use its best efforts
Licensee agrees to:
    produce _____ or sell _____ specified units
    produce _____ or sell _____ specified products
    invest specified amount
    satisfy demands of trade
    refuse no reasonable request for sub-license
Penalty for lack of diligence:
    License converted to non-exclusive
    Licensor may nominate licensees
    Licensor may terminate upon _____ days' notice
    in writing

Infringement
A. Licensed rights
    Past infringement by licensee:
        forgiven _____ not forgiven _____
        forgiven for payment of _____
    If infringed by others:
        Who will notify

Who will file suit
Who is in charge of suit
Costs: borne by _____ divided _____

B. Rights of others
No indemnity by licensor
Licensor indemnifies licensee

Who will notify
Who will defend
Who will pay costs
Costs: borne by _____ divided _____

C. Damages
Retained by _____ divided _____

D. Right to settle suit:
by licensor ____ by licensee ____
by licensor only with consent of
licensee ____

Right of Inspection
Licensee shall have the right to inspect licensor's:
research laboratory ____ development
laboratory ____
engineering laboratory ____ pilot plant ____
production plant ____ department relating to
product ____
Number of visits permitted per year
Number of persons
Licensor shall have reciprocal rights of inspection

Technical Personnel
Licensor shall provide technical personnel to
deliver know-how:
At licensor's expense ____ at licensee's
expense ____
Not more than   persons for not more than
days.
At a fee which shall be the salary, plus   per
cent.
Travel expenses ____ living expenses ____
borne by licensor ____
borne by licensee ____
Number and duration of stay of technical
personnel determined by:
Licensor ____ licensee ____ mutually ____

Confidentiality
No obligation ____ licensee obligated ____
both parties obligated ____
Without limitation as to time ____ life of
agreement ____
until published by owner ____
Obligations of confidentiality of employees ____
sub-licensees ____

Arbitration
No right of arbitration
Parties will use their best efforts
Parties agree to arbitration by:
specified body
three persons one selected by each party and a
third by the selected persons

Appeal from arbitration decision:
Not permitted, decision final and binding
Permitted to (specify tribunal)

Termination
By licensor:
If certain person incapacitated (name)
If certain person terminated connection with
licensee (name)
As specified time
Only upon breach after   days' written notice
By licensee:
At any time upon   days' written notice
On any anniversary date
At any specified time
Only upon payment of penalty of $
Only upon breach after   days' written notice
Upon termination, licensee assigns to licensor:
Trade marks ____ patents ____
sub-licenses ____
As to any specified patent or applications
As to any specified country
Of exclusive license with right to continue as
non-exclusive
Whenever any essential claim held invalid
Upon bankruptcy of either party

Force Majeure
Licensor has right
Licensee has right
Both parties have right
Nature of force majeure
Natural events: fire, floods, lightning, wind-
storm, earthquake, subsidence of soil, etc.
Accidents: fire, explosion, failure of equipment,
transportation accidents
Civil events: commotion, riot, war, strike, labor
disturbances, labor shortages, raw material
and equipment shortages
Governmental: government controls, rationing,
court order
Any cause beyond control of party
Assignment of Agreement and License
Not assignable by either party
Assignable by licensor, without consent of
licensee ____ with consent ____
By either party:
Upon merger
To successor of entire business
To any company of which a majority of stock is
owned
To any company of which a controlling interest
is owned
Binding upon heirs, successors and assigns

Most Favored Licensee Clause
Licensor required to notify licensee of similar
license
Licensee has option to take term of similar license
License changed to terms of more favorable
license
Licensee may terminate

Notices and Addresses
By registered air mail
Licensor's legal address for notice
Licensee's legal address for notice
Provision for deemed notice

Integration
This instrument is the entire agreement between parties
No modification effective unless written and signed by both
This agreement supersedes:
   all prior agreements between the parties
   the agreement dated

Language
The official language shall be English _____
   other _____ (specify)
Copy in _____ language shall be official _____
   unofficial _____

Law Applicable
To be construed according to the laws of

Signatures
For individual:
   "Hand and seal"
For corporations:
   By officer
   Title shown
   Corporate seal

Schedules
Patent list (inventor, number, issue date, official title)
Patent applications (inventor, serial number, filing date, official title)
Industrial designs (registration number and date)
Copyrights (description, registration number and date)
Trademarks (description, registration number and date)
Descriptions or copies of official documents, such as sub-licenses, assignment, prior license, etc.
Accounting procedures if any for determining sales, net sales, sale value of stock, or other property

---

Trademark Supplement

If the agreement is to include a trademark license, check the following items:

LICENSED TRADEMARKS
Trademark Application No. and date
Trademark Registration No. and date
Classes of goods (specify)
Goodwill of business (specify)

THE GRANT TO USE
Exclusive _____ non-transferable _____

Countries	Trademark	Registration No.	Date
_____	_____	_____	_____
_____	_____	_____	_____
_____	_____	_____	_____

Term of License

CONSIDERATION
Royalty: % of profits _____ of gross sales _____
   of net sales _____
Single sum of $ _____ Annual minimum $
Included in know-how fee _____ not included _____
Stock of licensee (name company)
   at market value _____ "book value" _____

PRODUCT QUALITY CONTROL
Mark to be used only on goods (specify)
Made under written specifications: attached _____
   to be supplied by licensor _____
No other trademarks to be used on same goods
Samples to be furnished upon request:
   quarterly _____ annually _____
Inspection of product manufactured by licensor permitted:
   when requested _____ quarterly _____
   annually _____
Liability for misuse:
   Licensor liable _____ licensee liable _____

TRADEMARK USE CONTROL
Licensor has right to approve, in advance, use of mark in:
   Advertising
   Labels
   Containers
   Registration notice
   Exhibits
   Speeches
   Publicity
   Corporate Signature

REGISTRATION IN TRADEMARKS OFFICE
Entire Agreement
Separate Registered User Agreement

Case 30

Ontario Flower Growers' Co-operative

On November 14, 1984, Harry Stueben was elected president of the board of directors of the Ontario Flower Growers' Co-operative (OFGC) of Mississauga, Ontario, at its annual meeting. He would hold the position for one year. He was aware of many of the issues facing the organization as he had already served on the board for a year, and he felt quite a bit could be done to build on the organization's strengths. Stueben's own major interest was in making the co-operative more attractive as a source of floricultural products. He saw his immediate task as deciding what his agenda would be for the board's next meeting on December 12, 1984.

The Co-operative

The OFGC was established in 1972 by a group of plant and flower growers with the assistance of the Ontario government to help Ontario growers sell their floricultural products. All were interested in providing a single location where growers could get together with buyers. Initially this was accomplished through an auction held in a rented industrial building in Georgetown, Ontario, but in 1974 the OFGC moved 30 kilometers to a rented building of 65,000 square feet in Mississauga on the outskirts of Toronto. Two other methods or programs for selling these products had been added recently: pre-sales and direct sales.

The OFGC had distinctive features because, as a co-operative, it was viewed as an extension of the growers' or farmers' enterprises. Each grower who wished to use the co-operative to sell his products had to become a member of it. He became one by providing part of the capital needed to operate it. As a member, he had equal voting rights with all other members no matter how much he used the co-operative. The profits generated by the co-operative were considered to be savings for the members who used it and were passed back to them each year as patronage dividends. These were not taxed at the level of the co-operative, but were part of the individual farmer's taxable income.

This case was prepared by Kenneth Harling and Alan DeRoo of the University of Guelph, Guelph, Ontario, Canada under a grant from the Small Business Secretariat of the Department of Regional Industrial Expansion, Ottawa. Mark Baetz assisted in the preparation of the case. Copyright © 1986 by Kenneth Harling and Alan DeRoo.

Exhibit 1: Grower Members' Sales through the Co-operative

	Year					
	1982		*1983*		*1984*	
Dollar Range of Individual Members' Sales	*Number of Members*	*Total Dollars*	*Number of Members*	*Total Dollars*	*Number of Members*	*Total Dollars*
none	28	—	27	—	27	—
$1–$250	5	$ 657	2	$ 179	2	$ 104
$251–$10,000	33	123,611	28	99,827	25	110,998
$10,001–$50,000	44	1,139,632	44	1,062,598	39	1,040,963
$50,001–$100,000	28	1,995,703	25	1,735,130	29	2,189,611
$100,001–$250,000	16	2,848,727	24	3,373,315	24	3,578,526
$250,001–$500,000	3	1,429,087	4	1,230,318	6	1,877,853
over 500,000	1	509,185	3	1,831,149	3	1,992,910
Total	159	$8,046,602	157	$9,332,516	155	$10,790,965

Source: Annual reports of the Ontario Flower Growers' Co-operative.

Membership

In order to qualify for membership of the OFGC, a grower had to be situated in Ontario. The co-operative's bylaws also required that members only sell product which had been in their greenhouse for 60 days or more through the OFGC. In recent years the board of directors had felt that more growers wanted to sell through the OFGC than there were buyers, so it had required that prospective members go through a trial year in which they had to regularly ship good-quality product to the OFGC. After one year of acceptable performance, they were made full members.

The sales of individual members through the OFGC ranged from nothing up to over $500,000 (see Exhibit 1). This variation was due to differences in both grower size and the proportion of business growers sent through the co-operative. In recent years, the larger growers had accounted for an increasing proportion of the volume.

Organization

The OFGC's organizational structure, presented in Exhibit 2, shows the two groups which affected the OFGC's activities: the board of directors and management. The board's seven directors oversaw the management of the OFGC. Each director was elected by the members to serve a two-year term but could be reelected an unlimited number of times. The directors did not always agree on what needed to be done. Personalities sometimes expanded these differences to the point that there was personal and emotional conflict among members. Further details on individual directors appear in Exhibit 3.

Exhibit 2: Organization of the Ontario Flower Growers' Co-operative

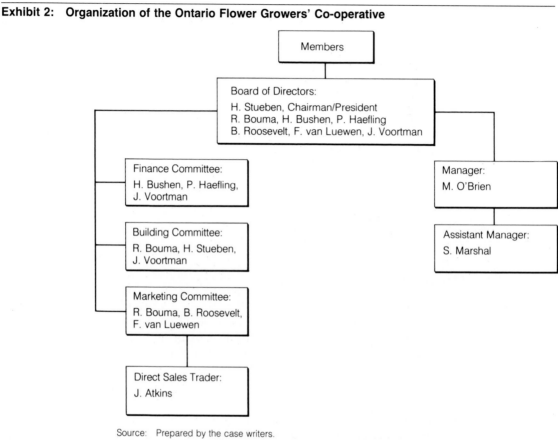

Source: Prepared by the case writers.

The executive positions on the board were allocated by the board in a private discussion following the election of the new directors. The board had several committees with each committee being served by directors who had an interest in the subject matter of the committee. The building and marketing committees were very active during 1984. The building committee was looking for land for a new building and arranging for an architect to draw up plans for it. The marketing committee was looking for ways to expand sales and had a particular interest in direct sales. The finance committee had done little because it had been waiting for the previous president, Bert Roosevelt, to come to an agreement with the finance committee's chairman, Pat Haefling, about how the new building would be financed. Roosevelt had wanted the OFGC to finance the building, while Haefling had wanted it to borrow the money from the members.

The directors were all active members who ran their own floricultural businesses. This meant that they were very interested in the daily operations of

Exhibit 3: Members of the Board of Directors

Name	Ron Bouma	Henry Bushen	Pat Haefling
Age	55	34	57
Role on the board	Member and serves on the marketing committee and building committee.	Treasurer and serves on the finance committee.	Member and serves on the finance committee.
Years on the board	4	2	5
Business interests	Cut flowers. $150,000 sales/year.	Potted plants. $120,000 sales/year. Sells 2/3 to wholesalers.	Imported tropical plants. $1,500,000 sales/year. Sells 1/2 wholesale and from his greenhouse.
Use of the OFGC	Sells all his product through the auction.	Sells 1/3 through the auction.	Sells 1/2 through the auction. Heavy user of the buyback mechanism.
Expressed interests	None.	None.	Would like to see volume on the auction increased and dumping prevented. Wants the auction to build its own building.

Name	Bert Roosevelt	Harry Stueben	Frank van Luewen
Age	55	59	54
Role on the board	Vice president (past president) and serves on the marketing committee.	President and serves on the building committee.	Secretary and serves on the marketing committee.
Years on the board	5	1	5
Business interests	Potted and tropical plants. $2,000,000 sales/year. Sells wholesale to all types of retailers.	Garden center and traditional florist. $500,000 sales/year.	Potted chrysanthemums. $700,000 sales/year. Sells 2/3 to retailers on a contractual basis.
Use of the OFGC	Sends 1/5 to the auction. Buys at auction occasionally to meet wholesaling needs.	Bought $500 at auction in the previous year. Has sold nothing at Co-op in recent years.	Sends 1/3 to the auction.
Expressed interests	Has been pushing hard for direct sales.	Wants to help the OFGC attract more buyers.	Wants direct sales expanded.

Name	John Voortman
Age	50
Role on the board	Member and serves on the finance committee and the building committee.
Years on the board	2
Business interests	Sells cut roses. $150,000 sales/year.
Use of the OFGC	Sends 1/2 to the auction.
Expressed interests	Wants the problem with the auction solved.

the OFGC and devoted much attention to how these operations could be improved. The directors often called on their own experiences and instincts when addressing problems arising in this area. Conflicts of opinion about what should be done were not uncommon at the monthly board meetings as each director promoted what he thought was best for the OFGC.

The OFGC functioned with a small staff of three management people: the manager, the assistant manager, and the direct sales trader. The manager, Mildred O'Brien, was responsible for the operation of the auction and reported to the board. Except for 1980 and 1981, she had been the manager of the OFGC since it had started. She relied on the board to "tell her what it wanted." The assistant manager reported to the manager and was responsible for the pre-sales program and providing support for the manager. The current assistant manager had been hired six months earlier, and his previous experience had been in operating a theatre. The direct sales trader was responsible for the direct sales program and reported to the three-member marketing committee. He had been in his job since the fall of 1983 and before that had been a grower and a salesman.

Activities

The OFGC participated in the floricultural industry which is described in the Appendix. The co-operative had the potential to act as an intermediary between any buyer and seller of floricultural products, though it had chosen, in fact, to limit its activities to helping member growers sell product to any potential buyers.

The OFGC fulfilled its role as an intermediary by providing markets where growers and buyers could come together and playing an active yet impartial role in helping transact sales at these markets. This was different from other marketing alternatives which required either the grower or the buyer to seek out the other and then to carry out the sales negotiations. The co-operative carried out its role through three programs: auction, pre-sale, and direct sale. Each program was viewed as a separate business because it attracted different sellers and buyers. The original and still the most important program was the auction—it was the only one in Ontario.

The Auction

The auction, as it was called, was really a series of frequent auctions carrying the full range of floricultural products. An auction was held every Tuesday, Thursday, and Friday and on other days during peak sales periods. It started at 6 or 7 in the morning and was usually over by 11. Growers would deliver their product prior to the auction in boxes and pails purchased from the OFGC. Buyers could examine it before or during the auction while it stood in boxes and pails on carts waiting to be taken into the auction. Buyers could identify who grew the product by looking at invoices attached to the carts on which the containers stood.

The auction was conducted in a tiered gallery with seats for 200 buyers. They sat at tables and looked down on the auction floor and a Dutch clock mounted on the wall behind it. Product was rolled in front of them on carts. Each box on the cart was considered a lot and was auctioned off separately although buyers could ask for more boxes when they had a winning bid. The Dutch clock behind the floor indicated the price of the product being auctioned. The clock started at the grower's asking price, and as the clock rotated, the price dropped until a buyer pressed the button on the table at which he sat to indicate that he would buy the product at the price indicated on the clock. At the back of the gallery were buttons which enabled growers to remove their product from the auction by "buying it back." Growers did so when they thought the auction price had dropped too low. Buybacks were treated as sales, however, and the grower had to pay the OFGC its sales commission on them as well as regular sales. The commission was around 10 percent of the value of the product sold.

A buyer could participate in the auction personally by renting a seat in the gallery either for the day at $35 if one was available or for the year by winning a competitive bid for it. If he did not want to participate personally, he could deal through a commission agent who sat at the back of the gallery and charged a 10 percent fee on the value of product bought. Most buyers had to pay cash for their purchases before they left the building. Before growers left the auction, they were given a cheque for the product they had sold that day.

The auction had attracted a variety of different buyers. The estimated purchases by customer type in millions of dollars were: wholesalers, $2.5; plant and flower shops, $2.5; greengrocers, $2; garden centers, $1.5; and florists, $1. Approximately 60 percent of the dollar volume was potted flowering and foliage plants: 25 percent, cut flowers, and 15 percent, bedding plants. No separate record of volume under the pre-sales program was kept, as it was minimal.

From the buyer's perspective, the auction had several positive and negative features. On the positive side: (1) a wide range of products were traded, (2) prices were observed by all present, (3) available quantities could be bought by anyone willing to pay the necessary price, and (4) prices on average were lower than those of terminal wholesalers. On the negative side: (1) prices and quantities could vary considerably from day to day, (2) the auction seemed to attract a disproportionate amount of poor-quality product during peak buying periods, (3) any buyer buying a large amount quickly raised the auction price, and (4) the buyer had to be a good judge of quality.

From the grower's perspective, the auction also had several positive and negative features. On the positive side: (1) growers were able to bring all varieties and qualities they had to sell, (2) growers were paid their cash immediately following the auction, (3) it was a fast way of selling product, and (4) prices were better than those of terminal wholesalers. On the negative side: (1) many buyers seemed reluctant to pay premium prices and (2) bringing a large quantity of product to the auction depressed auction prices.

Pre-Sales

The pre-sales program was introduced as a way of guaranteeing that buyers who definitely wanted a particular item would be able to get it when they wanted it. Under the program, a buyer was able to use the services of the OFGC to get a grower to supply him with a particular item of a certain quality. The buyer paid the OFGC nothing for this service while the grower paid a 5 percent commission. The grower was given a cheque when the product was sold. Growers charged higher prices on these sales because they knew the buyer wanted the product.

Direct Sales

The direct sales program was a new program similar to an earlier export sales program which had lost $73,000 over 1980 and 1981. The previous program had so angered some members that a motion had been passed at the 1981 annual meeting banning export sales. Nevertheless, members had agreed recently to the direct sales program as a way of pursuing buyers who were not using the auction or pre-sales program. It was also argued that this program would reduce the supply of product at the auction and thus improve prices there.

This program was run by a trader employed by the OFGC, the direct salesman. He would contact both growers and buyers to see what was available and what was wanted. When he had a match, he would arrange a sale with the identity of buyers and sellers being kept confidential. Thus sellers and buyers would have to continue to rely on the trader to set up further transactions, and sales would continue to be made through the OFGC. The program was different from regular wholesale operations in several ways. First, the trader acted as an honest broker between the buyers and sellers by helping each get a "fair" deal, rather than maximize the margin he made on the transaction. Second, by being continually in the market for both growers and buyers, he acted as a clearinghouse for sales, usually being able to provide a buyer or seller in the market for the product.

Shipments of product to direct sales program customers were all sent from the OFGC's building where product from several growers was consolidated and repackaged if necessary. This approach had proven useful because it permitted medium-sized growers to sell to large customers. The trader was also able to see the quality of product that the growers were shipping—an important factor to many buyers under this program. In this way, the trader was able to judge whether a certain grower was providing the quality desired by the customer. The buyer used his impressions of quality when deciding on which growers to include in future deals.

The cost for using this program was a 5 percent commission paid by the grower. Growers were paid when product was received at the OFGC's warehouse, and buyers paid the OFGC within 60 days of receiving the product. By mid-1984, sales through the program had been largely top-quality potted plants going to retail chains in the United States. These sales had been especially lucrative for the OFGC because growers had been paid in Canadian dollars at the time of the sale, and the OFGC had received payment in more valuable U.S. dollars later as the Canadian dollar decreased in value.

Buyers liked the program because they could negotiate the price, quality, and timing of a sale. Medium-sized and large growers liked the program for the same reason.

Finance

The permanent capital needs of the OFGC were not great. (The balance sheet information for the years 1982 through 1984 is provided in Exhibits 4 and 5.) The last large purchase by the OFGC had been $150,000 in 1983 for a new computer for use in the auction. No major assets were purchased in 1984, but in 1985 the OFGC planned to take delivery of a new electronic Dutch clock that would cost $130,000.

The building committee of the board was also negotiating the purchase of land as a building site for a building to replace the leased one that was presently being used. The decision to build its own building had been prompted by the landlord's asking for a new lease for the building in Mississauga starting in September 1985 at $250,000 a year for three years. After that he proposed that the rate increase at 6 percent per year—the estimated rate of inflation. Many members felt that having their own building would be a good investment: Why should someone else be getting rich owning a building they were paying for? The building committee of the board anticipated it would need a new building of 80,000 square feet. The cost of land and construction of the building would be $2.5 million while moving to the new building would cost an additional $100,000.

Until recently, equity had been sufficient to finance the limited capital needs of the OFGC. There were two components of equity in the OFGC: common stock and retained earnings. Ten common shares were sold to each member when he joined the OFGC. Early members had paid $500 for these shares while recent members had paid $3,000. Growers tended to view this purchase of stock as an entry fee as they were never required to make further contributions to equity. Retained earnings had never accumulated because each year the preceding year's earnings were distributed as a patronage dividend in order to avoid paying income tax at a rate of 46 percent per year.

Anticipating the decision to build a new building, the finance committee had asked the members in 1983 for financial contributions so it could make a down payment on the land needed. Members had been unwilling to provide further equity investment in the OFGC, so it had taken loans from shareholders. Initially each member had been asked for $2,000 on which the OFGC promised to pay market rates of interest. Some members contributed, but the poor response led the board to reduce the contribution to $400 for those who felt $2,000 was too

Exhibit 4

ONTARIO FLOWER GROWERS' CO-OPERATIVE
Balance Sheet
As of September 30, 1982–1984

	1984	1983	1982
Assets			
Current assets:			
Cash	$162,264	$120,809	$141,926
Term deposits	122,850	122,850	—
Accounts receivable—auction	36,570	41,197	36,054
Accounts receivable—direct sales	88,019	26,852	—
Carton and label inventory	82,542	41,279	42,901
Deposits and prepaid expenses	19,896	15,966	42,041
Total current assets	512,141	368,953	262,922
Fixed assets:			
At cost	473,173	438,808	290,308
Accumulated depreciation	303,159	243,031	186,774
Net fixed assets	170,014	195,777	103,534
Other assets	3,787	3,787	3,787
Total assets	$685,942	$568,517	$370,243
Liabilities and Equities			
Current liabilities:			
Accounts payable—auction	$ 37,330	$ 13,479	$ 33,831
Accounts payable—direct sales	29,068	4,097	—
Due on redeemed shares	—	—	2,800
Deposits on shares	21,000	15,000	—
Shareholder loan	144,831	144,831	—
Total current liabilities	232,229	177,407	36,631
Equity:			
Common shares	152,500	141,500	145,000
Retained earnings	301,213	249,610	188,612
Total equity	453,713	391,110	333,612
Total liabilities and equities	$685,942	$568,517	$370,243

Source: Annual reports of the Ontario Flower Growers' Co-operative.

much. Those who did not contribute were barred from selling through the OFGC for a year. In the end, the OFGC was able to raise around $145,000.

The manager had discussed the OFGC's financing needs with its banker and had been told that if the OFGC were to use a mortgage to build, it would have to raise $600,000 of equity for a $2 million mortgage at the long-term market rate of 13.5 percent. The mortgage would require an annual repayment of $293,000 of which $263,000 would be interest on average for the first five years. The

Exhibit 5

ONTARIO FLOWER GROWERS' CO-OPERATIVE
Statement of Retained Earnings
As of September 30, 1982–1984

	1984	1983	1982
Retained earnings, beginning of year	$249,610	$188,612	$204,318
Net income for period	301,903	239,172	176,294
	550,513	427,784	380,612
Less: Patronage dividend	249,300	178,174	192,000
Retained earnings, end of year	$301,213	$249,610	$188,612

Source: Annual reports of the Ontario Flower Growers' Co-operative.

depreciation charge on the building would be around $85,000 per year for the first five years.

Performance

The OFGC was profitable and had demonstrated continuing financial success for the year just ended (see Exhibit 6). The total value of product marketed through it had increased considerably over time, from nearly $5 million in 1976 to over $10 million in 1984 (see Exhibit 7). In 1984 total sales volume was greater than planned though auction sales, the principal component, were below plan. The actual volume of the auction was unknown because buyback sales were incorporated with regular sales through the auction. Moreover, while direct sales had failed to cover direct costs by $18,000 in 1983, these sales contributed $25,000 after direct costs in 1984.

Measures of performance other than sales volume which were also used by the board were commissions charged, patronage dividends, and the cost of marketing. Commissions were important because they provided around 90 percent of the co-operative's total revenues. Commission revenues were supplemented by seat rentals and interest on the OFGC's bank account. Patronage dividends had also been used to measure the performance of the OFGC. The cost of marketing through the OFGC was a calculation some growers made on their own. It reached its lowest point in 1984 when it only cost 6.1 cents for a grower to market a dollar of product through the OFGC.

The Issues

Most members felt that there were not enough buyers. Although the OFGC had a list of 500 buyers, only 75–100 usually attended an auction. Members felt that more buyers would have to be found so they could sell more volume through the OFGC. Members disagreed, however, over how these buyers should be sought. Some felt that the auction program should be promoted and efforts made to make

Exhibit 6

ONTARIO FLOWER GROWERS' CO-OPERATIVE
Income Statement
As of September 30, 1982–1984

	1984	1983	1982
Total sales:	$10,790,965	$9,332,516	$8,046,602
Auction sales*	9,870,007	9,282,319	8,046,487
Direct sales	920,602	49,697	—
Revenues:			
Auction:			
Commissions	915,169	847,953	775,604
Seat rental	59,093	51,394	36,579
Total	974,262	899,347	812,183
Direct sales:			
Commissions	46,073	3,696	—
Markup and foreign			
exchange	166,367	6,670	—
Total	212,440	10,366	—
Other	27,214	17,702	35,478
Total revenues	1,213,916	927,415	847,661
Expenses:			
Auction	383,371	346,034	526,913
Direct sales	183,351	27,824	—
Unallocated:			
Building rental	144,883	144,883	144,883
Other	200,408	165,333	—
Total expenses	912,013	684,074	671,796
Net income before taxes	301,903	239,172	176,294
Provision for taxes	—	—	—
Net income for the year	$ 301,903	$ 239,172	$ 176,294

* Auction sales include buybacks.
Source: Annual reports of the Ontario Flower Growers' Co-operative.

it a more attractive marketing alternative for buyers. Others felt that the direct sales program should be used to pursue the U.S. market.

Members interested in the auction saw various ways of improving it. One problem they saw was that some members were inconsistent users of the auction. They only brought product when they were unable to sell it elsewhere, and sometimes the amounts they brought were large. Moreover, these growers did not worry about prices they received at the auction because they had already made their profits from other sales. They would sell product for whatever they could get. The members referred to this practice as "dumping." The result was that prices on the auction for that day were seriously depressed. At present the manager was talking to these growers and asking them to "treat the auction like

Exhibit 7: Performance and Goals of the Ontario Flower Growers' Co-operative (dollars in thousands)

Year	Sales			Commissions	Patronage Dividend	Cost of Marketing through the OFGC (Percent)
	Auction and Pre-Sales*	Direct	Total			
Actual:						
1976	$ 4,704	—	$ 4,704	$421	$ 36	8.2%
1977	5,683	—	5,683	513	105	7.2
1978	5,409	—	5,409	496	61	8.0
1979	6,002	—	6,002	547	109	7.3
1980	6,492	$ 398	6,890	634	36	8.7
1981	7,303	66	7,369	706	192	7.0
1982	8,047	—	8,047	776	178	7.4
1983	9,283	50	9,333	855	249	6.5
1984†	9,870	921	10,791	961	302	6.1
Planned:						
1984	10,175	500	10,675			
1985	11,193	1,000	12,192			
1986	12,312	2,000	14,312			
1987	13,543	3,000	16,543			
1988	14,897	3,600	18,497			
1989	16,387	4,320	20,707			
1990	18,257	4,968	22,994			

* Includes buybacks by members.
† Cost of marketing through the OFGC assumes all savings are paid to members as dividends.
Source: Actual from annual reports of the Ontario Flower Growers' Co-operative while planned was a finance committee document.

a customer," in other words, bring amounts to the auction in line with their customer demands outside the auction. Several board members thought that the quantity of product delivered by members should be much more tightly controlled.

Another problem was the quality of products marketed at the auction. Some members complained about the poor quality other members would bring to it. One cause of poor quality was that members would sell their good quality through other marketing alternatives where they could get high prices and then try to sell their poor-quality product through the auction at low cost with minimum effort. The manager had used her "treat the auction like a customer" presentation on these growers as a way of minimizing this problem. Roosevelt, a member of the board and a grower of tropical plants, felt that another cause was that importers of tropical products were not holding the plants in their greenhouses for the 60 days required by the OFGC. He argued that the OFGC needed to enforce the 60-day requirement and seemed to have the support of several board members for such action.

Buyers at the auction also expressed concern about the quality of product.

Some buyers, mostly occasional buyers, found it difficult to judge and compare product. They wanted grading so they knew what they were buying. Van Leuwen, a member of the board, argued that quality was a subjective thing that should not be graded. He was very critical of a previous attempt by the OFGC to grade product on a rigorous set of standards. This attempt had ended with the OFGC leaving it up to each grower to grade his own product. Now buyers were complaining about the uneven quality in individual product lots as some growers would put several poor-quality pieces in with good quality. The result was that the buyer wound up buying poor-quality product he could not sell. Some members proposed that lots be graded to ensure that the quality of a lot was consistent.

Whether a direct sales program should be used at all was subject to debate even though one was already operating. Growers relying on the auction complained that the availability of top-quality product at the auction had decreased with the introduction of the direct sales program. They said that direct sales was taking only top-quality product, leaving less of it for the auction. These members felt that the direct sales should be discontinued. A second argument presented by these growers was that, based on their previous experience, they would have to pay for losses of a program they did not want. They saw losses as a distinct potential in the long run because they felt that the dramatic increase in exports to the United States was due to the weakness of the Canadian dollar against the American dollar. One American dollar had been worth $1.17 Canadian in 1979–80, $1.20 in 1981, $1.22 in 1982–83, and $1.30 in 1984. They thought that sales to the United States would be reduced considerably if the Canadian dollar strengthened. This would lower the value of sales to the United States and would also cause a glut of product as producers exporting to the United States would try to sell their product in Ontario.

Larger buyers and sellers both talked about the need for the direct sales program. They said that they had to limit their business through the auction because their large volumes altered prices significantly. Only by negotiating prices could they be kept in line with general market prices. Buyers illustrated the problem by the example of a large buyer from Buffalo, New York, who would come to the auction with a transport truck. As he always left with a full truck, many buyers said that they did not bother trying to bid against him because prices got driven too high.

Where the customers of the direct sales program should be had never been clarified by the board. Growers using the program liked the fact that it was selling product in the United States. They saw that market as having unlimited potential. Efforts by the trader to make sales in Canada had been limited by the manager of the OFGC. She felt that direct sales were hurting the auction. She had convinced the board that because the purpose of the direct sales program was to find new buyers, the direct sales program should sell only to new buyers. All existing buyers who wanted to set prices through negotiation were required to use the pre-sale program.

A final issue was the construction of the new building. This idea had captured the interest of the members. Haefling had been instrumental in persuading the members that it was ''common sense'' to invest in a building for the OFGC—he had said they stood to make lots of money investing in their own building. At the November meeting much time was spent discussing what features should be incorporated in the new building. During the meeting an outspoken member had asked, ''And just who is going to pay for this monument to the board?'' After the meeting, Stueben realized that the board had put little thought into either the marketing or financial implications of the new building.

As Stueben reflected on these issues, he wondered what he should do. Many members of the board and the OFGC were pushing for changes, and all felt they had valid solutions. Stueben felt that what was needed was a coherent set of changes that he could sell to the members as the appropriate plan of action for the OFGC.

Appendix: The Ontario Floricultural Industry

The floricultural industry was involved in the production, distribution, and retailing of flowers and plants. The three main types of businesses in this industry were growers, wholesalers, and retailers. Each type of business was linked with the others through sales transactions. The dollar value of product moving between the various businesses and final consumers is presented in Exhibit A–1. Details on each of these businesses for the period 1979–1983 follow.

Growers

Ontario growers produced cut flowers, potted plants (foliage and flowering), and bedding plants. The long-term trend in production had been a shift out of cut flowers and into potted and bedding plants. Overall production of cut flowers had declined by 1 percent per year over the past five years while that of standard carnations and chrysanthemums—the major products—had declined by 7 percent per year as the Canadian market had turned to foreign suppliers. U.S. and Columbian producers had lower costs and were able to supply product for a much greater part of the year. Ontario's growers had held volume in other traditional cut flowers. Imports of high quality and new products from Holland had also grown over time. Canadian growers started growing the new types of cut flowers about five years after the Dutch introduced them into the Canadian market.

Production of most potted flowering plants (chrysanthemums, poinsettias, lilies, hydrangeas, and azaleas) had increased by 10 percent per year over the last five years. Production of tropical or foliage plants had stabilized while production of hanging baskets had peaked in 1981 and was still declining. The different product situations seemed to be related to markets served with the product. Potted flowering products had been moving into the United States while the others had been sold only in Ontario. Production of bedding plants had increased at 7 percent per year over the last five years.

Exhibit A–1:   Major Actors in the Ontario Floricultural Industry and the Value of Transactions between Them in Millions of Dollars for 1983.

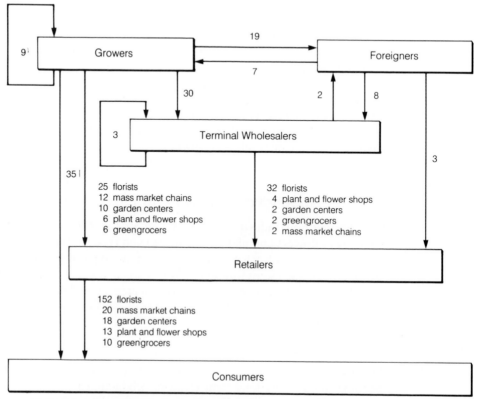

Source: An independent consultant to the floricultural industry.

Most growers specialized in producing a limited range of one type of product. They felt that this let them develop the specialized knowledge needed to grow each product although a grower could still experience growing difficulties. It also helped spread some of the price and market risks associated with specialization. Growers usually grew the same products for a long time because of the specialized production knowledge they developed, the long production cycle for some products, and the security in knowing their product would sell.

Nearly all the commercial production in Ontario was produced in greenhouses under controlled conditions. The publicly reported value of commercial sales in 1983 from Ontario's 3.6 million square metres of greenhouse space was $135 million. Only 2.5 million square metres were considered to be in commercial operation.

The two major areas of production were near the western ends of Lake Erie and Lake Ontario, that is, areas near major markets and with moderate climatic conditions due to the lakes. The average size of the 318 greenhouse growers in

Essex county near the western end of Lake Erie was 3,600 square metres, much larger than Ontario's industry average of 1,330 square metres. The area around the western end of Lake Ontario was the other major area of production. The 491 growers in this area had an average operation of 2,121 square metres.

Ontario greenhouses were largely family operations: 42 percent were sole proprietorships and 37 percent were family corporations. They used relatively small amounts of land. Thirty-eight percent of total greenhouse area was on farms with less than 9 acres, and 76 percent was on farms with less than 69 acres. The greenhouse enterprise was the primary or secondary activity on these farms. Most greenhouse owners were happy with this size of business and did not plan to expand. They felt that expanding their businesses beyond what they could handle as a family created both labour and quality problems in production. Thus increased size did not mean lower unit costs.

Growers had alternative customers for their products: (1) independent wholesalers, (2) other growers who wholesaled their own product along with that of others—such growers were known as grower-wholesalers, to be discussed in the next section, (3) retailers, (4) the public, and (5) foreign customers. Sales to these customers could be made in several ways: at the grower's or buyer's place of business or at one of two special market places, the auction of the Ontario Flower Grower's Co-operative or at the Food Terminal—a wholesale market on the outskirts of Toronto where farmers sold their products, mostly fruit and vegetables, to retailers.

A single grower rarely sold to only one customer or in only one way. He preferred to sell several ways so he could capture the advantages of selling to each. Selling to wholesalers provided some assurance of the amount and price of the product sold. Many wholesalers competed in southern Ontario, so the prices they paid were competitive among wholesalers. No grower relied on a single wholesaler, however, because the wholesalers' competitive situation had caused some to fail to meet their purchasing commitments to the grower or even go bankrupt. Most wholesalers were located close to growers and picked up product at the grower's greenhouse.

Selling through an auction provided growers with a ready market for any type, quality, or quantity of product. The auction required little time because it was held for a few hours several times a week. The grower got a feel for market prices and quality because all sales transactions were public knowledge. But prices at an auction could fluctuate considerably from one auction to the next depending on what growers offered and what buyers wanted.

Selling directly to retailers involved a lot of time and expense as the grower searched out buyers interested in what he had to sell. Nevertheless, the grower felt more secure with this method of marketing because he was seeking his own buyers for his product. Although prices were higher than selling to wholesalers, the gains were largely offset by high marketing costs, especially for the small grower.

Finally, selling directly to the public from the grower's greenhouse provided the highest profit margins and allowed the grower to stay at his site of production. Many growers liked marketing this way, but location near to customers and some merchandising ability were important requirements. The inability of many growers to meet these requirements had restricted the growth of direct sales to only 4 percent per year.

The most important characteristic determining how growers sold was the size of their business. Large growers tended to market their own products. Negotiated sales could be a time-consuming way to sell, but the grower only had to invest time and effort when he wanted to sell. Moreover, his large production quantities made it important that he find a customer for his production. Large growers had enough financial resources that they often extended credit to buyers. Most small growers relied on wholesalers and the auctions to help them market their products. They also sold from their greenhouses. Most did so because they would rather spend their time dealing with production than marketing, and they did not have the earnings to hire someone to market their product. Their limited financial resources also meant they liked to sell their products for cash. Finally, they wanted to be able to sell the small volumes of all qualities of product they produced.

Wholesalers

Wholesalers played an important role in linking supplies of floricultural products with retail demand. Several types of wholesalers carried out these activities. *Grower-wholesalers* grew and bought product they sold from other growers. They tended to be large growers who wanted to assure a market for their own product. While their marketing costs were similar to the wholesaler's 20–25 percent markup, they were more profitable because by growing their own product, they had assured supplies of products. They sometimes used other growers' product to complement their own product line and to fill in when their own production was not enough to meet their customer needs. *Terminal market wholesalers* specialized in collecting and distributing product from various growers to various retailers. Of the two types, the former was more profitable because it earned the margins from growing and always had some product available.

Most wholesalers were always searching all sources for top-quality supplies. They would bring them in from foreign sources if necessary although this meant the product was more expensive than local supply when it was available. Both types of wholesalers bought at the OFGC auction and competed with it by selling to retail customers who might buy at the auction. Those who grew all the product they wholesaled benefitted from the profits of both activities and removed themselves from buying activities in doing so. But most grower-wholesalers both bought and sold so the reasons explaining how they acted in both activities must be considered. When they bought product from growers they were able to line up deliveries of the desired quality of product in advance. They also were able to negotiate lower prices with growers because of their commitment to take the product. Wholesalers might meet part of their product needs by buying on spot markets. These markets were the Food Terminal, where they could negotiate on quality and price, and the OFGC's auction, where they could bid on available product. Sometimes they got very good quality for their money at the auction; other times good quality was scarce and available only at extremely high prices.

The main customers of wholesalers were retail florists. To satisfy florists' needs, wholesalers had to provide stable supplies of top-quality products at stable prices. By selling to florists, wholesalers got regular customers who paid premium prices. Serving florists was expensive, though, because they bought little each time and had to be dealt with individually in their place of business. Wholesalers also sold to mass-market chains. These chains wanted good-quality product but in large volume for holiday or seasonal selling. Chains also expected to pay lower prices because of the volumes they bought. Wholesalers sold to garden centres and other wholesalers as well. Here the conditions of sale were much more variable. One thing that stood out in all these transactions was that grower-wholesalers liked to sell good-quality product as their own and move their poor-quality products into markets where it would not hurt their product image.

A few of the largest wholesalers had been very active exporters of floricultural products in recent years. Virtually all exports went to the United States and were mostly potted plants. Ontario exports of these products had risen from $5 million in 1980 to $19 million in 1983—an increase of 57 percent per year. Reasons given for this dramatic growth were: (1) the high quality of Canadian product, (2) the low price of Canadian product, due in part to more advanced production technology and in part to the declining value of the Canadian dollar, and (3) the availability of Ontario product during peak consumer buying periods in the United States.

The overall growth rate of 7 percent per year in dollar sales was expected to continue in future. Growers wholesaling product were expected to continue to do so as long as they felt they could not find ready wholesale markets large enough to handle their large volumes without market prices declining.

Retailers

The retailing of floricultural products had changed considerably in recent years with changes in consumer tastes as well as changes in the retailing industry. The consumer market for floricultural products had been segmented by the retailers so that each segment was served by a particular type of retailer. The segmentation of retailing floricultural products had two implications for those providing retailers with products. First, each retailer attempted to buy products in the way most compatible with its retailing approach. Second, the fortunes of those serving each type of retailer would change as the size of the market segment served by that retailing approach changed. Details for each of the retailers follow.

Florists

Sales by retail florists in Ontario could be broken up into sales of cut flower arrangements (45 percent of sales), flowering potted plants (17 percent), loose cut flowers (14 percent), and foliage plants (13 percent). Non-floricultural products accounted for the remaining 11 percent of sales. This breakdown of sales seemed likely to continue.

The successful florist had traditionally provided his customers with high-quality products and many services. His customers were willing to pay high prices to get what they wanted. To keep them satisfied, the florist was also willing to pay a premium for quality and availability. The variability in sales over the year complicated his buying. High sales levels in May (Mother's Day) and December (Christmas) meant that his needs were not in concert with the production pattern of Ontario producers. Nor did the florist spend much time buying flowers and plants; his interest was in taking and filling customer orders.

Florists bought product from several different sources. Most florists bought cut flowers from three or four wholesalers whose trucks would come by the florist's shop. Traditional florists liked to buy from wholesalers because they would deliver product to the florist's store; they usually had a full line of products; they guaranteed their products; they sold for stable though high prices; and they gave credit. A few florists bought cut flowers directly from foreign sources to get top-quality product unobtainable from Ontario growers. This activity was facilitated by some wholesalers who, acting as agents for foreign suppliers, charged florists a 10 percent commission on the cost of purchasing and shipping the product to Canada's major airport at Toronto. Even when cut flowers were available locally, foreign products were sometimes cheaper and better quality. Florists bought most of their potted plants from local grower-wholesalers.

Some florists had shifted from the traditional to a cash-and-carry orientation. The buying behaviour of these florists is described in the next section. In recent years, dollar sales increases of florists had only been 4 percent per year.

Flower and Plant Shops

These shops grew out of the consumer interest in foliage plants in the mid-1970s. Flower and plant shops tried to sell high volumes by providing the customer with a large product range including cut flowers, foliage plants, and bedding plants—all at low prices. They kept down their costs by offering few services and selling primarily on a cash basis. They also devoted a lot of effort to buying floricultural products because the cost of product accounted for a large part of their revenue. They tried to buy only products that would sell quickly and wanted to pay as little as possible for them. They had started buying more of the better-quality products as their customers were becoming more sophisticated and starting to look for quality.

Shops bought from several different types of sellers. Many bought at the

OFGC's auction because it brought together many different varieties and qualities of product. Shop owners could compare the available product and get a good feel for what their competitors were paying. They felt that products tended to be cheap at the auction but that they had to be fairly knowledgeable about the products in order to buy well. Complaints they had about the auction included the requirement that purchases be paid for in cash, the variable quality of product in sales lots, and the limited availability of quality product. Some also bought at the Food Terminal. Here they had to negotiate their own deals. This allowed them to pick the quality and quantity they wanted, but they did not know what others were paying. Other problems with the Terminal were that floricultural products were sold for only part of the year and buyers had to work quickly to get the quality, quantity, and variety of products they wanted before they were sold. These shops were using wholesalers increasingly for unusual and high-quality items.

Flower and plant shops appeared to be fully able to maintain their past growth rate of 10 percent per year.

Garden Centers

Garden centers or nurseries were located in suburban areas. Some innovative ones had extended their original activities beyond bedding plants, shrubs, and trees into potted plants, cut flowers, plant accessories, and craft items. Their approach to business made them appear to be the suburban equivalent to plant and flower shops. These centers, as a result, approached buying the same way as plant and flower shops. They were different in several respects, however. They sometimes had greenhouses on the premises which let them buy larger quantities of potted plants than a plant shop could. They were also larger and could afford to carry buyers on staff. The overall result was that they preferred contractual arrangements with growers because they could negotiate lower prices due to the volume they bought, and they were able to buy product when they wanted it. They sometimes used the auction as a source for part of their needs.

These centers promised continuing growth as suburban areas in Southern Ontario continued to expand. In the past they had grown at 8 percent per year.

Chain Stores

Chain stores reportedly bought $9.8 million of floricultural products in 1982. Different types of chains marketed these products in different ways. Food chains marketed them as impulse items. A moderately priced potted plant fitted easily into the grocery budget as a single additional item which could be taken home with the groceries. Stores induced customers to buy these products by offering good-quality plants at low prices during the periods of the year when the public bought most flowers and plants. Other types of retail chains sold bedding plants in the spring as part of their outdoor departments' product line and other plants (usually foliage plants) as special promotions.

Chains had been very successful in buying what they wanted because sellers sought them out. The large volume they bought was attractive to sellers although sellers had to meet rigid product standards while receiving low unit prices. Chains sometimes required sellers to put their products in special packaging so that the product could withstand the extra handling that chains performed since shipments were delivered first to a central warehouse and then distributed from there to each store.

Chain stores sales had grown at 10 percent per year over the last few years, and they looked as if they had the potential for greatly expanded sales in the future if they could do two things. First, they had to improve product maintenance once it was placed in the store. Second, they had to develop customers' buying habits so that customers would purchase flowers and plants regularly.

Greengrocers

Greengrocers were small grocery stores with product lines similar to those of convenience stores. Most were owned and operated by ethnic families. They were found in the high-density urban areas of Toronto whereas food chains were mostly in the suburbs. Greengrocers, like chain stores, also marketed plants and flowers as an impulse purchase. They often displayed these products on the sidewalk in front of the store. They offered both flowers and plants of low to average quality at low prices.

Most greengrocers were only occasional purchasers and were not well informed about prices or qualities. When buying, they tried to buy product which looked like that of their competitors and was cheap enough that it could be competitively priced yet still provide a reasonable profit. Many bought at the OFGC's auction where they could see what other greengrocers were paying and could buy the amounts and qualities they thought their customers wanted. Many also bought at the Food Terminal seven kilometres south of the OFGC. They liked the convenience of buying flowers and plants at the same time they bought produce.

The dollar volume of greengrocer sales had grown at 12 percent per year, but it appeared that this rate would slow down as many greengrocers had found increasing competition was driving down the profits on floricultural products.

Case 31

Ontario Private School, Inc.

In December 1985 Mr. Benjamin Brown, a Toronto-based entrepreneur, contacted his former classmate, Mr. Kenneth Wong, to discuss the possibility of setting up a private high school in Ontario for foreign students. He asked Wong to come up with an overview report on private schools by March so he could decide whether he could set up a school—with Wong—and have it ready for September 1986 admission.

Brown and Wong had been university classmates 10 years earlier and had remained good friends since then. Brown obtained his MBA degree from the University of Toronto in 1976. He then worked for two years in an accounting firm and in 1978 decided to start his own business. He had had both successful and unsuccessful experiences in the past eight years. At the end of 1985 Brown owned three fast-food restaurants, four book stores, and three leather goods stores. Because of his leather goods business he had travelled to Brazil, Venezuela, Taiwan, and England.

Wong graduated from the University of Toronto with a bachelor of science degree in 1975 and a degree in education in 1977. He had worked since then in the education field. He had been involved in the development of two private schools—one of which was still in operation—as teacher and administrator and had travelled to most countries in Southeast Asia and Central America for student recruiting activities (recruiting about 100 students per year).

In response to the request from Brown, Wong prepared a report containing a detailed overview of the private school business situation in Ontario and the feasibility of setting up a private school in Toronto. The sections which follow contain excerpts from Wong's report, which examined the private school market, government regulations, possible school location, language barrier, foreign recruiting strategies, financial investment, and some of the technical problems associated with setting up a private school in Canada.

Setting up a Private School in Ontario

According to the Education Act (1974) a private school by definition is an institution at which instruction is provided at any time between the hours of 9 A.M.

This case was prepared by Professor Paul W. Beamish, School of Business and Economics, Wilfrid Laurier University. It is based primarily on an MBA report submitted by "Kenneth Wong"—who prefers to remain anonymous. Copyright © 1986 by Paul W. Beamish.

and 4 P.M. on any school day for five or more pupils who are of or over compulsory school age, in any of the subjects of the elementary or secondary school courses of study. The minimum number of students in any one school is five.

In order to set up a private school an application must be submitted to the Ministry of Education regarding the intention to operate a private school. After the submission of the application form and followed by an interview with a ministry official, approval will be granted if successful. The school will be given an official school number. With this number and the approval of the Federal Immigration Department the school can then recruit any students overseas, and student visas will be granted to those students who satisfy the requirements as stated by the department. The waiting or the processing period to get the approval by the Ministry of Education and the Federal Immigration Department will range anywhere from two to five months. An early decision and subsequent persistent followup after the submission of the application is required in order to start recruiting students in early summer. The letters from the Ministry of Education and Federal Immigration Department must be sent to the Canadian consulates or embassies in those prospective markets. A visit by a representative from the school definitely helps in developing the relationship with the officials in those consulates or embassies. It also helps to understand the requirements and regulations laid down by those consulates for visa students. The basic requirements are more or less the same from country to country, but there are also some differences (for example, language requirement, fund requirement, and so on).

The items required for the application interview are:

  a. The qualification of the school operator or the school principal and the school policy in terms of teachers' qualifications.
  b. A prospective school location and its facilities.
  c. A detailed summary on the philosophy of education written by the operator of the private school.
  d. The proposed school curriculum.
  e. A detailed course of study on those courses which will be offered by the school.

These preparations have to be made in a very short time in order to have them ready for the interview.

The purpose of setting up a private school is to provide students with a secondary school graduation diploma so they can apply to Canadian and American universities. According to the Education Act, any school granting such a diploma must be inspected to determine the quality of the standard of instruction in the subjects leading to the graduation diploma. An inspection fee is charged according to the total number of students and the location of the school. A transportation fee will be charged if the school is registered in Ontario but operating outside Ontario. Such an inspection can be requested by a private school operator. For a school of 250–300 students, a fee of approximately $300 could be expected. The frequency of the inspection ranges from once per year for schools based on a regular September–June school year to once per semester if a semester system is offered.

The inspection will not be carried out until the school is in operation, but preparation has to be made (for example, hiring the qualified teachers, development of school curriculum, development of English as a second language program, and preparation of a science laboratory). Hiring of qualified teachers is no problem since there are so many new or unemployed teachers in Ontario, but hiring of good teachers must start as soon as possible because good teachers usually get hired before summer.

Analysis of School Structure

The school should offer a secondary school program that offers courses in Grades 11–13 or a program that leads to Ontario Secondary School Diploma for the university admission requirement. According to the past statistics on secondary school students, about 55 percent of the visa students came for Grade 13, 30 percent for Grade 12, and 15 percent for Grade 11 or lower. The school should concentrate its program on the Grade 12 and 13 level.

In order to make the best use of the school facilities, the school year should be divided into three semesters. The three semesters are:

a. Fall semester: August to November.

b. Spring semester: December to March.

c. Summer semester: April to July.

The semester schedule may not be conventional, but this is the only schedule that provides the graduates from the school with their marks in time for university admission. Using the trimester system instead of the conventional semester system means the school can accommodate at least 20–25 percent more students. This will transform into more revenue and faster cash flow. This system is successfully offered by similar private schools.

The other major area that has to be considered is that many foreign students come from countries where English is not their first language nor their mother tongue. Their proficiency in English can be expected to be low and may not be acceptable to the school or Canadian Immigration Office. In order to solve this problem, it is suggested that the school should also offer an English as a second language (ESL) program. Those students whose TOEFL[1] marks are below standard or whose proficiency in English is judged below standard by the Canadian immigration officer will have to register in that program before they can be formally accepted into the regular secondary school program. According to

---

[1] Test of English as a Foreign Language, to be successfully written by overseas students as an admissions requirement for most Canadian universities.

estimates, the school can increase its revenue by 15–20 percent in offering this program. Students whose proficiency in English cannot meet the standard set out by the Canadian High Commission for secondary school admission can obtain a student visa if the school has an ESL program. About 20 percent of the applicants will be rejected if the ESL program is not offered by the school. Also, every year about 10–15 new immigrants to Canada (non-visa students) may pay to join this intensive program to smooth their transition into public schools, where the ESL program may be too advanced for their extremely limited command of English.

The possibility also exists for visa students already in Toronto to transfer to either a public or another private school after they complete their initial term in the first school. Such transfer can be facilitated by advertising in the local newspapers.

The school should also consider setting up a school accommodation facility in the future. Almost all visa students are new to Canada, and they would prefer the school to have its own residence. The ideal proposal is that the school act as accommodation agent for the students in the first year of operation and, as the school and the financial resources grow, then invest in a residence.

Analysis of School Location and Facilities

Many visa students enroll in high schools in Canada to improve their chances of entry into Canadian universities. Such enrollment not only provides an opportunity to adjust to the Canadian culture and English instruction but it offers students a chance to improve their academic grades in comparison with the tougher standards of many of their home countries. While not all are successfully admitted to university, in 1983–84 there were nearly 14,000 visa students enrolled in undergraduate Ontario universities (see Table 1 for an analysis by province, country of citizenship, and sex). In addition, graduate students added another 30 percent to this total. Since over 35 percent of foreign students had chosen Ontario because there are 15 universities in Ontario and because Ontario is not as cold as some provinces (such as Alberta or Manitoba), it is suggested that the school be located in Ontario.

The ideal location should be Toronto because it is a cosmopolitan city, and many students may find out that they have relatives or friends living in Toronto. This makes it a very attractive selling point to the students.

Recently at least 12 to 15 public schools have been closed in metropolitan Toronto, and it may be a good idea to lease one of these buildings. Since these buildings are school buildings and they have all the necessary school facilities, it should reduce the initial cost of renovation (a rough estimate is that it should reduce the renovation cost by $30,000 to $40,000). The school should have at least one library, 8 to 10 classrooms, one science laboratory, and three offices. Also, because visa students often enter math, computer science, and business, computer services and training would also be provided.

Analysis of Prospective Local and Foreign Competitors

Local Competitors

Local or national competitors are those that offer the same type of programs in Canada, but mainly those which offer the same program in Ontario. There are over 500 private schools in Ontario, most of which are religious affiliated schools, that is, Catholic, Jewish, Christian, and other faiths, which cater (to a varying degree) to students with certain beliefs. There are also some special trade schools, such as, dance schools, business schools, and so forth. There are at least 30 private schools in Ontario actively recruiting foreign students and about another 100 schools which accept foreign students but are not actively involved in overseas recruiting. Because of decline in enrollment in the public schools, public school boards have also actively been involved in recruiting students in the past. Directors of education of several of these boards have visited Hong Kong to recruit students, and some of them have set up agents and representatives in various countries.

In the past three years about 15 private schools have ceased business due to low enrollment, but at the same time 12 new schools have been started. Not all of these defunct or new schools have a visa student component, yet it appears that due to these changes, there has been a slight net loss in schools accepting visa students.

Foreign Competitors

Foreign competitors are those colleges or schools in other English-speaking countries which offer the same program and have plenty of higher education institutes for further education:

a. Australia.

b. United Kingdom.

c. United States.

Country	Population	Number of Universities	Number of Universities per Million
Australia	15.5 million	19	1.226
United Kingdom	57.0 million	46	0.807
United States	240.0 million	1,500	6.250
Canada	26.0 million	66	2.538

Table 1: Undergraduate Enrollment of Visa Students and Landed Immigrants by Province, Country of Citizenship, and Sex, 1983–1984

Country of Citizenship	Newfoundland Landed Immigrants	Newfoundland Visa Students	Prince Edward Island Landed Immigrants	Prince Edward Island Visa Students	Nova Scotia Landed Immigrants	Nova Scotia Visa Students	New Brunswick Landed Immigrants	New Brunswick Visa Students	Quebec Landed Immigrants	Quebec Visa Students	Ontario Landed Immigrants	Ontario Visa Students
1 Total non Canadian enrollment	162	146	34	27	593	1,538	274	585	4,502	4,250	12,775	13,864
2 Africa	4	15	2	2	21	152	12	101	351	1,740	410	557
3 Egypt	2	—	—	—	—	1	1	1	40	5	39	10
4 Ghana	—	1	—	—	1	8	—	1	6	11	17	32
5 Kenya	1	2	—	2	—	3	1	10	7	77	33	96
6 Nigeria	—	5	—	—	6	22	2	40	11	20	41	96
7 South Africa	—	—	—	—	2	25	2	—	2	3	105	11
8 Tanzania	1	1	—	—	—	1	—	2	1	3	69	48
9 Other	—	6	2	—	12	92	6	47	284	1,621	106	264
10 Asia	24	88	5	15	98	832	44	282	1,055	713	2,863	9,721
11 China, Mainland	—	—	—	—	1	12	—	—	28	22	87	93
12 Hong Kong	4	35	—	8	21	257	5	77	39	127	1,004	4,739
13 India	9	4	—	1	25	20	7	3	52	19	354	62
14 Indonesia	—	3	—	—	2	18	—	—	3	31	26	195
15 Iran	1	4	2	—	4	25	5	6	128	83	194	172
16 Israel	—	—	—	—	—	1	—	—	14	11	57	18
17 Japan	—	—	—	—	—	3	—	—	7	17	33	35
18 Korea, South	1	—	—	—	—	2	—	1	4	11	59	17
19 Lebanon	—	1	—	—	13	39	7	29	206	93	89	41
20 Malaysia	1	21	—	2	8	311	4	122	7	130	89	3,314
21 Pakistan	—	—	1	1	—	1	—	—	13	16	67	16
22 Philippines	1	1	—	—	3	3	1	—	18	2	173	32
23 Singapore	1	15	—	2	5	82	—	16	6	22	43	764
24 Taiwan	1	—	—	—	—	3	2	1	6	7	65	38
25 Turkey	—	—	—	—	—	7	2	1	29	12	44	9
26 Vietnam	4	—	2	—	11	1	9	—	402	2	326	1
27 Other	1	4	—	1	5	47	2	26	93	108	153	175
28 Europe	63	21	13	1	194	112	94	43	1,298	530	5,095	1,643
29 Belgium	—	—	—	—	2	—	1	3	81	8	30	9
30 France	—	—	—	—	6	2	—	3	411	163	83	48
31 Germany, West	2	—	1	—	10	6	11	1	66	20	316	61
32 Greece	—	·1	—	—	2	15	1	4	52	131	118	156
33 Ireland	4	3	1	—	4	—	2	—	12	2	137	16
34 Italy	—	1	—	—	—	1	1	1	96	9	411	25
35 Netherlands	—	—	1	—	10	1	6	—	32	10	173	32
36 Poland	—	—	—	—	10	—	1	1	57	7	185	13
37 Portugal	3	4	—	—	1	2	—	—	49	12	252	46
38 United Kingdom	48	10	9	1	125	73	65	26	274	136	2,952	1,142
39 Other	6	2	1	—	24	12	6	4	168	32	438	95
40 North America	68	17	14	9	239	420	111	98	1,159	1,101	3,012	1,462
41 Barbados	3	—	—	—	—	2	—	4	16	20	82	66
42 Bermuda	—	—	—	—	10	128	—	24	—	2	10	64
43 Haiti	—	—	—	—	—	2	1	1	445	22	31	12
44 Jamaica	1	—	1	—	3	2	—	2	22	22	383	75
45 Mexico	—	—	—	—	2	—	—	—	23	21	20	20
46 Trinidad and Tobago	1	3	—	—	5	16	1	33	79	44	535	609
47 United States	61	6	13	9	208	138	108	30	538	911	1,802	437
48 Other	2	8	—	—	11	132	1	4	36	59	149	179
49 Oceania	1	—	—	—	7	—	—	1	21	8	177	21
50 Australia	—	—	—	—	5	—	—	—	21	4	146	11
51 New Zealand	1	—	—	—	2	—	—	—	—	4	24	9
52 Other	—	—	—	—	—	—	—	1	—	—	7	1
53 South America	2	5	—	—	4	19	3	20	168	99	567	241
54 Brazil	—	—	—	—	—	1	—	—	6	2	35	11
55 Chile	—	—	—	—	1	—	—	—	65	5	49	7
56 Guyana	2	5	—	—	3	10	1	4	13	8	311	98
57 Venezuela	—	—	—	—	—	4	—	15	18	60	33	82
58 Other	—	—	—	—	—	4	2	1	66	24	139	43
59 U.S.S.R.	—	—	—	—	—	—	—	—	5	—	35	3
60 Not reported	—	—	—	—	30	3	10	40	445	59	616	216

Table 1 (concluded)

| Manitoba | | Saskatchewan | | Alberta | | British Columbia | | Canada | | | | | |
| Landed Immigrants | Visa Students | Landed Immigrants | Visa Students | Landed Immigrants | Visa Students | Landed Immigrants | Visa Students | Landed Immigrants | | | Visa Students | | |
								Male	Female	Total	Male	Female	Total
1,102	**2,005**	**581**	**646**	**2,232**	**1,432**	**2,543**	**1,397**	**12,547**	**12,251**	**24,798**	**16,324**	**9,566**	**25,890**
67	106	31	45	138	109	84	66	713	407	1,120	2,294	599	2,893
4	3	1	—	12	—	2	—	58	43	101	10	10	20
—	4	3	1	12	5	—	3	30	9	39	48	18	66
—	12	1	6	27	39	28	25	51	47	98	182	90	272
9	54	3	6	12	17	—	6	57	27	84	208	58	266
8	—	6	1	29	1	21	3	93	82	175	30	14	44
—	7	1	19	25	18	12	9	60	49	109	78	30	108
46	26	16	12	21	29	21	20	364	150	514	1,738	379	2,117
322	**1,675**	**116**	**503**	**551**	**1,083**	**616**	**983**	**3,483**	**2,211**	**5,694**	**10,205**	**5,690**	**15,895**
9	27	2	2	6	12	23	19	98	58	156	110	77	187
94	1,082	39	381	239	694	217	530	965	697	1,662	5,136	2,794	7,930
45	8	15	5	89	8	41	8	373	264	637	96	42	138
1	22	1	4	3	14	6	32	25	17	42	226	93	319
7	9	2	9	11	11	70	30	259	165	424	267	82	349
4	5	1	1	9	2	5	1	51	39	90	25	14	39
2	5	1	1	12	5	20	17	27	48	75	37	46	83
4	2	—	2	9	—	1	1	48	30	78	25	11	36
3	—	—	1	8	1	8	4	254	80	334	190	19	209
11	417	3	57	33	196	47	211	115	88	203	3,054	1,727	4,781
3	—	2	2	7	6	5	3	73	25	98	37	8	45
40	3	5	—	23	4	60	17	156	168	324	27	35	62
2	57	1	11	6	107	23	70	40	47	87	597	549	1,146
3	2	—	23	5	3	26	7	51	57	108	55	29	84
—	1	—	—	4	—	1	1	41	39	80	24	7	31
72	3	36	—	53	—	31	1	665	281	946	6	2	8
22	32	8	4	34	20	32	31	242	108	350	293	155	448
369	**88**	**175**	**51**	**790**	**125**	**943**	**163**	**4,100**	**4,934**	**9,034**	**1,683**	**1,094**	**2,777**
6	1	1	—	4	—	8	1	46	87	133	11	11	22
12	7	4	2	11	2	12	5	212	327	539	109	123	232
49	20	15	5	62	13	100	33	256	376	632	71	88	159
3	14	—	2	3	3	3	9	113	69	182	272	63	335
15	—	6	—	18	—	17	5	84	132	216	13	13	26
28	—	3	—	21	—	26	4	292	194	586	27	14	41
17	3	6	2	59	7	56	4	164	196	360	33	26	59
16	2	4	—	35	2	12	—	175	144	320	17	8	25
19	3	1	1	7	15	21	3	169	184	353	50	36	86
176	29	129	37	486	67	582	42	2,192	2,654	4,846	967	596	1,563
28	9	6	2	84	16	106	57	396	471	867	113	116	229
268	**113**	**152**	**37**	**585**	**84**	**633**	**147**	**2,764**	**3,477**	**6,241**	**1,652**	**1,836**	**3,488**
4	—	—	—	6	2	—	3	58	53	111	52	45	97
—	—	—	—	1	—	1	3	5	17	22	94	127	221
5	—	—	—	2	—	—	—	323	161	484	23	14	37
17	2	3	—	28	7	7	1	204	261	465	45	66	111
1	—	2	—	5	—	11	6	25	39	64	19	28	47
41	75	6	3	40	30	7	12	334	381	715	375	450	825
182	26	137	31	483	39	591	116	1,684	2,439	4,123	840	903	1,743
18	10	4	3	20	6	16	6	131	126	257	204	203	407
9	**2**	**14**	**1**	**62**	**11**	**102**	**18**	**160**	**233**	**393**	**32**	**30**	**62**
7	1	11	1	39	8	55	5	117	167	284	15	15	30
2	1	2	—	19	1	25	4	24	51	75	9	10	19
—	—	1	—	4	2	22	9	19	15	34	8	5	13
53	**17**	**28**	**6**	**69**	**20**	**44**	**16**	**554**	**384**	**938**	**235**	**208**	**443**
3	2	—	—	5	3	6	3	25	30	55	9	13	22
29	—	21	—	21	—	11	3	117	80	197	5	10	15
17	9	7	4	30	15	7	2	256	135	391	93	62	155
1	2	—	—	—	1	4	2	21	35	56	91	75	166
3	4	—	2	13	1	16	6	135	104	239	37	48	85
11	**1**	**2**	**—**	**17**	**—**	**6**	**1**	**40**	**36**	**76**	**4**	**1**	**5**
3	3	63	3	20	—	115	3	733	569	1,302	219	108	327

Second to the United States, Canada has the highest number of universities per capita. Due to a decline in the birth rate in the 1970s and 1980s, Canadian universities have ample spaces in many areas. Before 1980, visa students paid the same fees as Canadian students. At that time the tuition fees were the lowest compared to other English-speaking countries. In 1985–86 tuition fees for full-time foreign students at Canadian universities varied widely across discipline, school, and province. For example, while fees for undergraduate commerce students in Alberta were approximately $1,300/year, in most other parts of the country they were two to three times this amount, rising as high as $5,800 in Quebec universities. Canadian tuition fees were still comparatively lower than those fees charged by universities from other countries. All these factors make Canada still a very attractive place for further education.

There are many private schools in the United Kingdom and the United States that recruit and accept foreign students, and they can be treated as the primary international competitors. They are competing for students, agents, seminar spaces, and so forth in the same market. Due to apparent preferences of Asian students and a more restrictive national policy in Australia, the private schools in Australia are not as serious a competitive threat.

Market Selection

In order to select a potential market from which to recruit students, the market must possess some of the following criteria:

a. Politically unstable.

b. Economically wealthy.

c. Insufficient higher education facilities.

d. No foreign currency control.

e. Formal government relationship with Canada.

f. Proficiency in English.

g. No mandatory military service for citizens in 18–21 age range.

Analysis of the Prospective Markets

Malaysia

Malaysia is situated in the heart of Southeast Asia with a population of 14.2 million. About 55 percent are Malays and other indigenous people; 35 percent, Chinese; and 10 percent, Indians. They gained independence from the British government in 1955. Though the official language is Bahasa Malay, most people have a working knowledge of English, and English is more or less an official language in the business community. After the 1980 legislation, in which all text-books used in schools must be written in Malay, the level of proficiency in

English has been declining. Though there are seven universities and a few community colleges in Malaysia, people of Chinese origin and Indian origin and those living in East Malaysia are treated as second-class citizens in terms of gaining admission to universities. The racial discrimination, inadequacy of university facilities, no currency control, and no mandatory military service make it a very attractive market for recruiting students.

Singapore

Lying off the southern tip of Peninsular Malaysia, Singapore is a very small country, with a population of 2.5 million. The majority (75 percent) of the population is Chinese, and the racial tension is not as severe as in Malaysia. The republic has only one university, the Singapore University, which has several campuses. The mandatory military service at the age of 18 and an adequate supply of education facilities make it less attractive than Malaysia, but still there is a lot of potential in this country.

Hong Kong

Hong Kong is a British Crown Colony with a population of close to 6 million. Ninety-seven percent of the population is Chinese. This colony has two universities and a few community colleges, but it cannot satisfy the educational hunger of parents and students. This is reflected in the high number of students leaving Hong Kong every year to further their studies in other countries. The return of the colony to the Government of The People's Republic of China in 1997 is another major reason why parents send their sons and daughters away for futher education. Hong Kong is an ideal market to recruit students.

People's Republic of China

This is the most populated country in the world. With the open-door policy and the government taking a more liberal role in letting its citizens travel abroad, more and more students in China want to further their education in foreign countries, especially North America. Some students are funded by the government to attend universities. Those who want to further their education and are not selected by the government face the problem of foreign currency control and the lack of funds. The few who have relatives overseas may have an opportunity to leave the country. The other major problem is language—most Chinese students have little exposure to English. An intensive English program seems to be necessary for these students before they can meet the English proficiency standard set out by the school and the Canadian Immigration Office.

South Korea

South Korea has a population of over 39 million. There are 96 universities and 170 community colleges in this country. There are still many students who want to leave the country due to political instability and the fact that the ruler rules the country with an iron fist. This is reflected in the curfew that exists in South Korea after midnight. The English proficiency for most students is low. Very tight foreign currency control and compulsory military service place this country as a secondary market for student recruitment.

Middle East

Some countries in the Middle East have many students in foreign countries. Some of this is due to the political situation (for example, Iran) and some because of a desire for a different lifestyle or better education (for example, Saudi Arabia). After Khomeini assumed power in Iran, many students fled the country. During 1981–1982 several thousand students left Iran, but the student influx from these countries changes from year to year and may not be considered a reliable source.

Brunei

This is a country on the northern part of Borneo in between the two states of East and West Malaysia. It has one of the highest per capita GNPs in the world, mainly because of petroleum. The population was only 214,440 in 1983, and there is no university in the country. The government has provided many free scholarships to students who want to study abroad.

Taiwan

There are presently not many visa students in Canada from this country. Due to its geographic location, situated in the middle of Hong Kong, China, and South Korea, it can be treated as a tertiary market.

Venezuela

This is a country with a population of 17 million. It has 11 universities and 106 higher education institutes. The official language is Spanish, and the students' proficiency in English is low. In 1983, 166 visa students from this country came to Canada. This country can only be treated as a secondary market.

Trinidad and Tobago

This is a country with a population of 1.3 million. The standard of living is not very high and currency control is imposed on its citizens, but still there are quite a number of students holding student visas in Canada.

Table 1 provides a breakdown of the undergraduate enrollment of visa students (and landed immigrants) by province, sex, and country in 1983–84. Hong Kong was on the top of the list with 7,930 visa students, and Malaysia came second with 4,781. Singapore came fifth with 1,146 students. The United Kingdom and the United States were third and fourth, but few of these countries' students enrolled in Canadian secondary school programs prior to their university admission. Other countries that have higher numbers of visa students were Trinidad and Iran.

Setting up an International Recruiting Network System and Global Strategy

The school must have a global strategy for recruiting students, and the strategy can be formulated according to the classification of the market and its geographic location.

The network can be in three different categories:

(1) Subsidiary

Since Hong Kong is the largest market, it is reasonable to establish a wholly owned student services agency in Hong Kong. This agency can also overlook the activity of students from Taiwan, which has no formal government relationship with Canada, and Macau, which is a Portuguese colony a hundred miles from Hong Kong.

Assessing the political situation of Hong Kong, the future is clear and stable at least for the next 10 years. It is suggested that one person from Canada be sent to Hong Kong to set up an office and oversee the recruiting operation in Southeast Asia. This person should travel from country to country on a regular basis to ensure that the joint venture in Malaysia and all agents in other countries are performing.

(2) Joint Venture

Because Malaysians would rather believe a local than a foreigner, it seems logical to joint venture with a local educational institute in Malaysia. The ideal candidate for the joint venture will be a Malaysian private school or private college with campuses all over the country. The education in Canada can be treated as an extension of that school. This joint venture can have 50/50 control, with the local partner providing the management and local connections, the knowledge of local laws and customs, and personnel adapted to the local environment.

Also, since Malaysia is geographically divided into two parts, East and West Malaysia, it may be appropriate to set up agents in East Malaysia instead of using a joint venture because the population is much lower.

Since West Malaysia is much bigger than Hong Kong, the strategy should be to set up a main office in Kuala Lumpur, the capital of Malaysia, with branch offices in Penang, Ipoh, Kuala Trengganu, Malacca, and Johore Bahru. This office can also oversee the activity in Singapore.

(3) Agent

For countries which do not have a large number of potential students, agents seem to be the ideal policy. Those countries may include South Korea, Taiwan, Brunei, Iran, Singapore, Indonesia, Trinidad, Jamaica, and Venezuela. The ideal candidates for the local agent are: (*a*) educator—local private or public school educator and (*b*) previous graduates from Canadian university—they tend to know more about Canada as a country and its education system. They can be remunerated for their efforts by paying them a straight commission on tuition. The following schedule seems to be common practice among competitors:

1–20 students per year	10–12%
21–40 students per year	12–15
50 and above	15–20

The school should invite its representatives to visit its campus in Toronto so representatives can have more knowledge about the school, the city, the education system, and the country. The invitation should only be sent out to those representatives that have demonstrated good performance. Inviting them to visit Canada can act as an incentive or bonus for the representatives, since good agents were very difficult to find.

Impact on Canada

This business should have the support of the Canadian government because:

1. It increases the employment for teachers, a profession suffering from a high unemployment rate.

2. It stimulates the economy of Canada. It is the requirement of the Canadian Immigration Office that each student bring in a specified level of cash to Canada in their first year of study and that they show the same level as a balance in their bank account every year when they renew their visas. This level varies from country to country, averaging $10,000–$12,000 for the Southeast Asia area. According to an unofficial estimate from a *Toronto Star* newspaper article, every visa student brings in at least $80,000 to Canada during their stay in Canada, based on a five-year visit as follows:.

Tuition fee (five years at $4,000 each)	$20,000
Accommodation (five years at $4,000 each)	20,000
Food and transportation (five years at $2,500 each)	12,500
Books and accessories (five years at $1,000 each)	5,000
Clothes, expenses, and so forth (five years at $1,500 each)	7,500
Parent visit and expenses	10,000
Student trip to home country	3,000
Total	$78,000

3. It increases Canadian goodwill in the rest of the world; those students who graduate from a Canadian university will be in a middle- to senior-management position 5 to 10 years after their graduation. Their familiarity with Canada will definitely help to boost Canadian foreign trade in the long run.

Because of all the above benefits to Canada, help can be expected from the officers of the Canadian consulate and embassy. It is recommended that the representative from the school visit the Canadian consulate whenever the representative prepares to recruit students in that country, so the representative can learn about the local government attitudes toward foreign businessmen, the economic situation of the country, and general do's and don'ts.

Financial Analysis

The greatest advantage of this business is that all tuition fees are received in advance. Students are required to pay their tuition fee before Canada Immigration will grant a visa and allow entry to Canada. As visas are processed at varying speeds, these tuition fees could be received by the school from six months to almost immediately before the student arrives. Generally, it can be expected that a minimum of three to four months will pass between recruiter contact of the student and completion of necessary entry documents. Because of the advanced payment, it may be easier to control the budget than in other businesses.

Once the breakeven point is achieved, then the profit jumps quickly. According to the projected calculation, the breakeven point is roughly 250–280 students a year. This figure is not too difficult to meet provided the school has a good network of agents and good school program. But nothing is certain, especially since this business is affected by so many external factors. The average enrollment in existing Toronto private schools is 200–300 students.

Another major benefit of this business is that the upfront money can be invested through short-term loans in treasury bills. As well, the money might also be used as a down payment on a student hostel.

This is a very volatile business. Students will stay only for one to two years, actually two to four semesters. If the recruiting activity is well below expectation for three to four semesters, then it will seriously jeopardize the business.

Appendix 1 shows the projected revenue and expenses in the first year.

The breakeven point for this projection is 275 students per year. Before the breakeven point there is negligible profit, but it does generate cash on hand for a short period of time. Once it exceeds the breakeven point and reaches capacity, the profit margin can be as high as 40 percent. Until capacity reaches 450 students, there is very little increase in fixed costs. The only variable cost is teacher salary and agent's commission. Teacher salaries can be considered a fixed cost in the start-up phase, as a minimum of three to four teachers would be needed in order to maintain the required curriculum standards.

The cost in setting up an office in Hong Kong can be seen in Appendix 2. The cost for a joint venture in Malaysia can be seen in Appendix 3. Both operations are expected to recruit 100–120 students per year in order to break even. The performance of the agents plays an important role in creating profit for this business.

One of the major problems in this business is the transfer of funds from foreign countries to Canada. Some countries have currency controls; therefore, the agents in those countries have to help the students to obtain Canadian funds for tuition fees and ensure that money can be obtained by the Toronto office. The other problem is to ensure that both agents and subsidiary offices send their tuition fees to Toronto as soon as possible. Usually the Canadian High Commission recommends students pay their tuition fee before they go for their visa interview, that is, three to four months before the school term starts. Sending the money to the Toronto office early helps to increase the cash on hand and cash flow and to generate interest income.

Proposal Summary

1. The number one criterion for success in this private school business is the constant steady flow of students. The public school board can afford to close schools because of decline in enrollment, but the private school cannot. In order to have a constant steady flow of new students, the school must first establish its objectives, then develop its reputation. It should monitor the activities of its established markets and at the same time explore new markets. According to past statistics collected from other private schools, referral from former students is the number one source of recruiting new students; therefore, the school should provide a good, solid education to its students.

2. If the school wants to remain in business for a long period of time, it should save or invest its profit in good years in order to survive the bad ones. Decline in enrollment may be due to various factors:

  a. Economic recession in certain target markets.
  b. Poor performance of agents or agents being pulled away by competitors.
  c. Increase in competition.

d. Political reasons (for example, tighter currency control of some countries, tighter visa procedures in some countries).

e. Increase in tuition fees of Canadian universities.

f. Change in policy in Canada or foreign countries.

3. In order to ensure success in this business, the school should develop the following strategy:

a. Full control in the top two markets, that is, Hong Kong and Malaysia.

b. Set up a complete network of agents over the world.

c. Constant patrol of the existing markets and exploration of new markets.

d. The school must provide a good, solid education to build up its reputation.

e. The school must have a long-range plan in terms of investment (for example, student hostel, book store, and so forth).

f. The investors of this business must have the same philosophy in education, business attitude, and the long-term objective of the business in order to ensure success in this business.

g. The first year is very crucial to the success of the business. The owners should spend most of their time overseas to recruit students because these are the sources of revenue.

h. The school should be set up in Toronto because it is a cosmopolitan city where students can adapt more easily.

i. The school should look for a school facility which was declared as surplus by the public school board (that is, a small school with 8 to 10 classrooms to start with and space for expansion to 20 classrooms). The school should start with one science lab and one language lab and expand to two whenever the situation requires.

j. The school should establish an English as a second language program and charge about $1,000–$1,500 for each student. This four- to six-month intensive program is for those students whose proficiency in English is considered as below standard.

APPENDIX 1: Financial Analysis—Projected Cash Flow
(June 1986–June 1987)

	June	July	August	September	October
Cash flow:					
Tuition fees	$ 60,000	$123,000	$210,000	$ 30,000	$ 15,000
Application fees	500	1,025	1,750	250	125
Others	60,000				
Total revenue	120,500	124,025	211,750	30,250	15,125
Cash outflow:					
Salary	8,000	8,000	20,000	20,000	20,000
Rent	7,000	7,000	7,000	7,000	7,000
Maintenance	1,000	1,000	1,000	1,000	1,000
Utilities	700	700	1,500	1,500	1,500
Taxes	14,000				
Insurance	400	400	400		
Advertisement	500	500	500	500	500
Promotion	10,000	6,000	3,000		10,000
School supplies	1,500	1,500	1,500	1,500	1,500
Office supplies	300	300	300	300	300
Lab equipment	5,000	8,000	5,000	300	
Office equipment	3,000	400	1,000	800	800
School activities	500	500	500	500	500
Telephone	350	350	350	350	350
School improvement	3,000	10,000	6,000		
Bookkeeping	250	250	250	250	250
Administrative expense	3,500				
Professional fee	2,000				
Agent commission			21,000		
Overseas office	9,000	9,000	9,000	9,000	9,000
Miscellaneous	1,000	2,000	2,000	2,000	1,000
Contingency	2,000	2,000	2,000	2,000	2,000
Total expense	68,000	53,900	84,300	50,700	56,000
Cash balance	$ 52,500	$122,625	$250,075	$229,625	$188,750

Note: Tuition fee is based on $3,000 per student per two semesters. Financial estimates are based on attracting 250 students in the first year.

November	December	January	February	March	April	May	June
$ 30,000	$150,000	$ 39,000	$ 60,000	$ 60,000	$ 60,000	$ 15,000	$30,000
250	1,250	325	500	500	500	125	250
30,250	151,250	39,325	60,500	60,500	60,500	15,125	30,250
20,000	20,000	27,000	27,000	27,000	27,000	27,000	27,000
7,000	7,000	7,000	7,000	7,000	7,000	7,000	7,000
1,000	1,000	1,000	1,000	1,000	1,000	1,000	1,000
1,500	1,500	2,000	2,000	2,000	2,000	2,000	2,000
	16,000	16,000				16,000	
		400	400	400	400		
500	500	500	500	500	500	500	500
		10,000				10,000	
1,500	1,500	2,000	2,000	2,000	2,000	2,000	2,000
300	300	400	400	400	400	400	400
300	300	5,000	500	500	500	500	500
800	800	800	800	1,000	800	800	800
500	500	1,000	1,000	1,000	1,000	1,000	1,000
350	350	500	500	500	500	500	500
		10,000					
250	250	250	250	250	250	250	250
		1,000					
	6,000	24,000			20,000		10,000
9,000	9,000	9,000	9,000	9,000	9,000	9,000	9,000
1,000	1,000	1,000	1,000	1,000	1,000	1,000	1,000
2,000	2,000	2,000	2,000	2,000	2,000	2,000	2,000
46,000	52,000	120,850	55,350	55,550	75,350	80,950	64,950
$173,000	$272,250	$190,725	$195,875	$200,825	$185,975	$120,150	$85,450

APPENDIX 2: Projected Expense of Hong Kong Office for the Period June 1986 to May 1987

Expenses:	
Salary	$38,400
Rent	12,000
Maintenance	1,200
Advertisement	10,000
Office supplies	1,500
Printing	2,500
Telephone	2,000
Promotion	5,000
Total	$72,600

Note: Based on this expense then this office should recruit about 120 to 150 students in order to break even.

APPENDIX 3: Projected Expense for Malaysia Joint Venture Operation for the Period June 1986 to May 1987

Expenses:	
Salary	$40,000
Rent	12,000
Maintenance	1,200
Advertisement	10,000
Office supplies	2,000
Printing	1,000
Telephone	2,000
Travel	2,000
Promotion	5,000
Total	$75,200

Note: Based on this expense then this joint venture should recruit about 120 to 150 students in order to break even.

Sources

1. "Private Schools in Ontario," Research and Information Branch, Ministry of Education of Ontario.

2. "A World Survey," *The Europa Year Book 1985*, vols. 1 and 2.

3. "Malaysia in Brief," The Malaysia Trade Commission in Canada.

4. "Singapore in Brief," The Government of Singapore.

5. "The Licensing and Joint Venture Guide," Government of Ontario.

6. Stefan Robock and Kenneth Simmonds, *International Business and Multinational Enterprises*, 3rd ed. (Homewood, Ill.: Richard D. Irwin, 1983).

7. "Education Statistics," vol. 5 no. 5, Statistics Canada.

8. "Living Accommodation Costs for Full-Time Students at Canadian University, 1984–85 and 1985–86," Statistics Canada.

9. "Tuition Fees for Full-Time Foreign Students at Canadian Universities, 1985–86," Statistics Canada.

10. "Enrollment by Level, Home Province of Canadians and Landed Immigrants, Province of Study, Registration Status, and Sex, 1983–84," Statistics Canada.

11. "Undergraduate Enrollment of Visa Students and Landed Immigrants by Province, Country of Citizenship, and Sex, 1983–84," Statistics Canada.

12. "Graduate Enrollment of Visa Students and Landed Immigrants by Province, Country of Citizenship, and Sex, 1983–84," Statistics Canada.

13. "Private School Enrollment by Level and Province, 1972–73 and 1982–83," Statistics Canada.

14. "Student Visa Application Information," Canadian High Commission in Hong Kong.

15. "Higher Education in Canadian Colleges," Selangor Consumers' Association Executive Council.

16. The Education Act, 1974, The Government of Ontario.

17. "College and University Programs in Canada, 1984–85," Employment and Immigration Canada.

18. "Recognition of Degrees Given by Canadian University," High Commission of Malaysia in Canada.

19. James Van Horne, Cecil Dipchand, and J. Rovert Handrahan, *Financial Management and Policy,* 5th ed. (Englewood Cliffs, N.J.: Prentice-Hall, 1980).

20. Robert Anthony and James Reece, *Accounting: Text and Cases*, 7th ed. (Homewood, Ill.: Richard D. Irwin, 1983).

Case 32

Patent Protection and the Pharmaceutical Industry in Canada

In July 1983 the Canadian-owned companies in the generic drug industry in Canada were gathering for a meeting of their industry association, the Canadian Drug Manufacturers' Association (CDMA). The federal government had just announced it would be modifying Section 41(4) of the Patent Act which was a key piece of legislation governing patent protection for the pharmaceutical industry in Canada. The CDMA was alarmed that the kinds of modifications to the Patent Act being suggested would greatly assist the patent-holding multinationals and potentially spell the demise of the generic sector in Canada.

The federal government decided that before presenting specific amendments of the Patent Act to Parliament, it would go through a consultative process with various affected groups such as the CDMA. However, because all of the proposed changes to the Patent Act were seen by CDMA members as detrimental to their interests, the CDMA's government relations consultant, Ivan Fleischmann, recommended that the CDMA refuse to participate in the government's consultation process. Fleischmann justified his recommendation by noting:

> How can you have a consultation process when you do not consult on guilt or innocence, but rather on whether the victim (accused) should be hanged or electrocuted?

The CDMA members wondered if they should accept Fleischmann's recommendation, and further, if they did accept it, they wondered what else might be done to protect their interests.

In order to place the July 1983 CDMA meeting in context, this case will review the following:

1. The role of patents in the pharmaceutical industry and the case of Canada.

2. Events leading to the CDMA meeting in July 1983.

3. The case for retaining Section 41(4).

4. The case for changing Section 41(4).

This case was prepared by Mark C. Baetz and David W. Gillen of the School of Business and Economics, Wilfrid Laurier University. Copyright © 1986 by Wilfrid Laurier University.

The Role of Patents in the Pharmaceutical Industry and the Case of Canada

The "manufacture" of pharmaceuticals involved two distinct processes: synthesizing fine chemicals to produce the active ingredients of a particular drug and compounding the active ingredients into final dosage form. The marginal costs of manufacturing a drug were much lower than the front-end costs associated with invention. The invention costs included the research to identify and develop active ingredients with valuable therapeutic effects and the extensive testing to prove the drug was safe and effective. Because the front-end research costs were so much higher than manufacturing costs, and because lack of technical knowledge was not a barrier to manufacturing most drugs, research-based pharmaceutical companies had been one of the principal users of patent protection.

The Canadian Patent Act provided innovators with a patent term of 17 years. With respect to pharmaceuticals, patent protection in Canada applied to the manufacturing processes rather than on the product itself. In 1923 the Patent Act was amended to allow for compulsory license to manufacture pharmaceuticals. This meant that prior to expiry of patent rights, a firm in Canada could apply to the Commissioner of Patents for a license to manufacture and market a drug which had been patented in Canada, and the commissioner could grant the license even if the patent holder was against it (in which case it became a "compulsory" license as opposed to a "voluntary" license).

Despite the 1923 amendment there were very few compulsory licenses granted in Canada for two reasons. First, the industry in Canada was essentially foreign controlled, and most head offices decided to locate their manufacturing facilities in other countries to take advantage of more generous tax incentives. Second, to qualify as a manufacturer, a Canadian firm would have to synthesize fine chemicals to produce active ingredients, but there was no fine chemical manufacturing viable in Canada because of the substantial scale economies and the small domestic market.

The next, and more significant, change to the Patent Act occurred in 1969 when the act was amended with Section 41(4) to allow for compulsory license to import raw materials (that is, active ingredients) for the manufacture of patented drugs. In other words, the government had removed another obstacle to manufacturing under license in Canada by allowing importation of raw materials. The primary goal of this change was to respond to public pressure coming out of three major studies during the 1960s which expressed concern that drug prices were too high in Canada. The government expected that the presence of a larger generic industry would help to reduce the prices charged by the patent-holding companies.

Events Leading to the CDMA Meeting in July 1983

While there had been some debate throughout the 1970s about the efficacy of Section 41(4) of the Patent Act, it was not until 1982 that the pressure on the federal government to modify Section 41(4) intensified. This was because in 1982 a number of multinational pharmaceutical companies publicly announced that compulsory licensing was causing them to make major withdrawals of activity from Canada. Ayerst, McKenna and Harrison, Inc., announced that its basic research facility in Montreal, one of the largest drug research establishments in Canada, would be transferred to a major new R&D facility in the United States by the end of 1983. Hoffman LaRoche announced closure of its Montreal manufacturing facility and transfer of the remaining Canadian operations to Brampton, Ontario. Merck Frosst Ltd. and Syntex Ltd. also announced suspension of planned expansions. Following these corporate announcements, the federal government came under additional pressure to consider modifying the 1969 amendment to the Patent Act and began a consultative process to deal with the issue.

CDMA Concerns about the Government Consultative Process

While the CDMA members believed that their case for retaining Section 41(4) was far more convincing than the case for modifying or eliminating it, they were becoming increasingly concerned that their case was not being fully considered as part of the federal government's consultative process. This concern was a result of the following events:

- In late 1982 the CDMA learned that Consumer and Corporate Affairs Minister Andre Ouellet had instructed his staff to meet with the Pharmaceutical Manufacturers Association of Canada (PMAC), which represented the patent-holding companies, to work out proposals to accommodate PMAC demands that Section 41(4) be eliminated. The staff of the Department of Consumer and Corporate Affairs (DCCA) advised CDMA members that Ouellet had instructed them not to talk to the CDMA.
- In the spring of 1983 Ouellet retained Mr. Martin O'Connell, a former Liberal cabinet minister, to be a consultant to DCCA to advise the department on changes to the Patent Act. However, the CDMA believed O'Connell could not make an impartial assessment and was biased toward the PMAC position because he had been employed by the PMAC as a consultant and had also participated in writing the PMAC submission to Ouellet on this very issue.
- On May 27, 1983, Ouellet made the following announcement to the Standing Committee on Health, Welfare and Social Affairs:

  The government has announced, as a priority, its intention to stimulate investment and expansion in the high-technology sectors of the economy. The experience and concerns of various segments of the industry, such as the patent-holding companies, must be examined. It is time to evaluate trends and developments during the 14 years that compulsory licensing to import has been in effect. . . . To generate further growth in this industry, the Government of Canada has decided to change the Patent Act to rebalance the 1969 policy.

In a background paper presented to the standing committee, the minister outlined three general approaches for changing the Patent Act:

1. Variable royalty rates dependent on the level of research and development activity being conducted in Canada by the patent holder.

2. Periods of market exclusivity dependent on performance commitments by the industry and possibly combined with a price-monitoring scheme.

3. Company-specific exemption from compulsory licenses dependent on specific performance and price commitments.

The CDMA was surprised by Ouellet's unexpected announcement and believed that all three approaches suggested by Ouellet would have effects exactly opposite to the stated intentions. The CDMA also believed that if any changes were contemplated, they should be in a direction exactly opposite to those proposed. In particular, the CDMA supported: (1) total abolition of patents on drugs, (2) elimination of royalties on export sales, and/or (3) administrative changes at the Health Protection Branch to speed clearance of new generic drugs.

A Government Request for Consultation

As part of his May 27 announcement, Ouellet stated, ''The approach selected and the specific amendments to the act or regulations that may be chosen will depend on the outcome of consultations with the provinces, companies in the industry, those involved in the delivery of health services, and other interested parties.'' To facilitate such consultation, DCCA released a discussion paper entitled ''Compulsory Licensing of Pharmaceuticals: A Review of Section 41 of the Patent Act.'' A covering letter to this discussion paper which was sent to various industry representatives read as follows:

> The federal government has decided to modify the provision in the Patent Act that permits the granting of compulsory licenses to import pharmaceuticals. The objective of this review is to identify ways to stimulate growth of both patent-holding and generic pharmaceutical firms by creating a more attractive environment for increased research and development and drug manufacturing in Canada. It must be emphasized that in taking this initiative the government remains committed to the objective of maintaining reasonable drug costs.
>
> The enclosed report is intended to form the basis of a consultative process designed to seek the views of interested parties. This process will lead to the development of specific amendments to the Patent Act and will identify other changes that may be necessary to meet the government's objectives.
>
> Representatives of the industry, such as yourself, can play a major role in determining which changes are feasible and desirable. I believe that government/industry consultations can and must develop realistic targets for industrial expansion

in Canada along with a price-monitoring system that will provide reassurance to drug purchasers.

I have asked my deputy minister, Dr. George Post, to organize meetings with industry and company representatives and to review submissions over the course of the next several weeks. It is our objective to complete our consultations by late August with a view to prepare legislation for introduction during the fall session of Parliament.

What was perplexing to the CDMA was that the covering letter indicated a much greater commitment to change than the accompanying discussion paper, that is, the covering letter stated that the government "*has decided to modify* the provision in the Patent Act" while the discussion paper concluded that "the objective of industry expansion *may require modifications* to the Patent Act or Regulations." Furthermore, the 61-page discussion paper contained many of the arguments and data which supported the case for retaining Section 41(4). One journalist noticed this contradiction and wrote the following:

> It [the discussion paper] is remarkable because while it recommends a cutback in compulsory licensing, all of its preceding analysis of the industry is a carefully documented argument that such an action would be both regressive and futile.

A CDMA Response

The CDMA was alarmed that all three general approaches for changing the Patent Act being suggested by the government would greatly assist the patent-holding multinationals. Furthermore, it was felt that two of the options—market exclusivity and company-specific exemptions—would spell the demise of the Canadian generic industry. It was in this context that the CDMA government relations consultant, Ivan Fleischmann, prepared the following draft letter to be considered at the next CDMA meeting:

> Dear Mr. Minister:
>
> I have been asked by members of my association to respond to your request for government/industry consultations. I must regretfully advise that my association has instructed me that members of this association will not partake in the consultation process for the following reasons:
>
> (1) While we do not differ with the stated government objective of creating a more attractive environment for increased research and development and increased investment, we totally disagree with the concept that changes to Section 41(4) of the Patent Act would accomplish this purpose.
>
> (2) As we have stated to you and your officials previously, we do not believe that the process undertaken by your department is appropriate given the role of the Honourable Martin O'Connell in this process, and given the fact that you have indicated that changes would be made before the consultations have even taken place.
>
> We believe that this issue, with its ramifications in every sector of the Canadian

economy and upon the Canadian public, should be aired in a totally public forum, such as a royal commission.

The members of my association have asked me to express their views that they indeed wish to cooperate with the government in an unbiased process. They simply do not wish to embark upon a consultation process which is clearly aimed at their demise.

If you or your officials would care to discuss this matter with us, we would be most pleased to meet with you at your earliest convenience.

Yours very truly,

Luciano Calenti
Chairman of the Board
Canadian Drug Manufacturers' Association

cc: Dr. George Post
    Deputy Minister
    Consumer and Corporate Affairs

As further background for the CDMA meeting in July 1983 the remainder of this case will summarize the arguments which had been advanced up to July 1983 to support the case for retaining Section 41(4) and then the case for modifying or eliminating Section 41(4). The arguments in each section have been divided into the following categories: (*a*) prices, (*b*) research and development, (*c*) impact of compulsory licensing on brand-name multinationals, (*d*) impact of compulsory licensing on Canadian-owned small business, (*e*) dependence of generic sector on compulsory licensing, (*f*) Canadian trade deficit in pharmaceuticals, (*g*) job creation, (*h*) technology, (*i*) Canada's international reputation, (*j*) commitments by multinational brand companies.

The Case for Retaining Section 41(4) of the Patent Act

A. Prices

1. In March 1969 the Patent Act was amended to provide for compulsory licenses to import in order to reduce drug prices. From 1969 to 1982 the Commissioner of Patents granted 290 compulsory licenses for 62 drugs, and as of January 1983, 43 of the 62 drugs had been marketed by compulsory licenses. Various analyses both inside and outside government concluded that the presence of these generic products, combined with provincial substitution laws aimed at encouraging pharmacists to dispense lower-cost equivalent drugs, has lowered drug manufacturers' selling prices:

a. Fulda and Dickens compared Canadian and U.S. manufacturers' prices for a single dosage for 16 drugs.[1] They found that in aggregate, between 1970 and 1974, Canadian prices decreased 10.4 percent and U.S. prices rose 2.1 percent. (There was no compulsory licensing or price control legislation in the United States.)

b. Gorecki and Klymchuck reported in 1980 that Canadian competition programs had reduced pharmaceutical prices at the manufacturers' level (but the savings had not been fully passed on to the consumer by the pharmacists).[2]

c. Gorecki concluded that provincial government drug programs saved at least 20 percent because of the generic drugs.[3] (Provincial treasuries spent approximately $600 million yearly on these programs and another $240 million on drugs for hospital use.)

d. Gordon and Fowler concluded that Canadian prices of compulsory licensed drugs, based on price indexes, were 9 percent higher than the U.S. prices in 1968 (before generic competition existed) but 21 percent lower in 1976.[4] In another more recent study, Fowler and Gordon concluded that compulsory licensing legislation combined with provincial product selection legislation reduced the manufacturers' average price of compulsory licensed drugs sold to the pharmacist in Canada from about 86 percent of the U.S. price in 1968 to 45 percent in 1980. This was seen as a significant reduction because the price index for a large sample of drugs not affected by the legislation remained essentially unchanged.[5]

e. Kennett of the Department of Supply and Services concluded that between January 1979 and January 1982 the average price of a group of drugs subjected to compulsory licenses or sensitive to future licensing action increased by 5.4 percent, while drugs having only one source because of technical or economic factors increased 42.5 percent in price, and drugs with only one source because of physician and consumer demand increased 64.4 percent in price.[6]

---

[1] Thomas Fulda and Paul Dickens III, "Controlling the Cost of Drugs: The Canadian Experience," *Health Care Financing Review* 1 (Fall 1979), pp. 55–64.

[2] Paul Gorecki and Andrew Klymchuck, "Government Intervention, Regulation, and Competition in the Prescription Drug Market in Canada, 1968–1979," Paper presented at the Annual Meeting, Canadian Economics Association, Montreal, June 1980.

[3] Paul Gorecki, *Regulating the Prices of Prescription Drugs in Canada: Compulsory Licensing, Product Selection and Government Reimbursement Programs*, Technical Report No. 8 (Ottawa: Economic Council of Canada, 1981).

[4] Myron Gordon and David Fowler, *The Drug Industry: A Case Study in Foreign Control* (Toronto: Canadian Institute for Economic Policy, 1981).

[5] David Fowler and Myron Gordon, "The Effects of Public Policy Initiatives on Drug Prices in Canada," *Canadian Public Policy* X, no. 1 (1984), pp. 64–73.

[6] R. B. Kennett, *Profile of the Drug Industry in Canada* (Ottawa: Supply and Services Canada, 1982).

f. The Canadian Drug Manufacturers' Association concluded in a 1983 brief that brand-name wholesale prices in the United States of a "basket of essential drugs" were 510 percent higher than the generic Canadian prices. The CDMA also presented several estimates of annual savings to Canadians because of generic competition. These estimates ranged from $30 million (based on an estimate of the price differential between brand drugs and compulsory licensed drugs in Canada) to $165 million (based on reduction in price of single-source branded drugs with the presence of generic products). On two products alone, the CDMA estimated 1982 savings to consumers and hospitals of approximately $20 million.[7]

g. A 1983 study by the Department of Consumer and Corporate Affairs concluded that in 1982 Canadians saved $162 million on the 29 drugs for which licensees paid royalties. This study also found that drugs with no competition cost 21 percent less in Canada than in the United States based on list prices.[8]

In short, various studies concluded that drug costs in Canada were among the world's lowest because of Section 41(4), and this helped to minimize health care costs.

2. Because pharmaceuticals are essential products in the health care system, price must be controlled to ensure access to medicines at a reasonable cost. Furthermore, they are prescribed for a virtually captive consumer by a third party (the physician), who pays no part of the cost. Virtually all Western nations (with the exception of the United States and West Germany) regulate drug prices, and Canada has chosen an instrument—compulsory licensing—which minimizes direct government intervention because it enables market mechanisms to establish prices. A price-control system requires an expensive bureaucracy and complex review system. Furthermore, any price-control system is difficult to administer particularly for sole-source drugs introduced for the first time. Finally, there is no acceptable "basket" of drug prices from foreign countries for use in Canada because economic factors vary greatly, and multinationals can manipulate transfer prices, making it difficult to determine actual costs.

3. If compulsory licensing were eliminated, the cost of government drug programs would increase thereby diverting tax money to drug costs rather than to the causes of poor health such as poverty, poor nutrition, exposures to stress, environmental contaminants, and lack of access to information on disease prevention. Furthermore, the cost of drug reimbursement programs is expected to grow significantly over the next two decades as the Canadian population ages. Therefore, any significant increase in drug prices could

---

[7] CDMA, *A Case for the Retention of Section 41(4) of the Patent Act*, April 1983.

[8] Canadian Department of Consumer and Corporate Affairs, *Compulsory Licensing of Pharmaceuticals: A Review of Section 41 of the Patent Act* (Ottawa: Supply and Services Canada, 1983).

threaten the existence of subsidized drugs which in turn could mean that lower-income people would do without drugs they might need.

4. Removing compulsory licensing will increase drug prices because there is very little resistance to price-level increases. In Ontario, for example, more than 90 percent of households are covered by a prescription drug reimbursement plan. The insurance company typically has a cost passthrough agreement with the employer, so the insurer is not sensitive to cost increases. The employer's cost for the prescription plan averages only 3–4 percent of the total cost of employee benefit plans, so that there is little resistance to increased drug costs.[9]

B. Research and Development

1. Pharmaceutical research and development can be divided into four categories:

   a. Basic research—primarily academic in nature, seeking new concepts or totally new drug products; it is generally carried out in universities, by government, or by nonprofit agencies.

   b. Applied research—directs the findings of basic research toward a specific hypothesis; it tends to be done in central facilities to take advantage of economies of scale.

   c. Preclinical development—more product or market oriented than basic and applied research and less centralized than applied; it consists of preparation of clinical dosage forms and animal testing.

   d. Clinical evaluation—several phases beginning with limited testing in healthy humans and proceeding to specific tests on individuals suffering from the target disease.

   Preclinical and clinical evaluation is required to meet the regulatory requirements of health authorities. Very little basic or applied research is done or ever will be done in Canada by the foreign-owned sector of the pharmaceutical industry because of the following:

   a. Applied research which can involve up to $100 million for each drug is more efficiently conducted in large facilities which already exist in other countries.

   b. In some countries where drug prices are controlled, governments permit a company to charge higher prices if it increases its R&D activities; the size of the markets in some of these countries means that there is a great incentive to locate R&D in the country in order to capture greater revenues.

---

[9] Donald Thompson, "The Canadian Pharmaceutical Industry: A Business-Government Failure," *Business Quarterly*, Summer 1983.

c. Countries such as Scotland, Ireland, and Puerto Rico offer better tax incentives for fine chemical manufacturing than Canada.

d. Since R&D is so essential to long-term profitability, management may be reluctant to entrust the corporate future to branch plants particularly in countries such as Canada with no internationally competitive track record for success in the discovery of new chemical entities.

e. Some countries require R&D for the company to have access to the market (for example, France requires contractual arrangements from companies specifying R&D) and other investment commitments before prices can be negotiated.

f. Because of FIRA, (the Foreign Investment Review Act) and other factors, the Canadian investment climate is perceived to be hostile to foreign investment.

There are also other factors which discourage the multinational firms from carrying out preclinical development and clinical evaluation in Canada:

- Countries, such as Japan and France, ensure that significant research takes place domestically by accepting data for the health approval process only from domestic clinical research facilities; in Canada, drug submissions can be supported by data from reliable foreign sources.

- It is significantly easier and faster to clear drugs in countries such as Britain than in North America, thus providing faster return on investment.

Given the factors cited above, R&D expenditures by the multinationals have always been at a low level in Canada. In fact, R&D expenditure as a percentage of value of shipments in Canada has ranged between 3.5 and 4 percent during the 1960s and 1970s, which is less than half the U.S. percentage of 10 percent. Furthermore, none of the Canadian subsidiaries have facilities for basic chemical research, and only 5 of the nearly 140 Canadian subsidiaries conduct applied research.

2. There has been no decrease in R&D expenditures in real terms over the period of compulsory licensing. As a percentage of sales, R&D expenditures have remained relatively constant: 6.6 percent from 1964 to 1969, 6.3 percent from 1969 to 1975, and 7.2 percent from 1978 to 1981. Furthermore, Canadian R&D expenditures followed the same general trends as U.S. expenditures, that is, expenditures rose steadily in the 1960s, levelled through the mid-1970s, and began increasing in the late 1970s and early 1980s.

3. Canada pays its fair share of R&D for drugs, even with compulsory licensing. The multinational drug companies claim that the cost of developing a new drug is escalating and that it may be as much as $80–$100 million. However, the benefits are transportable and recoverable on a worldwide basis. Given that Canada's share of world drug sales is only 2

percent, Canada's share of development costs to be recovered over the market lifetime of each major patented drug should be no more than $1.6 to $2 million per drug, assuming $80–$100 million development cost. Although it is impossible to predict the effective market life of a particular drug, many drugs remain in regular use for 20 years or more. Given that in 1983 29 drugs faced 43 generic products introduced under compulsory license, these 29 drugs could at most be expected to recover in Canada between $45–$60 million worth of R&D costs for their patent holders over their combined lifetimes. However, in 1980 alone, Canadian sales of prescription drugs were $1.4 billion, strongly suggesting that Canada has more than paid its fair share of development expenses.

4. Canada has internationally renowned universities, hospitals, and research institutes in a stable political environment. Therefore, even with compulsory licensing, multinational brand companies will continue to be attracted to investing in preclinical evaluation of products and clinical testing.

C. Impact of Compulsory Licensing on Brand-Name Multinationals

1. During 1982 a number of Canadian subsidiaries made major decisions about their operations, but Section 41(4) was at most a small factor in these decisions. For example, Ayerst, McKenna and Harrison, Inc., announced that its basic research facility in Montreal would be transferred to a major new R&D facility in the United States by the end of 1983. However, the Ayerst president indicated in a public statement that Section 41(4) was not a factor in the move. Instead, the major reasons for the move (not all publicly announced) were: (a) corporate reorganization and consolidation of R&D, (b) lack of space for expansion in the Montreal site, (c) superior R&D incentives in the United States versus Canada, and (d) continuing difficulty for English-speaking firms in complying with Quebec language laws. Also during 1982 Hoffman LaRoche announced closure of its Montreal manufacturing plant and transfer of its remaining Canadian operation to Brampton, Ontario. The major contributing factors to this decision were not compulsory licensing but the need to rationalize North American operations because of a lack of new products in the marketplace and a strategic error in overexpansion of physical facilities to 400,000 square feet, much beyond corporate requirements.

2. From 1970 to 1982, 18 Canadian subsidiaries established or expanded Canadian research or manufacturing operations notwithstanding compulsory licensing.

3. Compulsory licensing by the generic sector has not significantly eroded the sales and profits of the multinational brand-name companies for the following reasons:

a. The brand-name multinationals have remained the major force in the overall market; generic products accounted for only 9 percent of total pharmaceutical sales in 1982.

b. Because the average lag between market introduction of the patentee's drug and the generic substitute has been eight years, the patentee enjoys a substantial period of exclusivity. Even after entry of the generic, the original patent holder typically retains the major market share; one study showed that in 1976 patent holders retained between 0 and 98 percent of the market for drugs facing generic competition, even though the generic prices were as low as one fifth of the U.S. price and brand-name prices were considerably above this level.[10]

c. Patent owners can recapture earnings lost to generic competition by charging higher prices on lower volume "service" products and specialized dosage forms which do not attract generic copies; as well, patent owners can charge higher market-entry prices for new product discoveries.

d. Because of a gentleman's agreement, the multinational brand companies have not taken out compulsory licenses on competitor's products, even though they are entitled to do so.

e. Patentees receive royalties of 4 percent from companies holding the compulsory license.

f. The administrative interpretations by the Health Protection Branch of National Health and Welfare sometimes accord the multinational patentees a form of protection; licensees under Section 41(4) are required, in some instances, to carry out clinical trials of copies of approved drugs in order to prove that they are bio-equivalents of the original; the replication of clinical studies by the generic importers can involve large sums ($100,000–$200,000 per drug) and substantial delays.[11]

g. In response to undesirable competition, patent-holding firms have saturated the market with brand-name labels by drastically reducing prices; one company—Hoffman LaRoche—was convicted in 1980 under the Combines Investigation Act for (*a*) its marketing practices ("practically giving away such tranquillizers as Valium to hospitals")[12] in an attempt to prevent any generic competition and (*b*) for conducting public campaigns questioning the quality of low-cost drug substitutes.

Because of these factors, industry profits, both before and after tax, increased almost yearly between 1965 and 1980 (exceptions occurred in

---

[10] Fowler and Gordon, "Effects of Public Policy Initiatives," p. 71.

[11] Douglas Hartle, "Federal Proposal to Restrict Competition in the Canadian Pharmaceutical Industry," *Canadian Public Policy* X, no. 1 (March, 1984), p. 82.

[12] Mayn Gallus, "Under the Sugar Coating," *The Globe and Mail*, April 21, 1984.

1976 and 1977).[13] As well, net after-tax profits calculated as a percentage of capital (10.3 percent in 1977), as a percentage of equity (11.6 percent in 1977), and on total income (4.7 percent in 1977) showed little variation over the 1968–77 period.

D. Impact of Compulsory Licensing on Canadian-Owned Small Business

1. Compulsory licensing has created a thriving generic sector, consisting primarily of small business entrepreneurs; in 1982 this sector employed 1,300 people in about 30 firms.

2. Compulsory licensing has created a Canadian-owned and controlled industry; two of the four largest generic firms are Canadian-owned, and most of the smaller generic companies are Canadian-owned.

E. Dependence of Generic Sector on Compulsory Licensing

1. Products produced under compulsory licenses constitute an important component of the growth of the generic sector, and therefore, without compulsory licensing, the generic sector would diminish, and the smaller firms (which are mostly all Canadian owned) would disappear.

2. The generic sector has reached a critical growth stage and with the continuation of compulsory licensing, various generic companies will reach sufficient size so as to make greater investment in R&D, fine chemical manufacturing, and export market development.

F. Canadian Trade Deficit in Pharmaceuticals

1. From 1975 to 1981 the Canadian trade deficit in pharmaceuticals increased from $112 million in 1975 to $301 million in 1981. However, as a percentage of the market the deficit has ranged only from 13.6 percent to 19.4 percent in that period.

2. A significant contributing factor to the deficit is the importation of pharmaceutical raw materials (active ingredients) which must be imported because Canada has had no domestic fine chemicals industry. However, importation of these chemicals by the generics has a smaller impact on the trade deficit than importation by the multinational companies. This is because the generics (who are primarily Canadian-owned domestic firms) purchase these chemicals on the international market in "arms-length" transactions, while the brand-name multinationals purchase these chemicals from their own plants at exaggerated intrafirm prices. A sample of 14

---

[13] The assumption here is that overall industry profits is a good indication of the profits of the multinationals, given that generic products accounted for only 9 percent of total pharmaceutical sales in 1982.

major drugs in Canada revealed, in fact, that these intrafirm prices were more than three times higher than the prices paid for the same drugs in the open market.[14]

3. Generic firms have become increasingly active in the export market. Exports by the generics have increased from $3 million in 1980 to more than $12 million in 1983.

4. At least one generic firm has plans to establish a fine chemical manufacturing operation. This will help the trade deficit by replacing imports and by increasing exports. In contrast, Canadian branch plants of multinationals cannot increase exports because they would be competing with other subsidiaries of their parent company. As well, Canadian branch plants must purchase their fine chemicals from company plants located in countries providing generous tax incentives.

G. Job Creation

1. Because the industry is not labour-intensive and because of productivity gains, the levels of employment in the pharmaceutical industry have remained relatively constant. For example, from 1975 to 1980 employment fluctuated between 14,200 and 15,800 (dropping from 15,000 to 14,200 from 1975 to 1977), despite a doubling of sales during this period (from about $700 million in 1975 to about $1.4 billion in 1980). This indicates that even without compulsory licensing, no significant increase in employment could be expected.

2. Although this industry is not labour-intensive, the generic sector has created some highly skilled jobs. Detailed investigation and evaluation of raw materials, including development of methods for identifying and measuring impurities, development of dosage form, stability testing, conduct of bio-equivalence, and quality control all require the employment of highly skilled scientific and technical personnel.

H. Technology

1. The highly competitive generic firms have installed some of the most modern efficient equipment in North America to produce drugs as efficiently as possible. In some instances, some of the expertise to build the equipment has been generated in Canada, and this knowledge is being exported to the United States.

I. Canada's International Reputation

1. Canada's international reputation has not been damaged by Canadian patent laws given that Section 41(4) is quite consistent with Article 5A of

---

[14] Canadian Department of Consumer and Corporate Affairs, "Compulsory Licensing," p. 16.

the Paris Convention for the Protection of Industrial Property. While the European Economic Community has questioned Section 41(4), there has been no attempt to refute Canada's position.

J. Commitments by Multinational Brand Companies

1. There would have to be costly bureaucratic machinery to set and monitor "reasonable" drug prices in Canada in the absence of competition and to enforce compliance with whatever R&D, chemical manufacturing, and export commitments the multinationals might make in order to gain various concessions, for example, market exclusivity or company-specific exemptions from compulsory licenses.

The Case for Modifying/Eliminating Section 41(4) of the Patent Act

A. Prices

1. If Section 41(4) were repealed or modified to give the multinationals longer patent protection, there would be no significant price increases for the following reasons:

   a. The present compulsory licensed generic copies would still be available because any change to the Patent Act would not be retroactive (from 1969 to 1983, close to 300 compulsory licenses were issued, covering close to 70 drug entities).

   b. The inventors' process patents on 20 top-volume drugs will expire in the period 1983 to 1990, and there are fewer new products being brought to market, so there will be a larger portion of the total market open to generic manufacture.

   c. The Pharmaceutical Manufacturers Association of Canada (PMAC), which represents the multinational brand companies, has offered to cooperate in the setting up of a price-monitoring system comparable with systems in similar developed countries.

   d. Pressure to increase prices on uncopied products will be reduced. In addition, any pressure on market-entry prices for new drug products will be reduced if the patentee receives a predictable period for investment recovery.

   e. International price comparison studies have shown that drug prices in Canada for products with *and* without compulsory licensed competition are generally lower than those in other similar developed countries.

f. Different drugs can be used to treat the same diseases. Existing alternative drugs place constraints on market-entry prices, and furthermore, new drugs resulting from research exert downward pressure on the prices of existing products in the marketplace.

g. Section 67 of the Patent Act will remain in force to provide for compulsory licenses in cases of patent abuse, such as price gouging.

h. Provinces will continue to enjoy effective price control through their drug benefit formulary listing policies, whereby they can abstain from listing or can delist products where prices or price increases are considered excessive relative to the product's therapeutic benefits or cost effectiveness.

2. The savings to consumers and governments because of compulsory licensing have been grossly exaggerated, given the following:

a. Some studies compare apples and oranges. For example, the best *multiple* quantity deal price of the lowest-price generic has been compared to the single bottle catalogue price for the originator's product to exaggerate the price spread. If the best selling price of the originator were compared to the catalogue price of the generic, the originator's product would be cheaper.

b. When comparisons are made of Canadian brand versus generic prices, based on manufacturers' actual selling prices, not artificial catalogue prices, and when comparisons are made of Canadian versus American manufacturers' selling prices for the same size and quantity, comparing generic versus generic, brand versus brand, it can be shown that Canadian consumers have enjoyed a marginal price advantage on patented *and* unpatented products, on copied and noncopied products, and before *and* after compulsory licensing was introduced. For example, a 1982 PMAC survey found that of 33 top drugs, 31 were lower priced in Canada, 1 was higher priced, and 20 of the 31 had no compulsory licensed generic copies. In other words, compulsory licensing was not the only factor leading to lower prices in Canada compared to the United States. Other factors such as provincial government drug plan policies, marketplace differences, and healthy drug competition in Canada play an important role.

c. Some studies on savings due to brand-generic price differentials in Canada do not take into account: (*a*) compensatory price increases by noncopied, single-source, or "service" products and specialized dosage forms and (*b*) augmented market-entry prices because of the threat of compulsory licensing. (The president of the Canadian subsidiary of one brand-name multinational, Smith, Kline and French (SKF), stated, "If I had known there would be a generic for Tagamet [a revolutionary new drug to treat stomach ulcers], I would have doubled the price of Tagamet in the first year.'')[15]

d. Published investigations have shown that only marginal savings, which may result from generic pharmaceutical copies, have been passed on to consumers or provincial Pharmacare budgets.[16] (The primary beneficiaries of compulsory licensing have been four generic importers, two of which are subsidiaries of foreign multinational companies.)

3. Prescription drug products account for only just over 4 percent of total health care expenditures in Canada, and therefore, it is unreasonable to hope to control increasing overall health care costs by controlling drug prices. Moreover, new drug products are extremely cost-effective and can reduce overall health care costs. When properly used, drugs can substantially reduce or avoid more expensive professional and institutional costs, while at the same time significantly reduce an individual's time lost from his/her place of employment. Therefore, the economic and social benefits of increasing pharmaceutical research and development by strengthening the patent system should be as much of a concern as out-of-pocket drug costs.

4. While generic drugs may come on the market at about two thirds of the innovator's price, over time generic prices increase to equal or even surpass the innovator's price.

5. In general, the patent system is capable of stimulating invention and investment in the development of new products, but it is inappropriate for price control; if special price control is believed necessary, means other than the patent system should be sought.

B. Research and Development

1. Section 41(4) has had a negative impact on pharmaceutical R&D in Canada given the following:

   a. Statistics Canada data showed a decline in the average annual growth rate of R&D from 18 percent in the 1963 to 1968 period (before compulsory licensing to import) to 7 percent in the period 1969 to 1983.

   b. In constant dollars, annual R&D expenditures as a percentage of sales declined from an average of 5.5 percent prior to 1969 to 2.7 percent from 1969 to 1983. This decline was more than twice as severe as that for the industry worldwide and also about twice as severe as that for other industries in Canada.

   c. An OECD comparative study showed that proportional to relative

---

[15] Joan Hollobon and Dorothy Lipovenko, ''Coat-Tail Ride for 'Pirates' Angers Major Drug Firms,'' *The Globe and Mail*, October 26, 1982.

[16] See, for example, Gorecki and Klymchuck, ''Government Intervention.''

market size, R&D investment in Canada has not kept pace with other Western developed economies.

d. Although several U.S.-based pharmaceutical companies more than doubled their research activities outside the United States during the decade of the 1970s, pharmaceutical R&D expenditures grew at only an average of 7 percent in Canada compared to 25 percent in the United Kingdom. (The U.K. abolished compulsory licensing in 1977.)

e. The loss of sales revenue because of compulsory licensing to generic companies has been identified as a major contributing factor, if not the primary reason, for the closure of research facilities in Canada by Pharma Research, Abbott, SKF, and Ayerst. The Ayerst decision represented 17 percent of total R&D investment in Canada and 20 percent of the 1,500 R&D scientists employed in Canada.

f. Less apparent than actual closures has been the halt of research expansion plans at Merck Frosst Laboratories and Syntex. Still more difficult to quantify are plans of other companies for research investment which were never initiated and represent lost investment and employment opportunities.

2. In 1982 a survey of PMAC members indicated that the 44 firms surveyed reported R&D expenditures of $44.3 million representing 3.8 percent of sales; 12.7 percent of these expenditures were categorized as "basic research," 47.5 percent were categorized as "development." As well, the survey indicated that R&D expenditure was fairly well spread among all sizes of companies surveyed and not just concentrated in large companies (companies with less than $2.5 million in sales spent on average close to 3 percent of total sales on R&D, while those with over $25 million in sales spent on average about 4 percent of total sales on R&D).

3. There are many benefits to pharmaceutical R&D:

   - Reduced total health care costs.
   - Increased quality of life.
   - Increased opportunity for preventing and alleviating human suffering and saving lives.
   - The quality of human resource employment is highest, for example, employment of scientists, university-trained personnel.

   These benefits are lost when R&D is reduced; a strong patent system helps justify R&D investments.

4. The generic companies do not generally engage in R&D activities directed toward new drug development, even though their size has reached and exceeded that of many of the major multinational Canadian subsidiaries.

5. Even with increased R&D tax incentives the multinational brand companies will be extremely reluctant to increase R&D (or manufacturing investment) in Canada as long as compulsory licensing exists, because this

would be viewed as indifference to compulsory licensing, which might encourage its extension to other political jurisdictions.

C. Impact of Compulsory Licensing on Canadian-Owned Small Business

1. Compulsory licensing has not helped to create a Canadian-owned small business generic sector. In fact, the generic sector is not synonymous with either Canadian ownership or small business given the following: two of the four largest generic companies—ICN and Horner—are subsidiaries of American firms; the four largest generic firms are not small businesses; they accounted for 84 percent of the $125 million in 1982 sales in the generic sector; Novopharm, the largest generic company, had the largest percentage of total prescriptions dispensed in Canada in 1982 and second largest sales growth (47 percent); Apotex, the other major Canadian generic company, had the 6th largest percentage of total prescriptions dispensed in 1982 and the largest sales growth rate (51 percent). ICN and Horner ranked 8th and 13th respectively in an industry of over 100 companies.

D. Dependence of Generic Sector on Compulsory Licensing

1. A generic sector will survive in Canada even without compulsory licensing, given the following:

   a. In the United States, which has perhaps the strongest pharmaceutical patent system in the world, the generic drug market is flourishing; during the 1970s generic pharmaceutical sales were greater than 40 percent of total pharmaceutical sales; it has been forecast that from 1983 to 1993 the generic drug market in the United States will more than double—from less than $5 billion to over $10 billion.

   b. Some of the growth of the generic sector in Canada is attributable to the sale of products where a patent is no longer extant; in the future, patents will be expiring on a number of major products which will be open to generic competition; a federal government survey in 1983 found that only 30 percent of generic manufacturers' total sales were represented by products produced under compulsory license.[17] (The president of the largest generic company stated in 1984, "We'll survive no matter what.")[18]

   c. Any change to the Patent Act would not be retroactive.

---

[17] Canadian Department of Consumer and Corporate Affairs, "Compulsory Licensing," p. 29.
[18] Gallus, "Under the Sugar Coating."

E. Canadian Trade Deficit in Pharmaceuticals

1. During the period 1964–1969 average annual growth in exports for the industry was 16.6 percent while imports were growing at an average of 10.2 percent. The trade deficit declined from 2.73:1 to 2.12:1. However, during the period from 1970 to 1981 this favourable trend in trade balance reversed. Import growth averaged 16.3 percent per annum, while export growth declined to an average of 10.7 percent per year. The industry's trade deficit increased from 2.12:1 to 3.89:1 because of the following:

 a. The multinational brand companies lost sales because of compulsory licensing leading to closure of manufacturing facilities; these companies then turned to more importation (for example, Hoffman La Roche estimated losses of $250 million in potential sales because of generic competition).

 b. Some multinationals cancelled plans for plant expansion because of the hostile environment created by compulsory licensing.

 c. In virtually all cases, generic firms have taken out compulsory licenses to import, not to manufacture.

 d. Generic firms cannot export to Canada's major Western trading partners without violating patent rights and laws of these countries.

2. Increased reliance on imports has placed Canada in a vulnerable position. Any shortages or problems outside Canada could threaten Canadian national security.

F. Impact of Compulsory Licensing on Brand-Name Multinational Companies

1. In the period 1969 to 1983 the brand-name multinationals have had a loss in sales revenue of approximately $670 million due to generic copies and a loss in profitability such that aftertax return on invested capital for the years 1974–76 averaged 8.6 percent. This return compares with average returns of 9 percent on virtually riskless investment in Canadian government bonds for the same period.

2. Because of generic competition the brand-name multinationals have closed both research and manufacturing facilities, reduced high-technology employment (500 jobs were lost in 1983 alone, representing a loss of $17.5 million in taxable wages and benefits), and cancelled plans for expanded investment in all phases of pharmaceutical research, fine chemical and finished product manufacturing, and export trade development.

3. Compulsory licensing has had the most negative impact on those companies investing the most in R&D. The more R&D-intensive the company, generally the more success in developing profitable, high-volume products, and in turn, the more the company has been adversely affected by compulsory licensing.

G. Job Creation

1. Prior to 1969 employment in the pharmaceutical industry grew at an annual average of 3.2 percent. From 1970 to 1980 average annual employment growth fell slightly to 2.5 percent.

2. While not labour-intensive, the industry is research-intensive, employing 1,500 R&D scientists in 1980. This represents the highest ratio of scientists to total employees of any industry in Canada. However, the number of scientists and others employed has dropped dramatically because of the closure decisions of Ayerst and Hoffman LaRoche.

3. Many employment opportunities are being lost while firms freeze investment plans anticipating possible changes to the Patent Act.

H. Canada's International Reputation

1. Canada's international reputation has been damaged by Canadian patent laws which follow the Third World approach of expropriating technology. This approach is demeaning to Canadian scientists and scientific institutions.

Port Weller Dry Docks Ltd.

In 1978 Duncan Maxwell, president and CEO of Port Weller Dry Docks Ltd., an Ontario-based shipbuilder, was at a crossroads with respect to the strategy of his firm. Port Weller had just experienced a year of resurgence, unmatched in the rest of the industry, and Maxwell was considering expansion of his production facilities. However, he was concerned about government policy with respect to the industry, and particularly he worried about any unilateral moves by Canada in allowing freer trade in the shipbuilding industry under the GATT. He also wondered if he could count on government assistance if he established a new major facility.

In order to appreciate the situation facing Port Weller, this case will review the following: (1) background on the Canadian shipbuilding industry; (2) Port Weller's strategy to 1978; (3) strategic options in 1978.

Background on the Canadian Shipbuilding Industry

Overview

In 1974 the Canadian shipbuilding and ship repair industry was about to fall from the crest of the wave of demand which had lifted its ''orderbook value'' from under $100 million in 1970 to over $400 million in 1974 (see Exhibit 1). It consisted of some 60 establishments of varying sizes, of which the 14 largest represented about 86 percent of the total value of production. Most of the Canadian shipbuilders were subsidiaries of large companies (see Exhibit 2). In 1974 the industry directly employed 16,344 people. It was estimated that two or three times that number of jobs were created in allied employment including component manufacturers (that is, between 32,000 and 49,000 ''generated'' jobs).

The industry had its roots deep in Canadian history but had received its real impetus during World War II, when Canada became, for the first time, one of the world's major builders of ocean-going merchant ships and warships. With the demise of significant naval construction after the war and the virtual extinction of the Canadian deep-sea merchant marine when government subsidies were removed in 1949, industry capacity rapidly dwindled. There was a revival of interest in the early 1950s, when the industry was regarded as a vital defence resource.

This case is based on a case and industry note by Randy Hoffman, York University. Edited by Mark C. Baetz, 1986. Copyright © 1986 by Randy Hoffman.

Exhibit 1:   Subsidy Payments and New Construction

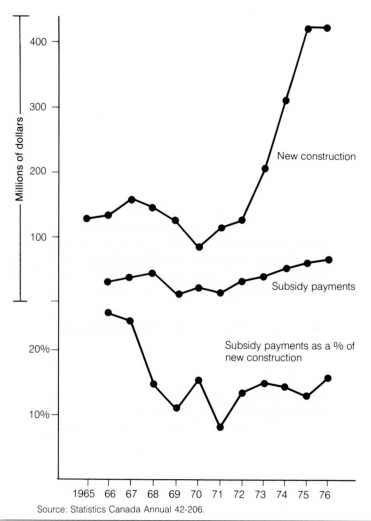

Source: Statistics Canada Annual 42-206.

Canada designed and built 24 destroyers and 3 large support ships for the Navy between 1940 and 1973, the Canadian Coast Guard expanded its Arctic fleet during the 1950s and 1960s, and subsidies for new construction of merchant ships were introduced at 40 percent from 1961 to 1963. From that point, the subsidy steadily declined to 14 percent in 1975. With the dwindling of the large-scale government ship procurement program, the Canadian industry concentrated on producing those few specialized vessels (such as Great Lakes carriers and ferries) demanded in the domestic market until about 1970.

Exhibit 2:   Relative Importance of Shipbuilding and Repair (S/B & R) Activity within Corporate Groups (dollars in millions)

Shipyard	Ultimate Parent	Value of S/B & R Sales (1)	Relative Importance (2)
Yarrows	Canadian Forest Products Ltd.	$50	D
Burrard Dry Dock	Canadian Forest Products Ltd.		
*Vancouver Shipyard	Genstar Ltd.	20	D
*Port Arthur	Power Corporation	40	D
*Collingwood	Power Corporation		
*Port Weller	Upper Lakes Shipping	20	B
Canadian Vickers	Vickers Ltd. (Britain)	15	D
Marine Industries	Societe Generale de Financement	75	C
Davie Shipbuilding	Soconav Ltee	75	A
*Saint John	Irving Group	60	C
Halifax Shipyard	Hawker Siddeley (Britain)	45	D
*Ferguson Industries	H. B. Nickerson	10	C
Marystown Shipyard	(Provincial Government)	12	A
*Newfoundland Dockyard	Canadian National	10	D

Notes: (1)   Approximate value of sales ($ million) in 1975, excluding nonmarine activities.
   (2)   Relative importance of shipbuilding and repair sales to total gross revenue of the group:

A—over 75 percent
B—25–75 percent
C—5–25 percent
D—less than 5 percent

*Indicates shipyards with associated shipowning companies (for example, Collingwood was owned by Canada Steamship Lines).

From 1971 to 1975, as part of a surge in demand for ships throughout the world, Canadian shipbuilders began to seriously penetrate the international market. By 1975 some 70 percent of Canadian-built tonnage was sold abroad. This penetration, however, came at a point when the world shipbuilding industry was teetering on the edge of a very severe slump. The boom in large bulk carrier construction (particularly oil tankers of over 100,000 deadweight tons), which began in 1963, had ended, leaving a huge surplus of these ships on the world market. The result was that the major shipyards of the world began to turn their attention to smaller and more specialized ships, thereby entering that sector of the world market in which the Canadian industry had been notably strong.

Shipbuilding and ship repair was relatively less labour-intensive than the construction industry (with which it largely competed for tradesmen). It was, nonetheless, relatively labour-intensive for the manufacturing field. The Canadian industry was forced to compete with a well-established, highly modernized world industry in which (except for the Western European industry) wages paid were a small fraction of those paid to Canadian workers. Furthermore, most countries with a shipbuilding industry also had a significant deep-sea merchant marine, and both the merchant fleet and the shipbuilding and ship repair industry were being heavily subsidized by their home governments in three specific ways to avoid massive unemployment:

1. Direct grants to shipbuilders to permit them to produce ships and sell them below cost (enabling them to offer prices up to 40 percent below the cost of comparable ships from Canadian yards) and similar grants on ship repair facilities.
2. Government loans or government-guaranteed loans to companies ordering ships from domestic builders which reduced financing costs to under 7 percent in some cases.
3. Restrictive legislation, such as the Jones Act in the United States, which restricts carriage of domestic (and in some cases imported) goods to ships built and owned in that country.

The Canadian industry, with only 0.8 percent of the international market and with only limited building and repair facilities (limited to less than 100,000 dwt[1]), faced severe problems in 1975. With no merchant marine and limited government subsidization, the industry could not compete financially. Furthermore, Canada, unlike other trading nations, had virtually no legislation preventing Canadian-owned ships from being bought offshore and registered under flags of convenience. Nevertheless, a 25 percent tariff was imposed on imported ships to Canada although this was considered inadequate by the industry. Potential Canadian shipowners also faced a unique situation of receiving no government assistance for purchasing *Canadian* ships (although they could often receive it from *foreign* governments for ships built in their yards), while *foreign* customers of Canadian yards could receive loans at 8 percent (or less) from the Canadian government's Export Development Corporation! Although owned and operated ships qualified for accelerated capital depreciation for tax purposes, such provisions did not exist for leasing arrangements—perhaps the most common modus operandi in the deep-sea trade.

These factors sent the Canadian industry into the latter half of the 1970s with a very bleak outlook indeed.

The Department of Industry, Trade and Commerce and the Ship Repair Building Industry

Direct subsidization of the industry began in 1961 under the Ship Construction Assistance Regulations. These subsidies dropped from 40 percent at the beginning of the program to 25 percent by the end. They were not designed to encourage exports—subsidized ships had to be kept under Canadian registry for at least five years. New regulations were instituted from the period of 1966 through 1975.

---

[1] dwt = dead weight tons.

Subsidy under these regulations was at a rate of 25 percent, decreasing to 17 percent, and the same Canadian registry provisions applied.

By 1970 domestic orders had fallen, but foreign owners had shown considerable interest in having ships built in Canada. The Shipbuilding Temporary Assistance Program (STAP) was implemented. It permitted subsidies of 17 percent (reducing to 14 percent in 1975) on ships built for export. The Canadian industry boomed temporarily, catering to a world market segment left unsatisfied by the concentration of major world yards on the highly specialized container trade and the huge bulk carriers.

In 1975 both programs previously in existence were replaced by the Shipbuilding Industry Assistance Program (SIAP), which provided for direct subsidies of new construction of 14 percent, reducing 1 percent per year to a continuing level of 8 percent. In addition to these direct subsidies on specific ships, a shipyard could obtain a grant of 50 percent of major capital expenditures on equipment which increased productivity, up to a maximum of 3 percent of the total subsidy granted that yard over an "orderbook period." SIAP also stipulated that components should be Canadian made, wherever such products were competitive.

SIAP was the comprehensive program provided by the department which included a total of 15 individual programs. Two additional programs were designed to promote research and development in Canadian industry in general. The first of these, the Program for the Advancement of Industrial Technology (PAIT), allowed a grant of up to 50 percent to a firm with a new product or process which incorporated new technology. The second, the Industrial Research and Development Incentives Act (IRDIA), provided for a grant of up to 25 percent on work done to research, develop, and test a new system which represented a potential *product* innovation but did not immediately incorporate a new technology in a commercial product to qualify for a grant under PAIT.

The slump in world markets which followed the 1975 peak called for more assistance from the department. In December 1976 ship conversions were made eligible for subsidization, and in March 1977 the subsidy was raised to 20 percent until the end of 1978. This subsidy was then extended to July 1980 at which time it was scheduled to drop to 9 percent.

The government had to determine if it wanted to continue subsidizing the industry and, if so, what direction this subsidization would take. The advantages of keeping a viable shipbuilding industry lay in its contribution to the national goals of enforcement of sovereignty, Arctic development, regional economic development, and employment.

National Sovereignty

Shipbuilding contributes to the sovereignty of the country by supplying vessels for its defence and for coastal as well as inland shipping. Without the capacity to build and repair ships, Canada would be extremely dependent on foreign industry.

Arctic Development

The Canadian Government announced that the development of the Arctic resources was to be for the benefit of all Canadians. Canada had gas reserves in the Arctic Islands estimated at over 16 trillion cubic feet which would keep 14 large gas carriers busy for 20 years. Using shipping instead of a pipeline would be advantageous in the following ways:

— It did not require each reserve to have a high threshold that would be required in order to justify building a pipeline to it.
— Whereas a pipeline required complete commitment from the beginning, tankers could be phased in, keeping risk lower.
— Tankers could deliver the gas to a number of receiving points without involving much additional expense.
— If other countries bordering on Arctic zones were also interested in developing their resources, the demand for gas carriers would increase. Once Canada had the ability to produce them, it would then be in a position to take advantage of this export market.
— While the building of a pipeline was a one-time activity, building ships provided long-term jobs in shipbuilding, ship repair, and shipping.

Regional Economic Development and Employment

The presence of shipyards in depressed areas of high unemployment contributed to the welfare of the people and to the industries located there. Shipyards provided direct employment for an estimated 134,000 workers and generated additional employment in industries which provided the materials and supplies.

The industry required government support to meet the above goals. For instance, Canada did not have dry-dock facilities to build ships of the size required to ship natural gas from the Arctic. This drawback also limited the ship repair jobs that could be done, as foreign ships trading in and out of Canadian harbours had to go elsewhere for repairs. The Canadian Shipbuilding and Ship Repair Association (CSSRA) predicted that an increase in the repair business as a result of having adequate dry-dock facilities would provide an estimated 600 man-years of work each year.

The shipping industry had been experiencing labour problems due to the instability of its demand. Industry fortunes went up and down depending on orders for ships. The best workers would get jobs in a more stable industry. Therefore, when orders were picked up, new labourers had to be hired and trained. Productivity may have been lower because the workers prolonged their work in the hope of avoiding layoffs. Stabilizing the industry would both ensure jobs and increase productivity.

Competition from the shipbuilding industries in other countries was affecting the Canadian industry. Britain, the northern European countries, and Japan heavily subsidized their industries, and regulations such as the U.S. Jones Act limited the market for Canadian ships.

The government could assist the domestic industry and overcome these problems in a number of ways. It could develop a "shopping list" of its future needs in reserve and place orders in periods of slowdown. An incentive program could be designed to increase orders from foreigners by making Export Development Corporation rates competitive with programs offered by other governments. Another option would be to provide loan guarantees to a lending institution, making it possible for the firm to offer the ship purchaser a lower interest rate on borrowed funds. This could reduce the overall cost of the ship and would be equivalent to a subsidy.

Also, some financial assistance would have to be provided for the building of adequate dry-dock facilities for Arctic vessels, as no private enterprise would be able to endure the heavy cost burden of such an endeavour.

As of early 1979 the government had responded to some of these needs of the Canadian shipbuilding industry and had already agreed to support three projects with funds:

—   The provision of a Synchrolift facility in St. John's, Newfoundland.
—   The extension of a graving dock in Saint John, New Brunswick.
—   The provision of a large dry dock in Vancouver.

The Department of Industry Trade and Commerce was also looking into the viability of its present program of general subsidies. It promised that a new program would be announced by early 1980. Indications were that this program would be aimed at concentrating government support in specialized areas of shipbuilding and facilities for repair.

The future support of the department was not enhanced, however, by the decision of the government, announced in January 1979, to not proceed with the creation of a Canadian deep-sea merchant marine nor by the failure to pass legislation restricting the Canadian coastal trade to Canadian vessels. In general the government's policy with regard to the Canadian shipping industry, even with regard to the needs of Arctic development, consisted largely of "encouragement" rather than legislation.

Port Weller's Strategy to 1978

Port Weller Dry Docks Ltd. was located at the northern end of the Welland Canal on Lake Ontario near St. Catharines. In 1975 it was eighth in employment among the major Canadian shipyards (3.7 percent) and the seventh in terms of sales (3.43 percent). It was wholly owned by Upper Lakes Shipping Limited, a Canadian corporation.

Under the guidance of President and Chief Executive Officer Duncan Maxwell (see Exhibit 3 for organizational structure), Port Weller had concentrated on domestic business since 1973 and resisted the temptation (unlike some of its sister

Exhibit 3: Port Weller Dry Docks Ltd. (A Division of Upper Lakes Shipping Ltd.)

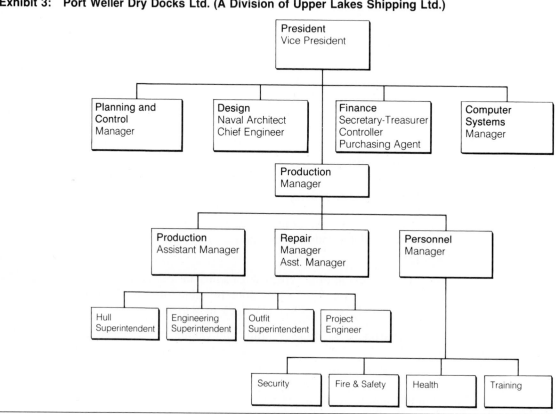

yards) to get into the "mass production" business of standard freighters and bulk carriers. Maxwell attempted to keep a stable, experienced work force of between 600–650 men employed and felt he could do this by "concentrating on what we know best," namely self-unloading bulk carriers (see Exhibit 4 for description of the carrier) and (since 1962) ice-strengthened ships for Arctic service. With the recent success of the yard's business, Maxwell was beginning to look more to the international scene: he was patiently laying the groundwork in Europe (through appearances at trade shows) to market internationally those preferred types of ships. While no firm orders had been placed, European countries—particularly those involved in the Baltic trade—had shown particular interest.

Port Weller had been a successful yard despite the "sea of troubles" generally facing the shipping industry. Reasons for the yard's success included:

1. Being owned by a shipping company, the yard had a more readily available source of orders than many others. (Upper Lakes Shipping was able to negotiate an important coal carrying contract in 1977.)

Exhibit 4

EVERYONE SAVES WITH SELF UNLOADERS

For Ship Owners. Self unloading bulk carriers provide substantial savings through:

- Greatly reduced turn around time. Unloading speeds are at least double those of shore facilities.
- Once docked, you start to unload when you want and at the speed you want without waiting for cranes to come to you.
- Shore based labour costs are cut to a minimum. No stevedores and no crane operators are required.
- Freedom from dockside labour problems.
- No more damage by grabs to cargo holds and side tanks.

For Port Operations. There are even greater savings for port operators.

- Expensive cranes are eliminated along with their maintenance and replacement.
- Without the weight of cranes and the width they require pier construction costs are reduced.
- The almost total elimination of crane operators, maintenance personnel and stevedores.
- Increased dockings per pier per year.

These savings result in lower dockage fees with no reduction in profits — an important incentive when ports are competing for business.

PORT WELLER DRY DOCKS
A division of Upper Lakes Shipping Ltd.
P.O. Box 3011
St. Catharines, Ontario, Canada 416-934-2581
L2R 7C1 Telex 061-5136

2. By concentrating on "what it knew best," the yard established a favourable reputation for quality work completed on time and had better costing information than the majority of yards.
3. Being situated on the corner of the Southern Ontario industrial area, the yard had better access than most to skilled tradesmen.
4. By its policy of keeping the work force relatively stable, the yard had enjoyed relatively good labour relations. Maxwell noted: "My essential idea was to keep a stable work force and keep introducing more work without necessarily increasing that work force substantially." (See Exhibit 5.)
5. The yard had been continually carrying out an orderly and selective program of improvements to facilities, which included equipment on the "leading edge" of shipbuilding and repair technology.

Prior to 1975 Port Weller had tended with the rest of the industry to live on a year-to-year basis. But in 1975 the yard found itself in the favourable position of having a $72 million orderbook stretching over 2½ years of guaranteed work. The

Exhibit 5: Employment at Shipyards with More than 200 Employees

		Employment		
Name of Company	Location	Late 1975	May 1977	Type of Production
Yarrows	Victoria	725	370	Tugs, barges, ferries, ship repair.
Burrard Dry Dock	Vancouver	750	800	Icebreakers, ferries, ship repair.
Vancouver Shipyard	Vancouver	600	260	Tugs, barges, ferries, ship repair.
Port Arthur Shipbuilding	Thunder Bay	250	210	Conversions and repairs.
Collingwood Shipyards	Collingwood	1,000	785	Lake vessels, ferries.
Port Weller Dry Docks	St. Catharines	600	660	Lake vessels, other cargo vessels, ferries.
Canadian Vickers	Montreal	500	685	Ship repairs only.
Marine Industries	Sorel	2,200	2,475	Cargo vessels, small tankers, ferries, ship repairs, naval vessels.
Davie Shipbuilding	Quebec	2,300	2,060	Large tankers, bulk carriers, naval vessels, ship repairs.
Saint John Shipbuilding	Saint John	1,500	1,620	Product carriers, naval vessels.
Halifax Shipyard	Halifax	1,400	1,075	Oil-drilling rigs, ship repairs.
Ferguson Industries	Pictou	350	235	Trawlers, patrol boats, other small vessels.
Marystown Shipyard	Marystown	400	350	Trawlers, tugs, ship repairs.
Newfoundland Dockyard	St. John's	300	300	Ship repairs.

bulk of this orderbook was in the form of a $40 million contract to build the M.V. *Arctic* (see Appendix), the world's first Ice Class II bulk carrier. In addition, a self-unloading bulk carrier was under construction for the parent company, Upper Lakes Shipping, and a tank-cleaning barge was under construction for the Department of National Defence. The yard had also booked $3 million of repair business.

By the end of 1976 the order backlog had fallen to some $42 million, and although repair work had increased $4 million and 15 months' work was assured for the yard's work force, no major new orders had been obtained. Nonetheless, the yard still was far better off than most (many others had been depending on an anticipated surge of federal government contracts for vessels and repairs which had not taken place), and Maxwell saw no need to change his firm's strategy. He noted:

> We try to be selective in our bidding. Maybe we won't tender because if at that time we have opportunities that are closer to our heart like the self-unloader or the ice-stiffened ships, we will try to select a bid on these. It is compatible with our flow of work in the yard, with the kinds of skills we have, and with the mix of labour that ties into that type of ship. If you have a resource mix such that you have so many thousands of tons of steel and so much outfitting, and you cycle it through the year, you get a more even distribution of work.

In 1978 with the negotiating of a coal-carrying contract by its parent and the increase in the federal subsidy back to 20 percent, two self-unloading bulk carriers were ordered, and the yard's orderbook increased in value to $100 million for the first time in its 30-year existence. Maxwell anticipated no change in the yard's product policy—he announced that he had no intention of getting involved in the bidding for new naval construction—but he increased his efforts to ease his yard's products patiently into the international market. Maxwell noted:

> There is a great growth of interest in self-unloading ships in Europe and elsewhere because of the fact that we may well go back to more coal being pushed around than recently. One of the great objections to self-unloading ships is that when you go into a port like Rotterdam, a major port with large land facilities, people don't want a self-unloading ship which employs no people. They want to employ all the same people and do all the same things, whereas a self-unloading ship goes in, drops off, and comes out and has no shore requirements at all. But if you have a short hull coming around, let's say, a coastal trade or dispensing that to further areas with a fast turnaround and no shore facilities, we really have the answer in this type of ship. So we developed this self-unloader; we've pushed it pretty hard at different shows.

Maxwell remained concerned about government policy with respect to the industry (notably about any unilateral moves by Canada in allowing freer trade in the shipbuilding industry's products under the GATT) and remained concerned lest any part of the naval construction program ''go offshore.'' Nonetheless, he affirmed Port Weller's guiding strategy—small, specialized, and stable.

There was great concern in the shipbuilding industry about the 20 percent subsidy (20 percent of the cost of all new construction was paid for by the federal government). The Liberal government had been phasing this subsidy out gradually. This was consistent with their stance that Canada could rely on foreign shipping lines and foreign production if need be. Both the opposition parties—Conservatives and New Democratics—favoured a domestic merchant marine and a domestic shipbuilding industry. With an election looming in 1979, it was not difficult to predict which political parties the shipbuilders favoured to win the election.

The government was asked for a two-year extension of the 20 percent subsidy level through to 1981. The industry was granted an extension to July 1980. One could presume that the Canadian Shipbuilding and Ship Repairing Association would lobby for further extensions. The president of this organization, Henry Walsh, made it very clear that this level of subsidization was necessary in order to compete with European and Japanese builders. Walsh noted: "If we are to get foreign orders we must continue to have that support."[2] Maxwell amplified as follows:

> It's a crazy world of subsidies. The present subsidy is 20 percent. It should have been 9 percent at this time. It was on a declining scale, but it was re-introduced back to 20 percent because everybody in the world was doing the same thing. We find that it isn't only the subsidy that is the problem. One of the biggest problems is financing terms. They are dedicated to the EDC (Export Development Corporation) rates which are standard, but they aren't really sufficient. In behind the scenes, there are other subsidies, the intervention fund in the U.K. is running at 25 percent and most of the shipyards don't make profits. We run at 20 percent and make a profit. What we're trying to do is keep it at 20 percent as long as other people are doing the same thing. If other international companies go back to zero subsidies, fine. But if you take the Japanese, who have so many hidden subsidies, where they have their own steel company tied into the shipyard, and tied into the engine works, the money is just turning about internally in the company, and supported by the government. It becomes very difficult to beat that kind of thing. Of course, there is a real world problem with recession in the world market. We are now seeing cutbacks in most major shipbuilding countries of 25–35 percent of the work force. . . . My feeling is that we'll put a proposition to the Poles, and the Poles will turn up their nose and say not good enough because it is not as good as they had from other countries and what they've had before. Their philosophy is: They build ships in Poland, sell them to other people to get dollars. They go out and buy their own ships elsewhere, and they demand 200 percent credit so that they can go out and buy other stuff as well. And they demand low terms and low interest rates. So, if you're really desperate to build ships, you do what the British did last year or the year before. They took on 20 ships for the Poles, gave them everything except the back shop, and then gave them financing conditions that were extremely good. Then the Poles said that's fine, we'll supply all the machinery and equipment and everything that goes in; so, none of your industries get any benefit from it, just your shipyards. We don't want that. If they

---

[2] *The Globe and Mail*, January 25, 1979, p. B13.

come here for ships, let's treat them fair and give them special terms if necessary, if that's what it'll take. But why give them special terms when you can give your domestic customers special terms and generate more business?

Strategic Options in 1978

With the shipbuilding industry's future precariously held in the hands of the politicians in Ottawa, Port Weller had been more successful than most firms in this Canadian industry. Vague promises existed from the federal government (and Petro-Canada in northern gas transportation) for a steady diet of projected Arctic and federal defence projects which would be designated for the Canadian industry. These projects were not to begin until the early 1980s. The outlook looked promising for Port Weller so long as subsidy rates could be maintained and the government continued to be a major customer to the industry.

With respect to future developments, Maxwell felt Port Weller had several options as follows:

1. It could continue its operations much as it did and remain profitable. This was a safe course of action and did not increase Port Weller's exposure to downturns in the market or reversals of government policy. Maintaining a stable work force would be an easier task under this plan; however, growth opportunities might be overlooked where it seemed that Port Weller was developing some competence.

2. Port Weller could attempt to expand its current site and increase the volume of production. Assuming that Port Weller had the ability to garner some European contracts with its unique product line, this strategy would enable it to service the increasing sales from that market.

3. It could go one step further and try to establish a new major facility. Despite its economic attractiveness, this strategy could not be accomplished without government assistance. The Province of Ontario had already taken the initiative in this regard. It had called upon Ottawa to establish a joint task force to investigate the possibility of constructing a dry dock capable of handling 1,000-foot lake vessels at either Port Weller, in St. Catharines, or at the Collingwood Shipyard in Collingwood. Maxwell saw certain problems there:

> We've made an engineering study of the possibility of a yard on Lake Erie for building 1,000-foot ships. . . . If we did produce the big yard with a flexible facility and a large capital investment, we would need all the business of Collingwood, Port Arthur, and ourselves. This would have social economic repercussions in these other areas. . . . You're talking about moving people from different towns, talking about shutting down the biggest industry in Collingwood and devastating its economy. . . . The government won't give me money that would shut down another place. . . . So we're trying to find a route that will solve all these problems.

Maxwell had to project the future so that his firm would be in the best position to take advantage of whatever came along. Maxwell knew that his long-term strategic decisions would directly impact on the firm's bottom line.

Appendix: The Motor Vessel *Arctic*

Pursuant to the passage of the Arctic Water Pollution Act in 1972, the federal government decided that Canada should develop, within five years, "operational excellence" in ice-covered waters. Additionally, it was decided that the first move in this development should be the design of a bulk carrier, capable of Canadian construction, which would be built as a joint project with the private sector. Officials of the Department of Industry, Trade and Commerce and the Department of Transport thus initiated the project which led, in May 1978, to the commissioning of the M.V. *Arctic*, a 28,000 dwt Ice Class II bulk carrier at the Port Weller Dry Dock.

The *Arctic* is a unique ship, the first of her kind in the world. Unlike other ships, which were ice-strengthened after initial construction and required icebreaker support in all ice-covered zones, she was designed and built from the keel up specifically to operate without assistance in ice up to two feet thick.

Montreal-based Federal Commerce and Navigation Company, a Canadian shipping consortium, accepted partnership in the venture. In conjunction with Caneat International Transportation Consultants of Montreal, Federal Commerce submitted a design for the ship, which qualified for a developmental grant under the PAIT. In late 1975 the contract to build the ship was awarded to Port Weller Dry Docks Ltd.

Although the *Arctic* would have qualified for a normal subsidy under SIAP, her cost (roughly twice that of a normal bulk carrier of similar size) and her experimental nature involved the Ministry of Transport as a direct partner. Consequently, the normal subsidy of 14 percent was waived. Port Weller did, however, qualify for grants under SIAP to improve productivity. It was able to introduce into the yard the "Autofon" equipment, a computer-controlled device for mold lofting (the full-size drawing of templates from which the ship is eventually constructed), which was one of the most modern of its kind, in addition to other yard improvements.

The contract for the vessel was of a cost-plus nature with an "adjustment clause" for about half the contract price (principally labour). The ship was delivered on time and within specifications.

Although under the terms of SIAP, components were required to be purchased from Canadian suppliers (this process was monitored fairly closely by DITC), the Canadian content remained fairly low outside of the hull itself. Of the 83 major equipment suppliers listed, only 29 were Canadian, and many of these were subsidiaries of foreign parents. Indeed, it was likely that (with the exception of the specialized steel plating) most of the major components were produced outside Canada although marketed through Canadian subsidiaries.

The ship operated in the Canadian Arctic from approximately June 25 to November 15 of each year. During the remainder of the year, she operated in more gentle climates. The latter area of operation served to increase foreign interest in the ship and to increase the possibility of European sales for Canadian shipbuilders (notably Port Weller). It was also hoped that 10 more such vessels would be built for Canadian registry.

The *Arctic* was operated by a consortium (Canarctic Shipping Limited), which was 51 percent government owned, under special leasing arrangements at a low rate (7 percent). Because of the expense involved in her construction, it has been noted that without this government financial assistance, the *Arctic*'s owners would likely have built her in Japan at a lower cost—if at all.

Case 34

Raytheon Canada (A)

As Bob Carpenter, contracts administrator for Raytheon Canada Limited (RCL), waited for clearance from Korea on the proposal to use Koshin as a supplier for advanced electronic components, he questioned the countertrade system of offsets. Even if Koshin were selected to fulfill the offset agreement, they were an unknown company in the United States. He had no idea whether their components would sell or whether they could be used internally by RCL. He had no doubt about the desirability of making the sale, but he wondered if the demands were becoming too stringent.

To put the decision regarding the countertrade system of offsets in perspective, this case will first provide the history of Raytheon Canada and its involvement with the Radar Modernization Project (RAMP). It will then discuss how it came to be involved with ground controlled approach systems in Korea.

Canadian Operations

RCL was incorporated in January 1956 as a wholly owned subsidiary of its American parent—Raytheon Company. Operations covered the fields of electronics, aircraft products, energy services, and major appliances in addition to several other lines. The company was among the nation's 100 largest industrial companies ranked by *Fortune* magazine each year. In 1984 sales were $6 billion with just under 50 percent of the total from the U.S. government. Raytheon Company's sales to customers outside the United States comprised 19 percent of revenues. Exhibit 1 gives a summary of the continuing operations for 1982 to 1984.

The head office of Raytheon Company was in Lexington, Massachusetts, and the firm had 12 major operating subsidiaries and more than 80 plants and laboratories in 26 states. The major overseas subsidiaries and affiliates were located in six countries with a principal one being RCL, which received a world product mandate from its parent to design, manufacture, and market air traffic control (ATC) systems worldwide. The RAMP project explained below was an integral part of this world product mandate and was to be completed in 1992. A second major commitment for RCL was their international radar program for air

This case was prepared by Professors J. Alex Murray and David L. Blenkhorn with special assistance from executives of Raytheon, Hyundai, and External Affairs Canada for the sole purpose of providing material for class discussion. Alterations of the facts were used to disguise events. Copyright © 1986 by Wilfrid Laurier University.

Exhibit 1:   Business Segment Reporting—Continuing Operations (dollars in millions)

Operations by Business Segments

Years Ended December 31	Electronics	Aircraft Products	Energy Services	Major Appliances	Other Lines	Total
Sales to unaffiliated customers:						
1984	$3,399	$723	$ 680	$797	$397	$5,996
1983	2,995	642	926	710	358	5,631
1982	2,656	568	1,124	565	304	5,217
Income from continuing operations before taxes:						
1984	431	6	14	61	33	545
1983	385	14	17	53	28	497
1982	319	61	65	22	23	490
Capital expenditures:						
1984	136	188	35	37	18	414
1983	103	83	34	21	13	254
1982	101	34	57	16	16	224
Depreciation and amortization:						
1984	81	27	36	18	12	174
1983	70	17	33	16	12	148
1982	63	10	32	16	10	131
Identifiable assets at:						
December 31, 1984	1,697	959	306	455	183	3,600
December 31, 1983	2,071	741	354	391	172	3,729
December 31, 1982	1,934	654	412	359	151	3,510

Operations by Geographic Areas

	Outside United States	United States (Principally Europe)	Consolidated
Sales to unaffiliated customers:			
1984	$5,450	$546	$5,996
1983	4,903	728	5,631
1982	4,419	798	5,217
Income from continuing operations:			
1984	327	13	340
1983	294	15	309
1982	273	30	303
Identifiable assets at:			
December 31, 1984	3,326	274	3,600
December 31, 1983	3,430	299	3,729
December 31, 1982	3,187	323	3,510

defense surveillance radars and ground control approach radars (GCAs). Typically, GCA systems were composed of three basic units: an airport surveillance
radar (ASR), a precision approach radar (PAR) to assure accurate approach on
landings, and a secondary surveillance radar (SSR) for systems operations. An

Exhibit 2: International Radar Marketing

Raytheon Canada Limited
Marketing Organization

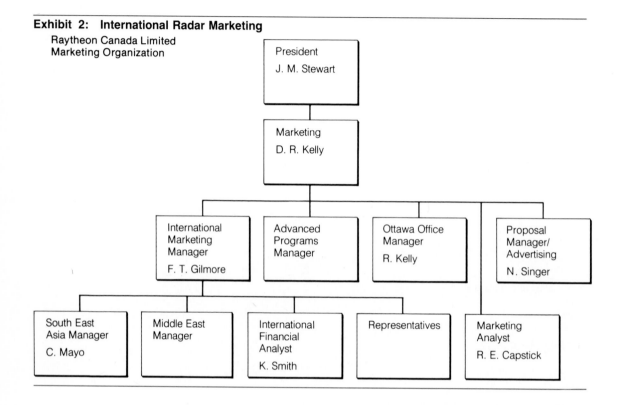

international radar marketing team had been organized with the president of RCL as team coordinator to sell GCA systems worldwide. Exhibit 2 gives an organizational chart for the Marketing Group.

The Radar Modernization Project (RAMP)

In 1978 the Canadian government developed a formal plan to update the present antiquated radar system in Canada. This plan was based on a conclusion of the specially appointed Dubin Commission of Inquiry on Aviation Safety that "radar equipment presently in use at Canadian airports was obsolete." The plan, known as CASP (Canadian Air Space Programs) was massive in scope with an expected cost totalling $3.5 billion by 1992.[1] Two years later, the federal government set specifications for the first of the new systems that made up CASP and made a request for proposals (RFP). Six firms responded with proposals for the project; RCL was one of these companies. In order to position itself competitively, RCL had increased its research and development on radar technology and by 1980 was

---

[1] Called RAMP/RSE (Radar Modernization Project/Radar Site Equipment), this first project covered the radar equipment (sometimes called sensors) at 41 sites and would be followed by an RFP for the RAMP DSE/RDPS (RAMP Display Site Equipment/Radar Data Processing System) about one year later.

well along on the development of the world's most advanced civil airport surveillance radar. Among other advances it featured solid state technology in the transmitter rather than the more conventional high voltage glass output tubes, and this was a factor in winning the contract valued at $390 million. It was the involvement with the huge RAMP project and being at the forefront in airport radar technology that put RCL in good contention for contracts in the international marketplace.

The Canadian Federal Government, through the Minister of Transportation, the Department of Supply and Services, and the Department of Regional Industrial Expansion were all actively involved with the RAMP negotiations. Canadian air traffic engineers had complained quite vehemently about the outdated system which had been in place for over 22 years. In order to upgrade the system and at the same time spread the benefits across Canada, three important requirements were included in the request for proposal (RFP):

1. The radar system should provide maximum safety for civil air traffic.
2. Many Canadian jobs should be created by the project.
3. Control of the technology should reside in Canada so that Canada could export the radar system to other countries.

Initially, the government had compiled a list of 27 national and international firms to which RFPs would be sent, early enough for international firms to find Canadian partners and qualify for the bidding process. The government established several criteria in order to evaluate different proposals:

1. Demonstrated experience in the field of radar systems.
2. Canadian entity; however, the government would accept a joint venture between a Canadian firm and an international firm contingent on there being an active Canadian component.
3. Financial stability of the company.
4. Evidence of good management.
5. Acceptable performance in past government contracts.
6. Present facilities or access to facilities capable of completing a project as large as RAMP.

The Raytheon Proposal

RCL assembled a team in order to present an integrated package for the proposal. In addition to an advanced engineering and technology system which would cover all the specifications listed by the RFP, RCL planned the following strategy:

1. RCL would own the radar technology.
2. RCL would export this and other technologies to other countries worldwide through world product mandates from their U.S. headquarters, Raytheon Company.

3. Jobs would be distributed throughout Canada so that all areas would benefit, not just southern Ontario. RCL estimated that employment would be created as follows:

> 242 person-years in the Atlantic region.
> 1,310 person-years in Quebec.
> 2,310 person-years in Ontario.
> 790 person-years in western Canada.

4. The U.S. and U.K. content would be 100 percent offset by Raytheon Company purchases in Canada.

5. The price would be competitive.

6. The building of a working model would cost approximately $1 million and would demonstrate the radar's effectiveness.

The RAMP contract was critical to the future direction of RCL; however, Westinghouse was a strong competitor. Both RCL and Westinghouse had existing products that were similar to that which was needed for RAMP. Their respective proposals, while meeting the rigid specifications of the Canadian government, were considerably different technically, in the management approach, and in the countertrade programs (socioeconomic benefits or SEBs). The role of SEBs in awarding the contract to a specified firm was given added weight as a factor in the award. The Canadian government had developed a unique set of offset procedures in which items not produced in Canada had to be balanced with exports of "like" products. It also developed that the Westinghouse bid had an appreciably higher price than the RCL submission.

International Radar Marketing

RCL was awarded the RAMP project on May 9, 1984. This was the world's largest and most comprehensive civil airport radar system yet implemented. Establishing a bid for this initial phase had required over $5 million of input funding over approximately three years. The major phase of the contract required the construction of 24 terminal surveillance radar (TSR) installations, providing primary and secondary surveillance radars at airports across the country. In 1985 RCL expanded its Waterloo, Ontario, plant to a 126,000-square-foot office and manufacturing facility on a 25-acre site. However, even before the RAMP award, RCL increased its export efforts to demonstrate its commitment to the Canadian government by undertaking the sale of its world mandate products to a number of foreign countries. Marketing strategies were initiated in the Pacific Rim, Middle East, Africa, and South America in order to implement a new ATC marketing plan. Of particular interest were Indonesia, Australia, Korea, Thailand, and Greece, in which the military was very interested in talking to RCL about its ground approach systems.

Ground Controlled Approach Systems

In mid-1983 RCL received a world product mandate from its U.S. parent for ground controlled approach radar systems (GCAs). Such GCA systems consisted of three separate units. The first was the airport surveillance radar (ASR) which provided for primary surveillance up to a range of 60 nautical miles. This unit displayed ''blips'' corresponding to approaching objects.

The second was the precision approach radar (PAR) which displayed all approaching aircraft and tracked as many as six aircraft on final approach. It displayed precise locations and other critical information needed to guide an aircraft into a landing. The third was the secondary surveillance radar (SSR) which addressed a transponder on the aircraft triggering a response that included an identification code, speed, and azimuth bearing. An integrated system of the above three units was first produced by the parent company as both a guidance for approaching aircraft and a surveillance radar system.

RCL identified three immediate overseas markets for the system—Korea, Thailand, and Taiwan—because of their need to provide both military surveillance of the skies and landing guidance for their own aircraft. Frank Gilmore, RCL's international marketing manager, pinpointed, in particular, the Korean need in 1983 for GCAs. The Korean Air Force had inherited a number of radars from the United States at the end of the Korean War in 1954 and had continued to periodically purchase new or updated equipment. They naturally went to the United States for their radar requirements when it became a priority. The only possible suppliers were those in the U.S. Armed Forces Inventory, that is, Westinghouse, ITT, Raytheon, and Texas Instruments. The Korean market appeared to be the most promising in 1983 since a general budget allocation had been designated for such general systems.

Raytheon's GCA systems were already used in South Korea by the U.S. Air Force because of their advanced technology. The Korean Air Force was familiar with the system, and this made it preferable as a military defense purchase.

The Korean government had committed 25 percent of its budget (6 percent of GNP, compared to 1 percent for Japan) to defense, and the military agencies were anxious to obtain the most sophisticated equipment available. Strained diplomatic relations with North Korea, China, and the USSR had placed a serious obligation on the government to assure a military alertness possible only with the most advanced systems.

The Republic of Korea

Korea existed as a part of various personal kingdoms and dynasties until 1910 when it was taken over by Japan. At the end of World War II, the struggle for its control escalated into the Korean ''Conflict'' when the country was divided, with the Communists ruling North Korea and an elected government in South Korea (The Republic of Korea). In 1961 Colonel Park Chung Hee seized military power and preached that the key to South Korea's economic success lay in exports. This commenced the move toward manufacturing for export, taking advantage of an inexpensive labour force.

Since 1980 Chun Doo Hwan, the current president, had taken a vigorous stand attacking inflation and improving living standards. He succeeded in reducing inflation from 25 percent to 4 percent, while the per capita GNP rose from $100 U.S. to $2,500 U.S. This was accomplished through rigorous fiscal control and zero-based budgeting for all departments of the government.

Korea had enjoyed five years of steady growth and social stability since the turmoil of 1980, when troops crushed an uprising in Kwangju. Unfortunately, this newfound wealth had not been broadly distributed with the resulting inequality lending support to the opposition efforts of Kim Dae-Jung, who returned from exile a short while later to make significant gains in recently held elections.

Contract Negotiations

Preliminary to successfully winning an order from the Republic of Korea for a GCA system, lengthy and involved negotiations were necessary. RCL's negotiation team consisted of two executives—Cy Mayo, project manager, and Bob Carpenter, contracts administrator, both from the Waterloo company.

Mayo had an extensive technical background and could keep all interested parties up-to-date with the capabilities of the equipment. He also could help explain the feasibility and expense of "peripheral" features in a system demanded by the Korean government. Carpenter was an expert negotiator and handled the commercial end of the negotiations.

The Korean negotiating team consisted of Lieutenant-Commander Choi from the Korean Navy as the senior negotiator, General Lee from the Defense Procurement Agency (DPA), and Major Chang of the Republic of Korea Air Force (ROKAF). DPA was RCL's immediate contact. The three were experienced and patient negotiators. Like negotiators in many Pacific Rim countries, they were not above using the tactic of threatening to cancel the negotiations and award the contract to a competitor if certain progress and objectives were not met.

The bargaining began when the field was narrowed to RCL and one of its traditional competitors. The other contenders did not have equipment which specifically met the Korean requirements, while RCL had produced such equipment and ITT had similar equipment in the developmental stage. RCL had a competitive advantage in that the U.S. Air Force used their system at its Korean bases.

From October 20 to November 17, 1983, representatives from each potential supplier met with the Korean bargaining team for all-day sessions. By mid-November offers and counteroffers had been proposed, discussed, and revised. Three major items of contention had been resolved.

First, there was an agreement on price. RCL's price was significantly higher, which was a major problem at the beginning since the Koreans were under a very strict budget and had many other items to procure with a fixed sum. Eventually it was agreed that RCL's price was acceptable. Since its competitors had never actually built the required system, cost overruns could be a problem or quality might suffer in order to meet the cost objectives.

Second, the terms of payment were another major hurdle which was overcome. The original plan called for payments in the first year which would exceed budget and was unacceptable to the Koreans. At the same time, RCL needed to ensure that working capital was coming in as fast as project expenses were going out. Finally, an agreement was reached to pay more money up front in return for add-on peripheral components being included in the package.

Third, performance bonds had presented a severe problem in the negotiations, but that issue too was eventually resolved. A compromise was struck, whereby complaints would be arbitrated by a panel of three—one independent and one appointed by each side of the contract.

Offset Agreements

In the world of international trade where goods are frequently bartered and countertrade among nations is commonplace, offset agreements are often used. An offset is broadly defined as a commitment by an international seller to do something that favourably impacts the economy of the buying country and describes a wider range of transactions than is usually referred to by the term *countertrade*. Offsets may be contrasted to countertrade in that in the case of offsets, the purchaser is a foreign government, the bilateral trade agreement covers a long period of time, and the transactions often include a technology transfer to the buying country as the items involved have a high value. Benefit packages, besides technology transfer, may include industrial spin-offs and guaranteed purchase commitments.

By the time the contract reached discussions of offsets in the spring of 1984, the Koreans were only beginning to develop an operational policy on the items and delivery to be included in any offset package.

The Raytheon Offset Proposal

When confronted with the offset requirement, John Stewart, president of RCL, decided to approach Korean companies presently doing business in Canada. His aim was to initiate importation to Canada of Korean products in order to satisfy the offset requirement. The government provided a list of candidates, three of whom were in Toronto. The international marketing manager was assigned the task of reviewing the candidates, the first on the list being Hyundai Canada Inc. of Markham, Ontario. They proved to be an $11 billion conglomerate with vast interests that included shipbuilding, construction, manufacturing, electronics, automobiles, and engineering.

Hyundai Canada's parent in Korea, Hyundai Engineering and Construction

Company Ltd., was founded in 1947 and grew from a small trucking firm. The company was also a major factor in the Korean financial and service industry including banking, insurance, marketing stocks and bonds, and hotels. The Hyundai motor division was one of the larger components of Hyundai Industries.

First discussions with Mr. Hyo-Won O, general manager and director, found that Hyundai were indeed interested and had plans to import the Hyundai Pony. They were presently negotiating with FIRA (Foreign Investment Review Agency) for permission to import the automobiles but needed something like the RCL proposal to make it happen. An agreement was signed, and for a fee, Mr. O agreed to make imports of Korean-made products that would satisfy RCL's 100 percent offset requirement. In turn, Hyundai would use the GCA contract to persuade FIRA to approve the import of Ponys. It was clear in the agreement that if insufficient Ponys were, in fact, imported, Hyundai would import one of its many other products. No difficulty was foreseen in the amount of imports required.

Counter Offers

By 1984 an offset program had been established by the Korean government, as detailed in the Appendix. The guidelines called for support of high-priority industries and attempted to offset with "like" products. The Koreans were seeking electronic product offsets to match the purchase of electronic equipment as an entry into the North American market. There was also a general feeling on the part of the Koreans that the Hyundai Pony would have succeeded without the help of RCL. Since the approval of FIRA had been expected, and sales were actually projected to be higher than the levels proposed by Raytheon, the Koreans felt that this was not a very advantageous offset and sought additional ones.

The ministry watchdog for promoting Korean high technology, the Defense Industry Bureau (DIB), wanted to negotiate the best offset contract to assist in technology transfers and employment to selected companies, particularly those firms the DIB felt had the most promise. RCL located and contacted Koshin,[2] a supplier to a large U.S. retailer of branded television sets. They agreed to be part of the offset arrangement. This left only two items on the agenda—the dollar amount needed to satisfy the additional offset requirement and the timetable for the offset purchase in order to satisfy the agreement.

By the fall of 1984 Bob Carpenter was ready to go back to the Korean government with these questions. He was prepared to purchase 5 percent of the contract's value (about $1 million U.S.) and take delivery over the next five years. The Koreans demanded 50 percent of the contract price in additional offset purchases (about $10 million U.S.) and delivery within the two-year span of the ASR agreement.

The Koreans said they would consider Koshin as a supplier for the offset, but

---

[2] Koshin, as the parent holding company, is in several industries such as pharmaceuticals and banking and, through one of its groups, had become a major exporter of electronic products and components.

to Carpenter's surprise, television sets could not be the product of the offset. He was told these were not considered "like" products under the guidelines. RCL would have to take electronic components (for example, integrated circuits) from a specified supplier in order to satisfy the terms of the offset agreement. This was the only line manufactured in Korea which was considered "favoured" by the government.

Appendix: Summary Guide for Korean Offset Program, Defense Industry Bureau, Ministry of National Defense, Republic of Korea

1. *PURPOSE*

   The purpose of this "Guide" is to outline definitions, objectives, basic guidelines and procedures in support of Offset Programs, directed by the Defense Industry Bureau (DIB), Ministry of National Defense (MND), Republic of Korea.

2. *SCOPE OF APPLICATION*

   This "Guide" applies to all agencies under the Ministry of National Defense and Korean industries as well as all foreign contractors incurring obligations under the Republic of Korea Offset Program.

3. *DEFINITIONS*

   A. Offset Program: The Offset Program is work, or the provision of work, or other compensatory opportunities, directed to the Republic of Korea by foreign contractors as a result of receiving, or in anticipation of receiving, a major order for equipment, material (including spare parts) or services in which the Government of the Republic of Korea is involved. There are two offset categories—direct and indirect. The determination of category, as well as project qualification, will be made by DIB, MND.

      (i) Direct Offset: Activities in the direct offset category are those which are directly related to the original purchase by the Republic of Korea, or foreign equipment, material or services. Direct Offset includes the following:

         (a) Transfer of technology to achieve the capability to manufacture and manage the production of parts and components to meet follow-on logistic support.

         (b) Provision of opportunities to manufacture and export parts and components related to the original purchase.

         (c) Transfer of technology to obtain a maintenance capability for equipment purchased within the Republic of Korea.

         (d) Assistance in obtaining maintenance opportunities in overseas markets for which the Republic of Korea has the technological capability.

(ii) Indirect Offset: Activities in the Indirect Offset Category are those activities which are not directly related to the production of equipment originally purchased. Indirect Offset activities include the following:

(a) Korean Industry Participation (KIP)

    (1) Activities in paragraphs 3A(i)(a) through (d) which are not directly related to the original purchase.

    (2) Opportunities to participate in major research and development projects.

    (3) Assistance in establishing industrial facilities and developing technological capabilities.

    (4) Assistance in creating new employment opportunities.

    (5) Any approved activity that will further Korean national, political, economic, military, and industrial interests.

(b) Counterpurchase: Counterpurchase activities include those which are related to the purchase of general commodities and financial assistance. It should be noted that general commodity purchases will not be indiscriminant and credit will only be allowed when a commodity purchase has been given approval from DIB, MND. Counterpurchase activities include the following:

    (1) Direct purchase by the contractor of Korean products or services.

    (2) Assistance in selling, or the direct purchase of, self-defense articles from original Korean sources.

    (3) Assistance in arranging sales to third parties from the original Korean manufacturer.

    (4) Efforts to obtain financial assistance for Korean products.

B. Memorandum of Agreement (MOA) for Offset Programs: An addition to the basic contract setting forth the obligations and understandings of foreign contractors and the Government of the Republic of Korea with respect to the Offset Program.

4. *OFFSET PROGRAM OBJECTIVES*

The primary objective of the Offset Program is to assist the Republic of Korea in developing and expanding its manufacturing and industrial capability. The goal of the program is to obtain new technology, provide design and development work, assist under-utilized sectors of industry, selectively stimulate sectors of the economy, and create new employment opportunities. The program is intended to increase technological and industrial capability with an emphasis on the area of National Defense.

5. *BASIC GUIDELINES*

A. The Offset Program will apply, on a case by case basis, to all major equipment, material and services purchased by the Government of the Republic of Korea for more than one million U.S. dollars.

B. The national goal for an individual Offset Program will be at least 50 percent of the basic contract value. At least 20 percent of the basic contract value will be in the Direct Offset Category.

C. The basic offset proposals will be considered on a competitive basis and foreign contractors will submit Offset Program Proposals to DIB, MND within a specified period of time. Offset Program Agreements will be an important factor in awarding the final contract.

D. The Memorandum of Agreement for the Offset Program will be part of, and attached to, the basic contract.

E. In executing the Offset Program, all values that exceed program goals will be credited to the foreign contractor for follow-on contract.

6. *EVALUATION CRITERIA*

A. The technological sophistication, the total dollar value and the length of time to complete the Offset Program will be major factors in the evaluation process.

B. It is expected that Korean equipment, material and services will be used to the maximum extent possible. Priority will be given to those Offset Program Proposals containing a greater amount of Korean material and services.

C. Some projects will not be approved by MND because they do not meet selection criteria.

D. The following categories are listed in order of importance: Activities of national high priority which promote political, economic, military and industrial development objectives:

(a) Participation in advanced technological development projects.

(b) Transfer of advanced technology and know-how.

(c) Creation, or improvement of, self-reliance in equipment purchased by providing for:

(i) Ability to produce equipment independently.

(ii) Ability to produce equipment jointly.

(iii) Ability to produce spare parts independently.

(iv) Ability to maintain equipment independently.

(d) Creation or improvement of self-reliance in related equipment/industry by providing for:

(i) Ability to produce related equipment independently.

(ii) Ability to produce related equipment jointly.

(iii) Ability to produce spare parts independently.

(iv) Ability to maintain related equipment independently.

Case 35

Redpath Industries Limited

In July 1978 Neil Shaw, president and CEO of Redpath Industries, was assessing the position he should take with respect to the future of a joint venture between Redpath and Labatt. The joint venture had been formed in December 1977 to conduct a feasibility study for constructing and operating a corn wet milling plant and starch conversion plant for the production and sale of starch-derived sweeteners including high fructose corn syrup (HFCS). Based on the feasibility study, the Labatt board of directors approved in early July 1978 a capital request to proceed with construction of the plant in a 50:50 joint venture with Redpath. It was now up to Neil Shaw to decide if he should recommend to the Redpath board that Redpath proceed with the project.

In order to place Shaw's decision in context, this case will outline the following: (1) background on the corn wet milling industry and the sugar industry, (2) history of Redpath to 1978, and (3) events leading to the formation of the joint venture.

Background on the Corn Wet Milling Industry and the Sugar Industry

Corn wet milling is the process of wet separation of the components of corn, that is, the germ, hull, gluten, and starch. The wet starch is further processed through a process known as starch conversion to yield a corn sweetener which can be used in a wide variety of foods. This sweetener is a corn syrup known as glucose. High fructose corn syrup (HFCS) is produced from glucose utilizing another process, glucose isomerization, and both HFCS and glucose compete in the sweetener market against sucrose and artificial nonnutritive sweeteners.

The origins of the glucose isomerization process were Canadian, but it was Japanese scientists who developed in the 1960s the enzyme to transform glucose (also known as dextrose) into fructose to yield a mixture similar to liquid invert sugar (see the Appendix for a further description of competitive sweeteners). Based on the work of the Japanese, two U.S. corn wet millers (Clinton and Staley) developed commercial processes utilizing immobiled enzymes. HFCS was the first commercially available natural product equivalent to sucrose. This was considered a major breakthrough.

This case was written by Mark C. Baetz with the assistance of Kenneth Harling and Ralph Troschke. Copyright © 1986 by Wilfrid Laurier University.

HFCS was originally made up of 42 percent fructose (hence, this type was referred to as HFCS-42) and 50 percent dextrose, and the remainder included various other types of sugars. Varying the combinations of dextrose and fructose allowed the mixture to be as sweet or sweeter than sucrose (dextrose was less sweet while fructose was much sweeter than sucrose). As technologies improved it became economically possible to manufacture higher fructose concentrations so that HFCS-55 became more popular than HFCS-42 in the United States. This trend to HFCS-55 occurred during the mid-1970s as Coca-Cola and PepsiCo started substituting HFCS for sugar. It was possible to add the HFCS-55 process on to an existing HFCS-42 facility since HFCS-42 was required in the manufacture of HFCS-55.

HFCS is a substitute for sugar. Its market success depended on it being sold at a discount to refined sugar since it was a relatively new product and because of the following limitations of HFCS: (1) it was available in liquid form only; (2) depending on the user, switching costs for storage tanks to house HFCS ranged from $50,000 to several hundred thousand dollars, and product reformulation was also necessary as HFCS behaved differently than sucrose when added to other ingredients; (3) HFCS-42 had to be stored and distributed at a warm temperature (100°F) to prevent possible crystallization; and (4) relative to sucrose, HFCS had a very short shelf life of several months.

Sweeteners were used as a major ingredient in the soft drink, fruit and vegetable canning, dairy, and confectionery industries. The impact of HFCS caused significant changes within the sweetener industry. Consumption of HFCS as a sweetener grew very quickly in the United States (see Figure 1 and Exhibit 1) and represented 25 percent of the total liquid sweeteners in 1975.

HFCS was introduced in 1973 in the United States during a period of high sugar prices. It was priced 10–15 percent below the price of sugar to quickly penetrate the liquid sugar market. In fact, by the end of 1977 a significant portion of the American liquid sugar market converted to HFCS. Per capita consumption of HFCS grew from 5 pounds in 1975 to an estimated 11 in 1977 with 16 forecasted for 1980. Declining sugar prices slowed its market penetration, but it was still expected that consumption would reach at least 2 million tons by 1980. Eight manufacturers of HFCS existed in the United States in early 1978, representing a

---

Figure 1: Corn Sweeteners Consumption

| | *Pounds per Capita* | |
Year	Canada	United States
1960	4	14
1970	7	19
1975	12	27
1976	13	30
1980 (E)	18	40

Exhibit 1: U.S. per Capita Consumption of Caloric Sweeteners

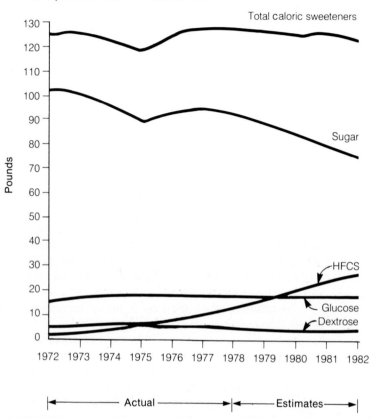

temporary overcapacity in the industry, but this was expected to disappear as sugar prices rose. New variations of HFCS were expected to push the market growth upward. In particular, the increased fructose content, in HFCS-55, had great appeal to the soft drink industry, especially to Coca-Cola and Pepsi-Cola.

The Canadian market was shifting toward products of corn wet milling as well but at a slower pace (see Figure 1). The corn sweetener used in Canada was mainly glucose which was manufactured in Canada by Canada Starch and St. Lawrence Starch. In 1977 HFCS was not produced in Canada and thus had to be imported; Redpath was the main supplier.

Growth in the usage rate of fructose in Canada would depend on the following:

1. High sugar prices creating a savings to buyers (net of changeover costs).
2. The percentage that sweeteners were represented as an ingredient in a buyer's product.

Figure 2: **Cost of Producing a Pound of Sweetener from Cane Sugar, Beet Sugar, and Corn**

	Cane Sugar	Beet Sugar	HFCS–42 Corn
Production costs per acre (dollars)	644	534	235
Production costs per pound of sweetener (cents)	9.8	10.8	5.8
Value of by-products per pound (cents)	.7	3.5	4.2
Processing and refining costs per pound (cents)	6.5	11.0	6.5
Total costs (cents)	15.6	18.3	8.1

Source: Merrill Lynch.

3. Availability of technical data demonstrating that HFCS was equal to or superior to sugar.

4. Acceptance by Coca-Cola Canada Ltd., and Pepsi-Cola Canada Ltd.

5. Refined sugar industry's reaction to the manufacture of fructose in Canada.

While production costs were difficult to calculate, according to one source, the production of HFCS had significant cost advantages over refined sugar (see Figure 2). Furthermore, the major input factor into HFCS, predominantly corn, was relatively stable in price (usually corn ranged between $2.00/bushel to $3.50/bushel) as compared to the price of raw sugar (to be further discussed). In addition, corn represented a very small portion of the total production costs of HFCS, and therefore, even when the primary input increased in price, there was little impact on the final HFCS production cost per pound. Figure 3 shows the relative price stability of corn in the United States from production year to production year and across producing states.

The process for the milling of glucose and HFCS-42 from corn involved many steps (Exhibit 2 presents a flow diagram illustrating the variety of steps for a glucose line). The corn in these cases has already been broken down into a wet starch before entering this process. Several key production factors or considerations should be kept in mind:

1. Poor-quality wet starch can lead to off-specification HFCS or glucose.

2. Plants must operate at high volumes to be profitable due to high fixed costs.

3. Product must meet customer specifications (that is, typically 15 specifications must be met).

4. HFCS can be stored only for several months before it discolours.

5. Demand tends to be seasonal.

The entire corn wet milling process led to three joint products: HFCS, glucose, and dry starches. The glucose market in Canada had been maturing, and growth was dependent on growth in sweetener demand. Annual demand in 1978 was estimated to be approximately 110,000 metric tonnes. Glucose was used primarily by canners, confectioners, jam and jelly manufacturers, and brewers.

Figure 3: U.S. Corn Price (dollars per bushel)

State	1976	1977	1978
Georgia	$2.31	$2.07	$2.45
Illinois	2.14	2.09	2.15
Indiana	2.10	1.97	2.15
Iowa	2.05	1.99	2.00
Kansas	2.12	1.99	2.25
Kentucky	2.22	2.19	2.35
Michigan	2.04	1.92	2.10
Minnesota	2.03	1.90	1.90
Missouri	2.27	2.05	2.15
Nebraska	2.06	1.97	2.05
New York	2.42	2.20	2.35
North Carolina	2.38	2.01	2,35
Ohio	2.10	2.01	2.15
Pennsylvania	2.37	2.32	2.45
South Dakota	2.18	1.83	1.80
Texas	2.33	2.16	2.40
Wisconsin	2.12	2.01	2.00
U.S. average	2.15	2.02	2.11

1 bushel = 56 pounds

Source: Sugar and Sweetener Report, Crop Production, January 1979.

Glucose did not compete directly with sugar as its applications were somewhat different, and therefore, its price was less sensitive to swings in sugar prices.

Starches were used in the packaging and paper industries. Little, if any, growth was expected for this segment into the 1980s. Annual demand in 1978 was estimated to be approximately 130,000 metric tonnes. Margins in this industry were very low, and overcapacity generally existed.

HFCS had become the main product of corn wet milling, and as has been noted, the growth potential was vast as the Canadian market had not witnessed much of a push on this product. To examine it in detail, one must consider the different segments of the market: soft drinks, fruit and vegetable canning, dairy, confectionery, and miscellaneous. Figure 4 shows the total consumption of all sweeteners by market segment in Canada.

The soft drink industry represented a huge potential market although it was expected that any sales of HFCS in the soft drink industry would come at the expense of sugar. HFCS was growing in usage in the American soft drink industry, and Coca-Cola was considering utilizing 50 percent HFCS-55 in place of refined sugar. Coke represented 10 percent of the volume of the entire sweetener market in the United States.

The fruit and vegetable canning industry was expected to grow at a steady 2 percent annual rate, and HFCS had been introduced to it. Sugar and HFCS would trade off with each other for gains in sales in this market.

Two other segments of the sweetener industry existed, but neither held much

Exhibit 2: Flow Diagram of Glucose Line

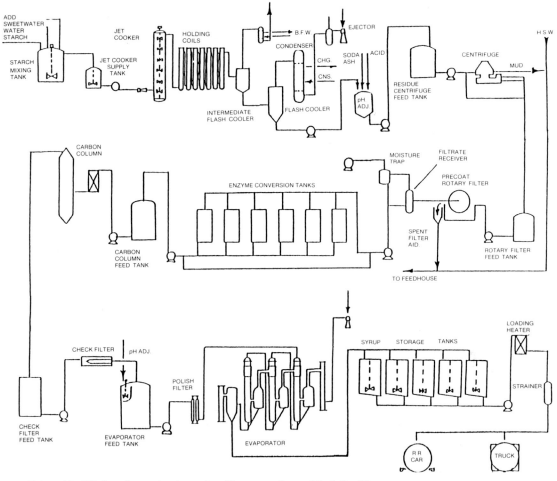

Notes: (1) This flow diagram has been altered to preserve the confidentiality of the process.
        (2) The HFCS line involved many more steps than the glucose line.

potential for HFCS. Segments of the dairy industry were closed to HFCS as the product was incompatible for technical reasons with the other factors in the production process, and in the confectionery industry, sucrose and glucose were the preferred sweeteners, not HFCS. Wineries, breweries, bakeries, and biscuit and cereal manufacturers represented the miscellaneous group of potential customers.

The Comparison to Sugar

As noted previously, the HFCS selling price was linked to that of refined sugar. Experience in the United States had shown that price was the first and foremost

Figure 4: Consumption of Sweeteners in Canada 1970–1977 (in thousands of metric tonnes,* dry solids)

Year/Segment	Sugar	Glucose	HFCS	Total
Soft drink:				
1970	154.8	—	—	154.8
1971	155.2	—	—	155.2
1972	161.5	—	—	161.5
1973	164.8	—	—	164.8
1974	166.6	—	—	166.6
1975	176.7	—	—	176.7
1976	173.1	—	—	173.1
1977	174.2	—	—	174.2
Fruit and vegetable canning:				
1970	93.7	1.4	—	95.1
1971	85.5	2.1	—	87.6
1972	66.7	5.0	—	71.7
1973	99.0	5.3	—	104.3
1974	97.0	9.3	1.0	107.3
1975	81.6	10.6	3.5	95.7
1976	80.2	8.9	5.5	94.6
1977	78.0	12.5	5.0	95.5
Dairy:				
1970	39.0	10.6	—	49.6
1971	38.9	11.8	—	50.7
1972	39.1	12.8	—	51.9
1973	56.2	9.5	—	65.7
1974	50.0	13.6	—	63.6
1975	52.8	15.2	—	68.0
1976	48.2	15.9	—	64.1
1977	54.9	14.9	—	69.8
Confectionery:				
1970	79.4	21.0	—	100.4
1971	78.0	23.2	—	101.2
1972	78.0	20.0	—	98.0
1973	78.3	20.6	—	98.9
1974	70.0	21.5	—	91.5
1975	56.0	16.9	.3	73.2
1976	60.4	18.5	.3	79.2
1977	57.0	19.1	.5	76.6
Totals for all segments[†]:				
1970	940	60	—	1,000
1971	1,020	66	—	1,086
1972	1,000	67	—	1,067
1973	1,060	83	—	1,143
1974	910	89	—	995
1975	890	95	4[‡]	989
1976	980	99	7[‡]	1,086
1977	996	110	7[‡]	1,113

* One metric tonne = 1,000 kg = 2,204.6 pounds.
[†] Includes other sweetener segments not represented.
[‡] Very rough estimates.
Source: Redpath estimates.

Figure 5:   Total U.S. Consumption—Caloric and Noncaloric Sweeteners (hundreds of millions of pounds)

Year*	Sucrose	HFCS	Dextrose and Glucose	Other†	Total Caloric	Saccharin	Aspertame	Total Noncaloric	Total
1975	192	11	49	3	255	13	—	13	268
1976	204	16	49	3	272	13	—	13	285
1977	207	21	48	3	279	15	—	15	294
1978	204	27	48	3	282	15	—	15	297
1979	201	34	48	3	286	16	—	16	302
1980	191	44	48	3	286	17	—	17	303
1981	182	54	49	3	288	17	—	17	305
1982	171	61	50	3	286	17	2	19	305
1983	166	71	50	7	294	17	5	22	316
1984	157	86	51	7	301	17	6	23	324
1985	150	92	51	4	297	17	12	29	326

* Actual figures are given for 1975–77; 1978–1985 are estimates.
† Refined sugar imports, honey, edible syrup, and so forth.
Source: U.S. Department of Agriculture Sugar and Sweetener Report.

consideration in the ability to sell HFCS. A significant discount had to be made to buyers to convince them to change over. Total U.S. consumption of sweeteners is shown in Figure 5. The trade-off between sucrose and HFCS should be noted as well as the leveling of demand for caloric sweeteners.

Even though only about 15 percent of world sugar supplies are freely traded, sugar is a commodity which tends to follow the rules of supply and demand. The supply of sugar adjusts very slowly to demand changes because of the long lead times involved in production (that is, sugar cane or beets are planted months before the actual demand is known). When demand fluctuates, the result is a very unstable price level for raw sugar. Year-end stockpiles usually dictate the world price. Therefore, the key to predicting sugar prices lies in evaluating the stock of world sugar. However, this is difficult to do as some of the major producers, such as the USSR, Cuba, and China, do not operate free market economies. This has produced a highly volatile market for sugar. Exhibits 3 and 4 reflect these relationships. Figure 6, listing the world's sugar producers, notes the relative importance of the three centrally planned economies and the insignificant amount produced in Canada.

The sugar market has often been called one of bull to bear. The bull market was related to shortages in supply of sugar, with the reverse for the bear market. Between 1950 and 1977 the bull market had an average duration of two years. The last bull market began in 1974–75.

Although the sugar market was highly volatile, it was possible to purchase long-term contracts in the futures market. This meant that sugar refiners, such as Redpath, could and did operate under a fully hedged position, where purchases of

---

Exhibit 3: World Sugar Stocks as a Percentage of World Demand versus World Sugar Price

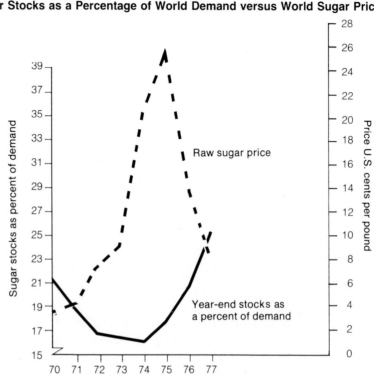

physical raw sugar were matched with sales of futures contracts in the commodity market. The purchase contracts could range up to 18 months.

In the United States the federal government had been supporting a floor price for sugar. In addition, import restrictions involving duties and import fees for raw sugar had been implemented to shield the American domestic sugar cane and beet producers against unusually low raw sugar prices. Canada did not have any floor for raw sugar prices but did have duties for raw sugar at the most-favoured nation (MFN) and British preferential levels. The lack of a price-support policy in Canada reflected the fact that Canada had no sugar cane production and only minimal sugar beet production in Quebec, Manitoba, and Alberta.

History of Redpath

As Neil Shaw considered his options in July 1978 with respect to HFCS, his firm was celebrating its 125th birthday. The company had its start when John Redpath built a small sugar refinery in Montreal. The firm was called Canada Sugar. It eventually merged with Dominion Sugar of Wallaceburg, Ontario, in 1930. Due to the development of the St. Lawrence Seaway, a refinery was built in Toronto in 1958. As of 1978 this refinery was one of the world's most efficient.

Exhibit 4:   World Consumption of Sugar versus World Production of Sugar and Raw Sugar Price

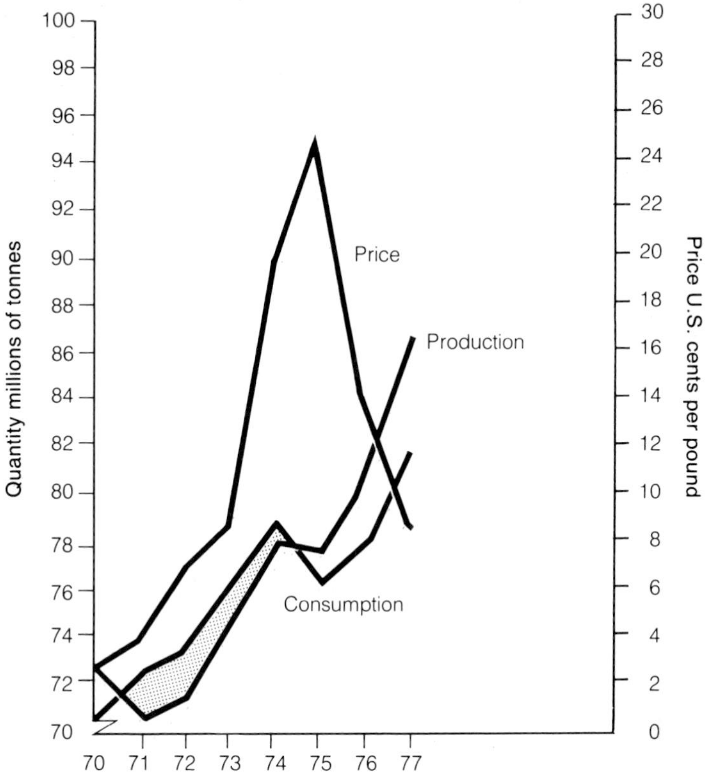

In the late 1960s a new reality hit home. There was a growing realization within the firm that the sugar market would soon be facing a no-growth situation and the Wallaceburg sugar beet processing plant had to be closed. In 1973 the name of the company was changed to Redpath Industries to reflect the beginning of a diversification program. Redpath had become involved in a diverse portfolio which included businesses in the agro-industrial industry, construction materials industry, packaging industry, and as of 1978 they were seeking active participation in the oil and gas industry. By 1978 Redpath Industries controlled 10 firms although sugar refining was Redpath's core business and vital to its profitability. In 1977, the agro-industrial division (representing sugar refining and a major engineering and construction contract to build a raw sugar facility for the government of the Ivory Coast) had 80 percent of the revenue and 85.5 percent of the net income, the construction materials division had 16.7 percent of the revenue and 11.6 percent of the net income, and the packaging division had 3.4 percent of the revenue and 2.9 percent of the net income. The controlling shareholder of Redpath Industries was Tate and Lyle, a major sugar refiner in

Figure 6: World Sugar Production

Continent and Country	1977 Production 1000 Metric Tons	Continent and Country	1977 Production 1000 Metric Tons	Continent and Country	1977 Production 1000 Metric Tons
North America (cane unless otherwise indicated):		Europe (beet unless otherwise indicated):		Mozambique	350
Barbados	102	Belgium and Luxembourg	755	Reunion	265
Belize	100	Denmark	516	South Rhodesia	230
Canada (beet)	118	France	3,913	South Africa	2,100
Costa Rica	213	Germany, West	2,740	Swaziland	210
Cuba	6,000	Ireland	195	Tanzania	120
Dominican Republic	1,400	Italy	1,190	Uganda	10
El Salvador	295	Netherlands	815	Zaire	60
Guadeloupe	95	United Kingdom	1,000	Other Africa	820
Guatemala	602	Total EC	11,124	Total Africa	6,457
Haiti	55	Austria	400	Asia (cane unless otherwise indicated):	
Honduras	150	Finland	90	Burma	135
Jamaica	350	Greece	350	China, People's Republic of (cane and beet)	2,750
Martinique	15	Portugal:		China, Republic of (Taiwan)	1,000
Mexico	2,880	Azores and Maderia	60	India	6,000
Nicaragua	250	Spain (cane and beet)	1,305	Indonesia	1,200
Panama	227	Sweden	340	Iran (cane and beet)	728
St. Kitts	36	Switzerland	87		
Trinidad and Tobago	200	Total W. Europe	13,756		

United States:	
Continental (beet)	3,000
Continental (cane)	1,400
Hawaii	1,000
Puerto Rico	225
Total North America	18,713
South America (cane unless otherwise indicated):	
Argentina	1,600
Bolivia	290
Brazil	8,600
Chile (beet)	230
Colombia	870
Ecuador	370
Guyana	335
Paraguay	95
Peru	960
Surinam	10
Uruguay (cane and beet)	123
Venezuela	500
Total South America	13,983
Albania	21
Bulgaria	290
Czechoslovakia	850
Germany, East	650
Hungary	450
Poland	2,200
Romania	725
Yugoslavia	717
Total E. Europe	5,903
Total Europe	19,659
USSR	9,300
Africa (cane):	
Angola	60
Egypt	665
Ethiopia	175
Kenya	197
Madagascar	110
Mauritius	715
Morocco	370
Japan (cane and beet)	574
Pakistan	745
Philippines	2,300
Thailand	1,800
Turkey (Europe and Asia) (beet)	1,200
Other Asia (cane and beet)	412
Total Asia	18,844
Oceania (cane):	
Australia	3,400
Fiji	300
Total Oceania	3,700
World total (cane)	54,778
World total (beet)	35,878
World total (cane and beet)	90,656

Source: U.S. Department of Agriculture, *Agricultural Statistics*, 1978.

Great Britain, which held a one-third interest in a European corn wet milling joint venture (including HFCS capability) in which Staley was also a partner.

One of Redpath's most important investments was Refined Syrups and Sugars Inc. This was Redpath's entry into the U.S. market in 1976. The U.S. plant was purchased for $6 million, and another $30 million was committed to it. This was considered a major investment on the part of Redpath.

The American refinery was to cause Redpath to experience a reduction in net income in 1978, although year-end figures were not yet available. The reduced income was due to lost sales while the plant was renovated and the product line changed from liquid sugar to granular sugar. The American refinery aside, income had been rising steadily since 1972. Figures 7, 8, and 9 show the financial picture of Redpath as of September 30, 1977.

Sugar refining is a relatively simple process of squeezing the sugar content out of sugar cane or beets and then drying the resultant mixture. Even though sugar refining was quite straightforward, there were differences in efficiency, and Redpath was more competitive in sugar refining than the rest of the Canadian industry. It had the most efficient manufacturing process and maintained sales volume in Eastern Canada in a declining market. Margins, however, had been reduced due to overcapacity in the refining industry. It was feared that in the long run this situation would inhibit the growth and profitability of Redpath's refining business as competitors cut prices to maintain production levels.

Events Leading to the Formation of the Joint Venture

In an effort to diversify its base and lessen its reliance on the sugar industry, Redpath was actively searching out other business opportunities. Redpath commissioned a study in 1976 to determine the viability of a HFCS-42 plant in Canada. Redpath noted that HFCS had characteristics similar to refined liquid sugar. As a result of this study Redpath decided to start importing HFCS into Canada but not to construct a plant. Redpath felt that its well-established sales force would be able to successfully market HFCS-42 to the Canadian market.

With respect to a HFCS plant in Canada, Redpath felt that the capital costs were too high, sugar prices were too low, the Canadian economy was too uncertain, Canadian market potential was undetermined, and the U.S. industry had excess capacity, making it possible to purchase HFCS at low prices in the United States. Nevertheless, the decision to import HFCS rather than produce it in Canada was not a final one. The company wished to gauge the success of their sales force with imported HFCS.

At the same time, John Labatt Limited was looking to continue its own program of diversification out of beer. Labatt had numerous holdings in various industries which were organized around three groups: Brewing, Consumer Products, and Agri Products. Figure 10 shows the performance of Labatt as a whole and its Agri Products Group in 1976 and 1977. The Agri Products Group,

Figure 7: Summary of Financial Performance of Redpath Industries Limited (dollars in thousands)

	1977	1976	1975	1974	1973	1972	1971	1970	1969	1968
Revenue (excluding equity in earnings of affiliate)	$271,319	$200,393	$270,934	$223,925	$128,217	$103,291	$85,135	$74,994	$64,578	$54,819
Income taxes	6,567	5,145	3,985	4,216	3,141	3,300	3,725	3,250	3,600	3,650
Net income (excluding extraordinary items)	8,571	7,531	7,343	5,712	5,244	4,300	4,392	3,836	4,243	5,380
Dividends	3,079	2,858	2,835	2,819	2,790	2,490	2,790	2,635	2,635	2,170
Working capital	43,963	29,067	13,106	10,132	10,879	10,944	12,574	13,669	15,356	16,273
Short-term investments	23,446	21,181	16,440	1,000	—	—	—	278	3,667	4,858
Short-term notes	20,358	20,558	32,019	12,117	16,035	10,211	3,830	2,474	910	743
Long-term debt	29,734	1,686	2,172	2,257	2,926	3,337	3,730	4,061	5,520	5,645
Shareholders' equity	70,170	64,625	59,916	55,014	52,121	49,276	47,766	46,113	44,586	42,978
Capital expenditures	9,180	5,555	3,623	5,230	4,634	4,927	2,020	1,803	1,926	617
Net income as percent of revenues	3.16%	3.76%	2.71%	2.55%	4.09%	4.16%	5.16%	5.12%	6.57%	9.81%
Net income as percent of shareholders' equity	12.21%	11.65%	12.25%	10.38%	10.06%	8.73%	9.19%	8.32%	9.52%	12.52%
Earnings per share	$2.69	$2.37	$2.33	$1.82	$1.69	$1.39	$1.41	$1.23	$1.37	$1.73
Number of employees	2,045	1,840	1,690	1,595	1,657	1,582	1,487	1,268	1,182	1,170
Number of shareholders	2,820	2,793	2,851	2,909	2,904	2,799	2,958	3,133	3,250	3,327

Source: Redpath Industries Annual Report, 1977.

REDPATH INDUSTRIES LIMITED
Balance Sheets
For the Years Ended September 30, 1976 and 1977
(in thousands of dollars)

	1977	1976
Assets		
Cash	$ 1,612	$ 2,004
Other current assets	102,905	75,962
Investments	13,788	6,110
Property, plant, and equipment	48,778	38,621
Other assets	2,677	548
Total assets	$169,760	$123,245
Liabilities		
Current liabilities	$ 60,554	$ 48,899
Long-term debt	29,734	1,686
Deferred income taxes	9,302	8,035
Shareholders' equity	70,170	64,625
Total liabilities and equity	$169,760	$123,245

Source: Redpath Industries Annual Report, 1977.

which would be responsible for HFCS, incuded a multiproduct milk manufacturer, a producer of pharmaceutical intermediates and other fine organic chemicals including nutritional additives for the agricultural and food industries, a large flour milling company, and one of the world's largest producers of gluten (used for baking, breakfast cereals, pet foods, and other foods) and wheat starch.

Labatt had budgeted $34 million for capital investments in 1978 alone and a total of $180 million over the next five years. Labatt was very much interested in expanding their Agri Products Group.

Negotiating the Terms of a Joint Venture

Neil Shaw, on behalf of Redpath, approached Labatt and proposed a joint venture which would initially investigate the feasibility of constructing a HFCS-42 refining plant. (The plant would be designed so that it could be upgraded to produce HFCS-55 as well as HFCS-42.) Redpath proposed an 80:20 ratio of ownership in the venture (80 percent for Redpath, 20 percent for Labatt). This proposal was made during the first quarter of 1977. However, as 1977 progressed, the probability of consummating a joint venture seemed to be decreasing. Labatt concluded it would prefer to go it alone, and Redpath seemed to be increasingly ambivalent about entering the corn wet milling business. In the fall of 1977 Labatt complained to Neil Shaw at Redpath about differing objectives, management approaches, and

Figure 9

REDPATH INDUSTRIES LIMITED AND ITS SUBSIDIARIES
Consolidated Statements of Income and Retained Earnings
For the Years Ended September 30, 1976 and 1977
(in thousand of dollars)

	1977	*1976*
Income		
Revenues	$271,319	$200,858
Expenses:		
Cost of sales and other operating costs	222,251	162,350
Selling, distribution, and administrative	25,766	19,829
Depreciation	4,357	3,644
Amortization	202	15
Interest—long-term debt	327	117
—other	3,278	2,227
Total expenses	256,181	188,182
Income before income taxes	15,138	12,676
Income taxes	6,567	5,145
Net income	$ 8,571	$ 7,531
Earnings per share	$2.69	$2.37
Retained earnings:		
Balance beginning of year	$ 41,772	$ 37,099
Net income	8,571	7,531
	50,343	44,630
Less: Dividends paid	3,079	2,858
Balance end of year	$ 47,264	$ 41,772

Source: Redpath Industries Annual Report, 1977.

Figure 10:   Summary of Financial Performance of John Labatt Limited and Agri Products Group (in thousands of dollars)

	1976	*1977*
Total business entity:		
Gross sales	$837,218	$922,194
Earnings	24,327	28,065
Cash income	45,639	50,860
Earnings per sales dollar (in cents)	2.91¢	3.04¢
ROA (after tax)	8.6%	9.4%
EPS	$1.89	$2.12
Agri Products:		
Gross sales	$196,629	$229,750
EBIT	7,675	11,019

Source: 1977 Annual Report.

commitments to a timetable for the venture. Labatt was perplexed at the stop-go-stop-go enthusiasm exhibited by Redpath. It seemed to Labatt that on one day Redpath would be resolved to enter the corn wet milling industry and then on another day would be against the idea. In Labatt's view, Redpath was unable to make up its mind on the matter and was stretching out the time frame for a decision considerably longer than Labatt felt was necessary. Shaw realized that Labatt was now seriously thinking of going ahead without Redpath, so efforts were stepped up to demonstrate Redpath's interest in the project.

Labatt wished to make the terms of a joint venture more favourable to itself and proposed that the ownership ratio should change to 50:50 from 80:20. Finally, the two firms publicly announced that on December 19, 1977, they reached agreement to enter into a joint venture on a 50:50 basis to study the feasibility of a corn wet milling plant in Canada. The two groups undertook to begin marketing and engineering studies so that the project's viability could be ascertained.

In terms of products and productive capacity, it was expected that the plant would be able to produce any combination of the three products—HFCS, starch, or glucose—to a total of 24,000 bushels per day of grind capacity with up to 17,000 bushels per day to HFCS. If desired, more than 50 percent of the output of the plant could be starch and glucose syrup. Beyond 30,000 bushels per day, the processing cost per unit flattened, although some U.S. plants had capacities of 300,000 bushels per day.

During the period of the feasibility study, the two firms each considered the following issues:

1. The Opportunity Presented by HFCS

HFCS was seen to have a raw material advantage over sugar. This was because corn, the primary input factor into HFCS, had reasonable price stability compared to raw sugar. Furthermore, Canada was seen as a growing market for HFCS because it was undersupplied since there were no Canadian producers. Nevertheless, it was generally conceded that Canada could support only one large-scale corn wet milling facility.

The American market for HFCS was a proven one, and success should be transferable to Canada. These items indicated an above-average return on investment.

2. Why a Joint Venture?

Redpath was seen as providing marketing expertise and a ready-made sales force since it was in the sugar refining business and had started to import HFCS. They would also bring their experience in blending facilities gained from the sugar refining process to this venture. Labatt would bring its extensive experience, including milling experience, from its Agri Products Group, and companies in

Labatt's Consumer Products Group could serve as a possible customer for the joint venture. In addition, Labatt's Brewing Group could be a customer if its breweries eventually made the switch from corn grits to high-maltose corn syrups. Generally, the Labatt group of companies represented significant market potential for glucose and HFCS products, although the Labatt business represented a minor portion of the proposed plant capacity and there were no commitments by Labatt to take any of the output from the joint venture. In any case, the Labatt participation might be necessary from Redpath's point of view to avoid FIRA since Redpath was British controlled and Labatt was Canadian owned.

Labatt was pleased that Redpath had the marketing and sales experience including knowledge of sugar users (for example, volumes, storage facilities) thereby minimizing the need to start up a marketing department. Both firms noted that this venture was a way to reduce capital commitment and risk, and it was apparent to Neil Shaw that Redpath would face Labatt as a competitor in this industry if they did not go in together.

3. Technical Considerations

A. E. Staley, one of the pioneers of this technology, was approached to provide process design, plant start-up, process control, access to R&D, and technical marketing support. It was concluded by both Redpath and Labatt that a Staley license would be too expensive and extremely restrictive. Staley had wanted a royalty of $1 million per year for a contract length of 15–20 years. Redpath and Labatt ultimately agreed that they were satisfied they could succeed in the business without purchasing the technology from an existing corn wet miller. The technology was considered to be well established.

Modern Process Design (MPD) of Dayton, Ohio, was contacted and was willing to act as an engineering consultant who would provide process engineering and operating know-how for a one-time fee of $500,000. They had designed one of Staley's plants. SNC, a large Canadian engineering consulting firm, would assume primary responsibility for project management and overall engineering. The MPD/SNC combination was expected to cost $500,000 more in engineering costs than the Staley proposal but would eliminate an ongoing annual royalty to Staley.

4. Sugar Prices

The variability of sugar prices and their impact on HFCS prices was the key to the profitability of the project. Refined sugar needed to be in the 15–20 cents price range before HFCS producers could make money and still offer the discount off sugar prices needed to encourage industrial consumers to switch to HFCS. The required price range for refined sugar was determined to be equivalent to a raw sugar price of 8–13 cents per pound. The price of raw sugar was 9 cents per pound in mid-1978. It was felt that due to depressed sugar prices, other world sugar producers would not be investing in this industry and thereby keep the sugar supply down. This would, in turn, force the price up. It was assumed that raw sugar would remain below 10 cents per pound until late 1978 at which time the price was expected to move to 10–15 cents by 1980.

During the period of the feasibility study (December 1977 to June 1978), world developments were quite favourable to a higher sugar price. A draft for an International Sugar Agreement with prices of 11 to 21 cents for raw sugar had been drawn up. This would have meant that Canadian refined sugar would be at least in the 18–28 cents per pound range. Redpath had estimated 17.5 cents per pound as the long-term minimum average price. In the United States the Carter administration went a step further than just import restrictions on raw sugar. They unveiled a plan to ensure that a refined sugar price of 19–20 cents per pound would prevail as of January 1, 1978. They, in effect, would legislate a minimum legal price for refined sugar in the United States.

5. Other Considerations

Labatt and Redpath agreed on the following conditions beyond the 50:50 partnership agreement: The venture, if it went ahead, was to be an entity on its own and free to sell HFCS to anyone; for tax reasons, the venture would be organized as a partnership; there would be a buyout agreement with a so-called shot-gun provision. Here partner A could offer to purchase partner B's interest, but then partner B could either refuse the offer and allow partner A to sell to a third party at that price, or accept it, or purchase partner A's interest at the same price offered by partner A. Redpath was able to get the Foreign Investment Review Agency (FIRA) to approve this shot-gun provision if Redpath was willing to acquire Labatt's share. Labatt intended to use nonrecourse financing so that the debt associated with the project would not appear on Labatt's balance sheet thus improving Labatt's financial leverage; nonrecourse financing also meant higher interest charges since there would be no recourse if the project went sour.

Feasibility Study Conclusions

The results of the feasibility study were made available in June 1978. Based on this study, which contained revisions to a study undertaken by Labatt prior to the joint venture feasibility study, the Labatt board of directors gave approval to the project on July 7, 1978.

The revised capital considerations and ROI are given in Figure 11. The $66.3 million investment was to be made over seven years with $64.4 million in the first three years. The ROI presented in the study was considered acceptable by Labatt even in light of the additional funding required to get the project on line. It was expected that the $59.7 million needed for fixed assets would be financed by debt at floating interest rates.

The study noted some inherent risks. It alerted the two parties to the fact that

Figure 11: HFCS-42 Viability

	Labatt Original Study	Joint Venture Study	Change
Capital ($ millions):			
Fixed	$51.4	$59.7	$8.3
Working Capital	5.0	6.6	1.6
Total	$56.4	$66.3	$9.9
Volume (thousand cwts— liquid basis)	2,360	2,700	340
By-product returns*	50%	55%	5%
DCF-ROI (before tax)	20.4%	18.5%	(1.9)%

* The percentage of the original cost of corn returned as by-products (e.g. corn gluten, corn gluten feed, germ).

they were making a major commitment to the agri-processing business. Earnings were likely to be cyclical, and there was some danger in tying together the two unrelated commodities of corn and sugar.

Seven leading experts in sugar were contacted during the study period. The consensus of this group was that the consumption of sugar would surpass production in 1980–81. In light of current depressed prices, sugar investment was down and thus production would fall. Current sugar prices were below production costs. The experts projected prices of raw sugar moving upward in 1979 and reaching a range of 10–13 cents by 1980–81 with a peak of 15–20 cents by 1983–85.

The group did caution that after the upward price trend, the cyclical nature of sugar would start on a downward trend. The price at the time of the study was 8.6 cents per pound, and this was the lowest price in 25 years. The group reasoned that since production costs were significantly higher in 1978 than in the 1950s or 1960s, a long-term floor would be established in the 12–16 cents range. Figure 12 demonstrates the sensitivity of profits to variation in sugar prices.

The study also reemphasized other issues that the two firms had already considered. Overall, Labatt was very optimistic about the success of the venture

Figure 12: Joint Venture's Sensitivity to Sugar Prices

	Prolonged Disaster	Conservative Estimation	Likely
Raw sugar (cents per pound)	10¢	13¢	14–15¢
Corn (dollars per bushel)	$3.00	$2.75	$2.50
By-product	50%	55%	60%
Capital	$70.3 million	$66.3 million	$64.3 million
Share of target market*	50%	60%	70%
DCF-ROI (before tax)	5.3%	18.5%	26.7%

* Sugar types distributed in liquid form.

Exhibit 5: Canada Starch News Bulletin

Montreal, January 4, 1978

The following announcement of our entry into the High Fructose Syrup market was released to the press today:

The Canada Starch Company Limited, Montreal,[1] has announced that it will be entering the High Fructose Corn Syrup market through a $12 million addition to its Cardinal, Ontario, plant. The new readily expandable facility embodying the latest in cost-efficient technology will have the capacity to produce in excess of 130 million pounds[2] of high fructose corn syrup per year. Construction will begin immediately with production scheduled in March 1979.

Canada Starch Company has been the major producer of products derived from corn since its establishment in 1858. This new expansion, with its accompanying basic grind increase, will maintain the Company's position as the largest wet miller of corn in Canada. Grind capacity has expanded steadily during the Company's history to meet an increasing demand through wider use of corn-derived products in both the food and nonfood manufacturing industries.

"High Fructose Syrup, though widely used in the United States, has thus far not been manufactured in Canada. Canada Starch will be the first domestic producer. The product, which utilizes a domestically grown raw material, provides its users a distinct cost advantage over sugar," a spokesman said.

The much publicized High Fructose Corn Syrup is a liquid sweetener, manufactured by the conversion of corn starch, and contains dextrose and fructose, both of which exist as natural sweeteners in many foods. It has the ability to replace sugar in the beverage, baking, and other food industries.

Corn, the raw material from which the syrup is made, has a history of price stability compared to sugar and is an important Canadian agricultural product.

Notes (not included in news bulletin):

[1] Canada Starch was owned by CPC International (formerly Corn Products Company) in the United States. CPC was the world's largest corn wet miller, and although it had historically dominated the U.S. corn wet milling industry, it was a minor participant in HFCS production in the United States.

[2] The bulletin did not reveal whether the 130 million pounds was on a commercial liquid basis or dry solids basis. If it was on a commercial liquid basis, it would be supplied by 8,000 bushels/day, and if it was on a dry solids basis, it would require 11,500 bushels/day.

---

even though a competitor (Canada Starch Company) had recently announced its intentions to build a similar facility in Canada (see Exhibit 5).

Despite Labatt's enthusiasm, Neil Shaw wondered about his ability to get his board's approval to go ahead with a full commitment to the new plant so quickly. The estimated returns of the project were less than Redpath expected, and the capital cost seemed to be much too high. Because Canada Starch would be expanding, it would be more difficult to gain a large market share. Finances would be difficult to get since the British parent of Redpath, Tate and Lyle, was very hesitant about committing large sums of money to investments in Canada. This was because Tate and Lyle had been experiencing problems with capacity rationalization in British sugar refining. As well, the Refined Syrups and Sugars venture into the United States, and its loss of money in 1977, had made Tate and Lyle somewhat gun-shy. Nevertheless, Shaw did not want to be left behind when faced with a competitive threat to Redpath's primary business.

Shaw felt he could possibly stall the issue for six to nine months, but he knew that was risky as Labatt really wanted to get going on the project. In fact, Labatt was quite clear: They wanted to hear about Redpath's intentions by the end of July.

Appendix: Sweeteners

Sucrose. Common table sugar, derived commercially from cane and beets. Composed of dextrose and fructose. It should be noted that in certain product applications, sucrose contributes functional benefits (for example, as a preservative) as well as serving as a sweetener.

Raw sugar. An extract from sugar cane composed primarily of sucrose. Traded as a commodity and refined to pure sucrose by a crystallization procedure.

Liquid sugar. A water solution of crystalline sucrose. Generally sold by railcar and tankcar at about 65 percent dry solids.

Liquid invert sugar. A water solution of dextrose and fructose derived from the hydrolysis of sucrose. Medium invert is from a partial hydrolysis, while total invert would be approximately 49 percent fructose, 49 percent dextrose, and 1 percent sucrose. There is a dry solids weight gain of 5 percent when sucrose is totally hydrolyzed (inverted). Liquid invert is sold in railcars and tankcars at a minimum of 65 percent dry solids.

$$\text{Sucrose} \ + \ \text{Water} \ = \ \text{Fructose} \ + \ \text{Dextrose}$$
$$\text{(342 tonnes) (18 tonnes) (180 tonnes) (180 tonnes)}$$

Glucose (commercial). Commercial glucose is corn syrup. Many varieties (compositions) are manufactured, and all are sold by railcar and tankcar lots. All products are prepared by acid and/or enzyme hydrolysis of starch. These products are sold at 80 percent solids. The products are extremely viscous. Sweetness varies considerably by product and is a secondary property. It should be noted that many corn syrup products are sold for their functional as opposed to sweetener properties.

Fructose. Commonly called fruit sugar. Fructose makes up one half of the sucrose (table sugar) molecule. On an equal weight basis, fructose is 75 percent sweeter than sucrose.

Dextrose. Known by the chemical name "glucose." Dextrose makes up one half of the sucrose (table sugar) molecule. On an equal weight basis, dextrose has 70 percent of the sweetness of sugar. Dextrose, prepared from an enzymatic hydrolysis of starch, is sold as crystalline or dry powder product.

HFCS-42. High fructose corn syrup (HFCS) containing 42 percent fructose. This product is sold in railcar and tankcar quantities at 71 percent dry solids. This product on a dry solids basis has the sweetness of liquid sugar. It is derived from enzymatic hydrolysis of corn starch to dextrose and conversion of part of the dextrose by enzymic means to fructose. HFCS-42 must be stored and distributed warm (including within the purchaser's plant) to avoid dextrose crystallization. Many recognize the process to produce HFCS as the most technically sophisticated food process. Its most important uses are in chewing gum and confections.

HFCS-55.   High fructose corn syrup containing 55 percent fructose. This product which has the sweetness of invert sugar on a dry solids basis is sold in railcar and tankcar lots at 76 percent solids. It is manufactured from HFCS-42 by a process which extracts the fructose and recycles the dextrose for further conversion to fructose. This isolated fructose is blended with HFCS-42 to raise the fructose concentration to 55 percent. (Higher fructose concentrations are possible.) HFCS-55 has the sweetness of invert sugar in all potential applications. The major use is as a sweetener for soft drinks, preserving, baking, brewing, canning, and fruit drinks.

Case 36

RM Industries Limited

On January 8, 1981, Lionel Rumm, president of a Canadian manufacturer of automobile flashers, wipers, and hose clamps, received a teletype that caused him a fair amount of concern. It was from the company's sales agent in Mexico City, L. Villanueva. The telex read:

> Rumour—highly dependable source—major U.S. competitor shortly to establish flasher and wiper manufacturing facilities here—will probably close Mexican market to RM—will update when info available.
>
> L. Villanueva

Rumm was disturbed by this report, since he had confidence in his agent's judgement. Villanueva was highly respected in the circles he frequented in Mexico and had personally been responsible for the success RM had experienced in the Mexican market. Villanueva presided over a staff of four people and in 1980 had an annual sales volume of approximately $15 million. He also acted as an agent for a number of U.S. automotive parts manufacturers. To initiate action, Rumm scheduled a meeting in four days' time, involving four key executives.

Agenda Mexico

On January 12, 1981, the meeting convened with Vice President Finance, C. Nash; Vice President Manufacturing, Z. Brixton; Vice President Sales (North America), S. Sellers; and President J. G. Castelli of RM International present. Rumm, as chairman of the meeting, read aloud the message he had received from Villanueva. He went on to say:

> It is safe to assume that within the year one of our major competitors intends to be manufacturing high-quality flashers and wipers in Mexico. It is my understanding that the Mexican government raises tariff barriers to imports of a product as soon as domestic production is sufficient to meet domestic demand. The net effect is that the borders are virtually closed to imports. This certainly appears to have been the case with clamps which we no longer export to Mexico. We currently sell close to $1.2 million worth of flashers and wipers to Mexican motor vehicle manufacturers (see Table 1). We are in danger, it appears, of losing this amount of future sales plus any potential sales expansion in the market. The way I see it, we have four options. We

This case was prepared by I. A. Litvak, York University. Copyright © 1984 by I. A. Litvak.

Table 1: RM Sales to Mexico

Total sales volume (1980)		$1.2 million
Sales composition:		
Flashers	80%	
Wipers	20	(Currently testing the Mexican market)
Clamps	0	(Exports ceased, since now produced in Mexico)
Total	100%	

can (1) continue exporting to our Mexican customers and eventually, in the near future, lose their business; (2) establish a manufacturing facility in Mexico ourselves; (3) work out a licensing arrangement with a Mexican firm to produce our products for us in Mexico; (4) establish a joint venture with a compatible Mexican firm.

As the senior executives in this firm who would be most affected by any of these options, I would like your opinions on the probable future significance of the Mexican market to our company and on what steps, if any, we should take to protect our best interests.

Castelli, president of RM International, was the first to speak up. He explained that on the basis of market surveys carried out on the Mexican auto-parts market and on conversations he had had with Villanueva, exports to Mexico by RM could be projected to reach easily over $4 million in less than 18 months if the company was willing to push aggressively into the market and to establish a warehouse in the Mexico City area. Castelli argued:

A rapidly growing auto-parts market exists which RM is in a position to tap. However, Mr. Villanueva's information seems to indicate that direct exports alone will not be enough to maintain any significant market share in Mexico. I would contend that it is best for RM to be first to establish itself in the Mexican market. If we are first into Mexico with our products, the border will be closed immediately to imports of similar items from other industrial firms, and Mexican car builders will be forced to use our products in the manufacture of their automobiles. This is how the law stands. If a product is made in Mexico they have no choice but to install that product in their car. So if RM were to manufacture in Mexico, it would automatically have a jump on the market.

Nash countered by arguing:

The immediate profit potential, based on my knowledge of the growth of the Mexican auto-parts market, is not large enough to justify us establishing a manufacturing plant in Mexico. Furthermore, I have heard that ownership restrictions are imposed in Mexico and that we would not be able to retain a 50 percent or even controlling interest in any manufacturing operation we might establish there. We probably would be restricted to a maximum 49 percent interest in a joint venture arrangement with subsequent loss of control, shared profits, and what appears to me to be a rather limited return on investment. As for a licensing arrangement, I am concerned about the protection of our technological know-how. We don't want our licensee in Mexico becoming our alter ego, in competition with us in other markets. Moreover, a licensing arrangement will garner us only 10 percent of gross sales, and as with a joint venture, I would not think that such a limited return would justify entry into what I have heard is a quite unstable market both economically and politically. Who knows, restrictions on capital leaving the country may be imposed by the government limiting even further our return from either a joint venture or a licensing arrangement.

Brixton tended to agree with much of what Nash had said and went on to say:

Even if the value of establishing a Mexican manufacturing facility could be proven to outweigh all other alternatives, I would be hard-pressed to find the time to involve myself in the setting up of a manufacturing facility in Mexico, whether wholly or partly owned. I would not want to leave the organization of the factory to a Mexican partner firm, as managerial talent down there is scarce and our production processes are rather specialized. On top of that, we are experiencing some excess capacity in our three plants here as it is. Loss of $1.2 million worth of sales to a new Mexican plant could have a very serious impact on the profitability of our Canadian operations. Perhaps we should look into increasing our exports to more easily accessible markets, such as Europe or the United States, before embarking on such a speculative venture.

As for licensing, I went to a few plants while I was down in Mexico on vacation last summer, and it was like going back 30 years in Canada. In many of the places I visited they had very antiquated methods. On the other hand, I must confess I did see a few specialized factories which were up to date. The question is, what kind of firms are really available? And if they are available, are they interested in a licensing agreement?

Sellers, in contrast to Nash and Brixton, was quite enthusiastic about moving right into the Mexican market:

I've seen the market surveys Mr. Castelli brought up a few minutes ago, and my understanding of them indicates to me that the Mexican market for auto parts is really ballooning. If we were to establish a manufacturing facility there, not only could we capture a large part of this rapidly expanding market but we would also put ourselves in a strong position to move into the rest of the Latin American Free Trade Association (LAFTA) market. Mexico, as you know, is a leading member of LAFTA, and establishing a facility there could open the door for us to the whole of South America. As far as I am concerned, setting up our own manufacturing plant is the way to go. I once worked for a firm that went the licensing route. We set up an existing similar product manufacturer to handle our product line. It seemed like a good idea at first since it had the appropriate production facilities, established distribution system, and market knowledge. But we soon found that there was a conflict of interest, that is, the foreign manufacturer would sell our product only when it could not sell its own.

Rumm then remarked:

It's clear that we don't have any consensus here on what our course of action should be. However, a tentative decision has to be arrived at, I think, without delay. Mr. Castelli, as you are and will be responsible for any Mexican operation our company carries on, I would like you to prepare for me a written presentation outlining the current commercial environment in Mexico. Keep in mind that moving into Mexico will likely have an impact on our company's involvement in other markets. I would like to have that report on my desk in three weeks.

Twenty-one days later, Castelli had his report on Rumm's desk (see Appendix 1). Upon reading the Castelli report, the president had copies of the report sent to Nash, Brixton, and Sellers. Attached to the report was the following memo:

To: Messrs. Brixton, Castelli, Nash, and Sellers

From: C. Rumm

Subject: Mexico

Scheduled all-day meeting for February 6, commencing at 8:00 A.M., to discuss the Mexican situation. Detailed letter from Villanueva indicates high likelihood that our major U.S. competitor will establish an affiliate operation in Mexico. What strategy should RM pursue? Have your written recommendations on my desk by 8:00 A.M. February 4.

The Company

Privately held RM Industries Limited was a 100 percent Canadian-owned company with its head office in Oshawa, Ontario. The company was founded in Toronto in 1930 by the grandfather of the current owner and president, Lionel Rumm. Its only product was stainless steel hose clamps, developed by the founder, manufactured at the RM plant in Toronto, and supplied to the Canadian motor vehicle industry. The company experienced modest growth until 1939 when it introduced the adjustable worm-drive gear clamp, and the demand for this product grew rapidly as a result of World War II. Growth continued modestly through the balance of the 1940s and 1950s for this one-product company.

By 1965 it became necessary to expand the manufacturing facilities, so a new plant was built on 30 acres of land in Oshawa and the Toronto plant was sold to a steel service centre. It was at this time that RM introduced the world's first electronic signal flasher. This product innovation offered a variable load flasher for the turn signals and hazard warning lights. It was ideal for cars pulling trailers and for most commercial vehicles. Two models covered 90 percent of the applications required. It then became apparent that the domestic market alone could not support RM's growth plans on such a small product base. RM spent the next four years trying to crack the export market by participating in government-sponsored trade missions.

While the export market was being nurtured and developed by RM's sales and marketing team, the engineering group was hard at work on the next new product. Having identified windshield-wiper blades as a desirable product area and having been thwarted by patents on metal wiper blades, RM originated, designed, and developed the world's first nonmetallic wiper blade and introduced it into the Canadian automotive aftermarket in 1970.

RM had three plants. Two were located in Oshawa—one manufactured clamps; the other, signal-light flashers. The third plant, in Whitby, manufactured the nonmetallic windshield-wiper blades and refills. RM was headquartered at the original Oshawa plant.

In recognition of the growing requirements for research and development, RM established a separate research and development facility at its first Oshawa plant. The engineering department grew from 5 persons in 1973 to over 30 by 1981. The Government of Canada was highly supportive of the company's research and development efforts.

Patents on the clamps, flashers, and wipers were held by RM. All three company products were high-cost, high-quality products that sold on the basis of quality and service against competitive products, which could be purchased at up to 55 percent lower cost from other producers. All three products were designed by RM to be compatible with motor vehicles manufactured by all the major original equipment manufacturers (see Appendix 2). The vast majority of sales were made to original equipment manufacturers.

Total sales in 1980 amounted to slightly more than $60 million, 60 percent of sales being clamps; 15 percent, flashers; and 25 percent, wipers, all of which were manufactured by the company's three plants. Approximately 70 percent of the total sales were realized in export markets (see Table 2). When RM first began to export in 1965, hose clamps were sold to American automakers under the Canada-United States Auto Pact, which allowed free trade in automobiles and parts. During 1981 RM expected to become the world's number one supplier of worm-drive gear clamps.

In 1977 the two-year supplier research program with Ford resulted in the acceptance of RM wiper blades on four of their 1978 model cars, representing 22 percent of RM's North American production. Ford expanded its use of RM wiper blades to include 11 of its 1979 models, representing over 50 percent of RM's North American production. Recently, Volkswagen (North America) and Nissan

Table 2:   RM Sales Composition

	Percentage of Total Canadian Dollar Value			
	Wipers	*Flashers*	*Clamps*	*Total*
Total sales by product	25%	15%	60%	100%
Domestic sales as percentage of total sales	5	10	15	30
Export sales as percentage of total sales	20	5	45	70
Export sales as percentage of sales of each product	80	33⅓	75	

(Datsun in Japan) had also accepted the blade. Chrysler, Honda, and Opel were testing it, and British Leyland was actively considering it for their aftermarket program. RM appeared to be on the verge of becoming a major world marketer of this product.

The signal-flasher product line, while it had been considered a stable product in recent years, was about to emerge as a significant growth product. Extension of its life cycle was made possible through identification of certain target "niche" markets.

Since 1965 two thirds of the company's exports were to the United States, the other one third going mainly to Europe, Japan, Australia, and Mexico. Mexican sales, consisting of flashers and wipers, totalled approximately $1.2 million in 1980. Clamps were no longer exported to Mexico because they were manufactured there by other firms.

RM Industries International Ltd.

In 1977 the company established RM Industries International Ltd. to act as the global marketing arm of the company. This subsidiary handled the marketing of the company's products in all markets except the North American market. It operated sales offices and warehouses in continental Euope, the United Kingdom, Asia, and Australia. There were also many warehouses in various locations in the United States, operated through the company's head office in Oshawa. RM International established RM (France) to serve continental Europe, RM (U.K.), RM (Asia) in Hong Kong to serve the Asian automotive market, and RM (Oceania) in Sydney, Australia. The rest of the world, except for North America, was served by RM International through the use of sales agents, as was the case in Mexico.

The company's outstanding export performance was based on the proficiency of its sales representatives and its network of warehouses, which were located in most of its major markets. The company had never felt compelled to establish manufacturing facilities outside of Canada because its products were small and light and so could be shipped at low freight rates all over the world. As a result shipping did not constitute a major export expense. Moreover, RM continued to receive assistance from the Export Development Corporation to finance its export shipments.

Appendix 1:   The Castelli Report on the Mexican Market

Background

The role of the government in the country's economic expansion is a dominating one. It identifies the growth sectors of the economy and then plans their development. Special treatment has been accorded to heavy industry, which the Mexican government considers essential for national development.

Trade and Investment Policies

The overall economic objective since 1940 can be described as the promotion of economic growth with a view to (1) improving the education, health, and welfare of Mexicans; (2) providing a basic industrial infrastructure for the economy (for example, transportation, communication, power, and water); and (3) replacing imports. Both objectives (2) and (3) impinge on the Mexican policy toward foreign investment. Certain industries are viewed as "basic" and are reserved either to government ownership or to majority Mexican ownership. Further, the extent of a foreign investor's reliance on imports will be a major determinant of the attitude of the Mexican government toward the investor. Associated with these three major objectives of economic growth, the movement toward independence from foreign investment has been a priority objective of all Mexican presidents.

Within this set of economic objectives, Mexican industrialization policy has centred on the concept of import substitution, linked to a high degree of protectionism, with very little concern for such other objectives as the efficiency of industries.

In general, Mexico pursues a unilateral approach to policies of protectionism and employs such instruments as the imposition of tariffs, the issuing of import licenses, the granting of subsidies, and the establishment of "official prices" for dutiable items. In 1947 tariffs were altered from a specific to an ad valorem basis with the government setting "official prices" for items on which the duty was levied, thus providing the government with greater administrative discretion in implementing its protectionist policies. Import licenses have been in use since 1947 and are now the main instrument of protection, although recently a policy of liberating items from the requirement of obtaining a prior import license has been followed. About 30,000 applications for licenses are received each month, of which about one third are approved. Each application has to be assessed against 37 criteria so that there are wide opportunities for arbitrary action and administrative discretion.

The level of tariffs set varies with the type of goods involved. For goods produced in Mexico, the tariffs are set after negotiation and agreement between the domestic manufacturers and the Ministry of Finance; for goods not produced in Mexico, tariffs are set high for luxuries and low for raw materials, machinery, equipment, and some essential consumer goods. Thus, the tariff policy is consistent with what are considered to be basic and necessary industries.

Two government departments are largely responsible for administering the protectionist policies: the Ministry of Finance for tariffs and the Ministry of Industry and Commerce for import licenses. Lack of coordination between these two departments and the wide range of discretion associated with both the setting of "official prices" and the issuing of import licenses have resulted in the high level of protectionism being administered in a very unwieldy manner.

Mexicanization and the Automotive Industry

Many companies have been taking advantage of the opportunities existing in Mexico, fully aware of the central concept of Mexico's development policy—"Mexicanization" (the aim of which is to make Mexican industry as self-governing and self-sufficient as possible). The policy of excluding foreign investment in one sector at a time has been supported by increasing the restrictions on foreign business. This has resulted in many investors accepting "Mexicanization" as a fact of life.

The case of the automobile industry is instructive. Since the early 1930s the automotive industry in Mexico has been burdened by government regulations. Foreign cars had been assembled in Mexico for several years when, in 1962, the authorities announced that in future, 60 percent of the value of their construction must come from local sources.

The objective of the 1962 decree was to bring about the conditions necessary for the manufacture of automotive vehicles in Mexico rather than merely for their assembly, as heretofore had occurred. The idea was to reduce imports and, consequently, the drain on dollar reserves. American, French, German, and Japanese companies willing to collaborate on these terms joined with Mexican groups in some nine companies. For those companies not in compliance with the 1962 law, assembly quotas were reduced and import of parts prohibited. There are currently eight companies manufacturing cars and/or trucks in Mexico, with Volkswagen being the sales leader. It was reported by the Mexican Automotive Industry Association (AMIA) that the automotive industry in Mexico in 1980 is expected to produce 550,300 cars and trucks, as compared with 368,700 in 1979 and 365,000 in 1978. The industry is expected to grow at a rate of 13 to 15 percent over the next three years.

AMIA reports that over the next three years Mexican public and private enterprise will invest over $1 billion (U.S.) each in the auto industry in an effort to raise vehicle exports from slightly under $900 million currently, up from $352 million in 1976, to over $3.35 billion and to create 52,000 new jobs.

In 1972 the Mexican government legislated the Auto Decree, which stated that all new auto-parts ventures must be 60 percent Mexican owned. The policy of the Mexican government is to allow imports of auto parts as long as there is no company producing the part in Mexico but to close the border to imports as soon as any firm begins to manufacture a sufficient output of the product to meet domestic demand. All Mexican automakers are then forced to purchase from the firm producing the part in Mexico.

In recent years the growth of Mexico's auxiliary or supplier automotive industry has put it close to the top of Mexico's manufacturing sector in terms of production volume, number of employees, and so forth. It was estimated in 1977, which is the latest year for which figures could be found, that the sector has an annual production value of P.15.5 billion, sold about P.21 billion in 1977, and employed some 73,000 people. The sector, which now consists of around 500 plants, up from 450 in 1977, has registered an annual growth of about 20 to 24 percent a year since the automotive integration decree of 1962, which assured domestic auto-part manufacturers of a captive and growing market.

The trend in the Mexican auto-parts industry has been toward a decrease in imports and an increase in exports of auto parts, engines, and accessories even though in the last 18 months a policy of liberating items from the requirement of obtaining a prior import license has been followed. The trend is reflected in Canada-Mexico trade figures in auto parts, which show that from 1975 to 1979 exports by Canada to Mexico of auto parts have decreased from $28.7 million (Cdn.) in 1975 to $9.3 million in 1979. Exports by Mexico to Canada have increased during the same period from $4.3 million in 1975 to $15.9 million in 1979.

Several other laws, passed within the last 10 years and which should also be of interest to the company, are discussed below.

Foreign Investment Law

Passed in 1973, this is intended to promote Mexican investment in the domestic market and to regulate foreign investment. Its main points are: (1) future foreign investment in any venture involved in the manufacture of auto parts is limited to a maximum of 40 percent participation; (2) the newly appointed National Commission on Foreign Investments, which consists of the ministers of the Interior, Foreign Affairs, the Treasury, National Patrimony, Industry and Commerce, Labour and Social Welfare, and of the Presidency, must authorize future foreign investments greater than 25 percent of a local company's capital or 49 percent of its fixed assets (the commission may veto any proposed foreign participation); (3) all foreign companies must register with the new National Registry of Foreign Investors and all foreign shares are to be nominative from now on; and (4) foreign administrative positions in Mexican companies must be in direct proportion to foreign equity holdings.

Specific factors or characteristics of foreign investment that are considered by the commission in its determination of whether an investment should be authorized are outlined in Exhibit 1.

Technology Transfer Bill

There are four main points to this bill, which came into effect in December 1972: (1) it calls for much greater coordination and regulation of foreign technology contracts; (2) it prohibits technology agreements that limit prices, local export possibilities, or local development of complementary technology; (3) it provides for a National Technology Registry to be run by the Ministry of Industry and Commerce—the registry must receive within 60 days of the signing of the contract complete technical details and contracts from all companies using or acquiring new technology; then it decides whether the given technology should be permitted and whether a fair price is being charged; and (4) under normal conditions it limits payments for technology to 3 percent of gross sales. The nature of the technology

---

Exhibit 1:   Factors Determining Foreign Participation

The following characteristics are considered by the National Commission on Foreign Investments in determining whether a foreign investment should be authorized:

1. The degree to which it supplements national investment.
2. The degree of displacement of national enterprises that are operating satisfactorily.
3. The beneficial effects the investments might have on the balance of payments and in increasing exports.
4. The effects it may have on employment, both as to the level of employment that will be generated and the remuneration that will be paid.
5. The use and training of Mexican technicians and administrative personnel.
6. The use of national raw materials and components.
7. The degree to which operations are financed from foreign sources.
8. The diversification of sources of investment and the need to promote regional and subregional integration in Latin America.
9. The contribution to the development of undeveloped zones and regions.
10. The occupation of a monopolistic position in the national market.
11. The capital structure of the existing area of economic activity involved.
12. The contribution of technology and to research and development of technology in the country.
13. The effect on the price level and quality of the products.
14. The preservation of cultural and social values of the country.
15. The relative importance of the activity in the national economy.
16. The identification of the foreign investor with the interests of the country and his relation to foreign economic decision-making entities.
17. In general, the degree to which the investment contributes to attaining the objectives and complies with the policies of national development.

---

is of significance in the evaluation of fees and royalties. The nature of the technology is determined by: its age (older technology may not be of significant benefit); its life expectancy (a higher royalty may be permitted for a short expectancy); and its contribution to developmental, balance-of-payments, and indigenous R&D goals.

A contract may be restricted further from a maximum time span of 10 years if the contract terms are deemed to be ''unreasonable.'' The reasonableness of the contract depends on the age and life of the technology and whether continuous improvements and innovation can be anticipated.

1977, 1978, 1979 Auto Decrees

These decrees generally reflect the objectives of the earlier decrees of 1962 and 1972 but strengthen the demands in the areas of foreign exchange generation and local parts integration in order to transform the auto industry into a net generator of foreign currency earnings and a contributor to equilibrium in the balance of payments. With respect to the terminal sector, the decrees set up an annual foreign currency budget for each company based on an initial authorized quota and on each firm's net exports. Timetables are to be set whereby companies will compensate for all their exchange requirements (imports, interest, royalties, and so forth) by export earnings. Local content by 1981 is to reach 75 percent for automobiles; 85 percent for trucks; 90 percent for tractor trucks and buses. At least 59 percent of a terminal producer's total exports must be made up of domestically manufactured parts and components. Terminal producers may use imported components instead of nationally produced ones if they can prove that parts manufacturers are unable to fulfil their needs without this affecting their degree of integration or having to compensate via exports. If local content levels are not met, production parts imports must be compensated for by exports on more than a dollar-for-dollar basis.

Auto-parts manufacturers continue to require at least 60 percent Mexican participation, and local content plus exports must be at least 80 percent by 1980. The Patrimony Secretariat has established lists of auto parts of domestic manufacture, which are required to be included by vehicle producers in vehicles manufactured for the domestic market. However, only components with at least 80 percent local content are included in the mandatory integration lists put out by Patrimony.

Tax incentives aimed at spurring the growth of the local auto-parts industry have also been established. They include up to 20 percent grants for investments in plants that make auto parts. To qualify for the incentives, companies must maintain an import-export balance in their foreign currency budgets to satisfy integration requirements. The Treasury Secretariat can then also grant a reduction of up to 100 percent of the import duty on machinery and equipment not produced in Mexico destined for the manufacture of vehicles or components. Although available to all such manufacturers, this incentive is normally extended only to auto-parts producers in certain geographical zones designated as eligible for incentives. With special approval, a 75 percent reduction can also be granted in non-eligible zones. Furthermore, the Commerce Secretariat can grant to component and terminal producers a refund of up to 100 percent of the indirect taxes on exported components and vehicles.

These tax incentives are part of a new national industrial development plan which was introduced by Mexico's Secretary of National Properties and Industrial Growth. One of the plan's chief aims is to give a rapid boost to Mexico's surging auto industry. The plan calls for maintaining at least an 11 percent annual growth rate in domestic car and truck sales while expanding exports by 25 percent a year through 1982. The government is hoping thereby to cut the country's $250 million deficit on auto trade to zero. To accomplish this, the government aims to spur the growth of the local steel and auto-parts industries through various fiscal incentives and grants and to attract further investment on the basis of the country's swelling domestic market, its export potential, and its cheap and abundant labour supply. When the plan was unveiled, policy statements by government officials asserted that, with the help of Mexico's new-found oil wealth, the strategy of import substitution was to be replaced by one of making production more efficient through the use of cheap energy and through broadening both internal and external markets. Priorities of the new industrial plan are said to be: production of basic consumer goods, seen as the real support for adequate compensation of labour; highly productive industries capable of competing in world markets; full use of Mexico's natural resources; and development of capital goods production. Although the immediate effects of this plan have yet to materialize beyond the lifting of many of the import license requirements, the long-run implications of such a policy shift may have interesting consequences on foreign investment in Mexico in coming years.

In summary, much of the above legislation reflects a nationalistic orientation, which might give rise to some concern. But it should be reiterated that the Mexican authorities are pragmatic—they are quite prepared to accommodate foreign interests when bending the rules can serve a useful purpose. Consider the following comments by the Mexican Minister of Industry and Commerce:

> Foreign investment will be welcomed insofar as it contributes to the improvement of our technology, promotes the development of new, dynamic industries, produces goods for export to the entire world, and contributes to the achievement of our national goals.
>
> Mexico is not interested in having foreign investors purchase already-established companies as this does not usually mean any net capital gain, nor does it lead to the transfer of technology, import substitution, or the creation of new sources of employment . . . foreign investment should not displace Mexican capital but complement it through association when this is considered useful.

Appendix 2: Product Lines

Hose Clamps

RM clamps come in seven series, each having its own special features such as size of band width and type of housing and screw. Each of five of the series is available in 27 diameter ranges, from ⁹⁄₁₆–1 up to 10⅛–11¹⁵⁄₁₆. The remaining two series are "micro gears" available in ⁷⁄₃₂–⅝ and ⅜–⅞ clamp diameters. All series and sizes are packaged in lots of 10 per box. Applications for these clamps include fuel lines, welding lines, and fluid and gas lines in industries such as automotive, marine, chemical, food processing, electrical, and plumbing.

Electronic Signal Flashers

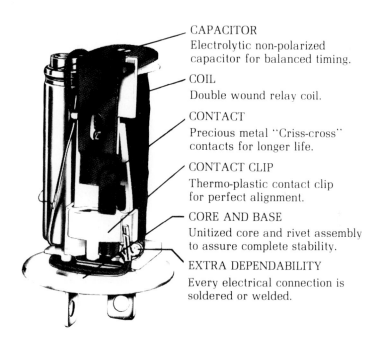

CAPACITOR
Electrolytic non-polarized capacitor for balanced timing.

COIL
Double wound relay coil.

CONTACT
Precious metal "Criss-cross" contacts for longer life.

CONTACT CLIP
Thermo-plastic contact clip for perfect alignment.

CORE AND BASE
Unitized core and rivet assembly to assure complete stability.

EXTRA DEPENDABILITY
Every electrical connection is soldered or welded.

The flashers are used for turn or hazard warning signals. Of the 10 models produced, three—HD12, HD13, and HD63—can service 90 percent of all vehicles. The HD12 replaces all 12 volt, 2 terminal flashers in North American cars; HD13 is used for 12 volt, 3 terminal flashers in North American commercial vehicles and European cars; and HD63 services 6 volt, 3 terminal flashers in North American and European vehicles. The other electronic flashers service 24 volt systems with 2 pin receptacles, 24 volt with 3 pin, and 36 volt systems with 2 pin receptacles. Alternating systems flashers are produced for 6 volts–3 pins, 12 volts–3 pins, and 24 volts–3 pins. RM's flashers have the fastest starting time for the first flash and use only one hundredth of the power required by other flashers. They also produce a clear sound signal and are dependable.

Wiper Blades

RM's line of wiper blades covers 99 percent of the market. The blades are packaged according to blade length. Each box contains the clip or clips needed to adapt the blade to most arm configurations. Blade features include easy installation, superstructures made of break-resistant polymer, specially-coated rubber squeegees to minimize friction, and construction that meets all federal and SAE standards. As well, RM offers a full line of wiper arms for all vehicles and special wiper blades and refills for trucks and buses.

The Buckeye Steel Waste Treatment Plant

In early March 1985, Art Miller, an independent consulting mechanical engineer based in Toronto, was considering whether he should become involved in a project to build a waste treatment project for Buckeye Steel Inc. of Ohio. The proposed project would require expertise from Grid Engineering Inc. which had sole rights to the technology. Grid had brought the project to Art because of his extensive experience and competence in engineering project management including industrial experience in fluid handling and general business skills. Art had also worked with Grid people on several smaller projects over the past few years and related well to them. Art and the principals of Grid would form a joint company to build the waste treatment plant on land that Buckeye would provide at no cost.

Buckeye Steel, located in the small community of Mansfield, near Columbus, Ohio, was small for a firm producing steel plate (sales of less than $50 million a year). Since the early 1980s it and hundreds of similar independent firms in the United States had been under severe economic pressure. Both sagging domestic sales and low-cost, imported products contributed to many bankruptcies and plant closures. So far, and due in large part to several loyal local customers and a nonunion work force, Buckeye had been able to remain in operation without shutdowns or layoffs. However, any considerable increase in direct or indirect costs could have a serious effect upon future profitability. Even without such a cost increase, there was always a small chance that business might decline to the point where a temporary shutdown or plant closure would become necessary.

How to deal with the industrial waste created by Buckeye's operations had recently attracted the attention of its top management. The company was highly interested in the new treatment proposal because the existing method of waste treatment involved a haulage firm which might be unable to find new storage sites when their contract expired in August 1986. Even if sites were available, there was the feeling that the contract might be renewed at additional costs of 10 cents to 15 cents per gallon of waste over the 25 cents per gallon they were presently paying.

Grid's method of waste handling was unique but chemically quite simple. The main treatment problem was spent acid which had been employed in "pickling" the steel. The process treated the acid with a special formula of readily available chemicals until it became inert (not capable of further chemical reactions). The

---

This case was prepared by Randy Hoffman, York University. Copyright © 1986 by Randy Hoffman.

resulting solid material could then be used as harmless landfill. The treatment plant was actually a lot of "plumbing" that any competent industrial contractor pr;could assemble. The main difficulty in the eyes of all parties was whether certification could be obtained from the U.S. Environmental Protection Agency for this method of waste treatment. In principle, this should not be difficult. Rendering toxic waste chemically inert was an ideal solution. In addition, U.S. President Reagan seemed to be favouring industrial over ecological and environmental concerns more than previous administrations. EPA approval, however, could only be obtained once a detailed plant design was completed. The agency also reserved the right to close the treatment unit if it did not appear to be performing up to expectations.

Although Art had a great deal of experience in project management and Grid had designed (but not built themselves) a similar plant in Canada which was in operation, Art felt that he had reasons to be worried about this project as follows:

1. Failure of the new joint company would involve substantial opportunity costs for Art Miller and Grid. Cash demands would be heavy because bank financing, secured by the waste treatment plant, would likely cover only the needs of the first 1½ years. The partners would have to supply any additional funds required. More important, concentration on the Buckeye project would force Art to neglect his consulting practice.

2. Buckeye Steel currently produced about 12 million gallons of waste and 585 tons of furnace dust per each million gallons (which was relatively easy to dispose of in any landfill on site). However, it did appear from historical records that any output between 6 and 15 million gallons was equally likely. Given the rate of closure of small U.S. steel plants, Art also felt that there was a 5 percent probability of Buckeye shutting down temporarily or permanently during any given year. On the other hand, Buckeye would benefit by the protectionist trade measures being proposed in the U.S. Congress (and opposed by President Reagan).

3. Although Art Miller and Grid Engineering jointly possessed the needed design and project management expertise, they realized that local Ohio contractors would have to be hired for the actual construction. Grid had the necessary design expertise but lacked the project management experience possessed by Art Miller. Unfortunately, only Grid personnel would be able to be in continuous attendance on-site. Ultimately, this might be limited to one person from Grid supervising the technical aspects of construction. A local contractor would have to be relied upon to complete the project on time and within budget. Art himself could spend about 20 percent of his time in Ohio. He worried about the cost estimates for the construction which were supplied by Grid. Engineers from Grid assured Art that the construction techniques were within the competence of any industrial contractor.

4. Art still was concerned about receiving the EPA license but not to a great extent. The semirural location of the plant meant that local opposition was not probable. Since the mid-Ohio region was mildly depressed, construction and operation of a waste treatment facility could also provide some local employment.

Art Miller Consulting Limited consisted of Miller himself, a full-time secretary, a draftsman, and one part-time employee (bookkeeper). The firm maintained a small suite of offices in Woodbridge, Ontario, giving a total overhead (excluding Art's salary) of about $80,000 per year. Undertaking the Buckeye project would mean that he could probably just cover his expenses with a little left over for himself through other small projects during the lengthy period before revenue would be received. Although Art would not be investing any personal (or company) funds, he estimated that the net opportunity cost for his efforts throughout the project's first 18 months would be $200,000 to $300,000 in net revenue as he would have to forego a large and more traditional project currently being offered to him. He felt this project would bring in about $360,000 of gross revenue to his small firm over that period.

The initial proposal was presented to Buckeye. (Excerpts are included in the Appendix.) They seemed very receptive but asked for a few weeks to consider it. Their only definite pronouncement was that they were "a steel company" and had no interest in purchasing the plant until 1991, if at all. By that time, the plant might require some extensive rebuilding to remain in operation. Art thought that he could negotiate a 40 percent share in the project (Grid would own 60 percent) but wondered whether it was really worth it.

In order to form some preliminary feeling as to the project's profitability and to ensure that a proposed line of credit of $2.4 million would be sufficient, Art Miller drew up a pro forma cash flow covering the first three years of the project. (See Exhibit 1.) Although the net revenue estimates began to look interesting, even by the end of the first year and one half, Art could see that the risk inherent in this project was not shown by this type of statement. He also knew that he would have to make his decision known to Grid immediately if he wished to withdraw.

Exhibit 1: Financial Prospects of Waste Treatment Project—Cash Flow/Capital Requirement/Projected Performance (beginning April 1985)

	Design		Construction			Testing(5)	August 1986 Operations					
	1st Quarter	2nd Quarter	3rd Quarter	4th Quarter	5th Quarter	6th Quarter	7th Quarter	8th Quarter	9th Quarter	10th Quarter	11th Quarter	12th Quarter
Disbursements:												
Construction costs (1)	$75,000	$75,000	$425,000	$560,000	$485,000	$380,000	Ø	Ø	Ø	Ø	Ø	Ø
Operation costs (2)												
Fixed						75,834	$113,750	$113,750	$113,750	$113,750	$119,438	$119,438
Variable @ (12 million gallons)						62,083	186,249	186,249	186,249	186,249	195,561	195,561
Variable @ 0 volume						Ø					Ø	Ø
Total operating costs						137,917	299,999	299,999	299,999	299,999	314,999	314,999
Interest on loan @ 14% (3)	2,625	5,250	20,125	39,725	56,700	69,921	148,260	148,260	148,260	148,260	148,260	148,260
Amortization of loan	N/A	N/A	N/A	N/A	N/A	N/A	declining balance of debt					
Receipts:												
From line of credit	77,625	80,250	445,125	599,725	541,700	379,505						
Cumulative	77,625	157,875	603,000	1,202,725	1,744,425	2,123,930						
Sales revenue @ 12 million gallons	N/A	N/A	N/A	N/A	N/A	208,333	625,000	625,000	625,000	625,000	625,000	625,000
Net cash (quarter)	Ø	Ø	Ø	Ø	Ø	Ø	176,741	176,741	176,741	176,741	161,741	161,741
Net cash (cumulative) (4)	Ø	Ø	Ø	Ø	Ø	Ø	176,741	353,482	530,223	706,964	868,705	1,030,446

Notes:
1. Construction costs include design, fabrication, and testing.
2. Fixed costs are included in construction costs until operations begin.
   Inflation of all costs included at 5% per annum beginning in 11th quarter.
3. Annual effective rate of loan = 14.93% (amortized over 20 quarters from August 1986).
4. No cash reserves while supported by line of credit.
5. No receipts during testing stage.
   The revenue projections do *not* reflect any "passing on" of inflation to Buckeye which was ultimately included in the proposal (in Appendix).

Exhibit 1 (*concluded*)   Yearly Costs of Waste Management to Buckeye Steel and to the Joint Company

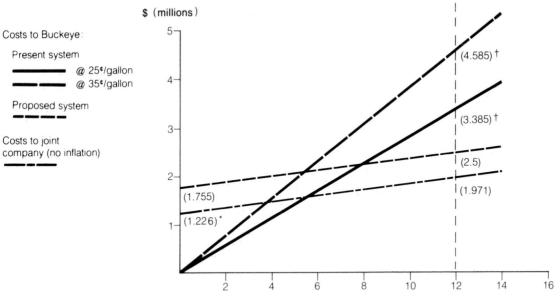

Costs to Buckeye:

Present system

━━━━━ @ 25¢/gallon
━ ━ ━ @ 35¢/gallon

Proposed system

━ ━ ━ ━

Costs to joint
company (no inflation)

━ ━ ━

Millions of gallons of acid with 585 tons of furnace dust per million gallons

* Includes $177,960 of contingency costs.
† Includes costs for disposing of furnace dust.

Appendix: Excerpts from the Proposal to Buckeye Steel

Subject: Waste Solidification Service   February 25, 1985

Gentlemen:

Art Miller Consulting Limited and Grid Engineering Inc. are pleased to present the attached proposal for the supply of a Waste Solidification Service at your Ohio facility.

The plant, to be owned and operated by Miller Consulting, will be designed and licensed by Grid Engineering Inc. and is to be erected on land provided by Buckeye Steel. The plant will produce a "delisted" inert material for local disposal from your present hazardous wastes, namely:

1. Electric furnace baghouse dust.
2. Spent pickling acid.

It is proposed that Buckeye Steel (or its designated subsidiary) enter into a five (5) year service contract with us (or our designated operating company) for the disposal of the hazardous waste from its Mansfield and area operations. The attached proposal details the terms of the service contract which will have the flexibility of being based in part on the amount of waste treated.

The financial benefits to Buckeye Steel of using this Waste Solidification Service are as follows:

1. Immediate substantial savings in waste disposal at the start of plant operations.
2. Elimination of the risk in the availability and cost of waste disposal in the future.
3. A purchase option that enables Buckeye to assume plant ownership at its option, and at a price comparable to the present value of the saving afforded through the use of waste solidification.

As official EPA approval may take as long as one year to obtain, it is imperative that design and pilot plant work be commenced quickly in order that approval would coincide with the Solidification Plant start-up (proposed for June 1986). Work to obtain EPA approval would start immediately upon receipt of a letter of intent from Buckeye Steel that the terms of this proposal were acceptable and that a formal contract would be negotiated. Any agreement would have to carry the clear understanding that in the event EPA approval was not forthcoming we would be reimbursed for "out of pocket" costs plus 10 percent, and Buckeye would assume ownership of the unfinished project.

Once you have had a chance to study this proposal in detail, we would appreciate the opportunity to discuss with you any questions that may arise. If you find the terms of this proposal acceptable, we should meet at your earliest convenience so that a letter of intent may be drafted to allow us to proceed with the work necessary to obtain EPA approval.

Yours very truly,

Art Miller, P. Eng.
President, Art Miller Consulting Limited

Proposal

1.0 INTRODUCTION

This proposal has been prepared as a result of the Engineering presentation made by Grid Engineering Inc. on June 21, 1984. At that time Grid demonstrated the possibility of combining the electric furnace baghouse dust and the spent pickling acid in a solidification process to reduce the cost of disposing of these hazardous materials. The economic sense of such an arrangement seemed apparent; however, no action was taken.

Upon review of this work, Art Miller Consulting Limited approached Grid Engineering Inc. to form an operating company which would design, finance, install and operate, under contract to and on the site of Buckeye Steel, a Waste Solidification Process Plant. This "service" arrangement, it is felt, would free Buckeye of the necessary capital and management commitments, while passing on the benefits and savings of an "in-plant" operation.

The following proposal outlines the terms under which such a plant may be built and operated under contract.

2.0 SOLIDIFICATION TECHNOLOGY

Solidification is a process technology which was developed to stabilize and render inert the metal components of wastes that are considered hazardous. It has a similar although limited effect on hazardous organic constituents, if present. The process is patented. Use of the process is possible only on a licensed basis.

The solidification process provides a means to dissolve the silicates found in many common materials (e.g., slags, clays, etc.). These "activated" silicates react with the metal constituents present in a given waste in specific proportions. The metal species and the activated silicates combine to form part of the silicate molecular chain structures. The chains provide an essentially inert substrate and do not allow the metals to redissolve under any current leach testing used to define hazardous substances. Since we are dealing here with positive chemical reactions and also with one of the most stable forms of material silicates, the end result is generally considered one of the best long-term solutions available for stabilizing hazardous wastes. Delisting of the end product is virtually assured by following the EPA procedures and testing.

The solidification technology used in this plant will be licensed from Waste Transportation Limited, Hamilton, Ontario.

3.0 COST OF THE WASTE SOLIDIFICATION SERVICE TO BUCKEYE

3.1 BASIC COST

The cost of disposing spent acids and dust is composed of a fixed and a variable component dependent on the amount of waste materials treated. With a start-up projected for June 1986, the total cost to Buckeye Steel Corporation for the first year of operations may be expressed as:

Fixed cost .... $1,755,000 plus

Variable cost* .... $ 62,100 per million gallons of spent acid

---

* It is assumed that there are approximately 585 tons of electric furnace dust for disposal for each million gallons of spent acid.

The following table is the schedule of costs for various annual volumes of waste to be treated:

Spent Acid Volume (millions of gallons)	Total Annual Cost (first year of operations)
1	$1,817,100
2	$1,879,200
3	$1,941,300
4	$2,003,400
5	$2,065,500
6	$2,127,600
7	$2,189,700
8	$2,251,800
9	$2,313,900
10	$2,376,000
11	$2,438,100
12	$2,500,200
13	$2,562,300
14*	$2,624,400

* Maximum plant capacity.

3.2   FIVE YEAR COST GUARANTEE

Art Miller Consulting Limited will protect Buckeye Steel against unreasonable increases in the cost of Waste Management for the five (5) year contract period. Specifically, your costs will increase only by the actual amount of the increase in our labour and material costs.

For example, should these costs increase by 5% in 1987, then the cost to Buckeye for disposing of 12 million gallons of liquid waste and furnace dust will increase by only $63,000.00 or 2.5%.

3.3   PLANT PURCHASE OPTION

Buckeye may, at its option from the third year of operation, elect to purchase the Waste Solidification Plant and assume its operation at any time during the remaining five year life of the contract. Following is a Schedule of Prices expressed in constant 1985 dollars:

Year*	Purchase Price
1988	$3,856,000
1989	$3,021,000
1990	$2,074,000
1991	$1,000,000

* As of June 1st of that year.

3.4 COST COMPARISON WITH PRESENT METHODS OF WASTE DISPOSAL

At a nominal volume of 12 million gallons of spent acid and 585 tons of furnace dust per million gallons, the yearly savings to Buckeye will be $885,000. If the cost of present disposal methods has risen to $0.35/gallon by the time (June 1986) that the plant is ready to begin operation, then the savings will be in excess of $2 million annually.

3.5 FIVE YEAR PRESENT COSTS OF WASTE DISPOSAL

Employing a conservative discount rate of 12%, the present cost of waste disposal to Buckeye Steel over the five year contract period may be represented as follows (in 1985 dollars as of June 1, 1986).

Current Method (@ $0.25/gal.)	Current Method (@ $0.35/gal.)	Solidification (at contract cost)
$12,203,000	$16,528,000	$9,768,000

The present value (employing a 12% discount rate) of the Solidification Plant for waste disposal to Buckeye is therefore $2,435,000 or $6,760,000 in comparison with the present disposal method at $0.25/gallon or $0.35/gallon, respectively.

Since it is extremely likely from present trends that the costs for the present method will increase faster than the general rate of inflation, the present value of this proposal is almost certainly greater than the conservative estimates given above.

3.6 SUMMARY OF FINANCIAL BENEFITS TO BUCKEYE STEEL CORPORATION

1. Immediate substantial savings in waste disposal at the start of plant operations.
2. Elimination of the risk in the availability and cost of waste disposal in the future.
3. A purchase option that enables Buckeye to assume plant ownership at its option, and at a price comparable to the present value of the savings afforded through the use of waste solidification.

The Grand Theatre Company

There is no better director than me. Some may be as good, but none better.[1]

In December 1982 the board of directors of Theatre London (see Exhibit 1) were considering a proposal to hire Robin Phillips as artistic director to replace Bernard Hopkins. The hiring decision was complicated by Phillips's ambitious plans for the theatre, which included a change from a subscription theatre to repertory, an increase in budget from $1.9 million to $4.5 million, and even changing the organization's name. The board had to act quickly as plans had to be made and actors hired for the next season.

Theatre in Ontario

Theatre is big business. In Toronto alone (including cabaret, dinner theatre, and opera) some 3.5 million people attended 120 productions in 1982, in 28 locations. There are 24 nonprofit professional theatres in Toronto and 18 in the rest of Ontario.

Virtually all theatre organizations are nonprofit (with rare exceptions like Ed Mirvish's Royal Alexandra) and are subsidized by local, provincial, and federal grants. Thus theatres compete for funds with charity, educational, and health care organizations. As shown in Exhibit 2, a third of revenue typically comes from government sources, and half of this comes from the Canada Council. Another 10 percent comes from individual and corporate donors and the balance from the box office. Because of the pressing need for box office revenues, most theatre companies sell subscriptions of five or so plays from October to May.

In 1982–83, audience size was 570,000 for the Stratford Festival, the largest arts organization in Canada, and 268,000 for the Shaw Festival, the second largest theatre company. According to a Stratford audience study, audiences break down into: (1) committed theatregoers (27 percent) who see a number of plays each year and who tend to be older and more educated and live in Ontario; (2) casual theatregoers (53 percent) who attend a theatre every year or two to see plays of particular interest; and (3) first-timers (20 percent). The challenge for these theatres is to develop these first-timers to be the audience of the future.

This case was prepared by Dr. Larry M. Agranove from published sources and interviews with numerous people in theatre, government, and arts organizations. Copyright © 1986 by Wilfrid Laurier University.

[1] Robin Phillips, quoted in *The Globe and Mail*, December 31, 1983, p. E1.

Exhibit 1: The Board of Directors, December 1982

J. Noreen De Shane	President of the Grand Theatre, and president of a stationery firm
Peter J. Ashby	Partner, major consulting firm
W. C. P. Baldwin, Jr.	President, linen supply firm
Bob Beccarea	Alderman and civic representative
Art Ender	Life insurance representative
Ed Escaf	Hotel and restaurant owner
Dr. John Girvin	Surgeon
Stephanie Goble	Representative of London Labour Council
Elaine Hagarty	Former alderman, active in arts community
Barbara Ivey	Active board member of various theatre groups
Alan G. Leyland	Entrepreneur
John F. McGarry	Partner, major law firm
C. Agnew Meek	Corporate marketing executive
Robert Mepham	Insurance company executive
Elizabeth Murray	Board member of theatre groups and Ontario Arts Council
John H. Porter	Vice president and partner, major accounting firm
Peter Schwartz	Partner, major law firm
Dr. Tom F. Siess	University professor
Dr. Shiel Warma	Surgeon

Exhibit 2: The Major Arts Organizations in Canada—Ranked by Size of Total Revenue for 1982–1983

Arts Organization	Total Revenue 1982–1983	Box Office and Earned	Government Grants	Private Donations	Accumulated Surplus/ Deficit End of 1982– 1983
1. Stratford Festival	$12,314,300	$9,678,285	$1,405,939	$1,230,076	$(1,731,492)
2. Toronto Symphony	9,480,503	6,020,112	1,893,100	1,567,291	(149,391)
3. National Ballet	7,271,616	3,233,810	2,943,856	1,093,950	(675,096)
4. Orchestre Symphonique de Montreal	7,071,886	4,048,749	2,164,350	858,787	(857,662)
5. Canadian Opera Company	5,969,077	2,668,698	2,029,100	1,271,279	(290,168)
6. Vancouver Symphony	5,189,041	2,488,690	1,784,315	916,036	(818,951)
7. Shaw Festival	4,801,700	3,848,200	586,000	367,500	(45,167)
8. Royal Winnipeg Ballet	4,021,263	1,884,339	1,611,463	525,461	343,639
9. Centre Stage	3,483,020	1,923,312	1,316,000	243,708	(212,108)
10. Citadel Theatre	3,541,911	2,097,096	1,117,733	327,082	(177,821)
. . . .					
18. Grand Theatre	1,990,707	1,277,625	390,000	323,082	0*

* Reduced by Wintario Challenge Fund.
Source: Council for Business and the Arts in Canada.

Theatre audiences tend to be well educated, with most having university education and slightly over 50 percent having attended a graduate or professional school. Those aged 36 through 50 make up 35 percent of the Stratford audience, and the 21 to 35 and 51 to 64 age groups each make up 25 percent. Visitors from the United States account for 35 percent of box office receipts at the Stratford Festival; Toronto accounts for 25 percent; and the remaining 40 percent come from elsewhere in Ontario. Twice as many women attend as men. It is understood that Shaw's market is similar, with slightly fewer coming from the United States.

A recent study[2] showed that while 42 percent of Ontario residents attended live plays and musicals in 1974, this grew to 55 percent by 1984. Some 24 percent of the Ontario population are "frequent attenders" (at least six times a year). They come from all age groups, but many are "singles," and many are university educated and affluent. In fact, while only 63 percent of Ontarians without a high school education attended live theatre, 94 percent with university degrees have attended live theatre.

There is some price sensitivity: 73 percent said they would attend oftener if tickets were less expensive. However, 77 percent (which included young adults and lower-middle income families) said they would accept a tax increase of up to $25 to support the arts.

The Organization of a Theatre Company

The Board of Directors

The board of directors is fiscally and legally responsible for the theatre. They may determine the theatre's artistic objectives then delegate the fulfilling of these objectives to the artistic director. However, any artistic plan has financial objectives, and the board's responsibility is essentially financial. Artistic directors generally demand, and are generally granted, a great deal of autonomy in such matters as programming and casting; to a large extent the board "bets" on the artistic director's ability to put on a season of theatre, subject to his accountability in meeting budgets and providing an appropriate level of quality.

Board members are typically expected to assist in fund-raising and to set an example by contributing generously themselves.

Board members often have business backgrounds. As a result, they may be—and are certainly often perceived to be—insensitive to the unique needs of an artistic organization. Artistic boards often include lawyers and accountants, who are often recruited to serve a specific function but who tend to remain on long enough to achieve positions of power.

Busy business people serve on boards for a number of reasons. They may perceive their serving as a civic responsibility. Others may see it as an opportunity

---

[2] Report to the Honourable Susan Fish, the minister of citizenship and culture, Province of Ontario, by the Special Committee for the Arts, Spring 1984.

to wield power at a board level, something they are not allowed to do in their own organizations. Membership on a board allows people to widen their social and business contacts; this can be important to lawyers and accountants, who are limited in their freedom to advertise. One common motivation for business people to join arts boards is the opportunity to mingle with luminaries in the arts. Here is one view of their performance:

> It has often been charged that many a hardheaded businessman loses his business sense on entering a meeting of an arts board. Lacking a profit motive to guide the affairs of the organization, businessmen who serve on arts boards sometimes feel unsure of themselves and their expertise. Compounding this problem is the inclination on the part of arts organizations to consider themselves a breed apart, outside the realm of normal business practice. But whether a company manufactures widgets or mounts exhibitions, the basic business concerns remain the same: strategic planning, good marketing, adequate financing, and competent management are essential to any enterprise.[3]

Theatre Management

In addition to the artistic director, whose role and relationship with the board were described above, there is usually a general manager who is responsible for the business affairs of the organization. Since artistic directors strive for maximum quality, which is expensive, and since business managers have to find and account for the money to run the theatre, conflicts often occur. Not surprisingly, boards often side with the business manager because of their similarities of culture and values. Typically, both artistic director and general manager report directly to the board.

Mounting a Production

The theatre company selects "products" to suit its objectives and audiences. For example, a theatre might select a playbill of classics or children's plays. A regional theatre might select a Canadian play (to satisfy government grant-giving agencies), a classic (to satisfy the artistic aspirations of the artistic director), a resounding "hit" from Broadway or England (to help sell the series), and one or more plays that have been successful elsewhere.

Each production requires a producer (who may be the artistic director) to act as the "entrepreneur" to put the show together. He acquires the rights to the play, if it is not in the public domain, for a fee of 7 to 10 percent of the box office revenue. He also retains a director, who may be on staff or who may be a free-lance director retained for the run of the play. In the latter case, minimum

---

[3] "Developing Effective Arts Boards" (Undated publication of the Council for Business and the Arts in Canada), pp. 28–29.

scale would be \$6,174.80 for a run of three weeks of rehearsal and three to four weeks of performance.

Casting is done, beginning with the major parts, on the basis of a uniform contract, which sets out fees (minimum of \$416.27 per week for a major company), starting date, billing, working time, and "perks" (for example, dressing room, accommodation).

Finally, a stage manager is contracted, as are designers for sets, costumes, and lighting. It is essential, of course, that all these people work well together.

The above describes the typical stock, or subscription, company. However, Stratford and Shaw operate as repertory companies, hiring a group of actors for one or more seasons and allocating roles among the members of the company. Repertory companies typically sell tickets for individual plays, while subscription companies sell their series at the beginning of the season with few single ticket sales.

Lead times are considerable; in Stratford, for example, plays that open in May are firmly cast by the previous December, and the entire session is planned by March, when rehearsals begin.

Theatre London

Background

The Grand Opera House was opened in London on September 9, 1901 by Ambrose J. Small, a Toronto theatrical entrepreneur and frustrated producer. It quickly became the showcase of Small's theatrical chain, opening with such attractions as the Russian Symphony Orchestra and later offering such performers as Barry Fitzgerald, Bela Lugosi, Clifton Webb, Sidney Poitier, and Hume Cronyn. Small sold his theatre chain in 1919, deposited a million dollars in his bank, and disappeared. There has been no explanation to this day; however, Small's ghost is said to haunt the Grand.

Famous Players bought the theatre in 1924, tore out the second balcony, and converted the theatre to a cinema. They sold to the London Little Theatre for a token amount in 1945, and the building housed an amateur community theatre till the spring of 1971. The theatre employed professional business management and a professional artistic director, but the actors were all amateurs. Some of London's leading citizens acted in plays, and some even displayed a high level of competence. The theatre was prominent in the social life of the city and attracted one of the largest subscription sales in North America, both as a percentage of available seats and in absolute terms. It also achieved a reputation for a very high level of quality, given that it was essentially an amateur theatre. Articles about the theatre appeared in such magazines as *Life*.

However, there was some concern in the theatre that the level of quality was as high as it was going to get as a company of amateurs and that the community deserved, and was ready to support, a professional theatre. Another local organization, the London Symphony, had engaged a conductor with an international reputation and was changing from an amateur to a professional orchestra. An active art gallery association was formed to work toward providing London with a major art gallery. Although strong objections were raised against the proposal for a professional theatre, particularly because of the increased financial burden, the risk, and the denial to many of the theatre's supporters of an opportunity to participate in their hobby of acting, London Little Theatre changed to Theatre London in 1971 under Artistic Director Heinar Piller. The progressives were vindicated, as theatregoers in London and area were treated to a decade of artistically and financially successful theatre.

Piller was succeeded, at the end of the 1975 season, by William Hutt, who had achieved great success as an actor at Stratford and was well known to Londoners. He served from 1976 to 1978. Bernard Hopkins arrived in 1979 and was artistic director till May 1983.

The Grand was attractively and authentically renovated at a cost of $5.5 million, reopening in the fall of 1978 after being closed for a full season. (The company had a reduced season during that time in small rented accommodations.) During the renovation, seating capacity was reduced from 1,100 to 845.

Theatre London ran successful stock seasons from 1979 to 1982. The 1981–1982 season was particularly successful, operating at 85 percent of capacity. Eighty percent of its tickets were sold through subscription to some 13,431 subscribers. Financial statements are shown in Exhibit 3.

The London Environment

London was founded at the forks of the Thames River in 1793 by Governor Simcoe with the intention of making it the capital of Upper Canada. Instead, it became the cultural and commercial centre of southwestern Ontario. Located on three railroad lines and on Highway 401 that serves the Quebec-Windsor corridor, London also has a major airport served by two airlines. London is two hours away (by car) from Detroit or Toronto; however, it is in a major snow belt. London is a major retail centre, with the second highest per capita retail capacity in North America. It serves as a trading area for almost a million people, although its own population is only 259,000. (See the Appendix.) There are four hotels near the core area and motels in outlying areas. Many interesting restaurants had opened with a great deal of excess capacity; a few restaurants closed or changed hands.

There is little heavy industry in London, but there is a major university, a community college, a teacher's college, and two small church-affiliated colleges. Four major hospitals serve a wide area and provide teaching facilities for the university medical school and dental school. In addition to being a retail centre, London is the home of major financial institutions and agribusiness firms, as well as a major brewery.

London is also a major cultural centre. In addition to Theatre London,

Exhibit 3

THEATRE LONDON
Condensed Five-Year Operating Results
As of June 30, 1979–1983

	1979	1980	1981	1982	1983 (Estimate)
Revenue:					
Productions:					
Ticket sales	$ 551,650	$ 585,938	$ 620,313	$ 664,058	$1,100,000
Sponsored programs	26,000	25,000	26,500	9,000	9,000
Program advertising	17,283	17,270	19,652	24,241	24,000
Total production revenue	594,933	628,208	666,465	697,299	1,133,000
Grants:					
Canada Council	145,000	163,000	173,000	185,000	210,000
Ontario Arts Council	145,000	152,000	160,000	170,000	180,000
Wintario	89,254	—	—	—	—
City of London	12,500	—	—	—	—
Cultural Initiative Program	—	—	25,000	—	—
Total grants	391,754	315,000	358,000	355,000	390,000
Other:					
Operating fund drive	41,222	27,462	182,559	183,188	160,000
Special projects	36,811	36,525	43,881	41,281	65,000
Interest	34,553	50,608	62,128	86,106	80,000
Concessions	33,500	75,073	69,581	62,065	78,000
Theatre school	8,720	17,687	19,481	—	—
Box office commissions	3,319	3,721	651	6,142	3,000
Theatre rental and miscellaneous	3,170	—	—	4,704	2,000
Total other revenue	161,295	211,076	378,281	383,486	388,000
Total revenue	1,147,982	1,154,284	1,402,946	1,435,785	1,911,000
Expenses:					
Public relations	179,880	128,502	139,907	177,267	270,000
Administration	91,973	115,798	162,723	167,749	330,000
Production overhead	190,911	237,606	282,270	339,474	350,000
Productions	466,906	414,644	416,440	421,151	780,000
Front of house, box office, and concessions	75,563	123,910	107,617	126,673	140,000
Facility operation	131,445	139,215	152,153	142,061	140,000
Theatre school	9,742	20,832	34,804	—	—
Total expenses	1,146,420*	1,180,507	1,295,914	1,374,375	2,010,000
Excess of revenue over expense	$ 1,562	$ (26,223)	$ 107,032	$ 61,410	$ (99,000)
* Salaries, fees and benefits	$ 658,507	$ 754,109	$ 791,954	$ 823,260	$1,000,000†
Supplies and expenses	487,913	426,398	503,960	551,115	911,000
	$1,146,420	$1,180,507	$1,295,914	$1,374,375	$1,911,000

† In addition, development costs for the establishment of a repertory company in the 1983–1984 season could be incurred which could be largely offset by federal and provincial grants.

Exhibit 3 (*concluded*)

THEATRE LONDON
Condensed Balance Sheets
As of June 30, 1979–1982

	1979	1980	1981	1982
Assets				
Current assets:				
Cash and term deposits	$351,010	$372,868	$325,631	$316,939
Accounts receivable	3,908	13,957	35,208	10,916
Inventory	7,463	7,146	6,050	—
Prepaid expenses	20,257	32,788	46,938	72,471
Total assets	$382,638	$426,759	$413,827	$400,326
Liabilities and Surplus				
Current liabilities:				
Bank loan	—	$ 25,000	—	—
Accounts payable	$ 26,253	24,041	$ 30,112	$ 67,198
Advance ticket sale	280,431	324,524	319,843	302,983
Advance grants	1,060	—	15,201	14,805
Payable to Theatre London Foundation	—	4,523	—	15,340
Total liabilities	307,744	378,088	365,156	400,326
Surplus	74,894	48,671	48,671*	—
Total liabilities and surplus	$382,638	$426,759	$413,827	$400,326

* In addition, there was equity of $453,080 from the Wintario Challenge Fund Program in 1981 and $807,289 in 1982. Under the terms of the program, Wintario will match two dollars for every eligible contributed dollar raised (during the three-year period ending 30 June 1983) in excess of 5.9 percent of the current year's operating expenses. All these matching contributions are placed in a separate investment fund for at least five years, although interest earned on the fund may be used for current operations.

London has a professional symphony orchestra and a couple of significant choral groups. The university has an active program of theatre and music, and the community is a centre for visual artists. There are various commercial art galleries, an art gallery connected with the university, and a major public art gallery located in the city centre. There are several museums, including a unique children's museum and a museum of Indian archaelogy. The latter two attract visitors from a wide area.

The Grand Theatre Company

In late 1981, a decade after the company had become professional, concern was again raised in the theatre that the level of quality had stagnated and the theatre would have to move in new directions. Bernard Hopkins was a superb actor and a competent artistic director. With some success he had directed a few plays, rather than have to pay for a free-lance director. However, some members of the board believed that he had taken the theatre as far as he was able, and there was no initiative on either side to extend Hopkins's contract beyond its expiry in May 1983.

A planning committee, under one of the board members, addressed the issue of continuing the growth in quality. They conducted a number of retreats and interviewed experts in professional theatre as well as officers of the Canada Council and the Ontario Arts Council. During the course of the investigation, they interviewed Robin Phillips. Phillips had been artistic director at the Stratford Festival and was well known to Barbara Ivey (who served on both the Stratford and Theatre London boards) and to other Theatre London directors. He also had directed, with considerable artistic success, two productions for Theatre London: *The Lady of the Camellias* and *Long Day's Journey into Night*.

Robin Phillips

Robin Phillips is a highly talented artistic director and a person of incredible charm. (In *all* of the interviews conducted by the casewriter, words like *charm*, *charisma*, and *talent* abounded.) Actress Martha Henry said, "Once you've worked with Robin, it's almost impossible to work for anyone else."

He came to Canada from England in 1974 to plan the 1975 Stratford season, although he would not direct any specific plays till 1976. His tenure at Stratford has been described as successful but stormy. When he was contracting to direct a production for the Canadian Opera Company in 1976, he said he would not renew his Stratford contract unless he had more evidence of support for his ambition to make Stratford the focus of Canadian theatre, with film and television productions as well as live theatre. He received a five-year contract to run from November 1, 1976; the contract could be terminated with four months' notice.

There was a series of resignations from, and returns to, Stratford starting in July 1978, until Phillips's departure in 1981. In addition to his Stratford activities, Phillips was involved with theatre in Calgary, New York, Toronto's Harbourfront, and Vancouver. He also filmed *The Wars*, a novel by Timothy Findley. It was generally understood that he was seeking a theatre in Toronto to serve as a base for his stage, film, and television ambitions. However, none was available.

The Phillips Plan. Robin Phillips had a plan for Theatre London, and would come only if he had a budget to fulfill his plan and complete artistic autonomy. His plan called for raising Theatre London from 18th place in Canadian theatre to third and changing its name to The Grand Theatre Company.

The plan required a budget of $4.5 million, up from $1.9 million. This included $400,000 of capital cost to improve the Grand's facilities. Box office and concessions would provide 73 percent of the budget; 18 percent would come from donations; 5 percent from the Canada Council; and 4 percent from the Ontario Arts Council. Revenue projections were based on playing to 80 percent of capacity; this was considered feasible because Phillips had surpassed that performance at Stratford, and Theatre London had been operating at 85 percent. The theatre requested a permanent tax exemption from the City of London; the deputy mayor described this request as "cavalier."

Three of the stage productions would be adapted for television and filmed by Primedia Productions of Toronto. This would provide some $100,000 of additional revenue for each production as well as audience exposure.

Robin Phillips strongly favoured a repertory company over a subscription policy. He believed, and often stated, that subscriptions denied audiences a choice, and audiences must learn to discriminate. A change had to be made to make the theatre different, special, and exciting. A repertory company would provide a company of salaried actors who could not be lured away during the season and who would be attracted by steady employment.

Another advantage of the repertory concept is the flexibility afforded patrons who may choose the dates they see a play and their seat locations. In a subscription series patrons are restricted to the same seat location on the same night for each performance. In repertory theatre, several productions are typically run simultaneously.

The Playbill.   Phillips proposed to offer these plays on the main stage (in addition to a children's program in a small, secondary theatre):

Godspell by John-Michael Tebelak	A rousing rock musical with audience appeal, especially for younger audiences.
The Doctor's Dilemma by George Bernard Shaw	An established classical "hit."
Waiting for the Parade by John Murrell	A Canadian play, with an all-female cast, showing what women did while their men were fighting World War II.
Timon of Athens by William Shakespeare	A little-performed, little-known Shakespearean play, ignored by Stratford.
The Club by Eve Merrian	A musical spoof of men's clubs, with a female cast playing the part of men.
Arsenic and Old Lace by Joseph Kesselring	A well-known classic comedy of American theatre.
The Prisoner of Zenda adapted by Warren Graves	A comedy of political intrigue and romance, set in a mythical Eastern European kingdom.
Hamlet by William Shakespeare	One of his best-known plays.
Dear Antoine by Jan Anouilh	A comedy by a leading contemporary French playwright.

Casting for these plays would not be a problem, as leading actors from Canada, the United States, and England were eager to work with Phillips.

Pricing.   Since the plan envisioned a box office yield of $3.2 million, up from the $1.2 million planned for the 1982–1983 season, revenue would have to be increased in two ways. The number of productions would be increased, with nine productions in the season instead of the previous six. There would be a record 399 performances instead of the 230 performances in the 1982–1983 season. Thus the plan projected an audience of 217,000, compared with the 137,000 planned for the 1982–1983 season. In addition, prices would be increased.

A subscriber in the 1982–1983 season could see five plays for $55 on weekends or $45 on weekdays. This pricing schedule was proposed for the 1983–1984 repertory season:

Number of Seats	Price	
	Weekdays	Weekends
178	$20.00	$22.50
245	14.50	15.50
422	10.50	12.50

Promotion. Since the theatre would require an expanded audience from a wider area, the plan envisioned a program of investment spending in major area newspapers: *The Toronto Star* and *The Globe and Mail*, the *Kitchener-Waterloo Record*, and the *Detroit Free Press* as well as the *London Free Press*. The advertising would be directed at a first-time audience.

Group sales would be stressed, particularly to schools. Hotel-restaurant-transportation-theatre ticket packages were projected. However, data on expenditures was not available.

The Decision

The directors were impressed by the charm and the reputation of Robin Phillips. The proposal to hire Phillips—and to accept his plan—was supported by board members who had sound business backgrounds and who had worked in theatre for some years. They had a comfortable, modern theatre, with a recently acquired computer to issue tickets. They had a proven record in selling tickets, as did Robin Phillips.

On the other hand, if Phillips were hired, his artistic strengths might not be matched administratively. There was an administrative director who had been there for only two years and a chief accountant but no controller. And Stratford, Canada's leading theatre, was less than an hour's drive down the road. Would this be an audience builder or a competitive threat?

Appendix

1983 Disposable Income by Census Metropolitan Area

	Income Rating		Per Capita Personal Disposable Income	
	Index	*Rank*	*Amount*	*Rank*
Toronto	117	6	$12,693	7
Montreal	103	11	11,212	14
Vancouver	118	5	12,793	6
Ottawa-Hull	118	5	12,796	5
Edmonton	126	4	13,668	4
Calgary	132	1	14,324	1
Winnipeg	111	8	11,997	9
Quebec	98	14	10,623	18
Hamilton	112	7	12,114	8
St. Catharines	103	11	11,223	13
Kitchener	101	13	10,974	16
London	106	10	11,462	11
Halifax	101	13	10,923	17
Windsor	107	9	11,602	10
Regina	130	2	14,056	2
Saskatoon	129	3	14,021	3
Oshawa	106	10	11,450	12
Thunder Bay	102	12	11,089	15
Canada	100		10,851	

Note: This list shows all 18 census metropolitan areas in which the principal city had a population of at least 100,000 in the 1981 Census.

London-Centred Seven-County Market Area Data

	Population June 1/83 (Thousands)	10-Year Growth Rate (Percent)	Households June 1/83 (Thousands)	Wage Earner Average Income 1981	Per Capita Disposable Income 1983	Per Capita Retail Sales 1983
Seven counties	838.5	5.7%	293.7	$14,522	$10,669	$4,238
Canada	24,886.6	12.0	8,335.0	15,141	10,851	4,153

Source: *Canadian Markets*, 1984, and 1981 income tax returns.

Victoria Heavy Equipment Limited

Brian Walters sat back into the seat of his Lear jet as it broke through the clouds en route from Squamish, a small town near Vancouver, British Columbia, to Sacramento, California. As the 51-year-old chairman of the board, majority shareholder, and chief executive officer, he had run Victoria Heavy Equipment Limited as a closely held company for years. During this time Victoria had become a worldwide force in the crane market, with sales of approximately $100 million. But in early 1986 the problem of succession was in his thoughts. His son and daughter were not yet ready to run the organization, and he personally wanted to devote more time to other interests. He wondered about the kind of person he should hire to become president. There was also a nagging thought that there might be other problems with Victoria that would have to be worked out before he eased out of his present role.

The Firm

Victoria Heavy Equipment began in Victoria, British Columbia, on the southern tip of Vancouver Island, as Victoria Logging Equipment, one of two pioneer manufacturers of log skidders. Victoria produced its first horse-drawn skidder in 1903 and in 1920 moved to Squamish, north of Vancouver.

Victoria was one of the first companies in the industry to add motorized skidders to its wide line of construction machinery. By 1935 its product line included cranes. In 1938 Victoria was the first company to include hydraulic controls in its cranes, an innovation later incorporated by the industry. Victoria had moved into crane manufacturing as a consequence of a clear industry need for means of moving heavy items (including logs) in a safe, efficient manner.

In spite of its record of innovation, Victoria was in serious financial trouble when Brian Walters, Sr., bought the operation in 1948. Under his direction the company continued to manufacture the full range of logging machinery, and with tighter financial controls and greater attention to productivity, he was able to turn the company around.

A major turning point in the history of the company occurred in the mid-1950s when two decisions were made:

This case was prepared by Professor Thomas A. Poynter, Massachusetts Institute of Technology, and Professor Paul W. Beamish, Wilfrid Laurier University. Case material has been disguised; however, essential relationships are maintained. Copyright © 1986 by T. A. Poynter and P. W. Beamish.

1. They would stop being a full range manufacturer of construction and log skidder machinery and concentrate solely on cranes and their attachments.

2. They would enter the international market for cranes.

By 1985 the Victoria Heavy Equipment Limited was well recognized in crane circles and was now an organization exporting to over 70 countries. Victoria was second in terms of market share only to the giant Washington Cranes in the crane market.

Victoria's sales for 1985 were just over $100 million, while crane production was approximately 213 units over the 50-week production period. Of the $100 million, approximately $6 million were sales of crane attachments made by Victoria. The average price for the cranes sold by Victoria was in the range of $500,000. Financial statements for 1981 to 1985 for Victoria Heavy Equipment Limited are in Exhibits 1 and 2. Sales figures varied considerably due to large government contracts, but Victoria's sales had, on average, exceeded the inflation rate since 1975. Approximately 925 people were employed in the Squamish operation with over 90 percent of them coming from the surrounding, mainly logging, area.

The Product

Mobile cranes were unique within the heavy equipment market because they were capable of moving quickly and easily from one construction site to another, had superb maneuverability, and could be manipulated skillfully and precisely on-site. This capability was instrumental in the development of a niche for the mobile cranes in the heavy equipment industry.

Mobile cranes could be divided into two major classes: hydraulic and conventional. The hydraulic crane, although limited in size, was quick to set up and could achieve normal highway speeds with ease. Conventional cranes had to be dismantled for transportation but were available with capacities as large as 300 tonnes.

The more important features of the crane were its capacity and on-board tip-height. Victoria primarily produced one series of cranes, the LTM 1000 series. Five basic sizes ranged from capacities of 25 tonnes to 125 tonnes and on-board tip-heights of 34 to 63 metres. Numerous options were available for these cranes which resulted in uncompromised site performance, precision moving capabilities, fast highway travel, and effortless city driving. Particularly because of the numerous choices available, Victoria preferred not to build cranes to stock. They guaranteed a 60-day delivery and "tailor-made" cranes to customer specifications.

Brian Walters had typically used a great deal of ingenuity to keep Victoria in a competitive position. For example, late in 1982 Walters had been notified by a close contact in the logging industry that a new tract of redwood trees had been opened for logging. However, the company contracted to move the logs was

Exhibit 1

VICTORIA HEAVY EQUIPMENT LIMITED
Balance Sheet
For the Years 1981–1985
(in thousands)

	1981	1982	1983	1984	1985
Assets					
Current assets:					
Cash	$ 3,642	$ 2,598	$ 3,889	$ 5,590	$ 5,842
Accounts receivable	13,486	14,362	15,187	14,222	13,809
Allowance for doubtful accounts	(293)	(310)	(287)	(297)	(316)
Inventories	10,153	12,425	11,698	11,626	11,345
Prepaid expenses	619	404	356	106	429
Total current assets	27,607	29,479	30,643	31,247	31,109
Fixed assets:					
Property, plant, and equipment	3,840	3,980	3,875	4,353	5,489
Total assets	$31,447	$33,459	$34,518	$35,600	$36,598
Liabilities and Shareholders' Equity					
Current liabilities:					
Notes payable	$ 6,645	$ 5,460	$ 6,420	$ 5,952	$ 6,212
Trade accounts payable	9,712	14,998	10,543	10,465	10,986
Accrued expenses	1,074	1,119	1,742	1,978	1,155
Progress billings	419	400	396	428	345
Income tax payable	545	692	612	420	516
Other	—	450	—	—	23
Total current liabilities	18,395	23,119	19,713	19,243	19,237
Long-term debt	1,284	1,110	1,020	1,005	1,114
Total liabilities	19,679	24,229	20,733	20,248	20,351
Shareholders' equity:					
Common shares	1,200	1,045	1,295	1,390	1,435
Retained earnings	10,568	8,185	12,490	13,962	14,812
Total shareholders' equity	11,768	9,230	13,785	15,352	16,247
Total liabilities and shareholders' equity	$31,447	$33,459	$34,518	$35,600	$36,598

encountering a few problems. Because the logs were heavier and above average in length, a crane with a larger-than-average on-board tip-height and heavier capacity was required to move the logs about on the tree plantation site. Up to this point, due to technological complications, this was not possible. However, Walters vowed that Victoria would arrive with the solution to this new problem in the industry and six months later had succeeded.

Although the LTM 1000 series provided almost all of Victoria's crane sales, a new crane was introduced in 1984 after considerable expenditure on design, development, and manufacture. The A-100 had a 70-tonne capacity and could lift

Exhibit 2

VICTORIA HEAVY EQUIPMENT LIMITED
Income Statement
For the Years 1981–1985
(in thousands)

	1981	1982	1983	1984	1985
Revenue:					
Net sales	$63,386	$77,711	$86,346	$94,886	$100,943
Costs and expenses:					
Cost of sales	49,238	59,837	63,896	68,318	74,698
Selling expense	5,470	6,994	8,635	10,437	11,104
Administrative expense	684	777	2,590	3,795	4,038
Engineering expense	342	389	432	949	1,009
Gross income	7,652	9,714	10,793	11,387	10,094
Income taxes (40%)	3,061	3,886	4,317	4,555	4,038
Net income	$ 4,591	$ 5,828	$ 6,476	$ 6,832	$ 6,056

loads to heights of 61 metres, a combination previously unheard of in the industry. Through the use of smooth hydraulics even the heaviest loads could be picked up without jolts. Also extra hoisting height could be added by rigging up lattice extensions. Another option featured was a ram-operated tilt-back cab designed for the comfort of the operator. This alleviated many problems the operators had with stiff necks when keeping an eye on high loads.

Sales of the A-100 to both contractors and governments had been somewhat disappointing. The normal price range for these machines was $600,000 to $700,000. However, as a result of the below-target sales, several of the six machines built had to be leased to customers at unattractive rates. The A-100 had, however, been a very effective crowd attraction device at equipment shows.

Manufacturing

Victoria maintained two manufacturing facilities with the main location in Squamish manufacturing approximately three units a week during 1985. The second facility, located in Sacramento, California, produced 1¼ cranes a week since its establishment in 1979. The U.S. facility served the U.S. domestic market (where Victoria had a 15 percent market share) and those foreign markets where sales were financed by U.S. aid or funding. All other markets were served by the Canadian plant.

Victoria had a policy of manufacturing approximately 85 percent of crane components in-house, a figure substantially higher than the competition. Even the more complex and demanding products were produced by Victoria and its subsidiaries. This strategy, Victoria argued, enabled them to control quality and supply.

Victoria's largest manufacturing facility consisted of machinery of various ages and utilized manufacturing techniques that were, in some cases, 50 years old. The firm had initiated a process of replacing less versatile and slower automatic machines with numerically controlled (NC) machines. Approximately 15 percent of the firm's machinery had been replaced with expensive $250,000 NCs.

Markets

There were two distinct market segments in the crane industry: the government and contractor sectors. Success in the government market (foreign, federal, provincial, state, regional, and municipal bodies) lay in the ability of the manufacturer to meet the buyer's specifications at the lowest price. Since government users did not have to contend with the high direct costs of downtime, a lower priority was given to parts and service availability compared to original capital cost.

In the contractor segment, the amount of equipment downtime could make the difference between showing a profit or a loss on a contract. Contractors were, therefore, very sensitive to machine dependability as well as parts and service availability. Most contractors consequently showed a willingness to pay major price premiums to ensure equipment reliability or to deal with a manufacturer who had a strong distribution network.

The worldwide market for all types of mobile cranes was estimated at $630 million for 1985 of which approximately 55 percent lay outside of North America. The crane market in 1985 in Canada was 16 percent of the North American market which was significant considering that the Canadian population was less than 10 percent of the North American total population. This difference was due to the need for cranes in the Canadian transportation, logging, petroleum, and construction markets and the large Canadian government market. There had been very little, if any, real growth since 1980.

Victoria's marketing strategy had been to seek government rather than contractor crane sales. The reason given was that Victoria could produce a custom-built crane with more features at a much lower price than their main competition, Washington Cranes. Washington's hold over the contractor sector, however, was quite secure. Washington's reputation for reliability, strength, and worldwide service and parts network gave it unquestioned leadership in the contractor sector. As a result only a very small percentage of Victoria's sales were to contractors.

Victoria generally competed worldwide on the basis of providing what was seen to be a medium to heavy load crane, an acceptable level of parts availability and servicing, and a lower price (when special features were required) than its main competitors. For example, in the medium weight class, Victoria's list price was approximately 75 percent of its two main competitors. The gap closed as the class became heavier, but even then Victoria's price was about 15 percent less than Washington's.

Victoria's marketing effort was divided into eight worldwide regions, plus the Canadian federal government market which was so important to Victoria that a separate sales effort (Craneco Sales Ltd.) had been created. This company actively pursued every Canadian tender for cranes and had acquired approximately 60 percent of the Canadian crane market worth approximately $27 million or 54 units per year. Of this, about two thirds was derived from sales to the federal government. Victoria's efforts had been so successful that the tender sheets sent out by the Canadian federal government tended to have Victoria specifications as the norm.

In the traditional sense Victoria pursued little or no advertising with the exception of regular exhibition at trade shows. Alternatively, the company made very extensive use of its executive jets to fly in prospective customers from all over the world. Victoria believed that the combination of its integrated plant, worker loyalty, and single product concentration evident in their Canadian plant produced a convinced customer. There were over 14 such visits to the British Columbia plant in 1985 including delegations from The People's Republic of China, Korea, France, and Turkey.

Competition

Victoria, as the second largest producer of cranes, faced competition from five major worldwide firms, all of whom were much larger and more diversified. The industry leader was the Washington Crane Company with 1985 assets and sales of approximately $150 million and $400 million, respectively. Washington had become a name synonymous around the world with heavy duty equipment and had been able to maintain a sales growth rate of over 15 percent per annum over the past five years. In the worldwide crane market, Washington had captured approximately a 50 percent share. It manufactured in the United States, Mexico, and Australia. Key to its operations were 100 strong dealers worldwide with over 200 outlets. They had almost 50 percent of Canada's construction market but a negligible share in the federal government market.

Next after Victoria was Texas Star, another large manufacturer whose cranes were generally smaller and sold through their extensive worldwide equipment dealerships. The next two largest competitors were both very large U.S. multinational producers whose crane lines formed a small part of their overall business. With the exception of Washington, industry observers suggested that crane sales for these latter firms had been stable (at best) for quite some time. The exception was the Japanese crane producer Toshio. They had been aggressively pursuing sales worldwide and had entered the North American market recently. Kato, another Japanese firm, had started in the North American market as well.

Management

The main motivating force behind Victoria's success in recent years has been its chairman, Brian Walters. Walters was a hard-driving entrepreneur who was a firm believer in "people power." He saw three basic elements to success:

1. A quality product.
2. Professional people.
3. Motivation to be the standard of excellence in their field of endeavour.

According to Walters, "Almost every element for success was dependent upon the competence and motivation of the people in the firm."

Walters saw Victoria continuing to grow by "being more entrepreneurial, by exhibiting greater dedication, and by being more flexible than its competitors." Walters perceived a competitive advantage in that cranes were only one part of a larger product line for most of his competitors. Line managers were accountable to a corporate superstructure where ". . . everything was done by the numbers, there was no room for an emotional plea, they couldn't look at losses to get into an area, they would turn the key on a loser." As a result, continued Walters, "they have bred [grey-suited] managers." In Victoria all effort was directed toward manufacturing and selling one product. According to Walters, decisions could be made quickly, with all managers aware of the qualitative as well as the quantitative aspects of the decision.

On the other hand, Walters was aware that Victoria's success had not gone unnoticed by its competitors. "We were at the top of Washington's hit list, and Toshio and Kato were going to be tough. As competition increased, and as sales grew, we had to be careful not to develop the same kind of organization as the big U.S. firms. In fact, Victoria's growth had already occasioned the need for organizational change."

Organization

The history of Victoria's management and organizational structure had been one of close family control. Brian Walters's uncle, James, took over when his father (Brian, Sr.) retired in 1968. The company continued to grow, but the James Walters's management style did not fit with a growing and increasingly complex Victoria. He exercised very close personal control of the operation, and eventually the load was such that his health began to fail. The solution was to create an assistant general manager, Mr. J. Rivers, through whom the tight supervision could be maintained while easing the work load. James Walters suffered a stroke, and Rivers became general manager in 1970. At the same time, Brian, the present chairman and chief executive officer, became head of the U.S. operation.

By 1973 the company was doing well in a few markets but not in the United States. Business came infrequently and in big lumps (50 cranes) that created an unstable production flow. It was necessary for Victoria to diversify its markets. In Brian Walters's words, "We would rather have crane orders of 10 each from 10 different countries than one order for 100." Consequently, the strategy was to widen distribution and increase market share in the United States.

At the time, Victoria was working through a distributor in the United States who was selling only 30–40 cranes a year. Walters thought he should be selling at least 150. To handle the problem, Walters and Rivers divided their responsibilities: Walters to handle the United States and Rivers to handle Canada and exports.

In 1975 the time came for the U.S. distributor to renew its agreement. Walters said he would give them a five-year term if they would guarantee 150 cranes a year. They couldn't, and so Walters bought the operation. In the first month he fired 13 of the 15 employees and cancelled most existing dealers. He then went to work to rebuild. He wanted small orders only. Orders for over 10 cranes would not be accepted. He wanted to sneak in and set a foothold and a reputation before the big U.S. firms even noticed him.

This strategy proved successful, and in 1976 Walters came back to Canada. As Rivers was still general manager there was not enough to occupy him for 12 months a year. People told him he needed a hobby so he started travelling three or four months a year. While he was still in the company in a major way, it was not a full-time involvement.

This policy worked until 1979 when a number of accumulating problems brought Walters back into the picture. Sales were growing well, but work loads were piling up and things weren't getting done. Walters saw the problem as stemming from the "pyramid organization" that had continued to exist and grow larger now with Rivers at the top.

Most of the functional managers such as manufacturing, employee relations, and marketing reported directly to Rivers who made most of the decisions. In Walters's view, "We had to change. If we wanted to grow further we had to do things." Walters saw the need for certain types of cranes and the adoption of policies such as profit sharing. These were communicated to Freeman, the company secretary, but were not implemented by Rivers. In addition, says Walters, ". . . we had to develop middle-line managers—we had no depth."

Between 1979 and 1982 Walters reorganized the firm by setting up separate operating companies and a large corporate staff group. In several cases senior operating executives were placed in staff/advisory positions, while in others, executives held positions in both operating and staff groups. Exhibit 3 illustrates Victoria's organizational chart as of 1983.

By early 1984 Walters was beginning to wonder "if I had made a very bad decision." The staff groups weren't working. Rivers had been unable to accept the redistribution of power and had resigned. There was "civil war in the company." Politics and factional disputes were the rule rather than the exception. Line managers were upset by the intervention of the staff VPs of employee relations, manufacturing, and marketing. Staff personnel, on the other hand, were upset by "poor" line decisions.

As a result the marketing and manufacturing staff functions were eradicated with the late-1985 organizational restructuring which is illustrated in Exhibit 4. The services previously supplied by the staff groups were duplicated to varying extents inside each division.

In place of most of the staff groups, an executive committee was established

Exhibit 3: Victoria Organizational Structure, 1979–1983

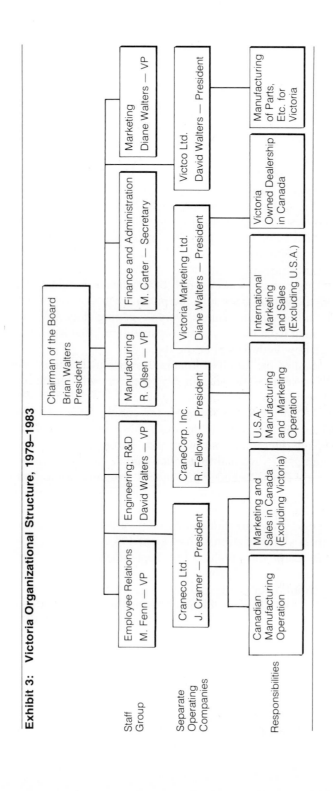

Exhibit 4:   Victoria Organizational Structure, Late 1985

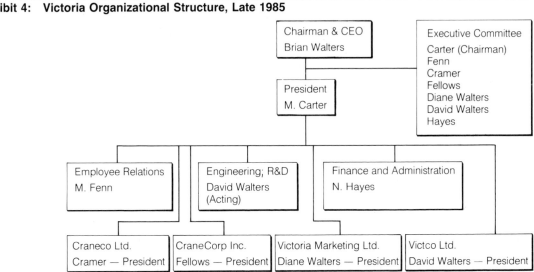

in 1984. Membership in this group included the president and head of all staff groups and presidents (general managers) of the four divisions. Meeting monthly, the executive committee was intended to evaluate the performance of the firm's profit and cost problems, handle mutual problems such as transfer prices, and allocate capital expenditures among the four operating divisions. Subcommittees handled subjects such as R&D and new products.

The new organization contained seven major centres for performance measurement purposes. The cost centres were:

1. Engineering; R&D (reporting to Victco Ltd.).
2. International Marketing (Victoria Marketing Ltd.).
3. Corporate staff.

The major profit centres:

4. CraneCorp, Inc. (U.S. production and sales).
5. Victco Ltd. (supplying Victoria with components).
6. Craneco (Canadian production and marketing).
7. Victoria-owned Canadian sales outlets (reporting to Victoria Marketing Ltd.).

The major profit centres had considerable autonomy in their day-to-day operations and were motivated to behave as if their division was a separate, independent firm.

By mid-1985 Brian Walters had moved out of his position as president, with

Michael Carter—a long-time employee close to retirement—being asked to take the position of president until a new one could be found.

Walters saw his role changing. "If I was anything, I was a bit of an entrepreneur. My job was to supply that thrust but to let people develop on their own accord. I was not concerned about things not working, but I was concerned when nothing was being done about it."

In the new organization Walters didn't sit on the executive committee. However, as chairman of the board and chief executive officer the committee's recommendations came to him, and ". . . they tried me on six ways from Sunday." His intention was to monitor the firm's major activities rather than to set them. He did have to sit on the product development subcommittee, however, when ". . . things were not working . . . there was conflict . . . the engineering group (engineering, R&D) had designed a whole new crane and nobody including me knew about it." Mr. McCarthy, the VP of engineering and R&D, called only five to six committee meetings. The crane his group developed was not to Walters's liking. (There had been a high turnover rate in this group with four VPs since 1983.) Recognizing these problems, Walters brought in consultants to tackle the problems of the management information system and the definition of staff/line responsibilities.

In spite of these moves, dissatisfaction still existed within the company in 1986. Diane Walters, the president of Victoria International Marketing, liked the autonomous system because it helped to identify the true performance of sections of the company. "We had separate little buckets and could easily identify results." Furthermore, she felt that there was no loss of efficiency (due to the duplication of certain staff functions within the divisions) since there was little duplication of systems between groups, and each group acted as a check and balance on the other groups so that "manufacturing won't make what marketing won't sell." Other comments:

> The divisionalized system allowed me to get closer to my staff because we were a separate group.
>
> We ended up with sales and marketing expertise that was much better than if we had stayed under manufacturing.
>
> If you [run the firm] with a manufacturing-oriented organization, you could forget what people want.
>
> In a divisionalized system there was bound to be conflict between divisions, but that was not necessarily unhealthy.

The views of staff and the operating companies' presidents varied considerably when they discussed Victoria's organizational evolution and the operation of the present structure.

Some executives saw the decentralized, semiautonomous operating company structure as a means of giving each person the opportunity to grow and develop without the hindrance of other functional executives. Most, if not all, of the operating company presidents and staff VPs were aware that decentralization brought benefits, especially in terms of the autonomy it gave them to modify existing practices. One senior executive even saw the present structure as an indicator of their basic competitive stance: "Either we centralize the structure and retract, or we stay as we are and fight with the big guys." Therefore, with minimal direction supplied from the CEO (Brian Walters), presidents were able to build up their staff, establish priorities and programs, and essentially, were only held responsible for the bottom line.

The policy had resulted in considerable dissension. Some conflict centered around the establishment of appropriately challenging budgets for each operating firm and even more conflict over transfer pricing and allocation of capital budgets. In 1985–86 even though requested budgets were cut equally, lack of central control over spending resulted in overexpenditures by several of the profit and cost centres.

The opposing views about the existing decentralized structure disagreed with the comment that there were ". . . no costs other than duplication of people." As one executive put it, "The semi-independence of the operating companies and the lack of a real leader for the firm has resulted in poor coordination of problem solving and difficulty in allocating responsibility." Pointing to two particular companies within the firm he noted how Engineering's response to Manufacturing was often slow and poorly communicated. Even worse, he noted, was how the priorities of different units were not synchronized. "When you manufacture just one product all your activities are interrelated. So when one group puts new products first on a priority list while another is still working out bugs in the existing product, conflict and inefficiencies have to develop."

This same opposing group argued that the present organization was more appropriate to a larger, faster growing, and more complex company. As one senior executive put it, "We're too small to be as decentralized as we are now. All of this was done to accommodate the 'Walters kids' anyway, and it's now going to detract from profitability and growth." One of these executives stated that rather than being a president of an operating company he would prefer to be a general manager at the head of a functional group reporting to a group head. "If we had the right Victoria Heavy Equipment president," he said, "we wouldn't need all these divisional presidents." Another continued, "Right now the players [divisional presidents and staff VPs] run the company. Brian Walters gives us a shot of adrenalin four or six times a year but doesn't provide any active leadership. When Brian leaves, things stop. Instead Brian now wants to monitor the game plan rather than set it up for others to run. As we still only have an interim president [Carter], it is the marketplace that leads us, not any strategic plan or goal."

The New President

Individual views about who would be the ideal new president were essentially determined by what each executive thought was wrong with Victoria. Generally each person knew that the new president would have to fit in with Brian Walters's presence and described role in the firm and the existence of his two children in the organization. They all generally saw Brian as wanting to supply ideas and major strategies but little else.

Concerning the new president, all but one agreed that the president should *not* get involved in day-to-day activities or in major decision making. Instead, he should "arbitrate" among the line general managers (subsidiary presidents) and staff VPs and become more of a "bureaucrat cum diplomat" rather than an aggressive leader. As another put it, "The company will drive itself; only once in a while he'll steer a little."

1986 Situation

By early 1986 it seemed as though Victoria was very much in the middle of a slow sales period. Profits for 1985 were down slightly from 1984, and production was expected to go down to 1980 levels during 1986. Approximately 75 people had been laid off from the shop floor, and the forecast was not significantly different.

Industry forecasts for 1986 showed a marked decline of about 30 percent in the North American market. The rest of the world was not expected to decline, but competition in the North American market was expected to affect sales. Overall the world market was at best stable and was expected to decline by about 10 percent from the 1985 market level of approximately 12,000 units.

Added to this was the possibility of low morale and loss of productivity in the work force. The reduction of the work force back to 1978 entry seniority levels helped increase the morale in the remaining work force who were very much aware of the production decrease. Reducing morale, however, was the ill-timed introduction of the profit-sharing plan and the increase in staff functions. The profit-sharing plan for all employees was introduced amid much fanfare in early 1985. It was not until October, however, that employees were told that no bonus would be given that year. Aggravating the problem was that the work force felt that while certain groups met their budget, others did not, and hence *all* were penalized. This arose because each bonus was based on overall as well as divisional profits.

Production cost trends were not very promising. While there was considerable improvement in 1985 over the previous year, factory door costs for the standard crane had risen by several percentage points more than the consumer inflation rate.

Many members of the shop-floor workers and the supervisory staff were not generally impressed with the additions to the central and divisional staff groups while at the same time the work force was being reduced. Even more so was the strongly held feeling that the paperwork these staff functions created was time-consuming and gave little if any benefit. They noted, for example, that there were four or five times as many people in production control in 1986 as there were in 1980 for the same volume of production. In addition they pointed out that despite all sorts of efforts on the part of a computer-assisted production control group, inventory turnover was the same or possibly worse than it was before the group's arrival.

Brian Walters's Plans

Earlier in the day before he started his flight to California, Brian Walters was outlining with great gusto and delight his plans for the firm to all senior executives in British Columbia. His goal was to more than double Victoria's market share in the Western bloc world to approximately 25 percent. This he intended to do by 1990.

Walters looked beyond this point as well, to sales of $250 million by 1999. This would require new moves after 1990, and he identified the "easy" ones as vertically integrating back into some businesses they had left years earlier. Other activities would have to come from new product/business areas—probably by purchase.

"The hazard for Victoria," Walters said as he looked out of his window toward the Squamish airstrip, "is that we could develop the same kind of bureaucratic, quantitatively oriented, grey-suited managers that slow down the large U.S. competitors." "But that," he said, turning to his audience, "is something I'm going to watch like a hawk. We need the right people."